# THE HISTORY OF
# THE NORTHAMPTONSHIRE REGIMENT
## 1934-1948

H.R.H. The Duchess of Gloucester, C.I., G.C.V.O., G.B.E.,
Colonel-in-Chief, The Northamptonshire Regiment

*(Dorothy Wilding Ltd.)*

*[Frontispiece*

# THE HISTORY OF THE NORTHAMPTONSHIRE REGIMENT : 1934–1948

*written by*
BRIGADIER W. J. JERVOIS, M.C.
*on behalf of the Regimental Council*

The Naval & Military Press Ltd

*Published by*

**The Naval & Military Press Ltd**
Unit 5 Riverside, Brambleside
Bellbrook Industrial Estate
Uckfield, East Sussex
TN22 1QQ England

Tel: +44 (0)1825 749494

www.naval-military-press.com
www.nmarchive.com

*In reprinting in facsimile from the original, any imperfections are inevitably reproduced and the quality may fall short of modern type and cartographic standards.*

# FOREWORD

*by*

## H.R.H. The Duchess of Gloucester
### C.I., G.C.V.O., G.B.E.

### COLONEL-IN-CHIEF OF THE REGIMENT

YORK HOUSE,
ST JAMES'S PALACE.

I am glad to provide a foreword to the Second Volume of the History of the Northamptonshire Regiment, of which I am proud to be Colonel-in-Chief.

This Volume, covering the period from 1934 to 1948, includes the story, not only of the years before the Second World War, when the Regiment carried out its various tasks with unobtrusive devotion to duty, but also of the critical years of that War, in which its Battalions added to their fame by their conduct in many theatres of operations. And, finally, it tells of the aftermath, in which took place the re-organisation which was necessary to meet the needs of a well-balanced, modern Army.

That this re-organisation greatly affected the Infantry of the Line is well-known, and we, in common with other Regiments, suffered the grievous loss of one of our Regular Battalions. Despite this, I am confident that the 1st Battalion, (48th/58th) will worthily maintain the traditions of the two old Battalions, the names of which are commemorated in its title.

In war, as this History tells, our 5th Battalion, of the Territorial Army, showed itself in every way the equal of its Regular brothers.

I am glad to see that due recognition has been given in this Volume, as in the first, to the deeds of those fine Battalions of the Commonwealth Forces with which the Northamptonshire Regiment is so proud to be allied.

I am sure that this record of past events and achievements will provide an inspiration to those now serving in the Regiment, and to those who will so serve in the years to come.

Alice
Colonel-in-Chief.

The Northamptonshire Regiment.

## PREFACE

*by*

MAJOR-GENERAL G. ST. G. ROBINSON
C.B., D.S.O., M.C.

### COLONEL OF THE REGIMENT

*THIS volume of our History is dedicated to those who served with the Regiment during the years 1934–1948.*

*That we are able to tell their story is due to several years of work by Brigadier W. J. Jervois, M.C., who undertook the task at the request of the Regimental Council. Thus, once again, we are indebted to an officer of the Regiment for recounting achievements of which we may well feel proud.*

*It has been no easy task to collect, and sift, the vast amount of material available after a war of six years' duration. Nevertheless I am sure that those who read this volume will agree that the Author has successfully overcome such difficulties, and has shown us, clearly and concisely, how well the spirit, discipline and traditions of the Regiment were kept alive during those critical war years.*

*On behalf of all ranks, past and present, I thank Brigadier Jervois most sincerely for what he has done.*

## AUTHOR'S NOTE

THE basis of a Regimental History must be the official records and war-diaries, but these, only too often, omit much that is of value and of interest. To do any justice to the subject the recollections of individuals who were present at the time that the events occurred are essential, and many have given the most willing help, both in lending me documents, diaries, and maps, and also in commenting on the drafts which I have produced from time to time. In all cases in which official and unofficial records differed I have accepted the evidence of the former, failing conclusive proof to the contrary. I have done my best to ensure that the lists of officers serving with battalions at various times, and of honours and awards, are complete and accurate. For any errors and omissions I make sincere apologies.

The list of all those who have assisted towards the production of this volume would be too lengthy to give in full, but, on behalf of the Regiment, I should like to thank the following individuals in particular:

Lieut.-Col. J. Rhoderick Jones of the Infantry Record Office, Warwick, for the loan of battalion war-diaries and for other information.

Mr. C. V. Owen, of the Historical Section of the Cabinet Offices, for access to the diaries of formations in which battalions of the Regiment served. And to one of his assistants, Mr. Lewis, once of the 58th, who provided me with many maps.

Lieut.-Col. W. G. A. Coldwell for much detail concerning the operations of the 48th in Waziristan.

Brig. D. E. Taunton, Lieut.-Col. P. de C. Jones, Majors T. R. Molloy and N. R. Ogle, Capt. R. A. Clayton and Mr. R. E. M. Hughes for details of, and comments on, the story of the 48th in Burma. In addition, special thanks are due to Brig. D. A. L. Mackenzie, Commander of the 32nd Indian Infantry Brigade, who lent me his personal narrative and many maps of the Burma Campaign, and who read, and made most valuable comments on, those chapters.

As regards the operations of the 58th in many theatres of war, I owe much to Brig. J. W. Hinchcliffe, Lieut.-Cols. C. J. M. Watts, J. A. W. Ballard and D. J. B. Houchin, Majors J. C. Denny, A. W. B. Symonds and R. S. Wallis. To the last-named, more especially, for permission to draw upon the *History of the 58th, 1939–1945* for many details.

For the story of the 4th Battalion much information was provided by

## AUTHOR'S NOTE

Lieut.-Col. W. C. Furminger. And for that of the 5th Battalion by Lieut-Cols. G. A. Anstee, T. A. Buchanan and R. K. MacMichael, and Majors D. V. Emmerton, J. H. Andrews, W. V. Marshall and J. H. W. Cobbing. Capt. I. A. McKee's *History of the 5th Battalion in Italy* proved invaluable, and the author has given much help in other ways.

Lieut.-Cols. A. St. G. Coldwell and J. K. Arthur, the late Lieut.-Col. W. E. Carrick and Major F. R. Wilford provided me with much material regarding other battalions of the Regiment and the I.T.C.

Lieut.-Col. N. J. Dickson produced most of the technical information contained in the appendix dealing with weapons and equipment of the period.

For the material contained in the brief summaries of the histories of our Allied Regiments I am indebted to Brig. M. J. Moten, formerly of the Australian 48th, Lieut.-Col. B. J. Callinan of the Australian 58th, the late Col. C. S. White of the North Auckland Regiment of New Zealand and Col. M. Jelley of the 585th Searchlight Regiment R.A. (T.A.). Major T. M. Hunter of the Canadian Army Liaison Establishment in London provided details concerning the Lake Superior Regiment. Much of the history of the Regiment de la Rey was gleaned from their publication *The Story of Men*.

Lieut.-Col. O. K. Parker and Major J. T. Ennals have answered many requests for help in various directions.

A great debt of gratitude is owed to Mrs. Gurney, assisted, latterly, by her son Mr. T. R. Gurney, for the drawing of the fair copies of the majority of the maps. In so doing she has continued the work which she undertook for the first volume of the Regimental History, written by her husband, the late Major-General R. Gurney.

Major-General H. Essame and Lieut.-Col. C. J. M. Watts undertook the preliminary reading of the manuscript, and produced many valuable suggestions for improvement. Lieut.-Col. Watts has also helped much in proof-reading, and, as Secretary of the Regimental History Committee, has borne the brunt of the task of production of the volume.

Finally I should like to express my personal thanks to the Colonel of the Regiment, Major-General G. St. G. Robinson, who, having entrusted the task of writing this history to me, has never failed to give me encouragement and helpful advice.

W. J. J.

# ACKNOWLEDGEMENTS

For kind permission to use certain copyright extracts the Regimental History Committee are indebted to:

The British Broadcasting Corporation for extracts from a commentary on the Trooping the Colour at Belfast; Mr. Harry C. Butcher and Messrs. Heinemann for an extract from *Three Years with Eisenhower*; 'Bartimeus' and Messrs. Chatto and Windus for an extract from *The Turn of the Road*; *The Times* for an extract describing the entry of the 78th Division into Tunis; *The Statesman* for an extract describing the Kyaukchaw battlefield; Mrs. Bambridge and Messrs. Macmillan for an extract from Mr. Rudyard Kipling's *From Sea to Sea*; Her Majesty's Stationery Office for extracts from various despatches published in the *London Gazette*; and the Air Ministry for the reproduction of an air-photograph of the Irrawaddy River.

The Committee also wish to express their gratitude to the *Northampton Chronicle and Echo* for having placed at their disposal the photographs from which the following illustrations were made: The visit of the Colonel-in-Chief to the Depot; the handing over of the 48th Colours at Northampton and of the 58th Colours in Berlin; and the ceremony of presenting the Freedom of the Borough at Northampton.

The colour illustrations of types of battle-dress were painted for the Committee by Mr. C. C. P. Lawson, who went to much trouble to ensure accuracy of detail.

# CONTENTS

**I      THE REGIMENT, 1934–1935**     1

*The 48th at Jullundur, 1934–1936—The 58th at Aldershot, 1934–1935—The 4th and 5th Battalions, 1934–1935—The Colours—The Colonel of the Regiment—The War Museum at Mons—The Locomotive 'The Northamptonshire Regiment.'*

**II      THE 48th IN WAZIRISTAN, 1936–1937**     10

*Razmak—The Move to Razmak—Operations of Razcol, November–December 1936—The 48th at Razmak, December 1936–March 1937—The Situation in Waziristan, March–May 1937—Operations of Razcol, June–August 1937—The 48th at Razmak, August–September 1937—Operations of Razcol, September–November 1937—Retrospect of the Campaign—The 48th leave Razmak.*

**III      THE REGIMENT, 1936–1939**     27

*The 48th at Dinapore, 1938–1939—The 58th at Ballykinler, 1936–1939—The 4th Battalion, 1936–1939—The 5th Battalion, 1936–1939—The new 4th Battalion, 1939—The Colonel-in-Chief of the Regiment, 1937—The Colonel of the Regiment—Alliance with the Regiment de la Rey, 1937—Liaison with Allied Regiments, 1936–1939—The Regimental Depot, 1936–1939.*

**IV      THE CAMPAIGN IN FRANCE AND FLANDERS, 1939–1940**     43

*Move of the B.E.F. to France—Shortcomings of the B.E.F.—Work on Defences—Completion of the B.E.F.—Situation in Europe, September 1939–May 1940—The Allied Plans—The German Offensive, 10th–18th May—'Frankforce' at Arras, 20th–24th May—The B.E.F. Triangle—The Belgian Surrender, 27th May—The Dunkirk Perimeter—The Evacuation from Dunkirk.*

**V      THE 58th IN FRANCE AND BELGIUM, 1939–1940**     51

*Mobilisation at Ballykinler, September 1939—The 58th at Aldershot, October 1939—The Move to France—The 58th in France, October 1939–May 1940—Operations in Belgium, 13th–19th May—The Battle of Arras, 20th–23rd May—The Move to Ypres, 24th–26th May—The Stand near St. Eloi, 27th–28th May—The Withdrawal to the Coast, 28th–31st May—The Evacuation from Dunkirk, 31st May–1st June.*

**VI      THE 5th BATTALION IN FRANCE AND BELGIUM, 1939–1940**     70

*Mobilisation, September 1939—Training, September–December 1939—The 5th in France, January–May 1940—The Move into Belgium, 13th–17th May—The Withdrawal to the Escaut, 17th–18th May—The Fighting on the Escaut, 19th–22nd May—On the Lys, 23rd–27th May—Withdrawal towards Ypres, 27th–28th May—Withdrawal to the Coast, 29th–30th May—Evacuation from Dunkirk, 31st May–1st June.*

# CONTENTS

**VII**      THE TRAINING YEARS, 1940–1942      80

*The Army's Problem—The 48th at Dinapore, September 1939–January 1940—The 48th at Jhansi, January 1940–March 1941—The Bi-centenary of the 48th, 17th January 1941—The 48th at Dinapore, March 1941–January 1942—Mobilisation, January 1942—The 48th in Ceylon, June–December 1942—The 58th in Scotland and England, June 1940–April 1941—The 58th in Northern Ireland, April 1941–January 1942—The 58th at Caterham, January–March 1942—The 4th Bn. in England, September 1940—The 4th Bn. in Northern Ireland, June 1940–December 1942—The 5th Bn. in England, June 1940–April 1942—The 5th Bn. in Scotland, April–October 1942—The 50th (Holding) Bn., June–October 1940—The 6th Bn., October 1940–December 1942—The 70th Bn., December 1940–December 1942—The I.T.C., 1939–1942.*

**VIII**      THE 58th IN MADAGASCAR, 1942      98

*The Voyage to Madagascar, 21st March–4th May 1942—The Landing at Madagascar, 5th May—The Attacks on Antsirane, 6th–7th May—Occupation, 7th May–10th June.*

**IX**      THE 5th BATTALION IN NORTH AFRICA, 1942–1943
THE LANDING, AND THE ADVANCE ON TUNIS, 1942      108

*The General Situation, 1942—Operation 'Torch'—The Plan for the Landings—The Voyage to North Africa, 26th October–7th November—The Landing at Algiers, 7th–8th November—Incidents after the Landing—Near Algiers, 8th–15th November—The Task of 78th Division—Advance of 'Hart Force'—The Country—The Forward Move of the 5th Bn., 16th–21st November—The Capture of Medjez, 20th–27th November—The Advance to Djedeida, 28th–30th November—The German Counter-offensive, 30th November–12th December—In Defence, 12th–21st December—The Last Attempt to Capture Tunis, 21st–27th December—Comments on the Operations, November–December 1942.*

**X**      THE 5th BATTALION IN NORTH AFRICA, 1942–1943
DEFENCE, AND THE FINAL ADVANCE TO TUNIS, 1943      132

*The General Situation, January 1943—The 5th Bn. in Defence, January–February—Rommel's Offensive, February 1943—Von Arnim's Offensive, February–March—The Beginning of the Allied Offensive, March–April—Advance in the Mountains, 5th–13th April—The Attack on Tanngoucha, 14th–15th April—The Final Offensive, 22nd April–13th May—The Attacks on Sidi Ahmed, 27th–29th April—The Advance to Tunis—Comments on the Campaign—The 5th in North Africa, May–July 1943.*

**XI**      THE 58th IN INDIA, PERSIA, IRAQ AND PALESTINE, 1942–1943      148

*The 58th in India, June–September 1942—The 58th in Paiforce, September 1942–January 1943—The Move to Egypt, February 1943—Training, February–June 1943—The 58th Embark.*

**XII**      THE 58th AND THE 5th BATTALION IN SICILY, 1943      153

*Background of the Operation—The Opposing Forces—The Allied Plan—The Landings—Landing of the 58th, 10th July—Capture of Syracuse—Capture of Priolo, 11th–12th July—Advance to Augusta, 12th–16th July—Progress of Seventh and Eighth Armies—58th Move to the Simeto, 16th–22nd July—General Progress of Operations, 31st July–2nd August—The 5th Bn. reach Sicily—Attack on Catenanuova, 30th–31st July—Capture of Centuripe, 31st July–2nd August—Capture of Bronte, 7th–9th August—Operations near Randazzo, 12th–14th August—Final Operations by the 58th, 1st–9th August—End of the Campaign—The 58th in Sicily, 9th August–2nd September—The 5th Bn. in Sicily, 15th August–21st September.*

## CONTENTS

### XIII THE CAMPAIGN IN ITALY, 1943–1945 — 168

*The Plan of Invasion—Italy Surrenders—The Landings at Reggio, September 1943—The Salerno Landing—Advance of the Eighth Army—Landings at Taranto—Advance to Foggia—Capture of Termoli—The Allies' Problem—Crossing of the Trigno, October-November 1943—The Sangro Battle, November-December 1943—Advance North of the Sangro—Situation, January 1944—Operations of the Fifth Army, January 1944—Operations at Cassino, February-March 1944—Plans for 1944—The May Offensive—Capture of Rome, June 1944—Advance to the Gothic Line, June-July 1944—Assault on the Gothic Line, August-September 1944—The Advance Continues, September-December 1944—The Final Offensive, April 1945—The Accomplishment.*

### XIV THE 58th IN ITALY, 1943–1945 — 179

*The Landing at Reggio, 3rd September 1943—Advance from the Beachhead, 3rd–14th September—To Foggia, 15th September–23rd October—Advance to the Sangro, 25th October–19th November—Maintenance of the Battalion—On the Sangro, 20th November–8th December—On the River Moro, 9th December 1943–2nd January 1944—Into the Fifth Army, 3rd–13th January—Crossing the Garigliano, 14th January–4th February—Advance to the Minturno Ridge, 23rd–28th January—Attack on Pt. 156, 29th January–2nd February—In Defence, 5th February–3rd March—In the Anzio Bridgehead, 3rd March–26th April—In 'The Fortress,' 27th April–6th May—Retrospect of 'The Fortress'—Crossing of the Moletta, 9th–31st May—Advance to Rome, 1st–5th June—The 58th leave Italy—In the Middle East, July 1944–February 1945—Return to Italy, 8th February–5th March—Departure from Italy, 6th March.*

### XV THE 5th BATTALION IN ITALY AND EGYPT, SEPTEMBER 1943–SEPTEMBER 1944 — 207

*Landing and Initial Moves, 21st–29th September 1943—Advance on Termoli, 30th September–3rd October—Capture of Termoli, 3rd–10th October—Across the Trigno, 23rd October–4th November—Advance to the Sangro, 5th–19th November—Fighting on the Sangro, 21st November–2nd December—In the Central Sector, 3rd December 1943–31st January 1944—Back to the Coastal Sector, 1st–11th February—To the Cassino Front, 12th February–21st March—In the Line at Cassino, 24th March–25th April—Resting at Capua, 26th April–13th May—Assault on the Gustav Line, 14th–24th May—Advance to Rome, 18th May–8th June—Northwards from Rome, 9th–15th June—Capture of Montegabbione, 16th–17th June—Fighting round Lake Trasimeno, 18th June–2nd July—Journey to Egypt, 4th–22nd July—In Egypt, 23rd July–9th September.*

### XVI THE 5th BATTALION IN ITALY, SEPTEMBER 1944–MAY 1945 — 228

*Back to the Italian Front, 15th September–12th October—The Situation—Task of 78th Division—First Attack on Pt. 508, 13th–14th October—Second Attack, 14th–15th October—Third Attack, 15th October—Fighting round Monte Spaduro, 21st–29th October—Reorganisation of the Battalion—In the Spaduro Sector, 1st November 1944–13th February 1945—Rest and Training, 13th February–25th March—Start of the Offensive, 26th March–15th April—Battle of the Argenta Gap, 16th–19th April—The Final Stages, 20th April–2nd May—Conclusion.*

### XVII THE 48th IN CEYLON AND BURMA THE DEFENSIVE, JANUARY 1943–NOVEMBER 1944 — 242

*Training, January–November 1943—Move to the Burma Front, December 1943—General Situation to December 1943—In the Kabaw Valley, December 1943–January 1944—The Japanese Position at Kyaukchaw—Preliminaries—Approach and Bombing—Attack on the 18th January—Attack on the 19th January—Attack on the 20th January—*

## CONTENTS

*Subsequent Operations, 21st–25th January—Postscript to Kyaukchaw—Round Kyaukchaw, 26th January–17th March—The Japanese Offensive—Withdrawal from Kyaukchaw, 18th March–1st April—Into the Naga Hills, 2nd–12th April—The Bishenpur-Silchar Track—Topography and Tactics—Task of 32nd Brigade—48th reach Bishenpur—Operations of No. 1 Company—48th Occupy Pt. 5846—Japanese Attempt to block the Track—Keeping the Track open, 1st May–8th June—Operations Elsewhere—First Attack on Dome, 10th–11th June—Second Attack on Dome, 13th–14th June—Final Attempt to block the Track, 16th–28th June—Last Days on the Track, 29th June–13th July—Silchar Track: Retrospect—The 48th rest and train, July–November 1944.*

### XVIII    THE 48th IN BURMA. THE OFFENSIVE, NOVEMBER 1944–MAY 1945    282

*General Situation in Burma—32nd Brigade's Problem—March to the Chindwin, 23rd–30th November 1944—Crossing the Chindwin, 2nd–5th December—Advance to Chingyaung, 9th–14th December—At Chingyaung, 15th–23rd December—Advance on Budalin, 24th December 1944–4th January 1945—Gaining of Contact, 4th–6th January—Capture of Budalin, 7th–10th January—Advance to Monywa, 13th–15th January—Fighting at Ywathit, 16th–19th January—Attack on Monywa, 20th–23rd January—The Advance Continues, 25th–28th January—The General Situation—The Plan—The 48th's Task—Resources—Preliminaries to the Irrawaddy Crossing—The Crossing, 12th–15th February—Japanese Attacks, 16th–17th February—Holding the Bridgehead, 18th–28th February—Relief of the Bridgehead—Advance to Kyaukse, 6th–19th March—Operations round Kyaukse, 23rd–30th March—Final Operations, 1st–25th April—The 48th leave Burma.*

### XIX    THE BATTALIONS AT HOME AND THE I.T.C., 1943–1945    321

*The 4th Battalion, February 1943–February 1944—Exercise 'Flake,' February–August 1944—Move to Cornwall, September 1944–January 1945—The 4th Mobilise, February 1945—The 6th Battalion, 1943–1945—The 70th Battalion, 1943—The I.T.C., 1943–1945—Death of Major A. Hill-Walker, V.C., April 1945—The Comforts Fund.*

### XX    THE 58th AND THE 4th BATTALION IN HOLLAND AND GERMANY, 1945    326

*The 58th move to Belgium, 8th March–15th April—Move into Germany, 15th–20th April—Operations on the Elbe, 22nd–30th April—The Elbe to the Baltic, 1st–6th May—The Aftermath of Victory, 6th May–1st July—The 4th move to Holland, 11th–16th February—On the Maas, 17th February–2nd March—Across the Maas, 2nd–6th March—Preparations for the Rhine Crossing—The Rhine Crossing—Various Tasks, 25th March–8th May.*

### XXI    THE REGIMENT AFTER THE WAR, 1945–1948    333

*The 48th in India, May–December 1945—The 48th in Malaya, January 1946–February 1947—Homecoming of the 48th, April 1947—Final Ceremonies—The 58th at Göttingen, July 1945–June 1947—The 58th in Berlin, June 1947–January 1948—The Return of the Colours, October 1947—The 58th move to Austria, January 1948—The 4th Battalion in Germany, May 1945–February 1946—The 5th Battalion move into Austria, May 1945—Occupation, July 1945–September 1946—Disbandment, September 1946—Re-formation of the 5th Battalion—585 Searchlight Regt., R.A. (T.A.)—The I.T.C., 1945–1946—No. 48 P.T.C., 1946–1948—The Depot—The Comrades' Association—Post-war Reorganisation—The Reasons—The Solution—The Revised Solution—The Colonel of the Regiment—The Regimental War Memorial—Freedom of the Borough of Northampton, 8th June 1946.*

NOTES ON CHAPTERS    353

INDEX    442

# APPENDICES

| | | |
|---|---|---|
| I | The Colonels-in-Chief and the Colonels of the Regiment | 393 |
| II | Biographical Notes on Colonels | 394 |
| III | Succession List of Lieutenant-Colonels | 395 |
| IV | Succession List of Adjutants | 397 |
| V | The Mess Plate | 398 |
| VI | Notes on Organisation and Conditions of Service, Uniforms, Arms and Equipment, and Wireless | 399 |
| VII | Regimental Shooting Records, 1931–1948 | 405 |
| VIII | The 585th Searchlight Regiment (Northamptonshire) R.A. (T.A.), 1937–1948 | 417 |
| IX | The North Auckland Regiment, 1935–1948 | 420 |
| X | The 48th and 2/48th Battalions, Australian Military Forces, 1934–1948 | 422 |
| XI | The 58th Battalion (Essendon Rifles), Australian Military Forces, 1934–1948 | 425 |
| XII | The Lake Superior Regiment, 1940–1948 | 428 |
| XIII | The Regiment de la Rey, 1934–1948 | 430 |
| XIV | Honours and Awards, Waziristan, 1936–1937, Second World War, 1939–1945 | 433 |
| XV | The Victoria Cross | 441 |

# ILLUSTRATIONS

## Colour

| | Facing Page |
|---|---|
| The Centre Device of the Colours | 56 |
| Soldiers of the 58th and the 5th Battalion in Battle-dress | 162 |
| Soldiers of the 48th in Jungle Battle-dress | 256 |
| Reproduction of the Title Deed conferring the Freedom of the Borough of Northampton, 8th June 1946 | 350 |

## Monochrome

| | |
|---|---|
| H.R.H. The Duchess of Gloucester, C.I., G.C.V.O., G.B.E., Colonel-in-Chief, The Northamptonshire Regiment | *Frontispiece* |
| | *Facing Page* |
| Silver Jubilee Royal Review, Aldershot, 13th July 1935. The 58th March Past | 6 |
| The 48th on the March from Bannu to Razmak, 1936 | 16 |
| The Colonel-in-Chief presenting the Coronation Medal to Major Alan Hill-Walker, V.C., at the Depot, 1937 | 38 |
| The 48th Guard of Honour at the unveiling of the King George V Memorial, Patna, 1939 | 82 |
| Major-General G. St. G. Robinson, C.B., D.S.O., M.C., Colonel of the Regiment | 122 |
| The 58th receiving their Colours in Berlin, 1947 | 192 |
| The Granting of the Freedom of the Borough of Northampton, 8th June 1946 | 324 |
| Handing over of the Colours of the 48th at Northampton, 1947 | 336 |

# MAPS

| | |
|---|---|
| Operations of the 48th in Waziristan | 12 |
| France and Belgium, showing Routes of 58th and 5th Battalion | *facing p.* 50 |
| The 58th at Arras | 58 |
| The 58th at St. Eloi | 64 |
| Operations of the 58th in Madagascar | 101 |
| The 58th Night-attack on Antsirane | 104 |
| General Map, Northern Tunisia | 116 |
| Operations of the 5th Battalion in Tunisia | 126 |
| The Invasion of Sicily | 155 |
| General Map, Italy | *facing p.* 184 |
| The River Garigliano Area | 188 |
| The 58th in 'The Fortress,' Anzio | 198 |
| Monte la Pieve | 230 |
| Monte Spaduro | 235 |
| The 48th in Burma | 245 |
| The 48th at Kyaukchaw | 248 |
| The Silchar Track, to illustrate Operations of the 48th, April–July 1944 | 262 |
| Panorama Sketch, the Silchar Track | 264 |
| Panorama Sketch, Dome Area | 273 |
| The Budalin Area | 291 |
| The 48th at Budalin | 293 |
| The Budalin-Monywa Area | 297 |
| Monywa Operations, 13th–25th January 1945 | 299 |
| The 48th at Monywa, 19th–20th January 1945 | 302 |
| The Irrawaddy Crossing, air-photograph and trace | *facing p.* 308 |

# PREFACE

THE first volume of this history told the story of The Northamptonshire Regiment from 1742, the year of its foundation, to 1934.

In the course of those one hundred and ninety-two years the British Army fought in many wars, which varied in size from small colonial expeditions to what is now known as the First World War of 1914–1918. The period was one of great military progress and of marked changes in tactics, weapons and dress. The line of Wolfe's days had given way to the section columns of 1934: the 'Brown Bess' musket to the magazine rifle: the ornate red frock-coat, knee-breeches and stockings to drab, but serviceable, khaki.

This second volume deals with a period of only fourteen years, for half of which the British Commonwealth was engaged in the greatest struggle it had ever had for its existence. It tells the story of the Regiment in those years of apparent peace, when some men realised that war with Germany was inevitable; it continues that story through the years of endurance to the years of victory; it ends with the story of the beginning of the reconstruction of the Army after those years, and of the effect of that reconstruction on the Regiment.

# CHAPTER I

## THE REGIMENT, 1934-1935

*The 48th at Jullundur, 1934-1936—The 58th at Aldershot, 1934-1935—The 4th and 5th Battalions, 1934-1935—The Colours—The Colonel of the Regiment—The War Museum at Mons—The Locomotive 'The Northamptonshire Regiment'*

### *The 48th at Jullundur,* 1934-1936

AT the beginning of 1934 the 48th were still stationed at Jullundur, in the Punjab, to which place they had moved from Egypt at the end of 1932.

Jullundur was a good station, its only drawbacks, from the point of view of the Battalion, being that one company was almost permanently on detachment at Amritsar, and that, apart from a battery of Gunners, there were no British troops nearer than Lahore.

The general routine varied little from year to year. At the start of the hot weather, early in May, Battalion Headquarters, two companies, and the married families, used to move to Dalhousie in the Hills. After three months, these companies changed places with those which had remained in the Plains. Then, when the cool weather began early in October, the Hill party returned to Jullundur, and there, apart from the Amritsar detachment, the Battalion remained concentrated for training until the following May. Only in 1935 did events interfere with this programme. In that year communal strife broke out between Sikhs and Muslims in Lahore, the cause being a dispute over the ownership of a mosque. In July, as there was a danger of the trouble spreading, the Hill party had to move to Jullundur at short notice. However, things soon quietened down, and within a month they were able to return to Dalhousie.

The intensively cultivated country round Jullundur was unsatisfactory for training purposes. As a rule, therefore, company and battalion training was carried out from a camp near Hoshiarpur, in the foothills twenty miles to the north, where the Battalion stayed for some six weeks in October and November. Here the training area was good, and exercises against a battalion of Gurkha Rifles, usually encamped nearby, gave plenty of scope for friendly tactical rivalry. In addition to this, during their time at

Dalhousie, companies moved in turn to camp at Dayan Khund, two thousand feet higher up in the Hills, where they could practise mountain warfare.

When stationed in Egypt the 48th had won some successes at shooting, but they had never managed to get near to winning the blue riband of the Army Rifle Association, the Queen Victoria Trophy. Now, at Jullundur, they set out to win it, and thus to prove that they were the best shooting battalion in India. They were fortunate in having good ranges close to their lines, and they made full use of these. How full is best illustrated by the comment of an officer of the Indian Cavalry, who, visiting the ranges with the idea of seeing some of his own men, went away and reported that the whole of Asia was apparently occupied by the 48th.

To cut a long story short, a story of much encouragement by Commanding Officers backed by the hard work and enthusiasm of all ranks, in 1933 the 48th rose to sixth place. In the following year they won the Trophy, and this was but the beginning of a series of successes. They were still the holders when they left Jullundur, as the result of another win in 1935, and, as later chapters will show, that was not the end of the story.[1]

It is sometimes argued that success in competitions is no gauge of the general shooting efficiency of a battalion, since only a few experts are called upon to take part. This is not so, for the various competitions which score towards the Queen Victoria Trophy demand the participation of a large number, of all ranks and lengths of service. And during those years there was a great improvement in the standard of weapon-training throughout the Battalion; more than a third classified as marksmen in the annual courses, and the number of second-class shots decreased every year; in the whole three years there were only two third-class shots, and their fate is not recorded.

The lack of any other British units at Jullundur meant that, apart from cricket and hockey, at which games the Indian excels, the Battalion teams could find no opponents against whom to get practice. Nevertheless, they managed to secure their share of successes.

In 1934 they won the District competition for the Punjab Commission Cricket Cup, but were defeated in the next round by the I.A.S.C. at Rawalpindi. At football they lost the final of the Lahore District competition to the 1st Bn. The Leicestershire Regt.

In boxing they were always to the fore. After winning the District Championship in 1935, they scored another victory against the 2nd Bn. The Royal Sussex Regt. in the quarter-finals of the All-India Army and R.A.F. Championship, but in the semi-finals they were defeated by the Somerset Light Infantry.

In 1936 they lost in the first round to the 1st Bn. The King's Regt. only by the odd fight, and it was some consolation that their opponents went on to reach the All-India semi-finals. One of the 48th team, Pte. H. Baulch, won the All-India Services' feather-weight championship of the year.

What with these and other successes, it can be said that during their time in the Punjab the 48th maintained their reputation as a battalion that could hold its own in most forms of sport.

The celebration of the Silver Jubilee of H.M. King George V in 1935 was marked by the award of a commemorative medal. Twenty-four of these were allotted to the Battalion, and on the 5th June the names of those selected for the award were published, together with the following Battalion Order:

> The disposition of these Medals is entirely in the hands of the Commanding Officer, but it is laid down that in selecting individuals for the receipt of the Medal, primary consideration will be given in every case to long and distinguished service during the reign.
>
> The Commanding Officer has made his selection on the consideration that the most distinguished service a N.C.O. or man can have is service in the field, where he has risked his life and his health for his King and Country. Length of service speaks for itself.[a]

On the 6th February 1936 Lieut.-Col. F. W. L. Bissett, D.S.O., M.C., relinquished command, on appointment as an instructor at the Senior Officers' School, Sheerness. He was succeeded by Major W. G. A. Coldwell, D.S.O., who joined the Battalion on the 29th February.

In 1935 the Battalion had been told that they would probably move to Dacca during the trooping season of 1935–1936. The prospect was not an inviting one, for this place, in the terrorist area of Bengal, had little in its favour as a station for a British unit. So no disappointment was felt when it was announced that this move would not take place, and that the Battalion would remain at Jullundur for a fourth year.

Then came the news that their next station would be Razmak, in Waziristan; that they would go there during the 1936–1937 trooping season; and that after a year there they would be stationed at Delhi. Consequently, training in 1936 was devoted to fitting all ranks for the mountain warfare that lay ahead. In May the Commanding Officer took a tactical advanced party to Razmak, where they stayed for a month studying the problems which would confront the Battalion; meanwhile, companies at Dayan Khund practised long marches in hilly country, and got much help and sound advice on the many aspects of mountain warfare from the 2/4th P.W.O. Gurkha Rifles.

On the 18th October the advanced party left for Razmak, followed, four days later, by the main body of the Battalion. Shortly before they left they were inspected by the Commander of the Lahore District, Major-General B. R. Moberly. In his address to the Battalion he said:

> It is not often that a District Commander has the opportunity of knowing units in his District very well, but in the case of the 48th I feel that I do know you well, as I have seen a lot of you during the past two seasons in Dalhousie.
> . I know you to be a thoroughly efficient battalion, and I congratulate you again on your outstanding A.R.A. successes of the last two years, which showed a record to be proud of.
> I know that you will put up a fine show in Razmak, and that you will come down to Delhi in fine condition next winter, in time to take part in the ceremonies connected with the Coronation.
> I am very sorry to lose you, and I wish you all the best of luck in your new station.

On the departure of the Battalion from Jullundur, the Brigade Area Commander, Brig. G. C. B. Buckland, C.B., D.S.O., M.C., published the following Special Order:

> It is with much regret that the Brigade Area Commander says Good-bye to all ranks of the 1st Battalion The Northamptonshire Regiment.
> Their discipline and soldierly bearing have been an example to all units in the Brigade. Their prowess on the range has brought them success for two years running in the Queen Victoria Trophy. I know that I am voicing the wish of all the Brigade in wishing them a third win.
> Should the 1st Battalion The Northamptonshire Regiment be called upon to take part in active operations in Waziristan, I am sure they will give a good account of themselves.
> The best of good luck at Razmak to all who have been with us here, and all success to the 48th wherever they may be in future.

As will be seen, the 48th did not fail to fulfil the expectations of these two Commanders.

*The 58th at Aldershot, 1934–1935*

Meanwhile the 58th were well settled down at Aldershot, still, as it had been for many years, the chief military centre in Great Britain. Life there was strenuous, for in addition to the normal unit training, followed by higher formation training carried out as a rule in an area away from Aldershot, there was a succession of such events as the Aldershot Tattoo, which had become a national affair, the Command Horse Show, and the Small-Arms Meeting, to say nothing of a multitude of competitions embracing every form of military and sporting activity. Rivalry was keen, and none but a thoroughly fit, well-trained and well-organised battalion could hope to hold its own. All the more, then, might the 58th be proud of their record during the four years they spent in the Command.

To present a complete picture, it is as well to hark back to the period covered by the final chapter of the first volume of this history.

In 1932, their first year at Aldershot—and, be it remembered, a unit's first year at Aldershot was invariably a trying one, for all Commanders were critical of the new arrival—the 58th had won the Command Boxing Championship and the Duke of Connaught's Challenge Cup, the latter a test of horses and horsemanship open to teams of the mounted officers of Infantry battalions.[2] At the Army Rifle Association's Meeting at Bisley they had run second in the Worcestershire Cup for Lewis gunners, and had been well represented in the individual events.[1]

In the following year they had again won the Duke of Connaught's Cup, thus creating a record, since never before had the same unit won it for two years in succession. At the Command Horse Show their transport and chargers had won the Farnborough Cup. At the Command Small-Arms Meeting their teams had won two major events, and had been placed sixth in the Inter-Unit Championship.[1] When presenting the prizes after the Meeting, the G.O.C.-in-C., General Sir Charles Harington, first congratulated the winners and then specially mentioned the improvement made by the 58th since the previous year. The object of these competitions, he said, was to improve the shooting of the Army; the 58th had shown the real value of the training at Aldershot, and he commended their example to other units.

Soon after this, Sgt. Marshall, who had done much for shooting in the Battalion, won third place in the King's Medal at Bisley. It was the third time that he had qualified to shoot in this event.[1]

The 58th had already achieved much, but they were to achieve more. In June 1934 they rose to third place in the Inter-Unit Championship at the Command Small-Arms Meeting.[1] Two days later their team won the Duke of Connaught's Cup for the third time. In the Farnborough Cup at the Command Horse Show they were runners-up to the 2nd Bn. The Coldstream Guards. And at Bisley, in July, they had eight representatives in the King's Medal and the Army Hundred.

The year 1935 began well, with another victory in the Command Boxing Championship. After this it was a disappointment that they failed to record a fourth successive win in the Duke of Connaught's Cup and had to be content with taking second place to the Coldstream Guards. However, now that mechanisation has made the horse virtually extinct from a military point of view, it is unlikely that the 58th's record of three wins and one second place in four years will ever be equalled, let alone surpassed. That they accomplished this without any expert assistance from outside in the way of trainers is a great tribute to the officers who formed the teams, and to the grooms of the Regimental Transport who were responsible for the turnout of the horses and saddlery.[3]

The Command Small-Arms Meeting of the year might well be described as 'all 58th,' since of the seventeen matches in which they competed they won four, were second in six and gained no place lower than ninth in any event. They won the Evelyn Wood Cup for the second time in four years, and, best of all, were the winners of the Inter-Unit Championship.[1]

Speaking after the Meeting, the G.O.C.-in-C. referred to 'the very wonderful performance' of the 58th. In the individual matches, he said, they had scored 409 points, while the next unit, the 2nd Bn. The Coldstream Guards, got only 191. One very noticeable thing was that the winning Young Soldier (Pte. Horn of the 58th) did better than the trained private soldiers. He was told that his bolt action was almost unique in its efficiency, which showed the effect of good elementary instruction on shooting.

At the Command Horse Show the Battalion Transport won the principal event, the Infantry Transport Competition. It was only right that, at the prize-giving, the shield for this event should have been handed to the Transport Sergeant by General Knox, the Colonel of the Regiment.

On the 8th May 1935 Lieut.-Col. G. St. G. Robinson, D.S.O., M.C., gave up command of the Battalion, and was appointed Assistant Commandant of the Small-Arms School. As he had also commanded the 48th for two years, in 1917–1918, there was much which the Regiment owed to his leadership, for under him each battalion had increased the reputation it already had, the one in war, the other in peace. Major O. K. Parker, M.C., succeeded him in command.

On the 13th July the 58th took part in the Royal Review at Aldershot and were led past the King by the Colonel of the Regiment. It was a tribute to their smartness that *The Times* of the following day should have used their photograph to illustrate the parade.

The time had now come for the Battalion to leave Aldershot, and on the 5th November they entrained for Ballykinler in Northern Ireland. As they left, the G.O.C.-in-C., General Sir F. Gathorne-Hardy, telegraphed, 'Best of luck in your new station; you leave Aldershot to everyone's regret.'

The end of this chapter in the life of the 58th is best closed by two quotations from their Annual Inspection Report for 1935. The Commander of the 1st Division wrote: 'A fine battalion, and in every way up to the best standards of British Infantry. The men are of exceptionally good

Silver Jubilee Royal Review, Aldershot, 13th July 1935
The 58th March past
*The Times*

physique and appearance, the officers of a good and keen type. I am sorry to lose this reliable and efficient battalion. Fit for war in all respects.' To which the G.O.C.-in-C. added: 'A battalion that I am very sorry to see leave Aldershot. A fine battalion with a good body of officers.'

In fact, the 58th left Aldershot with a record and a reputation which it would be hard to equal.

## *The 4th and 5th Battalions*, 1934–1935

In peace-time the Territorial Army received little share of the moderate amount of limelight that fell upon the Army as a whole. Its officers and men carried out most of their training at hours when others, who may have been equally patriotic citizens but were not prepared to devote some of their spare time to training themselves for a national emergency, were enjoying leisure and recreation. Only on rare occasions, such as during their annual camps or at civic functions, did the T.A. appear before the public eye. To this the 4th and 5th Battalions were no exception, and though this account of their activities during the years of peace may appear to be brief, it conceals a story of much hard, unobtrusive work.

When this period of their history opens, the 4th, with Headquarters at Northampton, were commanded by Lieut.-Col. W. R. Styles, M.C. Their strength of 570, only 15 below establishment, did them much credit, for it was a time when recruits did not come forward readily.

In March 1934 Lieut.-Col. Styles finished his tenure of command, and was succeeded by Lieut.-Col. H. N. Scott-Robson, formerly of the Royal Scots Greys.

During these years the 4th were always at, or near, the top in those competitions in military subjects which were such a feature of the T.A. Their chief successes were in the Divisional Signalling Test of 1934, when they were second out of thirty-four teams; and in the Lewis Gun Competition for the Trevor Cup of 1935, won by the teams from 'C' and 'D' Companies.

Like the 48th and 58th, the 4th always produced good boxers. In 1934 their team won the 54th Divisional Championship for the fifth time in seven years, and followed this up with another win in 1935.

In the meantime the 5th, based on Peterborough, were under the command of Lieut.-Col. A. H. Mellows, T.D. His six years of command were coming to a close, and in November 1935 he handed over to Major W. E. Green, D.F.C., who was the last of the officers who had served with the old Huntingdonshire Battalion, formed in 1920.

The 5th, too, held their own in competitions, and in 1935 they, and the 4th, were the only units in the Eastern Command to figure in the results for the Dartmouth Cup, open to the signallers of all the Infantry units of the Territorial Army.

While individual Battalions had been making their own history, there were other matters of Regimental concern which should be recorded.

*The Colours*

The first volume of the Regimental History told of the approval, in 1933, of a device of a sprig of three maple leaves as the centre badge of the Regimental Colours. Since then further information has become available, giving the reasons which led to the selection of this device.

The first device to be selected was the Castle and the Key. This was not approved, for reasons given to Col. Muirhead by Sir Gerald Wollaston, then Garter King at Arms. The King wished the new devices to be distinctive and particular to the regiment concerned, and since honours such as the Castle were borne by several regiments none would be allowed to include them in the new device for the Colours. On being told that both the 48th and the 58th had been present at the Battle of Quebec, and that in no other regiment had both battalions been present, Sir Gerald referred to the coat-of-arms of the city of Quebec, and undertook to evolve a suitable device from it. A painting of this, as eventually approved, was presented to the Regimental Museum by Col. Muirhead.

Early in 1935, two brass plates were put up in the Church of the Holy Sepulchre at Northampton, describing the Colours reposing there and giving the dates on which they were laid up in the church.[4]

It is believed that, with three exceptions, all the old Colours of the Regiment which are still in existence now rest in the church. The exceptions are the Colours of the 58th in the church at Hartfield, in Sussex, and in the War Memorial Museum at Auckland, New Zealand, and one Colour of the 48th which hangs in the Salle des Drapeaux of the Invalides in Paris.

In the Salle des Drapeaux are five British Colours. Four of these are in so bad a state of repair as to make it impossible to identify them, but the fifth, a fragment about eighteen inches square, bears the device of a crown above the inscription 'XLVIII Regt.' According to information supplied by the Baronne de Mareuil, one of whose ancestors presented the Colour to the Invalides, it was captured in the Peninsular War by Maréchal des Logis Chef, De Dion D'Aumont, of the French 10th Hussars. The fragment is all that remains, as the result of a fire which broke out at the Invalides during the funeral of Marshal Sebastiani in 1851.

It seems almost certain that this Colour was one of those of the 2/48th, captured by the French at the Battle of Albuhera on the 16th May 1811. The Regimental History records that, on that occasion, three battalions, including the 2/48th, were taken by surprise by a charge of French cavalry against their flank and rear, were practically annihilated, and their Colours captured.

# THE REGIMENT, 1934-1935

In the year 1820, the Colours of the 2/48th bore only two battle-honours, 'Peninsula' and 'Talavera.' Possibly the fact of the loss of the Colours at Albuhera explains why they did not bear that honour also.

## The Colonel of the Regiment

In January 1935 the Colonel of the Regiment, Lieut.-General H. H. S. Knox, was honoured by the King with the Knighthood of the Order of the Bath.

In the same year it was with regret that the Regiment heard of the death of Major-General G. FitzHerbert Browne, Colonel of the Regiment from 1910 to 1925.

## The War Museum at Mons

In August 1935, at the request of the Burgomaster of the town of Mons in Belgium, a set of regimental buttons and badges was sent there, for inclusion in the collection in the War Museum of the insignia of all the units which had fought in the Battle of Mons in August 1914.[5]

In reply to an enquiry made in 1947, the Burgomaster stated that they had managed to save the collection from the hands of the Germans, and from damage by air-raids, during the years 1940-1945.

## The Locomotive 'The Northamptonshire Regiment'

In October 1935 there took place at Northampton a ceremony which was without precedent in the annals of the Regiment.

At the request of the London, Midland and Scottish Railway Company, one of their locomotives of the 'Royal Scot' class was named 'The Northamptonshire Regiment.' The christening ceremony was carried out by Lady Knox, who, after unveiling plaques of the Regimental badge fixed above the name-plates, said: 'I name this engine "The Northamptonshire Regiment," and wish her good running, safe journeyings and God speed.' In a speech of thanks to the Company after the ceremony, which was attended by detachments from the 58th, the 4th and 5th Battalions, and the Depot, the Colonel of the Regiment said that the engine was an embodiment of controlled power, a fitting emblem for a British Infantry Regiment.

A scale model of the engine was later presented by the Company to the Regimental Museum.

## CHAPTER II

## THE 48th IN WAZIRISTAN, 1936-1937

Razmak—The Move to Razmak—Operations of Razcol, November-December 1936—The 48th at Razmak, December 1936-March 1937—The Situation in Waziristan, March-May 1937—Operations of Razcol, June-August 1937—The 48th at Razmak, August-September 1937—Operations of Razcol, September-November 1937—Retrospect of the Campaign—The 48th leave Razmak (*see* Map on p. 12)

### Razmak

RAZMAK lies in the centre of Waziristan, a mountainous country some 4,000 to 5,000 square miles in extent. To the west is Afghanistan, to the east the Durand Line, the border of what was then British India. Situated on the border of the territories of two great tribes, the Mahsuds and the Wazirs, it owed its establishment as a permanent station, in 1923, to a petition by the Wazirs who wished for British support to restrain Mahsud aggression. Starting as a perimeter camp Razmak developed, and by the time the 48th went there it possessed most of the amenities of a normal Indian station, except for the fact that there was no feminine society; no women were allowed there, and the married families of the Battalion were relegated to Dalhousie.

The garrison of Razmak normally consisted of a brigade of one British and five Indian Army Infantry Battalions, Tochi Scouts, Artillery, Engineers and Services. But though Razmak was nominally a peace station, the turbulence of the tribesmen frequently necessitated the transformation of the brigade into 'Razcol,' a column of all arms capable of moving out at short notice, and of staying out for an indefinite length of time, to deal with those who were causing trouble; on these occasions two battalions always remained behind to guard the camp.

So Razmak was a good test of a battalion's ability to march, shoot, fight and generally look after itself, more especially as the tribesmen were opponents who had to be treated with the greatest respect, for they were quick to take advantage of any error in tactics.

### The Move to Razmak

The 48th left Jullundur on the 22nd October 1936 in two trains, which took them to Mari Indus. Thence, after a day in the Rest Camp, they moved in three parties by narrow-gauge railway to Bannu, and, after spending the 27th in preparing for the marches which lay ahead, set forth for Razmak on the following day.[1]

The first two days took the Battalion the twenty-four miles to Mir Ali. The next three stages, to Tal-in-Tochi, Damdil and Razani, totalled thirty-six miles, and involved a steady, though easy climb the whole way. By now the troops were in excellent marching trim and, though the final stage of fourteen miles from Razani to Razmak meant a climb of some two thousand feet, the 48th entered the camp on the 2nd November as though they were on a drill parade, the Drums of the 1st Bn. The East Yorkshire Regt. and the Band of the 4/8th Punjab Regt. playing them in.

The physical fitness of the Battalion can be judged by the fact that, apart from nine cases of unavoidable sickness, only one man had fallen out on this seventy-four-mile march.

*Operations of Razcol, November–December* 1936

Having relieved the East Yorkshire Regt. and settled down in barracks, the 48th busied themselves in learning as much as they could about mountain warfare in a short time. For they had been warned to be ready to move out with Razcol on the 6th November.

On this occasion the intention was to exercise the right of the Government of India to move troops through the Khaisora Valley, under an agreement made in 1935 with the inhabitants, the Tori Khel tribe. Before Razcol started there were reports that the Faqir of Ipi, who was a perennial nuisance, was trying to create trouble, and it was thought that they might meet with opposition; according to plan they were to return to Razmak on the 29th, but this was to be one of those occasions on which things did not proceed as planned.

On this operation, besides the 48th, Razcol included the 5/12th Frontier Force Regt. (Guides Infantry), the 6/13th R. Frontier Force Rifles, the 1/9th Gurkha Rifles and the 22nd Mountain Brigade, R.A. Both the C.O. and his acting Adjutant, Lieut. Osborne-Smith, were in hospital when the column marched out on the 23rd November, and until the former rejoined on the 21st December the Battalion was commanded by Major Nailer, with Capt. Furminger officiating as Adjutant.

The first two days' marches, which took the column to Gardai Camp and then along the stony, sandy bed of the Khaisora River to Damdil Camp, were uneventful. Not so the next day.

Reports indicated that the Faqir was at Biche Kashkai, where he had collected a small following of Tori Khel Wazirs and some Mahsuds. Razcol was to move on this village from the west, while Tocol, the Bannu Brigade column, approached it from Mir Ali, to the north. Serious opposition was not expected.

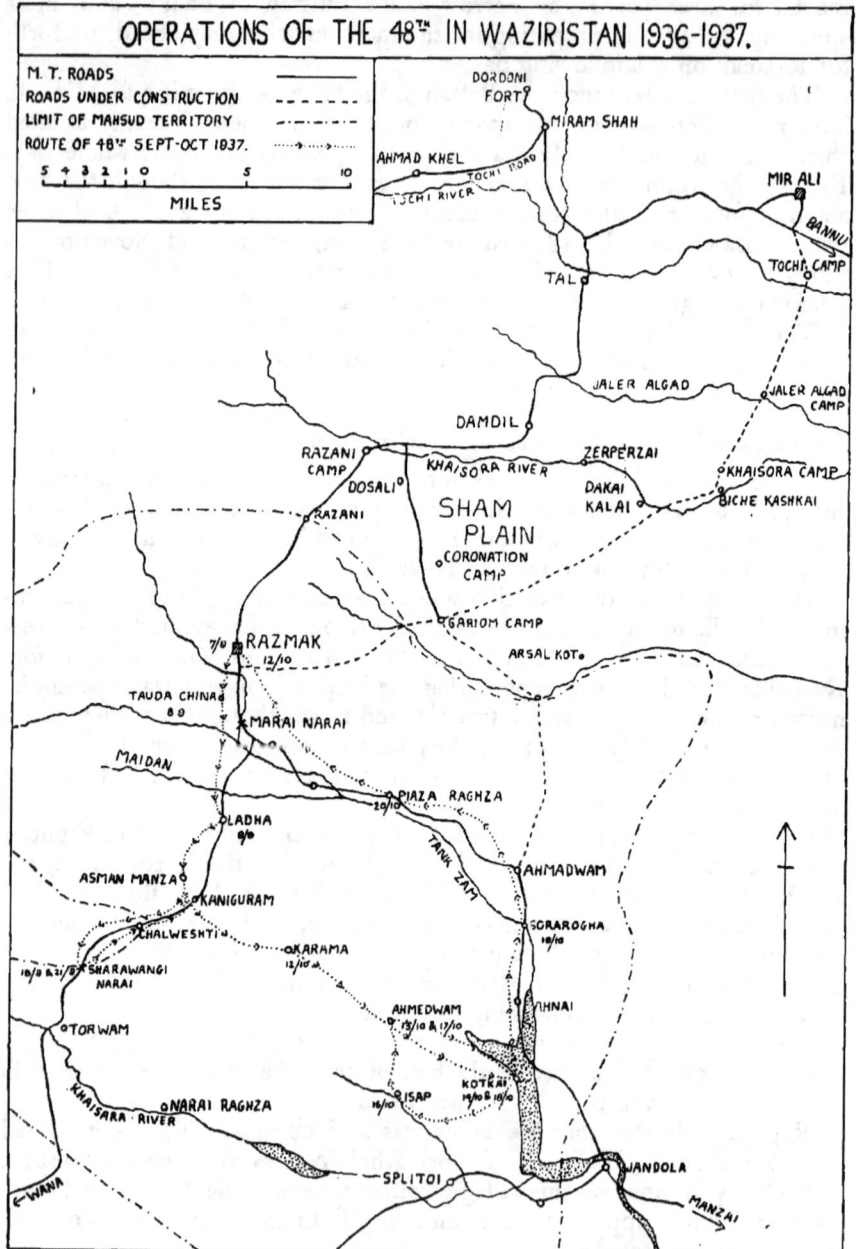

The next move started at 0800 hours on the 25th, the 48th being in the main body of the column. Three miles out from Damdil the sound of artillery fire showed that something was afoot. Shortly after midday the 48th were called upon to start piqueting, and Battalion H.Q. came under fire. At this point the valley was narrow and winding, with high, steep cliffs on either side, and tribesmen, very well concealed on both flanks, were making things unhealthy.

To begin with, 'A' Company, well covered by the Tochi Scouts, established four piquets. Then 'B,' assisted by the Scouts on a high ridge to their right and supported by observed artillery and machine-gun fire, successfully attacked and piqueted a steep feature. In doing this they had no casualties, but some had narrow shaves; Lieut. Bennett, only recently promoted, had one of his newly acquired stars shot from off his shoulder.

'B' Company had just started to consolidate the position when they were relieved by the Scouts, and the advance continued towards the village of Dakai Kalai. After the enemy had been shelled out of this, 'C' Company established piquets on the far side. In doing this the 48th incurred their first casualties, one man, Pte. Presland, being killed and three others wounded.

By this time the Battalion had been used up as piqueting troops, it was almost dark and Biche Kashkai was still three or four miles ahead. So Battalion H.Q. and 'A' Company (less Major Winkler, the Company Commander, and their original piquet) pushed on towards camp; the piquets which were still out would be withdrawn by the rear-guard, the 1/9th Gurkhas, by means of lamp and whistle signals, since the fall of darkness prohibited the use of the normal flag signals.

In due course all the piquets were got in without difficulty, except for one of 'C' Company's, commanded by L/Sgt. Wyatt. This was fired upon from both flanks, and had three casualties, none, fortunately, stretcher cases. By 2100 hours the whole Battalion was in camp.

Two of the Signallers attached to 'A' Company, Ptes. Rose and Millard, were awarded the Military Medal for their gallantry on this day. One piquet did not receive the order to withdraw, and these two men made their way, in the dark and through hostile and unfamiliar country, to the rear-guard, and then returned to the piquet with a verbal order for the withdrawal. It was only within the last twelve months that Pte. Rose had begun his man's service.

The 48th's first day in action in Waziristan had been a long one, but they finished it as they had begun it, in good heart. That they had done so well all that they had been called upon to do spoke much for their spirit and for the earlier training they had had.

The opposition which Tocol had encountered had prevented them from reaching the camp at Biche Kashkai on the 25th and they had been forced to halt for the night some four miles away. On the morning of the 26th two Razcol battalions went to help Tocol in, while the 48th stayed in camp and manned the piquets and part of the perimeter. In the afternoon they and the 1/9th Gurkhas took up positions about a mile outside the camp, covering a battery while it shelled Dakai Kalai, the focal point of most of the previous day's trouble, and returned after the village had been dealt with satisfactorily.

The next day's operations were to prove long and trying. Both columns were to move to Mir Ali, Tocol forming the advanced guard and Razcol the flank and rear-guard.

The 48th were given the task of protecting the left flank, and all went smoothly until they were about six miles short of Mir Ali, when they received orders to halt. The rear-guard was having a difficult time, and to assist it the 48th counter-marched, and occupied a high ridge with two rifle companies and the support company. Though all companies engaged targets they were not seriously involved, and after three hours the advance was resumed, Mir Ali being reached at 1930 hours. It had been a fourteen-hour day, they had been on their feet for fourteen miles of difficult going, and had fought in spasms with very little respite, and all were very tired by the time that they got into camp.

There was now an interlude from this type of operation. For centuries, the development of communications has been one of the principal means of ensuring control of a hostile country, and nowhere did this apply more than on the North-West Frontier. So, after two days in Mir Ali for cleaning-up and reorganisation, both columns started work on the construction of a road from there to Biche Kashkai.

The Battalion spent the next three weeks either in pick-and-shovel work —hard work too, for the ground was very rocky—or in taking their turn at protecting other units at work, or in guarding the camp. As the road progressed, so did the column establish more advanced camps, named Tochi, Jaler Algad and Khaisora; the dates on which these were occupied and their distances from Mir Ali, give an idea of the rate of progress of the road; 5th December—four miles; 9th December—ten miles; 18th December—thirteen miles.

The task of road-making was not as dull as it sounds. Before each day's work the road had to be 'opened up'—in other words, a considerable force had to go out and establish piquets on commanding heights, an operation which often involved fighting. The passage of M.T. convoys between camps necessitated similar operations, only in this case troops had to move out from both of the camps concerned, until they had made contact with each other.

The scale of operations can be judged from the fact that the original force proved to be inadequate, and another brigade, the 2nd, from Bannu, had to be brought in, and Razcol, temporarily assuming the name of

Khaicol, was strengthened by the addition of two battalions, the 2/11th Sikhs and the 2/13th F.F.R., and a company of light tanks. Life was hard, and to add to its unpleasantness the weather was very wet, sometimes for days at a time, and there was, of course, no artificial means of drying sodden clothing.

The whole affair was, in fact, just another example of those duties which the Army, and the other Services, have to carry out so often in 'peacetime,' unobtrusively, without the glamour of headlines in the Press, probably without even a mention. The only reward the knowledge of a task well done, strengthened perhaps by the commendation of a Commander, such as the words of the Brigadier to the C.O. of the 48th on the 15th December, after they had returned to camp on completion of one of their many days of piqueting duty: 'I want to congratulate your men on the excellent show they put up. I was watching your movements throughout the day. They went out of camp and took up their positions well and quickly, and they carried out the withdrawal excellently.'

With the completion of the road, the Tori Khel began to show signs of submission, and the time came for Razcol to move back to Razmak.

The Faqir was reported to have collected 250 followers, and opposition was expected, more especially at Dakai Kalai. The intention was that the 2nd Brigade, which had moved up to Khaisora Camp on the 21st December, should advance to this village on the day following. Razcol, now back to its original composition, was then to pass through, and advance along the Khaisora Valley to Damdil, fourteen miles away. Should this prove to be impossible during the hours of daylight, the column was to halt for the night at Zerperzai, four miles short of Damdil.

The 2nd Brigade reached their objective with little opposition, and Razcol, which had left camp an hour after them, at 0700 hours, duly went through. The advance was rapid, and after having safely negotiated a gorge where there might well have been trouble, the 48th hoped for a quiet journey. However, opposition was encountered farther on, and although this was soon overcome there were still four miles to be covered when Zerperzai was reached, and time was getting short. Some further resistance was dealt with by the machine-gunners, after which the remainder of the march was uneventful, and the last of the Battalion's piquets reached Damdil Camp at 1745 hours.

Leaving the rest of Razcol there, the 48th and the Guides then returned to Razmak in two stages, entering camp on Christmas Eve in a snowstorm, which made them all the more grateful for hot baths, fires and roofs over their heads, comforts they had not seen for a month. That night the two battalions took over the protection of Razmak from the 1/3rd Gurkhas and the 4/8th Punjabis, who had been 'holding the fort' whilst the column had been out, and who now went to rejoin it at Damdil.

So far as the 48th were concerned the Khaisora Valley operations were over, though fighting continued spasmodically until the 17th January, when Razcol returned to Razmak.

During their month on column the Battalion had lost one killed and fourteen wounded, out of a total for the whole force involved of 38 killed and 129 wounded. To offset this, the enemy were known to have had at least 119 killed and 186 wounded.

From the remarks of some of their Commanders it is clear that, in this 'Small War,' the 48th had added as much to the reputation of the Regiment as had any of their forebears in the past.[2]

*The 48th at Razmak, December 1936–March 1937*

The Battalion was now able to enjoy a spell of rest, though that word could not be taken too literally at Razmak. For the tribesmen never rested, and occasionally reminded the garrison of their presence by sniping at games of hockey and football. And, as a matter of course, the 48th had to take their turn at holding the piquets which protected the camp, a task which never stops on the Frontier.

Nevertheless, they managed to play off many of those inter-company competitions which mean so much in the life of a battalion. Their boxers were to the fore as usual. After winning the Peshawar District Tournament, they went on to beat the South Wales Borderers, the Rawal Pindi District champions, and so qualified to meet their old opponents, the King's Regt., in the All-India quarter-finals, but once more, after a series of close fights, the King's were just too good for them.

Before leaving Jullundur the 48th had fired some of the matches which counted towards the Queen Victoria Trophy. The two which were still outstanding were fired at Razmak early in 1937, and when the results came out the Battalion found that they were the winners for the third consecutive year. This was indeed a fine performance, all the more so because shooting at Razmak had to be done under active-service conditions, with piquets on the surrounding hills to protect the firers from the attentions of the tribesmen, and on a range where the wind varied in strength and direction from minute to minute. It was a real test of nerves and skill, and proved that they were not merely fair-weather shots.[3]

*The Situation in Waziristan, March–May, 1937*

The Khaisora Valley campaign had ended in the temporary pacification of the Tori Khel. The road had been built, and hostages and arms had been surrendered. But the Faqir of Ipi had not been evicted from his lair at Arsal Kot, and so long as he remained there he was a potential source of trouble. His policy was one of looting whenever and wherever possible, and since, on the Frontier, the word 'loot' had an irresistible attraction, the

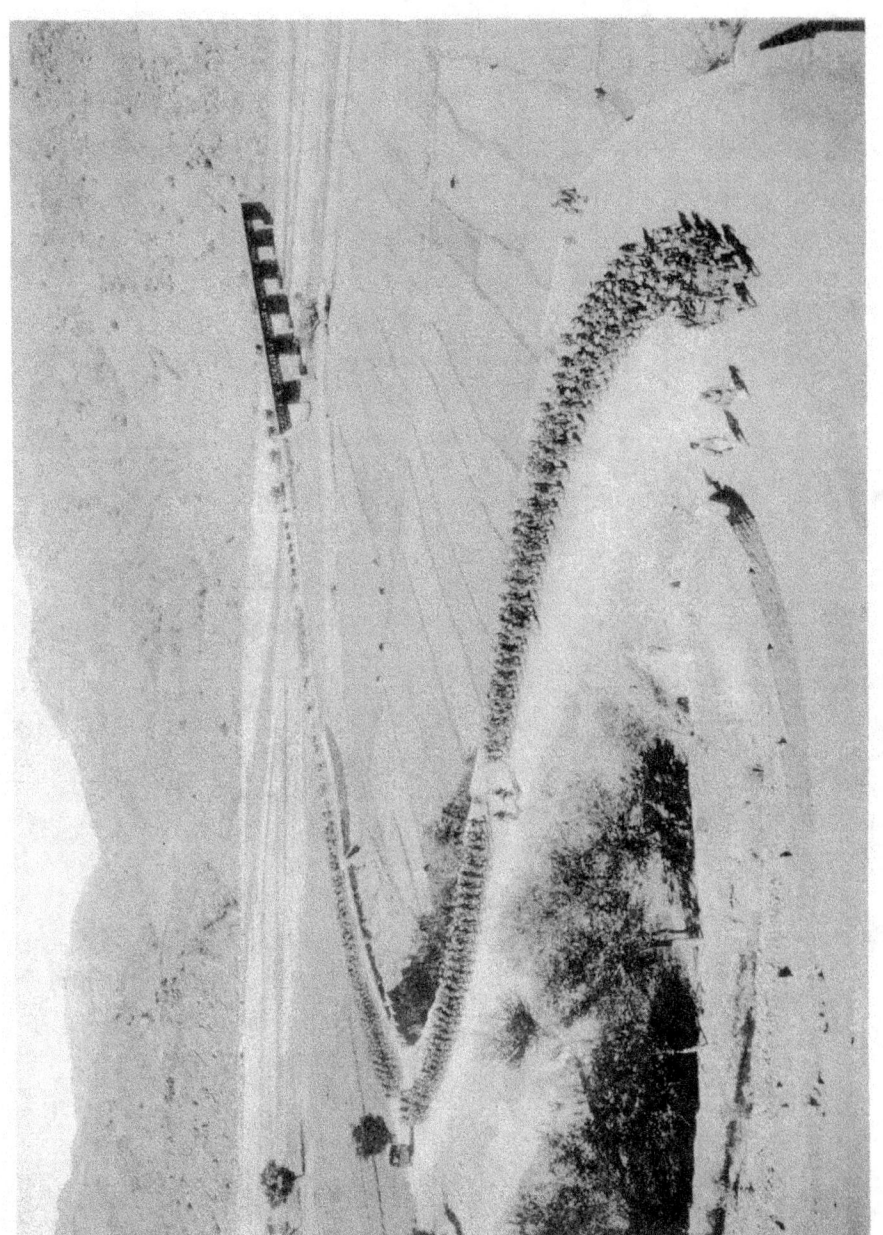

The 48th on the march from Bannu to Razmak, 1936

bad men of Waziristan, a certain number of Mahsud hotheads and a considerable following of Afghans, flocked to his banner.

Many hostile acts were committed, and the Bannu–Razmak road became the scene of murder and brigandage, and had to be closed to all military traffic other than escorted convoys. Reinforcements were sent to Waziristan from British India, and operations started on a larger scale than before.

At first convoys were run from Bannu and Mir Ali to Razmak, protected by troops from Mir Ali, Damdil and Dosali, the Razmak Brigade covering them almost daily on the last stage of their journeys. On the 29th March the 2nd Brigade met with stiff opposition from a lashkar of an estimated strength of 800 when they were opening the road towards Dosali. This, combined with the action of the Tori Khel in blowing up bridges and culverts, led to the closing of the Bannu road to all traffic, and Razmak's only means of road communication with the outside world was through Jandola and Dera Ismail Khan, passing through Mahsud territory.

On the 8th April a convoy left Razmak for Manzai, under the command of Major Nailer who was on his way to England. This was the last to leave the station for some time, for on the next day a convoy was attacked between Manzai and Wana and suffered heavy casualties, including several British officers. This action closed the only road remaining open to traffic, and, except for communication by air, the garrison of Razmak was now isolated. To add insult to injury the pipe-line was cut, though a well just outside the perimeter provided a strictly rationed supply of water. Continual attacks were made against the perimeter at night.

Throughout the second half of April, and May, Razcol was out on reconnaissance duty as often as four and five times a week. The 48th took part in most of these operations, and were fortunate to suffer no casualties.

In May the centre of interest shifted to the area round Damdil and Dosali. On the 12th of that month Tocol and the 1st Brigade moved by night towards the Sham Plain, occupying it on the next day and establishing a camp, suitably named Coronation Camp. This was too much for the Faqir and for some of his adherents; the plain was the largest grazing-ground in Waziristan for the flocks of the Tori Khel, and its occupation sent many of the tribe back to their homes. Furthermore, the Faqir had to leave Arsal Kot, and suffered much loss of prestige when, on the 28th May, the troops reached and burnt it.

In the meantime the daily piqueting from Razmak went on. Rumour had it that the road was to be reopened for convoys. On the 2nd June the 48th were out on road-protection duty, when a light tank hove in sight, followed by a string of lorries. The road was once more open, and it was a long time before the Battalion forgot the sight of the Derby Day procession into Razmak.

## HISTORY OF THE NORTHAMPTONSHIRE REGIMENT

*Operations of Razcol, June–August* 1937

After the success of the Sham Plain operation, it was decided that the next step was to send troops into Mahsud territory, with the object of demonstrating our ability to move therein at will. Though many of them had fought for the Faqir, they had been careful not to do so within their own territorial limits.

Consequently, on the 7th June, Razcol, composed of the 48th, the 1/3rd Gurkha Rifles, the 6/13th R. Frontier Force Rifles and the 5/12th Frontier Force Regt. (Guides), left Razmak and camped at Tauda China. The following day's camp, at Piazha Raghza, was an old one and there was little wall-building to be done, but water was a difficulty, mules having to fetch it from a nullah 500 feet below. Early on the 9th the 48th and the 1/3rd Gurkhas set out to piquet the road towards Sorarogha, to help Tocol in from that place. The day's piqueting was hard work, one platoon of 'C' Company taking a full hour to scale an almost inaccessible peak, a climb which involved the negotiation of a most difficult cliff face.

Razcol and Tocol now moved to Tauda China, where the camp had been enlarged to accommodate both columns, and on the following day Tocol left for Razmak. Their departure involved the reconstruction of the perimeter wall, an afternoon's work for the 48th and the 6/13th. Sniping had been a nightly occurrence at all the camps, a nuisance rather than a danger, but on this afternoon a burst of sniping hit six of the 48th's mules, and a tin of dripping upon which one of the cooks was seated. The artillery soon dispersed the snipers.

On the 12th June an early start was made for Ladha, and there Razcol remained until the 21st, conducting several reconnaissances towards Kaniguram and elsewhere, all without incident. Apart from the heat, Ladha was a reasonably comfortable camp, and tents were available. There was time for some sport, snow trout being found in the stream near the water-point, but the catches made with improvised rods, and, in a less orthodox way, with mosquito-nets, were not large.

Tocol had now returned to Ladha, and on the 21st piqueted Razol half-way to Chalweshti, Razcol doing the same for them on the next day. Both columns were then established there, in a camp which was muddy owing to recent heavy rain, and in which a large number of piquets were necessary on account of the commanding ground in the vicinity.

The plan for the next two days was for both columns to move to Torwam, some ten miles distant. The forecast was that resistance was to be expected, and this proved to be correct.

Early on the 23rd Tocol began to piquet Razcol out. The country, particularly on the left flank, was covered with thick scrub, limiting vision to ten or twenty yards in parts, and was very precipitous. This suited enemy tactics well, for it enabled them to lie up near to the road without the slightest chance of being seen. Fighting started within a few miles of Chalweshti, the enemy resisting stubbornly and showing a disinclination to allow themselves to be dislodged. Tocol, assisted by the South Waziristan Scouts, bore the brunt of the day's fighting, which cost the two columns some forty casualties. When Razcol passed through Tocol they met with considerably less resistance, and reached Torwam without much difficulty. Unfortunately, Lieut.-Col. Grant, commanding the 5/12th, was killed by a sniper on the Sharawangi Narai.

On the next day Razcol assisted Tocol into Torwam without incident, the 48th having one man wounded, and on the 25th the column from Wana joined the other two there.

The reason for this concentration of columns was that one Sher Ali was still in the area, with a lashkar about 250 strong, and it had been decided that it was time that he was taught a lesson. Accordingly, on the 29th June the three columns moved out of camp before dawn.

The plan was for Wanacol to advance along the road towards the Sharawangi Narai, with the object of attracting the lashkar in that direction. Razcol and Tocol were then to converge upon the enemy from the west and south respectively. To the 48th was allotted the task of taking Razcol's first objective, a long rocky ridge lying to the east of the road and commanding it, and separated from it by a broken, scrub-covered nullah. The 1/3rd Gurkhas were to secure the right flank.

The Battalion took their objective without difficulty, the enemy firing only a few shots. Machine-guns were then moved up to assist the further advance of the Guides and to cover the movements of the 2/4th Gurkhas (old friends of Jullundur and Dalhousie days) of Tocol on the left. They arrived at the right time, for a battery of mountain guns flushed the enemy from their hiding-places, and the machine-gunners were able to engage good targets in the open.

The 2/4th now advanced in the face of considerable fire, and hand-to-hand fighting ensued in which they inflicted many casualties on the enemy. The 48th were able to help them and that evening a note of thanks was received from their Commanding Officer for the 'timely and valuable help' of the machine-gunners.

Meanwhile the Guides had passed through the 48th to the ridges beyond and were engaged in mopping up small parties of tribesmen, and farther to the left Tocol were doing good work.

At about midday both columns began to withdraw. In Razcol the Guides and the 6/13th withdrew through the 48th, the 6/13th to a position from which they could cover the eventual withdrawal of the Battalion. Here they were joined by the 48th machine-guns.

When the time came, the 48th carried out their withdrawal without wasting time, since it was certain that the enemy would occupy their positions as soon as they had been vacated. Bullets soon started to splash round the feet of the troops, and one platoon might have been cut off but for the action of a local 'lay-back' which met an enemy outflanking movement with effective rifle fire. The artillery, and the machine-guns of the 48th, materially helped the Battalion to get across an extremely unpleasant and difficult piece of country.

The result of the day's operations was satisfactory. Sher Ali's lashkar was completely routed, 55 being killed and many more wounded, while the two columns only suffered 8 casualties, all among the Indian other ranks.

On the following day Razcol and Tocol carried out a reconnaissance to Turabez, seven miles west of Torwam, noteworthy for the fact that no white man had ever before entered this area. That night they received orders to return to Chalweshti on the 1st July.

The 48th, detailed as 1st echelon piqueting troops, were due to move off at 0500 hours, so tents were struck on the previous evening. As ill luck would have it, torrential rain fell that night, soaking everyone and everything. However, they moved out at the appointed time, and the negligible amount of resistance encountered, even at the Sharawangi Narai, showed how effective had been the action against Sher Ali. That evening, after they had got into camp, heavy rain again fell. The troops, true to type, sang.

Four days were now spent at Chalweshti, the only incident being an attack on one of the piquets held by the Scouts. On the preceding night this piquet had been held by the 48th, and an attempt had then been made to cut it out. Both attempts failed, with casualties to the enemy.

The 5th July saw both columns leaving the camp, with no regrets, for the ground was now a quagmire. Starting on the same road, Razcol branched off to Asman Manza, while Tocol continued by Ladha to Razmak. Razcol's new camp was sited on a high plateau overlooking the large town of Kaniguram, and was on ground which dried quickly after rain. The month they spent there was employed in minor reconnaissances and road-protection duties. There was little sniping of the camp, but that did not mean that the tribesmen were asleep. One night a most determined attack was made on a piquet held by the 1/3rd Gurkha Rifles. A lucky bomb disabled most of the garrison, and despite a most gallant resistance many were killed or wounded.

In due course Razcol and Tocol changed places. Razcol's first day's march, on the 7th August, was uneventful; the second was not. After a short halt at Tauda China, to water animals, the advance continued at noon. Soon afterwards the Guides and the 1/3rd Gurkhas took over piqueting duties from the 48th, and a burst of firing to the east soon showed that the tribesmen were on the alert.

It may seem strange that a strong column could have its advance seriously hindered by fifty or sixty Pathans. But each one of those Pathans was an expert at making use of ground and cover and was able to conceal himself on the highest and most inaccessible ground, often in thick scrub where his position could only be guessed and not seen, and was an excellent marksman. Add to these the difficulties of the country to the attacker, and the wonder is, not that the tribesmen could impose delay, but rather that trained British and Indian troops could defeat them on their own ground.

So it was in this case. There was some delay, then, with artillery and machine-gun support, the necessary piquets were occupied and the advance was resumed. By 1830 hours the column was back in Razmak. Casualties had been very light, Lieut. Green being the only one in the 48th, and he was able to remain at duty.

After nine weeks of hard living the Battalion appreciated the prospect of hot meals and hot baths. They had earned them, as they had earned further praise from their Brigade Commander.[4]

### *The 48th at Razmak, August–September* 1937

While Tocol had been in Razmak they had been working on the construction of a new road to Gariom. It was now Razcol's turn to carry on with this work, and for the next month there was little variation in the 48th's weekly programme. For four days they toiled with pick and shovel, after blasting had made the ground workable; for two days they protected the road; on one day, Sunday, they rested. And on every day there were the camp guards and piquets to be found as a matter of course.

### *Operations of Razcol, September–November* 1937

On the 7th September the 48th, the 1/9th Gurkha Rifles and the 4/8th Punjab Regt. received orders to move to camp at Tauda China, whence they were to carry out road-protection duties for about seven days. A few hours after they had reached the new camp, on the 8th, they were surprised to find themselves joined by the 6/13th, this adding force to the rumour that they would be away from Razmak for a considerably longer period.

After a night of heavy and continuous sniping the column started out early on the 9th for Ladha. The 48th were advanced guard, and by 1100 hours the road had been piqueted.

The enemy seemed determined to obstruct the advance, and No. 6 Platoon of 'B' Company, commanded by 2/Lieut. Meredith of the Unattached List, Indian Army, which was covering the Marai Narai bend in the road, received particular attention. Sniping was continuous and accurate, and it was not long before L/Cpl. Jarvis was mortally wounded. The country round the piquet was covered by thick scrub, and though individual tribesmen were difficult to locate accurately casualties were inflicted on them by rifle and light-automatic fire. The Gunners did all that they could to help, but the steepness of the ground, and the proximity of the enemy to our own troops, prevented their fire from being as effective as usual.

By the time the piquet had been under continuous fire for six hours they had suffered further casualties, Pte. Nind and a Jemadar F.O.O. of the 4th Mountain Battery killed, and four of the platoon wounded. They were due to start withdrawing at 1430 hours, but just as the rear-guard, the 1/9th Gurkhas, arrived on the road below a heavy storm blotted out visual communication for about ten minutes. Eventually the piquet received the permissive order to withdraw, by means of lamp signal, and were greatly helped by the fire of two light tanks which came into action for that purpose. The tribesmen were quick to follow up, but fell into a trap; a party of Gurkhas, well hidden in a fold in the ground, opened effective fire and stopped them. The other piquets were withdrawn without difficulty, and in due course the Battalion reached Ladha Camp.

Much praise is due to all the troops who took part in this action, more especially to the platoon of the 48th which had held its piquet for more than seven hours under extremely trying conditions. The awards received for gallantry were well-earned. One man, Pte. Letts, was awarded the D.C.M. Though wounded early in the day he insisted on staying with the piquet, frequently exposing himself to fire in helping to locate the enemy. When the Jemadar was wounded he fell in an exposed position, and Letts dashed out and brought him in to safety. In previous operations he had shown conspicuous courage. Two others, Ptes. Clarke and Lee, received the M.M. They were members of a L.M.G. section, of which Pte. Clarke took command after the section commander had been killed. Both men, though wounded, stayed with the piquet and kept their gun in action throughout the day, often in exposed positions, displaying complete disregard of their personal safety in their devotion to duty.

In addition to these men, 2/Lieut. Meredith and Lieut. Rawlins were subsequently mentioned in despatches for their good work on that day.

After a week in Ladha, during which the 4th found the Guard of Honour for the Army Commander when he held a jirga, the column moved to Asman Manza, their camping-ground earlier in the year, on the 17th September. There they spent the next few weeks on the usual tasks; helping Tocol in and out, opening the road to Ladha and making a passable track round Kaniguram. 'A' Company had a long day on the 10th October, when they were out from 0415 hours to 1900 hours, helping to piquet the road for the Army Commander's visit to Wana. There was no question of an eight-hour day in Waziristan.

While in this camp the immediate awards for the action of the 8th September were announced. The friendly feeling which existed between units was shown by the congratulations received by the 48th from the rest of Razcol; and by the invitation from the Gurkha officers of the 1/9th for the recipients of the awards, and other representatives of the Battalion, to celebrate the event in their Mess.

On the 12th October Razcol left Asman Manza for a cross-country tour. Since all ports of call were to be off the road, the Battalion travelled with the lightest possible scale of baggage and on hard rations. The first three days took them to Karama, Ahmedwam and Kotkai Scout Post, and were arduous; cross-country movement, combined with piqueting, was a strenuous affair, calling for complete physical fitness and, at the first two halting-places, the perimeter walls had to be built up from ground-level. So the observance of the 15th as a holiday was welcomed.

The next place to be visited was in the Jabil area, recently bombed by the R.A.F. to deter the inhabitants from the truculence of which they had shown signs. The 48th were flank-guard and had about the hardest march they had had for some time, and that was saying a good deal. And even when they reached Isap, work on defences was not finished until after dark, so they were glad of a quiet night.

Returning to Ahmedwam and Kotkai Scout Post, Razcol reached Sorarogha on the 19th. They now felt that they were heading well for Razmak, but the nine miles to Piaza Raghza on the following day involved much difficult piqueting; nor did the night allow of much rest, for the camp was viciously sniped and the 48th had one of their Indian followers badly wounded and lost several mules.

Only the last lap now remained. On the 20th October the 6/13th started piqueting the road by moonlight, and by first light Razcol was on its way, the 48th being rear-guard. There were fifteen miles to cover, mostly over rough and stony ground, but by the evening the column was back in Razmak.

The 48th had not quite finished. On the 28th November they moved out to Shawali Camp with two other battalions, their rôle being the protection of part of the route to be traversed by the Commander-in-Chief, who was touring the newly completed roads of Waziristan, a task which required the services of 10,000 troops in all. The piqueting was done on the 29th, and on the following day the column returned to Razmak. The distance was seventeen miles, at least ten of them uphill, and it was one of the toughest marches of the year; but not a man fell out, the Battalion covered the last four miles in fifty minutes, and marched into barracks with light hearts and the hope, which was fulfilled, that they had completed their last column in Waziristan.

*Retrospect of the Campaign*

The campaign of 1936–1937 in Waziristan had achieved much. How much can be judged from the Special Order of the Day, published on the 5th December by General Sir John Coleridge, the Force Commander:

> On the break up of Wazirforce I wish to express my high appreciation of the fine work done by all ranks throughout this arduous campaign. In battle the enemy has been so severely and so successfully dealt with that only a few small hostile bands remain in the field, and the majority of the leaders are either fugitives, or are in hiding. Our columns have penetrated the greater part of Waziristan to an unprecedented extent, and the country has been further opened by the construction of over 100 miles of motoring roads. . . .
>
> I am honoured by having commanded so fine a force, and thank you all . . . for your cheerfulness, your high sense of duty, and your unremitting efforts. This is a record of which you may well be proud.

It is interesting to compare some figures of the campaign with those of the Tirah operations in which the 48th had taken part forty years before.

In the Tirah, operations lasted for approximately six months; in Waziristan for nearly a year.

In the Tirah, some 52,000 combatant troops, followers and civilians in military employment were engaged; in Waziristan, 61,000.

In the Tirah, casualties in action totalled 288 killed, 853 wounded; in Waziristan, up to the end of October, 242 killed, 685 wounded.

Most striking of all are the comparative figures of deaths from disease, showing as they do the immense progress made in medical treatment and in the training of troops in methods of hygiene. In the Tirah, these amounted to 1,916; in Waziristan to 74.

It is in operations such as these that close friendship is made between battalions. More so, perhaps, on the Frontier than anywhere else, for the very nature of the fighting demands it, since, without close and friendly co-operation, there may well be swift disaster.

This applied to all the units of Razcol, but, as far as the 48th were concerned, more especially to the 1/9th Gurkha Rifles. This battalion had done all in their power to help the 48th when they first arrived in Razmak, and it was largely due to the way in which they had given the benefit of their long experience of Frontier warfare that the 48th had been able to accomplish what they did. The officers, both British and Gurkha, and the men of the 1/9th mixed with the 48th, both in barracks and in the field, in a way that the 48th will never forget.

This feeling of comradeship was commemorated. The officers of the 1/9th presented those of the 48th with a silver statuette of a Gurkha Rifleman.[5] In return, the officers of the 48th gave the British officers of the 1/9th a silver replica of the Mess Honorary Membership card, inscribed with the names of those who had served in Waziristan, and conferring the honorary membership of the 48th Mess for all time.

The Sergeants' Mess gave the Gurkha officers an inscribed photograph of their members, and received in return a pair of silver kukris.

It had been a hard year for the 48th. They had scaled, and held, hills which in any other part of the world would merit the name of mountains, often in the face of enemy fire, only to withdraw from them when, and not a minute before, they received the order to do so. They had covered close on 1,500 miles on their feet. They had been hot, cold, wet, hungry and tired. But they had never lost heart. Every member of the Battalion could be justly proud of the right he had earned to wear the ribbon of the Indian General Service Medal, with the clasp for 'Waziristan 1936–1937.'

*The 48th leave Razmak*

A month after their return from their last column, the 48th left Razmak for Bannu, *en route* for their new station, Dinapore. For unknown reasons this had been substituted for Delhi, to which place, it will be remembered, they had been told that they would move. The journey, by lorry, was not without incident, and at times they doubted if they had really seen the last of Razmak. On the 30th December, the day of their departure, a heavy snowstorm began and for a time it was uncertain if the road would be passable. However, they left soon after 0900 hours. Blinding snow was still falling and the road was very slippery and, in spite of slow driving, several lorries came near to disaster at dangerous bends; to help them to negotiate these the H.Q. Wing and two companies had to cover six miles of the stretch to Razani on foot. In the end all reached Bannu safely, after a bitterly cold journey of eight and a half hours.

Here they had to wait in a staging camp until the 5th January. The inhabitants of Bannu were not unique in fearing the worst of the possible behaviour of British troops, especially of those who had just returned to civilisation after a long absence from it. Their fears reached the ears of the Bannu Brigade Commander, who, after the Battalion had left, wrote to the Commanding Officer: 'These people were not only most agreeably disappointed, but viewed your departure with sorrow. Had I not heard so many flattering remarks about your men it would not have occurred to me to write to congratulate you and your men on giving a display of good discipline and behaviour that impressed everyone in Bannu.'

A day's train journey took the Battalion to Mari Indus, and from there they reached Dinapore, to relieve the D.C.L.I. on the 8th January, less one company which went straight to the detached station at Muzaffarpur.

So ended another episode in the history of the 48th, for which many individuals received honours.⁶ In Waziristan they left those who had fallen in battle, their memory honoured by a tablet in the Church of the Holy Sepulchre in Northampton. They also left behind them a name for work well done. Though the story which has been told speaks for itself, it may be summed up in the words of the G.O.C.-in-C. Northern Command: 'The Battalion did invaluable service during the recent Waziristan Operations, and has worthily earned a fine reputation.'⁷

# CHAPTER III

## THE REGIMENT, 1936–1939

The 48th at Dinapore, 1938–1939—The 58th at Ballykinler, 1936–1939—The 4th Battalion, 1936–1939—The 5th Battalion, 1936–1939—The new 4th Battalion, 1939—The Colonel-in-Chief of the Regiment, 1937—The Colonel of the Regiment—Alliance with the Regiment de la Rey, 1937—Liaison with Allied Regiments, 1936–1939—The Regimental Depot, 1936–1939

## *The 48th at Dinapore*, 1938–1939

THE 48th finished their long journey across India from Razmak to Dinapore on the 8th January 1938. There can hardly have been a greater contrast than that between their new station and the old, for Dinapore, some four miles from Patna, the capital city of the province of Bihar, lay in the flat, densely populated valley of the Ganges. The hot weather was humid and unpleasant.

Originally a Dutch settlement, in the days when the traders of that nation were penetrating the interior of India along the big waterways, Dinapore had later become one of the garrisons of the East India Company, and the stables for an Elephant Battery which had been stationed there were still standing in the barracks.

The Battalion occupied two separate barracks. Arrah, the old ones, lay close to the British cantonment and held one company; Victoria, which were more modern, accommodated Battalion Headquarters, the Headquarter Wing, one company and the Sergeants' Mess. The buildings were by no means bad, and there were adequate playing-fields, but apart from a narrow strip of land near the rifle range there was no training area at all, every inch of ground being cultivated. The greatest drawback, however, was the extent to which the Battalion was split up. One company was permanently on detachment at Muzaffarpur in North Bihar, the journey there involving a voyage up the Ganges and four hours by narrow-gauge railway. A second company was even more inaccessible, for it formed the British garrison of Port Blair in the Andaman Islands.

All things considered, it seems illogical that a battalion which had had a year of active service on the Frontier should have been sent to a station where training, sporting and social facilities were virtually non-existent.

The possible answer may be that thus it had always been, and thus it would always be, for the 48th were by no means the first to suffer from this strange whim of the powers at Delhi. Furthermore, the battalion at Dinapore was the only unit, British or Indian, in the whole of Bihar Province, and this, roughly the size of England and Wales, and very liable to communal disturbances, demanded the presence of really well-trained troops. Whatever the real reason, the 48th settled down to make the best of a bad station.

In these conditions, 1938 was a comparatively uneventful year for the Battalion. The detachments were relieved after they had spent about nine months in the outstations, so that all companies could have their fair share of the somewhat better amenities of Dinapore; and during the hot weather companies took their turn of a three months' spell in the Hills at Lebong, near Darjeeling, whence some of the more enterprising did treks up to the Tibetan border. Battalion H.Q. were less fortunate, for they were condemned to spend the whole of the hot weather at Dinapore.

With two companies permanently away and no other unit anywhere near, games were almost entirely limited to those on an inter-company or inter-platoon basis. The Battalion boxing team was defeated in the first round of the District event by the 1st Bn. The Cameronians at Calcutta; this, however, was no disgrace, for the Cameronians went on to win the All-India Championship.

In one important respect, however, 1938 was a red-letter year. The competitions for the Queen Victoria Trophy had been fired soon after the Battalion reached Dinapore, and when the results were published early in May it was found that once again the 48th led the field.[1]

With this victory they equalled the record established by the 1st Bn. The Rifle Brigade, who had won the Trophy for the years 1929 to 1932, and had previously been the only battalion to have achieved four consecutive wins since the competition had been started in 1903.

This success crowned the efforts of several years, which had seen the 48th rise steadily in the order of merit until, in 1935, they had won the Trophy for the first time. Many had contributed to this, from Commanding Officers to last-joined privates, but if one individual is to be selected it would be Major Winkler, whose knowledge of shooting and enthusiasm were so largely responsible.

In March the Battalion was reorganised as a Rifle Battalion, a year later than the 58th owing to their service in Waziristan. Being in India, however, none of the new weapons and vehicles which were being introduced at home were yet available for issue to them; the only sign of mechanisation was a derelict motor ambulance, issued for training purposes, which had long since ceased to be self-propelled and had to be drawn by bullocks from the railway station to the barracks.

## THE REGIMENT, 1936–1939

This reorganisation entailed the departure of the Indian Platoon, which had provided the mule-leaders for the machine-gunners. The 48th were sorry to lose these fine men, who had served them so well for five years.

At the end of the year Army Headquarters announced that the 48th would move to Nasirabad, in Rajputana, during the trooping season of 1939–1940, relieving the 1st Bn. The Lincolnshire Regt., who were to take over at Dinapore.

The year 1939 opened with yet another contest between the 48th boxing team and that of the Cameronians, won by the latter by the odd fight of the nine. It was the luck of the draw that, in two successive years, the 48th should have had to meet such formidable opponents in the first round; in this year the Cameronians did not meet with defeat until the final of the All-India Championship.

In February the G.O.C. Eastern Command inspected the Battalion, and took the salute at a ceremonial parade. Afterwards, writing to the C.O., he described the parade as excellent in every respect, and praised the smartness of the men. His concluding remark was: 'Altogether a first-class Battalion of British Infantry, well commanded and very ably administered, with outstanding N.C.O.s and fine personnel.'

The 48th suffered one great disappointment during the year. They had hoped to beat the record by yet another victory in the Queen Victoria Trophy, and the teams had put up good scores in the various competitions; but, by only a narrow margin, these were not quite good enough to beat that fine shooting battalion the 1st Bn. The 60th Rifles, and they had to be content with second place.

A small team was sent to shoot in the Central Rifle Meeting at Meerut, the Bisley of India, and achieved some successes, though it was the first time that the Battalion had competed at this Meeting.[1]

At the end of May, Lieut.-Col. Coldwell went to England on leave, pending retirement on relinquishing command on the 1st August. He was succeeded by Major W. J. Jervois.

During the summer of 1939 the effects of the expansion of the Army at home began to make themselves felt in India. Many Warrant Officers and N.C.O.s had to be despatched to England to help in the training of the enlarged Territorial Army, and this, combined with the demands of India and the Singapore base for others for extra-regimental employment, was to be a continual drain on the 48th from now onwards. They were a great loss to the Battalion, though their departure meant more rapid promotion for others.

These demands were not the only signs of impending war. Soon there arrived in the Orderly Room the outer cover of the *War Book*, a work intended to give instructions on the action to be taken in various emergencies. The instructions themselves followed at frequent and irregular intervals. At the end of August orders were received to hold other ranks to serve their extra year with the Colours, and discharges by purchase and premature transfer to the Reserve were suspended.

At 2215 hours on the 3rd September a telegram from District H.Q. at Calcutta announced that war with Germany had broken out, but that mobilisation had not yet been ordered in India.

## *The 58th at Ballykinler*, 1936–1939

The move of the 58th to Ballykinler went smoothly, the Regimental engine of the L.M.S. doing its first tour of official duty by pulling one of the trains which took them to Heysham, and the Battalion marched into their new quarters on the 6th November 1935.

Ballykinler differed from Aldershot in many ways. It was a one-battalion station, with no other unit nearer than Belfast. The barracks were a mixture of ancient and modern, in which the former predominated; the company lines, the dining-halls, offices, stores and married quarters were all in corrugated-iron or wooden huts of unknown age; the only brick buildings were some of the officers' quarters and the cookhouse, the latter equipped with really up-to-date aids. A major drawback from the troops' point of view was the thirty miles' distance from Belfast, the nearest place with amenities such as cinemas and shops. However, to counterbalance this, Ballykinler had good playing-fields and a private golf-course of sorts, and there was an excellent beach for bathing whenever the temperature of Northern Ireland was suitable.

The Battalion boxing teams soon got into their stride, and though the full team was narrowly beaten by the 1st Bn. The Welch Regt. in the District finals, the novices won their event, defeating the combined Depots of the Royal Inniskilling and Royal Irish Fusiliers.

At Aldershot there had been little time for athletics, but this was soon altered at Ballykinler. The Battalion team followed up a sweeping victory in the District Meeting in June 1936, when they won every track event except the hurdles, by being fifth in the Army Championships, run at Aldershot a month later. In the same year 2/Lieut. Anderson won the Ulster 100 yards and 200 yards championships.

The ranges at Ballykinler were good, and the 58th made the best use of them. After their successes at Aldershot, it was hardly surprising that at the 1936 N.I.D. Small-Arms Meeting they won the two main events, and, apart from these, out of the twelve competitions for which they entered, they won six and were second in the other six.[1]

At Aldershot the Battalion's time had been so fully occupied that they had been unable to make any serious bid for the Queen Victoria Trophy and so emulate the 48th in India. Now the programme was a little less crowded and teams were entered. Practice shoots went well, but the Regimental diarist records, with honesty, that when it came to the firing of the matches proper 'something went wrong,' and scores did not come up to expectations. However, they were undeterred and resolved to train all the harder for 1937.

Distance, and the cost of travelling, prevented the 58th from sending full teams to compete at Bisley that year. However, seven enthusiasts made the journey at their own expense, and two succeeded in getting into the Army Hundred. With commendable initiative, they made a post-entry for the Britannia Trophy, which required a team of six, and were rewarded by gaining third place.[1]

Collective training was carried out at the end of August from a camp in the country, but Brigade training, which was to have followed, was literally washed out by the weather.

The Army Estimates for 1937 made provision for all the Infantry at home, except the 4th Division, to be reorganised, either as Rifle or as Machine-gun Battalions, with mechanised first-line transport. Accordingly, on the 1st January of that year the 58th became a Rifle Battalion. The Support Company ceased to exist as such and was transformed into a fourth Rifle Company. In its place a Mortar Platoon and a Light Machine-gun Platoon were added to the Headquarter Wing, which was henceforth known as the Headquarter Company. At the same time the limbered G.S. wagons disappeared, their place being taken by tracked carriers.

The new equipment took time to materialise, but in the course of the year Bren guns and 2-inch mortars were issued, and mechanical transport replaced all the horsed transport.

These innovations necessitated much preliminary training by means of tactical exercises and weapon-training cadres, to ensure that, by the time collective training came round again, everyone would be capable of handling their new commands and their new weapons. For this training the 58th occupied the same camp as in 1936, and once again the weather put a stop to Brigade training.

It is a sad commentary on the state of recruiting for the Army, at a date less than two years before the outbreak of the greatest war in history, that for this training, owing to shortage of men, the four companies had to be telescoped into three, and even then one platoon of each was but a skeleton.

Judging by contemporary accounts, the winter at Ballykinler was usually bleak; but this does not seem to have induced the 58th to hibernate, as is shown by the record of their next year's achievements, due largely to winter preparation.

They began by winning the District Boxing, though beaten in the next round of the Army Championship by the Black Watch. Then, having won the District Athletics again, their team went to Aldershot for the Army Inter-Unit Team Championships, and put up a fine performance, finishing second to the 2nd Bn. The Cheshire Regt. The boys of the Battalion also distinguished themselves by winning the District Boys' Team Athletics, Football Cup and Boxing, while the full Battalion team won the District Football Cup.

From the shooting point of view, 1937 was a good year. The team of one officer and twenty men which went to Bisley were second to the Rifle Brigade in the most important event of the meeting, the King's Royal Rifle Corps Cup, which demanded a consistently high average in all the team and individual matches. Of their four representatives in the King's Hundred, one, L/Cpl. Gould, was one of the four 'young soldiers' to gain a place, and another, Pte. Pollard, got into the King's Fifty.

In the A.R.A. Non-Central Matches the 58th showed what could be done by hard training, for their efforts gained them second place in the Queen Victoria Trophy.

For the ceremony of the Coronation of King George VI and Queen Elizabeth on the 12th May, the 58th sent a detachment to London, the C.O. and seven other ranks taking part in the procession, while two officers and forty-three other ranks helped to line part of the route.[2]

A month later, on the occasion of the King's Birthday on the 9th June, the Battalion trooped the Colour at Ballykinler. The salute was taken by Viscount Craigavon, Prime Minister of Northern Ireland.

On the three days which followed this they carried out the same ceremony in the arena at Balmoral, on the outskirts of Belfast, the occasion being the athletic meeting of the Royal Ulster Constabulary, which was to Northern Ireland the equivalent of the Aldershot Tattoo to England. The Trooping and, at the end of each day, the entry of the 58th into the floodlit arena to take their place in front of the array of performers facing the royal stand, were recognised as the outstanding features of the display. After taking the salute on the final day, the Prime Minister congratulated all ranks on their magnificent drill which, in all his experience, he had seldom seen equalled. In a broadcast of the scene on the night of the 11th June, the commentator of the Northern Ireland station of the B.B.C. used these words:

'The Trooping of the Colour of the Northamptonshire Regiment was most impressive. . . . A magnificent display, which brought the crowd to its feet. . . . Every bayonet is exactly in a straight line, every arm straight. Seldom does one see marching like this in an ordinary Infantry Regiment. The order "Eyes Front" appealed to the crowd—every eye moved as if pulled by elastic, every head came round with a click. . . . The Grand Finale is a most impressive picture, with the Northamptonshire Regiment in front.'

Speaking after the final performance, the Inspector-General of the R.U.C. said: 'If there is another battalion that can handle its arms and

## THE REGIMENT, 1936-1939

march on grass as well as the Northamptonshire Regiment, I should like to see it.'

There were many events in that Coronation year of 1937 upon which the 58th could look back with justifiable pride.

The year 1938 was one of improvement as far as the barracks at Ballykinler were concerned, for brick-built Messes, married-quarters, orderly room and other buildings arose, not before they were long overdue.

Once again the 58th distinguished themselves at athletics. After winning the District Cross-country Running for the second year, their team was fifth in the Army finals at Aldershot. In the District Athletic Meeting they were again inter-unit champions, and the boys' team won the similar event open to them. In four events the 58th teams broke N.I.D. records, the figure for the long jump, 44 feet 4 inches, accomplished by Lieuts. Symonds and Anderson, exceeding the Army record. At the Army meeting at Aldershot, their team was again runner-up to the Cheshire Regt., Lieut. Symonds and Pte. Valentine establishing a new record of 225 feet 2½ inches in the discus throw.

Earlier in the year Lieut. R. A. Hofman had been the individual winner of the Modern Pentathlon competition, held at Aldershot. It was his second win in this event, his first having been in 1937 while he was still a cadet at Sandhurst. He was also one of the pair which represented Britain and defeated Holland in the first international match to be held in connection with the competition.

In the shooting world, the 58th eclipsed their previous year's performance.

The team which went to Bisley owed much to their hosts, the Grenadier Guards, at Pirbright, who went out of their way to make things comfortable and easy for them. Although they did not succeed in winning any of the principal team events they were second in three, and considering that in each case the winners were the 1st Bn. The Rifle Brigade, they felt that they had done well. In the Worcestershire Cup, for light-automatic teams, one of their pairs, Cpl. Malpas and Pte. Ludlow, was the champion pair of the Army, their score being a record for the meeting.

In the individual matches they did even better. The best performance was that of Cpl. Malpas, who won the Class 'B' Individual Championship, and with it the Manchester Cup. Second to him, and only one point behind, was Pte. Pollard. In the Army Championship (All Classes) these two were fourth and sixth.[1]

It is worthy of record that, as an E.Q.M.S. of the S.A.S. Corps, this same Malpas was winner of the King's Medal and the Championship of the Regular Army at home in 1947. To the 58th went the credit for having taught him to shoot.

When the A.R.A. Meeting had ended, the 58th team stayed on to compete in some of the matches at the meeting of the National Rifle Association, the first time that they had tackled these. This meeting is an even greater test of marksmanship than that of the Army, for it is open to the Forces of the Empire and to teams from every branch of the Services at home, in the Dominions and the Colonies. In spite of this the 58th acquitted themselves well, the pair who had done so well in the Worcestershire Cup gaining second place in the Lewis Gun Match, only eighteen points behind the Rifle Brigade.

Individually, too, they distinguished themselves; two were in the Revolver Thirty, and four, as members of the King's Fifty, shot for the Regular Army against the T.A., and for the team representing the English Regiments in the Methuen Cup.[1]

Meanwhile, in the absence of the most expert shots at Bisley, others had maintained the shooting reputation of the 58th in Northern Ireland. Competing in the Ulster Challenge Shield on a range they did not know, and in difficult weather conditions, their two teams were first and fourth out of ten competing. The shoot ended in a tie for first place with the holders, H.M.S. *Caroline*, but the decision went to the 58th 'B' team by virtue of their better score at the longer range.

Finally they fired the competitions for the Queen Victoria Trophy and, though not the winners of any, were placed second or third in every one, and were third in the Trophy itself.

Though they did not know it then, this was to be the last time for many a long year that the 58th were to be able to do any competitive shooting. But 1938 had raised them high on the roll of good shooting battalions.

For this year's training, the Battalion shared a camp at Ballywillwill with the South Wales Borderers. Whether due to the determination implied by the name of the camp or to other reasons, the fact remains that for the first time for eight years the weather allowed the District Commander's final exercise to be held.

Before 1938 was out, coming events were casting their shadows before. In September, when Hitler marched against Czechoslovakia, the 58th were ordered to take air-raid precautions and, as the months of 1939 passed, the atmosphere of crisis and the need for measures to meet it became greater. This being so, it was lamentable that early in January shortage of men forced the Battalion to organise into three companies. Of these, the Headquarter Company, now for the first time possessing a complete Bren Gun Carrier Platoon, was busily engaged in training with its new equipment; one company was finding employments and drafts for overseas; and one company was carrying out the training of recruits who, because of lack of accommodation at the Depot, had been sent to the Battalion before they had finished their initial training. By April it was possible to re-form all the companies, and the introduction of compulsory service compelled the

Depot to transfer the recruit-training company, complete with instructors, to Ballykinler.

On the 7th May 1939 Lieut.-Col. Parker completed his tenure of command and handed over to Bt. Lieut.-Col. E. G. Warren.

As war became more obviously inevitable, so did preparations to meet it increase. Batches of Reservists came up for training, as also did volunteers from the Reserve of Officers. At the same time the Battalion was called upon to provide a large number of officers and N.C.O.s to act as instructors for the many new units which were being formed.

At 1550 hours on the 1st September the 58th received orders to mobilise, war with Germany being imminent.

## The 4th Battalion 1936–1939

The years 1936 to 1939 were important ones in the history of the Territorial Army as a whole, much reorganisation and re-equipment taking place, and the 4th Battalion was affected more than most.

The beginning of 1936 found them only about thirty below establishment, and by July their strength of 585 other ranks was slightly above it, a tribute to the popularity of the unit and to the effectiveness of their efforts, and those of the Territorial Association, to induce men to join.

The annual camp was at Worthing and was noteworthy for the fact that the transport of the Battalion was mechanised, instead of having to rely upon hireling horses as in past years. The word 'mechanisation' may give a false impression, for it meant only the provision of hired vans and lorries; however, it was a beginning, and early in the following year two platoon trucks were issued.

On their return from Camp the 4th paraded, 500 strong, in the Market Square at Northampton and were inspected by their Honorary Colonel, Earl Spencer, accompanied by Sir John Brown and Colonel Muirhead, the Brigade Commander.

The Battalion had a successful year in other ways. The signallers won the Dartmouth Cup, in which they had had a fine record over a period of years, having won it in 1928 and 1929, being second in 1930, and since then having never been lower than tenth. In camp they won the Hampden Harter Cup for the unit gaining the most points in comprehensive tests, which involved platoon training, signallers and machine-gunners.

The year 1937 was one of many changes. To begin with, the Brigade of which the 4th had formed part for many years was broken up, and they found themselves transferred to the 143rd (Warwickshire) Infantry Brigade of the 48th (South Midland) Division. The reason for the transfer was the conversion of some battalions of the Royal Warwickshire Regt. into anti-aircraft units.

This was followed by a War Office letter which announced the decision to invite the 4th to undergo a similar conversion and to form an Anti-Aircraft Battalion R.E. (T.A.).[3] This meant that they would become part of the Corps of Royal Engineers, but though they would cease to be an integral part of the Northamptonshire Regiment they would still be affiliated to it and its name would be included in their new designation.

Before their conversion in this way, a detachment of three officers and twenty-eight other ranks helped to represent the Regiment at the Coronation ceremony in London.[2]

At midnight on the 30th September 1937 the old 4th Battalion died and from its ashes rose the 50th (Northamptonshire Regiment) A.A. Battalion R.E. (T.A.). Thus was partially severed a link which had existed for two hundred years, from the days of the first formation of a Volunteer Association in the county in 1744 to the time when, in 1881, the Volunteers became the 1st Volunteer Battalion of the Regiment and then, in 1908, the 4th Battalion (T.F.). Though the link was now to be severed in this way, the ties between the 50th Battalion and the Regiment would remain strong through affiliation.

## *The 5th Battalion*, 1936–1939

Meanwhile the 5th Battalion carried on. Their 1936 annual camp, held in Norfolk in June, was in the nature of an experiment, for this was about two months earlier in the year than usual; consequently it was a one-battalion, instead of a brigade, camp. Though it lacked the atmosphere of competition which brigade camps produced, there were compensations; employers seemed to find it easier to release men for training at this time of the year than later, and the numbers attending were, as a result, encouraging.

While a detachment from the Battalion was taking part in the Coronation procession in London,[2] the remainder gave a display at a Tattoo organised by the City Council of Peterborough. In spite of bad weather this was very successful, and there were hopes that one result might be to persuade some of the spectators to join the Battalion.

Together with the 4th, the 5th were transferred to the Warwickshire Brigade in 1937. Unlike them, their rôle was to be unchanged, and for the time being they were the sole T.A. battalion of the Regiment. There was some readjustment, the 4th taking over 'D' Company of the 5th at Fletton, while the 5th acquired the Rushden Company of the 4th.

Annual camp, near Cheltenham, produced training of greater interest than usual, since it was based on the new organisation, and dealt with innovations such as Bren guns and mortars—though in theory only, for the actual weapons were not yet available for issue to the T.A.

In the year's Dartmouth Cup Competition their signallers won them third place.

# THE REGIMENT, 1936-1939

All this time the strength of the 5th had been rising steadily. By the middle of 1938 it had reached 500, and it says much for the keenness of the men and of the employers who released them that fewer than fifty failed to attend the Annual Camp at Corfe Castle.

Earlier in the year Lord Burghley was appointed Honorary Colonel of the Battalion. He was then the Member for Peterborough and was, perhaps, even more famous as the best hurdler ever produced by England.

In the autumn of the year the crisis in the affairs of Europe brought much extra work, especially to the permanent staff of the Battalion, who found themselves busily engaged in polishing up schemes for mobilisation and passive air-defence, and, in their spare time, in digging shelter-trenches. The crisis also had a marked effect on recruiting, for by April 1939 the strength was 543, only 38 below their peace establishment, and by July it was 660; what is more, the majority of the recruits had joined before the introduction of compulsory service. Simultaneously with this influx of men the new weapons and vehicles started to arrive, so what with the initial training of the new recruits and the instruction of the older hands in the new weapons, there was not much time to spare for other activities.

Early in August the Battalion went into camp at Arundel, well up to strength. Accompanying them were the other two battalions of the brigade, the 7th and 8th Royal Warwickshires, and the newly formed 'duplicate' battalions which included the newly reborn 4th Battalion of the Regiment. It was a strenuous, though most successful, camp; the full fortnight was completed although war was so imminent, and on their return to Huntingdonshire the members of the Battalion dispersed to their homes.

About a fortnight later, even before the rear party had finished winding up the camp at Arundel, the order came for the Battalion to mobilise on the 2nd September. This was done by companies under their own arrangements, Battalion H.Q. and the H.Q. Company at St. Peter's College, Peterborough (the Drill Hall having been handed over to the Royal Artillery with whom it had been shared for many years), 'A' Company at Ramsay St. Mary, 'B' at Oundle, 'C' at Huntingdon and 'D' at St. Neots.

## The New 4th Battalion, 1939

It was not long before the Regiment's 4th Battalion was restored to it. In a praiseworthy, though belated, effort to raise an Army more nearly adequate for the country's commitments, the Government decided to double the strength of the Territorial Army. As a result, a War Office letter of the 20th April 1939 ordered the formation of a new 4th Battalion. A month later the Commanding Officer was appointed, Lieut.-Col. J. G. Lowther, D.S.O., M.C., T.D. He was no stranger to the Regiment, for he had commanded the old 4th from 1924 to 1928.

On its formation, the H.Q. of the Battalion consisted of one room in the Isolation Hospital at the Depot. The equipment can hardly be described as lavish, consisting of one four-foot table and one chair, but no doubt this soon increased, for the newly appointed Quartermaster was Lieut. F. R. Carrington, M.M., better known to the Regiment as a former R.S.M. of the 58th and one of their most distinguished shots. The difficulties with which he must have been faced are shown by the fact that in the first week in June the contents of the clothing store consisted of thirty-six sergeants' sashes, useful and decorative articles no doubt, but hardly ones which would have ranked high in the priority of requirements for a newly raised battalion.

Headquarters did not remain in this cramped accommodation for long and soon moved into a house in Langham Place, Northampton. The H.Q. Company, less a detachment at Long Buckby, was also in the town. 'A' Company formed at Kettering, 'B' at Raunds and 'C' at Wellingborough. 'D' at Rushden was a going concern, for it now came back to the 4th, from which, it will be recalled, it had been transferred to the 5th some two years earlier.

Before long the Battalion had a R.S.M.—in fact, he arrived before the Commanding Officer had been appointed—and three permanent staff instructors, while two more were on their way from the 48th in India. Thanks to their efforts, aided as they were by the N.C.O.s of the Depot, who gave a helping hand after they had finished their normal day's work, training went ahead steadily; it meant hard work, for within two months of its formation the Battalion was 346 strong.

Over 400 went to camp at Arundel in August and, though only a few had more than about four months' service, carried out a hard programme of training. Hardly had they returned from camp than, on the 24th August, they received orders for embodiment.

*The Colonel-in-Chief of the Regiment, 1937*

For the whole Regiment, the outstanding event of these years was the honour accorded to it when, on the 11th May 1937, H.R.H. the Duchess of Gloucester consented to become its first Colonel-in-Chief. In thanking her for this, the Colonel of the Regiment emphasised the value of the connection between the Regiment and the county, a connection which had existed for more than a hundred and fifty years. In her reply, the Duchess expressed her happiness that the Regiment belonged to her own county of Northamptonshire.[4]

The Colonel-in-Chief lost no time in showing her practical interest in the Regiment. On Sunday, the 4th July, the Comrades paraded at the Depot, 262 strong. Headed by the Colonel of the Regiment and giving the salute to Major Alan Hill-Walker, V.C., as they left barracks, they

The Colonel-in-Chief presenting the Coronation Medal to
Major Alan Hill-Walker, V.C., at the Depot, 1937

*(Northampton "Chronicle and Echo")*

marched to the War Memorial, where a wreath was laid. The Duchess attended the service which followed in St. Sepulchre's Church, and afterwards inspected the parade in barracks and presented Coronation Medals to several serving and retired officers and men, and the Dartmouth Cup to Lieut.-Col. Scott-Robson of the 4th Battalion. A visit to the men's dinners, and lunch in the Officers' Mess, was followed by a tour of barracks, and so ended a very memorable day in the history of the Regiment.

In December a brooch, in the form of a replica of the collar-badge, was presented to the Colonel-in-Chief on behalf of all ranks, past and present, of the Regiment.[5]

The appointment of a Colonel-in-Chief demanded the honouring of a special toast on Regimental guest-nights, after the toast of 'The King.' The initial proposal, that the toast should be preceded by the playing of a few bars of the National Anthem, was abandoned, since this music would already have followed the loyal toast. Then it was suggested that a portion of the Regimental Slow March, played in faster time than normally and preceded by the Regimental Call, should be adopted; this was approved by the Colonel-in-Chief, who signed the original copy of the music, which is now deposited in the Regimental Museum.[6]

*The Colonel of the Regiment*

None could have been more pleased than the members of the Regiment, when on the 15th May 1936 their Colonel, Sir Harry Knox, was promoted General. In December 1937 he relinquished the appointment of Adjutant-General to the Forces and in the following October was made Governor of the Royal Hospital at Chelsea.

*Alliance with the Regiment de la Rey, 1937*

In April 1937 the War Office informed the Colonel of the Regiment that the King had approved of yet another alliance with one of the Regiments of the Dominions, the Regiment de la Rey of the Union of South Africa Defence Forces.

In bygone years the 58th had seen much service in South Africa, and the present recruiting area of the newly allied Regiment had been the scene of many of their operations against the commandos of General de la Rey, known to them as 'the Lion of the Western Transvaal.' It was fitting therefore that the regiment bearing the honoured name of a former enemy should now be linked with a British regiment which had once opposed him in battle.[7]

*Liaison with Allied Regiments, 1936–1939*

As a rule liaison with the Allied Regiments is limited by distance to the exchange of letters giving news of mutual interest; but these years brought many visitors from overseas to Britain and the Regiment was glad to welcome them. In 1936 Major Cook, of the Lake Superior Regiment of Canada, visited the 58th at Ballykinler; he was the first of his Regiment to establish personal contact since the alliance in 1933, and was the bearer of a letter of greetings from his Commanding Officer.

In the following year all the Allied Regiments sent representatives to the Coronation and several of them managed to visit the Depot. Capt. Bruer, of the Australian 43/48th Battalion, brought with him a gift in the form of a boomerang bearing the signatures of all the officers of the battalion.[8]

Another member of the Lake Superior Regiment, Lieut. Keane, stayed at the Depot in 1938, and the 58th were glad to be able to entertain Lieut.-Col. Edgar, a recent Commanding Officer of the Australian 58th Battalion.

## The Regimental Depot, 1936–1939

The work of a Regimental Depot is liable to be taken for granted by those outside it, though its work is of such importance to the Regiment.

For most of the year the Depot at Northampton performed its main task, the training of recruits; but it came into prominence annually during the Regimental Week, the success of which was due so much to the work of the permanent staff of officers and N.C.O.s who undertook the organisation of the Regimental 'At Home,' the cricket matches, the Comrades' dinner and church parade and all that those functions involved.

At the beginning of this period the state of recruiting for the Army was at a very low ebb throughout the country. In Northamptonshire the number of young men who came forward to join their County Regiment was most disappointing, despite the best efforts of the Depot to attract them. There were several reasons for this, apart from the fact that the Army was the 'ugly duckling' of the three Services and the Infantry of the Line (not to be honoured by a capital 'I' for some years to come) was regarded as the least attractive in the least popular of the three. Among these were the small amount of unemployment in industry, the conditions of Army pay and accommodation, and the prospect of long years of service abroad. Furthermore, the local man was often deterred from joining his County Regiment by the fact that he would have to start his soldiering in a neighbourhood in which he had always lived, though this deterrent would not have applied had the public regarded the Army with greater esteem than they did.

To illustrate the state of affairs: in the first nine months of 1936 only 125 men presented themselves for enlistment to fill the Depot quota of 304, and of these fewer than 40 came from the county. In January 1937 the Depot had only one squad of twenty men under training and it had taken five months to fill that squad.

## THE REGIMENT, 1936-1939

Among the remedial measures taken by the War Office was one which ordered the holding of 'Depot Days,' on which the public were to be admitted to barracks and given an insight into the life of the soldier. On the first of these occasions, in July 1936, only about 600 of the public were sufficiently interested to attend; they were entertained by a programme which included various displays, tours round barracks and band concerts. The 600 must have spread the news that 'Depot Day' was attractive, for in the following year there were some 4,000 visitors.

As time went on recruiting did improve, and in March 1938 the Depot had 132 recruits under training, the largest number it had had for some time, though only 32 of them came from the county. It took the European crisis in the autumn of that year to bring about any marked boom. In the first quarter of 1939 the Depot received 238 recruits, of whom 22 were Supplementary Reservists who underwent a shortened course of training before being drafted to the 58th.

This influx of recruits created many problems, chief of which was that of accommodation. To solve this, several squads had to be sent to the 58th, there to finish their period of initial training.

The introduction of compulsory service complicated matters still further, especially as the arrival of the first batch of militiamen coincided with that of Reservists who had been called up for training and who had to be equipped and sent to join the 58th on the next day. However, the Depot staff took these difficulties in their stride, with some changes in organisation. In place of the former Administrative and Training Companies there were formed a Headquarter and Administrative Company, a Recruit Company, and a Militia Company in which the militiamen were to carry out the first two months of their training before being posted to the Home Battalion. Accommodation became an even more acute problem than ever and it was decided to build huts within the confines of the barracks. These, however, could not be ready till September so, as a temporary measure, the Recruit Company was sent to the 58th at Ballykinler. The additional training staff which this reorganisation demanded was supplied by the Regular Battalions and by utilising the services of some of the Reservists who had been called up.

Prior to all this increased activity a step had been taken which few who knew the barracks at Northampton considered overdue. In April 1938 it was announced that a new Depot was to be built at Wootton, two miles outside the town, at an estimated cost of £271,000. The intention was that these barracks should be completed by the spring of 1941, but circumstances beyond anyone's control were to prevent this.

Not to be outdone by the 48th and 58th, the Depot entered a team for the A.R.A. Prince of Wales Cup, open to Depots, in 1936 and 1937. In the first of these years they were placed sixth, but at their next attempt they gained second place.

On the 29th May 1938 a detachment from the Depot was present at the ceremonial opening by Major-General Sir John Brown of the Garden of Rest in Abington Square. On the walls of the garden are inscribed the names of the 2,906 citizens of the Borough of Northampton, many of them in the Regiment, who gave their lives whilst serving in the War of 1914–1918.

48th (South Midland) Division

## CHAPTER IV

## THE CAMPAIGN IN FRANCE AND FLANDERS, 1939-1940

Move of the B.E.F. to France—Shortcomings of the B.E.F.—Work on Defences—Completion of the B.E.F.—Situation in Europe, September 1939-May 1940—The Allied Plans—The German Offensive, 10th-18th May—'Frankforce' at Arras, 20th-24th May—The B.E.F. Triangle—The Belgian Surrender, 27th May—The Dunkirk Perimeter—The Evacuation from Dunkirk (*see* Map facing p. 50)

### Move of the B.E.F. to France

WHEN war broke out there was no delay in organising French ports for the reception of the British Expeditionary Force, for the necessary arrangements had been made well in advance. By the 21st September the concentration of the G.H.Q. Staff and of the essential Lines of Communication units had been completed and the fighting units of the 1st Corps began to disembark.

The sector allotted to the B.E.F. by the Supreme Commander, the French General Georges, lay some two hundred and fifty miles north-west of its assembly area near Le Mans. With its right at Maulde, it ran northwards along the Belgian frontier as far as Halluin and thence south-westwards along the River Lys to Armentières, enclosing within the salient thus formed the cities of Lille, Roubaix and Tourcoing.

Early in October the 1st Corps, consisting of the 1st and 2nd Divisions, moved up and occupied the right-hand portion of the sector. A fortnight later the 2nd Corps began to arrive from Le Mans, the 3rd Division taking over on the left of the 1st Corps and the 4th being kept in G.H.Q. reserve. Before long the arrival of more units enabled Lord Gort, the Commander-in-Chief, to form the 5th Division. A French division which had been lent to the B.E.F. was relieved by the 4th Division and at the end of December the 5th Division took over a sector to the left of that held by the 4th. It was in the 17th Infantry Brigade of the 5th Division that the 58th served throughout the campaign.

In January 1940 the 48th Division came from England, thus completing the first contingent of the B.E.F., which now consisted of two Corps, each of three divisions. The 5th Battalion was in this division, but was soon transferred to the 11th Infantry Brigade of the 4th Division.

## Shortcomings of the B.E.F.

The strength of the B.E.F. at this time was 220,000, considerably greater than that of its predecessor of 1914, though the actual fighting force was smaller. In 1914 the B.E.F. had increased from five to eleven divisions in the first five months of the war. In 1939, in the same space of time, the B.E.F. had only increased from four to six divisions; moreover, these had only three battalions in each brigade, as compared with the four of the brigades of 1914.

There were also other shortcomings. In his second despatch Lord Gort wrote:

> The situation as regards equipment, though there was latterly some improvement in certain directions, caused me serious misgivings, even before men and material began to be diverted by the needs of operations elsewhere. I had on several occasions called the attention of the War Office to the shortage of almost every nature of ammunition, of which the stocks in France were not nearly large enough to permit of the rates of expenditure laid down for sustained operations before the war.
>
> Equipment also was incomplete, especially as regards anti-tank guns.

Above all, the B.E.F., faced by the prospect of operations against the most strongly armoured force in the world, had no armoured division. The only one which was available was retained in England until after the German offensive of the 10th May and, when it did go to France, it lacked much of its proper equipment.

Once again in her history Britain had found herself unprepared for war.

## Work on Defences

Having taken over the sector, the British troops set to work to improve the defences.

The Maginot Line came to an end at Mézières, for the French had relied upon the strength of the Belgian defences to stop any German attack between that place and the Belgian-Dutch border. From Mézières north-westwards along the Franco-Belgian frontier there had been dug an almost continuous anti-tank ditch, covered by concrete pill-boxes designed to hold anti-tank guns and machine-guns. To complete these defences the B.E.F. had to add field works, a reserve position across the base of the Lille salient and another system farther in rear.

This work did not provide any real training for the troops so, by arrangement with the French, from December onwards British Infantry brigades took it in turn to occupy a sector on the Saar front, in advance of the Maginot Line. Here they were in contact with the enemy and were able to gain experience of patrolling. Early in May this detachment was increased to a division, the 51st Highland being the first selected for the duty.

*Completion of the B.E.F.*

Lord Gort had been led to expect the arrival of the 3rd Corps from England early in 1940, and arrangements had been made for it to take over the sector held by the French on the left of the 2nd Corps; but its departure was delayed because of the situation elsewhere in Europe, and it was not until February that the 51st Highland and the 50th Motor Divisions reached France, followed by the remainder of the Corps, the 42nd and 44th Divisions, at the end of March.

To complete the picture of the B.E.F. mention must be made of three other divisions: the 12th, 23rd and 46th. These had been brought out to France primarily for work in the L. of C. area. They were not, at the time, intended for combatant purposes, nor were they organised or equipped for them. They consisted of Infantry battalions and divisional engineers only; they had no artillery and their signal and administrative units and their transport and equipment were in skeleton form.

*Situation in Europe, September* 1939–*May* 1940

During the months of the so-called 'phoney war' in France events had moved fast elsewhere. While France was mobilising and the B.E.F. was in the process of being transported overseas, without the slightest interference on the part of the enemy, Germany, with some assistance from her Russian ally, had overrun Poland in a matter of weeks. In mid-September French troops had advanced into the no-man's-land which lay between the Maginot and the Siegfried Lines in the area between the Rhine and Luxembourg. At one time it seemed that they might occupy the German town of Saarbrucken, but a counter-attack forced them to withdraw and bad weather stopped any further major operations. The general effect of this French offensive was negligible as far as any interference with German plans was concerned.

Six months after she had occupied Poland, Germany struck elsewhere. The occupation of Denmark in April 1940 was followed by the invasion of Norway. Then, on the 10th May, came the 'blitzkrieg' against the Low Countries.

*The Allied Plans*

In the early months of the war plans to meet a German offensive had been worked out by British and French General Staffs. It was obvious that if Belgium were invaded the Allies would have to go to her assistance; but Belgium (and Holland too) was so determined to observe strict neutrality, hoping thereby to avert invasion, that she refused to discuss any plan of action or to reveal details of her own plan. However, enough was known to assume that she would occupy her frontier defences forward of the River Meuse and along the Albert Canal, and it was believed that she had prepared an anti-tank obstacle between Namur and Wavre.

Three courses of action had been considered by the Allies. The first of these was for the Allies to occupy the defences which they had prepared along the Franco-Belgian border, with a French Army holding the Messines Ridge and the line of the Yser Canal on the left of the B.E.F. Mobile troops would be pushed forward to the River Escaut. This plan was ruled out, for it would have left the Belgians and the Dutch to their own resources and, once they had decided to resist the common enemy, the other Allies could hardly have stood back.

It then became a question of how far into Belgium the Allies could advance. Under the project known as Plan 'E' they would have held the line of the Escaut, from where it crossed the frontier at Maulde up to Ghent, joining up there with Belgian forces extending the line as far as the coast. This was a wide frontage but, being within a day's march of the frontier, it had the advantage of ease of speedy occupation.

However, further information about the Belgian defences became available and the conclusion—which proved to be unduly optimistic—was reached that they would hold up the enemy for a considerable time. Accordingly a third plan, Plan 'D,' was studied, which visualised a deeper advance into Belgium, up to the River Dyle. This line would be shorter and stronger than that of the Escaut, but it had two disadvantages: its occupation would involve a forward move of sixty miles, by roads which could not be reconnoitred in advance, owing to Belgium's refusal to allow any action which might be deemed to compromise her neutrality; and the success of the operation would depend upon time, which would only be adequate if the Belgians could impose sufficient delay upon the enemy.

At a final conference held in November, it was decided to adopt Plan 'D.' The frontage allotted to the B.E.F. on the Dyle was to be from Wavre to Louvain, with three divisions forward—the 2nd, 1st and 3rd—and others disposed in reserve. To the right would be the French First Army, to the left the Seventh, the latter having an alternative task of advancing into Holland to help the Dutch if they were attacked. The understanding was that if the Belgian Army were forced to withdraw it would take up a line on the left of the B.E.F., between Louvain and Antwerp.

*The German Offensive 10th–18th May*

An hour after German bombing on the morning of the 10th May had announced the opening of their offensive, orders were issued putting Plan 'D' into effect. Zero hour was 1300 hours and at that time the armoured cars of the 12th Royal Lancers crossed the frontier into Belgium, followed by the forward divisions of the 1st and 2nd Corps. The advance went according to plan, in spite of enemy air attacks and difficulties caused by the streams of refugees on the roads, and on the 12th May the Dyle line had been manned.

The German offensive was carried out by seventy to eighty divisions, with another thirty to forty in reserve. Two armies attacked Holland where the Dutch forces, though gallant, were weak and unskilled. Not even the defensible nature of the country, with its numerous water obstacles, could make up for this and, by the 14th May, the German advance had split the country in two. Further resistance was useless and on the 15th the Dutch Army laid down its arms.

Farther to the south the Germans, moving through Aachen, overcame the weak defences of the Maastricht 'appendix,' the tongue of Dutch territory adjoining the northern portion of Belgium's eastern frontier. Then, largely by the use of parachute troops, they captured the strong Belgian frontier fortress of Eben Emael, thus creating a breach in the outer defence line on the Albert Canal. Simultaneously, the two southern German armies, composed mainly of armour supported by lorried infantry and ordinary-type divisions, crossed Luxembourg and the Ardennes, the spearhead moving at the rate of twenty-five miles an hour, and reached the Meuse.

Within a short time of the B.E.F. having reached the Dyle the situation on both flanks had become serious. On the left the French Seventh Army had reached Holland too late to stop the Germans from seizing the islands in the delta of the Rhine, and this had virtually turned the Belgian left flank. At the same time, on the other flank, 'as a result of incredible mistakes' (to use the words of M. Reynaud, the French Prime Minister) by the French Ninth Army, the Germans had been able to cross the Meuse at Dinant and between Mézières and Sédan. Then, driving westwards with ten armoured divisions, they made for the Somme, Abbeville and the coast. Once the opening had been made they were exploiting success in accordance with their doctrine.

Meanwhile, on the 17th May the 5th Division had been rushed from the area where it had just started a period of training into the line south of Brussels. And, in an attempt to close the gap which the enemy were making, the 12th, 23rd and 46th Divisions were hurriedly provided with some artillery and were moved into positions east and south of Arras.

By the morning of the 19th the B.E.F. had withdrawn from the Dyle to the Escaut. This had been forced on them by circumstances beyond their control, for they had held their own when attacked, though the full weight of the German offensive had not fallen upon them. It was the situation to the south that was causing anxiety. The gap had become a corridor along which the Germans were pouring. From Péronne, on the Somme, southwards the Allied line had ceased to exist, and the enemy were in Amiens. The defensive flank which Lord Gort was forming would not save the situation. The only thing which could do this would be a counter-attack against the flank of the German corridor.

*'Frankforce' at Arras, 20th–24th May*

With this object there was formed a force known as 'Frankforce,' from the name of its Commander, Major-General Franklyn of the 5th Division. This consisted of the 5th and the 50th Divisions, each of two Infantry brigades only, the 1st Army Tank Brigade, 'Petreforce,' consisting of battalions from the 12th and 23rd Divisions, and Lieut.-Col. Lumsden's force of the 12th Royal Lancers and the 1st Battalion The Welsh Guards. With the exception of the two divisions and the Army Tank Brigade, all these troops were already heavily engaged in the defence of the Arras area.

On the 21st May the counter-attack began, one brigade of each of the 5th and 50th Divisions and the tank brigade being engaged. The French 1st Light Mechanised Division* co-operated, but a promised simultaneous counter-attack on the left by two other divisions of the French First Army never materialised. Though the opposition was stronger than had been expected, the tired British troops gained the objectives of the day, but without the support of the French on the left further progress was impossible. The only alternative was to hold the ground gained and impose the maximum delay on the enemy, for time was vital to the B.E.F. But the enemy continuously threatened to outflank and, on the 24th May, the 5th and 50th Divisions were withdrawn into reserve near Lille.

By now the enemy penetration was so deep that it had severed all communications across the Somme. The B.E.F. was cut off from its base ports to the south and could no longer operate as a whole, since south of the Somme were the 51st Division, withdrawn from the Saar, portions of the 12th and 46th, the Armoured Division which had at last arrived in France, and all the L. of C. troops.

*The B.E.F. Triangle*

By the 24th May Lord Gort had managed to establish a line of defence facing south-west, the area then held by the B.E.F. forming the shape of a rough triangle. The northern side of this was the coast-line. The apex, held by French troops, was at Douai. The eastern side was approximately the Plan 'E' line of the Escaut, held as far as Halluin by the 42nd, 1st,

* A Light Mechanised Division (or D.L.M., i.e. Division Légère Mécanisée) would be better described as a Light Armoured Division. It comprised tank and lorry-borne cavalry units, armoured cars and mechanised artillery.

THE CAMPAIGN IN FRANCE AND FLANDERS, 1939-1940    49

3rd and 4th Divisions, and thence towards Ghent by the Belgian Army. The western side ran along the 'Canal' line from Douai to Gravelines, fifteen miles west of Dunkirk, and was held by improvised British formations as far as St. Omer and by the French thence to the coast.

On the 25th the Belgians on the River Lys were heavily attacked. It was clear that if this front gave way the B.E.F. would be in grave danger of being cut off from Dunkirk, its last remaining port, so the 5th and 50th Divisions were brought from reserve to extend the British line from Halluin towards Ypres, along the line of the disused Ypres–Comines canal.

The perimeter of the triangle was now too long for the available troops to hold and, on the 26th, arrangements were made to shorten it. On the same day the British Government authorised Lord Gort to prepare plans for the withdrawal of the B.E.F. by sea to England, after he had pointed out that even in the best circumstances this would inevitably lead to the loss of the greater part of the force and its equipment.

*The Belgian Surrender, 27th May*

Events now moved quickly. Hardly had it become evident that the Belgian Army would be forced back in a northerly direction instead of towards the Yser where they would have been in touch with the British, than late on the 27th May Lord Gort was informed that the King of the Belgians had asked the Germans to grant an armistice from midnight on that night. The message, delayed in transit, reached G.H.Q. barely an hour before the Belgian Army would have ceased to fight.

*The Dunkirk Perimeter*

Now the pressing need was to form a perimeter round Dunkirk to cover the embarkation of the troops. Its organisation had been begun on the 27th, under the orders of Lieut.-General Sir Ronald Adam, who had given up command of the 3rd Corps for the purpose. By the 28th he had succeeded in getting the perimeter manned by an assortment of units, mainly of the Royal Artillery. The right, from between Gravelines and Dunkirk to Bergues, was held by the French; from there to the left, at Nieuport, by the British.

While this was being done the main body of the B.E.F. was still outside the perimeter, the troops on both sides of the triangle fighting hard, and practically back to back, to keep the lane of withdrawal to Dunkirk open against ever-increasing German pressure. In this they were successful, and by the 30th May the whole force and the two Corps of the French Army were within it. It had been a near thing, especially on the left flank at Nieuport, where the enemy, pouring through the gap left by the Belgians, had managed to establish a bridgehead over the canal. Here they were stopped by a troop of the 12th Royal Lancers, until the breach was firmly sealed by the 4th Division.

## The Evacuation from Dunkirk

Throughout this time troops were being got away to England, and as they went so was the perimeter reduced in size. The departure of the 3rd Corps was followed by that of the 2nd, and by the morning of the 1st June there remained only the 1st Corps, now less than 20,000 strong.

At midnight on the 2nd Major-General Alexander, who had taken over command two days before when Lord Gort had returned to England on the orders of the British Cabinet, toured the beaches in a motor-boat with the Senior Naval Officer. After satisfying themselves that no British troops were still ashore, they left for England.

Dunkirk was not a victory. In some respects it was the greatest disaster ever suffered by a British force of the size of the B.E.F. In others it was a great feat of arms, of which Britain will always be proud.

Thanks to the work of the Royal Navy, of the crews of the 'little ships' and of the pilots of the R.A.F. who prevented the Luftwaffe from doing its worst, nearly a quarter of a million British and over a hundred thousand Allied troops were safely conveyed to England, where they could prepare to fight again. But the gallantry of the other Services would have accomplished little without one other thing—the discipline of the British Army and its refusal to admit defeat.

Towards the end of his despatch on the operations of the B.E.F. Lord Gort wrote:

> Most important of all, the Campaign has proved beyond doubt that the British Soldier has once again deserved well of his country.

True words indeed, and words to be remembered.

## CHAPTER V

## THE 58th IN FRANCE AND BELGIUM, 1939–1940

Mobilisation at Ballykinler, September 1939—The 58th at Aldershot, October 1939—The Move to France—The 58th in France, October 1939–May 1940—Operations in Belgium, 13th–19th May—The Battle of Arras, 20th–23rd May—The Move to Ypres, 24th–26th May—The Stand near St. Eloi, 27th–28th May—The Withdrawal to the Coast, 28th–31st May—The Evacuation from Dunkirk, 31st May–1st June (*see* Maps on pp. 58 and 64)

*Mobilisation at Ballykinler, September 1939*

THE order to mobilise reached the 58th at Ballykinler at 1550 hours on the 1st September 1939. Mobilisation procedure was started at once and, during the days which followed, a continuous stream of officers and men joined and left the Battalion. The war diary for the 3rd September records that arrangements were proceeding smoothly and that the N.C.O.s and men were cheerful. At 1115 hours on that day the Prime Minister broadcast the news to the nation that, as no reply had been received to the British ultimatum to Germany, a state of war existed between the two countries.

By the evening of the 12th mobilisation had been completed, except for some of the equipment and most of the transport, and the Battalion carried on with the training of the reservists who had joined; many of them had never seen the weapons which had recently been introduced into the Army.

*The 58th at Aldershot, October 1939*

Towards the end of the month the Battalion had orders to prepare to move. On the 3rd October, having handed over the barracks to the I.T.C. of the Royal Irish Fusiliers, they left for England via Larne and Stranraer, experiencing a bad crossing which made most of the troops seasick. Arriving at Aldershot on the 5th, they were met by Brig. M. G. N. Stopford, M.C., Commander of the 17th Infantry Brigade, in which they were now to serve. Col. R. Gurney, formerly of the Regiment, was to have commanded this brigade, but had, unfortunately, been found medically unfit for active service.

After a period of three days' embarkation leave there was much work to be done, especially for the M.T. Section, who had to paint the cars, trucks and carriers which arrived straight from the makers. The 3-ton lorries were a mixed collection, taken off the streets; many were in bad condition and were to be the cause of much trouble later.

On the 13th October the road party left for the port of embarkation, the name of which was veiled in secrecy; however, the postmark on a letter from the O.C. party, announcing their safe arrival, showed that guesses had been correct and that it was Southampton. Finally, there was a farewell visit from the Colonel of the Regiment, who was accompanied by two Chelsea Pensioners, members of the Regiment in bygone days; after inspecting the Battalion he read them a message of good wishes from the Colonel-in-Chief.

*The Move to France*

On the 18th October the 58th entrained at Farnborough. On reaching Southampton they embarked in the S.S. *Canterbury*, which sailed in convoy in the small hours of the 19th. After landing at Cherbourg seven hours later the troops were allowed to fall out, and soon showed the ability of the British soldier to make himself understood in any land by ordering large meals without the knowledge of a word of French.

*The 58th in France, October 1939–May 1940*

Throughout that night the Battalion travelled in one of those French troop-trains of which some had memories dating from over twenty years before. Then, early on the 20th, they detrained near Le Mans and went into billets. Battalion H.Q. were in the Château de Courtillolles, the remainder at Champfleur and Ste. Rigomer. Three days later the M.T. left by road for an unknown destination, followed the next day by the Battalion, by train. They had enjoyed their first experience of being billeted on French soil, not least the members of the Battalion H.Q. Officers' Mess who, before they left, were entertained at a champagne party by the Comte de Courtillolles and his family.

At the end of their journey the 58th detrained at Seclin, a few miles south of Lille, and went into billets in the village of Houplin. Here, throughout November, their task was the construction of strong-points in the Corps reserve line. Otherwise the month was uneventful, except that on the 12th a report of the imminence of a German attack on Holland and possibly on Belgium as well caused considerable activity; it was received with mixed feelings, the question being whether the occupation of wet trenches and periods of anxiety were preferable or not to dry billets and long spells of boredom. The answer was not yet to be forthcoming, for within a week the alarm subsided.

On the night of the 1st/2nd December the Battalion left Houplin by lorry convoy for Halluin, the northernmost point of the B.E.F. sector, and took over the 17th Brigade front from the French 310th Infantry Regiment; when the other units of the brigade arrived the 58th handed over to them all the defences except the pill-boxes and frontier-control posts, for which they were still to be responsible. Halluin was right on the Belgian frontier, so much so that in part of the town one side of a street was in France, the other in Belgium. This caused complications, for soldiers who strayed into Belgium on their unlawful occasions were liable to be arrested by the Belgian police and interned. It was to the credit of the 58th that none of them suffered this indignity.

Soon after their arrival the Battalion had their first visit from Major-General H. E. Franklyn, Commander of the 5th Division, which had just been formed and included the 13th and 17th Infantry Brigades.

At Halluin, as at Houplin, the defences required completion, particularly as regards the anti-tank ditch and the concealment of the pill-boxes. The latter was achieved by disguising them as chicken-houses, and the Battalion was congratulated upon the ingenuity of this, and upon their good work in general, when they were visited by the C.-in-C. of the B.E.F., General Lord Gort, accompanied by the Home Secretary, Sir Samuel Hoare and Lord Hankey. This party of distinguished visitors was but the first of many to this somewhat popular part of the British sector; the most distinguished party of all was possibly that which was composed of six Field-Marshals.

The first few weeks of 1940 saw the Battalion still working on the defences, though for days at a time the exceptionally severe weather seriously interfered with digging operations. On the 6th February Lieut.-Col. E. G. Warren was appointed to the command of an Infantry Brigade and was succeeded in the 58th by Major J. W. Hinchcliffe. Lieut.-Col. Warren, and Lieut.-Col. Jervois who was then commanding the 48th in India, were the last of the officers still serving regimentally who had gone to France with the 48th in 1914.

Soon after this all C.O.s in the 5th Division received a personal letter from the Divisional Commander warning them that the Division was to move to the United Kingdom in the near future, to refit before going to another theatre of war. Orders for the advanced parties to move were, in fact, given but, fortunately perhaps, events in Europe moved too quickly and the project was cancelled.

Early in April the Division was to have gone to the Saar to take its turn in gaining experience of minor operations in contact with the enemy, but this was cancelled; instead, towards the end of the month, the 17th Brigade was ordered to the Amiens area, there to do a period of six weeks' training; 'D' Company were already training in the Calais district. Before the Battalion left, the combined 58th/5th Battalion Drums beat retreat in

Halluin, a ceremony which was watched by many, including the 5th Division's Commander.

On the 29th April the 58th entrained for Poix, south-west of Amiens. On the following day the C.O. and some other officers who had travelled by road went to Poix railway station to meet the Battalion, but no one was more surprised than Lieut.-Col. Hinchcliffe when the train passed rapidly through the station and disappeared into the distance. In response to enquiries they were advised to look for the 58th at Yvetot, but it was at Bolbec, not far from Le Havre, that they eventually found them detraining.

The mystery was soon solved. The story of the six weeks' training was a myth, invented for security reasons. The truth was that the Division was concentrating for transfer to another theatre of war, which rumour said was Norway, and preparations were begun for a move by sea. On the 3rd May the projected move was cancelled and the M.T., which had gone to Le Havre to embark, returned. Three days later the Battalion did go to the Poix area, and started to get ready for training, but got no farther than preparations. On the 10th May the long-expected event happened. The German armies invaded the Low Countries.

The months of the so-called 'phoney war' were over, and the time had come for the B.E.F. to meet the enemy. It is doubtful if history will judge it to have been a well-trained force, either physically or mentally, at least not sufficiently so to oppose a German machine which had been preparing for this moment for many years.

In the days of peace the Regular Army at home had rarely been up to strength; training was thereby seriously handicapped and, generally speaking, lacked reality. This state of affairs was not improved when the reservists came back to the Colours on mobilisation, for most of them were considerably out of date as regards training and were less physically fit than the Regular soldiers. This might have been remedied to some extent had units had better opportunities for hard training during the months of inaction in France; but digging was the order of the day and, to cite one example, in the whole seven months the 58th had only had one week of battalion and one week of brigade training. However, even though the troops lacked training they did not lack courage.

*Operations in Belgium, 13th–19th May*

As the preceding chapter has shown, the 5th Division did not take part in the advance to the Dyle, which was the immediate action now taken by the B.E.F., but no time was lost in moving them forward. For three days, from the 11th to the 13th May, the 58th were on the march. It was a trying time for the troops, especially for the reservists among them owing to the previous lack of opportunity to practise long route-marches and to the hot weather. It would be untrue to say that not a man fell out on the line of march, but on the whole they stood it very well. For the first time since the war had begun the threat of attack from the air had to be taken seriously, but it was difficult to make the troops realise that the digging of slit-trenches must take priority over the making of tea or the removal of boots from tired feet.

After marching a distance of forty-nine miles the 58th reached the neighbourhood of St. Pol on the 13th; then, after a day's rest, events moved swiftly.

Very early on the morning of the 15th orders were issued for a rapid move into Belgium. At 1530 hours the Battalion embussed and, after passing through Béthune, Lens and Tournai, their movement greatly hampered by the stream of refugees going in the opposite direction, reached their destination, Ninove, at 1000 hours on the following morning. That afternoon the brigade began to move to an area west of the Brussels–Charleroi canal and north of Hal, but the transport to carry the 58th did not arrive till after midnight, so they did not reach their allotted position at Mekinghem, in brigade reserve, until 1000 hours on the 17th. Here they dug in, working till after darkness had fallen. They were repeatedly machine-gunned by low-flying aircraft and henceforth it was unnecessary to order the digging of slit-trenches; the lesson had been learnt.

Earlier in the day information had reached Brigade H.Q. that the enemy had penetrated the front of the 48th Division, which was withdrawing from its position east of the canal, and that German A.F.V.s were approaching Hal; this latter piece of information proved to be false, the A.F.V.s being in fact only a few motor-cyclists. The withdrawal of the 48th Division through the position held by the 5th Division proceeded without interference on the part of the enemy, and at 1530 hours, when the last of their troops had crossed the canal, the bridges were blown.

By 2030 hours the situation on the right of the 5th Division had deteriorated and a withdrawal became necessary. At 2200 hours the 58th were ordered to pull out as quickly as possible and to occupy a rear-guard position on the Enghien–Castre road, where they would find some anti-tank guns and machine-guns ready to support them. The other battalions of the brigade, the 2nd Royal Scots Fusiliers and the 6th Seaforth Highlanders, were to withdraw through this position to an area round Paricke, where the 58th were eventually to rejoin them.

It was a rush to get the Battalion on the move. The C.O. had been out visiting companies and did not return to his H.Q. until 2230 hours; soon after that Major J. R. Wetherall arrived from Brigade H.Q. with the orders, and then Company Commanders had to be summoned and they, in their turn, had to collect their men, who were dispersed over a wide area. However, by 2345 hours the 58th were on the move.

The route allotted to them consisted of tracks which were marked on the map, but the map proved to be most unreliable in this respect and there were some anxious moments during the march. Nevertheless, by a combination of good judgment and good fortune, the Battalion reached the destination at 0500 hours on the 18th and occupied defences on a wide front. Three hours later the other two battalions passed through the position and the 58th withdrew, collecting stragglers from many different regiments as they went. Near Grammont they were picked up by M.T. and, by 1500 hours, had concentrated at a village some six miles to the south of that place.

That afternoon it was decided that the 5th Division was to continue its withdrawal westwards as soon as possible. The 17th Brigade was to go to the Ronchin area, carried in sixty lorries of the Petrol and Ammunition Companies. The move was to begin at midnight.

The Brigadier did not get back to his H.Q. from the divisional conference at which these orders had been issued until 2200 hours; he then gave out his verbal orders to units, but owing, once again, to the inaccuracy of the maps and the difficulty of route-finding along country lanes, it was already midnight before unit guides for the M.T. had left Brigade H.Q. Half an hour later came news that only twenty-four, not sixty, lorries would be available, so battalions were ordered to start marching by the main road between Grammont and Renaix.

By 0130 hours on the 19th battalions had begun to reach this road, along which was also moving a double column of M.T. belonging to the troops holding the forward positions; then, to make matters worse, the convoy of lorries for the 17th Brigade arrived from the opposite direction, meeting the others head on. The road was soon completely blocked by marching troops and vehicles, but by some means order was evolved from chaos, the lorries were turned round and by 0400 hours the last of the troops had embussed. It had been an anxious time, for it had seemed impossible for embussing to have been completed by daybreak, and the congested road would have been very vulnerable to enemy bombing. As it was, the rest of the move passed off without incident, though progress was slow because of the refugee and other traffic. Units reached their new areas soon after midday, the 58th billeting in Ascq. All were very tired and glad to get their first rest since leaving St. Pol five days before.[1]

*The Battle of Arras, 20th–23rd May*

Next day the 5th Division was ordered to move to the Lens area, where it was to take part in the counter-attack by 'Frankforce' which, it was hoped, would stop or, at least, check the German drive towards the coast, now threatening to sever the lines of communication between the B.E.F. and its bases. The 17th Brigade was to debus at Lens and occupy a reserve position on the Vimy Ridge.

During the day the 58th marched from Ascq to Ronchin, where they

The Centre Device of the Colours
(See p. 8)

went into empty houses and waited for their buses to arrive. These were late in returning from transporting the other brigade of the division, so the Battalion did not get on the move again until 0200 hours on the 21st. Two hours later they reached Lens and marched to the Vimy Ridge, where they took up a defensive position facing south. Some of them occupied trenches of the First World War, preserved since then as a memorial, though they had to face in the opposite direction to the troops who had held them in those days; 'D' Company were in position round the great Canadian War Memorial.

The 13th Brigade had been given the task of trying to cross the River Scarpe at Athies, in conjunction with an attack by the 50th Division and an Army Tank Brigade, the object of which was to improve the situation at Arras where the British troops were being hard pressed. If this attack was successful the 17th Brigade was to advance and widen the bridgehead across the river; but, owing to lack of information on the progress of the 50th Division's attack, the operation by the 13th Brigade did not take place, so for the rest of the day the 17th Brigade remained on the Ridge, out of ground contact with the enemy though subject to constant attacks from the air.

At 0700 hours on the 22nd the Brigadier gave orders for the occupation of another position on the River Scarpe, facing south and excluding Arras, where 'Petreforce' was practically surrounded except for one avenue of approach by the Lens road. The brigade front was about six thousand yards wide and stretched from Maroeuil Wood on the right to Ste. Catherine on the left; in front of it the river formed an indifferent obstacle to tanks. The 58th were to be on the right, the Seaforth Highlanders in the centre and the Royal Scots Fusiliers on the left.

The Battalion started to move forward from the Ridge at 1000 hours. Preceding them were the C.O. and his Reconnaissance Group, with the Carrier Platoon to protect them, for the information was that there were no troops between them and the enemy; consequently they were pleased to find a detachment of French motor-cyclists on the new position. Later on the C.O. found a small group of French officers in the village of Maroeuil; they appeared to be slightly excited and, in reply to enquiries, stated that the Germans were quite close at hand advancing down the road and that they proposed to retire. The suggestion that, in the circumstances, the correct course of action was for them to stay where they were, did not meet with their approval and they departed, leaving the 58th Reconnaissance Group to their own devices. Investigations by 2/Lieut. Roche in one of the carriers soon disclosed that the alleged enemy were, in fact, British armoured cars; nevertheless, the C.O. was relieved when the Battalion arrived at about 1300 hours; on the way up they had been attacked by dive-bombers.

## HISTORY OF THE NORTHAMPTONSHIRE REGIMENT

Companies were soon in position and started to dig in. This was hard work on the heavy, chalky ground and, to make it harder, they had to start with entrenching tools, for the 'A' Echelon transport did not arrive till about three hours later.

The dispositions of the Battalion were as follows: On the right, in Maroeuil Wood, with an open right flank, 'A' Company (Capt. Melsome); in the centre, 'B' (Major Watts), responsible for holding a spur and

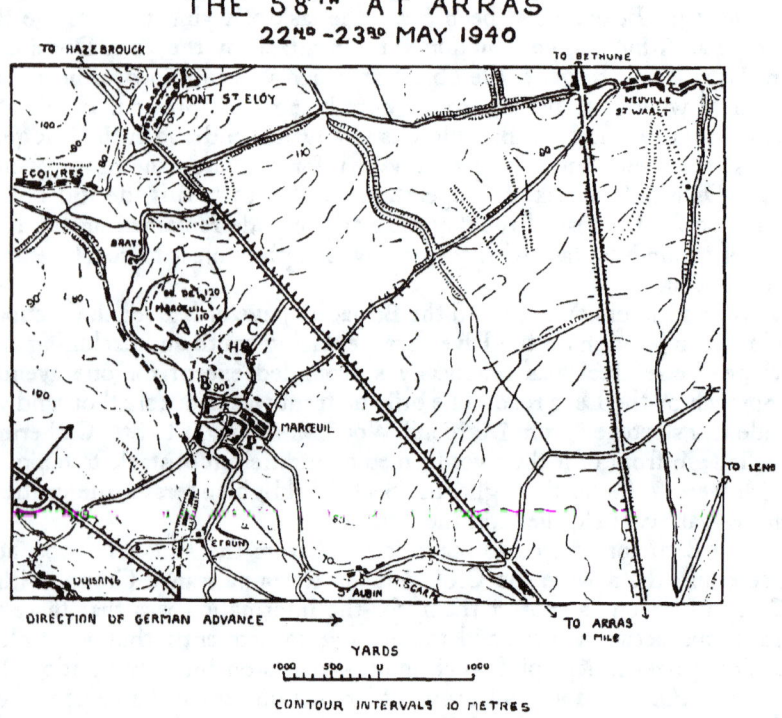

a re-entrant which ran back into the position; on the left, 'D' (Capt. Houchin), holding the village of Maroeuil. 'C' Company (Capt. Norman) were in reserve, and support was to be provided by a French Artillery Regiment.

To the right of the 58th lay Mont St. Eloi, a feature which dominated the whole of their position. It was essential that this should be firmly held, and the French 2nd Light Mechanised Division, who were there, assured the 17th Brigade that this would be done to the last.

Soon after the 58th had got into position considerable movement was seen at what was evidently an enemy headquarters on the forward slope of a ridge some three thousand yards ahead; though requests were made for artillery fire to be brought to bear on this target, it was not engaged. Before long Battalion H.Q. and the company areas were shelled and at 1530 hours the shelling increased on Maroeuil Wood and on the 'B' and 'D' Company localities. To avoid casualties 'A' withdrew from the wood and were placed in position to cover the re-entrant which lay between them and 'B' Company's area; after the C.O. and his Second-in-Command had gone up to ascertain the situation and had reconnoitred the wood, 'C' were sent forward to relieve 'A,' which then went into reserve.

During the night the right platoon of 'D' Company, commanded by P.S.M. Field, was approached by a party of enemy who came down the road in trucks. The platoon had closed the gates of a level crossing in front of the position and these stopped the trucks; the enemy got out and attacked, but were driven off, abandoning a truck; subsequent inspection showed that they had suffered casualties.

During the next morning, when on his way to visit the 58th, the Brigadier saw a few German tanks and about two hundred infantry advancing towards Mont St. Eloi from the direction of Acq; at the same time shelling and dive-bombing suddenly increased. Soon after 0800 hours there was considerable pressure on the 58th front and by 1000 hours an attack developed against the right flank; in the course of this a German tank was knocked out on the edge of Maroeuil Wood by the guns of the Brigade Anti-Tank Company.

Meanwhile, 'D' Company had arranged to tackle a German post which had been causing annoyance. Unfortunately, the 3-inch mortars which had been sent up to provide support could not register the post, so instead they carried out an area shoot on another one. This produced quick reaction by the enemy and one of the 58th mortars received a direct hit, putting it out of action and causing heavy casualties to its crew. Another direct hit on a house nearby partly demolished it, killing or wounding every man of the section there.

In the course of the morning the French withdrew from Mont St. Eloi, though they had not been heavily attacked and despite their previous assurances that they would hold it to the last. They informed the Brigadier that they were establishing road blocks of heavy tanks and dismounted cavalry to the east of the place, and that they would be prepared to counterattack should the enemy make any further progress. Later in the day, when asked to do this, they declined on the grounds that if they were caught on the move they would be engaged by the German artillery. To complicate matters still further, at 1030 hours the French artillery liaison officer at Brigade H.Q. announced that the guns supporting the Brigade were to be withdrawn; however, he agreed to have this postponed until

1300 hours, and the 5th Division promised to replace them with a British Field Regiment.

Enemy pressure now became severe all along the Battalion front. With Mont St. Eloi abandoned, 'C' Company were in an unpleasant position; for some time they had been under heavy shell-fire and, in the end, the enemy managed to enter the wood and force them back. At noon a tank attack was stopped, except in the re-entrant on 'B' Company's front, where one tank got a foothold and proceeded to shell Battalion H.Q. Major Watts and one of his men got an anti-tank rifle into action and engaged it, scoring hits but causing no apparent damage; however, after opening up with its machine-gun, the tank withdrew. During the incident five French tanks appeared at Battalion H.Q., but moved no farther forward, and, after a stay of an hour, went away.

'D' Company also had been having difficulties; at one time they had been forced out of Maroeuil, but had re-entered it and chased most of the Germans out; they continued to have trouble, mainly from enemy snipers who had got round their left and were in a tall factory building which commanded the area; as this flank seemed to be vulnerable, some of the carriers were sent up to protect it.

At 1415 hours the Brigadier heard from his liaison officers that the French tanks and cavalry had gone northwards to deal with an enemy threat in the direction of Souchez. This left the right flank of the Brigade even more completely in the air than it had been before and there was considerable danger that it might be surrounded, so he decided to withdraw to the line of the Arras–Béthune road.

It was no easy matter for the 58th to get out of their position, as many of the lines of withdrawal of the forward companies were commanded by the enemy; however, three of the companies managed it and moved some two miles back under heavy shelling and air attacks. Unfortunately, 'C' Company either failed to get the order to withdraw or were surrounded in the wood before they could do so; their Commander, Capt. Norman, was wounded and he, and many others, were taken prisoner. So henceforth the Battalion had only three rifle companies. Four carriers were put out of action by anti-tank bullets, and others had difficulty in withdrawing owing to tangled telephone wires which wound themselves round the tracks.

In the course of the day the 58th had lost some of their more important members. Lieut.-Col. Hinchcliffe, Capt. Green, the Adjutant and R.S.M. Goodall had been wounded by shell-fire at Battalion H.Q.; the Second-in-Command, Major J. R. Wetherall, in command for a matter of hours, had been hit when going to see if 'C' Company had got out. Major R. M. G. Wetherall took over command, with Major Watts as Second-in-Command and Lieut. Drew as Adjutant. Capt. Philpot-Brookes took over 'B' Company in place of Major Watts.

Having got back, the Battalion started to dig in on the new position, but at midnight received orders to move as quickly as possible to Douai, there to await further instructions.

So ended the first action in which the 58th were engaged in the war. As was the case in 1914, a small British force had opposed an enemy much superior in numbers and in equipment and had been forced to withdraw. The fighting had cost the Battalion 352 casualties, but in spite of this they had held the enemy where they had been ordered to hold him. Before he was wounded Lieut.-Col. Hinchcliffe had set a fine example to all, often going forward under heavy fire to find out the situation and take steps to deal with it; he was later awarded the D.S.O. for what he had done. 2/Lieut. Roche, commanding the Carrier Platoon, won the M.C.; throughout the day his command had been in action almost continuously, providing a reserve of fire-power where it was most needed and carrying out many liaison missions under fire.[2]

The counter-attack by 'Frankforce' did not achieve any decisive result, nor could it have done this without the French co-operation which, though promised, was never forthcoming. But the resistance which had been offered to the German advance had imposed some delay on the enemy and so gave the B.E.F. time to organise a defensive flank; this, assisted by the stand made by garrisons such as those of Arras and Doullens and by Brig. Nicholson's force at Calais, made it possible, ultimately, to withdraw the B.E.F. from France. So the Battle of Arras was not fought in vain.

*The Move to Ypres, 24th–26th May*

At 0100 hours on the 24th May the 58th moved off, breaking contact with the enemy without difficulty as the German patrolling was not active. About 150 men were carried in the Battalion transport, the remainder marching by compass across country, under Major Watts. In due course the M.T. came back down the Douai–Arras road to meet them; the leading truck, in which Lieut. Evans-Evans was travelling, drove past the post which had been placed on the road to stop the transport when it arrived, and went on towards Arras, where it, and its occupants, fell into the enemy's hands. The rest of the transport stopped, the troops got on board and by midday had rejoined the Battalion at Raches.

After a brief rest the 58th moved to positions covering the bridges over the canal north of Douai. At 2030 hours that night they were relieved by French troops and went by lorry to Templemars, near Seclin, arriving there at midnight in time to get some much-needed sleep.

The morning was spent in reorganisation, then came the news that the Brigade was to move, to hold a position south of Ypres, part of the line being organised to cover the withdrawal of the B.E.F. towards the coast. From 1900 hours the Battalion stood by, ready to move at half an hour's notice. Early on the morning of the 26th, as there was still no sign of the troop-carrying transport, Brigade ordered units to start marching, and at 0330 hours the 58th set out along the Lille road. After they had marched for some distance the transport picked them up, but progress was extremely slow and the column was still on the move when day broke. Passing through Messines they came under artillery fire, so they debussed and finished the journey on foot, arriving at St. Eloi at noon on the 27th.

*The Stand near St. Eloi, 27th–28th May*

The position which the Brigade was to hold was on the line of the Ypres–Comines railway, from east of Hollebeke to Zillebeke. The Royal Scots Fusiliers were to be on the right, the Seaforth Highlanders on the left; the 58th were to be in reserve behind them on the line of the canal, which was disused and dry and offered no obstacle to the movement of tanks.

The country was thickly wooded and, considering this, the front which the 58th had to hold was a wide one. To begin with, 'B' Company were on the right and 'D' on the left, but soon after they were in position there seemed to be a wide gap to the left of the latter which should, it was believed, have been held by another brigade; accordingly 'A' Company were sent up to prolong that flank, the Second-in-Command, 2/Lieut. Gibson, being sent to attach himself to the R.E. at the bridge which carried the Messines road across the canal, with orders to remain there until the bridge had been blown.

A liaison officer from the French Light Mechanised Division had reported to the Brigade that his division was holding Zillebeke, forward and to the left of the Seaforth, and that they would counter-attack should the enemy advance; but when Brig. Stopford went to see the Commander of the division he found that the headquarters had gone and that the last of the French tanks were withdrawing towards Ypres. No doubt this was in accordance with orders they had received, but the incident serves to illustrate the difficulties and the uncertainty of the situation.

In their reserve position the 58th spent a quiet night, but in the forward battalions' area German patrols were active. Early on the 27th increasing enemy pressure forced the left company of the Seaforth back from the line of railway. Later, as there was a risk of the Royal Scots Fusiliers being cut off, both battalions were withdrawn to the line of the canal, the Fusiliers prolonging the line held by the 58th towards the right, and the Seaforth going into brigade reserve.

The morning of the 27th was spent in improving the slit-trenches and in organising all-round defence for Battalion H.Q. Up to midday things were fairly quiet, apart from occasional shelling which twice drove 'A' Echelon transport from their cover in rear of the Battalion; 'B' Echelon, under the Quartermaster, were farther to the rear with the Brigade transport.

The 'Q' side of a battalion is liable to be taken for granted, but the story of this campaign would not be complete without reference to the work done by that of the 58th. At quite an early stage it was difficult to get the supplies to feed the troops; in the later stages, when the supply depots had been destroyed, it was even harder; but thanks to the work of the Quartermaster, Capt. Holmes, and his staff, and to the transport, first under Capt. Symonds and then, after he had taken over the H.Q. Company, under 2/Lieut. Fitzwilliam, the Battalion was fed. Petrol was a major difficulty and frequently P.S.M. Allen and his petrol clerk had to drive fifty miles or more, against a stream of military and civilian refugee traffic, to get it to the Battalion in time; but they always got it back, and the 58th transport was kept on the road long after that of many other units had had to be abandoned.

To resume the story of the battle. By the early afternoon the enemy had followed up the withdrawal of the two forward battalions, and were in contact with 'B' and 'D' Companies of the 58th, which maintained their positions. At 1630 hours 'A' Company could still get no contact with any troops on their left, so a section of carriers was sent to help to cover the bridge.

About an hour and a half later all the companies reported that the enemy was attacking strongly and that the situation on the flanks was critical. They got good support from the Gunners; for example, within ten minutes of the receipt from 'B' Company of the map-reference of an enemy mortar a 25-pounder battery just behind Battalion H.Q. had engaged the target and ten minutes later the company signalled 'Magnificent show! Men very pleased with R.A. Blown up men and mortar in wood.' The effect of this on morale was great.

At 1930 hours a determined attack developed on the right. The 13th Brigade was driven back and, to protect the flank of the 17th Brigade, the Royal Scots Fusiliers drew back their right flank. Meanwhile, 'B' Company had come under intense and extremely accurate mortar fire which had forced them out of their slit-trenches, and they then occupied part of a ridge near a farm some four hundred yards north-east of Battalion H.Q., the latter being situated south of St. Eloi on the Warneton road. 'D' Company were now under heavy bombardment and the enemy were infiltrating along the canal bank between them and 'A' Company, so they withdrew to the ridge on the left of 'B.'

Capt. Symonds was now sent forward to find out the situation on 'B' Company's front and flank. He had an adventurous journey, for on riding his motor-cycle through the archway of the farm in which he understood 'B' Company's H.Q. to be, he came face to face with Germans. Reacting more quickly than they, he turned round and got clear of the farm, managing to avoid being hit by the fusillade which followed him; but after covering about three hundred yards he was wounded by splinters from a shell which burst nearby; fortunately, he was not incapacitated and got back to Battalion H.Q. to report the gap which he had found to exist on the right.

To strengthen 'A' and 'B' Companies' positions, Major Watts then led up some details from Battalion H.Q. and some stragglers of another unit,

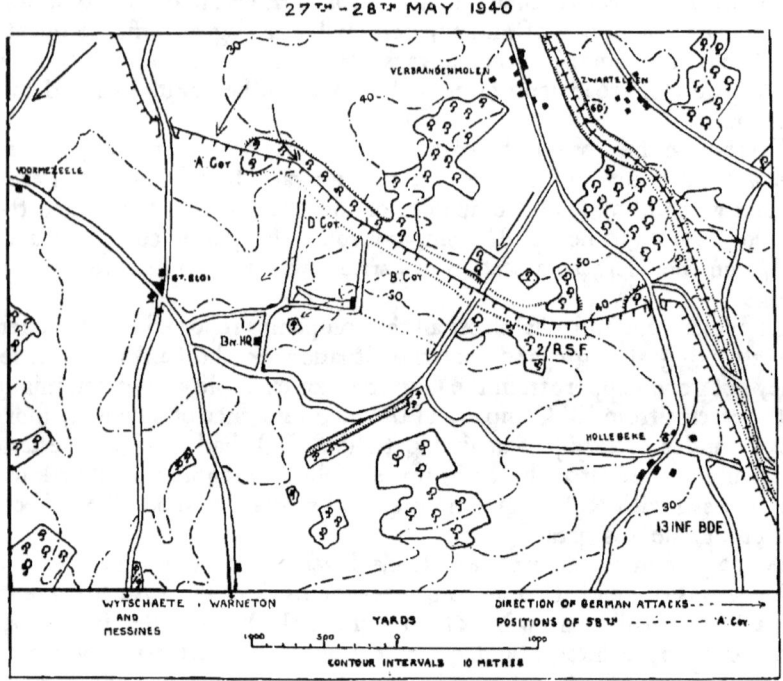

THE 58TH AT ST ELOI
27TH-28TH MAY 1940

reaching the ridge after incurring some casualties from machine-gun fire on the way. The C.O. and Major Watts set a fine example, walking about in the open and rallying groups of men of various units to strengthen the defence forward of Battalion H.Q.

By now companies were running short of ammunition, and it was only thanks to the fine work of R.S.M. Howard, who took supplies to them across a heavily shelled area, that they had enough with which to carry on.

For the time being the situation became stabilised, though there was a considerable amount of shelling, and the C.O. went forward in a carrier to investigate matters; a patrol under 2/Lieut. Reddy, sent to locate the Royal Scots Fusiliers on the right, encountered nothing but enemy.

By now everyone was intensely weary, but there was little chance of rest for the officers, who had to visit the men continually to ensure that they were on the alert.

At about midnight Brig. Stopford visited battalions and impressed on them that there must be no withdrawal, as the 5th Division had to hold on to protect the northern flank of the corridor through which the B.E.F. was pulling back towards the coast. At 58th H.Q., where, in the words of the 17th Brigade war diary, 'the Commanding Officer, Major R. M. G. Wetherall, appeared to have a good grasp of the situation and was unruffled,' he gave orders for the Battalion to try to regain the line of the canal before the Brigade was relieved by the 10th Brigade at dawn.

Acting on these orders, the C.O. ordered an attack, with the object of driving the enemy back over the canal. By the time that 'B' and 'D' Companies had started to advance it was getting light. Capt. Philpot-Brookes was killed almost immediately and, with the Germans holding the advantage in ground, little progress could be made; in the end the companies had to return to the ridge from which they had started, and there they continued to suffer heavy casualties from the fire of artillery, mortars and snipers. Once again, R.S.M. Howard did invaluable work in taking ammunition to the forward companies.

At 0600 hours Major Watts was sent to try to locate the 10th Brigade, but all he could find was one company of the D.C.L.I. An hour later the C.O. went out, alone, to visit the right flank of the Battalion. He was never seen again and it was not till some months had passed that it was known that he had been killed. His steadying influence, during a most trying time, had been great. Command now devolved upon Major Watts.

During the night Capt. Melsome had come in to Battalion H.Q. to report, leaving P.S.M. Turnbull in command of 'A' Company. Nothing more was heard of the company, which was in an isolated position on the left, until a long time afterwards, and then it was known that the P.S.M. and some twenty men had been taken prisoner after resisting for as long as they could.

At 0730 hours Battalion H.Q. came under very heavy shell and small-arms fire from a ridge to the right. The farm in which they were lay in a saucer-shaped depression and so long as the forward companies—or what remained of them—were still able to hold their positions it was practically immune to any fire other than that of artillery and mortars; but once the enemy could reach the lip of the saucer the building would become a death-trap. As it was evident that this was what was now happening and that the enemy had worked round the right, the ambulance, full of wounded, was sent away in charge of the M.O., Capt. Dowzer; as it moved down the St. Eloi road the German fire almost ceased, only to be renewed with greater intensity. Capt. Houchin now reported that his company had very few men left and the same applied to 'B,' commanded now by 2/Lieut. Reddy.

By 0900 hours there was still no sign of the relieving brigade and all communications to 11th Brigade had broken down. After two despatch-riders had failed to return, Major Watts set out in a carrier driven by 2/Lieut. Roche to report the situation to Brigade H.Q., which was near Wytschaete. As they went down the Messines road the carrier was repeatedly hit, clear evidence of the extent of the enemy's infiltration; however, they reached their destination, passing on their way the 10th Brigade having breakfast near Wytschaete, with no apparent knowledge of the fact that they were supposed to relieve the 17th. Having reported, they began their return journey, in the course of which they met some of the 5th Battalion moving into position.

Not long after Major Watts had left, the enemy's small-arms fire against the 58th H.Q. farm intensified; snipers were active and men were hit leaving the building. The men of H.Q. Company were engaging the enemy on a semi-circular arc, 'B' Company could see Germans debussing behind the right flank and others could be observed moving along the main road towards Messines and past the St. Eloi cross-roads. Ammunition was running very short, in spite of the efforts of the R.S.M. Those who could continued to fire on the enemy, one man in particular giving a magnificent demonstration of the result of previous training—Pte. Hasdell of H.Q. Company, who had served in Waziristan with the 48th, installed himself in a well-camouflaged position near the headquarters, filled as many Bren magazines as he could and did some very effective shooting at any enemy who came in sight for as long as his ammunition lasted.

At about this time the Intelligence Officer, Lieut. Brittain, went out on a motor-cycle to visit the companies, but was killed on his return journey.

Though it was impossible to get any news of the situation in the forward area, it was now clear that all effective resistance had ceased, for the enemy was closing in all round the farm. Going out to investigate, the R.S.M. was hit as soon as he got outside the door; one man, Pte. Neill, volunteered to make a dash to try to get through to Brigade to report the situation, though Capt. Symonds told him that his chance of getting clear of the farm was a very slender one; he had gone only a few yards on his motor-cycle when he was hit by a hail of bullets. As it transpired, he could never have got through, for the enemy were now a mile up the Messines road and a battalion of the East Surrey Regt. was fighting in a village well behind the 58th.

Suddenly a man came into the farmhouse and announced that the enemy had got into the farm buildings. At the same time the house itself became the target for every sort of weapon, including an anti-tank gun, the shells from which went through the walls as if they had been made of paper. Soon the enemy entered the house. With no ammunition left, and having obeyed orders and done their duty by holding on to the last, further resistance was not only impossible but would also have been useless. Those who were left—five officers, the wounded R.S.M. and twenty to thirty N.C.O.s and men—surrendered to save further waste of life, and were marched away as prisoners.[3]

North of Ypres and not many miles from St. Eloi the 48th had fought back the Prussian Guard of 1914. Now the 58th had stood against the even more formidable German Army of 1940 till they could fight no longer. Their resistance, and that of other units, was not unavailing, for the enemy had intended to advance farther towards Dunkirk on the 27th, and had been checked in their plans. The object, that of gaining time for the B.E.F., had been fulfilled.[4]

While these events had been happening, Major Watts and 2/Lieut. Roche had been returning from Wytschaete. After their carrier had been put out of action by an anti-tank gun they made their way on foot to within two hundred yards of Battalion H.Q., but there they were stopped by the intensity of the enemy's fire. There was no hope of getting any farther, so after collecting a few men they made their way back to Brigade H.Q., meeting Capt. Houchin on the way. 'B' and 'D' Companies had been outflanked on both sides and the barrage of fire behind them had prevented them from getting back towards the 58th Headquarters; thanks to the action of one platoon of 'D,' which stopped the enemy from coming on, some of them had succeeded in withdrawing by a route farther to the left. 2/Lieut. Reddy, who had been wounded, was taken prisoner when the Field Ambulance to which he had been removed was captured.

### *The Withdrawal to the Coast, 28th–31st May*

It was fortunate that the enemy could not push on on the 28th, for all that could be collected of the 17th Brigade at the time was about seventy men. At 1915 hours the 5th Division was ordered to withdraw northwestwards during the night; all unnecessary baggage was to be dumped and surplus supplies destroyed and, obeying this order, the C.O. of the 58th himself demolished two cases of whisky with a hammer. At 2130 hours the remnants of the Brigade, merged into one unit under his command, were on the move in M.T.; German aircraft were very active, dropping flares and bombs, and the roads were most congested, the result being that they did not reach Drieridders, between Poperinghe and Furnes, until 0500 hours on the 29th.

After a brief rest the 'brigade' took up a position on the Yser Canal between Stavele and the Ypres–Furnes road; this consisted of a series of widely dispersed localities covering likely crossing-places and there would have been little hope of stopping a determined attack. The forward troops, consisting of fragments of the Royal Scots Fusiliers and the 58th, now about a hundred and fifty strong, six carriers and a troop of 25-pounders, under the command of Major Watts, were deployed by 1400 hours; in reserve were the Seaforth, some two hundred strong; to the left the defence was continued by the 13th Brigade.

Later in the day orders came that the 5th Division was to hold the position until 0430 hours on the 30th, so as to give time for the 3rd and 50th Divisions to withdraw. At that hour the Division was to retire to an area within the Dunkirk perimeter.

The force began to thin out at 0330 hours, and at 0445 hours Major Watts was able to report that the last troops were leaving the canal without interference by the enemy. On the way back all vehicles were effectively put out of action by mixing sand with the engine oil and then racing the engines. The force spent the day under cover among the sand-dunes near Adinkerke and was there formed into the '17th Infantry Brigade Battalion,' 441 strong, under the command of Major Watts with the Adjutant of the Seaforth as Second-in-Command and 2/Lieut. Roche as Adjutant.

## *The Evacuation from Dunkirk*, 31st May–1st June

The day passed uneventfully, apart from strong air attacks against the beaches, which were met by intense A.A. fire from the ships lying offshore assisted by the troops on the beaches. At 1830 hours the battalion started along the road to Dunkirk. When they had covered half the distance they were met by some transport sent by the Brigadier; about half the troops were put into this and went on to Dunkirk where they embarked that night; the remainder marched on.

It was dark by the time that they turned off the road on to the beach at Malo les Bains. The approaches to it, and the beach itself, were crowded with troops patiently waiting for boats to take them off from a quay which had been improvised by driving lorries into the sea and placing duckboards over them. Earlier in the day the Brigadier had gone ahead with guides, and now, as the Battalion marched along the beach, they began to meet them; to the C.O.'s repeated call of '17th Brigade,' out of the darkness came the answer 'Straight on,' and each guide, having done his duty, fell in with the Battalion. In due course they reached the landward end of the Mole at Dunkirk, empty save for Brig. Stopford, Brig. Dempsey of the 13th Brigade and their staffs. Let it now be said that throughout the campaign the 17th Brigade owed much to their Commander, who was always calm and cheerful however black the situation, and to whose foresight was due the smooth progress of the move to the Mole.

Things were now fairly quiet, except for spasmodic shelling, mostly upon the town and the docks, and the occasional bomb from an aircraft. At the seaward end of the Mole stood an officer of the Royal Navy waiting to direct the embarkation of the troops. The tide was low and there was no sign of a ship, except for the wreck of one which had been sunk.

It was now one o'clock on the morning of the 1st June. It was cold, and time seemed to pass slowly to the little party as they waited, patiently and in silence. At length, after four hours, the tide had risen sufficiently to allow a destroyer, H.M.S. *Malcolm*, to come alongside, and they embarked by a plank stretching from the edge of the Mole to the ship's bridge, followed by the troops of the 13th Brigade and the two Brigadiers, about eight hundred all told.

The ship sailed and by eight o'clock had berthed in Dover harbour.

After the fighting at St. Eloi the 58th ceased to exist as a battalion, though those who were left carried on with the survivors of the other units of the Brigade. Many of the Battalion never returned; others, forced to spend the rest of the war as prisoners in German hands, did not come back until five long years had passed; but enough returned to England in June 1940 to rebuild a new 58th with the traditions of the old one which had died at St. Eloi.

5th Division

# CHAPTER VI

## THE 5th BATTALION IN FRANCE AND BELGIUM, 1939-1940

*Mobilisation, September 1939—Training, September–December 1939—The 5th in France, January-May 1940—The Move into Belgium, 13th–17th May—The Withdrawal to the Escaut, 17th–18th May—The Fighting on the Escaut, 19th–22nd May—On the Lys, 23rd–27th May—Withdrawal towards Ypres, 27th–28th May—Withdrawal to the Coast, 29th–30th May—Evacuation from Dunkirk, 31st May–1st June (see Map facing p. 50)*

### Mobilisation, September 1939

ON the evening of the 1st September 1939, a fortnight after their return from Annual Camp at Arundel, the 5th Battalion had the order to mobilise. This was carried out by companies in their own towns, Battalion H.Q. and H.Q. Company at Peterborough, 'A' Company at Ramsay St. Mary, 'B' at Oundle, 'C' at Huntingdon and 'D' at St. Neots. The process went smoothly, the most difficult part of it being the putting into operation of the Passive Air Defence scheme, which involved the digging of shelters and the shoring-up of buildings.

### Training, September–December 1939

A fortnight later the Battalion moved to Swindon, the concentration area of the 48th Division. Here it was brought up to war establishment in men and equipment; drafts were received from the I.T.C. at Northampton and from the I.T.C.s of the South Staffordshire and East Lancashire Regiments and of the King's Shropshire Light Infantry.

Route-marches and weapon-training occupied most of the next three months. Training also included the digging of a trench system, which savoured somewhat of the 1914–1918 War. However, it served a useful purpose in helping to get the men fit, especially as companies had to occupy the trenches during the very cold weather at the end of the year. Embarkation leave at the end of December was followed by a review of the Brigade by H.M. the King on the 2nd January. On the next day the Battalion was inspected by the Colonel of the Regiment.

# THE 5th BATTALION IN FRANCE AND BELGIUM, 1939-1940

## *The 5th in France, January–May* 1940

On the 11th January the 5th left Swindon by rail for Southampton, where they embarked in the *Ben-my-Chree*. The next morning they disembarked at Le Havre and, travelling by stages, arrived at Roost Warenden, near Douai, on the 17th. They did not stay there for long, for on the 29th they moved to Roubaix and found themselves transferred to the 11th Brigade of the 4th Division, commanded by Maj.-Gen. D. G. Johnson. This division was in the 2nd Corps, of which the Commander was Lieut.-Gen. A. F. Brooke, later to become Chief of the Imperial General Staff.

Throughout February the main task was work on the improvement of the defences in the Roubaix area. Then, early in March, the Brigade took its turn in the Saar sector of the Maginot Line.

After a few days near Metz the 5th relieved a battalion of the D.C.L.I. in the 'Ligne de Recueuil,' where they worked for ten days on improving the defences. Then, on the 23rd March, they took over a sector of the 'Ligne de Contact' from the 1st East Surrey Regt. Here they carried out active patrolling, but there was no contact with the enemy, the full moon restricting movement on both sides. On the 28th they were relieved by the 2nd Royal Warwickshire Regt. and returned to Tourcoing on the 31st. They had had the honour of being the first battalion of the Territorial Army in the front line.

Back at Tourcoing work on the defences was resumed and early in May the first of the companies went to Vimy to start a fortnight's training. They were still there and Lieut.-Col. Green was visiting them, when early on the 10th May news reached the Battalion that the German armies had entered Belgium and Holland. Transport was immediately sent for the company, which was soon back with the Battalion, as also were the 3-inch Mortar Platoon and the company 2-inch mortar teams, which had been at a French range some twenty miles from Tourcoing. It should be noted that this had been their first opportunity of firing the mortars on a range; even so, when the party was recalled only the 3-inch teams had practised. The 2-inch teams went into action without ever having fired live ammunition; however, as no 2-inch bombs were ever issued and were, apparently, unobtainable, they were not affected by the lack of practice.

## *The Move into Belgium* 13*th*–17*th May*

During the morning of the 10th the Battalion were warned that Plan 'D' was to be put into operation. The 4th Division was to be in Corps reserve and would not be required to move for four days, so the interval was spent in disposing of surplus stores and, generally, in preparing for action.[1]

On the evening of the 14th the Battalion embussed and, after passing through Tournai, Leuze and Renaix, reached Wemmel, north of Brussels, early the next day. It had taken about twelve hours to cover the seventy miles, an indication of the state of congestion caused on the roads by military and refugee traffic.

The rest of that day and the morning of the 16th were spent in reconnaissance; then came the news that the Dutch had capitulated and that the British were withdrawing from their forward positions on the River Dyle. The 5th were ordered to move into position and this they did late that night.

The position lay along the Charleroi Canal, just to the north of Brussels, and companies established themselves in posts in the factories and warehouses which lined the bank. The canal, some sixty yards wide, was almost full of barges so while the R.E. prepared the bridges for demolition the 5th collected the barges, and did their best to sink them by means of grenades and shots from anti-tank rifles. These efforts were unsuccessful and eventually the R.E. came to the rescue with more professional methods.

Work went on throughout the 17th, the bridges being blown when the forward troops of the B.E.F. had crossed them. At about 2000 hours the 5th made their first contact with the enemy on 'C' Company's front and, a little later, a German scout-car reached the canal opposite 'A' Company, but, apart from an interchange of small-arms fire, there was no serious engagement.

*The Withdrawal to the Escaut, 17th–18th May*

Late that night the Battalion were ordered to withdraw to Aspelaire, west of Ninove, and reached this place at between 0800 and 1000 hours on the 18th, not without some difficulty due to the inaccuracy of the maps. 'B' Echelon transport were lucky; they had been ordered to leave Wemmel at 0500 hours, but this timing did not take the enemy into account and the transport only just got away in time after coming under fire.

All were very exhausted when they reached Aspelaire. Few had had any sleep for the past seventy-two hours, and the twenty-mile march from Brussels had not been made any easier by the fact that, owing to the absence of the transport, the Battalion weapons had had to be carried by the men. There was not even time to organise a proper meal at Aspelaire, though use was made of any food that could be found locally abandoned by the inhabitants, for at 1130 hours, before all the companies had come in, orders came to move westwards again at 1200 hours. The journey by lorry was slow, and it was not until dusk was falling that the Battalion reached the hamlet of Dihaye, about four miles down the River Escaut from Audenarde. Here, with carrier patrols providing local protection, the troops managed to get a short night's rest.

## THE 5th BATTALION IN FRANCE AND BELGIUM, 1939-1940

*The Fighting on the Escaut, 19th–22nd May*

After reconnaissance at daybreak on the 19th the position, which extended for some two thousand yards on the west bank of the river, was occupied. In the main position 'C' Company were on the right, 'D' on the left in touch with the Queen's of the 44th Division. Covering these companies, and on the other side of the river, were the carriers, about a mile and a half to the south-east, and 'A' Company in the village of Berchem. 'B' were in reserve at Kerkhove and Battalion H.Q. in a house behind 'D' Company's front.

The rest of the day was spent in digging and wiring the position and in making arrangements for the withdrawal of 'A' Company across the river either by foot-bridges or boats. Units of the 3rd Division withdrew through the position and late in the day reports reached Brigade that enemy motorised columns were approaching Renaix, about five miles to the southeast. As a result of this the carriers were ordered to withdraw after daylight on the 20th and, as soon as they were over the river, the bridge on the right of the Battalion front was blown.

'A' Company were well hidden in scattered houses on the edge of the village, their Commander, Capt. Hart, keeping a watch down the road with binoculars for any sign of the enemy. At about 1100 hours a group of about twelve apparent refugees approached. To Capt. Hart it seemed that they were walking with a somewhat martial stride and his suspicions were confirmed when they were followed by about twenty cyclists, riding in pairs, and a lorry. The section covering the road held their fire until the cyclists were a good target at close range and then opened fire with Bren and rifles. The first burst of fire was effective, bringing down all the cyclists; whereupon the 'refugees' doubled off the road and opened fire with tommy-guns, while the lorry took cover behind a house, whence a mortar soon began to shoot. The Battalion 3-inch mortars were in action very quickly and some of 'A' Company advanced and took the 'refugees' in flank.

A more determined attack followed and was broken up by small-arms and mortar fire. At 1300 hours the Company were ordered to withdraw across the river into position behind 'D' Company and did so by boat without any interference from the enemy, having suffered only four casualties. In this, their first serious engagement, the 5th had taken the enemy by surprise and had given them more than they had expected. Capt. Hart was granted the immediate award of the Military Cross and Ptes. Sharpe and Herbert the Military Medal for their gallantry during the day's fighting.

Apart from some shelling and an attack on the front of the Queen's Regt. in which the Germans gained a foothold on the west bank of the river, from which they were soon ejected, the rest of the day and the night passed off quietly. But this state of affairs was not to last for long.

At noon on the 21st, 'D' Company and the Queen's came under very heavy artillery and mortar fire, and this soon extended to 'C' Company's front. After an hour and a half's steady bombardment of the front area the fire lifted on to buildings, including Battalion H.Q. and likely spots for reserves farther to the rear, cutting all line communications. At the same time an attack developed against 'D' Company.

It was evident that the enemy's intention was to force a crossing and establish a bridgehead. The rear of the Company area came under artillery (chiefly 5·9-inch) and mortar fire, and the front was swept by machine-gun fire from the right flank. Houses gave the attackers a covered approach up to within about fifty yards of the eastern bank of the river; but those fifty yards were open ground and, as soon as the German infantry emerged from the cover of the houses in parties of three, each party carrying a small folding boat, they came under most effective fire from the Company and from the machine-guns of a supporting platoon of the Royal Northumberland Fusiliers. After an hour of repeated but unsuccessful efforts to cross those fifty yards the attack died down, to be renewed at about 1530 hours. This time it extended over the whole of the Battalion front, but again the enemy could make no progress; and in five further attempts up to 2200 hours the result was the same, despite the fact that the 5th could get no artillery support owing to difficulties of communication by wireless, and had to rely upon the 3-inch mortars under 2/Lieut. Orr, which shot most effectively.

By about 1600 hours the enemy had managed to get across the river farther to the left. 'D' Company stood firm against many efforts to widen this bridgehead, but suffered considerable casualties from the enemy's fire and, by the end of the day, their effective strength was less than two platoons. 'C' Company had also lost about a third of their strength. Shortly before midnight, therefore, the Battalion front was readjusted. 'A' were moved up to the left of 'C,' and 'D' were withdrawn slightly to link up with the left of 'A,' the front then being roughly in the shape of a right angle with the left thrown back from the river to meet the threat caused by the withdrawal of the battalion on that flank. During the night the 6th Black Watch came up on the Battalion's left rear and so prevented the enemy from working round and surrounding them.

During the day's fighting Battalion H.Q. had been established in the cellar of a vicarage. This, though not the peaceful spot it should have been, had the virtue of strength, for it had withstood bombardment by 5·9s and 4-inch mortars reasonably well. However, with the readjustment of the front, this place was too far to the left, so H.Q. was moved to the edge of the village of Castre. At the R.A.P. the Medical Officer, Capt. Holloway, had been wounded and until a relief arrived for him a few days later the

Chaplain, the Rev. Quinn, acted as M.O. and was awarded the Military Cross for the work he did. In the course of the day Capt. Cobbing also had been wounded while carrying out a reconnaissance; but he remained at duty until the 23rd, when he was ordered to hospital.

Early on the 22nd reconnaissance patrols from 'A' Company found that the enemy who were across the river on the left were in considerable strength, estimated at not less than two companies. According to information from Brigade, a counter-attack was to be delivered by other troops against the enemy bridgehead, but this never took place.

In the afternoon, half an hour's heavy bombardment of 'C' Company's area was followed by an attack at 1330 hours; helped by good support from the artillery, the Company put up a stout resistance and the enemy made no progress. Unfortunately, after two hours, Company H.Q. had a direct hit upon it; the Company Commander, Capt. J. H. Johnson, was killed and there were many other casualties. Realising that 'C' were by now very reduced in numbers, the C.O. ordered the Carrier Platoon up to hold the enemy. They got into position and covered the withdrawal of the remnants of the Company, but suffered severely; any movement of the carriers attracted shelling directed by an aircraft which patrolled the front with impunity at a low height, and during the day the Platoon lost five of its vehicles and seventeen out of its twenty-eight men, eleven being killed. Twice in this action carriers found themselves surrounded and out of ammunition, and fought their way clear with hand-grenades.

Pressure now developed on 'B' Company. Here the enemy managed to penetrate into a wood just in front of the position, but the threat of a platoon advancing with fixed bayonets, led by Capt. Measures, induced them to withdraw.

At about 1630 hours a warning order was received from Brigade that a withdrawal would probably take place at about 2200 hours. On this, arrangements were made to get back some of the troops not immediately required, such as the Pioneer Platoon. At 1715 hours Lieut.-Col. Green left for a conference at Brigade H.Q., and Major Marshall, the Adjutant, went to reconnoitre a position at Teighem which the C.O. had selected as suitable to cover the withdrawal from the forward area, leaving Capt. Cobbing in command.

Shortly before this the enemy's artillery had opened up on 'A' Company's front. Hitherto the attacks in this area had taken the form of somewhat half-hearted rushes, supported by small-arms fire only, but obviously this was a more serious affair. At Battalion H.Q. it was difficult to find out what was happening, for line communication was continually cut by shell-fire and runners had to cross open ground swept by bullets. However, when the artillery fire lifted the Brens could be heard firing and the conclusion was that the Company was all right.

So the evening wore on, with pressure upon both 'A' and 'B' Companies which, though suffering casualties, were well supported by our own artillery and continued to hold back the enemy. But there was no sign of Lieut.-Col. Green. At 1850 hours Major Marshall returned to Battalion H.Q. with news that the C.O. had been wounded while reconnoitring the ground at Teighem on his way back from the conference at Brigade H.Q. As no one knew the orders for the withdrawal, Major Marshall went in search of Brigade H.Q., which had been shelled out of its previous location.

Just after this, Capt. Pashley of 'D' Company arrived at Battalion H.Q. and reported on the situation. It was clear that 'A' and 'B,' weak as they were, would be overwhelmed before long; accordingly Capt. Cobbing instructed him to tell them to hold on for as long as they could and, if they had to withdraw, to do so towards the north-west; Battalion H.Q. would cover them as they came back.

Before long, movement could be seen in the forward area and by 1940 hours it seemed that all the companies had withdrawn; so the Battalion H.Q. party, consisting of three officers and four men, with five wounded, left in a truck and a carrier to find Brigade H.Q. On the way they met 2/Lieut. King, who had been with the C.O. and had the notes on the Brigade orders, and he told them what had happened. He and 2/Lieut. Hill had been with Lieut.-Col. Green on the high ground near Teighem when a splinter from a shell bursting nearby hit the C.O. It was learnt later that he had died in the C.C.S. at St. Jean, near Ypres, to which he had been taken.

Shortly after this Capt. Cobbing met Brig. K. A. N. Anderson and told him of the situation. After he had been given the plan for the withdrawal, Capt. Cobbing arranged to meet the companies at a bridge over the canal which they would have to cross. Contact was duly made at this point, which was on the Courtrai road, and companies were ordered to make for Roncq, where arrangements were made to off-load the transport and send it back to lift the troops. By 0800 hours most of the Battalion had arrived there, though small parties which had got detached continued to come in for some hours.

The 5th had had a hard time on the Escaut. Eleven officers had been killed or wounded, 'C' Company came out less than forty strong and the other rifle companies could only muster sixty or seventy men apiece. The gravest loss was that of the C.O., who had commanded them for more than five years. But, despite their losses, they had shown an enemy who was superior in number and in equipment, and in the air, how a battalion of the British Territorial Army could fight. They owed much to the Royal Northumberland Fusiliers, whose supporting machine-guns had stopped the enemy from following up as the companies withdrew.

## On the Lys, 23rd–27th May

At Roncq the 5th were back in the positions which they had been digging in the earlier days of the war. Besides being very weak in strength they were, like most other units of the B.E.F. at this stage, very short of arms and equipment. They had but three carriers left, and the two 3-inch mortars which remained to the three battalions were brigaded under 2/Lieut. Orr. The Brigade diary mentions these as having done very good work one day when, in support of the 2nd Lancashire Fusiliers, they engaged many targets.

The Brigade was now facing north, forming part of the defensive flank which kept open the corridor leading towards the coast. The 5th were in reserve to the other two battalions which held a line on the River Lys, north of Halluin; so they managed to get some rest though subject to constant attacks by aircraft.

On the 25th Lieut.-Col. G. A. Anstee, M.C., of the Bedfordshire and Hertfordshire Regt., arrived to take command; Major Marshall then became Second-in-Command and Lieut. Hill, Adjutant. Almost his first duty was to have to tell the officers and the N.C.O.s that the B.E.F. was to withdraw from France. All documents were destroyed and the Battalion stood by for a move at short notice.

## Withdrawal towards Ypres, 27th–28th May

Throughout the 26th and 27th large numbers of enemy troops could be seen to the north of Halluin, moving westwards, but no attack developed against the front held by Brigade. German aircraft were active in dropping leaflets which gave what proved to be accurate maps of the Allied salient and called upon the troops to surrender.

On the 27th the Brigade Reconnaissance Group, under Lieut.-Col. Anstee, left to select new positions between Ypres and Poperinghe. At 2300 hours the Battalion, commanded by Major Lamplugh who had rejoined from H.Q. 4th Division, got on the move to follow them.

The marching troops of the Brigade were due to reach Vlamertinghe at 0600 hours on the 28th, but the Recce Group had no news of them until Lieut. Hilton-Johnson eventually discovered them at Wytschaete, some four miles south of Ypres, at about 1100 hours. They had had a long and trying march and, owing to lack of transport, all weapons had to be man-handled. The C.O. then returned to the Battalion, but the unit Recce Groups got no orders to rejoin because despatch-riders failed to reach them over roads under heavy fire. Eventually the 5th's Recce Group of twenty-three officers and men got back late in the afternoon, after travelling a considerable distance in one 15-cwt. truck and a civilian bus, which had been found and was driven by Lieut. Cawdell.

At Wytschaete the Brigade Commander had found the situation to be very confused. Elements of another brigade were falling back into the town and German infantry were advancing to the east of the road to St. Eloi. However, by about 1000 hours the 11th Brigade was in position astride this road, the Lancashire Fusiliers on the right and the 5th on the left. The latter now had only three rifle companies, 'C' and 'D' having been amalgamated.

Throughout the day the situation remained obscure and the fog of war was not made any clearer by the lack of any maps for the Company Commanders. The location of the enemy was unknown, though Ypres was thought to be still in British hands. The 5th Division, under whose command the 11th Brigade had temporarily been placed, was known to be at St. Eloi, about a mile to the east, and was to withdraw through the Brigade during the morning; but the Battalion saw only a few of the men of the 58th.

In the early afternoon enemy shelling and mortar fire became heavy and caused several casualties, among them four officers, Capt. Heard, Lieut. Stanley, the Rev. Quinn and the new Medical Officer. Wytschaete and the roads in the vicinity were heavily bombed.

*Withdrawal to the Coast, 29th–30th May*

In the evening a withdrawal was ordered to Coppernollenhoek, three miles north of Poperinghe. The Battalion was clear of its position shortly before midnight and there followed a long and difficult march of the type to which all were now accustomed. The roads were very congested and were the target for much bombing, especially in Poperinghe. Reaching the Brigade assembly area in the early hours of the 29th, they found a hot meal waiting for them, but they had not eaten this when orders came for them to be at half an hour's notice to move onwards in their unit M.T. only. To make room for the troops, all stores and equipment not required for actual fighting had to be jettisoned. Their destination was Furnes, but when about half-way to that place they were ordered to debus and continue the move on foot. All vehicles, except Company Commanders' trucks, were driven off the road to be destroyed under Brigade arrangements.

Arrived at Furnes the Battalion took up a position on the canal bank to cover the withdrawal of the 3rd Division across the only bridge which had not been blown. There was a considerable amount of sniping and shelling, but no attack developed. After relief by a battalion of the Coldstreams that evening, the Battalion moved to another position farther north, and here, by midnight, the 2nd Bn. The Grenadier Guards took over from them.

By 0600 hours on the 30th the 5th were in the sand-dunes on the coast near Oost Dunkirk, facing towards the Nieuport canal. The digging of defensive posts in the sand was difficult owing to the total lack of tools and material, and it was necessary to commandeer garden tools and even children's spades from the seaside villas, and to appropriate outhouse doors for revetting. The situation was not made any easier by the fact that there were many Belgian civilians about, and most of the houses were flying white flags which had to be removed from those which the Battalion wanted to occupy. By now the 5th had only two companies, but were not called upon to resist any attack, though they had to endure the usual shelling and mortaring, and suffered more casualties.

*Evacuation from Dunkirk, 31st May–1st June*

Early on the 31st orders were received to send off a party of one officer and fifty other ranks who were to return to England ahead of the Battalion in case it should prove impossible to evacuate the remainder. Lieut. Hunnybun, now the I.O., and specialists such as Signallers and Pioneers, left for La Panne and went from there to Dunkirk, where they embarked. The rest of the Battalion remained in the dunes, sending patrols up to the canal, where the situation was somewhat uncertain. Hostile fire continued to be heavy, but caused only a few casualties, thanks to the careful siting of the posts. At 1900 hours they began to thin out, and by 2330 had successfully withdrawn and were on their way to La Panne.

The intention was for the troops to embark at La Panne by means of improvised piers, but the number of boats available to take them from the pier-heads to the ships was very limited, so much so that on that night not more than three to four hundred men had been taken off the beaches out of a total of about eight thousand; so brigades were told to go either to Bray or to Dunkirk. Some seventy men of the 5th had got on board ship at La Panne. The rest of the Battalion, after a long wait while the beaches were heavily shelled, made their way to Dunkirk. There they were embarked and later on the same day, the 1st June, reached Dover, whence they went by train to Aldershot.

The story of the 5th Battalion in this, their first campaign, is the story of many other units of the B.E.F.—a long period of waiting, a rapid advance, a withdrawal before there had been any serious contact with the enemy, a stubborn fight against troops superior in almost everything except courage and refusal to give in, and then, through no fault of theirs, retreat to England.

In the fighting on the Escaut, the first major battle in their history, the 5th had shown the enemy what they could do. In the years ahead they were to have more opportunities and on more level terms.

# CHAPTER VII

## THE TRAINING YEARS, 1940-1942

The Army's Problem—The 48th at Dinapore, September 1939-January 1940—The 48th at Jhansi, January 1940-March 1941—The Bi-centenary of the 48th, 17th January 1941—The 48th at Dinapore, March 1941-January 1942—Mobilisation, January 1942—The 48th in Ceylon, June-December 1942—The 58th in Scotland and England, June 1940-April 1941—The 58th in Northern Ireland, April 1941-January 1942—The 58th at Caterham, January-March 1942—The 4th Bn. in England, September 1939-June 1940—The 4th Bn. in Northern Ireland, June 1940-December 1942—The 5th Bn. in England, June 1940-April 1942—The 5th Bn. in Scotland, April-October 1942—The 50th (Holding) Bn., June-October 1940—The 6th Bn., October 1940-December 1942—The 70th Bn., December 1940-December 1942—The I.T.C., 1939-1942

## *The Army's Problem*

WITH what remained of the B.E.F. back in England, it was only a matter of days before France gave up the unequal struggle against the Axis powers, leaving the British Empire to continue the fight alone until the treachery of Germany and Japan brought first Russia then the U.S.A. to its support.

For the first time since the Napoleonic Wars, England was in danger of invasion. The immediate threat of this, in the summer and autumn of 1940, was averted, thanks to the efforts of the Royal Air Force and Anti-Aircraft Command in the Battle of Britain and to the shield of the Royal Navy. They were helped, indirectly, by the miscalculations of the German Intelligence Service, which estimated the force available for the defence of Britain at thirty-nine divisions, twenty of which were supposed to be completely operational though equipped with only half their normal strength of artillery.

The possibility of encountering resistance from a force of that size, with an estimated million recruits of the Home Guard behind it, disturbed the German High Command, who were not to know that there were, in fact, only two or three properly equipped divisions. Nevertheless, it would have been dangerous to underestimate the threat and, though many months passed before it no longer existed, the Army was faced with many problems while it still lasted.

The units and formations which had composed the B.E.F. had been the best trained and the best equipped of the Army serving at home, and they had battle experience. But by the time that they had returned to England they had suffered considerable casualties and had lost the bulk of their equipment.

Men were available to bring units up to strength again, but these reinforcements and the survivors of the B.E.F. required training, and training was now an even more complex affair than it had been in 1939. Lessons had been learnt in the fighting in France and these led to new equipment and new tactics. The soldier had now not only to be a master of the rifle and the Bren gun: he had to learn to handle the Sten and the Piat; to learn new battle-drill and apply it at the schools which were soon organised to give 'battle inoculation'; to learn the technique of combined operations against the time when the offensive would be resumed.

The equipment lost by the B.E.F. was replaced comparatively quickly, but just as the need for the introduction of new tactics had been realised, so had the need for new types of equipment. These took time to produce and the delay further complicated the training problem.

In order to meet the threat of invasion, units had to be disposed tactically, and their stations were not necessarily those most suitable for training. Furthermore, they had to work day after day on the construction of defences and there were other distractions, such as the giving of help in the training of the Local Defence Volunteers, as they were called until their name, by a stroke of genius, was changed to that of the Home Guard.

So, faced by many difficulties and many conflicting tasks, the British Army trained, at first for the defence of the country, then for the operations which would lead to victory. The Northamptonshire Regiment was not among those which were represented in the Desert Army, at this time, under General Sir Archibald Wavell, showing the forces of the Axis that the Empire was not yet defeated. In the United Kingdom and in India its battalions were preparing for the day when they could play their part in other theatres of war, though not all of them were to have that privilege.

*The 48th at Dinapore, September 1939–January 1940*

Although war had broken out in Europe, it was to be a long time before India felt the full impact. Meanwhile, the 48th at Dinapore were not mobilised and carried on with their internal security duties. War did bring some variety to these, for almost immediately they were ordered to establish a temporary camp for the reception of the enemy aliens collected by the police in the province of Bihar. A block of condemned and disused married-quarters in Victoria Barracks was considered suitable for the purpose and, after it had been duly wired in and fitted with perimeter lights, it received twenty-one German civilians. These were almost equally divided between engineers, who had been engaged in the installation of plant at the Tata steel-works, and missionaries. Neither category caused any trouble and, within a fortnight, they were transferred to the big internment camp at Ahmednagar.

At the end of November the Army Commander, General Sir Douglas Baird, inspected the Battalion and took the salute at a march-past. Afterwards he wrote that he wished all ranks to know how very pleased he was with all that he had seen. He particularly commended the steadiness of the Battalion on parade, the good arms-drill and march-past, and the fit appearance of all ranks.

Shortly afterwards, on the 16th December, the Battalion provided a Guard of Honour at the unveiling by H.E. the Governor of Bihar, Sir James Stewart, of the memorial statue to H.M. King George V at Patna. The guard of a hundred rank and file, under the command of Capt. R. E. Osborne-Smith, with 2/Lieut. M. R. Haselhurst carrying the Colour, was composed entirely of men wearing the Frontier medal and was worthy of the occasion.

Early in September the 48th had received news that the projected move to Nasirabad had been cancelled. No one was sorry, for this would have been yet another single-battalion station, with detachments to be found; all were equally glad when they heard that they were to go instead to Jhansi, in January. In that month 'C' Company rejoined the Battalion from the Andaman Islands, on relief by a company of the 1st Cameronians, and on the 14th the 48th left Dinapore by train for the new station, having handed over to the 1st Bn. The Lincolnshire Regt.

Though Dinapore was a poor station for a British battalion, the reputation of the 48th had been well maintained there. In the city of Patna the troops had frequently been subject to great provocation and even to attack by the anti-British element there, so much so that they had to be forbidden to visit it in parties of less than four, and a patrol of Regimental Police had to be maintained on the road between the city and Dinapore, as a safeguard for men returning off pass. When the Battalion left, the C.O. received a letter from the Governor of Bihar, who had taken a great personal interest in the Battalion, in which he expressed his appreciation of their discipline and good behaviour.

*The 48th at Jhansi, January 1940–March 1941*

Reaching Jhansi on the 15th January, the 48th found themselves concentrated, with no detachments, for the first time since they had left Waziristan in 1937. In all respects the new station was a great improvement on the old; there was a large garrison and plenty of good training areas and ranges nearby; and though the hot weather was trying, practically all ranks, with the exception of those of Battalion H.Q., spent some weeks of it at the hill-station of Kailana.

The 48th Guard of Honour at the unveiling of the King George V Memorial, Patna, 1939

## THE TRAINING YEARS, 1940-1942

The other units at Jhansi included the three Indian battalions of the 10th Indian Infantry Brigade, under the command of Brig. W. J. Slim, M.C., later to become famous as the Commander of the Fourteenth Army in Burma. It was a disappointment to the 48th that when this brigade eventually went to the Middle East they were not included in it; but it contained no British battalion.

Advantage was taken of the facilities for training at Jhansi to make up for the deficiencies of Dinapore in that respect and, although the 48th had been unable to do any battalion training since 1935, they soon found themselves called upon to act as 'enemy' to the Jhansi Brigade in many exercises, usually in conjunction with Indian State Forces and units of the Indian Territorial Force.

Towards the end of 1939 Army H.Q. in Delhi had produced a very comprehensive programme for the mechanisation of units, which laid down the phases in which training and equipment with vehicles was to be carried out. Though no doubt admirable on paper, this programme worked out less well in practice. At Dinapore the first sign of mechanisation had been an extremely part-worn ambulance, issued for training purposes; but this, having been towed into barracks by a pair of bullocks, was of little subsequent value. At Jhansi the Battalion hoped for better things, but naturally the Indian units which were being prepared for service overseas were given priority. However, by means of some lorries of ancient pattern, some stripped chassis, one old motor-cycle and an assortment of spare parts from local garages, training did progress, and by the end of the year all the officers had done a course in driving and maintenance and had passed as proficient motor-cyclists, and about a hundred other ranks had been trained as unit drivers.

In other respects too, British units in India were far behind their counterparts at home. Mortars, anti-tank rifles and carriers had not been issued and few of the troops had any knowledge of their handling. A further drawback was that, though the Vickers-Berthier light-automatic, the equivalent of the Bren in India, was intended to be used in both the light and the medium rôles, no tripods were available; consequently, no men could be trained to use the gun in the latter rôle.

On the 1st February the Battalion received its first draft since the beginning of the war. Of the thirty-one men in it, twenty-two were Militiamen, the first to join the 48th. The draft was unlucky, for an outbreak of contagious disease on board their troopship led to their having to spend their first few weeks in India in monotonous segregation in the gymnasium of the barracks, an unfortunate introduction to the country.

At this time the first of the emergency commissioned officers began to join the Battalion from England, and the 48th were called upon to send home numbers of experienced officers, warrant officers and N.C.O.s to help in the training of the greatly expanded Army. They were a great loss and it was no easy matter to replace them by others of equal experience.[1]

Early in May Lieut.-Col. Jervois was ordered home at short notice to take up an appointment at the War Office. He left on the 20th and was succeeded by Major A. O. F. Winkler, who relinquished command, owing to ill-health, at the end of the year. The Battalion was then commanded by Major D. E. Taunton for two months until Major J. V. Brewin returned from a course and took over from him.

Towards the end of the year two companies at a time went into a training-camp at Raksa, eight miles from Jhansi, but battalion training had to be done from barracks. After the departure overseas of the Jhansi Brigade the 48th, with three other British battalions, were concentrated for a fortnight in a camp at Babina, sixteen miles away. It was claimed that this was the largest concentration of British troops in India since the days of the Mutiny. In this camp the training was designed to give units a change from their internal-security duties and to teach lessons derived from mobile warfare in country which was not unlike that of the Middle East. Exercises involved many long marches in hot weather, and the Battalion earned praise for its good marching powers and speed of movement across country. Service M.T. vehicles were lent to units during this training and, as this was the drivers' first experience of handling them in practice, it says much for the earlier training that the results were as satisfactory as they proved.

### The Bi-centenary of the 48th, 17th January 1941

Wartime inevitably prevented the full celebration of a great event in the history of the Regiment—the two-hundredth anniversary of the raising of the 48th in 1741. Telegrams of greeting were received from the Colonel-in-Chief and many others, and the members of the Battalion did their best to observe the 17th January in proper form. After an inspection on parade by Lieut.-Col. G. Horsfield, the Station Commander at Jhansi, the Colours were marched in slow time along the front of the Battalion; the troops then marched past the Colours by platoons and finally the inspecting officer took the salute. Later in the day the Colours and the Regimental Silver were displayed to all ranks, sports were held and the day ended with a ball.[2]

### The 48th at Dinapore, March 1941–January 1942

Towards the beginning of March there was likelihood of serious communal disturbances in Bihar and, at the request of the Governor of that Province, who had formed a high opinion of the 48th during their earlier stay there, two companies were despatched to Dinapore at the end of the month. Battalion H.Q. soon followed and, though the expected riots did occur, the troops were not called upon to take any drastic action.

For some months the Battalion was scattered in various detachments, but by November they were concentrated at Dinapore, except for two companies stationed at Allahabad. At this time they received their full complement of M.T. and a few carriers for instructional purposes, and it became possible to do some useful training; but owing to the lack of any clear directive as to what was required, it was difficult to achieve any continuity.

*Mobilisation, January* 1942

By January 1942 the Japanese armies had overrun Malaya and were beginning their advance northwards through Burma. At the end of the month the 48th had sudden orders to mobilise with the greatest possible speed. Stores and equipment poured in and three-quarters of the Battalion saw for the first time such weapons as the anti-tank rifle, the 2-inch and 3-inch mortar and the ·38 pistol. Time allowed of but the briefest instruction being given in the handling of these weapons, and even this was only possible because a recent draft had included men with the necessary experience.

Very soon the Battalion left for Calcutta and there found that they, the 1st Bn. The Welch Regt. and the 2nd Bn. The Border Regt., were to form a brigade destined for Rangoon, then threatened by the Japanese.

The three battalions, less their M.T. but with all their stores, ammunition and equipment, duly embarked in the S.S. *Jala Dirga*. This vessel, of less than 4,000 tons, had normally been engaged in conveying pilgrims to Mecca; the accommodation, which may have appeared luxurious to a pilgrim, was distinctly cramped for British troops, but the prospect of action after two years of inactivity in India stifled any complaints.

The ship sailed slowly down the Hooghly and reached the Sunderbunds. Then, after cruising about in an unpleasant swell for some hours, she returned to Calcutta; the troops disembarked and the 48th made their way back to Dinapore.

It was a great anticlimax and a bitter disappointment to all ranks that they had not reached Rangoon. Not till later was it known that the cancellation of the move was due to the evacuation of that city by the British and Indian troops in the face of overwhelmingly superior Japanese forces.

Though they could not appreciate it at the time, it was fortunate for them that they had got no farther than they did. Had they reached Burma then, they would have been fighting with weapons which were strange to them, in conditions of warfare for which they had not been trained; and the brigade of which they formed part was a hurriedly organised formation, with a Commander and two staff officers but no H.Q. Staff and no Signal

Section. In fact, it is difficult to see what influence this brigade could have had on the situation which existed at Rangoon, and they were better saved to fight another day.

## The 48th in Ceylon, June–December 1942

After their return to Dinapore the 48th were able to carry out intensive training in their new weapons and, as far as the flat, sparsely wooded country allowed, in jungle warfare.

In April morale rose considerably, for they were transferred to Secunderabad, to the 80th Independent Infantry Brigade which contained two other British battalions. Here the country resembled that of Libya and the training was for desert warfare, but this did not last for long.

Early in July the brigade moved to Ceylon, where it joined the 20th Indian Division. Soon after its arrival the order of battle of the division was altered, in order to conform with the policy under which each brigade was to be composed of one British, one Indian and one Gurkha battalion. The 48th were transferred to the 32nd Indian Infantry Brigade, commanded by Brig. Chappel, the other battalions in it being the 9/14th Punjab Regt. and the 3/8th Gurkha Rifles. The division was commanded by Major-Gen. D. D. Gracey, and it was under him that the Battalion was to serve for practically the whole of the campaign in Burma.

In Ceylon the 20th Indian Division relieved an Australian Division and took over the responsibility for the defence of the southern portion of the island against Japanese invasion. Consequently the 48th, with headquarters at Horana, were very dispersed, but despite this, training for jungle warfare started in earnest. In the course of this, during a river-crossing exercise in November, one officer, Lieut. Boshell, and eight private soldiers were unfortunately drowned.

On the 15th October Lieut.-Col. Brewin relinquished command and was succeeded by Major D. E. Taunton.

## The 58th in Scotland and England, June 1940–April 1941

On the return of the B.E.F. from Dunkirk the officers and men of the 58th were despatched to various reception camps, but within a fortnight the Battalion had assembled in a concentration area at Turriff in Aberdeenshire. Shortly afterwards they received drafts of ten officers of the Somerset Light Infantry and 320 other ranks from the 50th Battalion and moved into camp at Dalgaty nearby, where they reorganised and were issued with fresh equipment. By the end of the month they were up to strength again and went into another camp at Doune. On the 18th June Lieut.-Col. Hinchcliffe came back and resumed command. He and R.S.M. Goodall, who rejoined soon afterwards, had both recovered from the wounds they had received at Maroeuil in May.

The months which followed were spent in training and in practising the defence tasks allotted to the Battalion, but one notable event occurred on the 5th October. H.R.H. the Duchess of Gloucester paid her first visit to the 58th since she had been appointed Colonel-in-Chief of the Regiment.

Late in October the Battalion left Scotland and went into billets at Northwich in Cheshire. Here, on the 17th January 1941, they too celebrated the bicentenary of the Regiment. The band came from the Depot for the occasion, and on the 19th there was a commemorative parade service in Hartford Church. Heavy snow prevented the holding of a full ceremonial parade but, after the service, the Battalion marched past their Brigade Commander, Brig. Stopford. It was the last time that they were to be able to do this, for before the end of the month he was succeeded in command by Brig. G. W. D. Tarleton. The 58th were genuinely sorry to lose the man who had commanded the 17th Brigade since the beginning of the war; he was to gain much distinction in the years ahead in the campaign in the Far East.

In March the training, which had been progressing steadily, was interrupted for a short time. Liverpool had suffered a series of heavy air-raids and the Battalion was sent there for fire-watching duty. Their week's stay there was, however, uneventful and they returned to Northwich, but within a week they had orders to prepare to move to another station.

*The 58th in Northern Ireland, March 1941–January 1942*

On the 4th April the 58th embarked at Stranraer and marched into billets in Enniskillen, Northern Ireland, on the following day. Here they were close to the border with neutral Eire, and this soon caused complications. As a result of faulty map-reading the R.Q.M.S. aiming to visit Armagh, crossed the border and found himself detained by the Civil Guards. However, whatever the other shortcomings of Eire, her neutrality was reasonably benevolent and he was released after a few hours' detention. With the object of avoiding further incidents of this nature, steps were taken to have the course of the frontier line heavily marked on all maps.

While in Northern Ireland, advantage was taken of the opportunity to investigate the state of the property of the Officers' and Sergeants' Messes, which had been stored in Belfast when the Battalion went to Aldershot in 1939. It was found that the warehouse in which the property had been stored had been destroyed in the course of one of the enemy air attacks on the city, and that not a stick of furniture, nor a picture, remained. This was a grievous loss of many articles of historical and sentimental value which could never be replaced. The sole consolation was that the loss would have been even more severe had it also involved the Mess Silver, but this fortunately was still safe in the strong-room of a bank.

Training went on uninterruptedly, except in September when most of the Battalion were employed on gathering in the harvest. In the many exercises in which they took part, the 58th often found themselves opposing the 4th Battalion, whom they were also able to meet on more friendly occasions.

So the months passed, with the 58th becoming fitter every day for a more active rôle, till in January 1942 the warning order came that the 5th Division was to get ready to move.

### The 58th at Caterham, January–March 1942

On the 17th the Battalion left for Caterham. The M.T., which did the journey from the north of England by road, did not arrive there until the 26th, four days late, owing to snowbound roads, and it was to the drivers' credit that they lost none of their vehicles.

A week after their arrival the 58th were warned that all leave would be regarded as embarkation leave. This was significant, and the meaning was made even more clear when, on the following day, they heard that the division was to be prepared to go overseas, to a tropical country, and that mobilisation was to be completed by the 28th February.

By the appointed date the Battalion was ready. On the 4th March they were inspected by the Colonel of the Regiment, and a week later the 17th Brigade formed up on the Caterham bypass for a visit by H.M. the King.

Soon afterwards Exercise 'Snowdrop,' as it was called, started. The 58th left Caterham in two trains, reached Liverpool on the 20th and embarked in the *Duchess of Atholl*. They little knew then what countries they were to see before they caught sight of England once again.

### The 4th Bn. in England, September 1939–June 1940

For the first month of the war the 4th Battalion stayed in the county. The H.Q. Company had a short spell of guarding vulnerable points, such as Weedon Barracks and various railway tunnels, before moving into billets in Northampton. The other companies were at Wittering, Upwood, Peterborough and Wyton. After a very brief stay in billets near Wantage, where considerable difficulty was experienced in communicating with outlying companies as the Battalion had no proper transport or signalling equipment, the 4th moved to Talavera Barracks, Aldershot. The prospect of Aldershot was not welcomed, owing to the stories spread by old soldiers; however, when they had been there for a short time the majority of the men found that they preferred it to billets in the country. On the 13th October, the day after their arrival, an Adjutant's parade was held, the first occasion on which the Battalion had paraded as a whole since its re-formation in April.

Unfortunately, the 4th did not remain in Aldershot for long. At the end of October they moved to Wellingborough, on transfer from the 48th

## THE TRAINING YEARS, 1940-1942

to the 61st Division, but even then their wanderings were not over, for in January they were at Chesham and Datchet in Buckinghamshire. In April two companies went on detachment to Warminster and in June the whole Battalion was near Newbury.

Col. Lowther had left the 4th in March, at the end of his period of command. He was succeeded, temporarily, by Major R. A. Marriott, and later in the month Major J. Lingham was appointed permanently.

On the 20th April the Battalion celebrated the first anniversary of its re-formation. In an address to them on parade, the Honorary Colonel, Lieut.-Gen. Sir John Brown, reminded them that the day was also the anniversary of the birth of Adolf Hitler. It is doubtful if the 4th deemed this coincidence a matter for self-congratulation.

### The 4th Bn. in Northern Ireland, June 1940-December 1942

After being given forty-eight hours' notice, the Battalion left Newbury on the 18th June and arrived at Victoria Barracks, Belfast, on the next day. Here, at last, they were to remain undisturbed for some months, and it was a pity that they were not in a place better suited for training. It was a great improvement when, early in February 1941, they moved to Bellaghy, just west of Lough Derg. There the hutted camp was in the grounds of Ballyscullion House, which stood on the shore of the lake and housed the Officers' Mess. For miles around lay open country, well suited for the continuous training, including many lengthy exercises, which occupied the next nine months. The Battalion made great progress and acquired a very fine reputation for efficiency in the 61st Division.

At Ballyscullion House they celebrated their second anniversary, Sir John Brown and six officers of the 58th being present, and three days later they were honoured by a visit from the Colonel-in-Chief of the Regiment.

Early in November the Battalion moved to new quarters, to billets in Ballycastle on the north coast, marching the distance of forty-six miles in two days. The new station was regarded as one of the best in which they had been, but they were not to stay in it for long, for towards the end of February 1942 they were transferred to Omagh, in the south.

In April Lieut.-Col. Lingham was promoted to the command of an Infantry Brigade and was succeeded by Major W. B. Spencer.

At the end of May another move took place, to Walworth Camp near Londonderry, and there the Battalion remained for the rest of the year. In August Major M. F. F. Buszard took over command from Lieut.-Col. Spencer.

### The 5th Bn. in England, June 1940-April 1942

The Headquarters of the 5th Battalion was established at Lyme Regis two days after they had landed at Dover from Dunkirk, and parties of men soon began to arrive there from collecting centres throughout the country. By the 23rd the Battalion had re-formed and moved into camp at Hursley Park, Winchester, where training began. Here, too, they had to be prepared, at short notice, to counter-attack any attempted invasion of the coasts of Hampshire or Sussex. Training was interrupted on the 2nd July, when they were sent to Southampton Docks at short notice. Their task was, if necessary, to assist the Royal Navy, who were about to seize certain ships of the French Navy and ascertain if their crews wished to remain in England or return to France. In the event the Royal Navy dealt unaided with the problem, and the 5th were not called upon to help in this unpleasant proceeding.

September was a month of alarms. On the evening of the 7th the codeword 'Cromwell' was received. This indicated danger of enemy invasion and, in accordance with the plan, the 5th occupied battle positions and awaited further orders. Shortly before midnight the ringing of the church bells of Hursley and other villages by the Home Guard gave the approved signal that enemy parachutists were landing, but later it appeared that the signal had been given prematurely; some agents only had landed, from the air and from small seaborne craft. The invasion—as we now know—did not take place, though for some days the Battalion stood-by at thirty minutes' notice to move and had another 'Cromwell' warning on the 22nd. From then on things calmed down, and though an inspection by the Corps Commander, Lieut.-Gen. B. L. Montgomery, may have inspired some alarm of a different nature, it seems to have passed off well, his comments on the fitness and keen bearing of the Battalion being most favourable.

Towards the end of October the Battalion went into winter quarters in the barracks and in requisitioned buildings at Christchurch, Hampshire. Here, on the 30th, they welcomed a visit by the Colonel-in-Chief of the Regiment, who, before lunching in the Mess, saw companies carrying out training.

Apart from some comparatively brief intervals, the 5th were to stay at Christchurch for over a year and, as a result, training went ahead. Much attention was paid to increasing the fitness and endurance of the troops, a feature being platoon four-day marches covering up to eighty miles. There were also several major exercises, including 'Bumper,' in the course of which much distance was covered.

The Battalion's efforts were not wasted and they earned much credit. After his second visit at the end of March, General Montgomery again complimented them on their fitness. In August the C.-in-C. Home Forces, General Sir Alan Brooke, went some distance out of his way to inspect them, in the course of a very full day's programme. A special order published after his visit said that he had been delighted with the offensive spirit of the individual training he had seen; in particular, he had asked the

C.O. to congratulate the Battalion Battle Patrol on their performance in negotiating wire obstacles.

After a spell of duty in May and June in the defences on the coast of Dorset the 5th returned to Christchurch till the 1st December, when they moved into billets at Runfold, near Farnham. Here they spent Christmas, and the festival seems to have been celebrated well; the war diary, with one of those intimate touches usually lacking in these documents, records the expenditure of £80 on chickens, £22 on beer, £11 on cigarettes and £3 on minerals for the men's dinners on that day.

Soon after they had reached Runfold they had the first indication of what the future might hold for them when the C.O., and several other officers, went on a Combined Operations course. Suspicions were aroused still more when, at the end of January, the whole battalion spent a fortnight at the training centre at Inverary, practising the technique of assault landing operations.

On the 6th March, three weeks after they had got back to Runfold, the Battalion was honoured by a visit of H.M. the King, who watched a demonstration of cliff-climbing by the Battle Patrol and a platoon of 'C' Company. The King expressed his delight at the demonstration, the fitness of those taking part, their eagerness and offensive spirit. He was pleased to hear that cliff-climbing was not confined to the few, but was a regular feature of the training of the whole battalion. On leaving he asked Major McMichael, who was in command while the C.O. was on a course, to convey his congratulations to all ranks and, as he left, the Battalion, who had been spectators at the demonstration, broke into rousing cheers.

At this time the 5th carried out a novel form of exercise, appropriately named 'Nocturne,' which was to pay good dividends in the future. For a week all training was carried out at night; no lights were allowed except hurricane lamps; reveille was sounded at 1900 hours, dinners were at 0030 and teas at 0900 hours; the daytime was spent in bed.

On the 6th April the Battalion entrained for Catterick. After a night there under canvas they started a long march, much of it across country, via Bowes, Coupland and Carlisle, to Langholm in Dumfriesshire, which they reached on the 12th; everyone marched and not one fell out.

A week later Lieut.-Col. Anstee, who had commanded the 5th since Lieut.-Col. Green had been killed in France, left to take up a staff appointment. At his farewell parade he said that, as a Bedford, he was proud indeed of his close connection with the Northamptonshire Regiment. The Battalion owed him much for the way in which he had trained them. He was succeeded by Major A. A. Crook.

## The 5th Bn. in Scotland, April–October 1942

A six-day march early in June took the 5th to Callander, thirty miles north of Glasgow, where they continued training for the next four months.

Their Brigade, the 11th, commanded by Brig. E. E. E. Cass, now left the 4th Division and joined the 78th, which formed part of the 'Expeditionary Force.' This change came about as a result of the reorganisation of Field Force divisions, which were now to consist of two Infantry Brigades, one Army Tank Brigade and Divisional Troops. Another innovation introduced at this time was the equipment of Infantry Battalions with 2-pounder anti-tank guns.

The Commander of the 78th Division, Major-General V. Evelegh, was well known to the 5th, for he had commanded the 11th Infantry Brigade for the greater part of 1941.

The Battalion had just returned from a large-scale exercise called 'Dryshod,' in which the full detail of an assault landing had been practised on dry land, when rumour had it that they were soon to take part in another one in which real landing-ships and landing-craft would be used. Preparations started with the removal of the canopies from transport vehicles and the waterproofing of their engines. Then the prospect that something more real than an exercise lay ahead became evident from the holding of medical inspections, the marking of kitbags with a battalion serial number and colour, and the introduction of postal censorship.

The Dieppe raid had not long passed, and the outcry for the opening of a 'Second Front,' chiefly by those who knew full well that they would never be called upon to take part in such an operation, was in full swing. So while there were some in the Battalion who suspected that active operations were pending there were many who did not, basing their disbelief mainly on the fact that no embarkation leave had been granted. The only ones who knew the truth were the officers of the C.O.'s Order Group, who had been told in strict confidence that an operation which would be known as Exercise 'Torch' was about to take place. What no one in the Battalion, and only a few outside it, knew was the nature of the objective.

On the 23rd September the Colonel of the Regiment paid the 5th a visit, as he always did whenever one of the battalions was about to go overseas, and took the salute on a ceremonial parade. After this preparations still went on and early in October two officers of the United States Army joined the Battalion, ostensibly as observers of the exercise. As a matter of history, their names should be recorded—Major D. V. Rosen and Capt. J. M. Swanley.

Soon some of the transport left to be loaded on board ship, and a week later, in the early hours of the 15th October, the Battalion started for Glasgow, leaving behind it 'R' (the reinforcement) Company and such transport as had been designated as not required for purposes of the 'exercise.' At Glasgow the 5th embarked in a 19,000-ton Dutch ship, the *Marnix van St. Aldegonde*, together with the 6th Bn. The Royal West Kent Regt.

The ship left dock on the 18th, only to moor in the Firth of Clyde. The

Battalion were told that they were to carry out a landing exercise soon, so the next two days were spent in practising the art of descending and ascending the scramble-nets rigged on the ship's sides to allow of embarkation in landing-craft. The exercise, which began with an assault landing on the shore of the Firth on the night of the 20th/21st, was followed by a march of eighteen miles. The troops then re-embarked and the ship remained at anchor, more and more vessels, many of them carrying American troops, collecting round her as the days went by.

On the 25th the troops were paraded on the mess decks for a talk by the Convoy Commander and any remaining doubts that a large-scale operation lay ahead were soon removed. Only the question 'Where?' could not yet be answered.

After dark on the next day signal lights flashed from the ships, anchors were weighed, and the forty vessels of the convoy steamed out of the anchorage. The 5th had begun the journey which, for some but not for all, was to end in Austria.

### The 50th (Holding) Bn., June–October 1940

A few days after Dunkirk the Regiment acquired another battalion. On the 12th June 1940 the 50th (Holding) Battalion came into existence at Beccles in Suffolk, under the command of Lieut.-Col. W. C. Furminger, in place of No. 9 Infantry Holding Battalion.

The early days of the Battalion's life must have been difficult ones. At 2100 hours on the day of its formation it received a draft of 361 men from the Depot. Two hours later a warning order was received to prepare to despatch large numbers of men to other battalions on the following day, and despatched they were; 200 men to the 5th Battalion and 320 to the 58th. For the next week there was a succession of orders to move, and counter-orders, and eventually, on the 24th, the Battalion did move to Halesworth and Redisham. The state of affairs was not made any the easier by the arrival of three Army Class intakes in the last ten days of June, when the Battalion consisted of hardly any but untrained recruits.

Within a fortnight they were again uprooted to camp in Euston Park, near Thetford, where they were responsible for the defence against invasion of a coastal sector. The defence scheme of the time gives a sidelight on the state of training of the troops and the general weakness of the country. One company, named the 'Operational Company,' was to man certain defended localities; the remainder were to defend their camp, and 'if men had not reached the stage of training whereby they could shoot they would use the bayonet to the best of their ability.' The words speak for themselves. However, much progress must have been made in a very short time, for in the defence scheme issued at the end of August all companies were given an active rôle and no mention was made of men who were unable to use their rifles. And when, in September, the 'Cromwell' alarm was given, the Battalion was in its allotted position in the 'stop line' within forty minutes of receipt of the order to move.

## The 6th Bn., October 1940–December 1942

On the 9th October the Battalion was rechristened the 6th Bn. The Northamptonshire Regt., a Regular Battalion on the higher establishment of 22 officers and 776 other ranks. The latter figure was very elastic, for at the end of November the strength was 920, fluctuating as time went on and as drafts came and left.[3]

In the middle of the month the 6th were moved to Clacton-on-Sea, in the rôle of support battalion to the brigade holding the beach defences. Before long they took over a sector and found the defences in a most unsatisfactory state. Many of the pill-boxes were untenable, owing to high tides, and were strung out over a wide front; one platoon was responsible for a front of half a mile—with no depth and very inadequate wire. So the Battalion set to work and made great improvements in the next seven months, besides laying several minefields.

During this time they were visited by the Colonel-in-Chief of the Regiment, on the 21st November, and by General Sir Alan Brooke, on the 26th March 1941. The latter described the Headquarter guard as the best he had seen for a long time.

A brief interval for training at Colchester early in the summer of 1941 was followed by a return to the defences at Clacton, where they were unlucky to lose two men of 'D' Company, killed by an explosion whilst laying a minefield on the golf-course.

Towards the end of July the 6th were relieved by the 1st Bn. The Royal Irish Fusiliers and moved a short way to Much Hadham, where they spent the remainder of the year in training and in the construction of a camp which they occupied at the end of November. Late in the following January they were transferred to Upminster in Essex, then, after four months, to Felixstowe, and finally, in September, to Sheringham in Norfolk.

While at Upminster, one of the Battalion, Pte. A. A. Pack, was mentioned in Command Orders for his gallant conduct in attempting to rescue the R.A.F. pilot of an aircraft which had crashed and burst into flames.

After nearly two years in command, Lieut.-Col. Furminger left the Battalion in May for a Staff appointment, and was succeeded by Major P. F. A. Growse.

## The 70th Bn., December 1940–December 1942

The formation of a 70th Battalion of the Regiment was authorised by the War Office on the 9th December 1940, the date on which it was to form being the 29th of that month.

# THE TRAINING YEARS, 1940-1942

The Battalion was one of several raised at this time, known as 'Young Soldiers' Battalions' and numbered as the 70th of their regiments. They had many duties, chief of which were the training of N.C.O.s and men for Field Force units and the selection and pre-O.C.T.U. training of potential officers. In addition they had the operational rôle of guarding airfields against attack. It was hoped that they would eventually be capable of taking their place in Field Force brigades.

The birth of the 70th was a slow process. The nucleus consisted of twenty-four W.O.s and N.C.O.s from various regiments and a Quartermaster, who appeared at the end of December. These were followed at intervals during January by ten 2/Lieutenants from the I.T.C. at Northampton, a C.O., Lieut.-Col. W. E. Carrick, who was to remain in command throughout the Battalion's existence, and several other officers. By the end of that month the strength was 90, of which 62 were permanent staff and training cadre and 28 were recruits, organised into one company.

Up to the beginning of February 1941, the Battalion was attached to the 70th Bn. The Leicestershire Regt. at Kettering, but from then on became an independent unit. By the end of the month the strength had risen to 245 and a second company had been organised, but training was as yet far from easy, for there were no rifles for the recruits and they had to use those of the employed men. However, early in May, 400 rifles were issued and this was just as well since, by the end of that month, the Battalion had four companies and a strength of 660. Matters were also simplified by an order under which all recruits were to train for two months at the I.T.C. before being drafted to the Battalion.

In the middle of July 1941, the 70th moved to Truro, and it was there, and at other places in Cornwall, that they were to spend the rest of their existence.

They were now one of the four battalions of the 73rd Independent Infantry Brigade and were fully employed in airfield defence, with training only at intervals. As time went on they became more fitted for operational duties, Signal, Carrier and Mortar Platoons having been formed early in 1942. At the end of that year, when they numbered 32 officers and 1,123 other ranks, organised into five operational companies and one training company, they were carrying out the rôle of a Field Force unit at Newquay.

## *The I.T.C.*, 1939-1942

The scheme of mobilisation on the outbreak of war included a plan by which Regimental Depots would change their names and undergo a great expansion. So it was that, in September 1939, the Regimental Depot was renamed 'The Northamptonshire I.T.C.' or Infantry Training Centre.

Under the new organisation, the Centre consisted of the following:

A Headquarters, a H.Q. Company about 400 strong, and a Depot Company which held the trained men, varying in strength from 200 to 600.

A Specialist Company, responsible for training in M.T., Mortars, Signalling and the like.

Training Companies, 200 to 300 strong, two in number to start with, but rising to four in 1940, in which recruits were given eight weeks' elementary training and a similar period of tactical training.

The old barracks in Northampton were naturally far too small to accommodate this large number of men, but before the war, with the help of the Borough Police, the necessary billets had been earmarked, and in these most, if not all, of the Training Companies were housed.

Mobilisation went smoothly. There was an immediate influx of officers from all categories of the Reserve and Reservist other ranks, and at the same time the peace-time Depot Staff was augmented by instructors from the Regular Battalions. Simultaneously, drafts were made up and despatched to various units. There were also various vulnerable points in the county for which guards had to be found.

So the work of the I.T.C. went on, until its smoothness of working was interrupted by an entirely unforeseen event.

Late in May, the I.T.C. Commander, Major A. St. G. Coldwell, was playing golf on a Sunday afternoon when he was informed that a telegram bearing the word 'Dynamo' had been received. This was the code-word signifying that the evacuation of the B.E.F. from Belgium was about to begin. History does not record whether, like Drake, he finished his game, or whether he returned to Barracks immediately. Anyhow, it was not long before the situation was disclosed to Company Commanders, and the I.T.C. prepared to receive the 2,500 troops they had been warned to expect.

In due course, over a period of about three days, five train-loads arrived at Northampton, bringing more than 4,000 men of various units and of all arms of the Service. On arrival, each man was given a hot meal, was issued with towel, soap and bedding, and had a bath. Then, when they had been sorted, they were despatched to join their units at centres notified in a special location statement.

Mention should be made of the outstanding example of good discipline provided by two men of the Welsh Guards. These two failed to parade for the meal with the rest of their train-load, and a search disclosed them—dirty, hungry and exhausted though they were—cleaning their arms and making up their quarters before reporting for food. Their behaviour was in marked contrast to that of the 480 troops of the French 9th Army, who were ragged and undisciplined, and left their billets in an indescribably dirty state.

The completion of operation 'Dynamo' throughout the country in a matter of about eighteen days was a triumph of rapid organisation in which the Northamptonshire I.T.C. played its allotted part well.

After Dunkirk, when invasion seemed so likely, the I.T.C. had to undertake many duties additional to its normal ones. Among these was the training of the Home Guard and the County Police in the handling of their weapons and in elementary tactics. Operational tasks included the guarding of vulnerable points such as the Rugby Wireless Station, and the recapture of certain airfields should they fall into enemy hands. The I.T.C. disposed of little fire-power or transport and, though schemes were worked out in detail, the success of such operations might have been somewhat doubtful.

At this time the I.T.C. was called upon to produce 6 officers and 150 men as the nucleus of a new battalion of The Buffs—the 6th—and can thus be regarded as the foster-parent of the unit.

On the outbreak of the war, the Bandmaster and bandboys of the 58th joined the I.T.C. Applications for a band to be included in the establishment were unsympathetically received, but regardless of this a band was formed, increasing from thirty to fifty-two players during 1940. Thanks to the hard work of the Bandmaster much progress was made, and the band not only proved its value for parades, but also visited battalions of the Regiment and gave local concerts. Eventually its existence did receive official recognition.

In the spring of 1941 the I.T.C. moved into Talavera Barracks, a hutted camp which had been built on the Northampton Racecourse. Then, in August, considerable amalgamation of I.T.C.s took place, and the Northamptonshire I.T.C. was ordered to Norwich where, with that of the R. Norfolk Regt., it formed No. 2 I.T.C. Lieut.-Col. Coldwell and several officers and warrant-officers remained behind at Northampton where, for another six months, they helped in the training and organisation of No. 1 A.T.S. Training Centre, which took over Talavera Barracks.

# CHAPTER VIII

## THE 58th IN MADAGASCAR, 1942

The Voyage to Madagascar, 21st March–4th May 1942—The Landing at Madagascar, 5th May—The Attacks on Antsirane, 6th–7th May—Occupation, 7th May–10th June (*see* Maps on pp. 101 and 104)

### *The Voyage to Madagascar, 21st March–4th May 1942*

ON the afternoon of the 21st March 1942, the *Duchess of Atholl*, with the 58th on board,[1] moved out of the Gladstone Dock at Liverpool and moored in the Mersey. Two days later she got under way and when, on the morning of the 24th, the ship joined a convoy of some forty others, including several destroyers, a cruiser and the aircraft-carrier *Illustrious*, no one could fail to appreciate that the Battalion was involved in an expedition of some size. Furthermore, it could be seen that many of the ships carried assault landing-craft on their davits in place of lifeboats, so the nature of the operation to come became obvious. But security had been excellent and not a single member of the Battalion knew the objective.

While on board the ship in Liverpool docks, Lieut.-Col. Hinchcliffe had been surprised at a visit of two officers from the War Office who had given him a bundle of Army Forms and an order to produce a complete stowage plan for the ship. Soon afterwards he was provided with a Staff officer who had been trained in the duties of an Assault Landing Officer. Now the 58th had carried out a comprehensive training programme during the past two years, but the one operation of war which they had not practised was assault landing. So when he saw the A.L.C.s in the other ships of the convoy, the C.O. told the Adjutant to produce the 'Manual of Combined Operations' which was at the bottom of the secret and confidential office box, and spent much time in studying the technicalities of this form of warfare before the ship touched land again.

For all except the C.O. the first part of the voyage was uneventful. The sea was calm, the weather became warmer as the ship got farther south and, apart from physical training, the troops had an easy time. In the light of subsequent events it is of interest that one evening the officers held a debate, the motion being 'That it is criminal foolishness to say that we must invade Europe from the West in 1942.' The advocates of a 'Second Front' defeated this motion by twenty-five votes to seven. Those seven were wiser than they realised at the time.

When the convoy entered Freetown harbour on the 6th April to refuel, the C.O. was summoned to the Brigade H.Q. ship and was informed that they were to take part in a combined operation, of which the objective was Madagascar. This information was passed on to Company Commanders three days later, when the convoy set sail again, though the objective was not disclosed. For the next fortnight the ship was a hive of activity. To get the men fit, physical training was intensified, route-marches were held round the deck, in full equipment and, to the horror of the ship's Captain, in boots, and the organisation of a platoon in an A.L.C. was practised in a mock craft built of planks and forms. This drive towards physical fitness was to pay later, and it also had its immediate effect, for in the ship's boxing competition the 58th team beat both a Field Regiment R.A. and the R.A.F.

Land was sighted again early on the 22nd. The convoy entered Durban harbour, the ship berthed soon after noon, and that evening the troops were allowed ashore. There was much to be done during the next week. The ship had to be completely unloaded and restowed on an operational basis, a task which often involved parties working all night, carriers had to be waterproofed, and route-marches were held ashore. But it was not all hard work and there was time to enjoy the hospitality so freely offered by the people of Durban. A feature of the visit was a ceremonial parade, in the course of which the three battalions of the Brigade marched past the Lord Mayor at the Town Hall.

By the 28th all the necessary preliminaries had been completed and the convoy sailed, joined by H.M.S. *Ramillies*. On the 30th orders were issued for the operation, but the destination was still kept secret and all place-names were camouflaged as Scottish ones. Before long, however, maps were issued, all ranks were told of the destination of the force and dress rehearsals of serial assembly were held. On the 4th May all ranks were told the plan; goodwill messages were received from the G.O.C. and the Admiral; and the afternoon was spent in organised sleep. The next day was to be zero day.

*The Landing at Madagascar, 5th May*

The force taking part in the landing at Madagascar went by the name of 'Force 121,' and was under the command of Major-Gen. Sturges. It comprised the 13th and 17th Infantry Brigades, the 29th Independent Infantry Brigade, and No. 5 Commando. Air support was provided by the aircraft of H.M.S. *Illustrious* and *Indomitable*.

The initial object was the capture of the French naval and air base at

Diego Suarez, near the northernmost point of the island, in order to secure it against possible Japanese seizure. To achieve this the plan was for an assault landing to be made on the north-western coast by the 29th Ind. Inf. Bde. and No. 5 Commando. Their task was to capture the coast-defence batteries at Courrier Bay and exploit to Diego Suarez; to seize Antsirane and its airfield and take possession of any ships in Antsirane harbour; and to exploit to clear the enemy from the Orangea peninsula, which lay to the east of Diego Suarez and commanded the entrance to the main anchorage.

The 17th Inf. Bde. was to be in reserve and the 13th in floating reserve. Of the 17th Inf. Bde., the 58th were to come under command of the 29th Ind. Inf. Bde. when they landed and were to be prepared to support the advance, or to continue it if it were held up. The 2nd R. Scots Fusiliers had the task of defending the main landing beach and the beach maintenance area.

As regards the enemy, the information was that the garrison of this part of the island consisted of about 2,500 troops, of which 500 were Senegalese, good fighters, and the remainder of the Régiment Mixte de Madagascar, of doubtful value. The French disposed of only some thirty-five aircraft. There was a considerable amount of information about the fixed coast defences, but less regarding the existence of any trench systems farther inland.

At 0430 hours on the 5th May No. 5 Commando landed on Red beaches and in little more than an hour had captured the two adjacent coast-defence batteries. Meanwhile the 29th Brigade had got ashore on Blue beaches and had started to advance on Antsirane via Anamakia. At 0758 hours 17th Brigade H.Q. intercepted a signal from the French commander, ordering Diego Suarez to be defended to the end, in accordance with the traditions of the French Army and Navy. So it could be assumed that there would at least be some show of resistance.

While action was in progress ashore, the 58th waited patiently on board ship for landing-craft to be available to transfer them to the beach. At 1250 hours the Beach Working Party went ashore, soon followed by Major Houchin and his Landing Staff. Then, at 1535, 'A' Company began to embark in A.L.C.s, followed by the C.O.'s reconnaissance party and 'B' Company, but rough seas prevented the remainder of the Battalion from landing till some hours later, so it was not until about 0100 hours that night that the whole Battalion were ashore.

Meanwhile, at 2000 hours, the C.O. and some of the officers of the Battalion H.Q. had set out on motor-cycles to make contact with H.Q. 29th Brigade, which they reached about four hours later, after a hazardous ride over very bad roads. Just as they had started, 17th Brigade had ordered the two companies which were then ashore to start marching

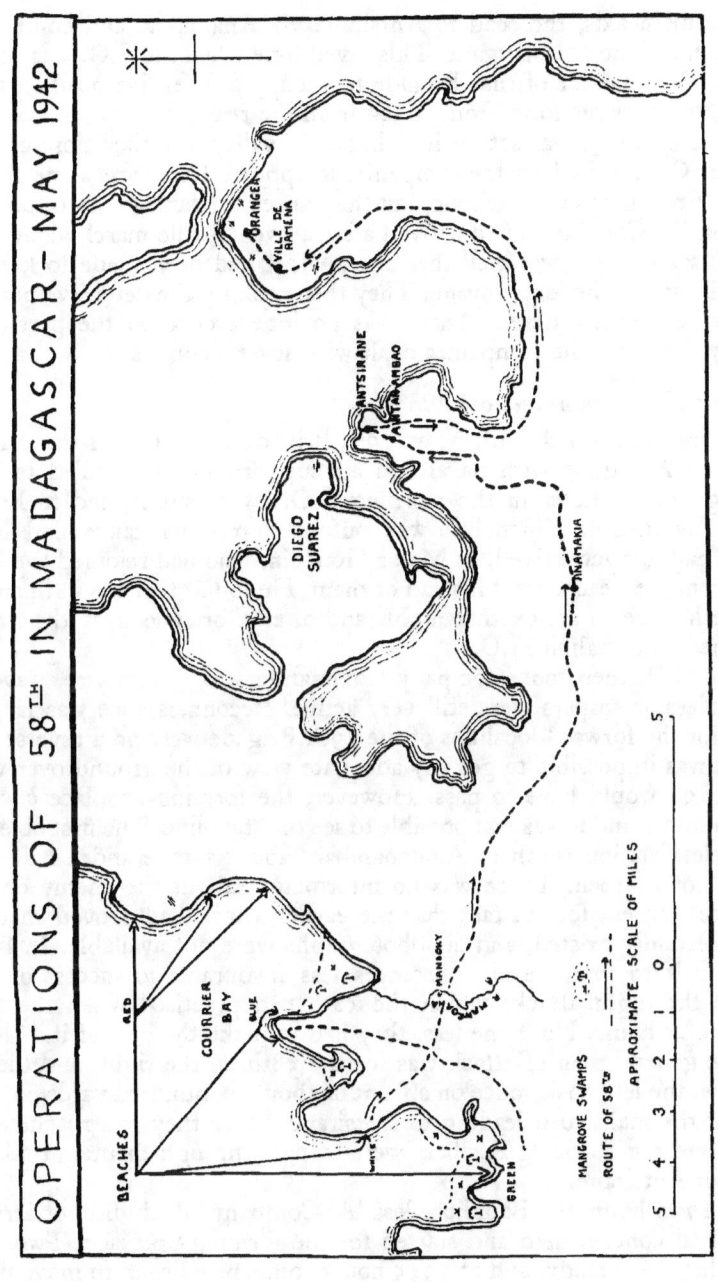

up the main axis, the road to Antsirane via Anamakia, and come under command of the 29th Brigade. This saved time when the C.O. was ordered by the Commander of that Brigade to occupy a defensive position facing south, to cover his force from attack from the rear.

Battalion H.Q. was set up in a hut in a valley in rather close country, and the C.O. waited for the companies to appear. There was some shelling by the French 75s at Antsirane, but this caused no damage. By 0800 hours 'A' and 'B' Companies had arrived after a twenty-mile march along a bad and dusty road; it was well that every effort had been made to keep the men fit during the long voyage. They then took up the defensive positions which had been ordered. There was no interference on the part of the enemy, but later the companies dealt with several snipers.

*The Attacks on Antsirane, 6th–7th May*

At first light on the 6th May, 29th Brigade had attacked the defences south of Antsirane with naval and air support, but had failed to break through them. Later in the morning C.O.s were summoned to Brigade H.Q. Lieut.-Col. Hinchcliffe was out on a reconnaissance and Major Hunt had not yet arrived, so Major Houchin, who had rejoined the Battalion from the beach, went instead of them. He found that the 58th and the Seaforth were to attack that night, and after a brief look at the ground returned to Battalion H.Q.

The C.O. then took Company Commanders to reconnoitre, travelling in carriers as snipers were still very active. Reconnaissance was far from easy, for the forward localities of the 29th Brigade were on a reverse slope and it was impossible to get any adequate view of the ground over which the attack would have to pass. However, the forming-up place could be reconnoitred and it was just possible to see the start-line. The first objective, a wireless station south of Anatanambao, about a mile and a half away, could not be seen. There was no information about the enemy or their defences, except for the fact that the earlier attack had proved that they most certainly existed, and air photographs were not available. In fact, it is difficult to imagine circumstances less favourable to success or more unlike the night attacks which the 58th had practised when they were training at home. None the less, they had to make the best of it.

The general plan of attack was for the 58th on the right, and the Seaforth on the left, to advance on a front of about six hundred yards on either side of the main road leading to Antsirane. Once they had reached their objectives the R. Scots Fusiliers were to pass through them and take the town of Antsirane.

By 1700 hours the Battalion, less 'A' Company which did not arrive in time, had concentrated and started for the forming-up place. Two hours later they were ready, and at 1945 hours companies began to move up the road to the start-line, a track which ran at right angles to the road. Here they got into formation for the advance, 'D' Company on the right, 'C' on the left and 'B' in reserve, and waited for zero hour. This had originally been fixed for 2000 hours, but had been postponed for half an hour to allow of a diversion in the shape of the landing of fifty Royal Marines at Antsirane. This diversion, a most dashing affair, proved to be most successful. The destroyer, H.M.S. *Anthony*, rushed the entrance to Diego Suarez harbour at 32 knots and landed the party on the quay almost before the French realised that anything was happening. The destroyer commander did not know if the harbour was mined, but he took the risk and won.

At 2030 hours the leading companies of the 58th crossed the start-line and, after passing through some dense bush country, came out on to the open plain south of Antanambao.

The defences which the Battalion had to overcome are shown on the sketch-map on the next page.

On the right was a pill-box, mounting a machine-gun which covered the length of an anti-tank ditch running across the front and some two hundred yards in front of the main position.

On the left two pill-boxes, one containing a 75-mm. gun, the other a machine-gun, formed a strong road-block.

Between the two pill-boxes ran a sytem of trenches manned by riflemen, machine-guns and mortars.

In addition to these, slightly to the right of the flank of the 58th and to the left of the Seaforth, were two forts. Although these had been built when Marshal Joffre was Governor of Diego Suarez in 1910, their position was apparently unknown to the British.

The night was very dark. The time available for preliminary reconnaissance by junior leaders had been extremely short, and this had not been possible for any below Platoon Commanders. No one had been able to get any view over the line of advance, a drawback which air photographs would have helped to overcome had they been available. Consequently, it was not surprising that difficulty was experienced in maintaining contact and direction. The latter, especially, was complicated by the fact that in their advance the companies encountered a road, not marked on the map, which ran diagonally across the front. However, they pushed on in the face of the fire of machine-guns, mortars and 75-mm. guns, missing the fort on the right by good fortune and some two hundred yards.

On reaching the enemy trenches, 'C' Company and a platoon of 'D' which had become detached from its own company made several efforts to capture the pill-box near the main road, in the course of which Major Anderson was wounded. By now Major Houchin had arrived on the scene. He had been left behind at the forming-up place to arrange for the evacuation of some wounded and had then made his way forward with a few

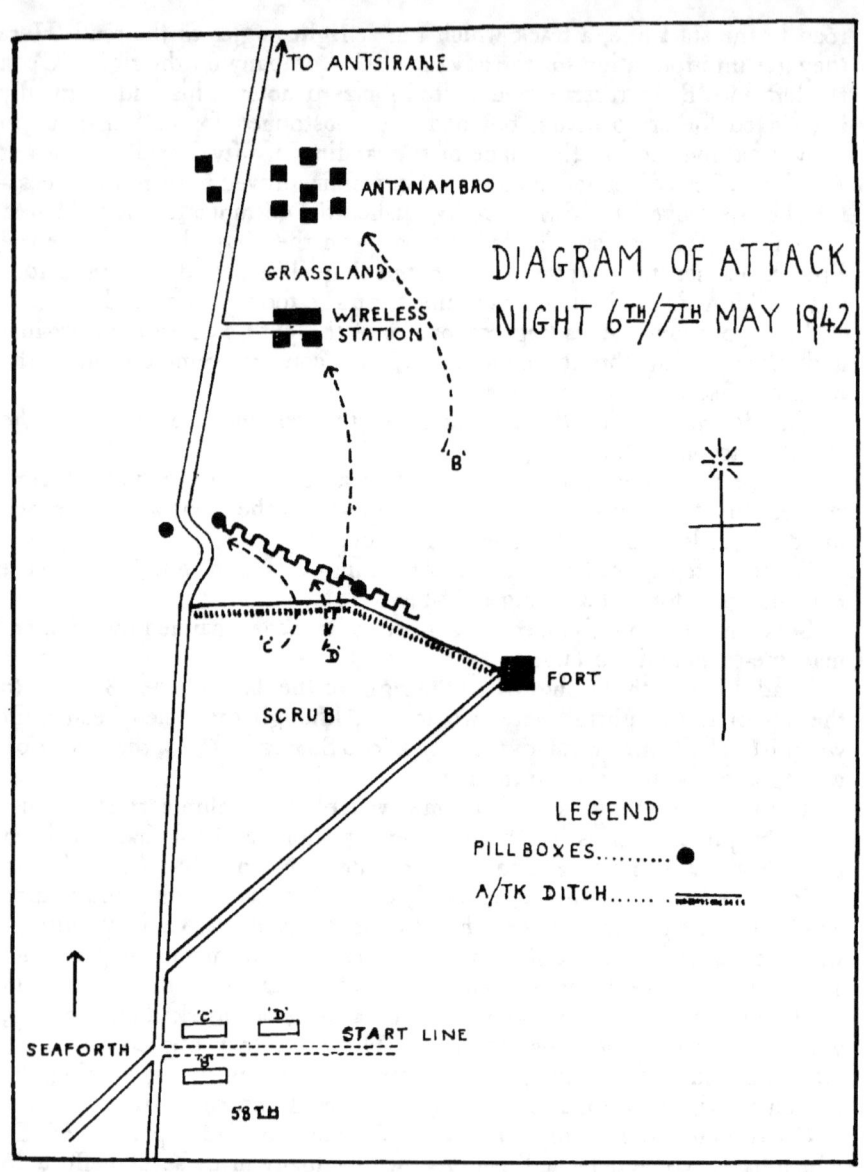

men; at one time his party found themselves behind the enemy trenches. Whilst organising another attack on the pill-box he was wounded in the head by a grenade; however, in the end the pill-box was captured. Major Houchin was later awarded a bar to his Military Cross.

Meanwhile, Capt. Purton had reorganised the remainder of 'D' Company, about forty men, and led them towards their final objective, the wireless station. A strong machine-gun post held them up for a time, but they captured this and continued to advance. They were now joined by the C.O., who had come forward with a few men. Unfortunately, just before this the Adjutant, Capt. Wood, had been severely wounded; he died later in the day. On reaching the wireless station an attack was organised, and after some resistance the garrison surrendered. Capt. Purton was subsequently awarded the Military Cross for his gallantry during the night.

During this confused fighting in the dark, 'B' Company, who were to go through and take the village of Antanambao, had followed a line of advance which took them too far to the right; they were probably misled by the diagonal road which had troubled the other companies. As a result they encountered a trench leading east from the right-hand pill-box, but they took this, went on to the line of the wireless station, where they sent up the success signal, and then proceeded to occupy Antanambao.

By 0330 hours on the 7th, Battalion H.Q. had been established in the wireless station and companies were reorganising. The situation as regards any enemy in the area was obscure, and there seemed to be some opposition over to the right of the Battalion. At 0600 hours 'B' Company was despatched to deal with this. It proved to be a battery of 75s which surrendered when the Company Commander, Capt. Hickson, had entered into negotiations with the French commander.

This was the last of the resistance in the Antsirane peninsula, which was occupied by other units without further difficulty.

A considerable amount of action had been compressed into the thirty-six hours which had elapsed since the 58th had landed on the afternoon of the 5th May as part of the first combined operation of the war. The resistance of the French was not, it is true, very determined, and the Battalion had only suffered thirty-two casualties, of whom one officer and three other ranks were killed, but they had successfully carried out a difficult night attack after others had failed. Their Brigade Commander summed it up well in the message of congratulation which he sent them. He pointed out that the attack had been carried out after the troops had been on board ship for some seven weeks and after they had completed a hot and dusty march of some twenty miles from the beaches. The operation was an example of what well-trained, well-disciplined and fit troops, determined to carry out the job, could do in the face of difficulties.

*Occupation, 7th May–10th June*

Later in the morning of the 7th the Battalion moved with the rest of the 17th Brigade to occupy the Orangea Peninsula. The march was halted, however, after they had gone two miles, while negotiations proceeded between a Liaison Officer from Force H.Q. and the commanders of two French batteries which showed signs of wishing to oppose the advance. Eventually one of the batteries surrendered, and was accorded the honours of war as they marched to barracks in Antsirane, but as the other remained adamant the Brigade returned to its starting-point.

During the night the remaining battery agreed to capitulate and was met by the Brigade on the outskirts of Antsirane with appropriate ceremonial. The Battalion spent the next night in bivouac in the south of the peninsula, as the batteries on the coast were not due to march out before the next morning. When they did so, they arrived unexpectedly early in the 58th lines and the honours of war had to be accorded to them in a somewhat impromptu manner. The Battalion then marched into Orangea, where H.Q. were established in the barracks, and companies were allotted positions for the defence of the coast.

The next few weeks were spent in miscellaneous peaceful duties. These included the evacuation of French officers and their families to Antsirane; the taking over and running of the local farm; rest leave, spent on board a ship in the harbour; bathing, and visits to inspect by daylight the battlefield of the night of the 6th/7th May. Amenities were fairly satisfactory considering the circumstances; the Battalion war diary relates that on the 22nd the first canteen supply of cigarettes and beer arrived, and adds, 'nothing further of importance.' The health of the troops was, on the whole, good, though there was a certain amount of sandfly fever and malaria. At Orangea, 'R' Company (the reinforcement company) rejoined the Battalion. Under the command of Capt. Whitaker they had been employed from the 6th to the 18th in unloading ammunition and supplies on Red Beach, and had been congratulated by the Naval Officer in charge for the excellent work they had done there.

The 30th May was a red-letter day, for the first mail arrived, six weeks out from England. Rejoicings at this were, however, somewhat shortlived, for within a few hours the Battalion received the alarm code-word, and stood-to. A flash was seen in the direction of the anchorage and for several hours during the night the explosion of depth-charges could be heard and felt. As far as the 58th were concerned nothing happened and, at 1120 hours on the 31st, they were allowed to stand-down.

The cause of the disturbance had been a Japanese two-man submarine which had entered the harbour, had damaged H.M.S. *Ramillies* and sunk a tanker with torpedoes. The crew got ashore and were rounded up and killed by Commando troops.

## THE 58th IN MADAGASCAR, 1942

Early in June the Battalion was warned to prepare for another sea-voyage. On the 6th four troopships arrived, packed with African troops, and an advanced party from the 5th K.A.R. began to take over the defences of the area. This battalion had fought in the Abyssinian campaign and was well fitted for operations in the bush country of Madagascar.

The relief was completed by the 10th, and the 58th embarked from the beach in the *Winchester Castle*, an Infantry Landing Ship. On the next day they began to steam across the Indian Ocean, leaving to others the complete occupation of Madagascar, for which they had helped to lay the foundation.

Cap Button, 1948

# CHAPTER IX

## THE 5th BATTALION IN NORTH AFRICA, 1942–1943
## THE LANDING, AND THE ADVANCE ON TUNIS, 1942

The General Situation, 1942—Operation 'Torch'—The Plan for the Landings—The Voyage to North Africa, 26th October–7th November—The Landing at Algiers, 7th–8th November—Incidents after the Landing—Near Algiers, 8th–15th November—The Task of 78th Division—Advance of 'Hart Force'—The Country—The Forward Move of the 5th Bn., 16th–21st November—The Capture of Medjez, 20th–27th November—The Advance to Djedeida, 28th–30th November—The German Counter-offensive, 30th November–12th December—In Defence, 12th–21st December—The Last Attempt to Capture Tunis, 21st–27th December—Comments on the Operations, November–December 1942 (*see* General Map of Tunisia on p. 116 and Map of the Operations of the 5th Bn. on p. 126)

## *The General Situation*, 1942

MANY months of 1942 were to pass before there was any indication that the year would merit the name given to it later—the decisive year of the war.

The Axis plans for that year were ambitious. Germany and Italy, and Japan who had joined them in the previous December, intended to knock out either Britain or Russia, or both, before America could raise, equip and train her forces. So the summer months saw four great enemy offensives in full swing.

The first of these was carried out on all the seas, though mainly in the Atlantic, and was aimed at those vital supply-lines which brought food and munitions from Canada and the Americas to the British Isles; which maintained our forces on so many fronts, all of them dependent on sea-power; and which kept Russia supplied until her new factories could replace those overrun by the enemy.

The second was in the Far East. By May the Japanese controlled Singapore and were reaching out westwards to try to cut our communications with India and the Middle East via the Cape.

The third was against Russia, and had as its objectives the seizure of the Caucasus and the oil-wells on the Caspian Sea.

The fourth was in the Western Desert, where Rommel hoped to start by driving the British Armies out of Egypt and the British Fleet out of the Eastern Mediterranean, and then, having captured Malta, to move still farther into the Middle East.

All of these four great offensives seemed destined to succeed. All were held.

On the seas, thanks to the magnificent work of the Allied navies and air forces and of the merchant seamen of many nations, communications were just—and only just—maintained.

In the Far East the Japanese drive westwards never fully materialised. An attempted attack on Ceylon was driven back, and Madagascar was secured by the British before the enemy could try to seize it; but it is doubtful if these successes could, by themselves, have stopped Japan if she had concentrated all her strength towards the west. As it was, her fear of the naval strength of the United States induced her to turn towards the south, in an attempt to defeat the American fleet and cut Australia off from American help. The result was the two biggest naval battles of the war up to date, those of the Coral Sea early in May and of Midway Island a month later. Both battles made naval history, for they were fought, not by the guns of the ships, but by carrier-borne aircraft at a range of two hundred miles or more. Both ended in defeat for the Japanese, who thenceforth were forced to abandon the offensive in the South-west Pacific.

In Russia the German armies advanced for many hundreds of miles, till they were held at Voronesch and Stalingrad and failed to reach their objectives.

Finally, in the Western Desert, Rommel drove the Eighth Army back to within sixty miles of Alexandria. There, on the Alamein line, General Auchinleck stopped the withdrawal and when, at the beginning of September, Rommel again attacked at Alam Halfa, the Eighth Army under General Montgomery held him.

So it was that the United Nations held their own whilst their armies and their air forces were being trained and equipped, and while the ships required for the counter-offensive were being built. September 1942, the beginning of the fourth year of the war, marked the high-water of Axis success and the turning of the tide.

*Operation 'Torch'*

As matters stood, the decision to plan a landing on the coasts of French North Africa—Operation 'Torch'—was a bold one, for while planning was in progress and even at the time that the operation was launched, the situation in all theatres of war gave little cause for optimism.

The main object of the operation was the securing of French Morocco and Algeria with a view to the earliest possible occupation of Tunisia. For its success it depended, partly on surprise, partly on the amount of opposition, or assistance, which might be offered by the French forces in North Africa. The attitude of the French Army was uncertain; that of the Navy less so, for they had not forgotten the sinking of some of their ships at Oran by the Royal Navy in July 1940. In both cases, national pride would probably demand a show of resistance, if nothing more.

This unknown factor directly influenced the plan. It was desirable that British forces, with their longer training and their more recent experience in battle, should play a leading part in the landings. On the other hand, the U.S.A. had maintained diplomatic relations with the Vichy Government, whereas Britain had supported the Free French movement under General de Gaulle. So, in the hope that American forces would receive a more friendly welcome than British, the whole expedition was placed under the command of Lieut.-Gen. Eisenhower, with a British officer, Lieut.-Gen. K. A. N. Anderson, as Commander of the Eastern Task Force. It was also planned that American troops should play a leading part in all the initial landings, and that General Anderson should not assume command in his area until that phase of the operation had ended.

*The Plan for the Landings*

The landings were to be made on a wide front. On the right, the U.S. 2nd Corps, under Major-Gen. Patton, was to cross the Atlantic from the U.S.A. and land at Casablanca. In the centre, a U.S. task-force was to capture Oran, supported by American paratroops flown from England, who were to secure airfields. On the left, the British 78th Division and two Commandos, and the U.S. 34th Division, all from England, were to land at Algiers.

The Algiers landing was to be carried out under the command of Major-Gen. Ryder, Commander of the American Division; once it had been completed, the First Army, mainly British but including some American troops, was to establish a base at Algiers, and occupy eastern Algeria and Tunisia as rapidly as possible.

*The Voyage to North Africa, 26th October–7th November*

When we left the 5th Battalion they had just sailed from the Clyde on the 26th October.[1] From there the convoy steamed out into the Atlantic. Few knew the secret of their destination until the 1st November, when the C.O. addressed the Battalion and explained the plan for the landing.

There was now much to be done. Maps were issued on a very adequate scale—more than adequate, in fact, from the officers' point of view, for the number to be carried ashore amounted, in theory, to more than a hundred apiece. Many of these had to be studied, as also had air photographs and very comprehensive Intelligence Summaries; plans had to be explained to junior commanders with the aid of an excellent scale-model of the beach—'Apples White'—on which the 5th were to land; talks had to be given to the troops on the country, climate, and peoples of North Africa; the com-

# THE 5th BATTALION IN NORTH AFRICA, 1942–1943

plicated landing-tables had to be prepared. So the days at sea passed quickly.

Shortly before the convoy reached the Straits of Gibraltar it split in two, part going south and part turning east for the passage of the Straits. On the morning of the 6th November the 5th Battalion found their ship steaming along the north coast of the Mediterranean, surrounded by an armada of warships; the convoy was now in the danger zone for attacks by submarine or aircraft, but three bombing attacks resulted in only slight damage to one ship.

## The Landing at Algiers, 7th–8th November

The night of the 7th/8th November was warm and starlit and there was hardly a ripple on the sea. At about 2000 hours there could be seen in the distance a mass of twinkling specks of light. This was a good sign, for it showed that the secret of the operation had been well kept and that Algiers at least had not been forewarned.

As the *Marnix van St. Aldegonde* steamed slowly ahead, on a course which was now parallel to the African shore and seven or eight miles from it, zero hour approached. At 2145 hours the officers and men of the 5th assembled on the mess-decks, 'Mae West' life-savers under their equipment, haversacks bulging with forty-eight hours' rations. Then 'C' and 'D' Companies and Capt. Cook's assault party of twenty men, forming the first wave, filed slowly up on deck, where each boat-load paraded facing the allotted L.C.A.

At 2330 hours the troops began to step across from the deck-rails into the assault-craft which hung on the davits. Then, to those watching, there was an anxious moment as the craft were lowered towards the water; there had been some doubt if the davits would stand the strain and rehearsal had been forbidden. However, all went well; one by one they were safely seaborne and cruised in circles until their numbers were complete; then throttles were opened and they sped away into the darkness towards the shore.

The rest of the Battalion could now only wait. The ship steamed slowly towards the coast until, about a mile from it, the engines were stopped and she drifted in silence. Faint booms could be heard from the direction of Algiers, twenty miles to the east, where the Americans were landing, but from the coast-line ahead there was not a sound. At 0330 hours the first of the L.C.A.s returned to the ship, followed by others; the remainder of the Battalion went down the scramble-nets into them without a hitch, and bicycles, wireless sets and even the four patrol dogs were lowered without damage. The earlier training had been well learnt.

In the meantime, the first wave had landed unopposed on the appointed beach between Zeralda and Castiglione. The only casualty was Lieut. Villis,

Second-in-Command of 'C' Company, who, in his keenness to be the first ashore, had jumped from a landing-craft into deep water, had been struck by the hull and had disappeared. His body, found later, was buried in Zeralda cemetery.

Once ashore, the two companies quickly formed a bridgehead and at 0400 hours the 2nd Lancashire Fusiliers landed and passed through them on their way to capture Blida airfield.

Ninety minutes later the rest of the 5th landed without incident near Castiglione and soon reached their rendezvous, a short distance inland. Local protection was at once organised, all telephone wires were cut and every Frenchman and Arab in the neighbourhood was arrested, though permission soon came for their release.

At about 0800 hours Battalion H.Q. moved a quarter of a mile inland and the C.O., visiting the forward companies, found them in the exact positions to which they had been detailed when on board ship. By now American troops, who had been landed some fifteen miles away from their correct beaches, were streaming through the Battalion area on their way to Algiers. There was no information of the situation, but the lack of any fire from the fort of Sidi Ferruch, the guns of which commanded the beaches, showed that the Commandos had captured it.

*Incidents after the Landing*

In a military sense the landing had been without incident, but it was followed by incidents which were not devoid of humour.

Soon after the 5th got ashore the Second-in-Command and Major Rosen, one of the attached American officers, were sent by Brigade H.Q. to interview General Maist, Commander of the French Algerian Division. Setting off in a car which had appeared at Battalion H.Q. and had been impressed into British service, they found on meeting the General that it was in fact his car and that he had sent it to meet the British when they landed. In the course of conversation he commented on the slowness of the landings and said that, as a result, there would be unnecessary casualties in Algiers and that the race for Tunis would be lost. How right his forecast was will be seen in due course.

Shortly afterwards it was necessary to make contact with the American forces. The Adjutant had a somewhat adventurous journey for, after being fired at several times by French armoured cars, he had to spend the night in a ditch without food or water. However, he returned the next day none the worse.

Major Hill-Walker and Major Rosen were more fortunate when they visited Algiers. On reaching the outskirts there were many American troops to be seen, but no information could be got from them about the situation, though at times there was the sound of slight machine-gun and rifle fire and of the explosion of an occasional grenade. While the civil population were continuing their normal occupations, some form of battle seemed to be in progress and at every street corner stood American soldiers with their rifles at the ready. Eventually a British Gunner F.O.O., found in a villa, stated that the opposition, which was only slight, came from Fort L'Empereur.

At that moment an orderly announced that there was a French general outside in a car carrying a white flag, and the occupants of the villa were just in time to see his departure with General Ryder, who had suddenly appeared, with a French bugler blowing the 'Cease Fire' from the seat beside the driver.

What was not known at the time was that when the French general had first arrived—he was none other than General Juin—he had asked to see the senior American officer. Major Rosen, who had stayed outside the villa, had been pointed out to him, whereupon, saluting, he had tendered the formal surrender of Fort L'Empereur and had departed. But Major Rosen, who understood no French, was oblivious of the importance of the message he had received.

The sounding of the 'Cease Fire' and the surrender of the fort had no immediate effect—in fact, the volume of firing at unknown targets seemed, if anything, to increase; so the Second-in-Command and Major Rosen made their way back to the Battalion.

*Near Algiers, 8th–15th November*

During these incidents the 5th had moved nearer to Algiers, and there 'A' Company had a stroke of luck. Five large cars drove into the village they were occupying, were stopped by the N.C.O. and two men manning a road-block, and were found to contain six German officers and nineteen N.C.O.s, all fully armed. These proved to be members of the German Armistice Commission in Algeria trying to make good their escape. Their capture was of considerable value, for they carried documents which were of great importance to the Allied Intelligence.

Another short move early on the 10th took the Battalion to Bir Mandreis, on the outskirts of Algiers, and there they were warned to stand by to deal with Fort L'Empereur, the garrison of which was still being obstructive, if Admiral D'Arlan had not accepted the Allied armistice terms by 0900 hours. By that hour nothing had happened, so they moved to the Fort prepared to take action, only to find the garrison piling arms voluntarily. At noon Admiral D'Arlan decided to sign the terms, and the Battalion went back to Bir Mandreis.

Part of General Maist's forecast had already come true. Thanks to the slowness of some of the landings the pro-Vichy element in Algiers had been able to recapture places which had been seized by the Patriots and to release Admiral D'Arlan and General Juin, who had been locked up, and as a result the Americans had met with some sharp resistance. However, this ceased completely when the armistice terms had been signed.

*The Task of 78th Division*

With the attitude of the French more or less settled, the time had come to start the drive eastwards. The spearhead was to be the two brigades of the 78th Division which were the only complete British formations yet landed.

The initial tasks given to the Division were the occupation of the airfields at Bougie, Djedelli and Bone by the 11th November, and the reinforcement of the garrison of Bone with a mobile force.

Forward airfields were all-important if the advance on Tunis was to be properly supported. From Algiers to Tunis was 400 miles, whereas from Sicily, where the Germans had air-bases which could easily be reinforced from Italy, the distance to Tunis was only 150 miles. Consequently it was to be expected that the Germans would not be slow to build up their strength in Tunisia, both in the air and on the land, and this expectation was fulfilled. The landings in North Africa had come as a complete surprise to them, but on the 9th November the first German troops reached Tunis by air. Unlike the Allies at Algiers, they met with no opposition whatsoever from the French.

To carry out the allotted tasks, the 36th Infantry Brigade, kept in floating reserve during the landing, was sent by sea to Bougie, and got ashore unopposed on the 11th November. But the battalion detailed to take the airfield at Djedelli was prevented by the rough seas from landing there and had to march from Bougie. This delayed the capture of the airfield until the 13th and, before British fighter aircraft could be established on it, the enemy carried out a raid on Bougie harbour. Several ships were sunk, losses of equipment were considerable and, as a result, the units of the Brigade had for some time to operate with what the troops could carry.

*Advance of 'Hart Force'*

The airfield at Bone had been seized by two companies of paratroops and, on the 12th, No. 6 Commando Force, to which were attached two sections of the 5th Battalion's Anti-Tank Platoon, landed from the sea and secured the port.

To support these troops a small mobile column was organised. Known as 'Hart Force' from the name of its Commander, Major W. V. Hart of the 5th Battalion, this was composed of 'B' Company (Capt. Truckle), the Carrier Platoon and two mortar detachments from the Battalion, and two sections of m.m.g.s. All the available transport of the 11th Brigade was pooled to carry this force, which left Algiers on the 11th and reached Bone on the 13th. The force did much valuable work before it was disbanded a fortnight later.

Three days after 'Hart Force' had left, the 5th marched to a village twenty miles to the south-east of Algiers. On the afternoon of the 15th they got orders to prepare to move as fast as possible towards Tunis, and that evening a platoon of troop-carrying lorries of the R.A.S.C. reported to them. This platoon had come straight from landing at the docks at Algiers and the drivers had only time to swallow a cup of tea before the Battalion embussed.

*The Country*

At this stage some description of the country is necessary, for the race to Tunis was decided as much by the advantages which it gave to the enemy in defence and by the climate as by anything else.

The distance from Algiers to Tunis by road was over 560 miles. There were two roads, both of them narrow and in a bad state of repair, which climbed through ranges of precipitous mountains and descended into richly cultivated valleys. In those valleys the rain, which began at the outset of the campaign, turned the soil into sticky, chocolate-coloured mud, impassable to any vehicle.

The one railway was short of rolling-stock and had to be kept supplied with coal from England. It, and the two roads, were the last links in lines of communication which originated thousands of miles away in Great Britain and America.

Tunisia is a country of steep, rugged mountains and rocky hills which are mostly covered with forests of cork-trees and thick, breast-high scrub; a country in which a comparatively weak defence could, if well placed, hold up a much stronger attack. The areas suitable for the employment of armoured forces were extremely limited; in the north, the valley of the Medjerda River; in the centre, the plain which lay between Tebourba, Goubellat and Pont du Fahs; and the Kairouan plain which stretched southwards from the central mountain group to the coast. Access to these areas was by passes easily dominated by an enemy, and the roads over the passes ran through long defiles commanded by the heights on either side. In such country command of the air was essential, for without it movement by day could only lead to trouble.

The Medjerda valley formed the gateway to Tunis, and Medjez-el-Bab, commanded on all sides by hills, was the gate. Many centuries earlier Hannibal had said, 'He who holds Medjez holds Carthage,' and those words still were true.

*The Forward Move of the 5th Bn., 16th–21st November*

Before the 5th left Algiers, progress was being made farther forward. The 36th Brigade, still operating on assault scales of transport, had pushed

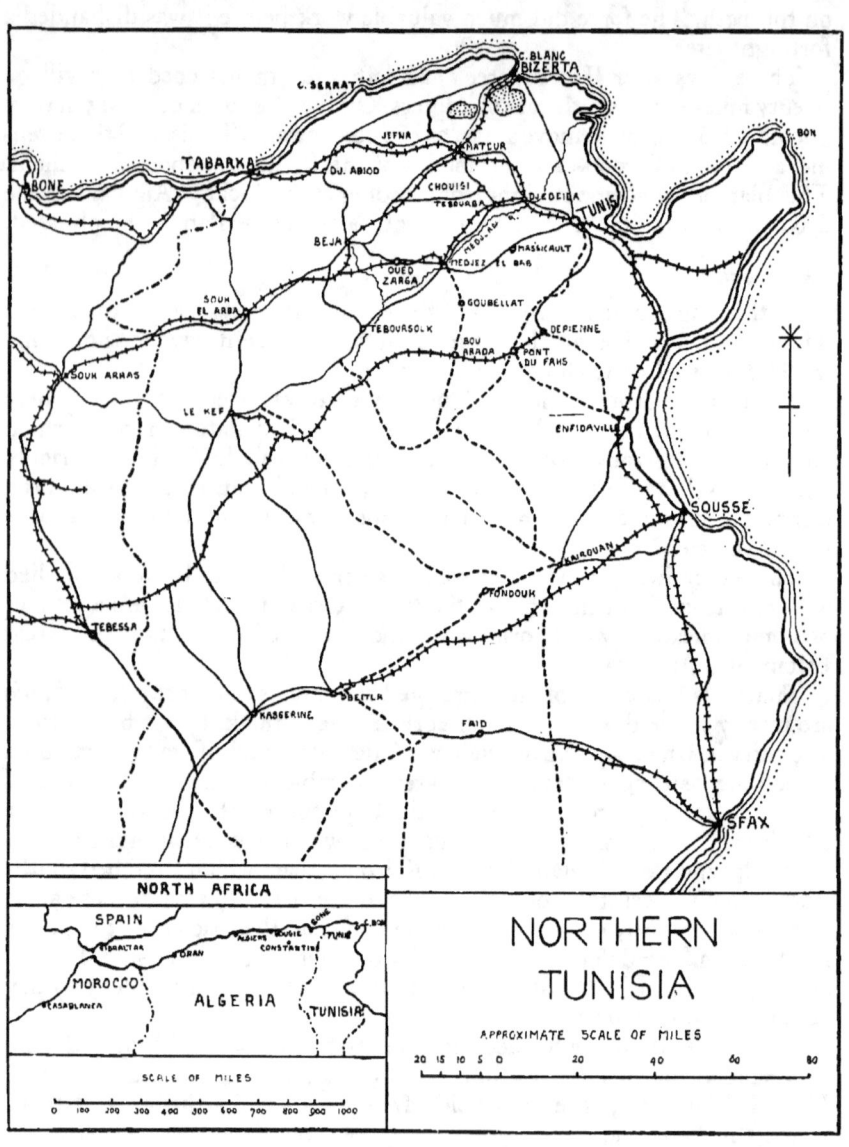

on; by the 15th the advanced guard had reached Tabarka, and three days later an enemy attack at Djebel Abiod had been repulsed.

'Hart Force,' which had led the advance throughout, was operating to the east of that place, and the carriers and reconnaissance cars working well forward were cut off by the German advance; but although they lost their infantry transport the remainder managed to rejoin the Brigade on the 19th. 'B' Company of the 5th took to the hills and got back two days later after conducting a successful guerilla campaign against the enemy's rear.

The 36th Brigade then advanced slowly on Jefna, where several attempts to dislodge the enemy from strong positions failed, with heavy losses.

Farther to the south the 1st Parachute Battalion had been dropped on the Souk-el-Arba landing-ground and was engaged with the enemy northeast of Beja. 'Blade Force,' the 17/21st Lancers' Regimental Group which had landed at Algiers from the follow-up convoy on the 13th, had been sent eastwards without delay and, by the night of the 20th, elements of the force were holding Oued Zarga, west of Medjez.

At Medjez, the French, having rejected a German ultimatum, had repulsed two attacks, but without air and tank support they could not hold on and withdrew westwards on the night of the 20th.

The 5th began their long journey on the 16th November. Their route, through Setif, Constantine and Souk Arras, took them across the frontier of Tunisia to Souk-el-Arba on the 19th. They had traversed the Tell Atlas range, with its steep gradients, grim scenery and weather which varied from blizzards to brilliant sunshine. In some of the towns and villages they had received a tumultuous welcome; in others there was no enthusiasm, and the attitude of the French, both civilians and soldiers, was not helpful, for they were afraid of possible German reprisals.

A tribute is due to the R.A.S.C. drivers of the T.C.V.s, which carried the Battalion on this long journey of 413 miles in four days. The column had to move over bad and twisty mountain roads, often without lights, but there was not a single accident and the march discipline was excellent. It was a fine performance, especially for men who had only landed in the country a matter of hours before they were called upon to start the journey.

On their arrival at Souk-el-Arba the 5th came under the command of 'Blade Force.' 'D' Company relieved the Parachute Company at Beja, weary after three days of continuous fighting. The enemy were within four miles of the place, but were inactive and, though 'D' had their first experience of a Stuka attack the next morning, they were prepared for it and suffered no casualties.

*The Capture of Medjez, 20th–27th November*

The 78th Division had been ordered to advance on Tunis and destroy the enemy forces as soon as its forward concentration had been completed.

The French had undertaken to cover the concentration to the best of their ability and to protect the right flank of this advance.

By the 21st November the enemy had withdrawn to the east bank of the river at Medjez, but the 78th Division was not yet strong enough to press the advance and was ordered to wait until it had sufficient forces and supplies to give a reasonable chance of reaching the objective.

On the 20th the other two battalions of the 11th Brigade had come up from Algiers; the 2nd Bn. The Lancashire Fusiliers at Oued Zarga and the 1st Bn. The East Surrey Regt. at Beja. Four days later the forward concentration of the Division and of 'Blade Force,' reinforced by light tanks from the 1st U.S. Armoured Division, was complete, and a resumption of the advance was ordered, with the line Tebourba–Mateur as the first objective.

Meanwhile, the 5th, now under command of the 11th Brigade, had moved first to Le Kef, then to relieve two French battalions astride the Beja–Oued Zarga road, then to near Teboursouk and finally, on the 24th, to a farm some eight miles south-west of Medjez.

Medjez was to be captured at first light on the 25th. The 5th Battalion was to advance on the town from the south-west, the Lancashire Fusiliers from the north-west. An American field battery was to support the 5th.

Lieut.-Col. Crook duly issued his orders in the extremely dirty sitting-room of the farm which, besides the eight or nine officers, contained the Italian farmer and his family of seven, some in bed, others in various stages of undress. Orders issued, those who could find some straw upon which to lie tried to snatch a few hours' sleep.

After moving a short distance in T.C.V.s the Battalion debussed at midnight, in bright moonlight, some four miles from Medjez. They had been on the march for less than an hour when the advanced guard, 'A' Company, was fired upon by machine-guns as it rounded a bend in the road. The enemy post, which commanded about 500 yards of the road, was sited on a small feature to the east. A platoon worked round the enemy's left, and, after softening the post with grenades, went in with the bayonet and disposed of the twelve Italians in it. Unfortunately, the German occupants escaped, taking their weapons with them. This minor engagement, the first of the campaign for the 5th, cost them two killed and about fifteen wounded.

The advance continued without more opposition for about a mile, when further orders were issued. 'C' Company were to capture a farm reported to be held by the enemy and were then to occupy the high ground overlooking the road leading south from Medjez; 'D' were to seize a hill, known later as 'Grenadier Hill,' which commanded the roads leading into Medjez from Tunis and Goubellat. 'A' Company formed the only reserve, for 'B' and the Carrier Platoon were still with 'Hart Force.'

The advance proceeded. 'D,' which had to make a lengthy approach march, gained its objective without opposition, while 'C,' having investigated the farm, went on steadily across country on the left.

While the advance by the 5th had been progressing, that of the Lancashire Fusiliers had been less fortunate. They had found the enemy determined to resist and were still in an exposed position north-west of Medjez when daylight came. Going on, they had reached the deep bed of the Medjerda River when German tanks appeared behind them and forced them to withdraw.

Shortly before noon six PzKw.IIIs—possibly those which had worried the Fusiliers—came in sight from the direction of Medjez and made for 'C' Company's line of advance. Two of the Battalion's anti-tank guns came into action right in the path of the tanks, but they and their transport were soon knocked out, and still the tanks came on. Fortunately, 'C' Company had seen them and withdrew in good order; the tanks then stopped and contented themselves with shelling Battalion H.Q. at a range of about two thousand yards. Meanwhile 'D' Company were in an awkward position, three miles away and without any anti-tank defence, but escaped by withdrawing along the bed of a watercourse.

That night the Battalion stayed concentrated and very much on the alert near Battalion H.Q. Early the next morning a dull boom was heard from the direction of Medjez, and it was suspected that the enemy had blown up the Roman bridge which carried the main road over the river and into the town, as a preliminary to a withdrawal.

Before daybreak on the 26th a squadron of General Grant tanks of the 2nd Bn. U.S. 13th Armoured Regt. arrived at Battalion H.Q. They would have been a welcome sight on the previous day, but they had then been on the other side of the river. Plans were at once made for a resumption of the advance.

In due course the tanks, with 'D' Company on board, went forward. It was found that Medjez had been vacated by the enemy so, after crossing the Tunis road, the tanks halted and the Company took up a position from which to watch the approaches to the town. 'C' Company went on into it and found that a weak battalion of Tirailleurs Algériens had been hanging on to the western outskirts. The Royal Engineers soon got to work and replaced the demolished bridge with a Bailey. It was not long before Stukas attacked this and the tanks, but caused no damage.

While in their position some of 'D' Company were misled by the similarity of the German steel helmet to that worn by the Americans, and allowed a motor-cyclist patrol, which they believed to be friendly, to pass through their lines. The patrol soon realised the situation and took to the open country towards Grenadier Hill, but here No. 2 Platoon made no mistake. The motor-cycle combinations were a welcome addition to the Battalion's scanty transport.

After occupying tank-proof localities covering the approaches to Medjez from the east, the 5th were relieved on the morning of the 27th by a French battalion and concentrated at a point north-west of the town. Here they were rejoined by the detachments which had been with 'Hart Force' and it was learned that these had suffered a number of casualties during their adventurous wanderings, including Lieut. Needle killed and Capt. Truckle taken prisoner.

### *The Advance to Djedeida, 28th–30th November*

By now the 36th Brigade was in the neighbourhood of Djebel Abiod, and 'Blade Force,' with the 1st Parachute Battalion and a U.S. armoured battalion, had moved on to the plain south of Mateur. From there, on the 26th, a successful raid had destroyed a number of Stukas on Djedeida airfield.

In the 11th Brigade sector the East Surrey Regt. had gone through and had occupied Tebourba on the night of the 26th. On the following day German tanks tried to get into the town behind them, but were stopped by the very gallant action of the 132nd Field Regt. R.A. which knocked out seventeen of them at ranges varying from one hundred to thirty yards and lost six of its eight guns in the process.

On the night of the 27th/28th the T.C.V.s took the 5th Battalion to within three miles of Tebourba and, from a hill to the east of it, a reconnaissance was made for the attack on Djedeida.

The view was magnificent. Below, and about three miles away, lay the town. Between it and Tebourba the country was fairly open for about two miles, though broken by ridges and gullies; then there were vineyards and fields enclosed by cactus hedges. In the distance, sixteen miles away, could be seen minarets flashing in the sun—the minarets of the mosques of Tunis.

In and around Djedeida there was no sign of enemy movement and this seemed to confirm the information that if it was held at all it was held by a weak force only; but the Luftwaffe was active and there were many attacks on the Tebourba area by Stukas and Messerschmitts, which could bomb with impunity since there was still no Allied air support whatsoever.

The reconnaissance made and orders issued, at 1300 hours the advance began from the olive-groves of Tebourba. 'A' and 'D' Companies rode on the nineteen American tanks, 'C' and 'B' followed on foot, three hundred yards behind. Meagre artillery support was provided by a troop of 25-pounders, firing concentrations on selected targets. A second troop was kept in hand to deal with possible tank counter-attack.

The advance followed the line of the railway, and for two miles proceeded steadily without any opposition. Then, after the tanks had crossed a ridge and were making their way across open country towards a cactus hedge on

## THE 5th BATTALION IN NORTH AFRICA, 1942–1943

the outskirts of Djedeida, a number of anti-tank guns and heavy machine-guns opened fire. Immediately, five tanks were hit and burst into flames and the remainder withdrew to hull-down positions behind the ridge. 'D' Company took up fire positions in the open, while 'A' and 'C' pushed on, but the enemy were holding the outskirts of Djedeida strongly and all attempts to work round the right flank were met with heavy machine-gun fire.

To those on the spot it was evident that no attack could succeed without more artillery support, and that to attempt to continue without it was merely to court unnecessary casualties. It soon became obvious that air support also was essential; for the remainder of that day and for the whole of the next the 5th were the object of almost continuous dive-bombing, low-level bombing and cannon fire from aircraft whose bases were only fifteen miles away.

As soon as darkness fell, 'D' Company was withdrawn from its exposed position and the Battalion organised defence for the night about two thousand yards from Djedeida.

Casualties had been fairly heavy and had included Major Hart killed. He was a very fine soldier and a great loss to the 5th. He had distinguished himself during the Battle of France, when he had won the Military Cross, and again in Tunisia with the force which bore his name.

Late that evening a Liaison Officer arrived with a message from Brigade H.Q. ordering the Battalion to attack and capture Djedeida by midnight and then to exploit towards Chouigi, up the Mateur road. It was obvious that this order could not be carried out; there was insufficient time to organise such an operation and the necessary reconnaissances could not have been made in the dark. So, after the C.O. had represented the facts by wireless, the order was cancelled. In the early hours of the 29th the Brigade Commander arrived at Battalion H.Q. and ordered another attack to be put in at dawn.

The attack was launched at 0645 hours. In the face of intense fire, 'C' Company advanced almost up to the road leading into the village, but was forced back after its Commander, Capt. Beagley, had been wounded. So heavy was the fire that it was only by Lieut.-Col. Crook and the C.O. of the American tank squadron going out in a tank that he could be brought in. In the centre, 'A' Company had fared no better, and on the left 'D,' after taking a ridge which dominated the country from the north-east, had disappeared out of sight over the crest. An hour or so later, all that could be seen of the latter company were a few stray men making their way back.

The enemy, who had evidently been reinforced since the previous day, made no attempt to counter-attack on the ground; but the air attacks went on and, though they did not cause many casualties, their effect on tired men who still saw no sign of British aircraft, was far greater than was realised by those who had not had to suffer such attacks for hours on end.

Casualties in the attack had been heavy, especially in 'D' Company, whose Commander, Major Wright, was missing. They might have been heavier had it not been for the conduct of the crews of the American tanks. Inexperienced as these were, in spite of their exposed positions, and regardless of dive-bombing, they were always ready to engage the enemy. Without their support the day would have gone even harder for the 5th, who also owed much to Lieut.-Col. Crook for his personal example and disregard of his own safety.

The Battalion had failed to capture Djedeida, but not without honour, for, to quote the words of General Anderson's despatch, 'On the 28th November 11th Brigade and the 2/13th Armoured Regt. were on the outskirts of Djedeida. We had attained the nearest point to Tunis that was reached until the final stage of the campaign.'[2]

On the night of the 29th the Battalion was relieved by the 2nd Bn. The Hampshire Regt. and went into reserve near Tebourba.

This battalion, which belonged to the 1st Guards Brigade, had been placed under command of the 11th Brigade to replace the Lancashire Fusiliers, who had gone north to assist 'Blade Force' in an attempt to take Mateur. After relieving the 5th they were attacked by the Germans for four days, finally charging the enemy with fixed bayonets. Only four officers and 120 men came back alive and unwounded. In the history of the Tunisian Campaign they will rank as second to none for their gallantry in this action.[3]

*The German Counter-offensive, 30th November–12th December*

It was now evident that the enemy intended to fight along the whole front. Having seized the ports and the airfields at Tunis and Bizerta the German forces, backed by the complete air superiority which they had at the time, advanced to secure the mountains on the Algerian frontier, in order to prevent the Allies establishing themselves on the plains of Tunisia.

When the first contact had been made, towards the end of November, the German forces were a mixture of units, many of them originally intended as reinforcements for Rommel's Army in Libya; their fighting strength was about 15,500, with 130 tanks and 60 field-guns. During the first half of December the 10th Panzer Division was completed and the Italian Superga Division arrived, both formations losing some of their equipment at sea on the way. There were also 'Reinforcement Battalions,' which fought as units, and later in the month the German 334th Division began to appear. This was a poor-quality formation and had no artillery until January. An important arrival during this period was the 501st Heavy

Major-General G. St. G. Robinson, C.B., D.S.O., M.C., Colonel of the Regiment

*Lambert and Weston)*

Tank Battalion, half of its tanks being the formidable Mark VI 'Tigers.'

In the first week of December German tank and infantry attacks forced 'Blade Force' back from Chouigi. It was withdrawn westwards and the defence of the forward area was entrusted to the 11th Brigade and the Infantry of Combat Command 'B' of the 1st U.S. Armoured Division, which had been brought up to act in a defensive rôle. Both they and the 11th Brigade were heavily attacked on the 3rd December and succeeding days. The 5th Battalion, south-west of Tebourba, did not come into this fighting, but their transport suffered from dive-bombing and lost precious lives and vehicles.

Although the 5th were not attacked, they had one uncomfortable moment. On the 1st December enemy tanks were reported to be approaching their position, and that evening a patrol located twenty-seven of them harbouring in some trees less than a mile away. Fortunately, orders came for the Battalion to withdraw that night and they slipped away without interference. They had to leave behind them an air O.P. aircraft, which was parked close to their H.Q. The Gunner pilot, determined to save his plane, elected to remain behind and, after the moon had risen, managed to take off and return safely to his base although he had no night-flying instruments.

Four days were spent in the new position, in a narrow gap between the mountains and the Medjerda River, astride the Medjez railway to the west of Tebourba. Intermittent shelling and dive-bombing caused further casualties to transport men and vehicles. The other units of the brigade withdrew through the 5th on their way to an area near Medjez, and when they were clear, on the night of the 5th/6th, the Battalion was relieved by the 8th Argyll and Sutherland Highlanders and moved back in M.T. to Longstop Hill. This, in reality the twin features of Djebel Ahmerah and Djebel Rhah, commanded Medjez from the north-east and was later to become famous as the scene of bitter fighting.

With few tools, no wire and a very scanty supply of mines, the 5th began to put the hill in a state of defence. The rains had now begun in earnest and the men had to work soaked to the skin, while vehicles and supplies had often to be man-handled across the countryside, which had become a sea of mud. They could now muster only some 350 men ('D' Company, which had lost heavily at Djedeida, had been re-formed by the transfer of men from other companies and had been renamed 'V' Company), but were well supported by a troop of 6-pounders and an American battery of 25-pounders, and across the river to the right was a number of light and medium tanks of Combat Command 'B.' So the Battalion felt confident of its ability to smash any German attack, and some enemy tanks which appeared on the 10th were, in fact, well dealt with by the American artillery.

On that same day the garrison of Medjez, which included four French battalions, was reinforced by the 1st Guards Brigade, preparatory to the withdrawal of the 11th Brigade and Combat Command 'B' to refit. That night the 5th left Longstop Hill, after lifting all the mines they had laid so carefully, and embussed for an area in the hills north-west of Oued Zarga. On withdrawal they found patrols to secure the river bridge and cover the movement of Combat Command 'B,' but unfortunately the Americans took the wrong route, got bogged in the mud, and had to abandon a large number of their tanks and vehicles.

*In Defence, 12th–21st December*

On the southern portion of the Allied front there was now a salient, of which Medjez formed the apex, Testour and Oued Zarga the other corners.

In their new area the 5th had hoped for time to reorganise and re-equip, but Oued Zarga guarded the approaches from Mateur and they had to prepare positions and send out constant patrols against a possible German advance through the mountains.

To begin with, the patrols reconnoitred the valleys north of, and parallel to, the Medjez–Tebourba road, penetrating to a depth of five or six miles. They gained no contact with the enemy, so on the 12th 'A' Company went out to Toukabeur, whence a patrol was pushed forward to Chaouach. No enemy were seen, but the wheel-marks of a German armoured car indicated their presence in the neighbourhood, and this was confirmed by the disappearance of a despatch-rider on his way to the company.

On the 15th Lieut. Rickett and five men set out on a three-day patrol into the mountains. Next day two pairs of the men returned with reports that the patrol was making good progress, and early on the 18th the fifth man came back with the news that he and Lieut. Rickett had encountered an enemy patrol at a farm, that the officer had been wounded and had ordered him to make his way back with the information. Another patrol which was sent out found enemy still in the farm and was told by the farmer that he had seen Lieut. Rickett being taken away in a cart and that he had been able to give him a written message, which he had handed over to some French troops. This message eventually reached the Battalion; written just before Lieut. Rickett had been captured, it gave valuable details of the track which the patrol had followed.

Two days after this occurrence, a standing patrol from 'C' Company had a brisk engagement with about thirty German motor-cyclists, killing three and capturing some of their vehicles.

There had been a short interval of fair weather and then the rains had started again. Owing to the isolated position of the Battalion and the absence of any roads, the M.T. officer had to change his vocation and organise a train of forty mules with Arab leaders, to bring supplies and water from 'B' Echelon, about five miles away.

Though life was fairly hard at this time there were some consolations. 'R' Company had arrived from the Base, bringing much-needed reinforcements, and the Battalion was issued with four Vickers machine-guns, which would be a better match for the German heavy machine-guns than were the Brens. The N.A.A.F.I. produced soap and razor-blades—up to now men had been sharing blades in the proportion of one blade to ten men—and whisky, the first seen for two months. And on the 18th came the first mail from home.

*The Last Attempt to Capture Tunis, 21st–27th December*

In mid-December the 5th Corps had been warned to prepare to resume the advance on Tunis. A preliminary to this was to be the capture of Longstop Hill, not, unfortunately, held by the Allies after the 5th Battalion had withdrawn from it. Then the 78th Division and the 18th Regimental Combat Team of the 1st U.S. Infantry Division were to advance astride the Medjerda River on Tebourba, while the 6th Armoured Division occupied the high ground at Massicault to the south. Both were then to drive straight to Tunis.

As the days passed the heavy rain caused anxiety, for cross-country movement was becoming more and more difficult. However, the Army Commander decided that the risk must be taken and the preliminary operations were arranged to start on the night of the 22nd/23rd December. D-Day for the main advance was to be the 24th.

On the evening of the 21st the Battalion received the operation order, which gave a very detailed programme of the course which events were to take. The rôle of the 5th was to move to a concentration area near Heidous, in the mountains north of Medjez, on the night of D-2/D-1. On the next night they were to advance from there, capture the feature Pt. 259 and block the gap between the hills and the Medjerda River with mines. At 1800 hours on D-Day they were to be relieved there by a French unit and rejoin 11th Brigade, which was to go through to Djedeida on that night. The object was, in short, to create a diversion which would assist the main advance by threatening the enemy's right near the Arret de Taullerville on the Medjez–Tunis railway.

For the initial operations, the 5th were to be under the command of the 18th Combat Team, and the orders were that they were to make contact with one of its battalions on the night D-2/D-1. But the Combat Team did not arrive in the area in time for any preliminary arrangements to be made with them; and the orders imposed wireless silence until the main advance started twenty-four hours later—an important factor in subsequent events.

Time was inadequate to make all the many preparations for such an

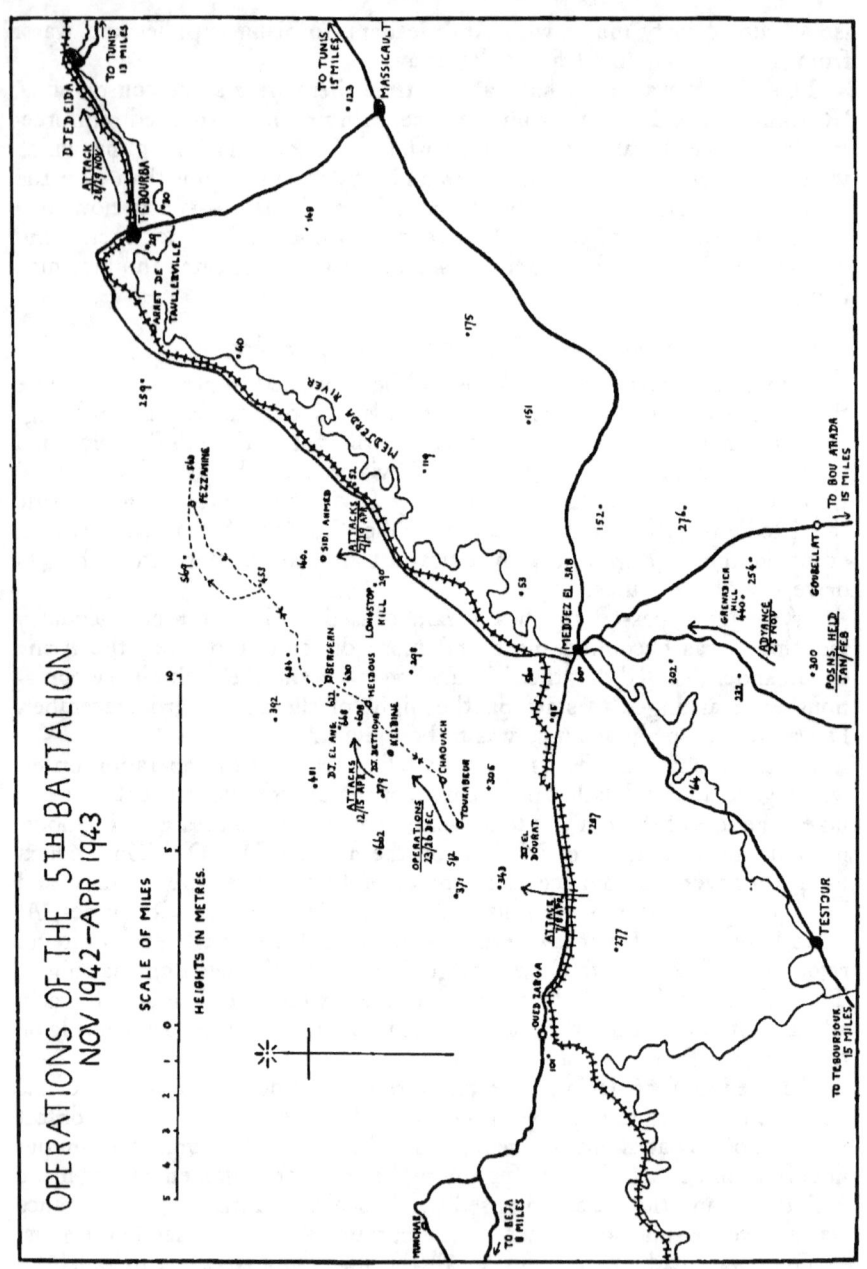

operation. There could be no question of using M.T. in the mountains, and rations for forty-eight hours, ammunition, signalling equipment, 3-inch mortars and m.m.g.s were all to be mule-borne. This, at least, was the theory. In practice, the Battalion was supplied with an assortment of ponies, donkeys and mules, led by Arabs. To load pack-animals fitted with the proper saddlery is an art, and few, if any, of the troops had been trained in that art; apart from this, the pack-saddles were of the native pattern, held together by pieces of rope or string. So the 5th looked forward to Christmas Day when, so the orders said, their own transport would meet them at the Arret de Taullerville.

Time did not allow of any proper reconnaissance, but the C.O., very wisely, despatched an officer to reconnoitre as much as he could of the route. He returned twenty-four hours later and reported that the route laid down was frequently little better than a goat-track and that the going throughout was bad.

On the 21st it began to rain and this continued at intervals all that night and the following day. Using all available M.T. in a shuttle-service, the Battalion completed its preliminary concentration in the olive-groves at Toukabeur shortly after nightfall on the 22nd.

Soon after midnight the advance started, the Battalion moving in single file, which was all that the track allowed. Each pack-animal, and its Arab leader, was in charge of a soldier, for the Arabs had soon shown that they would decamp at the first opportunity. The going was very heavy and slippery; it was necessary to grasp bushes in order to ascend some of the steep slopes and not more than a mile could be covered in the hour. Several of the pack-animals soon collapsed from sheer exhaustion—their loads, if weapons or ammunition, had to be changed in the dark; if rations, they were abandoned.

As dawn broke on the 23rd the Battalion reached its appointed jumping-off place, a plateau 2,500 feet up on the bare mountain-side a little way beyond Heidous, and there lay up, as ordered, throughout the hours of daylight. There was a drizzling rain and it was very cold. Below, and to the right, sounds of firing could be heard, but nothing could be seen because of the mist, and wireless silence prevented any information being obtained.

While the 5th had been on the move through the mountains, the 2nd Coldstream Guards had attacked and captured Longstop after severe fighting, and had then been relieved by a battalion of the 18th Combat Team. On the morning of the 23rd torrential rain had begun to fall, turning the country into a quagmire. Liaison officers went out from 78th Division H.Q. with the message that D-Day had been postponed for forty-eight hours (later it was postponed indefinitely) and that the 5th Battalion was to return to Oued Zarga. An entry in the 11th Brigade diary for the 23rd reads:

1530. Northamptons, however, were found to be out of touch temporarily owing to wireless silence, and steps were taken to get into touch with them and prevent them moving forward on their own into the hills.

Throughout that day the 5th were at the appointed jumping-off place, but the steps taken to get in touch with them failed. This was not surprising, for they were some twelve miles from Brigade H.Q. and, of that distance, less than half could have been covered on a motor-cycle; the remainder would have had to have been traversed on foot and very slowly. So they never heard that the operation had been postponed and continued to carry out their orders, even though they had failed to get in touch by patrols with the Combat Team at the arranged rendezvous.

None of the Battalion was sorry to get on the march again at dusk on the 23rd, for all were cold and stiff after lying out on the mountain-side without movement in the chilling rain. The track had become worse than ever and the streams that crossed it were now rushing torrents.

At midnight the C.O. ordered an hour's halt and the Signal Officer tried to get in touch by wireless with Brigade H.Q. and the Combat Team, but the attempt failed, probably because of the screening effect of the mountains.

After the halt they moved on, the track becoming steeper as they neared the crest of the ridge which ran towards the village of Fezzanine. A quarter of the pack-animals had now been lost, and the supply of rations and, more important still, of ammunition had been seriously depleted as a result. Almost more serious was the loss of the No. 19 wireless set; the mule carrying it had fallen down and it had been damaged beyond repair, so the Battalion had lost its only means of communication with the outside world.

An hour before dawn on Christmas Eve the top of the ridge was reached and, moving fast down the far slope, the Battalion reached a valley before daylight came and hid in the scrub. Between it and the objective there was now only one more mountain.

While breakfasts were being eaten the C.O. went ahead to reconnoitre and on return issued his orders. To start with, 'V' Company were to occupy the summit of Pt. 562 and so gain observation on to the objective below it, and then a further plan would be made.

The Company began to advance at 1300 hours and soon came under fire from a German machine-gun; pressing on, they took the objective, which proved to be an artillery O.P., with only slight casualties. Then the mist came down, making observation impossible, but it provided cover under which the rest of the Battalion was brought up. As they were getting into position there was a roar overhead and through a break in the mist appeared an aircraft, flying low. Attempts to attract the pilot's attention were apparently unsuccessful—in fact, it would have been a miracle if they had succeeded—and the aircraft was swallowed up in the mist.

The Brigade war diary for the 24th gives a sidelight on this incident:

> 1205. Efforts were made to establish wireless communication with 5 Northamptons. Last night's attempts to get in touch with them through American troops (18 Combat Team) and through French troops attached to 1 Guards Bde proved unsuccessful. Later in the day 5 Northamptons rear party established a base at Toukabeur, from which a patrol went forward to contact the bn. Air recce failed to locate them.

Soon after this episode, word came from 'A' and 'V' Companies' forward patrols that the enemy could be heard forming up below them. The Battalion stood-to and prepared to fight it out, though it was realised that shortage of supplies would render prolonged resistance to determined attack out of the question. At the same time, an officer was despatched to report the situation to Brigade H.Q., though, as this involved a difficult walk of about twenty miles to Munchar, it is doubtful if any action to help the 5th could have been taken in time to be of any use.

The first attack, on 'A' Company, came at 1900 hours and was repulsed, as were two others which followed at hourly intervals. Luckily, they were made without artillery or mortar support.

The C.O. now decided that as there was no sign of the main operation coming into effect, and as supplies were running low, there was no alternative but to withdraw. The wounded and the twenty remaining pack-animals were got back into the valley in rear and the companies withdrew from their positions, 'V' Company acting as rear-guard.

At midnight the enemy put in a strong attack, with a force estimated at two companies, against 'V' Company, with which were the C.O., the Adjutant, the I.O. and the Defence Platoon. Fire came from three sides of the hill and the fight went on for an hour and a half in bright moonlight, with rifles, grenades and automatics, often at a range of a few yards. In the end the Germans gave it up, after they had suffered heavy casualties. One prisoner, of the 69th Panzer Grenadier Regt., was taken.

After this the rear-guard rejoined the rest of the Battalion near the village of Fezzanine. All the remaining rations and ammunition were issued to the men, so as to free the few pack-animals for the carriage of the more seriously wounded, and stretchers were improvised from rifles bound together by telephone cable.

In the two hours before daylight the 5th managed to reach a gully, where they hid in the scrub, unable to move about or brew tea as they were in sight of the enemy, who had occupied the position from which they had withdrawn. That afternoon the mist came down again, and they were able to get on the march, slowly because of the wounded; by dusk they had reached the village of Bergern and spent another bitterly cold night there.

They were hungry too, for the ration for the day had been a slice of bully beef and a biscuit.

Many of the wounded owed much, possibly their lives, to the devoted work that night of Capt. Kerr, the Medical Officer. Almost without rest he journeyed up and down the hillside, in his efforts to get them into the most comfortable spots he could find. For this, and for his other work, he was awarded the Military Cross.

The 5th were now nearly at the end of their journey. Moving on again early on the 26th, they reached Heidous at 1000 hours and were greeted by 'A' Company of the East Surrey Regt., sent there on the previous day to establish a base for their return.

After a rest and much-needed meal, the Battalion went on to Toukabeur, where ambulances were waiting for the wounded and another meal and a change of clothing for the remainder. Then they slept, till late that night T.C.V.s took them back to billets at Munchar, where they had the few days' rest they well deserved.[4]

The Divisional Commander, Major-General Evelegh, lost no time in paying them a visit. Addressing the Battalion, he told them of the efforts which had been made to get in touch with them immediately after the operation had been cancelled and only a short time after they had started. Patrols and five aircraft had been despatched to search the mountains. He congratulated all ranks on their achievement and on their turnout on parade.

An 11th Brigade account of the campaign notes that two days after the 5th had returned from their adventure they had reorganised and cleaned up, and showed no signs of their gruelling experience.

To complete the story of events. The American troops which had taken over Longstop Hill had been heavily counter-attacked on the 23rd December and, mistaking their orders, had withdrawn from the crest. This was recaptured by the Guards Brigade on the next day, but was again lost on Christmas Day, and then, owing to the difficulty of operations in the mud, was left in the hands of the enemy. The original positions round Medjez were then occupied and withstood all further German attacks.

Any more attempts to reach Tunis were now out of the question until the weather improved, and it was realised that when the time came the offensive would have to be much stronger if it was to overcome the greatly increased opposition of the enemy.

*Comments on the Operations, November–December* 1942

The Allied forces had accomplished some of the objects of Operation 'Torch.' They had secured Algeria and French Morocco. But they had not achieved the principal object, the occupation of Tunisia and, more especially, the seizure of the ports of that country.

Some of the reasons for this are fairly stated in a book published later:

It was not an army that set off to smite its way across the mountains and the mud of Tunis. It was not even a corps; it was a division at assault strength, and the infantry went forward and fought for weeks in deluges of rain with nothing more to fall back on than what they carried in their packs, wearing the clothes they had landed in.

Yet had the Resident General in Tunis resisted the German demands —even for a day or two—that dauntless 78th Division would have been in Tunis by Christmas. But Christmas Day found them held, not so much by the enemy as by the sleet and the mist and the mud, 15 miles from their goal, after six weeks' bitter and incessant fighting.[5]

Credit is due to others not mentioned here, who also played a great part in those early days—British and American armour, Commandos and Paratroops. However, when all is said and done, it was upon the 78th Division, and upon the Infantry of that Division, that the brunt fell. And the 5th Battalion had done its full share.

Through no fault of theirs they had failed to take Djedeida; but they had penetrated farther on the road to Tunis than any other unit. Through no fault of theirs they had set forth on an operation which, in the circumstances, might have led to complete disaster; but they had carried out their orders and, thanks to good leadership, fitness and high morale, had accomplished a difficult withdrawal, bringing their wounded with them.

They had good reason for holding their heads high for the part they had played in operations which, though failing in their main object, had brought much glory to the Infantry.

## CHAPTER X

### THE 5th BATTALION IN NORTH AFRICA, 1942–1943
### DEFENCE, AND THE FINAL ADVANCE TO TUNIS, 1943

The General Situation, January 1943—The 5th Bn. in Defence, January-February—Rommel's Offensive, February 1943—Von Arnim's Offensive, February-March—The Beginning of the Allied Offensive, March-April—Advance in the Mountains, 5th–13th April—The Attack on Tanngoucha, 14th–15th April—The Final Offensive, 22nd April–13th May—The Attacks on Sidi Ahmed, 27th–29th April—The Advance to Tunis—Comments on the Campaign—The 5th in North Africa, May-July 1943.

### The General Situation, January 1943

WITH a halt called as far as any major offensive was concerned, the policy of the Allied Command in North Africa was to contain the enemy by constant pressure and by means of limited attacks to seize ground which would facilitate later operations; to help the French forces in the southern sector as much as possible; and to push on with the construction of airfields, work which the experiences of 1942 had shown to be vital to success.

Active patrolling and the strengthening of defences were therefore the order of the day and were very necessary, since the enemy were far from inactive.

Early in January the Germans took the heights round Mateur, and this led to the abandonment of that place and of Tebourba. Later in the month local attacks by the 36th Brigade and the 6th Armoured Division were followed by a strong attack against the latter down the Bou Arada valley and against the French to the south. Newly landed mountain troops and tanks of the 10th Panzer Division took part and, against the French, some of the 'Tiger' tanks made their first appearance in action. The attack on the British was stopped dead after heavy fighting, but the French resistance was overwhelmed and the situation was only stabilised after British and American troops had been sent to reinforce.

The result of this fighting was to bring the Allied front back to the line Bou Arada–Medjez-el-Bab–Sedjnane. And since operations had shown that, with Commanders of three different nations sharing responsibility for their conduct, proper control was lacking, General Anderson was

# THE 5th BATTALION IN NORTH AFRICA, 1942-1943

allotted the responsibility for the employment of American troops and the French Corps was placed under his command.

## The 5th Battalion in Defence, January–February

After four days' rest, the 5th Battalion, quite recovered from their Christmas adventure, took over part of the 11th Brigade position in front of Munchar. After a fortnight there without incident, for it was a quiet sector, they heard that they were to be detached from the Brigade and were to move to the hills south of Medjez and west of Goubellat.

The Battalion moved by M.T. on the 15th January and relieved the London Irish Rifles. In the new sector they came under the command of the 18th Regimental Combat Team which, in turn, was under the 6th Armoured Division.

The position was an important one, overlooking the Goubellat plain and commanding the entrance to an approach which, if lost, would open the road to Beja to the enemy. The Battalion front was held by three companies, two on exposed hills which flanked the sides of the entrance to the plain, the third between them and on a lower hill which blocked the entrance.

There was much to be done to make the position really strong and tank-proof. In front, a big minefield was laid by the Sappers; behind this each company constructed its own perimeter defence of triple wire, liberally sprinkled with booby-traps; all approaches likely to be used by the enemy were sown with grenades, adjusted to react to the weight of a man. In addition to its own anti-tank guns the Battalion was protected by sixteen 6-pounders, two 17-pounders (the latest anti-tank weapon) and a battery of 25-pounders, so when they had finished their work they felt that they could stop any attack. The only drawback was a gap of five miles on the right, which was never filled, and another of three miles on the left, which remained unoccupied for about a month.

The enemy held the hills near Goubellat, five miles away across the plain, and the 5th's patrols were very active, both by day and by night, with the object of gaining information from the Frenchmen who still worked the various farms which dotted the plain, and of dominating the wide no-man's-land. To begin with, the German regiment opposite showed little initiative, but when it was relieved by the Hermann Goering Regt. a more aggressive attitude was shown.

At first the daylight patrolling was done in carriers, but later on mounted patrols were employed. Ponies were obtained from farms, and patrols were organised under the supervision of P.S.M. Dumais, one of four representatives of the Canadian Army who had arrived for attachment to the Battalion. A French-Canadian, he was of the greatest assistance in getting information, for, dressed as a farmer, he would visit the farms on the plain and obtain news of enemy movements from his apparent compatriots.

There were several minor engagements during this period, and in one of them a patrol which was trying to locate the enemy forward localities encountered a considerably stronger enemy patrol, with the result that Lieut. Tighe and eleven men were missing.

The enemy made several attempts to penetrate the Battalion's position. On one occasion they attacked a 'B' Company standing patrol and in the ensuing fight Lieut. Nicholson was killed; two of the enemy were accounted for. On another occasion an attack on one of 'V' Company's forward localities resulted in a twenty-minutes' fire fight.

Only once, however, did the enemy succeed in making their way round behind the forward companies. There was a standing order in the Battalion that line communications to each company were to be tested at half-hourly intervals throughout the night, and one night no answer came from 'S' Company, well in rear. A line-party, sent to investigate, found a grenade attached to the cable. Companies stood-to, and presently movement was heard in the valley below Battalion H.Q. Fire was opened, and returned, but the enemy got away by a small re-entrant which ran between two of the forward company localities. A sequel was the destruction of a truck by a Tellermine which had been laid on a rearward track, so dispositions were altered and minefields laid in order to stop further inroads of this nature.

The troops lived and worked hard. A lucky platoon occasionally found itself posted in a farm, but this was the exception; the majority had to get what shelter they could from the wintry weather by means of groundsheets and gas-capes. Despite this there was very little sickness, and occasional relief from the rigours of the forward area was available at the Battalion Rest Camp, established at 'B' Echelon under the Quartermaster, and at Divisional Camps farther back. The fact of being under American command had its advantages, such as shower-baths hidden in a wadi, cigarettes and chewing-gum; what would have been appreciated, but was not forthcoming, was a change from the eminently practical, but intensely monotonous, 'Compo ration,' on which the Battalion had lived ever since they had landed.

Most of these amenities disappeared when, in the middle of February, the Combat Team left to rejoin its division and was replaced by the rest of the 11th Brigade from Munchar. At the same time a battalion of Algerian troops came in to fill the gap on the left of the Battalion front.

*Rommel's Offensive, February* 1943

The Eighth Army had occupied Tripoli on the 23rd January and had then continued to advance until, by the beginning of February, it had driven the enemy out of Libya and was approaching the defences of the Mareth Line, a strong position built by the French along the southern border of Tunisia in the years before the war. Behind this Rommel with-

## THE 5th BATTALION IN NORTH AFRICA, 1942-1943

drew, leaving two divisions to delay the pursuit. His arrival in Tunisia seriously affected the balance of strength there.

In the north was the British First Army, fully occupied in holding von Arnim's forces. In the centre and south the French and Americans were stretched thinly along a front of 150 miles, only able to hold their own against the limited force which von Arnim could throw against them from time to time. Now the Allies were faced by a much strengthened enemy, including such formations as the 21st Panzer Division, with great experience of warfare and with high morale, in spite of the battering it had had at the hands of the Eighth Army.

Rommel knew that it was vital to oppose the advance of the Eighth Army, but he appreciated that it would take that Army time to pierce the Mareth Line and that, in the interval, he and von Arnim could strike in Tunisia.

On the 14th February Rommel put in his attack, for which he had concentrated, among other formations, both the 10th and the 21st Panzer Divisions.

The attack, directed against Gafsa and the Kasserine Pass, was supported by heavy dive-bombing, against which the Allies could not bring their now adequate air strength to bear as many of the airfields were out of action because of recent heavy rains. It hit the American 2nd Corps at an unfortunate moment, just after it had relieved the French in the area, and drove it back with heavy losses in tanks and guns.

Counter-attacks failed to stop the German drive; by the 18th February, Sbeitla, one of the gateways to the north, was in their hands, and the Americans, to avoid being cut off, had been compelled to abandon their positions on the line Gafsa–Feriana–Kasserine; two days later the important Kasserine Pass was lost. The situation was now serious, for a break-through beyond the pass would enable the German armour to threaten the whole Allied position in Northern Tunisia.

It was fortunate, in view of the danger that existed, that a recent reorganisation in the chain of the higher command had taken place, for this enabled rapid action to be taken. General Sir H. Alexander had been appointed Deputy C.-in-C. to General Eisenhower and, in addition to assuming control of both the First and the Eighth Armies (then renamed the 18th Army Group), he was given the responsibility for the conduct of all land operations. The British and French forces in Tunisia remained under General Anderson's command.

The First Army was now more worthy of the name for, besides the 5th Corps (46th, 78th and 6th Armoured Divisions), it included the 9th Corps, the 1st Division of which was then landing from England at North African ports.

General Alexander acted quickly to check the enemy's 'desperate bid to break through the iron ring closing round him in North Africa.'[1] The 1st Guards Brigade, the 26th Armoured Brigade and Churchill tanks were sent to deal with the situation at the Kasserine Pass and Sbeitla. At the former place Rommel made a determined effort to break through towards Le Kef, at that time Advanced H.Q. of the First Army and a vital point on the lines of communication, but on the 22nd the German drive was stopped, only twenty-two miles from Tebessa. At Sbeitla the enemy was held.

By now the German armour had suffered heavy losses and Rommel could go no farther. Leaving an Italian rear-guard, in accordance with the usual German practice, he withdrew his force through the passes. The Allies followed, much hampered by minefields, retook the Kasserine Pass on the 26th and found the enemy digging in on a line between Faid and Gafsa in order to protect their flank while they turned to oppose the Eighth Army.

*Von Arnim's Offensive, February–March*

Rommel's offensive in the south was the forerunner of a series of determined attacks by von Arnim at various points on the First Army front, and also on the French west of Pont du Fahs. The main effort was made in the areas of Goubellat, Medjez, Sidi Nsir and Jefna.

From the 11th Brigade positions in the hills greatly increased activity was observed behind the enemy front, east of the Bou Arada–Goubellat road on the 25th February, and all units were warned to be particularly alert.

Before daylight the next morning the sound of firing from the French positions on the left of the 5th Battalion was at first thought to be caused by a patrol encounter. Half an hour later the left company, 'B,' commanded by Capt. Rayment, opened fire on a number of Germans in a gully immediately to their front, and a strong patrol from 'V' Company, led by Capt. Hertzberg of the Canadian Army, was sent out to intercept what was still believed to be an enemy patrol.

By 0600 hours the firing had intensified and it was evident that something more than a patrol action was afoot. A platoon of 'C' Company and a 3-inch mortar were sent to reinforce 'B' and efforts were made to recall the 'V' Company patrol, but contact by wireless could not be made. Two hours later 'B' were still engaging the enemy in the gully, their small-arms fire and the fire of the mortars stopping several attempts to attack and inflicting heavy casualties. German artillery was seen getting into action near a mosque on the plain and was engaged and dispersed by the British guns. At about this time a report that eleven enemy tanks had been seen at a spot known as 'Tally-ho Corner,' five miles south-east of Testour and well in rear of the position, caused the withdrawal of 'B' Echelon to Teboursouk.

Soon after 0900 hours the firing slackened and numbers of the enemy were seen surrendering to the French; the artillery O.P. reported that many Germans could be seen retreating across the plain and were being harassed by fire. The attack had evidently been broken and the enemy were given no encouragement to renew it; the artillery continued to engage any parties to be seen on the plain, and a 25-pounder was brought into action in 'A' Company's area, whence it could fire over open sights. Spitfires worried areas which the guns could not tackle. By 1830 hours all firing had practically ceased, and the Battalion settled down for the night, keeping a vigilant watch.

A carrier patrol sent out to search the plain on the 28th found one wounded man, Pte. Tovey, of the missing patrol and the bodies of Capt. Hertzberg, two N.C.O.s and five men close to the mosque. They had evidently sold their lives dearly when they had found themselves in the midst of very superior numbers of the enemy.

Immediate awards of the Military Cross to Capt. Rayment and of the Military Medal to C.S.M. Wade and Pte. Tovey were made for gallantry during the battle.

Elsewhere the success of the German attack had varied. At Medjez it had been defeated with heavy loss, though in places the German infantry had penetrated deep into the British gun-lines. Farther to the south a strong party of infantry and tanks had reached a point several miles behind the front, and 78th Division's H.Q. had only been saved by the timely arrival of some Churchill tanks.

By the 2nd March the situation was well in hand, though fighting went on for another fortnight. In the end the British had to give up Sedjnane, but Beja and Medjez, the enemy's main objectives, were still held.

*The Beginning of the Allied Offensive, March–April*

The 5th Battalion remained in the position for another three weeks and then, having been in the line for sixty-seven days without relief, handed over to the 2nd North Staffordshire Regt. on the night of the 23rd March. Marching back across the base of the Medjez salient, they took over defences south of the Oued Zarga–Medjez road.

The new positions were in a range of steep-sided hills which ran parallel to the road, north of which the enemy held similar positions. For the time being the Battalion's task was to improve the defences, to check the layout of the minefields and to patrol with the object of testing the strength of the enemy defences, reconnoitring approach routes, and obtaining identifications.

The weather soon began to improve and, early in April, preparations began for a resumption of the offensive.

In the second half of March the Americans had advanced from Tebessa, retaken Gafsa and pushed on to the east and south-east. On the 28th of that month the Eighth Army had driven Rommel from the Mareth Line and, moving northwards, had made contact on the 7th April with the leading troops of the American 2nd Corps south-east of Gafsa. The two Armies had at last met.

In the meantime the First Army was beginning to exert pressure against von Arnim in the north. Advancing eighteen miles in four days, the 46th Division recaptured the area from which it had taken the Germans three weeks to drive them at the beginning of March; Sedjnane and Cap Serrat were taken, and the northern flank was thereby cleared.

The next part of the programme was to evict the enemy from their command of the Beja–Medjez road. This task, entrusted to the 78th Division, was far from easy; the Official Despatch describes the country in these words:

> This mountain land is a vast tract of country, every hill in which is enough to swallow up a brigade of infantry, where consolidation on the rocky slopes is very difficult, in which tanks can only operate in small numbers, where movement of guns and vehicles is very restricted, and where the division had to rely on pack-mules for its supplies and to carry wireless telegraphy sets, tools and mortars.
>
> The general impression is one of wide spaciousness—a kind of Dartmoor or Central Sutherlandshire, but with deeper valleys and steeper hills.

The 5th were no strangers to this type of country; but on this occasion they hoped that they would be taking the offensive with all possible support, both on the ground and in the air, instead of with virtually none as they had done in the past.

*Advance in the Mountains, 5th–13th April*

On the 5th April the Battalion handed over its defences to a battalion of the R.A.F. Regt. and withdrew to a concentration area to make final preparations for the offensive. On the next day Lieut.-Col. Crook explained the plan of attack to as many of the Battalion as could be assembled under the cover of an olive-grove. Briefly, the operation was to begin with a night attack to drive the enemy from their positions north of the Beja–Medjez road. Then the attack was to wheel to the right and clear all the mountains as far as a point north of Medjez, so that the road, an essential line of communication for any advance on Tunis, would no longer be commanded by the enemy. All three brigades of the Division were to take part, the 11th on the right. The 5th Battalion was to be the right battalion, with the East Surrey Regt. on its left.

For the first phase of the attack the Battalion was to be commanded by Major Buchanan, who had come as Second-in-Command early in February, since Lieut.-Col. Crook was to be left out of the battle in accordance with divisional instructions. The 5th were, in fact, fortunate not to lose the C.O. for a longer time, for that night the car in which he and the Quartermaster were travelling hit a mine on the road; neither officer was hurt, but the driver was seriously wounded.

After dark the Battalion Intelligence Section taped the start-line on the road while the remainder were moving up. By 0030 hours on the 7th the Battalion had formed up, 'V' Company providing a protective screen north of the road; 'C' Company were on the right, 'B' on the left, 'A' in reserve.

It was a clear, starlit night, with no moon. The ground to be covered on the way to the German positions, about a mile and a half away, was undulating, becoming steeper as it approached them, and interspersed with cornfields and stone walls.

At 0100 hours the advance began. When about three-quarters of the distance had been covered, 'V' Company began to move half-right towards its objective on the western end of Djebel Dourat; 'C' continued straight ahead towards a saddle which joined this feature to Pt. 343, the latter being 'B' Company's objective. 'A' and Battalion H.Q. moved to take up a position on the reverse slope of a small hill behind the forward companies.

By 0350 hours the companies were creeping noiselessly and carefully towards their objectives. And then the artillery opened fire with a crash. The 5th had been told that the artillery support would be the strongest yet produced in the campaign, and as they lay and watched the flashes of the guns lighting up the sky above the hills behind them and heard the shells bursting on the German positions ahead, it seemed terrific. Months later, after the Sangro and Cassino, many of them wondered why.

At 0410 hours the artillery fire lifted off the objectives and the forward companies rushed the few remaining yards. In five minutes' time success signals from 'V' and 'C' Companies showed that they had taken their objectives. 'B' were held up, short of the objectives, by heavy mortar fire on the gully which was the line of approach, and all efforts to get on, gallantly led by Major Rayment, were without success. Though wounded in the face early in the day, this officer refused to leave his Company, and later in the morning he was killed instantaneously by a sniper's bullet. In him the Battalion lost a brave man.

In time it became clear that as the element of surprise had been lost no useful purpose would be served in continuing to try to take this portion of the objective without a fresh fire-plan. 'B' Company were withdrawn at 1100 hours to near Battalion H.Q. and a Churchill tank held the position they had reached until 'A' Company took it over.

The gains were now consolidated and the Battalion settled down for the night, during which heavy mortar fire, which had come down on the whole area as soon as the attack had gone in, continued at intervals.

At 0900 hours the next day, 'A' Company, with the support of a company of the East Surrey Regt. and tanks of 'A' Squadron 142nd R.A.C. attacked and captured Pt. 343, taking more than fifty prisoners of a Mountain Regt. In this attack Capt. Morgan, the Company Commander, was fatally wounded. While the Company consolidated, 'V' Company went on eastwards, cleared the Djebel and occupied a position at the extreme end of it.

In the hard fighting of these two days, the Battalion had had just over eighty casualties, including two officers and nineteen other ranks killed.

After daybreak on the 9th the Battalion advanced eastwards, meeting with no opposition and finding much abandoned enemy equipment, signs of a hurried withdrawal. After crossing the Medjez–Toukabeur road they took up positions in the mountains, from which the ground fell away to the Medjez plain, with Longstop Hill looming to the north. Here Lieut.-Col. Crook resumed command after his enforced rest.

During the day the 5th lost one who had served them well throughout the campaign. The Quartermaster, Lieut. McLoughlin, was mortally wounded by a booby-trap whilst reconnoitring a farm in which to install 'B' Echelon.

The three days which followed were spent in resting and reconnaissance. One night patrol had the misfortune to get into an anti-personnel minefield, losing its leader, Lieut. Burkley, and five men. Next morning the O.C. Pioneer Platoon and his sergeant, Sgt. Young, made a gallant attempt to recover the bodies of the dead, but in doing so the sergeant was killed and the officer wounded.

On the evening of the 12th the Battalion marched along a mountain track through the villages of Toukabeur and Chaouach to an assembly area at Kelbine, which they reached early the next morning. Here they were not allowed to dig in, for fear of arousing the suspicions of the enemy, and had an unpleasant day while the Germans searched the valley with shell and mortar fire, causing twenty casualties. Reconnaissances were made for an attack that night against Bettiour, a mountain feature 2,000 feet above sea-level.

'A' and 'V' Companies crossed the start-line at 2330 hours and advanced steadily, covered by heavy concentrations of artillery fire which came down on the objective twenty minutes later. By 0115 hours the enemy had been driven off the height and it had been occupied; 'C' Company were then moved from reserve to guard the left flank. The rocky top of Bettiour was under direct enemy observation and was the target throughout the day for heavy mortar fire, which killed Lieut. Woolvern of 'A' and wounded 2/Lieut. Clarke of 'B.'

From the top of Bettiour the Battalion could look down upon Heidous. Beyond Heidous, and linked to it by a buttress of rock, lay the squat, pyramid-shaped peak of Djebel Tanngoucha. From this westwards a saddle of moorland ran to Djebel Ang. Eastwards lay Longstop Hill.

Before the exits from Medjez could be freed, Longstop had to be taken. Before Longstop could be taken, the enemy had to be driven off Tanngoucha.

*The Attack on Tanngoucha, 14th–15th April*

On the morning of the 14th April the Brigade Commander, from his H.Q. at Chaouach, ordered Lieut.-Col. Crook by wireless to confer with the C.O. of the 2nd Lancashire Fusiliers, and make a plan for the capture of Tanngoucha that night. The Fusiliers had moved up on the left of the 5th Battalion earlier in the day, and two of their companies were already committed, helping the East Surrey Regt., who had achieved only partial success in their attack on Djebel Ang, carried out at the same time as the 5th's attack on Bettiour.

The two C.O.s decided to leave one company holding Bettiour and to attack round the left of it with four companies, two from each battalion, under the command of Major Cook of the 5th. The objective was Pt. 622. on the saddle between Djebel Ang and Tanngoucha.

As soon as the companies started to move, at 1530 hours, they came under heavy mortar fire which caused many casualties, including Capt. Wilkinson of 'C' Company, who was killed. The force pressed on and managed to reach their objective, but before they could dig in they were forced off it by machine-gun and mortar fire, Capt. McNeill, commanding 'V' Company, being wounded.

It was now decided to by-pass Pt. 622 and to organise a night attack directly on Tanngoucha with one company of the Lancashire Fusiliers and 'A' and 'B' Companies of the 5th, all under command of Major Hudson of the Fusiliers.

The advance began at 2130 hours, the companies having to make their way over extremely steep, rugged ground, skirting Heidous and climbing Tanngoucha by the rocky wall which led from the village to the summit. After marching for less than half an hour the companies suddenly found themselves enveloped in a dense mist, and contact between them was lost. 'B' Company failed to find the objective and, when daylight came, discovered themselves surrounded by the enemy. Many were taken prisoner, though some managed to escape in the confusion caused by British shelling of the area, taking with them some twenty Germans they had captured. For some hours the Company Commander, Capt. Beagley, was missing, known to have been seriously wounded, but later he was found and brought in by the Battalion's medical sergeant.

Meanwhile the other two companies had gained a foothold on the slopes of Tanngoucha, but by 0900 hours on the 15th touch could no longer be got with them by wireless and the fact that the enemy could be seen moving about on the hill gave cause for uneasiness. Later in the day a few men managed to return and reported what had happened.

'A' Company had reached Tanngoucha shortly after midnight, after a very difficult approach during which touch with the Lancashire Fusiliers company had been lost. However, at about 0400 hours the latter arrived and the two Company Commanders decided that, as most of the hill was under direct observation from positions held by the enemy, the best solution was to try to find some cover, dig in and hope.

After dawn, when visibility increased, the Lancashire Fusiliers' position became the target for constant close-range fire and soon after 1000 hours it was overrun.

The enemy then turned their attention to 'A' Company, with sniping and heavy mortaring, and conditions became worse at about noon when the British artillery put down a heavy concentration of fire on the hill. As soon as this had lifted, the Germans rushed the position and took prisoner all those who had survived an extremely trying experience.[2]

So, as far as the 5th Battalion and the Lancashire Fusiliers were concerned, ended the attempt to take Tanngoucha, an attempt which did not fail for lack of courage. The 5th had lost more heavily in this two-day battle than in any of their previous actions; their casualties totalled 170, of which number 100 were missing. To these must be added the considerable losses of the Fusiliers. This was a large bill to pay for an attack which, had its difficulties been fully realised, the Battalion would probably never have been ordered to carry out without more time for reconnaissance and preparation.

That night, the 15th, the Battalion was relieved by the 2nd London Irish Rifles and went into brigade reserve. An enemy counter-attack on Bettiour, which developed when the relief had been nearly completed, was repulsed. Early on the following morning, the Chaplain, the Rev. E. Elworthy, who had spent the night searching for the wounded, was himself hit.

In the course of its advance since the 6th April, the 78th Division, moving on a ten-mile front, had penetrated to a depth of ten miles into the enemy positions, helped by concentrated artillery fire and close-support bombing by the R.A.F. But, in General Anderson's words:

> It was chiefly an infantry battle, fought by units who had been in continuous contact with the enemy without a break since November. In all, during these nine days, 1,080 German prisoners were captured in a series of extremely fierce hand-to-hand fights, including much night work. . . . I consider the 78 Division deserves high praise for as tough and prolonged a bit of work as has ever been undertaken by the British soldier.[3]

## The Final Offensive, 22nd April–13th May

In the meantime, the Eighth Army had been moving up the coast. Rommel had made one last attempt to stop them at Wadi Akarit but had failed, and though the Allied forces had broken through at Kairouan they could not quite cut off the retreating Afrika Corps, which continued its withdrawal northwards. Before the end of March Rommel went sick and returned to Germany, leaving von Arnim in command of all the Axis forces in Tunisia, which were soon holding a front of 125 miles on two sides of a rectangle, with the sea on the other two sides.

In a final effort to postpone defeat, von Arnim launched a strong attack against the 9th Corps, between Medjez and Goubellat, with five battalions of the Hermann Goering Division and seventy tanks. Thanks to a stout defence, this attack was beaten back with heavy losses and caused a delay of only four hours in an attack which was on the point of being launched by the 46th Division.

D-Day for the start of the final Allied offensive was the 22nd April. The 46th Division attacked between Bou Arada and Goubellat, on the only part of the front on which armour could, at that time, operate. The 6th Armoured Division then went through, followed later by the 1st Armoured, but, after two days of heavy fighting, they were held up by the enemy, who had concentrated all their three armoured divisions in the sector, and were ordered to stand fast.

Farther to the north, the 1st, 4th and 78th Divisions of the 5th Corps began to fight their way forward through the hills north and east of Medjez, on both sides of the Medjerda Valley, with the object of gaining room for the deployment of armoured forces to the east of the river.

After a rest of two days the 5th Battalion had come under command of the 38th (Irish) Brigade, and on the 21st had taken over defences on Djebel Ang. Here they received eight officer reinforcements, but they were still badly in need of men; 'A' Company, for example, was only about thirty strong, having been re-formed from the few who had got away from Tanngoucha and others who could be spared from H.Q. and 'S' Companies. So they were relieved when they heard that they were to go back on the 26th to Toukabeur, for what they hoped would be a longer rest. They were soon disillusioned, for hardly had they had time to enjoy baths when a reconnaissance was ordered for a divisional attack on Longstop.

The assault on the hill was to be carried out by the 36th Brigade; the 38th was to advance through the hills north of it; and the 11th was to be in reserve to exploit success.

On the night of the 26th the 5th Battalion moved in T.C.V.s and then on foot to an assembly area. The attack on Longstop by the 36th Brigade and the East Surreys of the 11th Brigade was successful and, before dawn, Lieut.-Col. Crook and his Company Commanders were at the Argyll and

Sutherland H.Q. on the hill. Orders were soon received for the Battalion to advance and capture the mosque of Sidi Ahmed, in the valley a mile ahead of Longstop.

*The Attacks on Sidi Ahmed, 27th–29th April*

The feature on which the mosque stood was strongly defended, and the approach to it was over open country devoid of cover; yet no barrage or tank support was provided for the attack. In order, therefore, to give the companies some measure of support, the Carrier Platoon was ordered to move forward by a track leading to the mosque from the right, while 'B' and 'C' Companies advanced across the open to the left.

The carriers, under Major Hunt, got on well and one section reached the mosque, but soon they, and the rest of the platoon which had halted north of the main road, came under very heavy and concentrated artillery fire, and were forced to pull back. The Battalion I.O., Capt. Emmerton, who had gone up to the carriers with the C.O., was wounded.

When the companies had gone about a quarter of a mile the German artillery switched on to them, and this fire was thickened by that of mortars. They had many casualties and were held up. Early in the afternoon, 'C,' and 'A' which had come up on its left, made another attempt to reach the objective, but could not do so. 'B,' meanwhile, were pinned down in the open by machine-gun fire.

From his Command Post on Longstop Hill the C.O. could see what was happening below and, as the open plain was obviously untenable, he ordered 'B' and 'C' to withdraw at dusk. He was unable to communicate with 'A,' as the operator of their wireless set had become a casualty; however, they, now only about 25 strong, found cover in some old trenches and, in default of orders to the contrary, decided to remain there for the night.

Meanwhile, the remainder of the Battalion concentrated on the south side of Longstop, and there Lieut.-Col. Crook left them. Having led them with such energy through so much since the landing six months earlier, it was hard that he was not to see them through to final victory. Major Buchanan took over command in his place.

At 0930 hours on the 28th, half an hour after Lieut.-Col. Crook had handed over, the Battalion was ordered to attack again, and moved to a forming-up area, where it was joined by 'A' Company. The advance began at 1430 hours, and 'C,' 'A' and 'V' were held up in turn by mortar and machine-gun fire. After dark 'C' and 'V' managed to get on, and by 2030 hours the latter had secured Pt. 160, and were joined by 'C.' During the night the enemy put in a strong counter-attack and almost surrounded the companies, but they managed to withdraw, taking with them seven Germans, including an officer.

That night the 5th were relieved, and moved back to an area east of

Medjez. The casualties in the three days' fighting had been 79, including 4 officers.

## The Advance to Tunis

Strong enemy counter-attacks at various points had by now halted the advance of the infantry, though none of the ground gained had been lost. The 5th Battalion dug in in a reserve position and awaited events, heartened by the sound of loud explosions behind the enemy lines, caused by the blowing-up of ammunition dumps.

As a preliminary to the final blow, General Alexander had transferred the American 2nd Corps from the south to the north, and the First Army had been strengthened by two divisions from the Eighth, the 4th Indian and the 7th Armoured, both veterans of the desert fighting. At the same time, von Arnim, who expected an offensive by the Eighth Army, had moved troops to meet it, thus weakening his centre and right. Taking advantage of this, the American 2nd Corps advanced and captured Mateur on the 3rd May.

Then, before daybreak on the 6th May, the 4th British and the 4th Indian Division attacked on a very narrow front astride the Medjez–Massicault road, with extremely strong artillery and air support. The measures which had been taken to mislead the enemy as to the point of the main attack were most successful, and by 1130 hours the two divisions had taken all their objectives, penetrating to a depth of 5,000 yards into the enemy positions. The 6th and 7th Armoured Divisions went through the gap and took Massicault before dark. On the next afternoon the 7th Armoured entered Tunis, and to the north the Americans captured Bizerta.

That morning the 5th moved forward a few miles and, in the evening, was warned to get ready to go into Tunis, prepared for street-fighting.

Early on the 8th they embussed for a concentration area on the outskirts of the city and, after a short halt, marched on into the centre of it, the first troops to enter on foot. They kept a careful look-out for snipers, but instead of bullets they were received with bouquets, and instead of fighting Germans they had to fight their way through cheering crowds of Frenchmen and Arabs. This welcome continued throughout the day, and made the Battalion feel that the long months of struggling against the weather, the mountains and the enemy had been worth while.

Of this occasion the Special Correspondent of *The Times* wrote:

> The 78th Division did not take part in the final attack on Tunis. It was a grief to them that they could not have had a chance of getting there first; but they had been fighting incessantly for 29 days—some of them for 39 days—and it was a job for fresher troops. . . . But there did

fall to them the honour of occupying Tunis the day after the armour had entered it, and of being the recipients of the French population's almost hysterical gratitude. Though the French may not have known it, they were thanking the right men.

The 5th had some work to do in the way of searching buildings and collecting stray Germans. They were also able to welcome back two of 'A' Company who had been taken prisoner at Tanngoucha. Most of those captured had been shipped to Italy before the fall of Tunis, but Lieut. Dupre had not gone with them, being wounded, and had managed to escape from a ship in the harbour the day before she sailed. The other, C.S.M. Keilthy, had been left behind because he was a native of Eire, and the Germans, with their fondness for acting—on occasions—in accordance with the strict letter of the law, had come to the conclusion that he should be regarded as a neutral.

After bivouacking for a night north of the city, the 5th marched to a point on the Bizerta road where they blocked the efforts of any Germans to escape. On the 10th they moved on to Protville, where they pitched a camp.

To complete the story of the campaign. By dawn on the 11th May the 6th Armoured Division had sealed the mouth of the Cape Bon peninsula, into which the Axis forces had been driven. On the next day von Arnim and his Staff surrendered, and all that remained to be done was to round up the Germans and Italians as they gave themselves up. A quarter of a million were taken prisoner; only 663 escaped by sea to Italy.

General Alexander was now able to report to the Prime Minister that he had carried out the instructions given to him before the Battle of El Alamein, that the Tunisian Campaign was over, that the Allies were masters of the North African shores and that he now awaited further orders.

*Comments on the Campaign*

The North African Campaign might well be called a campaign of 'ifs.' If the French had not delayed the Allies by their show of resistance to the landings at Algiers, if they had resisted, even for a day, the German landings at Tunis and Bizerta, if the weather and other circumstances had not combined to prevent the giving of air-support to the forward troops in the early stages, Tunis might have fallen into the hands of the Allies in December, and the First Army would have been spared those months of fighting in the mountains.

Nevertheless, had matters gone as they might have gone, it is unlikely that the First Army would have gained the fame which, in the event, it did.

The campaign for Tunisia had been begun by inexperienced troops. It ended with a disaster to the enemy second only to that which they had suffered a few weeks before at Stalingrad, inflicted by those same troops, now seasoned by months of hard fighting and reinforced by some of the formations of the Eighth Army who had fought their way from El Alamein.[4]

Of all the divisions which took part, it was the 78th which had borne the brunt, and they might justifiably have added to their Battleaxe sign, the motto 'Per Ardua ad Tunis.' The officers and men of the 5th Battalion had done their full share towards earning a lasting name for the Division. They had made a reputation for themselves and they had, in some measure, avenged the setbacks of 1940. But the price they had paid was not small.[5]

### The 5th in North Africa, May–July 1943

At Protville the Battalion was able to relax for a short time, recreation including trips to Tunis, bathing at Carthage and visits to such familiar spots as Djedeida, Tebourba and the Goubellat plain. The Allied victory was celebrated on the 20th May by a march through Tunis, at which General Eisenhower, accompanied by General Giraud, took the salute. Those who represented the 5th Battalion in the divisional column were, as far as was possible, men who had been through the whole campaign. That evening the 5th played the East Surrey Regt. at football in the local stadium, and won; the proceedings were most suitably enlivened by the music of a captured German band!

At the end of the month the whole brigade moved, via Mateur and Tabarka, to Guelma, where three weeks were spent in training, broken by a parade on the 17th June for the visit to the division of H.M. the King. Then they moved again, to Hammamet on the coast east of Tunis.

On the 1st July the Battalion paraded for a visit by General Montgomery. After some of the officers had been introduced to him the parade ceased to be a formal one for, with his usual technique, he called the troops to close in round his car. For a quarter of an hour he delighted them by his informality, asking many questions, telling stories and exchanging 'wisecracks' with his audience. He told them that they were now in his Eighth Army and, when he left, he was given a genuinely spontaneous ovation. In those fifteen minutes he had made the Battalion feel that he was the man under whom they would like to serve.

A week later they moved down the coast to Sousse and began once more to prepare for action. All the preliminaries for embarkation were put in hand and long route-marches were almost a daily occurrence, often to the sea to give the men the chance of a bathe.

On the 10th July, troops of the British Eighth and American Seventh Armies landed in Sicily. On the following day Lieut.-Col. Buchanan told the 5th of the probable future rôle of the Battalion.[6]

# CHAPTER XI

## THE 58th IN INDIA, PERSIA, IRAQ AND PALESTINE, 1942-1943

The 58th in India, June-September 1942—The 58th in Paiforce, September 1942-January 1943—
The Move to Egypt, February 1943—Training, February-June 1943—The 58th Embark

### *The 58th in India, June-September 1942*

THE voyage of the 58th from Madagascar was uneventful, and the opportunity was taken to give the Battalion a rest. The health of the troops had been generally good and there had only been thirteen hospital cases of sandfly fever and malaria while they had been in Madagascar, but some were still suffering from minor malaria and dysentery.

The ship reached Bombay on the 21st June, but remained outside the harbour until the 25th, when she berthed at Ballard Pier. Two days later the Battalion entrained, and arrived on the 30th at Barkha Khana, whence trucks took them to Ranchi, nearly fifty miles away. After their train journey across the plains of India, it was a relief to reach their destination in the hills of Bihar.

The first ten days were spent in pitching camp near the village of Barambe and in making it habitable by laying brick floors to the tents and digging drains; the monsoon rains made the area a sea of mud. Little training was done, as the Battalion was undergoing a course of antimalaria treatment and the time was spent in sports and leave to Calcutta.

At the end of July Major J. A. W. Ballard appeared from South Africa, without warning, to join the Battalion, and soon afterwards three officers who had been wounded in Madagascar, including Major Houchin, rejoined from convalescence at Durban.

### *The 58th in Paiforce, September 1942-January 1943*

At the beginning of September the 58th heard that their wanderings were to start again; they were to take part in Exercise 'Character,' in which the 5th Division was to join Paiforce, the abbreviated name for the troops in Persia and Iraq. These two countries were important from the point of view of the Allies, for they, and their oil-fields, might be threatened if the German drive through the Caucasus progressed; also it was necessary to safeguard the communications which traversed them, carrying supplies to Russia.

The Battalion left Ranchi by train on the 8th September, embarked at Bombay two days later in a ship shared with the 2nd Royal Scots Fusiliers, and sailed on the 13th.

Before leaving Ranchi a party had been sent hurriedly to Delhi to collect new carriers, to replace their old ones which had been handed over to the K.A.R. in Madagascar. Otherwise the Battalion was devoid of transport, for with the exception of a few vehicles they had not seen theirs since they left Caterham. The M.T. had arrived at Karachi from Madagascar, but it never got farther into India. When Exercise 'Character' was ordered, the original plan was for all the transport of the division to move overland, through Afghanistan—a move never before attempted—but this had to be cancelled owing to the flooding of the Indus. In the end it went by sea to Basra, and thence up-country by road, and did not rejoin its units till another month had elapsed.

The ship carrying the 58th anchored off Basra on the 20th; two days later the Battalion disembarked and went by train to the camp at Shaibah. Here, in the sandy desert south-west of Basra, it was very hot, but thanks to the instruction given to the troops during the voyage there were no cases of heat-stroke and they gradually became acclimatised. They also became wiser as to some of the peculiarities of the country; initially it was a frequent occurrence for men to ask permission to go and bathe in 'the lake,' but these requests ceased after they had discovered that the water was but a mirage.

A fortnight later the Battalion entrained again; a hot and dusty journey took them to Baghdad and thence, on the morning of the 5th October, to Khanaqin station. Apart from four railway tracks, on which stood goods trains, which stopped abruptly in the desert, there was little to indicate that this was railhead.

Moving north-east in lorries and crossing the border of Persia after about four miles, the Battalion was not sorry to leave the desert behind as the road climbed up into the mountains; at the staging camp in the Pai Tak valley, where they halted for a night, a mountain stream gave them water for the coldest ablutions they had enjoyed for many months. An early start on the 6th took them to Kermanshah that evening; after skirting the town they began to see other units of the Division, and thirty miles farther on they reached the 17th Brigade area and met their long-lost transport. The 58th were now complete for the first time since they had left Caterham six months ago.

The site of the camp adjoined a bare valley and the pitching of tents was not easy, as most of the site lay on a mountain-side; in spite of difficulties, within a week the Battalion had both football and hockey grounds. The climate was good—like the English summer by day but cold after sundown; battle-dress had to be worn by night-guards.

Two days after their arrival, the 58th were visited by the C.-in-C. Paiforce, General Sir Maitland Wilson, and the Corps Commander, Lieut.-General D. F. Anderson, whom they had last seen when he was commanding in Northern Ireland.

Very early on the 28th orders came for a move. 'A' and 'D' Companies went ahead in T.C.V.s that day; the rest of the Battalion followed in the brigade convoy on the 29th and, after two night halts, reached Qum, south of Teheran, the capital, on the 31st. There they found 'D' Company; 'A' had gone on to Teheran to assist in the maintenance of law and order, bread riots having broken out in the city.

After various alarms the 58th moved on towards the capital on the 10th November, and pitched camp about fifteen miles away from it. The ten days which followed were spent by the Battalion in training and by the C.O. in attending a series of conferences at the British Legation in Teheran.

Only a few knew the secret of what was afoot at the time. Briefly, the cause of the trouble was that the Persian authorities refused to sanction an increased issue of paper currency by the State Bank and, as a result, the troops were unable to spend any of their pay, for sufficient notes were not available. To overcome this impasse, the scheme was for the 58th, with the help of a squadron of armoured-cars, a troop of 25-pounders and a section of R.E., to surround the Bank, enter it (with the aid of the Sappers' explosives if necessary), remove from it the required number of notes and lodge them in another bank.

The plan was made—and then the Government decided to give way and issue all the money that the British wanted. From the point of view of international relations it was probably just as well that a friendly solution was found; but from the point of view of the 58th it was a pity that they were not able to add large-scale official burglary to their other achievements. So they returned to Qum, there to receive the praise of the Corps Commander on the way in which they had carried out their move and their duties.

A week later the Battalion heard that Lieut.-Col. Hinchcliffe had been appointed to command the Teheran Sub-Area. When he left on the 28th the Battalion lined the road through the camp and gave him a rousing send-off; he had commanded them practically continuously for over two and a half years, in two campaigns and in many countries, and they owed much to his leadership. Major J. A. W. Ballard was appointed to command in his place.

For the next two months training was the order of the day, from section exercises to brigade exercises. One company was kept at Teheran on internal-security duty, and smaller detachments were sent to guard G.H.Q. at Baghdad and Tenth Army H.Q. at Sultanabad. In mid-December the 'little cold' began with two inches of snow, and before long fur-lined jackets and gloves were issued.

At the end of the year the 58th lost one who had served them well. Capt. Dowzer, the Medical Officer, was evacuated, sick, to hospital. He had been with them ever since they first went to France in 1939.

*The Move to Egypt, February* 1943

Towards the end of January 1943 the Battalion heard that the whole of the 5th Division was to carry out a long move. On the 2nd February they entrained at Qum, and after passing through Ahwaz reached Kurramshah on the morning of the 4th. Here the Battalion embarked in river-craft and moved up the Tigris for three hours, then entrained again, reached Baghdad shortly after noon on the 5th, and marched into Lancer Camp just as the first vehicles of the brigade road convoy arrived.

The wheeled transport of the 58th had left Qum on the 29th January under the command of Capt. Hornsby. They had had a long journey through Sultanabad, Malayir, Hamadan, Kermanshah and Khanaqin, part of it over snow and ice-bound mountain roads, and it says much for the drivers' skill that all vehicles arrived at Baghdad safely and on time.

The Battalion had a day's rest before starting on the next lap of their journey, then for five days they travelled in T.C.V.s, across the Syrian desert, through Rutbah (well remembered by a few who had been with the 48th when they had been flown from Ismailia to Baghdad in 1932, the first battalion to be carried by this means), Transjordan, and over the Jordan into Palestine. On the 12th they entrained again, and on the next day, after crossing the Suez Canal, reached Kabrit, a few miles north of Suez.

*Training, February–June* 1943

At Kabrit was the Middle East Combined Training Centre, and although the 58th could pride themselves on having taken part in a real combined operation, a thing which few, if any, of the staff of the Centre had done, neither they, nor any of the other units of the division, were excused any of the training. This began with a week of 'dryshod' training, including landing-craft drill, cliff-scaling, assault drill and practice in crossing wire obstacles—a good test of physical fitness—and was followed by a week of 'wetshod' training in real landing-craft.

On the 18th March the Battalion left Kabrit by train and journeyed to a camp at Qatana, twelve miles south of Damascus. There, throughout March and April, dryshod training was continued, culminating in an exercise which was, in fact, a rehearsal for their next operational rôle.

The first week in June found them back near Suez, this time at El Shatt. From there, on the 8th, they embarked in the L.S.I. *Duchess of Bedford*, and carried out landing exercises from her in the Gulf of Aqaba for a week. They then returned to El Shatt, where on the 26th General Montgomery personally welcomed the Battalion to the Eighth Army.

### The 58th Embark

On the 29th June the 58th re-embarked in the *Duchess of Bedford*, which sailed on the following day through the Canal to Port Said, where she anchored.

Meanwhile the M.T. party, which had remained behind when the Battalion went to El Shatt, had been busy waterproofing vehicles and loading them on board ship at Haifa and Beirut. Certain vehicles, such as the carriers and anti-tank guns, went by road and rail to Benghazi and thence by landing-craft to Tripoli. At the appointed time and place they were to rejoin the Battalion, whose ship sailed from Port Said in convoy on the 5th July.

Operation 'Husky' had started.

115th Independent Infantry Brigade

# CHAPTER XII

## THE 58th AND THE 5th BATTALION IN SICILY, 1943

Background of the Operation—The Opposing Forces—The Allied Plan—The Landings—Landing of the 58th, 10th July—Capture of Syracuse—Capture of Priolo, 11th–12th July—Advance to Augusta, 12th–16th July—Progress of Seventh and Eighth Armies—58th Move to the Simeto, 16th–22nd July—General Progress of Operations, 31st July–2nd August—The 5th Bn. reach Sicily—Attack on Catenanuova, 30th–31st July—Capture of Centuripe, 31st July–2nd August—Capture of Bronte, 7th–9th August—Operations near Randazzo, 12th–14th August—Final Operations by the 58th, 1st–9th August—End of the Campaign—The 58th in Sicily, 9th August–2nd September—The 5th Bn. in Sicily, 15th August–21st September (*see* Map on p. 155)

## Background of the Operation

AFTER the surrender of the Axis forces in Tunisia there was, inevitably, some delay before Operation 'Husky,' the invasion of Sicily, could be launched. Shipping had to be collected and the former German airfields in North Africa had to be made serviceable, but the time was not wasted, for after the reduction of the Italian islands of Pantellaria and Lampedusa, mainly by air action, the weight of the sea and air offensive was turned upon Sicily to pave the way for landings.

The operation was described by Mr. Winston Churchill as one of many 'operations of a peculiar complexity and hazard,' a true description indeed. Two all-important factors had to be considered, timing and weather conditions. Miscalculation of the one, misfortune as regards the other, might have made all the difference between success and failure.

Timing was far from easy, for the invasion force of the British Eighth and American Seventh Armies was to arrive off the shores of Sicily from several widely dispersed bases. Of the British Divisions, the 51st Highland was to come from Tunisia, to be joined at sea by the 5th and the 50th from Egypt, the 7th Armoured from Tripoli, and the 1st Canadian from England. The 78th was, at the outset, kept in reserve in Tunisia. Of the Seventh Army divisions all but one were in North Africa, this one coming direct from the U.S.A. via Oran.

The concentration of these forces could be achieved by good staff work, but this could not affect the weather, and the Mediterranean was subject to gales which might arise suddenly, without warning, and would seriously interfere with landings on open beaches.

## The Opposing Forces

The Allies' ten Infantry, one Armoured and two Airborne divisions varied in experience. Four of the British divisions had fought their way to Tunis, either through the desert or through the mountains, but of the other two, the 5th, though much travelled, had not met German troops in battle since 1940 and the Canadians had had no battle experience. Of the American divisions, only two had seen much fighting.

Against these, on the day of the invasion, the garrison of Sicily consisted of twelve divisions. The ten Italian divisions were of poor fighting value, especially the five coastal divisions, which were, in addition, widely dispersed. Consequently, the brunt fell upon the Germans, whose two divisions were the Hermann Goering and the 15th Panzer Grenadier. These had inherited the names of their predecessors, captured when Tunis fell. In addition there was a number of German parachute, air and garrison units, and it was not long before reinforcements arrived in the shape of the 29th Panzer Grenadier and the 1st Parachute Divisions.

## The Allied Plan

The Allied plan was for the Eighth Army to land to the north and west of Cape Passero, the southernmost point of the island, and to advance thence to the east and west of Mount Etna. The Seventh Army was to land farther to the west, mop up the central and western portions of the island, swing eastwards along the north coast, and link up with the Eighth Army as it came northwards past Mount Etna. Airborne landings, to capture certain important points, were to precede those which were seaborne.

## The Landings

On the night of the 9th/10th July, parachute and glider-borne troops of the British 1st and American 82nd Airborne Divisions landed at various points. The weather was far from ideal for them. The high wind caused their dispersal and, in addition, the inexperience of the pilots of some of the tug-aircraft led to many of the gliders descending in the sea. Nevertheless, the divisions gained many of their objectives, created confusion among the defenders and hindered their efforts to concentrate against the beach landings.

Some hours later came the seaborne troops, an operation which involved the use of about 3,000 vessels carrying 160,000 men, with 1,800 guns, 600 tanks and 14,000 transport vehicles.

The order of landing of the Eighth Army was as follows, from east to west. The 5th Division, some ten miles south of Syracuse; the 50th, near Avola; the 51st, on the eastern side of Cape Passero, and the 1st Canadian on the western side of the Cape. Farther to the west, Lieut.-General Patton's Seventh Army landed at Gela and Licata.

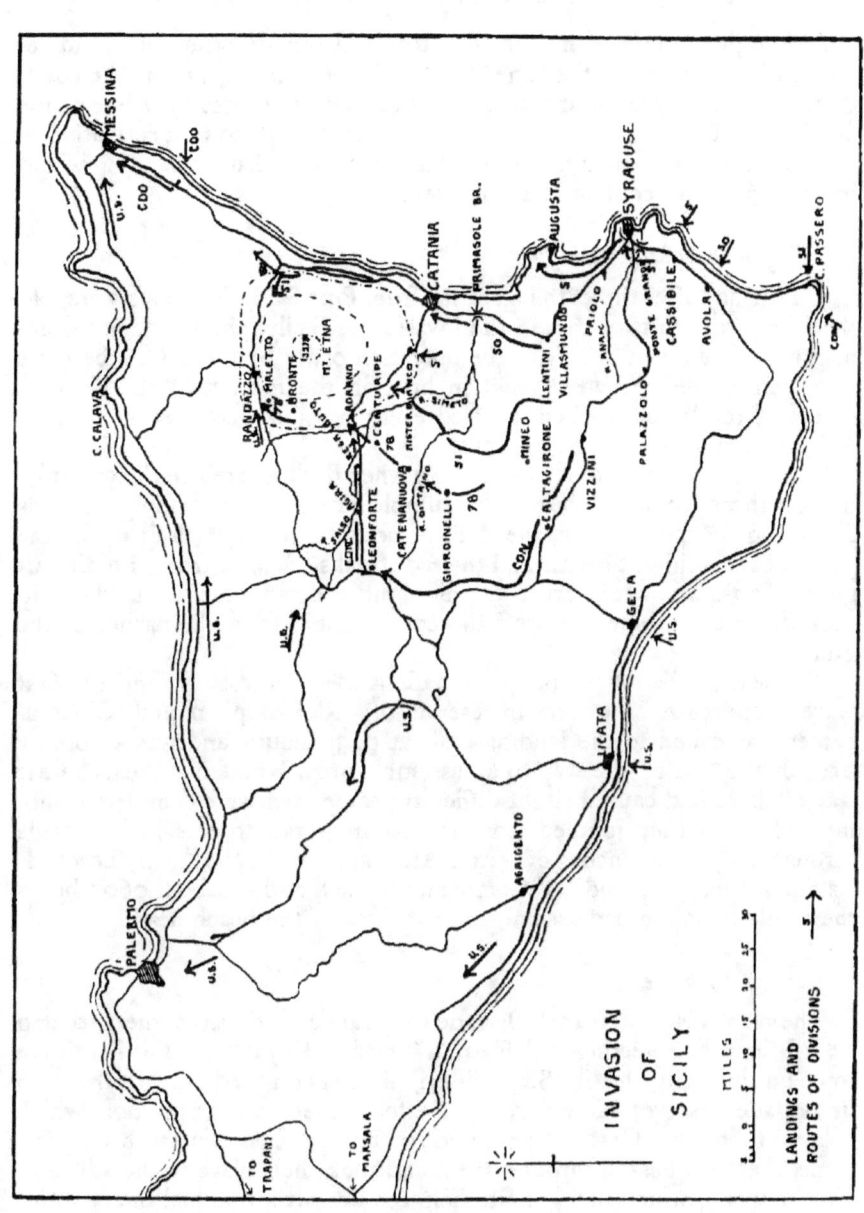

Although the high wind that had troubled the airborne troops had decreased in strength by the time that the Allied armada was off the coast, there was a heavy swell at sea, and this caused difficulties for some of the landing-craft. However, this helped indirectly, for it led to a relaxation of the vigilance of the enemy, who could hardly believe that any landing would be attempted under such bad conditions.

*Landing of the 58th, 10th July*

On the day after the 58th had sailed from Port Said, the troops were told that they were to take part in the invasion of Sicily, and Company Commanders were given details of the operation order by the C.O.; the three days which followed were spent in briefing the men, with the aid of a model of the beaches which showed every possible detail, even down to individual enemy machine-gun posts.

The ship was still out of sight of land when darkness fell on the 9th July, but overhead could be heard the rumble of aircraft streaming towards Sicily and, in the distance, the thud of bombs; the sky was lit up by the pencils of searchlight beams and the red streaks of tracer from anti-aircraft guns. Breakfasts were served at midnight and, an hour later, the ship dropped anchor some miles off the coast, visible from the flashes of the guns.

The leading battalions of the brigade landed successfully and the first wave of the 58th, who were in reserve, the 'R' Group, 'B' and 'C' Companies was called to the landing-craft at 0230 hours, and was ashore by 0500 hours and on the way to an assembly area. Numerous shoals a little way offshore had caused slight difficulty; some men were completely submerged when they jumped from the landing-craft, others had to wade through only a few inches of water. After an interval the L.C.I. beached; Battalion H.Q., 'A' and 'D' Companies landed, and by about 0600 hours the whole battalion had assembled in its area of the beach-head.[1]

*Capture of Syracuse*

The plan was for the 17th Brigade to advance northwards, the 13th and 15th Brigades protecting its left flank. The 2nd Royal Scots Fusiliers were to be on the right, the 6th Seaforth Highlanders on the left, with the 58th in brigade reserve. However, the Seaforth met with opposition which delayed them near Cassibile and, at 0930 hours, when this had been overcome, the 58th passed through them and took their place in the advance. 'A' Company, which had gone to help the Seaforth, rejoined the column; 'B,' which had been despatched to complete the capture of a battery of medium guns a few miles inland, did not get back to the Battalion until noon. At this stage the transport and the supporting arms had not arrived, their landing-craft having had trouble with a false beach, but the Battalion managed to collect an assortment of farm-carts, animals and bicycles.

The road by which the 58th advanced ran straight for several miles and, thanks to air photography, the position of the enemy's defences was clearly marked on the maps; consequently, preparations could be made to deal with these before they were actually met. To begin with, resistance was slight and confined to occasional sniping; this was largely due to the earlier action of the Airborne troops, groups of whom were met at intervals along the road. After they had covered about three miles the advanced guard, 'C' Company (Major Gibson), dealt with an enemy post which gave them some twenty prisoners, machine-guns and a couple of anti-tank guns. 'D' Company (Capt. Roche) then took the lead and, in due course, approached a main position which, from air photographs, appeared to be strong; through the Naval F.O.O. with the company the fire of the ships' guns was turned on to this and, when the advance continued, the position was found abandoned.

By 1600 hours the advance had reached the edge of the plain, which stretched for four miles south of Syracuse, and here a number of Italians with field-guns and transport were observed, apparently forming up to counter-attack. The Battalion now had some support, two sections of carriers, some mortars and self-propelled guns having come up, but the artillery could not open fire as the Italians had with them about sixty Airborne troops whom they had captured. However, the enemy were engaged by the mortars and by small-arms fire and, at an opportune moment, No. 18 Platoon (Lieut. Webb) attacked. As a result, the Italians surrendered, the guns were captured, the prisoners were rescued, and the 58th acquired some very useful transport.

The light was now beginning to fail, and the Battalion pushed ahead with all speed, the carriers dealing with enemy posts which had been by-passed but were still holding out, and securing the Ponte Grande, the important triple bridge south of Syracuse which, for the greater part of the day, had been held by a small party of Airborne troops who had prevented its demolition.

At about 1830 hours the advanced guard, with some Sherman tanks, entered the town, simultaneously with the Royal Scots Fusiliers who came in from the right. There was no resistance; in fact, the place appeared to be deserted until, by degrees, the populace started to emerge from air-raid shelters and other hiding-places, and gave the troops a rousing welcome.

That night the 58th occupied positions on the western outskirts of the town and, after orders for the next day had been issued, got the rest which they needed after having been on the move for nearly twenty hours. Syracuse had been taken at little cost, for the Battalion had had only nine men wounded and had taken prisoner more than a hundred Italians.

*Capture of Priolo, 11th–12th July*

The advance was resumed at first light on the 11th, the objective being Priolo. The 58th led the brigade, the carriers moving ahead, followed by 'B,' 'A,' 'C' and 'D' Companies; in rear, tanks of the Westminster Dragoons were in support.

Progress across the plain north of Syracuse was rapid, and the first encounter with the enemy was about a mile south of the woods below Priolo. A German lorry and a half-tracked vehicle which came down the road were engaged by Lieut. Adams's carrier; the Bren gunner, Pte. Owens killed his opposite number, and the rest of the enemy, including an officer, surrendered. They belonged to the Hermann Goering Division, so it seemed likely that the advance would meet with stiffer opposition than that shown, up to now, by the Italians.

At this stage, 'B' Company (Major Purton) began to enter very close country, orchards with dense undergrowth in which the enemy had taken up well-concealed positions; tanks could not operate off the road and the artillery O.P.s could not see to direct the fire of their batteries, so the battle became one in which much depended upon the leadership of Section Commanders. In one encounter a Section of 'B' Company, commanded by Cpl. Mead, attacked a machine-gun post; he was killed, but Pte. Wilks crawled forward, recovered his dead leader's tommy-gun and grenades and, with the two remaining men, assaulted and destroyed the garrison. For this deed he was awarded the Military Medal.

As 'B' Company worked their way through the woods, enemy mortar and artillery fire increased and it became clear that the defenders were in considerable strength, so 'A' Company (Capt. Hornsby) were put in on their left. The Seaforth, who were trying to attack Priolo round the left flank, were meeting with similar opposition.

'A' Company managed to make progress on the left of the road and reached the edge of the woods in front of Priolo, where they engaged an anti-tank gun till a German tank appeared and gave it shelter; but efforts to advance into the open only resulted in casualties, and the platoons had to be withdrawn into cover. On the extreme left, patrols reported that the edge of the village was strongly held and that the approaches to it across open country were swept by machine-gun fire.

Meanwhile the supporting tanks had done their best to find an approach round the flanks, but the stone walls and the dense olive-groves had defeated their efforts. One anti-tank gun on the road had been knocked out by the first shot from the troop-leader's tank; later on another of these guns covering the road approach to the village was engaged by the Shermans, but when they opened fire another concealed gun destroyed three of them.

'C' Company, now put in on the right of the road, reached the edge of the wood and tried to outflank the enemy by the right, but the defence was too strongly entrenched among the houses on the outskirts of the village, and the Company had to abandon the attempt after two of the Platoon Commanders, Lieuts. York and Mossop, had been killed.

In a final effort to capture the objective, 'D' Company were sent farther round, to try to force a way into the village from the east, but the attack across open ground failed, Lieut. Webb being killed, and they had to withdraw.

The position at dusk was that 'D,' 'C' and 'A' Companies were holding an arc of a circle within a few hundred yards of the village; 'B' were farther back in the wood near the main road. The day's casualties had been about five officers and fifty other ranks, and it was evident that a staged attack with artillery support was necessary to take the objective. After dark the forward companies were withdrawn slightly, so that artillery could register on the enemy's positions.

Plans were made to attack the village at first light the next day on a two-battalion front, supported by an artillery barrage and air-bombing. Before daylight a patrol under Lieut. Gaze could find no signs of the enemy, so he led his platoon into the village, which had been evacuated. The barrage was cancelled, but there was not time to stop the bombing; fortunately, however, this was upon the northern part of the place, so the platoon escaped it.

The 58th could congratulate themselves on the result of their first action in Sicily, all the more because they had quickly adapted themselves to fighting in close country, very different from the open desert in which they had been training.

*Advance to Augusta, 12th–16th July*

The Royal Scots Fusiliers were now ordered to pass through and continue the advance with Augusta as the objective; the 58th went into reserve.

The enemy were keeping Priolo and the approaches to it under heavy and accurate mortar and artillery fire, and had not withdrawn very far. After the Fusiliers had debouched from the village they met with stiff opposition, but had overcome this by midday and then made fairly rapid progress against many odd pockets of resistance.

By about midnight the Seaforth, on the left, had occupied the high ground north of Augusta, the Fusiliers were on the southern outskirts, and a Commando had landed in the port area. The 58th were ordered forward to complete the clearance of the town, occupy a position to the north of it and establish touch with the Commando. By 0830 hours on the 13th, 'B' Company reported that the peninsula on which Augusta and the naval base lay was clear of the enemy; apart from some sniping there was no resistance until about 1000 hours, when a machine-gun in the cliffs overlooking the town became annoying. This was soon dealt with by 'C' Company and a 3-inch mortar detachment.

The 50th Division now took up the running while the 5th had a rest, but there was still work for the 58th. On the 14th the whole battalion patrolled forward over an area of ground north of Augusta which had not yet been mopped up. The day's bag was 350 prisoners, all Italians, and on the next day this was increased by 65, including six of the crew of a submarine. The only shots fired were by a party of Italians who adopted this means of advertising their wish to surrender.

Referring to the operations carried out up to date, the 5th Division's war diary says:

It is perhaps worth noting that 17 Inf. Bde. had, during three days, 10th, 11th, 12th July, made an opposed landing and, advancing with only fifty per cent. of the transport expected (all of which was late owing to a very soft beach and difficult exits from it), captured Syracuse by 2100 hours on the 10th against fair opposition.

In order to accomplish this, the troops had covered up to 20 miles and had fought a battle all the way to the town. Despite this they continued their advance early on the 11th, fought a hard battle at Priolo and another at Augusta, which was captured in three days. At this period some battalions had covered over 100 miles on their feet, in boots which had been sodden with salt water.

*Progress of Seventh and Eighth Armies*

While the 5th Division had been moving up the coast to Augusta, operations elsewhere had not stood still. On the Eighth Army front, the 50th Division had captured Noto and was advancing on Catania, via Lentini, having sent one brigade ahead to secure the important Primosole bridge which had been taken by the 1st Parachute Brigade; on the left the 51st had gone through Palazzolo and was advancing across the plain of Catania; and the 1st Canadian Division, still farther inland, had taken Vizzini and Caltagirone. The Americans of the Seventh Army were pressing across the heart of the island, with detachments fanning out to the west and north-west to capture ports such as Marsala, Trapani and Palermo. The invasion was progressing well.

*58th Move to the Simeto, 16th–22nd July*

On the 16th July the 58th were warned to prepare to carry out a landing on the coast in the rear of the enemy positions on the Catania plain, to assist the operations of the 50th Division. Preparations were at once put in hand, including the collection of all available 'Mae Wests' from the beaches at Cassibile, but within a matter of hours the operation was cancelled. This was perhaps as well, for a landing from L.C.I.s on a mined beach would have been a hazardous performance.

Early the next day the Battalion was on the move again. A hot and tiring five hours' march took them to Villasmundo, and thence to Lentini by the late evening of the 18th. On the night of the 19th/20th they moved into an assembly area south of the River Simeto, from which they were to pass through the 15th Brigade, which was attacking, and exploit success. This attack was, however, held up short of its objective by strong opposition, and the 58th were halted after one company had crossed the river. The Battalion was in a very exposed position and had to disperse to avoid casualties; after dark they were withdrawn with the rest of the 17th Brigade to an area slightly farther south.

The resistance of the enemy on the 13th Corps front was now stiffening; farther to the left the Canadians were making good progress, so the 5th, 50th and 51st Divisions were ordered to hold the positions they had gained, while the success elsewhere was followed up.

On the night of the 22nd July the 17th Brigade relieved the 13th, in part of the Simeto bridgehead; the 58th on the right were in contact with the Durham Light Infantry of the 50th Division. Here their main task was the domination of no-man's-land in the plain by vigorous patrolling, and they succeeded in their object. One patrol was unlucky; 2/Lieut. Wardell, who had only joined the Battalion on the previous day, went out by day to reconnoitre a house, accompanied by two N.C.O.s. He crawled forward, with the others covering him, but eight Germans converged on him and took him prisoner, while the two N.C.O.s, who came under fire, had to make their getaway, in accordance with their orders.

*General Progress of Operations, 31st July–2nd August*

The 1st Canadian Division had taken Leonforte on the 22nd July, Agira on the 28th and were pressing on towards Regalbuto. This was one of the outposts of the Axis line constructed to cover Messina, their port of withdrawal to Italy.

This line, eighty miles in length, ran to the south and west of Mount Etna, and thence northwards to the coast. It was very strong, for the country in which it was sited was rugged; roads were few, easily blocked by mines and demolitions, and commanded from the high ground. At its eastern end Mount Etna dominated the narrow coastal approach from the south towards Messina. It therefore gave the enemy every facility for imposing the maximum of delay on the Allies while his troops were being withdrawn.

The keystone of the system was Adrano, for on this place depended the communications of the whole of the line to the east; once it fell, that part of the line would become untenable. Before Adrano could be threatened

Centuripe, the main outpost of the position, had to be taken, and it was defended by the Hermann Goering Division reinforced by a Parachute Regt., probably the best German troops in Sicily.

By this time the Seventh Army had overrun western and central Sicily and was in touch with the Canadians' left, so the two Armies could now concentrate on breaking the enemy line.

The first pressure came from the Canadians, who established a bridgehead across the River Dittaino, and thus made it possible for the 78th Division to be brought in from reserve to help to crack the strongest position yet encountered in Sicily.

*The 5th Battalion reach Sicily*

Back in Tunisia the 5th Battalion had been training and waiting for the day when the 78th Division would be wanted in Sicily. Their Brigade Commander had addressed them on the 17th July and had told them that the Division was in reserve to the Eighth Army, but that they were not yet required because operations were progressing even better than had been expected.

Three days later the warning order came that they were to be prepared to embark at short notice. On the 22nd and 23rd the M.T. and the marching troops went aboard ship at Sousse, and the whole Battalion landed at Cassibile on the 25th.[2]

The 5th was the first battalion to get organised after landing. In a matter of hours they were on the move, through Palassolo, Vizzini and Mineo to south of Palasonia and, on the next day, to the Giardinelli area. Here, on the 30th, 'B' Echelon suffered severely when they were attacked by fighter-bombers. The Quartermaster, Lieut. Beardsall, R.Q.M.S. Steadman and six men were killed, R.S.M. Maloney and two men seriously wounded. Direct hits were scored on petrol and ammunition trucks, and the Orderly Room truck, containing all the Battalion documents, was also destroyed.

*Attack on Catenanuova, 30th–31st July*

That night the Battalion was put in to attack a formidable rocky hill which overlooked the village of Catenanuova. Objectives were reached by first light without opposition and patrolling was then carried out towards the village, a difficult process which entailed the scaling of cliffs.

The 5th then came under the command of the 1st Canadian Division. The Canadians were to attack Catenanuova, supported by some of the 5th's carriers and all their anti-tank guns, while the Battalion took a high feature to the west.

Acting on the information obtained by patrols and the Intelligence Section, the 5th carried out a silent attack by night and took their objective

Soldiers of the 58th and the 5th Battalion in Battle-dress
*(From the painting by C. C. P. Lawson Esq.)*

without difficulty, while the Canadians, with full artillery support, captured the village. The carriers experienced much difficulty from an obstacle which was new to them, standing corn which got into the bogies and immobilised the vehicles.

Later in the day the Battalion passed through the Canadians and took up positions on the northern edge of the village.

*Capture of Centuripe, 31st July–2nd August*

The 5th Battalion now reverted to the 78th Division, which was about to tackle its first major task in Sicily—the capture of Centuripe.

This task was a tough one, as is shown by the following extract from the Divisional war diary:

> The town stands on a hill block at the western end of the Catania plain. This block has been caused by an outcrop of hard rock and the formation of two great river valleys on each side which drain the snows of the central highlands and Mount Etna. Thus it has gained the dominating position which it has held for centuries.
> It was the key to the whole German position.
> The hillsides below the town were very precipitous, and every few yards the ground was terraced for cultivation, which meant that any deviation from the path was extremely wearying. Vineyards and light scrub provided ideal cover for snipers and odd machine-guns.
> The outline plan of attack was for the 11th Brigade to hold a covering position north of the village of Catenanuova from which the 36th Brigade would carry out the assault. The 38th Irish Brigade was in reserve to exploit success.

This seems to indicate that the rôle of the 11th Brigade was to be somewhat passive, but this was not the case, for it had to secure features the capture of which was vital to the success of the whole operation.

On the 1st August the 5th led the advance of the Division, astride the road to Centuripe, the vigorous action of the companies preventing the enemy from destroying the bridges which were prepared for demolition. Two important ridges were taken, despite heavy mortar and machine-gun fire, which caused 46 casualties, including 2/Lieuts. Domminey and Metson and eight other ranks killed.

During these attacks the 36th Brigade had made progress on the left of the road, and on the following day, just short of the town, where the road began to climb steeply, the Battalion was switched to capture a hill to the right and slightly in rear of the town. This was taken, with a few prisoners, at small cost and that night Centuripe fell to the 36th Brigade.

A few days later Major-Gen. Evelegh showed General Montgomery round the area, and explained to him the course of the battle. In a message to all ranks of the Division, the Army Commander stated that he considered that they had performed a wonderful feat of arms in capturing the position and that he doubted if any other Division in the Eighth Army could have carried out the operation successfully.[3] This was praise indeed, and showed that the 78th had not forgotten the lessons which they had learnt in the hard way in the mountains of Tunisia.

## *Capture of Bronte, 7th–9th August*

The 5th Battalion now had a day's rest and then, before daylight on the 7th, moved forward again through Adrano. This town, flattened into dust by bombing, had been abandoned by the enemy when threatened on the one flank by the 78th Division, on the other by the Canadians.

The East Surrey Regt. were in the town, the Lancashire Fusiliers in contact with the enemy on the northern edge of it. To begin with, the 5th were in reserve, but as dusk began to fall they were ordered to advance astride the road, passing through the Fusiliers, as advanced guard to the Brigade. They moved off shortly before midnight and, despite the fact that they had had no time for reconnaissance, made good progress, dealing successfully with the light rear-guard opposition which was encountered from time to time.

At first light on the 8th, as they were approaching Bronte, the opposition stiffened and 'B' (Major Hunt) and 'C' (Major Cook) had some hard fighting to overcome it. Finally, these two companies attacked the town itself, while 'A' made a detour round it. 'B' and 'C' got through the town successfully and linked up, as planned, near the railway station to the north, but 'A' met with stiff resistance which had, eventually, to be dealt with by the East Surrey Regt.

Soon after the town had been captured, Battalion H.Q. and the reserve company, 'D,' came under heavy fire from Nebelwerfers—the German heavy, multi-barrelled mortars—which severely wounded Major Wherry, the Company Commander, Lieut. Mayhew, the I.O., Lieuts. Smith and Vickers. This was followed by another stroke of misfortune; as the C.O. and his runner were visiting the company positions they came under fire, with the result that Lieut.-Col. Buchanan was severely wounded and his runner was killed.

The 36th Brigade now took up the advance, while the 5th Battalion occupied positions covering Bronte under Major Connolly who had assumed command. Apart from intermittent shelling, which lost them yet another Company Commander, Major Hunt, wounded, the next few days passed uneventfully. From the Battalion O.P. American troops could be seen on the left, advancing in the direction of Randazzo.

# THE 58th AND THE 5th BATTALION IN SICILY, 1943

*Operations near Randazzo, 12th–14th August*

On the night of the 12th August, the 5th Battalion moved with Brigade through Maletto towards Randazzo. Steady progress was made by the marching troops, but the transport moving in rear was delayed by the mines which had been thickly laid along the route. At 0300 hours on the 13th, a halt was called until daylight, after which the Battalion moved across country with the object of outflanking Randazzo and securing positions to the south-east of it. Wheeled transport could not go with them, since the ground was covered with lava rock, but mules were provided to carry the No. 22 wireless set and supplies of ammunition. There was no resistance on the part of the enemy and by 1600 hours companies had reached their objectives. Two hours later a further advance on Passo Piscira was equally uneventful, and by midnight the Battalion were established there.

As far as the 78th Division was concerned, the campaign in Sicily was over. The Allied front had now contracted and between the northern slopes of Mount Etna and the coast the final drive on Messina was left in the hands of the Americans.

*Final Operations by the 58th, 1st–9th August*

As soon as Centuripe was taken, Regalbuto fell and with it the whole of the Axis line to the east had to give way, for the German forces were then split in two.

Over on the right of the Allied front the 58th had been relieved in their positions in the Simeto bridgehead on the night of the 1st August and had gone into reserve. Late on the night of the 3rd the enemy were reported to be withdrawing, and on the following morning the Battalion advanced towards Misterbianco as the right battalion of the Brigade.

The road along which they had to move had been thickly sown with mines and booby-traps and was heavily cratered, so the speed of advance was entirely dependent upon the work of the Pioneer Platoon and a section of a Field Company R.E., which led the way. These did valuable work in clearing the mines and making diversions round the craters, but the Battalion's rate of progress, governed by the speed with which the anti-tank guns and 3-inch mortars could be got forward, was slow and they had to halt for the night three miles short of Misterbianco.

Next morning the Battalion was ready to move at 0530 hours, but again the time taken for mine-clearance delayed matters. Eventually the carriers passed the starting-point seven hours later, but were held up after they had gone a quarter of a mile; soon after 1500 hours the marching troops went ahead of them and entered Misterbianco that evening. Battalion H.Q. set themselves up in the Town Hall and the companies went into billets and bivouacs at the exits to the town.

This was the end of operations for the 58th and for the 5th Division; all that remained for them to do was to carry out protective patrolling and to accept the surrender of numbers of Italian troops.

## End of the Campaign

In the closing stages of the campaign, the enemy, favoured by the country with its precipitous slopes and many easily destroyed bridges, were able to impose on the Allies delay out of all proportion to the strength of their rear-guards. Randazzo was held till the last possible moment and did not fall to the Americans till the 13th August; three days later the U.S. 3rd Division entered Messina from the east and was joined within a few hours by British Commando troops who had made a landing on the coast to the south twenty-four hours earlier.

The conquest of Sicily was complete, and though it did not end in disaster for the Germans comparable to that which had been inflicted on them in Tunisia, they had been decisively defeated and had lost 24,000 in killed alone; the majority of the 200,000 prisoners taken by the Allies were Italians.

The success of this thirty-eight-day campaign was, to a great extent, due to the degree of surprise achieved by the Allies, which led to their landings being virtually unopposed, and to their command of the air. But the battles were won by the troops, who refused to be deterred by the difficulties of fighting in country of a type which many of them were experiencing for the first time.

## The 58th in Sicily, 9th August–2nd September

The 58th now overhauled their organisation and their equipment, and began training so as to be ready for whatever the future might hold in store for them. Cases of malaria began to occur, legacies of their time on the Catania plain, but the spread of the disease was checked by the adoption of precautions, including the daily dose of mepacrine.

They had not long to wait for news of operations to come, for on the 19th August the C.O. heard that the Battalion would take part in another assault landing in the near future. Two days later the Battalion was pleased to hear that he had won the D.S.O. for his leadership during the campaign and that three other ranks had been awarded the Military Medal.[4]

In due course officers were told of the outline plan for the coming operation; no briefing of other ranks was allowed until after they had embarked.

Between the 30th August and the 1st September various officers, men and vehicles were embarked in the appropriate landing-craft, L.S.T.s or L.C.M.s, and a personal message from the Army Commander, addressed to all ranks, revealed the broad objective.[5]

# THE 58th AND THE 5th BATTALION IN SICILY, 1943

On the morning of the 2nd September the 58th moved to the docks at Catania and got on board L.C.I.s, a process which was disturbed by two German aircraft; however, these were shot down by gunfire before they could do any damage. As soon as the troops had embarked, they were briefed on the part they had to play in the invasion of Italy.

*The 5th Battalion in Sicily, 15th August–21st September*

After operations had come to an end, the 5th Battalion had a rest, which included leave to the Divisional Rest Camp and a visit to the 58th at Misterbianco. On the 29th they moved to near Cape Calava, on the north coast of the island, and there started a period of serious training, which included a special course for the Battalion Battle Patrol of five sergeants and twenty-five men.

Once again the 78th Division had to wait for a time before it was required, and had to be content with getting ready and following the course of the invasion with keen interest.

However, in due course, on the 21st September, the Battalion moved by M.T. to a beach near Cape Milazzo, farther along the coast towards Messina, and embarked in H.M.S. *Prins Albert*.

61st (South Midland) Division

# CHAPTER XIII

## THE CAMPAIGN IN ITALY, 1943-1945

The Plan of Invasion—Italy Surrenders—The Landings at Reggio, September 1943—The Salerno Landing—Advance of the Eighth Army—Landings at Taranto—Advance to Foggia—Capture of Termoli—The Allies' Problem—Crossing of the Trigno, October-November 1943—The Sangro Battle, November-December 1943—Advance North of the Sangro—Situation, January 1944—Operations of the Fifth Army, January 1944—Operations at Cassino, February-March 1944—Plans for 1944—The May Offensive—Capture of Rome, June 1944—Advance to the Gothic Line, June-July 1944—Assault on the Gothic Line, August-September 1944—The Advance Continues, September-December 1944—The Final Offensive, April 1945—The Accomplishment (*see* General Map of Italy, facing p. 184)

### The Plan of Invasion

BEFORE the end of the Sicilian campaign, preparations for the invasion of Italy—the start of the attack on the 'soft under-belly of the Axis'—were well advanced, for it was obviously desirable to give the enemy as little breathing time as possible. The plan of invasion contained two separate operations. Early in September the Eighth Army was to cross the Straits of Messina and land on the 'toe' of Italy. The object of Operation 'Baytown' as it was called, was to secure a bridgehead which would free the Straits for the passage of Allied Naval forces; should the enemy withdraw, he was to be followed up and engaged as closely as possible.

About ten days later the American Fifth Army, which was in fact half British for it included the 10th Corps, was to carry out Operation 'Avalanche,' a landing in the Bay of Salerno, on the west coast of Italy, the immediate object being the capture of the port of Naples.

### Italy surrenders

Political events had considerable influence on the Allied plan. In July Mussolini had paid a visit to Hitler to plead for German help against the invasion which was obviously about to take place. He received little encouragement and, on his return to Italy, was expelled by the Fascist Grand Council from his post as Dictator and was placed under arrest.

A Provisional Government was then formed under Marshal Badoglio and, after much secret negotiation, agreed to Italy's unconditional surrender. Armistice terms were signed on the 3rd September, but the news of this was only to be broadcast, by the Allies and the Italians simultaneously, just before the 'Avalanche' landing, when the Italians would order their troops to cease all resistance. It was hoped that the German garrison of some fifteen divisions would then find it impossible to remain in the country, and that they would have to withdraw from it.

## The Landings at Reggio, September 1943

Before the end of August, artillery of the Eighth Army had begun to bombard the eastern coast of the Straits of Messina. At the same time some of the small reconnaissance parties which went across found the coast deserted; but others failed to return, so it was decided to take no risks and to launch a full-scale assault.

At 0430 hours on the 3rd September the leading divisions of the 13th Corps, the 1st Canadian and the 5th, landed near Reggio under cover of artillery and air bombardment. No German troops were encountered, resistance by the Italians was negligible and, by the evening, the two divisions had reached San Stefano and Scilla respectively. During the days which followed, the 5th Division was opposed by German troops, and mines and demolitions on both axes of advance delayed progress, but by the 10th the advance had reached the narrowest part of the foot of Italy. There a short halt had to be called, for a hundred miles had been covered in seven days and the damaged roads were causing maintenance difficulties.

## The Salerno Landing

On the 9th September General Mark Clark's Fifth Army began to land at Salerno. The Italian surrender did not deter the Germans from resisting and, for a week, the ability of the Allied force to remain ashore, in the face of heavy shelling, bombing and counter-attacks, was in the balance.

## Advance of the Eighth Army

There were two ways in which the Eighth Army could help the Fifth; by keeping up their pressure, and so preventing the enemy from transferring reinforcements to the Salerno front; and by advancing as rapidly as possible, thus threatening the German flank and rear.

In spite of administrative difficulties the 13th Corps went ahead. By the 19th the Canadians had occupied Potenza and the leading troops of the 5th Division had reached Auletta, their patrols having made contact with American patrols at Vallo three days earlier. Thanks to the Eighth Army's advance of nearly three hundred miles in seventeen days, the enemy opposing the Fifth Army had to withdraw, and the situation at Salerno became easier.

### *Landings at Taranto*

In the meantime the British 1st Airborne Division, minus any supporting artillery and with very little transport, had been conveyed by sea to Taranto, had landed there unopposed on the 9th September and had sent patrols some forty miles inland. Within six days they had occupied Brindisi and Bari, and units of the 78th Division and the 4th Armoured Brigade, both of the 5th Corps, began to land at the latter port on the 22nd.

### *Advance to Foggia*

The Eighth Army's next objective was Foggia, where the Axis had established a group of airfields which the Allies wanted for the use of their strategic air forces. So, the Salerno bridgehead being now secure, the Army regrouped; the 13th Corps (1st Canadian, 78th and 4th Armoured Brigade) was to advance on Foggia, with the 5th Division in the Potenza area under its command and acting as a link with the Fifth Army; the 5th Corps (8th Indian and 1st Airborne Divisions) was, initially, to be in reserve near Taranto. At this time the main factor limiting operations was the difficulty caused by the switching of the Army's administrative axis to the ports in south-eastern Italy.

The enemy withdrew under pressure, and by the 26th patrols of the 13th Corps had reached the River Ofanto; after some delay, due to demolitions, the advance was resumed through Foggia, and by the 1st October the Gargarno peninsula had been reported clear of the enemy.

### *Capture of Termoli*

The 13th Corps now went on towards the line Termoli–Vinchiaturo, with the object of securing the Foggia plain; the 78th Division was to follow the coastal road, the Canadian Division to move through the mountains farther inland. The flank and rear of this advance was to be covered by the 5th Corps, and the 5th Division was moved up to the Foggia area.

The operation started well. A Commando landing at Termoli on the night of the 2nd/3rd October achieved complete surprise; the port was secured and a bridgehead established over the River Biferno, and this success was followed by the landing of a brigade of the 78th Division at Termoli.

The enemy lost no time in counter-attacking with a Panzer division transferred from the Fifth Army front, and at one time managed to penetrate into Termoli itself; but by the 7th the situation had been restored, with the aid of another brigade of the 78th Division which had been landed. The enemy then fell back to positions covering the next obstacle, the River Trigno, but administrative difficulties prevented a rapid follow-up.

Meanwhile, the Canadians, moving through difficult country against strong opposition, had got to within fifteen miles of Vinchiaturo by the 3rd October, but several days then elapsed before it was in their hands.

The 13th Corps was now operating on an ever-widening front; so the 5th Corps took over the responsibility for the coastal sector with the 78th Division, while the 13th continued on a two-divisional front with the Canadian and 5th Divisions.

On the other side of Italy, the Fifth Army had captured Naples on the 1st October and had gone on to cross the River Volturno, to which the Germans had retired on the 17th.

*The Allies' Problem*

The Fifth Army's next main objective was Rome and, for the Allied Armies in general, the road which ran thence to the Adriatic coast at Pescara.

It was evident that, unless the city could be taken soon, the winter weather would impose an added strain on the already strained administrative situation; many of the rivers would be in flood and would cause bridging difficulties, and snow and mud would render movement off the main road impossible.

Under any conditions the country in this part of Italy is ideal for defensive purposes, and it was now certain that the enemy intended to resist to the utmost; the German forces had been reinforced, and now amounted to some twenty-four divisions. The fact was that, though the defeat of Italy had been achieved, the hoped-for sequel, the withdrawal of the German armies, had not followed. Consequently the Allies found themselves committed to a course of action which had not been foreseen; they had not the resources which might have enabled them to exploit their initial successes, and the demands of the coming invasion of Normandy, especially in shipping and landing-craft, now prevented those resources from being made available; so there was nothing for it but to fight their way forward with those which they had.

*Crossing of the Trigno, October–November 1943*

On the Eighth Army front there was a pause until the night of 22nd/23rd October, when a battalion of the 78th Division managed to establish a bridgehead across the River Trigno.

North of this river was a plain, some two miles wide, ending in a ridge on which lay the German main positions. The intention was to obtain a firm hold on this plain, but heavy rain prevented the enlargement of the bridgehead and, for the same reason, a diversionary attack by the 5th Division towards Isernia had to be postponed. Eventually this started on the night of the 29th/30th, and ended in the capture of Cantalupo, but further progress was slow because of stiffer enemy resistance, difficult country and demolitions.

After several postponements, due to the weather, the 5th Corps attacked across the Trigno on the night of the 2nd/3rd November, and on the morning of the 4th the enemy had begun to withdraw along the whole of the Corps front. On the next day the 78th Division passed through Vasto and the 8th Indian took Palmoli; to the left, Isernia had fallen to the 5th Division. By the 8th, two brigades of the 78th were on the high ground overlooking the River Sangro, with the 8th Indian coming up on their left.

*The Sangro Battle, November–December* 1943

The main German position lay on a steep ridge, north of the River Sangro and separated from it by a low-lying plain. Naturally very strong, it had been made even stronger by the defences. The river itself was in flood and, though it was fordable in places, the depth of water was liable to vary by as much as six to seven feet in a day, according to the amount of water coming down from the mountains. Owing to the weather, the attack on the position was subject to many postponements and alterations of plan.

During the second week in November, the 78th Division managed to establish a small bridgehead across the river and, by the 24th, this had been extended to a depth of about 2,000 yards on a frontage of 10,000 yards. On its left the New Zealand Division had cleared the enemy from the south bank and, farther still to the west, the 13th Corps had made progress and had held its gains against strong counter-attacks.

At last there was an improvement in the weather and, on the 27th November, about a hundred tanks of the 4th Armoured Brigade and much transport were got across the river. The assault began after dark on the following day, but demolitions prevented the tanks and supporting weapons from getting forward; consequently, the 8th Indian Division, which had made good progress, had to give ground against a German counter-attack at dawn. However, that night it went forward again, the armour went through, and then tanks and infantry, turning outwards, helped by very strong air support, began to clear the ridge in the face of very strong opposition. By the end of the 29th the Eighth Army had broken into the Germans' 'Winter Line'; on the 30th the 5th Corps widened the breach and by dark the whole of the ridge was in British hands.

*Advance North of the Sangro*

The 78th Division, very tired after continuous fighting, was now relieved by the 1st Canadian, and went into reserve in the 13th Corps area; but this Corps, which included the 5th Division, was very soon transferred to the coastal sector, leaving the 78th to hold the inland flank in the mountains under command of the Army.

From the Sangro ridge the advance continued towards the north-west, and by the 10th December the Canadians had a bridgehead over the River Moro and were pushing on towards Ortona. On their left were the 8th Indian Division and the New Zealanders, and the 17th Brigade of the 5th Division was brought in to fill the gap between these two. The two Corps continued to advance against very stubborn resistance; by the end of the year the Canadians had taken Ortona and the New Zealanders had outflanked Orsogna, while in between them the 8th Indian and the 5th Divisions had made progress.

At this stage in the campaign General Montgomery left the Eighth Army to take command of 21st Army Group in England, and was succeeded by Lieut.-General Sir Oliver Leese.

*Situation, January 1944*

There were two approaches to Rome; Highway Six, through the valley of the River Liri, the key to which was Cassino, guarded by the formidable Monastery Hill, supported in turn by Monte Cairo and other mountains; and Highway Seven, nearer to the coast, which passed through the flooded Pontine Marshes.

Winter conditions prevented any large-scale operations on the Eighth Army front—now stabilised on the River Moro, where it remained with little change until the spring—or in the mountainous central sector, so operations were virtually confined to the Fifth Army front to the south.

*Operations of the Fifth Army, January 1944*

In January, after hard fighting, the Fifth Army had crossed the Garigliano, an operation in which the 5th Division transferred to the 10th Corps took part; but it could not penetrate into the Liri valley. In order to outflank the right of the German lines, on the 22nd January four divisions made a landing at Anzio, seventy-five miles farther up the coast and thirty miles from Rome. The Germans, who had just moved three divisions from the Rome area to reinforce the Garigliano front, were taken by surprise, and the Allies quickly established a beachhead; but strong counter-attacks followed in the next six weeks and, though these were held and the line firmly consolidated, it was impossible to break out.

*Operations at Cassino, February–March 1944*

Meanwhile, at Cassino, the battle for the mountain bastions which commanded the entrance to the Liri valley had started. On the 4th February American troops took part of the town, but could not capture the vital Monastery Hill. Then the temporarily formed New Zealand Corps—which included the 2nd New Zealand, 4th Indian and 78th Divisions, transferred from the Eighth Army, besides American formations—

attacked, but it too failed, in spite of an extremely heavy air bombardment which shattered the monastery. Towards the end of March it was decided to give up the assault for the time being. The New Zealand Corps was broken up, its British formations passing to the 13th Corps, and the Eighth Army took over the Cassino front.

In the two months which followed, operations were confined to patrolling and reconnaissance. The Armies suffered much discomfort; from wet, cold, and mud during their spells in the line; from lack of shelter when out of it, for towns and villages had been devastated by the enemy in the track of his withdrawal.

*Plans for* 1944

Broadly speaking, the Allies' plan of campaign for the spring and summer of 1944 had the same object as it had had for 1943—to engage as many German forces as possible; but with this difference, that the offensive was to be timed so as to coincide with the landings in Normandy. General Alexander's aim was to break through in the south, so that forces pushing up the Liri valley could join with those in the Anzio beach-head, and together advance on Rome.

Marshal Kesselring had eighteen divisions opposing the Allies, of which all but two faced the Fifth Army. The Allies had complete air superiority and were slightly superior in numbers, though this was offset by their lack of homogeneity; in addition to British, Commonwealth and American formations, their forces included others composed of Poles and Free French and were soon to include detachments of Greeks, Brazilians and Free Italians.

*The May Offensive*

On the night of the 11th May the offensive began, started by the Polish 2nd Corps with the object of pinching out Cassino. By the 13th it had a bridgehead over the River Rapido, north of the town, and on the next day General Juin's French Corps had breached the Gustav Line farther to the south and was thrusting towards the mouth of the Liri valley. The whole German front towards the coast began to give way, and the left of the Eighth Army swung up behind Cassino; but it was not until the 18th that it was finally given up by the German Parachute Division which had defended it for so long.

The whole of the southern front was now on the move. After three days of heavy fighting the 1st Canadian Division forced its way through the Adolf Hitler Line on the 23rd May. On the same day the Allied force in the Anzio beachhead began to break out, and on the 25th its patrols met those from the other portion of the Fifth Army, which had advanced up the coastal plain.

### Capture of Rome, June 1944

While the Eighth Army moved up the Liri valley, the Fifth had heavy fighting in the Alban Hills, where the Germans were making a last attempt to bar the way to Rome. By the morning of the 5th June the way was clear; that night the Fifth Army was in Rome, with advanced guards crossing the Tiber bridges in pursuit of the retreating enemy.

The fine achievement of the armies in Italy in breaking through the enemy's immensely strong positions to capture Rome, an achievement only made possible by the transfer of the bulk of the Eighth Army right across Italy from the Adriatic coast, was overshadowed by events elsewhere. For on the 6th June the Allied forces from Britain began to land on the coast of Normandy.

### Advance to the Gothic Line, June–July 1944

The German armies had suffered heavily in the battles in front of Rome, and took time to recover; so the Allied pursuit, turning northwards along the line of the Tiber through more open country, went ahead. Within a week the Fifth Army was in Viterbo, but the left of the Eighth had been delayed by mines and demolitions in the difficult Apennine country and had only reached Avezzano. On the Adriatic coast the enemy began to withdraw, abandoning Pescara.

The forward zone of the German main line of defence in northern Italy, known as the Gothic Line, ran through the Apennines to the north of the River Arno, from its mouth at Pisa to Florence, thence through the mountains to the source of the River Metauro and along the line of that river to the Adriatic. Time was needed to complete the defences, so Marshal Kesselring ordered his right, reinforced by four fresh divisions, to stand on a line running from Cecina on the coast, through Siena to Lake Trasimene.

Along this line and to the south of it, there was heavy fighting in the last week of June; by the end of the month the right of the Eighth Army had reached the area Macerata–Camerino, the centre and the left had secured the Lake Trasimene district, and the Fifth Army was nearing Siena and Cecina. In the six weeks since the fall of Cassino the Germans had been driven back a matter of two hundred miles, but had managed to pull back their exposed right flank and avoid the cutting-off of any of their divisions.

In July both the Allied armies were again on the move, and by the 17th had reached the line Ancona–Gubbio–Arezzo–Poggi-Bonsi–Leghorn. Heavy rain then delayed operations, but by mid-August they were up to the River Metauro in the east and to the River Arno, from east of Florence to Pisa, in the west, and were in contact with the forward edge of the Gothic Line defences.

## Assault on the Gothic Line, August–September 1944

General Alexander now switched the weight of the Eighth Army back to the Adriatic sector. This was a stupendous undertaking, for only two good roads were available—on one of which no fewer than sixty-three temporary bridges had to be built—for a move which involved the use of a fleet of 80,000 lorries, to say nothing of tanks and guns. However, the move was completed by the end of August, and all was ready for the assault on the eastern end of the Gothic Line.

The preliminary attack was launched across the River Metauro on the 26th August, on a twenty-mile front, paving the way for the main assault on the 31st. Three days later the whole of the eastern portion of the Gothic Line was in Allied hands, in spite of the resistance put up by three German supporting divisions and three others which were brought up to reinforce.

Even though the Line had been broken, very severe fighting followed—how severe can be judged from the fact that up to this date no fewer than twelve German divisions had been flung into the battle and defeated—and it was not until the 21st September that the Greek Brigade in the coastal sector was able to take Rimini, and British troops on its left to clear the territory of San Marino. On the 25th the 1st Canadian and the 56th Divisions forced a passage of the River Rubicon, north of Rimini and established bridgeheads beyond it.

## The Advance continues, September–December 1944

Meanwhile, to the west the Fifth Army and the British 13th Corps had made steady progress; by the end of September they had reached the Futa Pass, thirty miles from Bologna in the plains beyond, and were north of Pistoia and Lucca.

The valley of the River Po, a major obstacle, was still far ahead. In the Adriatic sector there was always one more river to cross, and in the centre one more mountain ridge; furthermore, the French Corps and several American divisions had been withdrawn from Italy, before the attack on the Gothic Line, to take part in the Allied landings in the south of France on the 15th August. As a result General Alexander lacked the strength which would have allowed him to drive through to the Po. And, in addition, operations were hampered by an exceptionally wet and stormy autumn.

As soon as the weather improved, the Fifth Army pushed on, reaching Livergnano, ten miles from Bologna, about the middle of October; but this was the limit of progress in this sector for many months. During this fighting the 78th Division again distinguished itself in the fighting for Monte Spaduro and other heights.

Towards the Adriatic coast the Eighth Army continued to advance steadily towards Bologna along Highway Nine. Forcing the enemy first from the River Savio and then from the River Ronco, Forlì, Faenza, and, to the north, Ravenna, fell in turn. At the end of December, when winter put a stop to major operations, the line of the River Senio had been reached.

At this stage Field-Marshal Alexander assumed command of the Mediterranean Theatre, General Mark Clark replacing him as Commander of the 15th Army Group. Early in January the Eighth Army was depleted by the transfer of the Canadian Divisions to 21st Army Group on the Rhine, and they were soon followed by the 5th Division, which had left Italy in July for a period of training in the Middle East.

*The Final Offensive, April* 1945

Early in April, just after the Allied armies in north-west Europe had crossed the Rhine, the 15th Army Group was ready for the final offensive. The object of this was to clear the whole of the valley of the Po and Northern Italy, and to destroy the two opposing German armies. The latter was no easy task, for the right of these armies rested in the western mountains and the left was entrenched behind the Rivers Senio, Santerno, Sillaro and Idice. The positions were strengthened by a maze of dykes and flooded fields and behind were the Rivers Po and Adige, and other rivers and mountains all the way to the Austrian frontier.

On the 2nd April the Eighth Army made the first thrust, forcing a passage of the Senio. A week later the defence line on that river had been broken. Farther to the right the 5th Corps aimed at Argenta, the key to a gap five miles wide between areas of flooded ground to the west of Lake Comacchio. Argenta was taken by the 78th Division, the gap was forced by the 19th April, and on that day the 6th Armoured Division burst it wide open. Overcoming all opposition, they cut the railway between Bologna and Ferrara, an important one to the enemy, and, by-passing Ferrara, reached the Po on the 23rd.

Meanwhile, on the 20th, American troops from the south and Polish troops from the east met in the streets of Bologna, from which city the Germans had retreated to avoid being cut off. On the 24th the Americans were in Mantua and the main columns of the Eighth Army were crossing the Po, bridged with speed in spite of great natural difficulties.

To all intents and purposes the German forces had been destroyed south of the River Po. The bulk of their equipment had been either destroyed or abandoned, and from now on resistance practically ceased.

On the 28th April the Eighth Army, headed by the 56th Division, entered Venice by way of Padua. Next day the 6th Armoured reached the River Piave and the New Zealand Division crossed it. Then the 6th Armoured moved swiftly east, to link up with the Yugo-Slavs who had occupied Trieste, while other divisions secured Udine and Vittorio Veneto.

On the Fifth Army front the right, advancing through Verona and Bolzano, had secured the Brenner Pass, which carried the main road and railway to Austria; the centre had passed through Milan to the Swiss frontier at Como; and on the left a column moving up the coast had taken Spezia, Genoa and Turin.

On the 2nd May the German High Command in Italy signed the document of unconditional surrender. The remains of twenty-two German and six Italian Fascist Divisions laid down their arms.

*The Accomplishment*

From the first the campaign in Italy was a secondary one to the main Allied invasion of Europe and, as a result of this, the 15th Army Group was continually depleted of troops and material required elsewhere. Consequently, in a country which favoured the defence to such an extent, the campaign was abnormally prolonged, lack of resources often preventing the fullest advantage being taken of success.

Nevertheless, the Allied operations in Italy contained a large number of the best divisions in the German Army, which would otherwise have been available to fight elsewhere; and the troops who fought their way from the toe of Italy to the Austrian frontier, over the mountains and across the rivers, through snow and mud, could pride themselves that they had contributed as much to the final defeat of Germany as had those who fought from Normandy to the Baltic.

# CHAPTER XIV

## THE 58th IN ITALY, 1943–1945

The Landing at Reggio, 3rd September 1943—Advance from the Beachhead, 3rd–14th September—To Foggia, 15th September–23rd October—Advance to the Sangro, 25th October–19th November—Maintenance of the Battalion—On the Sangro, 20th November–8th December—On the River Moro, 9th December 1943–2nd January 1944—Into the Fifth Army, 3rd–13th January—Crossing the Garigliano, 14th January–4th February—Advance to the Minturno Ridge, 23rd–28th January—Attack on Pt. 156, 29th January–2nd February—In Defence, 5th February–3rd March—In the Anzio Bridgehead, 3rd March–26th April—In 'The Fortress,' 27th April–6th May—Retrospect of 'The Fortress'—Crossing of the Moletta, 9th–31st May—Advance to Rome, 1st–5th June—The 58th leave Italy—In the Middle East, July 1944–February 1945—Return to Italy, 8th February–5th March—Departure from Italy, 6th March (*see* Maps on pp. 188 and 198 and facing p. 184)

### *The Landing at Reggio, 3rd September 1943*

ZERO hour for the landing of the 17th Brigade in Italy was 0430 hours on the 3rd September, but the 58th,[1] who were in reserve, were not due to land just south of the village of Gallico Marina until an hour later. There were probably few who had the time to realise that it was at Reggio, nearby, that the 58th had embarked for Sicily a hundred and thirty-seven years before, after they had fought in the Battle of Maida against the French.

'B' and 'C' Companies were put ashore according to plan, but 'D' was not landed until 0610 hours, north of Catona, and 'A,' also put ashore on the wrong beach, had the misfortune to incur six casualties, including the C.S.M. and C.Q.M.S., from long-range shelling. The terrific artillery support from the Sicilian shore caused thick dust and smoke, and this, added to a light sea-mist, had made visibility so poor that the navigational aids, such as vertical searchlights, were of little use; consequently it had been extremely difficult to make accurate landfalls. However, by 0730 hours the Battalion had reached its assembly area, and carriers, anti-tank guns and M.T. were beginning to arrive.

### *Advance from the Beachhead, 3rd–14th September*

At 0930 hours the Battalion began to advance inland, along a winding road flanked by high hills which had to be piqueted by companies in turn. There was no opposition, and mines and demolitions caused no delay, so in less than six hours Sambatello was reached, overlooking the beach and a few miles inland from it. A monitor of the Royal Navy was in direct support and, communications and fire-control being excellent, it was disappointing that lack of targets prevented her being used for any except harassing fire.

The 58th now came temporarily under command of the 13th Brigade, and 'A' Company, with artillery and mortars in support, were sent forward to occupy the village of San Stefano. Road demolitions eventually stopped the progress of any vehicles, and by 2015 hours the advance was held up by German troops. The company could get no support, the F.O.O.s being unable to get in touch with their batteries because of the screening of wireless, so took up a position for the night and patrolled forward. During the night the enemy withdrew, and early on the 4th the advance was resumed, the Battalion being now under the direct command of the Corps. 'A' Company were soon held up by a demolition a hundred yards long, and the R.E. pronounced that it would take two days to fit the road for M.T.; however, the company went on and entered San Stefano at 1700 hours. Those who had carried the 3-inch mortars and ammunition up some fifteen miles of steep mountain road deserve special mention. Shortly afterwards troops of the 1st Canadian Division arrived from the south and took over the place as arranged.

The Battalion now reverted to the 17th Brigade on the coast at San Giovanni, where 'A' Company rejoined them. Two days later they embarked in L.C.I.s and, after two hours' voyage, landed at Gioja a few miles up the coast.

On the 8th a mobile column was formed, composed of one company from each battalion in the brigade and the three 3-inch mortar platoons, the whole moving in carriers and under the command of Lieut.-Col. Ballard. His task was to assist another column which was relieving the pressure on the 231st Brigade (the former garrison of Malta), which, having landed on the west coast, was heavily engaged near Pizzo. Moving off that evening the two columns established contact the next day, and, having completed its task, the Ballard column was disbanded.

Meanwhile the 58th had followed a few hours later, hearing the news of the capitulation of Italy before they started, and, after a short halt on the night of the 8th, reached a point north of Pizzo by the next evening. In the two days which followed they marched, or were ferried in the vehicles of a Field Regiment, to Nicastro. There they were glad to rest until the 15th, for in the eight days which had elapsed since the landing they had covered nearly a hundred miles, mostly on their feet.

*To Foggia, 15th September–23rd October*

On the 15th September the 58th took to the sea again, a six-hour voyage ending in their disembarkation at Scalea, where the transport had already arrived by road. Here the 15th Brigade went through to carry on the advance; the necessity for speed was no longer so great, as the situation at Salerno had improved and the Americans were now firmly established there. A two-day journey in T.C.V.s then took the Battalion to Nemoli and Buonabitacoli, the road twisting along the mountain sides, often with a drop of many hundreds of feet below; the number of burnt-out German vehicles by the roadside bore witness to the accuracy of the Allied bombing. Then, on the 21st, they marched to Atena, where they stayed till the end of the month. Apart from patrolling to reconnoitre roads and to gain contact with the 82nd U.S. Airborne Division, the days were spent in training; the Battalion was now up to strength in men and only lacked a few vehicles.

The beginning of October found them on the move northwards again and, after staging nights at Avigliano and Minervino, they reached Troia on the 5th. They were now in reserve to the Brigade, which was covering the left flank of the Eighth Army, but soon had to undertake another duty. The town of Foggia, where Allied Military Government had not yet been established, was the scene of much looting, and the Battalion was ordered to carry out Operation 'Peasoup' and police it. This was a compliment, for the orders stated that they had been selected for this duty by the Corps Commander on account of their high standard of discipline. 'B' Company moved into Foggia on the 6th, followed by the rest of the Battalion on the next day, and by the 10th, when they were relieved by another unit and returned to Troia, their street patrols had restored order.

At this stage the 58th lost Lieut.-Col. Ballard, who left them to go to the American Staff College. After a short period of temporary command by Major Houchin, he was succeeded by Lieut.-Col. J. W. A. Stephenson of the Middlesex Regt. Another change was that of the Brigade Commander, Brig. A. D. Ward relieving Brig. G. W. B. Tarleton, under whom the 58th had served for over two years in many countries and in many campaigns.

*Advance to the Sangro, 25th October–19th November*

The period of rest and training at Troia ended on the 25th October, when the 58th moved in T.C.V.s to east of Vinchiaturo. There they got in touch with a Canadian battalion which was in contact with the enemy in Boiano. After two nights in this area, they moved across country as reserve battalion to the Brigade, and on reaching the outskirts of a mountain village received orders to occupy a feature, Pt. 1385, on the next day, and then to go on and take the town of Macchiagodena. However, heavy rain and bad roads delayed the arrival of the artillery to support the attack and there was a twenty-four-hour postponement.

In the meantime, three British officers who had escaped from a prisoners-of-war camp made their way into the Battalion lines. One of them was Lieut.

Truckle of the 5th Battalion, who had been captured during the Tunisian campaign.

Before daybreak on the 30th, the 58th moved up to their start-line. 'A' Company and a company of the Seaforth Highlanders then advanced and secured Pt. 1385 without opposition. At 0940 hours, after an artillery concentration, No. 14 Platoon of 'C' attacked another feature, Pt. 1102, forcing a small party of enemy off it; the rest of 'C' and 'D' Companies then advanced on to adjacent heights, while 'B' occupied Pt. 1102. In the course of the afternoon 'C' and 'D' were heavily shelled, incurring some thirty casualties, which included ten killed and four officers—Capt. Parratt and 2/Lieut. Northfield of 'C,' and Lieuts. Walker and Hofman of 'D'—wounded.

The Battalion spent a cold, wet and miserable night in positions about four thousand feet above sea-level. The only means of getting up supplies was by mule, across four miles of rough going, and this was made more difficult by a dense mist which made it impossible to find Forward Battalion H.Q., which had moved. However, thanks to the efforts of Major Houchin and R.S.M. Batchelor, the Battalion got its supplies, while admirable work by the M.O., Capt. Lamb, and Sgt. Lee overcame the difficulties in the evacuation of the wounded. The administrative lessons which were learnt were the foundation for the organisation which worked so well in later operations.

Early the next morning patrols found Macchiagodena strongly held by the enemy, but a few hours later the fighting patrol under Lieut. Hamer reported it clear, and, by 1040 hours, 'B' Company had occupied it without fighting. The Battalion then took up positions on the high ground to the east of the town, while the Seaforth attacked a feature to the north. The 58th spent a more comfortable night, for blankets could be got up to them, and they were heartened by a message from the Divisional Commander, congratulating them on the manner in which they had taken their objectives in the previous day's fighting.

On the night of the 2nd November a patrol from 'A' Company, skilfully led by Sgt. Hayman, entered the village of St. Angelo, high up on a rocky peak, and reported that there were signs that the enemy were preparing to withdraw from it. Next morning the Battalion occupied it, pushed on to Castelpetroso, and took up positions round the town; thence a platoon of 'A' Company, under Lieut. Richards, advanced as far as Carpinone, and found that the enemy were carrying out extensive demolitions, indicating a further withdrawal to be likely. After a few days spent in patrolling and in the repairing of demolitions, work for which they earned further praise, the Battalion concentrated in Castelpetroso on the 6th, and remained there for a fortnight, occupied in training, in overhauling weapons and vehicles, and in patrolling to keep touch with the Canadians.

## THE 58th IN ITALY, 1943-1945

*Maintenance of the Battalion*

Even after the Battalion had left the mountainous country, maintenance by mule transport was still necessary. The demolition of bridges rendered the road from Macchiagodena impassable to any other form of transport, and a jeep road which had been constructed could not be used until the enemy had been driven from positions which commanded it.

To meet the new administrative situation, some reorganisation was carried out within the Battalion. Under the new arrangement, the Forward Element consisted of Battalion H.Q., R.A.P., Signal Platoon, a mule-borne portion of the Mortar Platoon and the Pioneers, and the Rifle Companies; the Forward Administration Element, or 'Admin. Post,' under the O.C. H.Q. Company, contained the essential first-line vehicles, including all jeeps; behind this was the Rear Administration Element, with the Quartermaster in command of 'B' Echelon and the M.T. Officer in command of all transport not required forward. The Second-in-Command acted as the link between Battalion H.Q. and the Admin. Post, and organised the forward despatch of all supplies, either by mules or by carrying-parties.

The feeding of the Battalion was indeed a problem, for enemy observation prevented the movement of mules by day, and by night the mountain tracks were difficult to find and to negotiate; it was only by taping the route from the main road to Battalion H.Q. that the delivery of supplies could be ensured.

*On the Sangro, 20th November–8th December*

The forward troops of the Eighth Army had, by now, reached the River Sangro, and plans were made for the crossing. The main attack was to be made to the north but, with a view to deceiving the enemy, a left hook was to be made in the central sector.

On the 20th November 'A' Company (Major Purton) moved forward, to act under the command of the 2nd R. Scots Fusiliers, while 'B' (Capt. Careless) came directly under the Brigade Commander. The objective of the attack was Alfedena.

On the night of the 20th/21st, while 'B' took up a position to protect the left of the advance, 'A' went forward with the Fusiliers. The move to the start-line involved a climb to a plateau along a rocky path up a cliff-face some eight hundred feet high, a test of fitness, since all loads, including rations for twenty-four hours, had to be carried on the man.

Initially, 'A' Company were in reserve, but in the afternoon were called upon to tackle Pt. 1086, a hill with steep, rocky sides. Passing through heavy defensive fire at the foot, the Company scrambled up the slopes and, in little more than an hour, were consolidating the summit; digging was difficult and the defences had to take the form of sangars. During the next two days patrols made contact with the enemy and gained valuable information.

A week later the Battalion moved to Rionero and were rejoined by 'A' Company. On the night of the 28th they relieved the 1st York and Lancaster Regt. in the forward positions, 'A' being in Castel di Sangro, where Tac. H.Q. were located, 'C' and 'D' on features overlooking the town.

Castel di Sangro still contained many of its civil population, and the Padre was appointed Town Major. The 58th's efforts on behalf of the civilians were appreciated, witness the following letter, addressed to H.Q. Eighth Army by the Mayor after their departure:

> The representatives of the town of Castel di Sangro and all the population feel it their duty to express to the C.O. of Y68, and to all officers, their profound gratitude for the able work on behalf of the civil population which was carried out by this unit during its residence in the town.
>
> It has been confirmed that, during this period, there were five deaths among the population and more than thirty cases of severe wounds; all of these received sympathetic and careful attention from Capt. Dr. Lamb and Capt. the Rev. Evans.

Evidently the soldiers of Y68—the 58th vehicle number in the 5th Division—had been true to the British soldier's reputation for chivalry towards the people of a defeated nation.

'B' Company were still detached, under command of the Seaforth, and carried out active patrolling about six miles to the west of the town, reverting to the 58th on the 2nd December.

In front of the position held by the Battalion ran the flooded Sangro River. On the other side of it, and about a thousand yards away, were the German positions.

During the next ten days patrols did much good work, gaining information of the crossing-places over the river and of enemy dispositions, and generally establishing control of no-man's-land. In this work Lieut. Hamer and the Battalion Fighting Patrol were particularly successful. On the 30th November they waded through the icy waters of the Sangro and set up a base in a farmhouse, whence they operated by night over a wide area, communicating with the Battalion by line and 38-set. After they had been there for a few days Lieut.-Col. Stephenson and Major Purton went down to the crossing-place to see Lieut. Hamer, but by then the river was in spate, the water too deep and the current too strong for them to cross; in fact, a signaller who tried to do so was nearly swept away, and was only rescued by the C.O. manning a lifeline. Forty-eight hours later the patrol was running short of food; attempts by a ration party to get a line across the river failed; then the C.O.'s proficiency as a cricketer proved of service, for he hurled across a machete with a line attached to it, and by this means the patrol drew over rations in haversacks. On the evening of the 7th the patrol came in, crossing the river on horseback with the aid of an Italian farmer.

Another patrol of three men, led by Lieut. Richards towards Roccaraso, was less fortunate. On the night that they left, two of the patrol returned reporting that they had crossed the river without trouble, but that the patrol had then been challenged and fired upon, and had then split up. Early the next day the third man, Pte. Raisborough of 'A' Company, returned, wounded in the hand. After being fired upon, he and Lieut. Richards had hidden for a short time and had then tried to work their way back towards the river. As they did so grenades were thrown at them; he was wounded, and so, apparently, was the officer; but after crawling to the place where he thought he was he had failed to find him, and so had returned with the information.

On the night of the 7th December the 58th were relieved by the 2nd Inniskilling Fusiliers of the 13th Brigade, and went back to billets in Isernia.

*On the River Moro, 9th December* 1943–*2nd January* 1944

The Battalion had hoped to rest at Isernia and began to make arrangements for Christmas celebrations; but their hopes were soon dashed. In the Adriatic sector the 5th Corps had crossed the Sangro and had captured the ridge to the north of it, thus breaking into the enemy's 'Winter Line'; but the divisions were very tired after much continuous fighting, so the 13th Corps, which included the 5th Division, was transferred to that sector to continue the advance.

The 58th moved in T.C.V.s on the 10th and, after an uncomfortable night in bivouac, arrived at Atessa on the 11th. Here their brigade came under command of the 2nd New Zealand Division and received orders to move across the Sangro on the next day to an area where their task would be the protection of that division's right flank as it advanced towards Orsogna.

The 58th duly took over from the 5th R. Gurkha Rifles of the 8th Indian Division and got ready to attack. The New Zealanders were to advance on the night of the 14th/15th, with the object of cutting the Orsogna–Ortona road and the 58th were to help them by securing the line of the River Moro to the north of the Sangro, and the spurs beyond it, before dawn on the 14th.

At 2130 hours on the 13th 'B' Company crossed the muddy ditch which was all that was left of the Moro after the bombardments it had had. Ahead the ground rose sharply to the German positions, which included the village of Poggiofiorito. By 0100 hours on the 14th the Company were established on the objective, and remained hidden, according to orders, for the hours of daylight.

Shortly before midnight the other three companies followed. At 0100 hours the barrage for the New Zealanders' attack came down on the left, and forty minutes later 'C' Company, with a platoon of machine-guns, passed through 'B's' forward localities. There was some l.m.g. fire, but they soon reported that they had reached their objective, just short of the village; this was a mistake for, in actual fact, they were several hundred yards from their objective. By now the enemy were thoroughly aroused and there was heavy shelling of the Roman Road which was the Battalion's axis of advance; despite this, the 6-pounder anti-tank guns were got forward, a very necessary precaution as there was good tank country ahead.

The day was uneventful, except for enemy shelling, though heavy concentrations on the company areas after dark indicated that the enemy were preparing something.

Before daylight on the 16th heavy machine-gun and mortar fire opened from the direction of the village; the Battalion's Brens replied, defensive fire was brought down and no attack materialised. A prisoner, captured later by a patrol under Lieut. Hamer, confirmed that three companies of Panzer Grenadiers were to have attacked at 0415 hours, but that they had been caught in the defensive fire as they were forming up and that this had broken the attack. For this the 58th had to thank the prompt response of the 156th Fd. Regt. R.A.

Early the following morning it was seen that the tower in Poggiofiorito had disappeared and patrols discovered that the enemy had withdrawn. The 58th soon occupied the village and the high ground near it, the left company gaining touch with a New Zealand battalion. That afternoon the fighting patrol went forward to the railway station where, after overpowering a sentry, they captured all the five soldiers of a post of the 67th Panzer Grenadier Regiment. This was the hundredth patrol to be led by Lieut. Hamer since the Battalion had landed in Sicily, and earned him the Military Cross.

Subsequent patrols located the enemy holding two villages ahead in strength, so the 58th consolidated the positions they had reached. On the 21st they were relieved, and after a long march through the night reached Lanciano; there, though the billets were poor, they managed to enjoy Christmas. A draft of reinforcements from England arrived on the 29th and brought the Battalion up to nearly full strength.

*Into the Fifth Army, 3rd–13th January*

The year 1944 came in with heavy snow and many rumours about the future employment of the Division, these varying from a move to England to prepare for the invasion of Western Europe to a transfer to the Fifth Army on the other side of Italy. It was not long before the latter proved to be the more correct.

All possible precautions were taken to disguise the transfer of the Division. Before leaving Lanciano on the 3rd January, the divisional 'Y' sign and unit signs were removed from clothing and transport; on the next day's move, from Casalbordino on the Adriatic coast to Lucera, the route was marked with the 'TT' of the 50th Division, and from then onwards a plain '7' was used for both route and vehicle marking.

After crossing the Apennines, via Ariano and Avellino, where the heavy snow made the going difficult, the 58th had a few hours' rest at Cicciano, east of Naples, and then on the 6th reached the Mediterranean coast at Mondragone.

That evening they set off on foot for Cellole, ten miles to the north. It was a march which many will remember, for the road ran along the coast and was swept by an icy wind carrying dust which filled both eyes and mouth. At Cellole they were in reserve behind the 56th Division, who held the line of the River Garigliano. Before long an address by the 10th Corps Commander made it clear that there was 'one more river to cross'—and that by no means the last one—and in due course the 58th went back to Capua, to practise the use of assault boats on the River Volturno.[2]

*Crossing the Garigliano, 14th January–4th February*

On the 14th January 'A' and 'C' Companies took over positions on the Garigliano. These were about a thousand yards from the river and lay on the flat coastal plain which stretched inland for some five miles. Across the plain ran Highway Seven, which crossed the river about a mile and a half from its mouth. To the south-east the plain was bordered by a range of mountains, and any movement forward of these came under the observation of the enemy beyond the river, holding a 500-foot ridge on which were situated Trimonsuoli, Minturno and Tufo; behind this ridge the 5,000-foot peak of Monte Petrella dominated the whole area. So, for nights on end, guns, ammunition and equipment were brought forward after dark and concealed in any natural cover that existed. Meanwhile patrols refrained from abnormal activity, in order to prevent the enemy from realising that an offensive was impending.

The objective of the 5th Division's attack was the ridge beyond the river. The 13th Brigade was to cross the Garigliano on the right and attack the ridge from the Tufo end; the 17th Brigade was to cross at the estuary and advance on Minturno. The whole attack was to be a silent one, without any preliminary bombardment.

In the 17th Brigade the R. Scots Fusiliers were to make a landing from 'dukws' to the north of the estuary; the Seaforth were to cross the river at

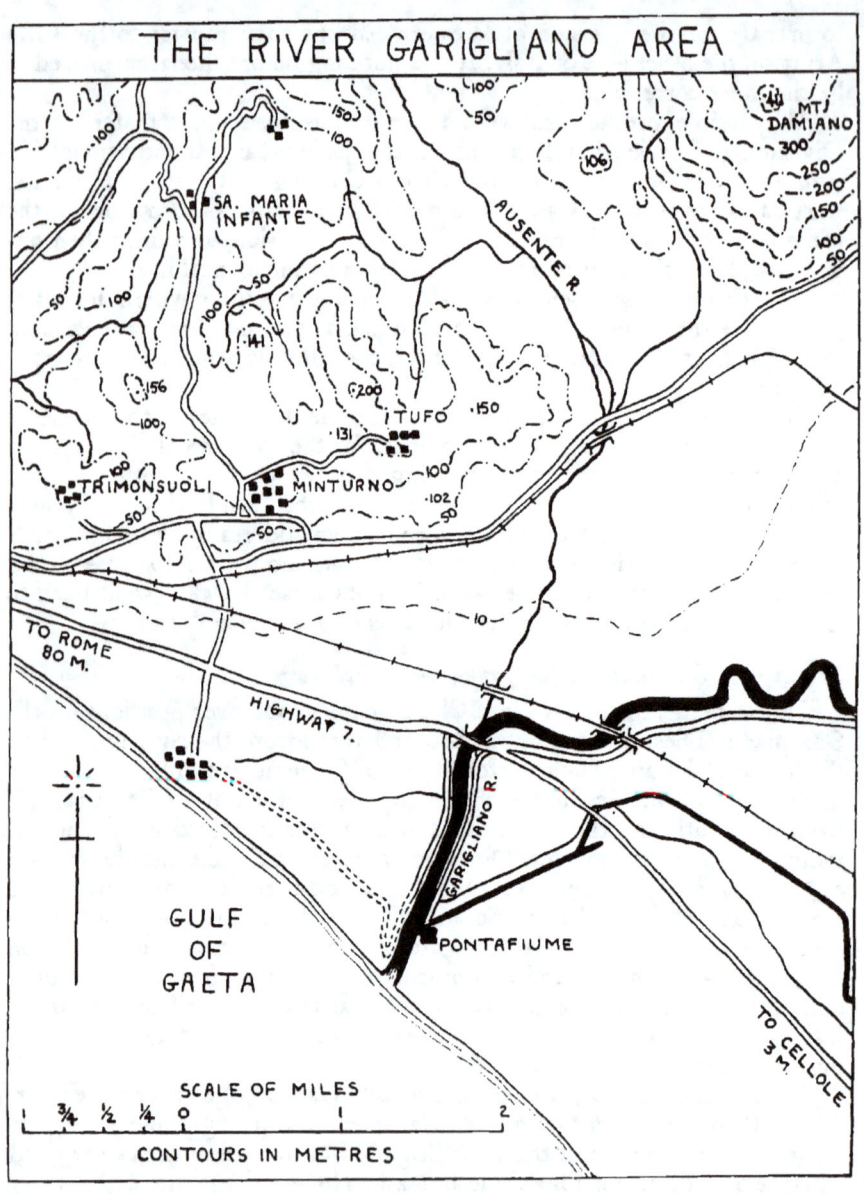

Pontifiume, and establish a bridgehead from which the 58th were to launch an attack upon Minturno and then upon Trimonsuoli.

Soon after dark on the 17th January the Battalion left Cellole and followed the taped route through the sand-dunes towards the river bank. When short of the river they halted and 'B' Company, who were responsible for ferrying the Seaforth across, went ahead.

Before long it was evident that the crossing was not going according to plan. A considerable volume of machine-gun fire was sweeping the river, the Seaforth had run into unexpectedly extensive minefields on the south bank and the crossing had been delayed. By 2315 hours only three assault-boats were serviceable; however, a few more were obtained and at 0200 hours 'D' Company of the 58th began to cross, followed by the rest of the Battalion.

On the north bank, even more extensive minefields had given the Seaforth much trouble as they passed through them and, owing to inadequate taping of the gaps, the 58th also had many casualties, including Major Roche and Lieut. Syddall of 'D' wounded by the same mine.

Strong counter-attacks soon developed against the Seaforth and there was no information of the progress of the Fusiliers' landing. It was known afterwards that the programme of the latter had gone astray owing to faulty navigation; the first troops to be put ashore had been a detachment of a Field Ambulance and a stores party under Major Houchin of the 58th, while the supporting tanks and anti-tank guns had been landed on the wrong side of the river mouth.

However, the two battalions managed to hold their ground, though attacked by tanks, and by first light the 58th, less 'B' Company which had been ordered to remain behind and dig in, had been ferried across the river. The original plan could not be followed, since their start-line had not been made good; instead, they were ordered to establish a small bridgehead north of the river.

The situation was far from pleasant, for the Germans still in occupation of the ridge had good observation over the river, and all attempts to get guns and vehicles forward were met by harassing fire. The minefields were also an obstacle, made the more difficult by the fact that the detectors could not locate the mines in the sandy soil.

At 0830 hours news came that the 13th Brigade attack was going well and was nearing Tufo, and that the 15th Brigade from reserve was to pass through them and exploit success. This was good news, for this advance would relieve the pressure on the 17th Brigade.

At about this time the Brigade Commander and Lieut.-Col. Stephenson had gone forward to reconnoitre and had been fired on by a German strong-point which had escaped being mopped up. 'A' Company were ordered to deal with it, and the attack which they put in was an excellent example of platoon tactics.

At 0900 hours No. 9 Platoon, commanded by Sgt. Bell, moved off from the river line. When the leading section had reached a point about 250 yards from the house held by the enemy it was met by heavy Spandau fire. Supported by the fire section and by a smoke-screen laid by the 2-inch mortar, the two assault sections moved to within fifty yards of the house, using the waterlogged ditches and sparse undergrowth to assist their approach. The smoke-screen, laid by Pte. Nicholls, was so effective that the sections suffered no casualties from the enemy's fire.

Ordering the fire section to a point where they could prevent the escape of the enemy, and the mortar to change to high-explosive fire, the Platoon Commander launched the assault sections against the strong-point. As the smoke-screen thinned, Cpl. Manners led his section in to the attack, hurling a 36-grenade followed by a 77-grenade as he did so. They had soon forced their way into the strong-point, where Sgt. Bell directed the mopping-up of the house and its consolidation.

The message 'strong-point ours' which came back from the platoon at 1000 hours was a modest description of an admirably led little action. Seven prisoners, all wounded, had been taken and one German had been killed; five light machine-guns had been captured; two wounded British soldiers who had been in the enemy's hands were released.

For their gallantry and leadership in this action, Sgt. Bell was awarded the D.C.M. and Cpl. Manners the M.M.

That night patrols tried to locate 'D' Company of the Seaforth, but, evidence of the hard fight they had put up against the German counter-attacks, they could find only dead men. Next morning 'A' Company moved forward, through a heavily mined area, to the blown bridge which carried the road across the river; 'C' and 'B' advanced, and the 58th took over the right sector of the Brigade front.

The mortar and anti-tank platoons were not complete, for it was not yet possible to throw a bridge across the river and though a ferry was in operation its capacity was limited. Until a bridge was built at the point where Highway Seven crossed the river, 'A' Company had to be supplied by means of two Wellington bomber inflatable boats which the enemy had left behind, carefully booby-trapped; but river traffic was made possible during the hours of daylight only by a periodical smoke-screen laid along the bank.

In the course of the day the 58th received encouragement, and a reminder of the presence off the coast of the Royal Navy, in the shape of a signal from H.M.S. *Laforey*, Northampton's adopted ship, which read: 'To our adopted Regiment. Best of good fortune to you all.'

*Advance to the Minturno Ridge, 23rd–28th January*

After two days of patrolling and considerable trouble from mines and booby-traps, which caused so many casualties in vehicles that it became necessary to sandbag them, the 58th moved up to the foothills of the Minturno ridge on the 22nd January. By that date the combined attacks of the 13th and 15th Brigades had taken the three places on the ridge and had held them against violent counter-attacks.

On the 23rd, the R. Scots Fusiliers and the Seaforth Highlanders of the 17th Brigade attacked two features, Pts. 156 and 141, which lay west and north, respectively, of Minturno. The 58th were to pass through them and capture the village of Santa Maria d'Infante at first light on the 24th, but this was later cancelled, as the two attacking battalions were forced back by tank and infantry counter-attacks. Instead, the 58th remained in the foothills, sending patrols forward every night to reconnoitre the route to Pt. 156 and to locate the enemy's defences there. They found that the main defences were on the reverse slopes of the feature, in accordance with the normal German practice, but that at night the forward slopes were held by strong standing patrols. The garrison was estimated to be not less than 150 strong, with a high proportion of automatic weapons.

*Attack on Pt. 156, 29th January–2nd February*

At last preparations were complete for another attempt on Pt. 156, and at dusk on the 29th January the Battalion moved to an assembly area below the ridge. As they did so the Intelligence Section under Lieut. Batiste taped the start-line, from which the Pioneers had cleared many Italian box-mines.

The attack was to be carried out on a three-company front. The start-line for 'D' and 'C' was just east of Minturno, that for 'A' farther to the west, so as to start that company squarely to its objective. All three companies had different axes of advance, but this unorthodox method of attack proved to be most successful.

The artillery programme consisted of a 'Chinese' barrage, lifting along the line of the earlier unsuccessful attacks, with Bofors guns firing tracer in the same direction, the whole being designed to induce the enemy to imagine that the attack was coming from the east and not, as in fact it was, from the south. The enemy positions were to be engaged by concentrations from 4·2-inch mortars and the Battalion 3-inch Mortar Platoons.

At one minute after midnight on the 30th the guns and mortars opened fire. The enemy reacted strongly, Minturno and the forming-up places used in the previous attacks being heavily shelled. Unfortunately, harassing fire also fell on 'C' and 'D' Companies as they waited on their start-line, the fragmentation of the shells on the rocky ground causing many casualties. Among these was Major G. M. C. Anderson, commanding 'D,' who had only just returned to the Battalion after recovering from the wounds he had received at Madagascar; severely wounded, he died later. 'A' Company, farther to the left, escaped this fire.

At 0130 hours the companies advanced. As they did so, the Intelligence

Section laid a tape to mark the main battalion axis behind 'C' Company, and another behind the leading platoon of 'A,' to aid direction-finding in the difficult mountain country. Parties from the Carrier Platoon and a Pioneer unit stood by to follow the advance, carrying ammunition in rucksacks.

An hour later the attack was going well, though movement up the terraced slopes was difficult, the troops having to surmount high banks topped by stone walls. On 'A' Company's front the going was somewhat easier; they had crossed the valley without casualties, keeping close to the barrage.

By 0330 hours 'C' and 'D' were encountering mortar and shell fire, and 'A' were forming up for the final assault on the feature. As No. 8 Platoon advanced to seize a spur which ran down from Pt. 156 they met a section of Germans moving up the slope to counter-attack. Charging them, they took twelve prisoners and went on to capture two machine-gun posts. Meanwhile, Nos. 7 and 9 Platoons were clearing the western end of the objective, and in the end the Company took more than thirty prisoners, at a cost of about twenty wounded, mainly from heavy artillery fire while they were consolidating the position.

The C.O. went forward at 0400 hours, and found 'C' Company still moving up the hill; they were now commanded by Capt. Kitchin, who had taken over after Major Gibson had been wounded. Owing to the darkness and the difficult going, platoons were finding great difficulty in keeping in touch with each other. There was no sign of 'D,' now commanded by Major Greaves, but they were making good progress.

Within less than two hours 'C' had cleared the summit of Pt. 156, 'D' was on its objective and a company of the Seaforth was moving on the cemetery farther to the right. By 0630 hours the three companies had dug in, with No. 14 Platoon of 'C' on a spur slightly in advance. 'B,' in reserve, were dug in about half-way up the hill to the rear.

At noon Pt. 156 was heavily shelled and mortared, and an hour later a strong body of enemy was seen forming up in front of 'C' Company. Then a box-barrage came down round the two left-hand sections of No. 14 Platoon and a section of machine-guns of the Cheshire Regt., and they were attacked by thirty or forty Germans. The Platoon Commander, who had been at Company H.Q. when the attack developed, returned, but by the time he reached the platoon the sections had been overrun by sheer weight of numbers and had lost eighteen men taken prisoner. The remainder of the platoon had been unable to help by fire, for fear of hitting their comrades.

At this stage No. 12 Platoon of 'B,' commanded by Lieut. Hamer, which had been moved up in rear of 'C' Company, went forward to restore the situation, and by 1430 hours their energetic action with the bayonet had driven the enemy from the position. Lieut. Hamer won a bar to his Military Cross for his fine leadership.

The 58th receiving their Colours in Berlin, 1947
(See p. 340)

(Northampton "Chronicle and Echo")

The rest of the day was fairly quiet, but at first light on the 31st, and throughout that day, the spur was heavily shelled. At 1615 hours there were signs that the enemy were about to stage another attack and defensive fire was called for. After machine-gun and mortar fire on No. 12 Platoon, the enemy was seen approaching. They were engaged by light automatics and did not succeed in setting foot on the spur. Subsequently, patrols found more than sixty enemy dead at the spot where they had been caught by the British fire.

The attack on Pt. 156 and the defence of the captured position had been carried out well and with determination, but not without cost to the 58th. Their casualties during the two days' fighting amounted to about a hundred, mostly wounded; of the officers, in addition to Major Anderson, Lieut. Cushion had been killed and Lieut. Ahlquist wounded. Capt. Kitchin and Capt. Garner were awarded the Military Cross for their gallantry.

On the night of the 1st/2nd February the 58th were relieved and moved back south of the Garigliano for a few days' rest. Reinforcements had not arrived and they were now rather short of men, so they reorganised into three rifle companies, 'D' Company H.Q. being retained as a nucleus for the training of drafts when they arrived.

## In Defence, 5th February–3rd March

The 58th were back in the line again on the 5th February, when they took over positions on the high ground east of the village of Tufo from the 2nd Bn. The Wiltshire Regt. Between their right and the left of the 56th Division was the valley of the Ausente and a gap of nearly a mile; this was covered by the Carrier Platoon working dismounted, and a section of anti-tank guns.

Soon after they had taken over they were ordered to prepare for a night attack on the Bracchi feature. The country on the approach to this was most difficult, as reconnoitring patrols discovered, so no one was sorry when the project was cancelled. It was to have formed part of an advance of the whole Army, from Cassino to the sea, but this was postponed when the efforts to take Monte Cassino had failed.

The Battalion now concentrated on the defences, putting up much wire and laying extensive minefields. One of the latter was, unfortunately, laid just too late to prevent the enemy attacking one of the Carrier Platoon's posts and taking five men prisoner.

On the night of the 18th the 58th handed over to the 2nd Scots Guards and went back for a few days' rest prior to taking over a sector of the line previously held by the 56th Division.

The new positions lay on the crest and the western slopes of the bare, dome-shaped Mount Damiano. Apart from patrols into the valley of the

Ausente the time in the line was uneventful, but there were many administrative difficulties to be overcome.

The only route up the mountain was a narrow track, strewn with slippery boulders. In some of the company areas there were no landmarks of any sort and the only sure way of reaching the forward platoons was to use the signal cable as a guide. It was fortunate that casualties were few, for it took at least six hours to convey a wounded man from a forward post to the R.A.P. and another hour and a half from there to an ambulance at the foot of the mountain.

For supply purposes an Admin. Post was set up in rear, where C.Q.M.S.s split the rations, packing them in sandbags, each of which held a section's share. These were marked with wooden labels, of a different shape for each company, so when the column of Indian porters reached Battalion H.Q. it was easy for the R.S.M. to direct them onwards by the correct route to the appropriate company. At Company H.Q. all that was necessary was to despatch four sandbags to each platoon.

Water-supply presented its own problem. The normal day's ration was eight gallons per platoon, little enough in all conscience considering that this had to serve for both cooking and washing; but platoons did not always get even this quantity, for human nature being what it is the porters had a habit of making their loads lighter by emptying half the contents of the tins.

Theoretically the Battalion was on hard rations, but the Quartermaster, Lieut. Goodall, by the exercise of that ingenuity which is the hallmark of a good Quartermaster, managed to provide a small quantity of bread as well as biscuits. To add variety, the Cook-Sergeant and his team produced prefabricated dishes, such as partially cooked porridge which, sent up in gallon containers, only had to be heated on a tommy cooker to be ready for consumption; and jam-tarts and cakes, packed in empty mortar-bomb boxes. So, in spite of the mountain, the 58th were as well fed as conditions would allow.

On the night of the 2nd March they were relieved by a battalion of the 34th U.S. Infantry Regt. and marched back to the banks of the Garigliano.

*In the Anzio Bridgehead, 3rd March–26th April*

From the Garigliano the Battalion went back in T.C.V.s to Pozzuoli, west of Naples. They knew that they had seen the last of the sector in which they had spent the previous two months, for it was to be held permanently by the Americans; the next day they heard that they were destined for Anzio, where the Fifth Army, which had landed there in January, was still holding a comparatively shallow bridgehead.

For the next few days the 58th were busily engaged in sorting their stores and vehicles, most of which were to be left behind and exchanged for those of the battalion of the 56th Division which they were to relieve. But there was time for many to pay a visit to Naples.

The advanced party left on the 6th March, under Major Purton who had become Second-in-Command when Major Houchin had left to take command of another battalion in the Brigade. The Battalion, still only three companies strong, followed in L.C.I.s and reached Anzio on the 9th. The whole of the beachhead was within range of the German artillery, and they found the vehicles they took over dug in up to bonnet height, as a protection against shelling.

On the next night the 58th took over a sector of the western portion of the perimeter, known as 'Starfish,' between the main road to Rome and the coast. The flat countryside was intersected by deep, narrow, 'wadis' to which the 56th Division had clung when driven back by the strong German counter-attack which had followed the landing, leaving the enemy in possession of the higher ground above them. Any movement by day was hazardous and by night the open ground was constantly harassed by enemy artillery, mortar and machine-gun fire.

The sector offered great opportunities for sniping and, as was right for a battalion of a regiment which prided itself on its ability to shoot, the 58th encouraged this form of offensive activity. A competition was started, in which snipers had to report their claims to Company H.Q., who would judge if the evidence justified the award of a hit, entitling the sniper to make a notch on his rifle-butt. Prizes were to be awarded by the C.O., the first to be won by the man scoring ten verified hits. 'A' Company, commanded by Major Denny, were first off the mark and 'C' soon followed suit; by the 20th March they had registered seven kills between them.

Enemy shelling was a daily occurrence, and on the 19th an attack by the Seaforth drew heavy defensive fire on the wadis, resulting in the wounding of the Signal Officer, Capt. Clark and four men at Battalion H.Q. 'C' Company lost C.S.M. Day and three stretcher-bearers killed, and its Second-in-Command, Capt. Large, wounded.

After ten days the Battalion had a short spell out of the line, spent in the 'B' Echelon area, where, though regularly bombed and under artillery fire, they were able to rest and have an occasional bathe in the sea.

On the night of the 25th they relieved the 1st York and Lancaster Regt. in the 'Lobster Claw' sector, to the left of 'Starfish' and even more unpleasant. The enemy localities were, in places, only thirty to fifty yards away and there was continual harassing fire from rifle-grenades and light mortars. On the other hand, the forward posts got no shelling, owing to the proximity of the enemy.

In the line opposite the 58th were troops of the German 4th Parachute Division, who showed themselves to be tough but clean fighters. One of the features of the fighting in this sector was the strict observance of the

Geneva Convention. When there was a casualty to be taken to the rear, the Red Cross flag was raised and the stretcher-bearers were able to cross the open ground to the ambulance jeep without being fired on; the enemy used a half-track vehicle, which drove close up to the forward localities. As soon as the stretcher-bearers had re-entered their slit-trenches firing recommenced.

The 58th were now very short of officers and the war diary for the 25th mentions that the three rifle companies had only eight between them. This state of affairs soon became worse, for as a result of very heavy mortar concentrations on the 27th and 28th, Capt. Adams, Second-in-Command of 'B,' and the C.S.M., Beard, were mortally wounded; Major Wallis, commanding 'C,' was wounded, and Capt. Whitaker, who went from the Support Company in his place, was hit within twenty-four hours. Between the 10th and the 31st the 58th had 56 casualties, including several N.C.O.s, many of them Platoon Commanders who could ill be spared.

The days passed in mortaring and being mortared, in wiring, minelaying and patrolling. Four times did 'B' Company try to search a small, battered building lying a short distance from their forward platoon in the hope of capturing the enemy who were believed to lie up in it, but without success. Finally it was shelled in daylight by an American tank-destroyer; twelve Germans were bolted from it, the Company accounting for two of them.

After five days out of the line the 58th were back in the 'Lobster Claw' on the 12th April, relieving the Cameronians. They were still very much below strength, two companies only could muster their full complement of platoons, 'C' had but a platoon and a half.

This tour brought more heavy bombardments, and nightly grenade battles were another feature. One night an enemy patrol leader, a sergeant-major of the 11th Parachute Regt., was killed on the wire of the locality held by Lieut. Newby's platoon of 'A' Company.

A week later the Battalion was relieved for another short rest, and reinforcements arrived which brought the three companies nearly up to strength; but of the six officers who now joined, five were casualties within a month.

At this time Brig. Ward left the Brigade to take command of the 4th Division, and was succeeded by Brig. Finlinson.

*In 'The Fortress,' 27th April–6th May*

The Battalion's next task was to hold 'The Fortress,' regarded as the nastiest sector of the whole Anzio beachhead and important because, if lost, it would have afforded the enemy a means of approach into the heart of it.

Broadly speaking, the sector consisted of a wadi, roughly T-shaped, up to forty feet in depth, from two to five yards wide at the bottom, and with sides that were nearly vertical. Just above the junction of the strokes of the T was the forward company locality—the 'Fortress' proper—in which the foremost platoon, limited in strength to two sections and a skeleton Platoon H.Q. because of lack of space, was over a ridge, out of sight and of fire support by the other platoons and surrounded on three sides by the German positions. Slightly in rear of this and to the left was another platoon, from whose locality the ground rose gently for about thirty yards to a hedgerow on the crest, behind which were enemy posts. From this platoon another, farther to the right, was hidden from view by the undulating, scrub-covered ground. Near the head of the vertical stroke of the T was a second company; farther to the rear and astride it, two reserve companies; and farther back still, Battalion H.Q.

The forward posts consisted of slit-trenches, each holding two or three men, half open and half provided with log and sandbag head-cover. No movement was possible by day in the forward platoons, as they were under direct enemy observation. Headquarters were in chambers dug into the sides of the wadi. The approach to the whole position was by a jeep track and then across about six hundred yards of open country.

The 58th took over 'The Fortress' on the night of the 27th/28th April. 'C' (Major Kitchin) was the forward company, with two platoons of 'B' under his command; behind it was one platoon of 'B' and 'B' Company's H.Q. (Capt. Hamer), acting as rear H.Q. to the forward force. 'A' (Major Denny) was in reserve to the west of the wadi and 'A' Company of the 6th Seaforth, under command of the 58th, on the other side of it.

As was natural, with the enemy at such close quarters, the grenade and the light mortar were the most useful weapons and, on their first day in the line, 'C' Company fought a duel with them against the enemy. Snipers were active too, 'A' Company losing three men; Lieut. Meager, commanding the forward No. 14 Platoon, was mortally wounded whilst helping a signaller to repair a cable.

After two nights sections of Lieut. Cowan's No. 13 Platoon relieved those of No. 14. At 1000 hours on the next day, the 30th, the sound of heavy mortar and l.m.g. fire was heard coming from the platoon's area. Artillery and mortars opened fire on their S.O.S. tasks and for some time the situation was obscure, as touch could not be gained with the platoon either by line or by wireless.

During this time the left forward platoon had engaged movement along the hedgerow to their front. Before long Germans could be seen forming up and several began to crawl forward through a gap in the hedge. Accurate defensive fire was brought down, causing confusion and casualties among the enemy, but some managed to infiltrate between the left and the centre platoons.

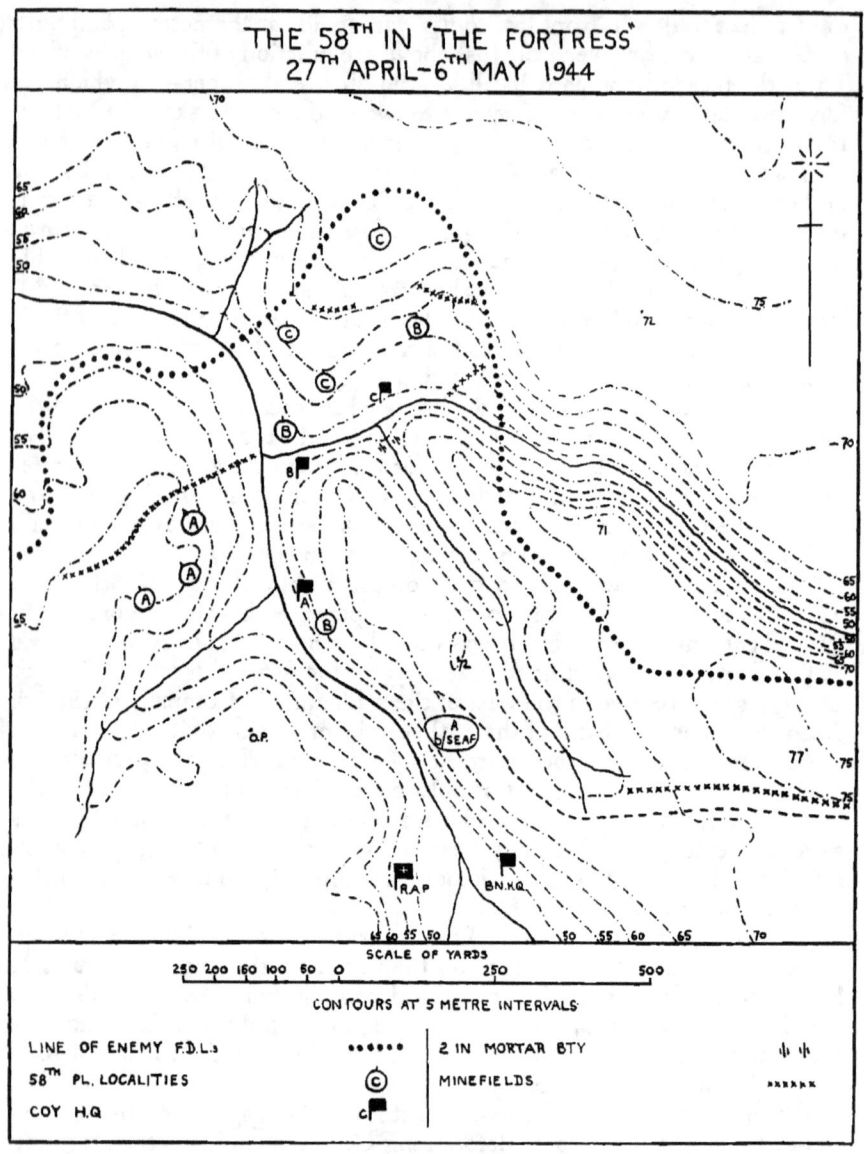

Meanwhile Brens could still be heard firing from the forward platoon locality, but it was discovered that it was the enemy who were firing them, to give the impression that the platoon was still holding out, whereas in fact it had been overrun.

Under cover of a smoke-screen on both flanks No. 11 platoon now put in a counter-attack. Firing as they advanced they threw back the enemy who had infiltrated and reached the ridge ahead; but the Germans had been quick to consolidate the locality they had captured and the attempt to drive them out failed, though not until every man of No. 11 Platoon had been either killed or wounded.

By 1315 hours the situation had been stabilised; the forward locality had been lost, but the attempt to penetrate the main position of the company had been defeated.

Half an hour later a second counter-attack was launched by a platoon of the Seaforth, under cover of a box-barrage. By now there was little chance of achieving surprise, especially as the enemy had observation right into the British positions, and, as the platoon formed up and advanced, it came under intense fire from every type of weapon. By 1400 hours this effort had failed, but a further attempt at infiltration by the enemy from the left was beaten back. A third counter-attack at 1555 hours by one platoon of 'C' and one of the Seaforth was also unsuccessful.

That night the C.O.s of the 58th and the Seaforth planned another attempt. This time, the attack by two platoons of a second company of the Seaforth which had been brought up was to be done in two waves with full artillery and mortar support.

By midnight on the 30th the platoons had moved up the wadi, past 'C' Company H.Q. and had reached their forming-up place. A quarter of an hour later the barrage opened. The enemy replied with l.m.g. fire, and then, as there was no news of the progress of the attack, the barrage was prolonged for an extra ten minutes. At 0040 hours small-arms fire could still be heard, but no news came back as all lines had been cut by heavy mortar fire. At 0200 hours the Seaforth Company Commander reported that the Commander of his second platoon had returned with fourteen men; they had reached the enemy positions but had then been driven back. There was no sign of the leading platoon. At 0330 hours patrols of the 58th came back reporting that the Germans were still very much on the alert, and that there was no trace of the missing Seaforth platoon. It was then decided to abandon further counter-attacks for the time being, and the survivors of the Seaforth company returned to their reserve area.

The rest of the day passed fairly quietly until after nightfall, when the enemy made another bid to penetrate 'C' Company's area from the left; this was defeated. Meanwhile, detailed plans were being made for yet another counter-attack to regain the lost ground.

It was not possible to attack on a frontage of more than one platoon, since wire obstacles and mines made a bottle-neck of the only approach to the objective. The plan was for a party of men of 'B' Company, under Sgt. Organ, to move to this bottle-neck, and protect the assaulting troops as they passed through the wire. The assault was to be carried out by two parties from 'A' Company, each fifteen strong, under the command of Sgt. Heward and Sgt. Hayman. There was to be complete silence until the last possible moment, and only when surprise had been lost and 'A' Company called for it was a box-barrage to come down round the assaulting parties. A model of the area was prepared and all the men were briefed in detail.

At 2300 hours on the 2nd May the parties moved to their forming-up place. All was quiet. Zero had been fixed for 2330 hours, and five minutes after that time there was still complete silence, except for the sound of sawing coming from the area of the objective.

At 0005 hours 'A' Company made a call for fire support urgently. The leading wave of the attack had almost reached the enemy position, apparently unobserved, when it was checked by the wire which the enemy was putting out and was met with a shower of hand-grenades and heavy mortar and small-arms fire. Pressing on, most of the two parties got into the position, where they engaged in fierce hand-to-hand fighting against stubborn opposition.

At 0011 hours a reserve party, composed of men from 'B' and 'C' Companies, under Sgt. Underwood, moved up and went into the attack, guided by Sgt. Hayman. It was hoped that this reinforcement would swing the balance in favour of the 58th, but after passing the forming-up place the party ran into the enemy's mortar barrage and smoke, which limited visibility to a few yards, and could make little progress. There was still no news of Sgt. Heward's party, but the R. Scots Fusiliers reported that red tracer could be seen coming from the area. As this, fired vertically, was the success signal, it raised hopes that some of the attackers had got into the enemy position and were holding it, but at 0050 hours there was still no news. By now the whole Battalion area was under heavy mortar fire.

Ten minutes later O.C. 'A' Company reported that another reserve party, under Sgt. McTighe, had gone in but had failed to reach the enemy's position as a body; the few men who had done so had all been killed or wounded, mostly by the enemy's mortar barrage. He asked for all fire, except counter-battery and counter-mortar, to be stopped, as a patrol was being sent out to try to discover what had happened to Sgt. Heward's party. The air was now so thick with smoke that it was almost impossible to move about the wadis.

The C.O. left the final decision on the action to be taken to the Company Commander on the spot. He decided to leave the remainder of Sgt. McTighe's party in 'C' Company's area, to collect casualties and to send out reconnoitring patrols to clear up the situation. Throughout the night the wounded were evacuated from the forward area, and after day broke the stretcher-bearers of the three companies were able to bring in the bodies of all the dead, under cover of the Red Cross flag. There were no missing. Of the attacking force of approximately fifty men, nine, including Sgt. McTighe, had been killed, and thirty-seven, including the other three sergeants, wounded.

Their great gallantry earned the D.C.M. for Sgts. Heward, Organ and Underwood, and the M.M. for Pte. McDonald, a signaller.

No words can more fittingly describe this action than those of the Commander of the battery supporting the 58th: 'The attack was as near success as some very gallant men could possibly make it.' Equally could the 58th praise the 156th Field Regt. R.A. who, as always, had given them magnificent support.

Any further attempt to recapture the position now could only have led to unnecessary loss of lives, so it was decided to seal off the area by minefields and wire, and this was done by the Pioneer Platoon commanded by Capt. Roberts. After another forty-eight hours, spent in the usual grenade and mortar battles, the Battalion was relieved by the 1st K.O.Y.L.I. and went back to the rear area for a short rest, badly needed by all, and not the least by the men of 'B' Echelon who, though not directly engaged in the battles, had supplied the nightly parties—averaging 150 strong and including clerks, cooks and M.T. fitters—for carrying up supplies and ammunition, usually through heavy fire. The cool determination of Sgt. Dodman, who led these parties, was rewarded by the Military Medal.

*Retrospect of 'The Fortress'*

In the Anzio beachhead the 58th took part in the hardest fighting they had yet experienced in Italy, and of all the sectors in which they were engaged it is 'The Fortress' which will remain the longest in the memory of those who were there. In the words of the Divisional Commander: 'It has become a name which we shall remember with admiration for those who held it.'[3]

Their eight days in 'The Fortress' had cost the 58th one hundred and eighteen casualties; of these, one officer and nineteen other ranks had been killed, six officers and ninety-two other ranks wounded. This was a heavy price to pay, but had they, or any of the other battalions which held this sector in turn, failed in their duty the whole beachhead might have fallen.

Every member of the Battalion played his part in this gallant defence, but special mention is due to the N.C.O.s, the signallers and the medical staff.

Reference has already been made to the acute shortage of officers in the Battalion at this period, and as a result practically every platoon was commanded by an N.C.O., often a comparatively junior one. Their responsibility was heavy, for platoons were, as a rule, isolated from each other and from Company H.Q. It was often out of the question for anyone to visit them in daylight and enemy bombardments made line communication a very uncertain quantity. The strain on these N.C.O.s was great, but they stood it as true 'Steelbacks.'

The signallers, too, had a hard task. Enemy mortar fire played havoc with line-communications, and as it was hardly ever possible to repair the old line the signallers usually had to run out a new one, across the open and under heavy fire. It was a great tribute to their work that only rarely were Company H.Q.s out of touch for any length of time.

Last, but not least, praise is due to the Medical Officer, Capt. Lamb, wounded when his R.A.P. received a direct hit, the Padre, the Rev. Jones-Evans, and the stretcher-bearers, who carried out their difficult and dangerous task with the utmost devotion to duty and to their comrades.

*Crossing of the Moletta, 9th–31st May*

On the night of the 9th/10th May, the 58th relieved the 2nd Wiltshire Regt. in the coastal sector of the beachhead. Deservedly they had a quiet time. The enemy were on the other side of the River Moletta and were some five hundred yards away, except at one point in front of an advanced post of 'A' Company where they were considerably closer. Apart from shelling, the days passed uneventfully, until the 23rd.

At dawn on that day the 1st Green Howards, supported by tanks, made a local attack on the small village of Americano, north of the river, 'A' Company of the 58th forming a firm base for the attack.

The Green Howards made good progress until they were checked by heavy fire and an unexpected minefield. At 1130 hours 'A' Company was ordered to send two platoons across the river, to come under command of the attacking battalion. That evening the enemy, taking advantage of a smoke-screen which had been laid to cover the withdrawal of the tanks, launched a counter-attack in force; 'A' Company's positions came under heavy mortar fire and by 2100 hours the enemy had managed to infiltrate between the leading companies of the Green Howards.

At this stage the 58th were told that the Seaforth Highlanders were side-stepping to the left and would take over a part of their front. The relief began at 2200 hours, and there followed a succession of orders and counter-orders from Brigade H.Q., caused, it seems, by a fear that the enemy might attempt to press forward across the river in the sand-dunes near the coast. Eventually the C.O. issued orders which had the effect of concentrating 'B' and 'C' Companies on the left and to the rear of 'A.'

In the meantime the situation north of the Moletta had deteriorated, and the Green Howards were ordered to withdraw behind the river at dawn on the 24th. Throughout the night the two forward platoons of 'A' Company had been engaged in close fighting among the sand-dunes and had inflicted severe casualties on the enemy. No. 9 Platoon, commanded by Sgt. Bell, D.C.M., was given the task of covering the final withdrawal across the Moletta. Meeting the enemy in fierce hand-to-hand fighting, the platoon held off a numerically superior force, and, having done its duty, withdrew. 'A' Company had lost several men killed and wounded by mines or by shelling.

Many had displayed great gallantry in this action, and this was recognised by the award of the Military Cross to Major Denny, and of the Military Medal to Sgt. Bell, D.C.M., Cpl. Wilford and Cpl. Doubleday.

On the 25th the Anzio beachhead was relieved, contact having been made with the troops which had at last broken through at Cassino and penetrated up the Liri valley. The 58th were withdrawn into rest, leaving 'B' Company behind on the Moletta, to be relieved on the next day by a squadron of the Reconnaissance Regt.

It was now thought that the enemy were about to withdraw, and the R. Scots Fusiliers were ordered to cross the Moletta and attack the high ground beyond it. The 58th moved into position behind them, ready to pass through and continue the advance, but the Fusiliers' attack was stopped by heavy fire on the plain north of the river, and on the night of the 29th the Battalion took over their positions. 'C' Company immediately got two platoons across the Moletta, and, patrols reporting the country ahead clear of enemy, the whole Battalion followed and established themselves in a wood called Boscoe Wood. This consisted of small scrub, and was completely overlooked by the enemy, receiving much attention from their artillery, especially when the anti-tank guns and m.m.g.s were being moved up to it by carriers in daylight. It was not long before the enemy made a vicious attack on a company of the Seaforth to the left of the 58th, practically wiping it out, and thereafter a fighting patrol under Lieut. Hamer took the precaution of patrolling the area nightly, to guard against surprise.

*Advance to Rome, 1st–5th June*

Before long, the 58th patrols found signs that the Germans might be withdrawing from the River Torto, the obstacle next ahead. A considerable obstacle it was, too, seventy feet wide and with sheer banks; added to this there were large fields of wooden anti-tank mines, difficult to locate, and the enemy were still holding Camp Jemini which commanded the approaches to the river.

During the night of the 3rd/4th June, patrols found a footbridge across the river. 'C' Company crossed, unopposed, by 0900 hours, followed three hours later by 'B,' and the R.E. were able to start the construction of a Bailey bridge. At midday the two companies were relieved and the Battalion concentrated, with T.C.V.s ready to move them towards Rome.

The C.O. had earlier been warned to make plans for the operation of a mobile column, which was to advance as soon as the Torto had been bridged and secure crossings over the River Tiber. There were two possible routes—the coastal road and another farther inland—and it was not till noon on the 4th that he heard that he was to use the former.

With the 5th Reconnaissance Regt. ahead, and a Field Battery, a troop of anti-tank guns, a platoon of m.m.g.s and a detachment of Divisional Signals under command, the column started, the rifle companies moving off at 1330 hours. The race to Rome had begun, but though the whole area was clear of Germans demolitions caused some delay, especially at a canal south of the Tiber where a diversion had to be made over which jeeps and trailers could pass. Eventually, by midnight the 58th came to a halt just short of the Tiber; patrols from 'A' and 'B' Companies reached the banks of that river, and one, under Lieut. Henderson, succeeded in crossing it.

By now other troops had entered Rome and the city had fallen, a few hours before the Allied troops began to land on the beaches of Normandy. The 58th were relieved by troops of the 88th U.S. Division and moved back to a wooded area twenty-five miles to the south of Rome.

*The 58th leave Italy*

Within a few days the Battalion heard that they were to leave Italy and go to the Middle East for a period of rest and training. A fortnight was spent near Naples, where stores and vehicles were handed in, and they then moved by train to Taranto. On the 5th July they sailed eastwards, under the command of Major Purton, Lieut.-Col. Stephenson having left them a few days before to take up an appointment in England. His energetic leadership had encouraged the 58th to great achievements during his nine months in command.

The 58th were to see Italy again but, though they did not yet know this, they were not destined to take any further part in the fighting there. The 5th Division had earned a great reputation since the landing at Reggio, and towards this the Battalion had contributed its full share in the course of ten months of bitter fighting in which an enemy, determined to hold on to every inch of ground and helped by mountainous country and an inhospitable climate, had been slowly but surely driven back.

*In the Middle East, July 1944–February 1945*

A crowded but uneventful voyage landed the 58th at Port Said on the 9th July. A short stay at Helwan was followed by a move to the Gaza area, and here Lieut.-Col. Ballard returned to them and resumed command.

After a few days spent in cleaning up, individual training began; full advantage was taken of the ranges near the camp, and as a result, and as was only proper, the Battalion won the Brigade Rifle Meeting.

Early in August they were on the move again, this time to near Baalbek in Syria, and here they came to rest for some weeks.

Their strength had fallen to as low a figure as 22 officers and 546 other ranks on the 7th May when they had come out of 'The Fortress,' but by early August it had risen to over 40 officers and between 950 and 1,000 other ranks. Many of the reinforcements came from disbanded Anti-Aircraft units of the Royal Artillery, compulsorily transferred to the Infantry; naturally they required considerable training to accustom themselves to their new arm of the Service, but they soon became acclimatised.

At the end of September the Battalion marched to the coast, covering the seventy-eight miles in a week. The men were fit, there were only a few cases of sore feet, and on the 3rd October they marched past General Sir Bernard Paget, C.-in-C. of the M.E.F., in fine style. After a day's rest on the coast they went on by M.T. to Pardes Hannah, near Haifa, where exercises involving long cross-country marches were a feature of the training.

Early in November the prospect of a return to Italy seemed to loom ahead.[4] A C.O.'s memorandum dated the 8th opened with the words: 'We are going to finish the party off'; went on to say that advanced parties would leave in a fortnight and that, as the Battalion would probably be operating in a mountainous country, the few weeks left would be used to train with this in mind; and closed with a reminder of the need for security in dealing with this information, which was to be imparted to all ranks.

However, time went on without a sign of a move, and early in December, when the Battalion had returned from a four-day exercise in the mountains of Syria, it became known that they would spend Christmas in Palestine.

On the 10th January Lieut.-Col. Ballard addressed the whole Battalion, warned them that they would really move soon and gave them to understand, in guarded terms, that their destination would indeed be Italy. The advanced party left and preparations for the move went ahead, interrupted but slightly by a draw for vacancies for a month's leave in England; the ten fortunate individuals departed on the 29th.

*Return to Italy, 8th February–5th March*

Early in February the 58th moved to Haifa, embarked in H.M.T. *Champollion* and sailed at midnight on the 10th. Disembarking at Taranto on the 15th they went by train to Bari, where they settled down in the Rest Centre and awaited developments.

They did not have long to wait. Two days later the Divisional Commander, Major-General Hull, addressed the Brigade and, from what he said, it was evident that the 5th Division was destined for North-west Europe. The advanced party, which had gone to Perugia some miles to the north of Rome and had taken over stores and vehicles from a unit of another division, now had to hand most of them back and move to Salerno, where it was joined by the rest of the Battalion on the 1st March.

*Departure from Italy, 6th March*

Here the 58th spent five days in tents on the beach, confined to camp except for exercise in the form of hill-climbing. Then on the 6th they embarked at Naples in the *Ville d'Oran*. Early the next morning the ship sailed and that afternoon the C.O. made it generally known to the Battalion that they were now under the command of Field-Marshal Montgomery, and were about to join his 21st Army Group.[5]

77th Division

# CHAPTER XV

## THE 5th BATTALION IN ITALY AND EGYPT, SEPTEMBER 1943–SEPTEMBER 1944

Landing and Initial Moves, 21st–29th September 1943—Advance on Termoli, 30th September–3rd October—Capture of Termoli, 3rd–10th October—Across the Trigno, 23rd October–4th November—Advance to the Sangro, 5th–19th November—Fighting on the Sangro, 21st November–2nd December—In the Central Sector, 3rd December 1943–31st January 1944—Back to the Coastal Sector, 1st–11th February—To the Cassino Front, 12th February–21st March—In the Line at Cassino, 24th March–25th April—Resting at Capua, 26th April–13th May—Assault on the Gustav Line, 14th–24th May—Advance to Rome, 18th May–8th June—Northwards from Rome, 9th–15th June—Capture of Montegabbione, 16th–17th June—Fighting round Lake Trasimeno, 18th June–2nd July—Journey to Egypt, 4th–22nd July—In Egypt, 23rd July–9th September (*see* Map facing p. 184)

### *Landing and Initial Moves, 21st–29th September 1943*

THE voyage of the 5th Battalion from Sicily passed off without incident, and after disembarking at Taranto on the morning of the 22nd September and spending two days there while they waited for the arrival of the vehicles, which had to come by road from Reggio, they entrained for Giovinazzo, west of Bari.[1]

After a few days of company training and route-marching, on the 29th they marched on with the rest of the 11th Brigade by the coastal road to Trani.

On that day Brig. R. K. Arbuthnott, took over command of the Brigade from Brig. Cass. He was to be the Battalion's guide and friend through many actions during the next fifteen months.

### *Advance on Termoli, 30th September–3rd October*

Next day the 5th were ordered forward and moved eighty miles by bus to just north of San Severo, where they came under command of the 4th Armoured Brigade. Early on the following day this Brigade received orders to advance and capture the town of Serracapriola. The plan was for the attack to be led by tanks of the 3rd County of London Yeomanry and the 56th Recce Regt., with the infantry following up the road in support in T.C.V.s.

The Battalion began to move at 0800 hours, at which time the tanks could be seen moving steadily forward without opposition. Before long, however, a bridge collapsed under the weight of the leading T.C.V., so they debussed and continued on foot along a valley leading to the town, in which heavy explosions had been occurring. The tanks engaged enemy guns and vehicles, and the 5th entered the town, receiving an hysterical welcome from the inhabitants, who had dealt with the small groups of Germans left behind when the main body had withdrawn during the morning.

Next day the advance continued, with the high ground between Portocannone and San Martino as the objective. Progress was again slow, owing to cratered roads and blown bridges, and eventually the Battalion had to debus and move across country to the objective, which was reached without meeting any opposition. Before leaving that morning the transport had twice been attacked by fighter-bombers; the second attack had been dealt with by Spitfires. Portocannone and San Martino were found to have been evacuated by the enemy and were occupied by platoons on the morning of the 3rd October.

*Capture of Termoli, 3rd–10th October*

The plan for the next operation, the capture of Termoli, was that the 11th Brigade was to advance by the coastal road from the south. Meanwhile a Commando Brigade was to be held in readiness at Bari to land and secure the town. When this had been done, the 36th and 38th Brigades of the 78th Division were to be ferried round by sea from Barletta.

In the early morning of the 3rd machine-gun fire could be heard at Termoli and landing-craft could be seen approaching the coast. The Commandos took the town after a short, sharp engagement and that night the 36th Brigade landed and took over the sector from them.

On the 5th October, after two days spent in patrolling and mine-lifting, the 5th Battalion were placed under the command of the 36th Brigade, separated from it by the River Biferno across which the R.E. had not yet built bridges. It was not long before the enemy launched a determined counter-attack with infantry and tanks along the ridge held by the Brigade, which had to give some ground, but in the end the attack was beaten off with the aid of two squadrons of tanks which managed to get across the river. Meanwhile all that the 5th could do was to watch the battle from their hill positions and make anti-tank arrangements.

After a short tour in the line near Larino, where their patrols were active across the Biferno, the Battalion were relieved on the 19th by the 1st Royal Fusiliers of the 8th Indian Division, and went back for a few days' rest in the reserve area at San Martino. Here they were able to welcome Lieut. Rickett, who had been wounded and taken prisoner while on patrol in Tunisia nearly a year before, and had escaped from a prisoners-of-war camp.

*Across the Trigno, 23rd October–4th November*

On the 23rd the Battalion moved forward again. The 38th Brigade was in front, south of the Trigno, with the 11th Brigade in rear; the 5th covered the extreme right at Pettacciato, in positions giving good observation over the river valley at its mouth, and guarding against possible enemy approach between the coast and the railway. The 38th Brigade then forced a crossing of the Trigno, and on the 3rd November the 36th Brigade went through and captured San Salvo.

On the evening of the 2nd the 5th Battalion concentrated closer to the Trigno. Next day they were ordered to move up and prepare for a night attack on the hills north of San Salvo. They marched off at 2030 hours, crossed the river where it was shallow, and reached a point south of the village at 0230 hours on the 4th, after a four-and-a-half-mile march. They then learnt that the 36th Brigade attack had not been completely successful and that the enemy still held positions covering the northern exits from the village, so the night attack was cancelled and the Battalion occupied defensive positions.

In the course of the morning they received orders to advance and capture a road junction on the high ground about four miles north of San Salvo. The start-line was to be secured by a preliminary attack by the 6th R. West Kent Regt., and at 1130 hours the 5th moved across country by a covered approach in rear of that battalion. At one stage the open country and enemy shelling forced them to open out into extended order.

The attack was to be carried out under cover of a barrage by 'C,' 'A' and 'B' Companies, from right to left, with two squadrons of the 44th R. Tank Regt. in support.

The advance began at 1400 hours, the tanks supplementing the barrage by giving covering fire over the heads of the infantry. Much of the ground was wooded and afforded cover, but in the early stages the advance was down a forward slope under the observation of the enemy. As soon as they crossed the start-line companies came under heavy mortar and machine-gun fire which caused some casualties, but they pushed on and by 1700 hours had gained all their objectives. 'A' Company took eighteen prisoners belonging to the 64th and 79th Panzer Grenadier Regts.

Some of the 6-pounder anti-tank guns were at once sent up to cover the position, and while moving on to the ridge encountered a group of enemy occupying a house. The Germans were engaged by the guns, but the crews were forced by heavy and accurate light-automatic fire to withdraw, after their Commander had been seriously wounded. 'A' Company then attacked and drove the enemy out, taking two more prisoners, but in the interval the enemy had driven away two of the guns and four portees.

During the day the Battalion had lost two warrant-officers and six men killed, and two officers (Capt. Emmerton and Capt. Coullie) and twenty-five other ranks wounded.

### Advance to the Sangro, 5th–19th November

On the next day the 1st East Surrey Regt. advanced and captured Cupello. While they were doing this the 5th Battalion took a short-cut across country and secured some high ground; then, as there was no opposition, the C.O. decided to push on, supported by the 50th R. Tank Regt., and take the town of Monteodorisio. This was accomplished without difficulty, the enemy having quitted the town, and the troops received the usual tumultuous welcome from the inhabitants.

On these cross-country moves it was the rule for 3-inch mortars and machine-guns to be man-handled; furthermore, up to forty-eight hours' rations, in addition to the emergency ration, were carried on the man, since the normal delivery of supplies was so often delayed until roads had been cleared of mines and other obstructions.

The 4th Armoured Brigade now led the advance to the River Osento, with the 11th Brigade following. At dawn on the morning of the 8th 'A' Company crossed the river, climbed a steep slope and established themselves in a position in which the rest of the Battalion soon joined them; meanwhile the other two battalions of the Brigade were occupying high ground to the right. The Brigade was on the right of the divisional front, and there was a wide gap of mountainous country between it and the 8th Indian Division, which was advancing on Atessa, captured on the 12th.

Heavy rain now fell, preventing the cooks' 15-cwt. trucks from getting forward. They had to be unloaded in rear and their contents taken forward by a ferry service of jeeps, the only vehicles which could negotiate the tracks.

On the 15th the Battalion marched in heavy rain to Casalbordino, south of the River Sangro, where most of them were in billets. They made the most of their few days there to rest and clean up, and a mobile cinema provided entertainment.

During the past six months the 5th had received drafts of men of many different Regiments. An entry in the war diary now records:

> During the recent actions men who have joined from other units came through the ordeals extremely well, and have shown themselves to be keen and enthusiastic soldiers. One notable instance was when a former member of the East Yorkshire Regt., asked to what Regiment he belonged, promptly and proudly replied 'The Northamptonshire Regiment, of course.'

A good augury for the future.

## Fighting on the Sangro, 21st November–2nd December

In this sector of the front, the German 'Winter Line' consisted of strong positions on the high ground north of the River Sangro. By the middle of November the 78th Division had established a small bridgehead across the river not far from its mouth.

On the morning of the 21st November the 5th Battalion moved up to the river, preparatory to relieving the 5th Buffs after dark. This battalion had one company over the river and the remainder on the high ground to the south of it. Before the relief began there were sounds of heavy firing across the river and during the next few hours remnants of the Buffs company, mostly wounded men, managed to reach the south bank. The relief was cancelled and the 5th were ordered to attack, recapture the ridge from which the company had been driven, and establish a stronger bridgehead.

Throughout the day the German positions were dealt with by bomber aircraft and artillery, while the Battalion made preparations for the attack.

At 1730 hours they moved off along the tracks to the river fording-places which had been reconnoitred. Guides of the Buffs were stationed along the route, but the move was a difficult one, since the night was dark and the troops were heavily loaded as they had to be self-contained for forty-eight hours, possibly more. However, the fording-places were reached successfully and the troops began to cross the river, about forty yards wide and three to four feet deep, with a fast-running current. To keep in touch and to prevent themselves from being swept away by the stream, each man held on to the belt of the man in front of him; so, thoroughly wet, they reached the far bank of the river, where there was a short halt while platoons checked their numbers and weapons.

So far the advance had been unobserved by the enemy, but the objectives were still 1,200 yards away, on the lower slopes of the strongly defended ridge which was another half-mile farther on. Presently the advance started, across boggy country intersected by deep, wide ditches. 'D' Company was on the right, 'B,' followed by Battalion Tactical H.Q., in the centre and 'C' on the left; 'A' occupied a position to the right rear, guarding 'D' from flank attack.

About five hundred yards from the objectives, enemy machine-guns opened up. At first the fire passed overhead, but before long 'B' Company and Battalion H.Q. were heavily engaged by small-arms and grenade fire from a small hill. An attack on this by two platoons of 'B' just failed to succeed, owing to darkness and the strength of the defences. Meanwhile 'D' and 'C' had got on without receiving too much attention from the enemy, but in their turn were held up for similar reasons.

It was evident that the attack could not succeed without further preparation, so the Battalion dug in at the foot of the ridge and remained there during the 22nd. They were comparatively undisturbed, the enemy making no attempt to counter-attack but devoting all their attention to the Bailey bridge which the R.E. had rapidly thrown across the river during the night.

Throughout the day the enemy positions were kept under continuous artillery and air bombardment, and at 1800 hours, after a ten-minute concentration by the whole of the Corps artillery, the 5th attacked again. The shelling had done its work and the objectives were reached without difficulty; inspection of the German positions showed that it was not surprising that the earlier attack had not been successful, for the trenches were deep and well camouflaged, and the wire and minefields were strong.

Rain fell incessantly on the 23rd. It was bitterly cold and everyone was soaked to the skin and, after forty-eight hours without hot food or drink, the arrival of a carrying party, provided by 'S' and H.Q. Companies and bearing hot food, was extremely welcome. These parties had a hard journey, for the ground was a quagmire in which the men sank almost to their knees in liquid mud.

During the next day patrols failed to make contact with the enemy, and that night the 5th were relieved by the East Surrey Regt. and went back across the river into reserve.

The right flank of the British positions was somewhat vulnerable to counter-attack. Accordingly, on the night of the 26th/27th, 'A' Company made a landing from 'dukws' on the coast to the north of the mouth of the Sangro and occupied some buildings a short distance inland, suffering a few casualties from mines in the process. On the following night one of their patrols had a clash with the enemy, in which Lieut. Morgan was killed.

On the morning of the 28th 'A's leading platoon was attacked by a strong force of enemy under cover of a heavy bombardment. Though practically surrounded, the platoon managed to withdraw to the Company H.Q. area as arranged, incurring only two casualties. Mortar and artillery fire then forced the enemy to retire.

In the final stages of the fighting on the Sangro 'D' Company had relieved 'A' with the task of distracting the enemy's attention from the main attack. This drew heavy fire on to them, but the ruse succeeded; the enemy were surrounded by tanks appearing from an unexpected direction, and 'D' Company received the thanks of the Brigade Commander for the way in which they had carried out their task. The Sangro bridgehead was now securely held, the enemy having had a terrific battering and lost over eight hundred prisoners and large numbers of guns, mortars and machine-guns.

On the 1st December the Battalion moved up to the ridge between

Fossacesia and the sea. It was a scene of great desolation, for every house had been damaged, and all trees had been cut down by the enemy and used, in conjunction with mines and booby-traps, to block roads and tracks. On the next day the 5th were relieved by the 1/48th Highlanders of the 2nd Canadian Brigade, and marched back to Casalbordino.

*In the Central Sector, 3rd December 1943–31st January 1944*

After little more than twelve hours at Casalbordino the 5th embussed late on the 3rd and, after an all-night journey, reached billets in villages in the Campobasso area the next afternoon. Here they were to rest, reorganise and train for a month, but within a week they were warned to prepare to move again to Montenero, near Forli di Sangro.

The new sector, in which the Battalion relieved the 2nd Wiltshire Regt. of the 5th Division on the 10th December, lay in the centre of the Allied line across Italy. The mountains varied in height from 3,000 to 5,000 feet, and the rugged country made it necessary to use mules for the conveyance of supplies and ammunition to the forward companies; two platoons, each of seventy-five mules, were attached to the Battalion, and the daily journey by a difficult mountain track took upwards of an hour. Wounded had to be carried on stretchers, each manned by eight bearers, over three miles of treacherous country.

The forward positions and some ten miles of the road to the rear were under enemy observation from the high ground on the other side of the river; consequently, it was the practice for the forward companies to withdraw to the reverse slopes during the daytime, leaving out observation posts only, and to reoccupy their prepared positions at dusk. There was much patrol activity on both sides, and owing to the wide front enemy patrols were able at times to penetrate between the company localities.

For the second year in succession the Battalion had to spend Christmas in the line, but in spite of all difficulties the occasion was celebrated in the proper style; the rear companies had their dinners at Montenero on the 25th, and the forward ones followed suit two days later, after they had been relieved.

At the end of December the 38th Brigade took over the sector and the 5th went to Campobasso, a fine town where there were many amenities in the way of cinemas, theatres and clubs. Their enjoyment of these received a slight setback on 5th January, when they were warned to despatch advanced parties to a new area. However, heavy snow made the roads almost impassable and they had a brief respite, but eventually the advanced parties left on the 7th. The Battalion was now nearly up to strength, having received a large draft just before Christmas. They had more officers than they had had since Sicily, these including four from the South African Forces.

Four days later the 5th moved nearer to the front, to billets in Pescolanciano and neighbouring villages. Training, especially that of the officers in the operation of the No. 22 wireless set, was carried out, and on the 18th the Battalion was inspected by the new Divisional Commander, Major-General C. F. Keightley, who had succeeded Major-General Evelegh.

On the 21st the Battalion moved by M.T. to relieve the unit in the forward area, their journey considerably hampered by snowdrifts.

The area was an extensive one and included three villages—Capracotta, San Pietro and Vastogirardi—each garrisoned by one or more companies. For purposes of communication each garrison was provided with a No. 22 set, which could be used for direct communication with Brigade or Divisional H.Q. if necessary.

The first two of these villages stood at opposite ends of a ridge which sloped gently down to the River Sangro, some three miles away; a similar ridge, north of the river, was held by the enemy, so no-man's-land was about seven miles wide and formed a happy hunting-ground for patrols. Some of their activities deserve mention.

On the 23rd January one from 'A' Company left Capracotta, crossed the river dryshod on mules provided by local farmers, and established a base near Ateleta. Next morning Lieut. Beynon, with two Carabinieri and an interpreter, carried out a reconnaissance to the north-west, and that night a fighting patrol found the village of Petrelli unoccupied; lying up there during the 25th they captured two Germans who walked into the place and returned to Ateleta that evening; the whole patrol went back to Capracotta on the following day.

This success was followed quickly by others. On the 27th Lieut. Terry of 'A' led a patrol of twenty men to Ateleta and registered a bag of one German killed, one wounded and one taken prisoner. On the 28th a 'B' Company patrol, under Lieut. Jewell, went out with the mission of securing identifications, to return on the morning of the 31st or as soon as they had completed their task. On the final day they wirelessed for permission to stay out for another day. This was granted and on the 1st February, the day after the Battalion had been relieved and gone back to Agnone, they returned to San Pietro with two Germans whom they had ambushed on a track.

*Back to the Coastal Sector, 1st–11th February*

In a very short time the 5th were on the road again, moving to Lanciano, north of the Sangro in the coastal sector. Here they came under command of the 5th Canadian Armoured Division, their rôle being to counter-attack should the Canadians be driven from the ridge which they were holding in front of Orsogna.

Lanciano, some seven miles behind the front, was comparatively undamaged, and plenty of entertainment was provided for the troops. Life was not entirely without its excitements, for on one afternoon the Signal Platoon, playing a game of football in a field in front of the town and oblivious of the fact that they were in full view of the distant enemy, was forced to disperse when shells began to burst round the ground.

*To the Cassino Front, 12th February–21st March*

The Battalion's next moves took them a long way. As a preliminary, an eight hours' run in T.C.V.s on the 12th took them the 111 miles to Castelnuovo, near Foggia. Three days later they were on the road again. Weather conditions were bad, with rain, snow and sleet alternating; consequently, they expected a difficult journey and they were not wrong.

The first check came at Lucera, where the column was held up for two hours; then, as the road climbed into the mountains, conditions became worse, and finally a halt was called that evening in the mountain town of Motta. Here billets were quickly found and within ten minutes not a man was to be seen. A comfortable night was spent in front of large fires.

When daylight came on the 16th it revealed what Field-Marshal Montgomery, when an instructor at the Staff College, would have called 'a scene of intense military confusion.' Vehicles were lying about in every direction, as Scammel tractors did their best to get them on the road again. Their efforts were successful, and on went the column, through Vinchiaturo and Isernia, until at 2200 hours it reached Alife, on the secondary road to Capua. The journey was marred by an accident to a T.C.V. carrying machine-gunners of 'S' Company, the vehicle going down a steep bank into a field and overturning, resulting in the death of one man and injuries to others.

It was thought that Alife was the final destination, but on reaching it orders were received to go to Capua, thirty miles farther on. However, the night was pitch dark and by now the convoy was very scattered, so the C.O. went ahead with a few vehicles, leaving the remainder to follow when they had reassembled. Throughout the night trucks continued to arrive at the collecting-point; the journey was resumed at dawn on the 17th and by noon the Battalion had concentrated in the village of San Secondino, north of Capua.

The whole of the 78th Division had been transferred to this area, and it was not long before an address by the Divisional Commander revealed that rumours as to the future had been correct. The Division was to prepare for the operations which were to break through into the Liri valley and open the road to Rome; so the 5th settled down to training, with special emphasis on mine-clearance and night operations.

Highway Six, the easternmost of the two main roads to Rome, passed through Cassino, and parallel to and south of it ran a main railway line.

With their usual thoroughness, the Germans had torn up the track and demolished the embankments at bridges and culverts. However, the embankment had been repaired and the former railway had been converted into a road, known as the 'Speedy Express,' used for the supply of the troops dug in on the banks of the River Rapido and opposite Cassino station. On the 23rd February the Battalion moved forward to the Mignano area, through continuous rain and hail-storms, and found themselves accommodated alongside 'Speedy Express.' It was a dismal area and, as but little tentage was available, shelter had to be improvised. One company in particular excavated homes for themselves underneath the arches of an old aqueduct; in the course of time the open sides were boarded up, stoves were installed and even electric light, and finally life beneath the arches was so comfortable that the company declined to move into tents when these became available.

Within a few days details of the forthcoming operations were made known; reconnaissances were carried out and the use of assault-boats was practised.

At this point the anchors of the Gustav Line were the Monastery of Cassino,[2] overlooking the town, and, north of it, the great 5,000-foot Monte Cairo. Forward of these ran the River Rapido, a deep, fast-flowing stream, with steep banks.

The plan of operations was for the Monastery, and its garrison, to be demolished by intensive air-bombing. The New Zealand Division was then to advance through Cassino and along the western bank of the Rapido; as soon as it had succeeded in doing this, the 2nd Lancashire Fusiliers and the 5th Battalion were to force a crossing of the river near San Angelo and clear up any remaining enemy resistance.

Throughout February and into March rain came down with monotonous regularity. The offensive had to be postponed, and the 5th were used to provide working-parties to assist the R.E. in the construction of passable tracks to the river. Then, suddenly, on the 15th March the Battalion was paraded for an address by the C.O. D-Day had arrived, the bombing was to start that morning, and the 5th were to get ready to move forward.

Soon the first wave of bombers appeared, flying high above Cassino, and those watching saw the bombs go down and heard them crash upon the target. Wave followed wave of aircraft for three hours, and at 1830 hours, just before the bombing ceased, the Battalion advanced to the assembly area. Arrived there, companies carried out last-minute preparations and then proceeded to watch and wait.

In the days which followed there came a succession of rumours of success and failure. The battle for Cassino went on furiously, and a few thousand yards away the 5th Battalion continued to wait for the time to come for them to play their part. They were little worried, except for occasional shelling, one shell hitting 'B' Company's headquarters and seriously wounding the Commander, Major Rosser of the South African Forces. Eventually, after a week of desperate fighting, the attack was abandoned; the New Zealand and Indian Divisions had fought with the utmost gallantry, but weather conditions, the obstacles created by the intensive bombing and the determined resistance of the German 1st Parachute Division, prevented them from gaining more than a few yards of churned-up ground. The 5th returned from their assembly area to Mignano, and the 78th Division got ready to relieve the 4th Indian in the mountains between the Monastery and Monte Cairo.

*In the Line at Cassino, 24th March–25th April*

In a blinding snowstorm on the morning of the 25th March eighty T.C.V.s took the Battalion northwards along Highway Six, thence by a road bulldozed through the olive-groves, till in the evening they debussed at the village of San Michele, had dinner and loaded kit on to pack-mules. Then they marched on across the Rapido, past the landmarks of the Plasterers' Arms and Cairo village, and up along a tortuous mountain track. Thoroughly exhausted and full of strange oaths, they reached their assembly area, the 'Bowl,' just before midnight.

The 'Bowl' was aptly named, consisting as it did of a deep, steep-sided valley in the midst of a range of hills. Though by no means immune from enemy shelling, it provided a certain amount of cover, and was the site of Battalion H.Q. and large dumps of supplies and ammunition for the forward troops.

After dark on the next day companies set out at two-hourly intervals to relieve those of two battalions of the 4th Indian Division which had been in the line for thirty-five days. In spite of the pitch-darkness the relief was completed smoothly, and after a heavy morning mist had lifted companies were able to take stock of their positions.

The ground was bare and rocky and the posts were in stone-built sangars, of the type familiar to any who had been in Waziristan. The position lay on a false crest, well concealed from the enemy; in front was a ridge, held by the Germans; to the left and beyond another ridge ran Highway Six; across a valley and farther to the left lay the Monastery, and to the right rear Monte Cairo overlooked the whole area.

Holding the dominating positions they did and only ninety yards distant from the British forward posts, the Germans could employ snipers with good effect; any movement in the sangars by daylight was certain to attract their attention. No cooking was possible, except such as could be done on tommy cookers, but a hot meal, prepared in a derelict farmhouse which also contained the R.A.P., was taken up nightly.

The comfort and morale of the forward troops depended much upon the working of the administrative machine, and despite the difficulties they were well served. Supplies, drawn daily at Mignano, arrived at San Michele at 0800 hours. There, in a clear space among the pine-trees, the ration-party, mainly composed of the Anti-Tank Platoon, laid them out in mule loads, mail in metal boxes to keep it dry, water in tins. The experience the Battalion had had in North Africa was invaluable.

During the afternoon jeeps and trailers were loaded with rations and ammunition for the Mortar Platoon, which was located at the foot of the hills occupied by the companies, and in the evening the mules of the Pack Transport Company, with Indian, Arab or Italian muleteers, arrived for loading. Then, jeeps leading, the fifty or so mules following, the convoy would start on its three-and-a-half-hour journey, down into the valley and then up to Cairo village, where they divided, the jeeps going on by the road, the mules across the fields. The road was a favourite target for the enemy's artillery, especially at the Plasterers' Arms corner, which the jeeps would often take on two wheels in the hope of getting round it before the next shell arrived. The mules' cross-country journey was shorter and safer, though on one night nearly forty were lost by shell-fire. On reaching the foot of the hills the mule convoy began to climb the steep track to the 'Bowl.' Sure-footed as they were they usually negotiated this without difficulty, but on one occasion Major Wasey, the Second-in-Command, tripped over a rope stretched across the track; feeling his way along it in one direction he encountered the head of a mule, in the other an Indian striving to pull the animal up. At the 'Bowl' the mules were off-loaded and returned to San Michele as fast as their drivers could drive them, while the rations were divided for issue to companies.[3]

The evacuation of casualties was made easier by the respect accorded by both sides to the Red Cross flag; even so it was difficult enough, the stretchers having to be carried down the hill from the forward posts by relays of men stationed at two-hundred-yard intervals. Despite this, casualties were back in hospital, nearly a hundred miles away, within twenty-four hours.

The 5th worked hard on improving the defences, and apart from sniping there was little activity, except on one occasion. Before dark on the evening of the 1st April two parties of enemy advanced on 'D' Company's positions; fire was withheld until they were only fifty yards from the sangars, then the company opened up on them and, after hurling grenades, the Germans bolted for cover in a small gully between the lines. This was engaged by the 2-inch mortars and the enemy withdrew. Thereafter they showed no desire to come to close quarters.

After a week in the position a system of reliefs by companies of the East Surrey Regt. was arranged, command of the sector alternating between the two C.O.s according to which had the greater number of companies forward. This enabled the troops to have a periodical spell of four days in the 'Bowl.' Their rest there was only slightly disturbed by shelling and by the occasional crashing of large stones from the top of the sides to the bottom, the latter causing more amusement than alarm.

Three weeks after the 5th had gone into the line advanced parties from the 1st Polish Battalion of the 3rd Carpathian Division arrived, and on the 25th April, in spite of language difficulties, this battalion took over the sector. The 5th marched out, embussed, and reached their camp near Capua in pouring rain the following morning.

*Resting at Capua, 26th April–13th May*

The site of the camp at Capua was a pleasant one. Situated as it was in green fields, in a valley leading down to the River Volturno, with hills covered with mauve flowers rising on either side, few places could have made the 5th forget the bleakness of the 'Bowl' more quickly than this. True, to begin with the camp was a sea of mud, but in two days the sun appeared and shone for the next fortnight. With the warmer weather khaki-drill was taken into wear, but the sun also brought out the mosquitoes, so all precautions against malaria, such as the daily dose of mepacrine and the wearing of long trousers after sundown, had to be taken.

After a week's rest the Battalion went into serious training and a fortnight later they were ready for the next battle.

*Assault on the Gustav Line, 14th–24th May*

On the 11th May the assault on the Gustav Line by the Fifth and Eighth Armies began, and, back at Capua, the 5th Battalion could hear the rumble of the bombardment and see the flashes of the guns reflected in the sky.

On the morning of the 14th May the Battalion moved in the brigade column up Highway Six towards Cassino. After a night in a concentration area, south of the Rapido, they made their way down the slopes to the Bailey bridge which spanned the river. A short distance to the right lay Monastery Hill, but the Germans' observation from it was completely blinded by a smoke-screen; so effective had this been that the enemy had not observed the launching of the initial attack by three divisions.

North of the river the Battalion halted under cover, at a point where tanks were lying behind the crest of the hill. The Cassino–Pignataro road was the start-line for their attack, due to begin at 1600 hours, but lack of information led Lieut.-Col. Connolly to decide to take no risks and he issued orders for a preliminary attack against it.

The Tank Squadron Commander could not be found, so at 1315 hours the attack started without armoured support, with 'B' Company on the right and 'D' on the left. Both companies came under considerable fire, but just after 1330 hours the leading platoon of 'D' reached the objective, where it had to deal with heavy fire from medium machine-guns. Later on it located a self-propelled gun shooting at the tanks which had by now come up. L/Cpl. Allkin and Pte. McGill went forward with a Piat and fired two shots, both of which hit the gun and forced the crew to abandon it.

At 1530 hours 'D' Company suffered one of those accidents which are inevitable in the confusion of battle. They were lined up in a ditch beside the road, waiting for the main attack to start, when they were dive-bombed by six Kittyhawks and soon afterwards friendly artillery fire killed two men of Company H.Q. and destroyed the wireless set.

The attack had to be postponed and 'A' and 'C' Companies were ordered up between the other two. Just short of the road 'C' were held up by heavy mortar fire and sniping, but a final assault took the position from the well-entrenched enemy. Unfortunately, when consolidating, Major Cook was killed by a sniper. He had commanded 'C' Company with much gallantry throughout the campaigns in North Africa, Sicily and Italy, and was a great loss to the Battalion. He was buried by the side of the road where he fell, with two of his men beside him.

Meanwhile, 'B' Company had been active. Seeing a party of Germans moving towards a feature which dominated his platoon position, Lieut. Hillian charged, firing a Bren gun from his hip, and killed or wounded five of them, after which he led his men forward and occupied the feature. He was awarded the Military Cross for his bravery and initiative.

During the day's fighting the Battalion took 126 prisoners, 84 of these falling to 'C' Company alone. This was a large number from an area which was, supposedly, but the starting-place for a bigger attack, and fully justified the C.O.'s foresight in mounting an organised attack upon it.

All companies experienced heavy mortar fire throughout the night, but this did not prevent 'C' from moving across the road and capturing a house which had been causing trouble. During this attack two of the Company were taken prisoner by a German patrol; the Germans, however, marched them off by a road which led to 'D' Company's position, and a standing patrol of that Company proceeded to capture the patrol and release the prisoners, who rejoined their fellows none the worse for their experience.

During the 16th the Battalion endured the heaviest shelling and mortaring that they had ever experienced; a large shell landing near main Battalion H.Q. brought down the walls of their house and caused considerable casualties among the Signallers. Many of the wireless sets were destroyed and the H.Q. was temporarily out of action, but replacements were soon provided by Brigade.

In the course of the day 'A' and 'D' Companies made a further advance, taking 49 prisoners at a cost of 3 killed and 14 wounded. Then, in the evening, heavy concentrations of mortar fire came down on all the Company areas, when the enemy put in a strong counter-attack against a battalion

## THE 5th BATTALION IN ITALY AND EGYPT, 1943-1944

of the Black Watch on the right. This was beaten off with the assistance of tanks. By nightfall the situation had become normal, and the 1st East Surrey Regt. and the 2nd Lancashire Fusiliers went through, continuing the advance towards Highway Six, north of Cassino.

By now the Monastery had been captured by the Polish Division, and the sight of it, no longer shrouded in smoke, produced a feeling of great pride of achievement. The Gustav Line had been broken and it now remained to break the Adolf Hitler Line, which here ran through the town of Aquino.

*Advance to Rome, 18th May–8th June*

On the evening of the 18th the 5th Battalion moved forward to a concentration area and got ready. By the 23rd May the 1st Canadian Division, helped by intense artillery support, had broken through the line, and at daybreak on the 25th the Battalion started to advance. 'D' Company rode forward on tanks, the remainder marching, but the first tank which tried to cross the River Aquino broke the bridge, so all continued the advance on foot. Moving eastwards to Aquino they found the area completely blasted by the artillery bombardment, and the only Germans found, except for the many dead, were two who were captured by the Padre; one of these was literally caught with his trousers down, for he was riding a motor-cycle minus those articles of dress.

By 1100 hours all companies were on their objectives. Orders then came for the Battalion to prepare to form a bridgehead over the River Malfa, and they moved forward; but the plan was cancelled and a concentration area was occupied for the night. German aircraft were unpleasantly active, but the 5th suffered no casualties from their bombs; the few casualties during the day had all been from mines and booby-traps.

The River Malfa was duly crossed without any opposition, and the Battalion settled down for a short rest in some of the deserted houses until the time came to advance up Highway Six on the 30th.

By this time there was no organised resistance on the part of the enemy; they were only able to fight rear-guard actions, and occasionally a pocket of resistance had to be cleared up. On the 2nd June the Battalion left the main road, moving towards Alatri, which was being cleared by the 36th Brigade. In order to secure the left flank the 5th moved up a valley, at the head of which they consolidated for the night. Here R.S.M. Surkitt fell in with some Italian partisans and went off with them and his batman to stalk a German 88-mm. gun about three miles away. Having lobbed a grenade among the crew, the party dispersed; the gun was later found abandoned, and the partisans, meeting the R.S.M. next day, announced that several of the Germans had been killed or wounded before they blew up their gun and fled.

A few days' rest in the village of Fumone, where the Intelligence Section undertook the interrogation of Fascists suspected of collaboration with the Germans, ended on the evening of the 8th June, when the 5th resumed their journey up the Highway. After passing through Valmontone there was much disappointment when their convoy took to a by-pass road which would have avoided Rome, disappointment which was understandable in any case, and even more in the case of a battalion of the 78th Division which had fought, sailed and marched its way there from Algiers. However, they were diverted from the by-pass through the centre of the city, and were able to get a fleeting view of it in the bright moonlight.

*Northwards from Rome, 9th–15th June*

After their all-night journey the 5th arrived at Rignano at first light on the 9th, and spent most of the day in sleep. The Allied armies were now in full cry after the retreating Germans, and the limitations of roads, not improved by wet weather, had strained the administrative services; consequently the Battalion enjoyed another two days' rest, during which inter-company football matches were played.

One of the platoons had an interesting task, that of guarding Field-Marshal Kesselring's former H.Q. This place consisted of a labyrinth of tunnels stretching into the solid rock of a mountain-side and giving access to air-conditioned offices, living-rooms and kitchens.

Just after midnight on the 13th the Battalion set off northwards in convoy. It was an inky black night and twice the column took the wrong turning, on one occasion completing a circle, with the head overtaking the tail. After passing through Viterbo they halted for the night, and were rejoined by Sgt. Thirkill, who, captured in December, had escaped when the train in which prisoners were travelling had been bombed by the R.A.F. and had lived with Italian peasants for over five months. Moving on again on the next evening the column passed Orvieto and moved into the hills north of the River Chiani. There they were greeted by some air-bursts right over the Battalion, a reminder that they were once more in contact with the enemy.

*Capture of Montegabbione, 16th–17th June*

At 0400 hours on the 16th June the Battalion set off by march route along the road through the village of Ficulle. 'A' Company rode on the tanks of the Wiltshire Yeomanry, who were in support, and followed with the carriers after a blown bridge had been cleared. Later in the morning they had to halt on the road and were attacked by four Allied fighter-bombers which, seeing a traffic-block, must have assumed that it belonged to the enemy. Although they went up and down the column for twenty minutes they caused only four minor casualties, though a later report to

Division from Allied Air Force H.Q. announced that an enemy column had been routed.

Meanwhile 'A' Company, leading the main body of the Battalion, had encountered machine-gun and sniper fire from Montegabbione, east of the road, and at 1330 hours an attack was staged, supported by tanks, artillery and mortars of the Brigade Support Group.

'C' Company advanced directly on the town, with 'A' on the left, supported by tanks. The country was close and a covered approach was available for the first two thousand yards, but this also made co-operation with the tanks difficult. On emerging from the close country some casualties were caused by small-arms fire from Montegabbione, which overlooked the area, but steady progress was made towards the hill upon which it stood.

A group of houses on the western edge of the town, on 'A' Company's front, seemed to be the key-point of the defence, and individual buildings were selected as platoon objectives. As soon as the barrage lifted, No. 8 Platoon, under Lieut. Terry, forced its way into the school, while No. 9 entered a large house farther to the right, engaging the enemy who fled from it.

Company H.Q. now joined the platoon in the school and immediately afterwards the building became the target for rifle and machine-gun fire coming from houses about forty yards away on the other side of the street. These houses were on a bank above the level of the school, consequently the enemy were able to shoot downwards into the narrow passages which ran along the front of the school on both floors. The narrowness of these passages made it impossible for the defenders to stand back from the windows, which had no shutters and were therefore vulnerable to grenade attack. Company H.Q. was set up in a large lecture-room on the ground floor, and there the wounded, both British and captured Germans, were tended; this was not made any the easier by the bursts of machine-gun fire which penetrated the barricaded front door and showered the occupants of the room with plaster as the bullets hit the walls.

The party was then joined by Major Crocker, Commander of 'S' Company, who was carrying out a reconnaissance, and from the back windows of the school the Padre, the Rev. Elworthy, was seen wandering about coolly with two stretcher-bearers, apparently oblivious of the enemy's mortar and machine-gun fire. His attention was attracted and he entered the school by a back window—the only safe, and certainly the most popular, means of entrance.

The enemy now made an attempt to reach the school under cover of smoke, obviously intending to lob grenades through the windows, but were checked by Bren and grenade fire and never succeeded in getting across the road.

Major Crocker then decided to return to Battalion H.Q. with a list of the Company's requirements. There was some debate as to the most satisfactory route, as bursts of fire were periodically sweeping the rear of the building. Eventually the Padre, who also wanted to return, volunteered to lead the way and, showing good judgment of ground, dropped from a window and made a dash for cover, quickly followed by Major Crocker in an interval between bursts of fire.

The shooting-match continued, and then, suddenly, the occupants of the school were amazed to see the decorative façades of the enemy-occupied houses crumbling under the intense fire of 75-mm. guns. Major Emmerton and his men could not understand the origin of this bombardment, which missed them yet hit the enemy positions with such accuracy, and it was some time before they discovered that they owed it to Major Crocker, who had directed the fire of the tank squadron in the valley far below.

Meanwhile, in No. 9 Platoon's area, Lieut. Pulleyn had led a party to attack an enemy post and had been badly wounded in both arms, but his platoon consolidated the building they had seized and linked up with 'C' Company, which had penetrated a short distance into the town.

No. 7 Platoon then moved round by the left and occupied a small house opposite the school, but before they could consolidate it they were engaged by a party of Germans firing at them from an upper verandah. To complicate things still further an incendiary grenade set fire to part of the house, so the Platoon Commander, between the devil and the deep blue sea, decided to vacate it. This was not easy, for the sole means of exit was a verandah, thirty feet from the ground, at the back of the house. The first man to leave descended at considerable speed by a drain-pipe and wrenched it down in the process, so the rest of the platoon had to jump; however, they got away successfully, having lost one man killed and one wounded in the building.

By nightfall 'A' Company were established in the eastern outskirts of the town, 'B' to the south and 'C' on the south-eastern edge. Eight Panzer Grenadiers had been taken prisoner and the Battalion had lost one officer, Lieut. Mattinson, and six other ranks killed, and four officers and forty-nine other ranks wounded or missing.

During the evening Lieut. Pearson of 'C' Company and his runner, Pte. Barnacle, stalked a self-propelled gun which had been seen holding up the tanks. They killed one of its crew and wounded two, and when the Company advanced into the town the next morning and occupied it—the enemy having withdrawn during the night—the gun was found abandoned. Moving in that afternoon, Battalion H.Q. were surprised by the surrender of two German Artillery officers and three men, escorted in their own car by one of the Regimental Police.

The Lancashire Fusiliers now passed through and continued the advance. The 5th stayed the night in the town which had been the scene of one of the most brisk actions they had fought.

### Fighting round Lake Trasimeno, 18th June–2nd July

Early the next morning, the 18th, the 5th embussed, and after passing through Piegaro, taken by the Lancashire Fusiliers, continued on foot, with a hill south of Panicale as their objective. 'C' Company, leading, were held up, and the approach of darkness and heavy rain forced them to dig in for the night.

At 0615 hours on the following morning the advance was resumed, 'B' Company under Major Wasey, with a troop of tanks, were detached and made a wide move round the right flank; the remainder advanced directly on Panicale, 'C' Company taking some prisoners and finding a number of abandoned machine-guns and much mortar ammunition on the way, and before noon the two forces met in Panicale, whence they watched a tank battle in progress on the plain ahead of them.

In the afternoon they pushed on towards the next village, Panicarola, with 'B' Company protecting the right flank. Heavy rain hampered movement and it was not until nightfall that contact was made with any enemy. The village was taken and the Battalion secured the line of a canal to the north of it. Here they remained for three days, while the 38th (Irish) Brigade continued the advance.

On the morning of the 24th the Battalion moved up the shore of Lake Trasimeno, giving right-flank protection to the advance of the 38th Brigade. The brunt of the fighting fell upon 'C' and 'D' Companies, which took thirty-eight prisoners at slight loss to themselves. After a further advance that night the 5th had more than twenty-four hours of heavy shelling and mortaring, until the front was taken over by the 36th Brigade and they were withdrawn on the evening of the 26th out of the shelled area.

A forward move to Piana on the 30th, over bad, dusty roads, was followed by an attack on the following day. After a heavy artillery concentration 'B' and 'C' Companies gained their objectives by 0030 hours on the 1st July. They then went on and occupied two villages without opposition, after which 'D' went through and established bases from which patrols were sent as far as the River Spina, which ran into the northern end of the lake.

This was the 5th Battalion's last action for some time to come. Some days earlier an advanced party had left for a destination which was unknown, but the information was that the Division was to be taken out for a rest. Early on the 2nd July the Battalion was relieved and went back to its old billets in Panicarola.[4,5]

They deserved a rest, after nine months of hard living and hard fighting. They also deserved their share of the congratulations which Lieut.-General

Sir Oliver Leese, Commander of the Eighth Army, who had paid them an informal visit on the 3rd July, had conveyed to the 78th Division after the fall of Rome.[6]

*Journey to Egypt, 4th–22nd July*

On the 4th July the Battalion embussed, travelled along the roads up which they had so recently fought, and arrived at Tivoli, a few miles east of Rome. Here they overhauled arms and equipment and checked stores and vehicles, which were handed over to another unit. There was time for sight-seeing in Rome, and representatives were included in a party of 4,000 members of the Division who were accorded an audience with the Pope.

Entraining on the 11th, their route took them past Cassino, along the 'Speedy Express,' now a railway once more, across Italy to the Adriatic coast and through Bari to near Taranto, where they went into a camp overlooking the harbour. The journey was marred by an accident at Roccasecca: some men jumped off the train at a halt, and there was an explosion in a German ammunition dump alongside, killing four and wounding eight, of whom one died later. The bodies of the dead, so unlucky to be killed in this way after all that they had gone through, were draped in Union Jacks and taken on to Caserta where they were buried.

On the 17th the Battalion embarked in the *Britannic*, together with the remainder of the Brigade and several other units, including an Indian Army battalion. The ship sailed the next day, and after a crowded but calm voyage reached Port Said on the 22nd.

*In Egypt, 23rd July–9th September*

After disembarking, the Battalion moved by road alongside the Suez Canal to a camp at Qassassin, on the banks of the Sweet Water Canal. Though a tented one the camp was excellently organised, and in spite of the heat life was enjoyable; the Battalion was allowed leave, in four parties, to Cairo and other health resorts, and enjoyed it in spite of lack of money aggravated by the extortionate prices charged by the Egyptians.

On the 11th August there was another move to Beni Yusef, near Cairo. The hutted camp here was situated on the fringe of the desert, among sand-hills from which the green valley of the Nile could be seen.

Here the 5th welcomed a draft of 13 officers and 250 men of the Royal Artillery, who had been manning anti-aircraft defences until the Luftwaffe was no longer a threat, when their units had been disbanded and they were used as much-needed reinforcements for the Infantry. This brought the Battalion up to strength in all respects, since within a few days of landing a complete issue of stores and vehicles had been made. Training now started, and in the course of it the Battalion was inspected

## THE 5th BATTALION IN ITALY AND EGYPT, 1943–1944

by General Sir Bernard Paget and Major-General D. C. Butterworth, who had taken over command of the 78th Division from Major-General Keightley, appointed to command the 5th Corps in Italy.

The Battalion's well-earned rest was nearly over. On the 28th August the first convoy of vehicles left for Port Said, and four days later only two trucks remained. These were usefully employed as a means of transport to the fleshpots of Cairo. Then, on the 9th September, the 5th embarked in the *Monarch of Bermuda* and sailed westwards.[7]

78th Division

# CHAPTER XVI

## THE 5th BATTALION IN ITALY, SEPTEMBER 1944–MAY 1945

Back to the Italian Front, 15th September–12th October—The Situation—Task of 78th Division—First Attack on Pt. 508, 13th–14th October—Second Attack, 14th–15th October—Third Attack, 15th October—Fighting round Monte Spaduro, 21st–29th October—Reorganisation of the Battalion—In the Spaduro Sector, 1st November 1944–13th February 1945—Rest and Training, 13th February–25th March—Start of the Offensive, 26th March–15th April—Battle of the Argenta Gap, 16th–19th April—The Final Stages, 20th April–2nd May—Conclusion (*see* Maps on pp. 230 and 235)

### Back to the Italian Front, 15th September–12th October

THE *Monarch of Bermuda* reached Taranto on the 15th September, and next day the 5th Battalion disembarked and went into the camp which they had left two months before. Ten days later they set off along the Adriatic coastal road, arriving at Fano after a tiring seventy-two-hour journey. A four days' rest here, and on the 3rd October they were on the road again to join the Fifth Army. An all-night drive took them first southwards, then through Perugia and past Lake Trasimeno, till they came to a halt at Figline, twenty miles south-east of Florence; thence they moved northwards by shorter stages till on the 12th they reached a point north of Castel del Rio, and heard the sound of the guns once more.[1]

### The Situation

The situation at this time was that the 38th Brigade had relieved part of the American 88th Division astride the Imola road. The Americans were preparing to drive a salient into the German lines towards Bologna, and were to attack the features of Gesso, Monte della Tombe and, ultimately, Monte Grande. The last-named, a massive slab of rock, resembled Monte Cassino in many respects.

To secure the American advance beyond Gesso it was imperative that their right flank should be cleared of the enemy; this involved the capture of the heights of Pieve di Gesso (Pt. 508) and Monte Spaduro (Pt. 396). The former was a rocky outcrop which reared up from a continuation of the Gesso ridge, the direct line of advance towards it ending in a cliff-like face. The Spaduro feature consisted of a long, razor-backed ridge, running parallel to the Tombe ridge in the direction of the River Sillaro. Between these two ridges was a valley, dotted with houses which were to play an important part as the action developed. The River Sillaro and the Castel San Pietro road ran across the funnel-like mouth of the valley, and beyond the road lay Monte Grande.

### Task of 78th Division

The task which lay before the 78th Division was summed up in an Order of the Day issued by the Divisional Commander:

> I wish every man in the Division to understand that the operation which is to start tonight (12th October) is one of the first importance.
>
> The Pieve feature (incl. Pt. 508) is one which the enemy is determined to hold. Its importance to him lies in the fact that, so long as he can hold it, the salient that the U.S. Corps are driving towards Bologna is bound to remain narrow and restricted, and their task of breaking into the plain so much more difficult.
>
> The task of the 78th Division is to break this corner-stone of the enemy's defence by capturing Monte Pieve and then moving on to Monte Spaduro. Owing to the nature of the country, once the attack has been launched, the result must rest largely with the regimental officer and soldier, especially of the infantry. Each one must be prepared to play his part to the utmost, employing every weapon to the full and all his courage and skill. Companies and Platoons must be prepared to operate by manœuvre by day as well as attack by night. Relentless pressure on the enemy (334 Division, whom you have already met and defeated at Lake Trasimeno) will bring about his defeat again.
>
> The 78th Division has a reputation second to none in the British Army. The U.S. Divisions on our flank rely upon us to play our part and will be watching us. We have the weapons, the skill and the courage to achieve success. Let us use them to the full.

### First Attack on Pt. 508, 13th–14th October

It fell to the lot of the 5th to be the first battalion to be committed against Pt. 508. On the evening of the 13th October they moved up to a valley behind the East Surrey Regt., who were holding a feature known descriptively as the 'Twin Tits.'

The general picture at this time was that the 351st U.S. Infantry Regiment had taken Gesso after extremely severe fighting, had exploited eastwards along the ridge to Pt. 462 and were pushing northwards towards Monte della Tombe.

The plan was for 'A' Company, under Major Emmerton, to take over from the Americans at Pt. 462 and to form a firm base there from which 'D' Company, under Major Hunt, were to capture Pt. 508. When this had been secured 'B,' with a squadron of tanks, were to swing to the right and take another feature, Pt. 473, 'C' were to be in reserve near Battalion H.Q. at the 'Twin Tits.'

The ground was dry and the weather favourable, but the advance was to be over open plough-land, affording little cover. The top of the ridge

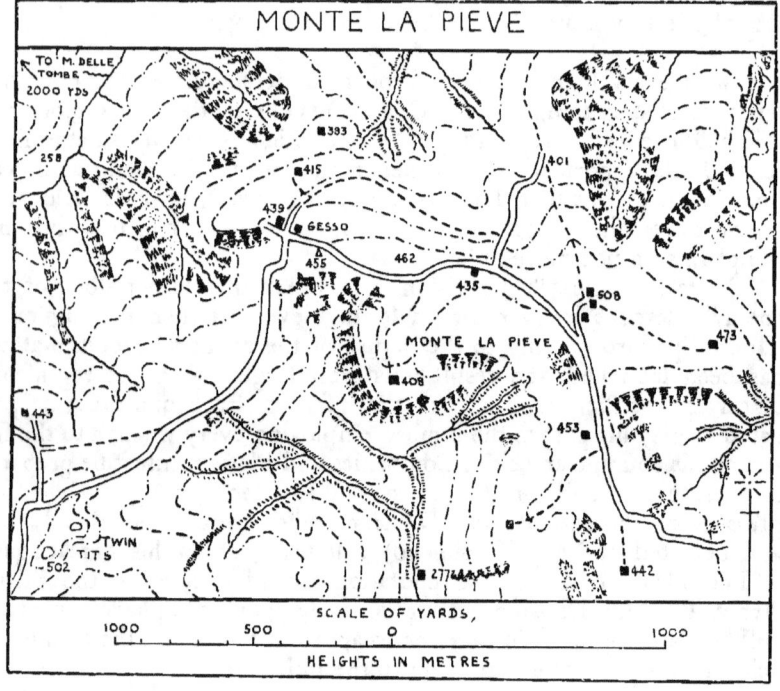

was very narrow and allowed little room for deployment, but the track which ran along it provided a useful means of communication. According to the information, the enemy were not holding the position in strength and were disorganised by the pressure applied by the Americans, but the 5th were to discover that this was, to say the least, optimistic.

On the night of the 13th 'A' Company moved up the track to Gesso. They had one officer and nine men wounded by anti-personnel mines beside the track, but completed the relief of 'K' Company of the 351st Regt. by 2100 hours, although the whole area was lit by the glare from a burning haystack.

After 0200 hours on the 14th there was a noticeable increase in the amount of hostile artillery and mortar fire on the Battalion area, but 'D' Company passed unscathed through this and by 0345 hours were dispersed near the track at Pt. 462. The night was clear, and from the start-line Pt. 508 looked like a massive ant-hill towering over the surrounding countryside. The attack was to go in from the north-west, the western and southern slopes of the hill being too steep to scale.

Zero hour was at 0420, and fifteen minutes before this the barrage opened, moving along the ridge towards the east. Unfortunately, just as the Company started to advance, shorts from the barrage began to fall among them, and at the same time there was heavy fire from the enemy's artillery, mortars, and machine-guns. In a short space of time six men were killed and twenty wounded, and four Bren guns and two wireless sets were put out of action; the combination of circumstances completely disorganised the start of the attack and, as it was rapidly getting light (the attack had been launched at a late hour in order to take advantage of the moonlight) it was clearly impossible to execute the original plan. 'A' Company were ordered to withdraw to the area behind Battalion H.Q. and 'B,' with two troops of tanks, were moved forward of Gesso.

*Second Attack, 14th–15th October*

During the morning plans were made for a fresh attack. 'C' Company were to tackle Pt. 508 and 'A' were to deal with Pt. 401, a hill to the left from which heavy mortar and machine-gun fire had interfered with 'D' Company's earlier attempt. 'B' supported by tanks were then to attack another feature, Pt. 453, and 'D' were to hold Pt. 462.

At 1930 hours, as a preliminary, a platoon of 'B' Company patrolled forward from Pt. 462 to Pt. 435, cleared the enemy from some houses which they must have occupied since 'D' Company's attack, and returned with two prisoners.

The attack started at 2300 hours, under cover of a barrage. Two platoons of 'A' advanced to within a hundred yards of their objective on Pt. 401, but were then held up by extremely heavy fire from posts in the building on the crest and from others on the flanks. They were unable to make any further progress, and had to withdraw to Pt. 462.

They had, however, carried out an important part of their task, since they had distracted the enemy's fire from 'C.' This Company had got a foothold on the lower slopes of Pt. 508 and adjoining ridges and, while the barrage rested on the summit, had been exchanging small-arms fire with the enemy. When they went on they met with stiff opposition from mortars and machine-guns, but by 0100 hours their forward elements had got to within eighty yards of the crest and were engaging the enemy posts with Bren fire and Piat bombs.

By now 'C' were running short of ammunition, so two platoons of 'B' were sent to reinforce them and to take up supplies. Before this, 'B' had had to deal with an enemy patrol which had approached Pt. 462 from the north of Gesso.

At 0200 hours on the 15th the situation was that two very depleted platoons were occupying the buildings on the crest of Pt. 508, having taken eleven prisoners; but they were only thirty-eight strong and very short of ammunition. A platoon of 'B' was fighting its way up the hill to get the much-needed ammunition to the gallant few on the summit, and other platoons were half-way up the feature and at the bottom of it. The enemy still clung to positions on the reverse slopes, and harassing fire tasks were carried out by the Artillery and mortars to keep them at arm's length while efforts were made to put the captured ground in a state of defence. But all this was unavailing, for soon after 0500 hours a determined counter-attack, in which portable flame-throwers were used, dislodged our troops who, now only twenty-five strong, were forced from the summit.

*Third Attack, 15th October*

Twenty minutes before the last men of 'B' Company had been forced off Pt. 508, the C.O. had ordered 'D' Company, with two troops of the 12th Canadian Tank Regt. in support, to relieve the pressure on them. There was only time for Major Hunt to have a hurried conference with the Tank Commander, at which it was arranged that the Shermans should move along the track—the only possible way—and get as far as they could up the slopes of Pt. 508, while the Company moved on their right.

At 0550 hours the troops began to advance from Gesso. The tanks attracted intense artillery fire as soon as the enemy saw them, and this and heavy machine-gun fire caused some delay at Pt. 462. However, the Company went on, down a bare forward slope and then up towards Pt. 508, the leading platoon reaching a small house at the foot where it was held up by intense and accurate fire; the second platoon tried to pass through towards its objective, but was in turn pinned down. It was now fully light, and there was much sniping from Pt. 401.

Meanwhile 'A' Company, which had been unable to get in touch with the tanks before starting, began to attack Pt. 401 under cover of smoke. At 0730 hours, soon after they had crossed their start-line, they ran into the fire of machine-guns shooting on fixed lines. No. 8 Platoon, led by Lieut. Hodgkiss, made a dash down the hill and across the open ground to the nearest cover at the foot, losing three men killed as they did so. This platoon was followed by another and by Company H.Q., which also suffered casualties. The Company eventually got to within sixty yards of the top of Pt. 401 in two parties—one under Major Hunt and Lieut. Hodgkiss, the other under the Second-in-Command, Capt. Ballam, and

C.S.M. Eassom—but by then only eighteen men could be counted; the wireless set had become detached from Company H.Q. during the advance and the situation could not be reported to Battalion H.Q.

While 'A' Company's attack had been going in, the tanks had been doing all that they could to help 'D.' Advancing down the track and firing continuously, they reached the position where the two leading platoons were held up; they then demolished a building, from which the enemy bolted, but engine trouble brought the leading tank to a standstill and, owing to the broken ground, the others in rear could not pass it. However, they continued to give covering fire. Communication with the tanks was not easy, for there had not been time to net with their wireless sets, so the only means of conveying requirements was by hammering on the turret until one of the crew put out his head to see what was wanted.

'D' Company were only two hundred yards from the objective, but the enemy's fire was taking a steady toll of efforts to advance; there were too few men left for any prospect of success, so the forward platoons were ordered to make for cover in the gullies to the south, while the remainder withdrew to Pt. 462 and Gesso.

Earlier in the morning 'A' Company of the 1st East Surrey Regt. had been placed under the command of the 5th Battalion. At 0730 they had been ordered to pass through 'D' and make another attack on Pt. 508, under a smoke-screen and with the support of tanks, but before they could get under way the attack was cancelled on orders from Brigade H.Q.

Three of the companies were now back in the area between Gesso and Pt. 435, weak from casualties and from the fact that a number of men could not rejoin from the positions they had reached until after dark. The position of 'A' could not be ascertained, owing to lack of wireless communication, but the tanks reported that they believed them to be on Pt. 401. Actually they were just short of the summit, and there they stayed, engaging the enemy at close range until nightfall, when they rejoined the rest of the Battalion, bringing their wounded with them.

Early on the 16th the East Surrey Regt. took over, and the 5th moved back for a few hours before relieving the Lancashire Fusiliers in a quiet sector on the ridge running south from 'Twin Tits.'

The Battalion had done its utmost to take Pt. 508, finally occupied on the 18th by another Brigade of the Division, and had suffered heavily in the process. The two days' fighting had cost them one officer, Lieut. Hillian, and ten other ranks killed, four officers and sixty-nine other ranks wounded, and twenty-one other ranks missing.

*Fighting round Monte Spaduro, 21st–29th October*

The Lancashire Fusiliers had by now taken over from the Americans positions on a feature which ran from the southern end of Monte della

Tombe ridge to Casa Oppio, a battered farmhouse lying south of the main valley. From here their patrols had probed the defences of Monte Spaduro and had found them held in strength.

The Americans were planning to capture Monte Grande, the last feature of importance before the Bologna plain could be reached and on the night of the 19th/20th they attacked and held it against fierce enemy counter-attacks. Simultaneously the 38th Brigade attacked Monte Spaduro, but was driven off it. A plan was now made for the 11th Brigade to take it, zero hour being fixed for 2230 hours on the 23rd October.

On the night of the 21st the 5th Battalion relieved the Lancashire Fusiliers on the eastern slopes of Monte della Tombe; here they were disposed very much in depth, with 'C' holding the forward position at Casa Oppio, at the end of a long ridge completely overlooked by the enemy a thousand yards away.

On the night of the relief 'C' Company had the task of capturing three houses ahead of their locality and on the lower slopes of Monte Spaduro; this they did efficiently, taking prisoners in the process, and as a result secured the start-line for the attack by the East Surrey Regt. and the Fusiliers. On the appointed night these two battalions formed up, climbed up the difficult slopes of Monte Spaduro and took their objectives and 125 prisoners.

To exploit this great success the 5th were ordered to capture Pt. 362, a hill on the ridge beyond Spaduro, so the 24th was a busy day for them, with reconnaissances to be made, routes and start-line to be taped and signal lines to be laid.

The general lie of the ground was very similar to that between Gesso and Pt. 508, except that the ridge along which the advance had to be made was even narrower; on either side of the ridge and east of Spaduro were two buildings, Casa Maletto and Casetta di Maletto, and these were dominated by Pt. 362 and another slightly lower feature, Pt. 336, or 'Barney's Knob,' lying to the north. The plan was for 'D' Company to capture the two buildings in succession, and for 'B' then to pass through them and take the two features, the whole attack to be supported by artillery and mortar concentrations.

The advance of the companies to the start-line was helped by 'artificial moonlight,' a device new to the 5th, by which a naturally dark night was lit by the reflection of searchlight beams directed on to the clouds. By 2245 hours 'D' had climbed Spaduro and were on the start-line; the other companies, following behind, suffered casualties from the enemy's fire which came down upon the reverse slopes.

When 'D' began to advance at 2300 hours they saw that their first objective, Casa Maletto, was ablaze, the glare of the flames lighting up the ridge and helping them to keep direction. They soon reached the house and cleared the area. Exploiting their success to the top of the feature they came under machine-gun fire which killed Lieut. Prinsloo, the commander of the leading platoon.

The position was consolidated and attempts were made to clear Casetta di Maletto, but an entrance could not be forced owing to fire from the buildings and from the ridge leading to Pt. 362, so the Company pulled back to a more suitable position from which they could engage the latter.

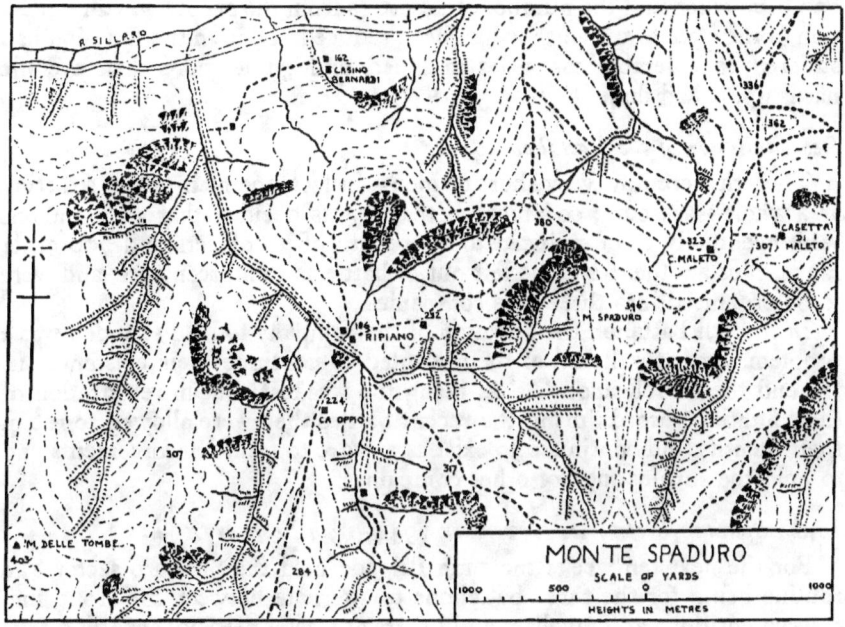

Meanwhile 'B,' moving below Casa Maletto, had attempted to take Pt. 362 from the left flank, but could not get near it because of the steepness of the climb and the enemy's accurate cross-fire. As it was clear that the attack could not succeed without the support of attacks on the flanks, and as the ground gained was untenable in daylight, a withdrawal was carried out before dawn to positions behind the Lancashire Fusiliers on Monte Spaduro. Casualties had been light, one officer and one other rank killed, nine other ranks wounded; six prisoners had been taken in addition to others who had passed back through the Fusiliers.

Torrential rain which started to fall on the 26th made any movement extremely difficult and put a stop to any further attempts to advance. Conditions became so bad that the Brigade war diary for the 31st mentions that the roads were rapidly disappearing and that, unless the Division moved forward, they would shortly find themselves to be a Division without an axis.

On the 19th November the Divisional Commander sent a message to all battalions, commending their achievements during the past three weeks. He drew attention to the capture of four important features, including Pt. 508 and Monte Spaduro, and to the fact that they would also have taken Pt. 362 had the weather not broken. Over four hundred prisoners had been taken and the number of deserters from the enemy was an indication of the state to which they had been reduced. Though the Division had suffered considerable casualties and had undergone more than average hardship, it had done its duty.

*Reorganisation of the Battalion*

The 5th were now very short of men—in fact, the man-power situation as a whole was acute; so much so that it was decided that all battalions were eventually to be reduced to a strength of 30 officers and 700 other ranks, plus another 40 to be left out of battle as reinforcements, and were to be organised into three rifle companies.

In the 5th Battalion the selection of the company to be disbanded was a problem, for naturally all of them wanted to continue their existence. In the end the lot fell upon 'A,' as being the weakest; but in recognition of their fighting record during the recent battles they were allowed to retain their identity and continued to exist as a cadre to train reinforcements and to hold the surplus men of other companies.

*In the Spaduro Sector, 1st November 1944–13th February 1945*

For the next ten weeks the 11th Brigade held the Spaduro sector, the routine being for the three battalions to alternate between the front line, reserve positions at Travellata and others at Castel del Rio, spending four days in each. By this arrangement none suffered unduly from the hardships of the weather, and at Castel del Rio there were amenities, such as a cinema and a canteen.

In the line all three companies were forward, but the positions were held only thinly during daylight and every man was able to spend three hours a day at some houses in rear, where hot meals and a drying-room awaited them.

Much time was spent in improving and maintaining the defences, the life of a trench being short owing to the damage caused by the weather; but the most important work was that carried out by the fighting patrols.

Two of these in particular deserve mention. On the night of the 13th/14th November a patrol led by Lieut. Hodgkiss followed a route carefully reconnoitred on the previous night. When they reached the area of a pond which lay between Casa Maletto and Pt. 362 they saw a party of eight Germans moving towards their trenches, oblivious of any danger. The patrol moved into position to deal with them, and, when the enemy were only fifteen yards away, opened fire. Every German was seen to fall and the patrol then withdrew.

A week later another patrol approached an enemy position which had been located previously. As Lieut. Kennedy and Pte. Mercer were crawling forward the sound of heavy breathing was heard from a trench. Drawing back the blanket which covered the trench they revealed two sleeping Germans, who resented being pulled out and started to shout for help. They had, therefore, to be shot, and though they could not be preserved for interrogation a paybook provided an identification of Intelligence value.

The effect of the aggressive patrolling by the 5th and the other battalions of the Brigade was twofold: it established complete supremacy over the ground in front of Monte Spaduro and it made the positions held by the Germans most unpopular, evidence of which was provided by the number of deserters who gave themselves up to the British.

This period saw two changes of Commanders. On the 19th December Lieut.-Col. Connolly had to relinquish command of the 5th on account of ill health. He had led the Battalion since the days of Sicily and, to quote the words of their history of the Italian Campaign, 'during 18 months of campaigning his cheerful personality was always a source of inspiration to every member of the Bn. It was due to his kind-hearted and sympathetic treatment of, and his absolute fairness to, every man that the Bn. was such a happy one.' An officer of the Buffs, he had in every way identified himself with the Northamptonshire Regiment, and in his farewell message to the 5th he expressed a hope that any who saw him in the future would go up and speak to him, even though he should be wearing different buttons and badges.

Major Wasey was in temporary command until the 29th December, when Lieut.-Col. Houchin, who had been commanding a battalion of another regiment since he had left the 58th, arrived and took over from him.

The other change of command occurred in November when Brig. Arbuthnott, who had guided the 11th Brigade through so many actions, was promoted to command of the 78th Division, and was succeeded by Brig. G. E. Thubron.

*Rest and Training, 13th February–25th March*

The last tour of the Battalion on Spaduro was a hard one; the snow was deep and it was bitterly cold, but winter-proof clothing gave protection from the weather and snow-camouflage suits from the enemy.

On the 13th February they handed over the positions, after a longer sojourn in the sector than in any other in Italy, and went back to a pleasant village near Florence. Ten days later they moved north-east, across the Apennines to Forlimpopoli and there, billeted in various villages, began vigorous training for the spring offensive. This included one novelty, training with 'Kangaroos'—Sherman tanks converted into armoured troop-carriers.

Here 'A' Company was re-formed, the decision to reduce battalions permanently to a three-company basis having apparently been rescinded.

*Start of the Offensive, 26th March–15th April*

On the 26th March the 5th moved forward to positions east of the River Senio. These were peculiar, for the section posts were dug into the flood-bank of the river, with the enemy in similar posts on the other side—at one point 'D' Company was only five yards from them—observation had to be made through periscopes or through holes dug in the bank. There was much grenade and mortar activity, the Intelligence Section fired propaganda leaflets into the enemy's lines and broadcasts were made through loud-speakers mounted behind the flood-bank. The whole of this front was extremely quiet and the 5th were unlucky to lose Lieut. Clarke, killed on the 30th.

After a week in this sector the Battalion moved to Russi and took over defences from a battalion of the Italian 22nd Regt. of the Cremona Group. In this position the Battalion lost the last officer they were to have killed in action, Lieut. Bennett, who lost his life whilst on patrol on the 8th April.

Here, on the 9th, as waves of aircraft passed overhead on their way to bomb the area west of Lugo, the C.O. addressed every member of the Battalion who could be spared, telling them of the Eighth Army offensive which was to begin that afternoon. Afterwards he presented eighteen Divisional Marks of Esteem to those to whom they had been awarded. These emblems, in the form of a black and gold bar to be worn on the shoulder below the divisional sign, had been instituted by the Divisional Commander to indicate that the wearer had performed gallant or meritorious service in the field. In no sense did they replace official honours and awards which emanated from H.M. the King, and if these were awarded, the Divisional Mark was no longer to be worn; they were tokens of the esteem in which the individual was held by his comrades in the Division, as one who had, by his conduct, proved himself to be a worthy wearer of the battle-axe sign. By the end of the campaign forty-one of the Battalion had received this award.

Attacking at 1930 hours on the 9th, the New Zealand Division crossed the Senio, the flame-throwing 'Wasps' of the 5th Battalion's Carrier Platoon giving support by burning out enemy positions on the far bank.

Next day 'B' Company moved forward against very slight opposition and, by last light, were established just short of Senio; the enemy had apparently abandoned their positions on the river bank as a result of the British attacks farther to the right, since patrols beyond the river did not make contact. In the four days which followed, the Battalion made a series of short moves and received many orders and counter-orders. Then, after crossing the River Reno on the 15th April, they were in position to start what was to be their final battle.

### Battle of the Argenta Gap, 16th–29th April

The German left rested on Argenta, a small town on Highway Sixteen. Through the western outskirts of the town ran a canal which joined the River Reno; some five miles to the east lay the shores of Lake Comacchio, a large expanse of water connected to the sea. Large areas of country had been flooded by the Germans, and Argenta, strongly protected by minefields, was the key to the only gap and had to be captured before the advance could proceed northwards.

The object of the initial attack on the 16th April was to clear the approaches to the town. It was carried out by 'D' Company moving up the line of the railway, 'B' along Highway Sixteen and 'A' by the canal bank, supported by tanks and flail-tanks to clear gaps through the minefields.

'D' Company's advance was delayed by their being mistaken by troops of another division for a strong German patrol. However, once the error had been rectified they went ahead and gained their objective without difficulty. 'B' encountered stiff opposition from snipers, and from two strongpoints which were dealt with by fighter-bombers, but in due course they linked up with 'D,' who then went on and by 1615 hours had reached the cemetery. There a halt was made for the night, patrols finding that the railway station was strongly held. Forty-three prisoners had been taken during the day, mostly belonging to the 42nd Jäger Division, and the Battalion had had only seven men wounded.

Shortly after noon on the next day 'D' Company, with tank support, began to probe the enemy's defences on the southern outskirts of the town, in order to distract attention from the east where the main attack was to be put in later. This succeeded, for after the cemetery had been entered through holes blown in the walls by a Piat, there was strong opposition.

At 1730 hours 'C' Company crossed their start-line for the right-flanking attack on the town. No. 14 Platoon, with a troop of Churchill tanks, led, followed by No. 13 Platoon, Company H.Q. and a troop of flame-throwing 'Crocodile' tanks; then No. 15 Platoon and a troop of 'Crocodiles,' with a third troop bringing up the rear.

No. 14 Platoon had taken the first objective, the station, by 1820 hours and formed a firm base there with the Churchills, while the other two platoons and the 'Crocodiles' cleared the eastern half of the town against slight opposition; they then advanced along Highway Sixteen, meeting with resistance from well-concealed riflemen with whom the 'Crocodiles' dealt quickly. By nightfall the Company had consolidated a road-junction north of the town, while the town itself was occupied by 'D' Company. Ten prisoners of the 29th Panzer Grenadier Division had been taken; the Battalion had lost two killed and seven wounded, and one carrier blown up by a mine.

At 0230 hours on the 18th the enemy delivered a counter-attack down Highway Sixteen with two tanks and about fifty infantry. One tank and some of the infantry penetrated as far as the road-junction, where they were stopped by the accurate fire of No. 13 Platoon; at first light one dead German was found three yards from their position. No. 14 Platoon was cut off from the rest of the Company, but held firm. An enemy tank commander was killed by a direct hit from a Piat, but ammunition ran short and the tank managed to get away, despite efforts to stop it with No. 36 grenades. Artillery fire dispersed the rest of the enemy's infantry, and the Company held the positions intact.

Argenta was now secured, as evidence of which the divisional dance-band played there that afternoon and there was a cinema performance in the evening. The 36th Brigade passed through to continue the advance.

### The Final Stages, 20th April–2nd May

On the 20th April 'D' Company were detached under command of the 4th Hussars of the 2nd Armoured Brigade in the town of Portomaggiore, where the 56th Recce Regt. had been held up by a strong pocket of enemy. After the Squadron Commander of the Hussars had become a casualty Major Rawlins took charge of the operation; by 1500 hours the town had been cleared, and the Company went on to capture Croatia, a mile to the north-west, receiving very effective support from aircraft which dropped their bombs only a quarter of a mile ahead of the leading troops. The day's bag was forty prisoners.

The rest of the Battalion had meanwhile moved northwards, giving flank protection on the 21st to an attack of the 38th Brigade across the San Nicolo canal. The three companies advanced up the railway behind a barrage and took their objective by first light, in spite of heavy shelling and mortar fire which caused the death of two other ranks and the wounding of one officer and fourteen other ranks. In the course of the advance 'C' Company captured a German Company Commander and thirty-two of his men, practically all of the occupants of a locality.

Marching onwards, 'D' Company having now rejoined, the Battalion reached the River Po di Volano on the night of the 23rd. 'A' and 'B'

Companies crossed by assault boat and established a bridgehead without opposition; the rest of the Battalion joined them by raft after daylight, and by midnight the R.E. had built a bridge which allowed the passage of tanks.

On the 24th two companies went forward to clear the Correggio area, meeting with some resistance from well-sited snipers and machine-guns, and losing one man killed and six wounded, the last casualties the Battalion was to incur in action. Later in the day the other two companies went out to provide flank protection to the 2nd Armoured Brigade.

When these tasks had been completed the Battalion concentrated, and moved on the 25th to take over a very long stretch of the south bank of the River Po, to prevent enemy infiltration across it. Very soon other divisions had cleared the ground north of the river and the vigilance of guards could be relaxed.

For all practical purposes the German armies had been destroyed south of the Po, the quantity of abandoned equipment being visible evidence of this. The pursuit went on to the north, but this was a task for swiftly moving forces and it did not fall to the lot of the 78th Division, which had been so well up in the hunt from Taranto to the River Po, to be in at the death. It was in small villages south of the river that they heard, on the 2nd May, that the German forces in Italy had surrendered unconditionally to the Supreme Allied Commander, Field-Marshal Alexander.[2]

*Conclusion*

The fight, begun in France in 1940, continued through North Africa and Sicily, and then up and down and across the Italian Peninsula, had been a hard one. For five long years the 5th Battalion had done their duty in a way which their predecessors of the Territorial Army in the First World War—the old 4th Battalion, who had gained their laurels on Gallipoli and in Palestine—would have been the first to admire.

The congratulations which they now received from the Colonel-in-Chief of the Regiment, from the County of Huntingdonshire and from their Commanders had been well and truly earned.[3] All had played their part, from the Commanding Officers who had led them so well down to the men who loaded the mules, but, as General McCreery said in his message after the victory had been won, the decisive factors were the magnificent fighting qualities of the soldier and the skill of the junior leader.[4,5]

# CHAPTER XVII

## THE 48th IN CEYLON AND BURMA
## THE DEFENSIVE, JANUARY 1943–NOVEMBER 1944

Training, January–November 1943—Move to the Burma Front, December 1943—General Situation to December 1943—In the Kabaw Valley, December 1943–January 1944—The Japanese Position at Kyaukchaw—Preliminaries—Approach and Bombing—Attack on the 18th January—Attack on the 19th January—Attack on the 20th January—Subsequent Operations, 21st–25th January—Postscript to Kyaukchaw—Round Kyaukchaw, 26th January–17th March—The Japanese Offensive—Withdrawal from Kyaukchaw, 18th March–1st April—Into the Naga Hills, 2nd–12th April—The Bishenpur–Silchar Track—Topography and Tactics—Task of 32nd Brigade—48th reach Bishenpur—Operations of No. 1 Company—48th occupy Pt. 5846—Japanese Attempt to block the Track—Keeping the Track open, 1st May–8th June—Operations Elsewhere—First Attack on Dome, 10th–11th June—Second Attack on Dome, 13th–14th June—Final Attempt to block the Track, 16th–28th June—Last Days on the Track, 29th June–13th July—Silchar Track: Retrospect—The 48th rest and train, July–November 1944 (*see* General Map of Burma on p. 245, Sketch Maps of Kyaukchaw on p. 248 and Silchar Track on p. 262)

## Training, January–November 1943

WE left the 48th in Ceylon, and there they remained for several more months, carrying out defence tasks and absorbing the technique of jungle warfare. Then came the time for their Division, the 20th Indian, to move to India for a final tuning-up before it went into action in Burma.

The Battalion embarked at Talaimannar on the 13th August and, after a short sea-crossing, travelled on by train to Ranchi, reached a week later. The state of Namkum Camp, their new quarters, was not impressive. The Battalion war diary describes it as being 'in a disgustingly insanitary state; flies and mosquitoes were everywhere, cookhouses were unusable, the ground around them being fouled,' to say nothing of other more unpleasant shortcomings which are duly recorded. However, a few days' hard work put it into a fit state for habitation, though it was still necessary to enforce full anti-malarial precautions, and then training began.

Early in October the Battalion reorganised into three rifle companies, and the H.Q. Company was divided into two, an H.Q. Company and an Administrative Company.[1]

At the end of the month Brig. D. A. L. Mackenzie took over command

THE 48th IN CEYLON AND BURMA. DEFENSIVE, 1943-1944 243

of the 32nd Indian Infantry Brigade, and under his leadership the 48th were to serve throughout their time in the 20th Indian Division.

*Move to the Burma Front, December 1943*

At the beginning of December orders came for the Division to move to the Burma front. The 48th entrained on the 6th of that month, and after a long journey, which included two river-crossings by ferry and several delays due to the idiosyncracies of the Indian engine-drivers, reached a transit camp at Dimapur, the railhead in North Assam, on the 11th.

Two days later lorries arrived early in the morning; as these were loaded with troops or with baggage, they were despatched on their way. The first reached Imphal in the late afternoon, but owing to breakdowns on the road it was not until midnight that the whole battalion had reached the transit camp there.

*General Situation to December 1943*

The full story of events in Burma cannot be told in this history. It is sufficient to say that by the beginning of March 1942 the Japanese had occupied Rangoon, and that by the end of May practically the whole of Burma was in their hands, despite the gallant resistance of British, Indian and Chinese troops against greatly superior numbers.

At the beginning of June the Allied forces were disposed on three fronts —in the south, in Arakan, a country of comparatively low, though steep, hill ranges, paddy-fields and scrub; in the centre, in Manipur State, where the jungle-covered mountains guarded the approaches to India proper from the valley of the River Chindwin through Assam; and in the north, guarding the approaches to China. Of these, the first two were held by British and Indian troops, the last by Chinese under the command of the American General Stilwell.

At this stage the monsoon rains began to fall and continued to do so for five months. The Japanese advance came to a standstill, since they were just as unprepared as the Allied forces were to conduct operations under these conditions. So the Allied Command had a breathing-space in which to build up and train its forces, and to construct communications behind the various fronts through country in which roads and railways were, to all intents and purposes, non-existent.

In December, as soon as the weather permitted, the first Allied offensive opened, British and Indian formations advancing southwards in Arakan with the object of capturing the island and the port of Akyab. They made some progress before being checked by the Japanese defences. A second attempt, in March, suffered the same fate, and eventually a strong enemy counter-offensive forced the attackers back to the positions from which they had started six months earlier.

Apart from this, the only major operation completed in 1943 was that in which Wingate's brigade of Chindits crossed the Chindwin and penetrated some two hundred miles into enemy-occupied territory. This was a gallant venture, and though the original intention that it should coincide with a Chinese advance from the north had to be abandoned, it achieved much. For, apart from confusing the enemy and damaging their communications, it provided lessons of great value for the future. Meanwhile, on the central front troops of the 4th Corps had been carrying out offensive patrols and, after the 1943 monsoon, small-scale offensive operations. In November the front was held by two divisions: the 17th Indian, based on the Imphal–Tiddim road, north of Tiddim; and the 23rd Indian, with headquarters at Tamu, soon to be relieved by the 20th and withdrawn for rest and training. The general plan was to take action to dominate the area west of the River Chindwin, as a preliminary to a large-scale offensive early in 1944.

*In the Kabaw Valley, December 1943–January 1944*

Three days after the 48th had arrived at Imphal, the reconnaissance party left for Moreh, near Tamu, followed on the next day by the advanced party. At Moreh the 32nd Brigade was to establish a strongly defended base, while the other brigades of the Division patrolled towards the Chindwin.

On the 18th December the Battalion got orders to move at 0300 hours on the 19th. Although this was two days earlier than they had expected, they were ready to move within three hours of receipt of the order. That night the M.T. arrived, having taken three weeks to cover the journey from Namkum Camp.

Despite some breakdowns the last vehicle of the convoy carrying the Battalion had reached Moreh by 1630 hours. It had not been a pleasant journey, for the road was often flanked by a precipice descending for some hundreds of feet, and the majority of the troops decided that, rather than travel by it again to go on leave, they would prefer to wait until they had reached a seaport, and go by ship.

Within twenty-four hours the 48th heard that they were to be placed under command of the 100th Brigade and that they were to undertake the capture of a strong position which the Japanese had established on the River Yu, at Kyaukchaw. This was about twenty miles south-east of Tamu by the map, though in the Burma hills distances measured by this means bore little relation to the mileage which the man on foot would have to cover, or to the time required to cover it. All surplus equipment and personal belongings were dumped, since from now on it was a matter of travelling light and kit had to be limited to a change of clothing, personal necessaries, a ground-sheet and two blankets per man.

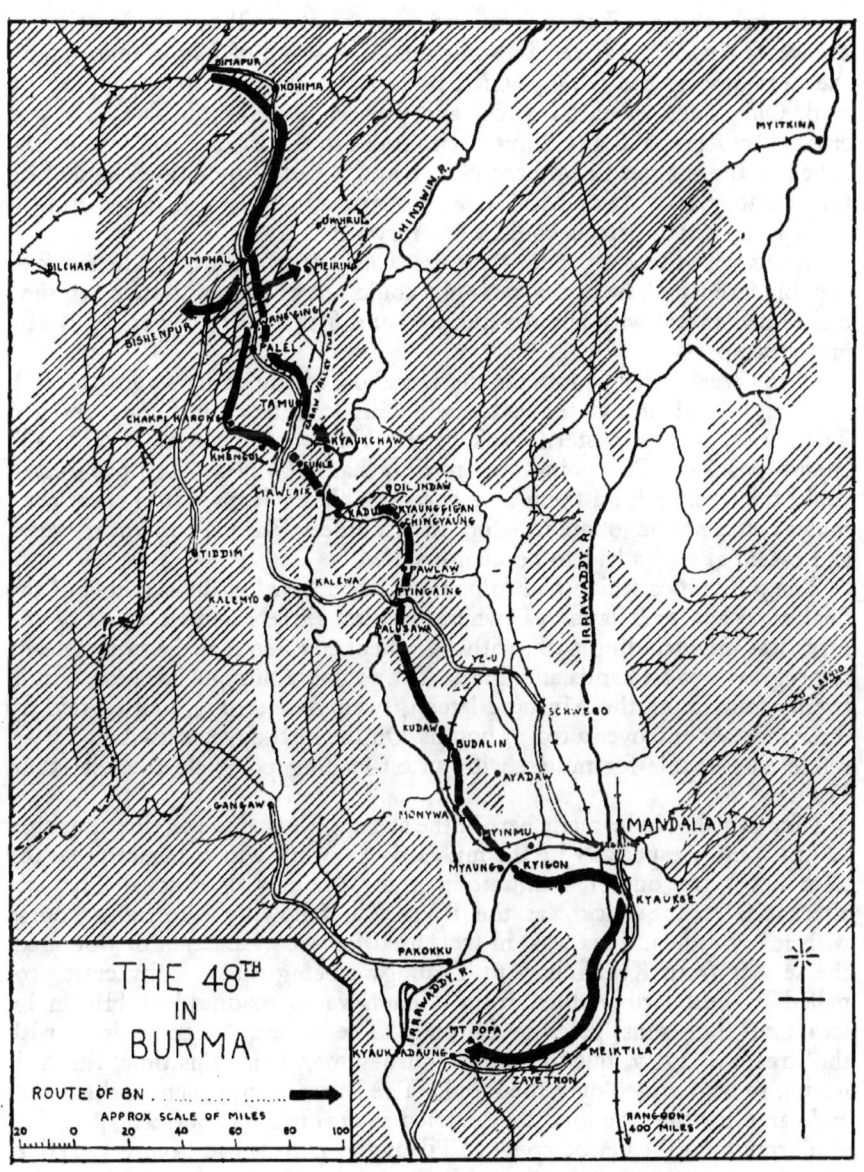

On the 22nd the Battalion moved forward to roadhead at Hlezeik, on the west bank of the River Yu some ten miles south of Tamu, followed on the next day by the M.T., which returned to Moreh after dropping its load. Only a few essential trucks and jeeps were retained. The river was crossed by ferry, and at Chinywa, two miles to the east, a 'box' was established in the jungle. From here Nos. 1 and 2 Companies, commanded by Capt. Cubey and Major Molloy, were sent south-eastwards to set up firm bases from which patrols could work forward.

In this wise the 48th spent their first Christmas in Burma. The stock of suitable fare which had been arranged could not be got up to them, so they had to be content with about a hundred and fifty ducks, delivered alive by mule transport.

In the week after Christmas the Battalion advanced by stages through the jungle and across the extremely hilly country, until they reached Tilaungwa, on the eastern bank of the Yu about three miles from the enemy position. The going was terribly hard. Only as they progressed could the track behind them be made passable for jeeps. Until then, even mules could not negotiate it before the Engineer Platoon had got to work, and essential stores had to be man-handled.

The difficulties which had to be faced are shown by the example of the final approach to Tilaungwa, where the first three hundred yards of the carry was up a winding path, with a gradient so steep that the safest means of progress was on hands and knees. Yet, to quote but one instance, within twenty-four hours the Mortar Platoon, twenty-six strong, had carried up three mortars and over a ton of bombs. On the next day the track had been rendered passable for mules, with an off-loading point close to Battalion H.Q.

Mention should be made here of the sterling work done on this appalling L. of C., more especially by the mule drivers, work which ensured that the 48th never ran out of ammunition, mortar-bombs or rations. The sole alternative to the track was the River Yu, following a tortuous course with many rapids. This was, in fact, used for the evacuation of wounded, the service from Kyaukchaw to Tilaungwa being operated by craft propelled by outboard motors, from Tilaungwa to roadhead at Hlezin by local craft (lundwins) poled by Burmans. The latter could come down with the stream in a day, but the return journey took twice this time, the craft having to be dragged over the rapids. The Burmese boatmen worked well, and cared for the wounded they carried as devotedly as nurses.

Throughout the period spent at Tilaungwa patrols had been very active, reconnoitring the Japanese positions and watching enemy movement. Their success was a tribute to the soundness of the earlier training in Ceylon and India. First contact was made by a patrol from No. 1 Company on the 29th December, but first blood was drawn by a composite patrol of the 48th and the 2nd Border Regt., which located an enemy post and laid an ambush. The full effect of this was spoilt by the premature firing of a shot, but the Japanese were known to have suffered five casualties. One lance-corporal of the 48th was wounded. Before this, the failure of a patrol commanded by Lieut. Hincks to return at the appointed time had caused some concern. However, eventually the patrol came in, forty-eight hours late, with valuable topographical information and firm believers in the compass as an aid to jungle navigation.

*The Japanese Position at Kyaukchaw*

The Japanese position lay on the bank of the River Yu, and was protected in front and in the rear by two natural obstacles, Jensen's Chaung and Dathwekyauk Chaung. 'Chaung' is the Burmese name for a small stream, sometimes deep, sometimes shallow, often with quicksands, running as a rule between high steep banks.

Between these two chaungs the country was undulating and covered with high teak forest. At this time of year the trees had lost their leaves and the undergrowth was not very thick; in fact, the general effect was that of an English oakwood. Along the line of the two main chaungs and of several smaller ones which ran into them, there was much denser jungle undergrowth.

According to the information available, the enemy position was in three parts. On the east bank of the river and opposite to the mouth of the Dathwekyauk Chaung was a platoon post. On the west bank were two others—one known as 'Bath,' between the two main chaungs, the other as 'Wells,' in the angle east of the Dathwekyauk Chaung where it joined the River Yu.

A sketch-map captured in December showed two further positions in the area, one to the north of 'Bath,' near Jensen's Chaung, and the other about two hundred yards to the south-west of it. All the positions were shown as being provided with bunkers and foxholes and all-round wire obstacles.[2]

The whole position was of considerable importance to the Japanese, for it covered the junction of two tracks—one leading east to the River Chindwin, one south down the Kabaw Valley—which were valuable as means of communication.

*Preliminaries*

It was originally intended, in the light of the information outlined above, that the enemy position on the east bank of the River Yu should be dealt with by No. 2 Company. Accordingly, on the 2nd January, Major Molloy set out on a three-day reconnaissance patrol in order to select a line of advance, forming-up place, and so on, and, if possible, to observe the

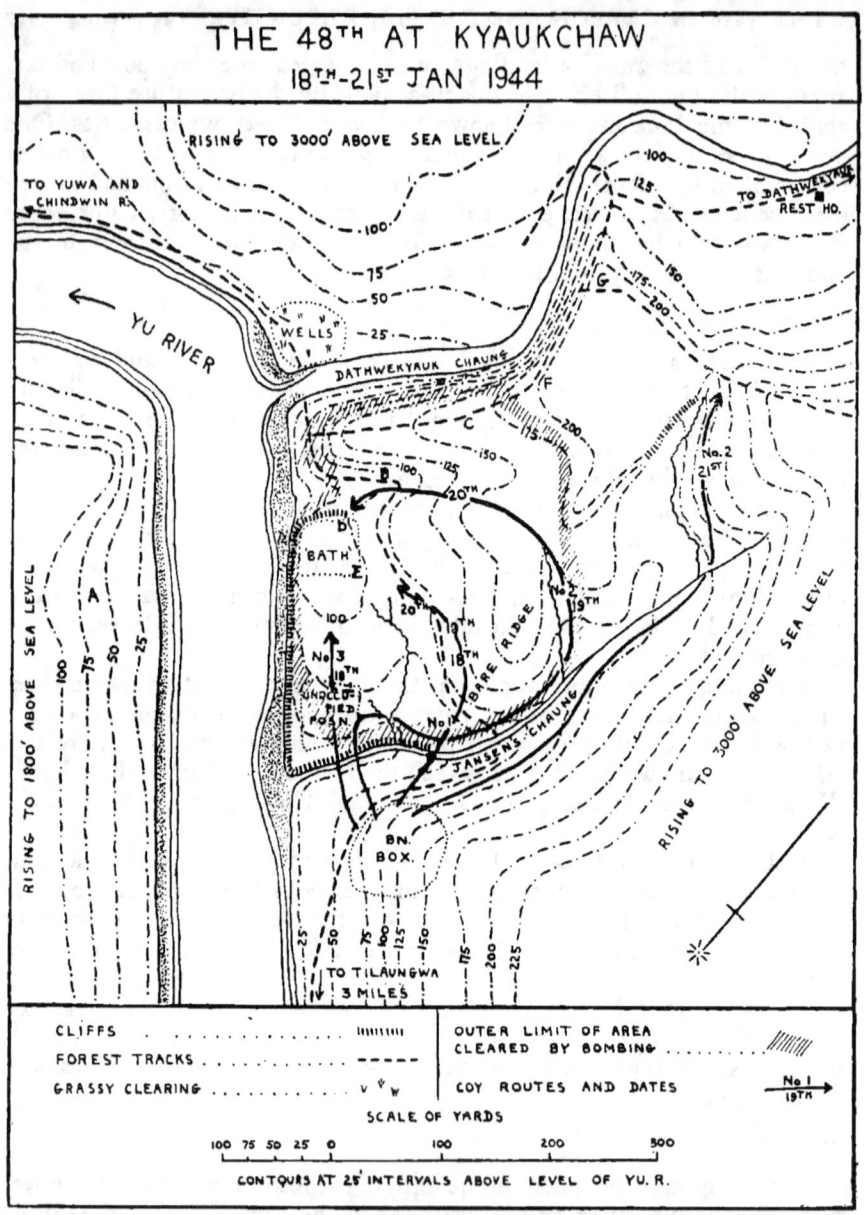

A—Platoon No. 2 Coy. B—Pt. reached by Lieut Hughes's patrol 19th. C—Ridge recced by L/Cpl. Walters's patrol 19th. D—Bunker attacked by No. 2 Coy. 20th. E—Pt. at which Lieut. Horwood was killed. F—Recce by C.O. and Major Molloy 21st. G—Enemy position unlocated until 21st.

position itself. He established the fact that the position did not exist, but much noise was heard coming from 'Bath,' where the building of bunkers was proceeding and there was considerable movement. From the area of 'Wells' there was neither noise nor movement.

Other patrols tried to obtain information about 'Wells,' but none succeeded in penetrating far enough. This was not surprising, for though the distance on the map from Tilaungwa was only about three miles, many days would have been necessary to carry out a thorough reconnaissance in the difficult country. Furthermore, it was most important that the enemy should not be forewarned of the attack.

So it had to be assumed that 'Wells' existed and was occupied, an assumption which influenced the course of the battle considerably.

Meanwhile, other preparations were being made. Mountain guns were brought up, and boats and bridging material were floated down the river, to be hidden in the jungle until they were wanted. The drill for destroying bunkers was rehearsed and in deep nullahs, well away from possible enemy interference, the 48th and the Sappers practised the use of demolition charges.

D-Day for the attack had been fixed for the 10th January, but bad weather caused a five-day postponement. Then, on the 11th, came a report from Brigade that a party of forty Japanese, with six elephants, had been seen moving away from the direction of the Kyaukchaw position. As the plan of attack included a preliminary bombardment by aircraft of the Strategical Air Force, the first occasion for such action against positions in thick jungle, the Higher Command wanted to make sure that the effort would not be wasted on unoccupied positions. The report could only be confirmed by patrolling and the work of one patrol in particular earned the commendation of the Brigade Commander. Under Lieut. Hughes, of No. 2 Company, this patrol lay up on the east bank of the River Yu for twenty-four hours, watching the enemy position at 'Bath.' They were able to listen to the Japanese having their early morning parade, which consisted of a sunrise roll-call and a salute to the Emperor with shouts of 'Banzai.' They could also watch the enemy troops coming down to the river to bathe and to do their washing, and an estimate of the strength of the garrison was obtained by counting the number of mess-tins brought down to the water to be cleaned by the Burmans who were employed as cooks. So the patrol was able to return with the information that the position was certainly still occupied, and with other valuable details.

The weather led to further postponements of D-Day, then, on the 16th, a signal notified that it would be on the 17th. When the written confirmation arrived it was found that the scale of bombing had been reduced, and that it would be carried out on the 17th only. This was a drawback, for it meant that the enemy would have twenty-four hours in which to recover from its effects, or to withdraw if they wished, before the infantry attack went in on the 18th. The change of plan was, however, unavoidable, for the river valley was filled with mist until after midday, making early bombing impossible. Consequently, there would not have been enough time for the Battalion to carry out the difficult approach and to attack before darkness fell at about 1800 hours.[3]

*Approach and Bombing*

At noon on the 17th January the Battalion began to cross from the east to the west bank of the River Yu, using rafts which carried twenty men at a time, and moved into an assembly area north of Jensen's Chaung. One platoon of No. 2 Company remained on the east bank, with the task of protecting the mountain guns, which were under Lieut.-Col. Taunton's command.

As the Battalion lay there, about a thousand yards from the enemy, they heard the Liberators approaching, and soon the bombs began to fall on the Japanese positions, the first of twenty tons which were dropped in a space of ninety minutes. The noise was most heartening to the waiting troops, and after dusk patrols reported that fires were burning in and round the positions and that the enemy showed signs of nervousness, keeping up small-arms fire for some time. It should be noted that, in jungle country, patrols rarely operated at night; these therefore deserve mention for achieving their object.

It had been necessary to indicate the targets to the R.A.F. by plotting on to air photographs the position of each individual bunker, and it is a tribute to the earlier work of the patrols of the 48th and other units that, in the event, only one defended area had not been located and this, as will be seen, was only revealed after three days of fighting.

Only when the attack began was it realised that in this type of country bombing had its disadvantages. Most of the large trees were not affected by it, but the undergrowth had been blasted and, as a result, though the attacking troops could see what confronted them, the enemy had a clear field of fire of from 200 to 250 yards between the tree-trunks.

*Attack on the 18th January*

Early on the 18th the 48th moved up to the attack, and at 1100 hours the mountain guns opened fire on the enemy positions. Three-quarters of an hour later Major Keily, commander of the left attacking company, No. 3, signalled back that he believed that they were on their objective, 'Bath.' This was not, in fact, the case, but in the circumstances the mistake was a pardonable one. In reality they had reached the position shown on the captured sketch-map as being south of Jensen's Chaung, but it was unoccupied by the enemy. Continuing to advance, as they topped the ridge ahead they came under heavy small-arms and grenade-discharger fire from 'Bath.' They mounted an attack, but by 1415 hours this had been brought to a halt. Two officers, Lieuts. Bucher and Hincks, and two platoon sergeants had been wounded, Lieut. Hincks being missing until the following morning, when he made his way back to Battalion H.Q.

No. 3 Company had managed to locate the flank of 'Bath,' so, while they kept the enemy garrison engaged, No. 1 Company were ordered to try to work round farther to the right. By 1630 hours, however, they too were held up, mainly by grenade and sniper fire. Lieut. Andrews, commanding a platoon which had moved by the western end of Bare Ridge, was killed.

The C.O. now decided to pull the two companies back into the Battalion area north of Jensen's Chaung, so as to allow the artillery to harass the enemy during the night. The withdrawal was not hindered by the Japanese and was helped by accurate fire from the mortars, directed by Lieut. Horwood, the Mortar Platoon Commander, an officer of the Queen's Royal Regt. who was serving with the 48th. Throughout the day he had done excellent work, advancing with No. 3 Company and establishing a forward O.P. from which he controlled supporting fire.

*Attack on the 19th January*

At 1030 hours on the morning of the 19th the guns and mortars again bombarded the enemy position, and at noon No. 1 Company advanced across the eastern end of Bare Ridge. Reaching a second ridge beyond it they were stopped by heavy and accurate fire from 'Bath.'

Meanwhile, No. 2 Company had moved into the unoccupied position south of Jensen's Chaung. They were now ordered to move round the outer flank in order to attack 'Bath' from the west. Under cover of Bare Ridge the Company moved to the head of a small chaung which ran out of Jensen's Chaung. From there, across about one hundred and fifty yards of ground which was open except for the trunks of the teak-trees, they could clearly see the loopholes of two of the Japanese bunkers. The enemy, who had been silent for some time, remained silent. Major Molloy began to think that the position had been vacated, and reported so by wireless to the C.O. Soon afterwards fire was opened and at first it was thought that this came from another company, but when grenades from a discharger began to fall it was clear that the Japanese were still there.

Darkness was now approaching, so Major Molloy took up a position astride the chaung and made preparations to attack on the following morning. A patrol under Lieut. Hughes was sent to reconnoitre a line of approach round the rear of 'Bath.' On reaching the thick undergrowth at the head of the small chaung leading into the River Yu and passing the southern edge of 'Bath,' their movement was heard by the enemy and two men were wounded by grenade fire. However, Lieut. Hughes was able to return and report that he had found a good line of approach. A second patrol, sent to investigate the ridge above the Dathwekyauk Chaung, unfortunately lost its leader, L/Cpl. Walters, killed by a burst of long-range fire.

During the day Lieut. Horwood had again done conspicuously good work. After setting up an O.P. within seventy yards of the wire surrounding 'Bath,' he had directed mortar fire, moving about on the ridge in full view of the enemy and indicating their positions to the attacking troops.

*Attack on the 20th January*

The 20th was a day of great effort and much gallantry. The plan of attack was for No. 1 Company to attack 'Bath' from the west, while No. 2 did so from the south by the route reconnoitred by Lieut. Hughes. As it was still believed that the enemy had a position at 'Wells,' No. 3 Company were ordered to protect the rear of No. 2 from possible counter-attack from that direction. The whole assault was to be preceded by a mortar bombardment.

When the attack began No. 1 Company failed to make any headway, owing to the openness of the ground and the obstacle presented by a steeply banked chaung into which the enemy were able to roll grenades.

No. 2 Company waited for some time for No. 3 to appear, but they failed to do so, having mistaken the chaung they should have followed and moved by one farther to the west. Eventually Lieut. Walton's platoon of No. 2 was ordered to carry out the protective task and also to assist the attack by fire and by a 2-inch mortar smoke-screen.

Lieut. Hughes's platoon was detailed to try to neutralise the bunker at the south-western corner of 'Bath,' and if possible to gain a foothold within the position. Support was a problem, for it was difficult to find any opening in the tree-tops through which the 2-inch mortars, with their instantaneous-fused bombs, could fire effectively. The smoke-screen, however, was of assistance and Lieut. Hughes managed to reach the enemy wire unobserved. Cutting it, he crawled through, but then something attracted the enemy's attention and they rolled grenades down the steep slope which existed at that point. A number of men, including every one of the section-commanders and all but one of the demolition party of the 92nd Field Company R.E., were wounded, two dying later of their wounds.

Although the element of surprise had been lost, the presence of No. 2 Company seemed to have neutralised the bunker, less than ten yards away from the wire. Major Molloy hoped that a further effort might gain a foothold in the position, and Lieut. Walton's platoon was brought up for the purpose, but the enemy were still on the alert and more showers of grenades reduced numbers to about fifteen. Lieut. Walton was severely wounded in the head by a bullet, and Lieut. Hughes and his platoon-sergeant, Sgt.

## THE 48th IN CEYLON AND BURMA. DEFENSIVE, 1943–1944

Hatcher, received grenade wounds but stayed at duty. A final attempt by L/Cpls. Harris and Houston to rush the nearest foxhole also failed, both being wounded immediately they moved forward.

It is possible that, had No. 2 Company disposed of its full strength, another effort might have succeeded, but the third platoon was still detached on the other side of the River Yu. Anyhow, at this stage they had to stop, for the fire which accompanied an attack on 'Bath' from another direction forced them to keep their heads down.

After the failure of No. 1 Company to make any progress, Lieut. Horwood, convinced that the enemy's resistance would weaken, got leave from the C.O. to lead another attack. Under his command, at 1600 hours a party composed of men from No. 1 Company, the G(R) Platoon of the 3/8th Gurkha Rifles and two detachments from the 92nd Field Company R.E., began to advance.

Crossing the small chaung between Bare Ridge and 'Bath,' the wire was reached. A bamboo Bangalore Torpedo inserted beneath it failed to explode, but on the left the Gurkhas were doing well, keeping the enemy bunkers under fire and hurling grenades into the communication-trenches. Lieut. Horwood, standing in the wire, was directing covering fire and efforts to work through the obstacle when, just as it seemed that the assault would succeed, he was killed by a burst of machine-gun fire.

So died a very gallant officer. For three days and two nights, displaying remarkable endurance and complete disregard for his own safety, he had set an example of cool bravery which had inspired all who were near him. The Victoria Cross, awarded after his death, was a fitting recognition of his valour.[4]

Deprived of Lieut. Horwood's leadership the attack came to a standstill, and after a period during which no progress was made the troops were withdrawn. In conducting the withdrawal of his men the Jemadar of the Gurkhas behaved with great gallantry and was the last to leave the enemy wire.

By now the Battalion had incurred about a hundred casualties, mostly wounded, and companies were very thin on the ground. So they were all withdrawn into a battalion 'box,' of which one side was held by a company of the 3/8th Gurkha Rifles, about four hundred yards from 'Bath.' The night was quiet, the enemy, who were engaged with harassing fire, showing no offensive inclinations. The depleted strength had its compensations when the rum ration of one water-bottle full per section was issued, for in at least one platoon every man received a pint.

*Subsequent Operations, 21st–25th January*

Early on the morning of the 21st a patrol drew no fire from 'Bath,' but there were signs of movement so the position was kept under mortar and artillery fire. With a view to mounting another attack, Lieut.-Col. Taunton, Major Molloy and others carried out a reconnaissance of the flank and rear of the position. An excellent observation point was reached, on the ridge north of the Dathwekyauk Chaung, and there the party spent more than thirty minutes, memorising routes and features and making plans.

That afternoon, No. 2 Company moved to establish a block on the track to Dathwekyauk, the route which Japanese reinforcements for 'Bath' would probably take. When they reached a point about a hundred yards from that from which the earlier reconnaissance had been made, they came under heavy fire and were forced to dig in. A Japanese counter-attack was pinned to the ground, mainly by mortar fire accurately directed by Major Molloy. Patrols then discovered an enemy bunker position within forty yards of the spot from which he and the C.O. had viewed the approach to 'Bath.' There seems no doubt that this was occupied at the time, and it is little short of a miracle that the party should have escaped as they did. It was a good example of the capacity of the Japanese to lie 'doggo' when they wished.

In the evening Capt. Cherrington of No. 2 Company went with Pte. Saunders, a company cook who had volunteered to go with him, to verify that the bunker was still occupied. Entering the wire Capt. Cherrington saw the top of a steel helmet protruding from a nearby foxhole, and after exchanging shots—both of which missed—he and Saunders beat a retreat. Later it was discovered that had they gone a few steps farther they would have come into the line of fire of the bunker, up to then masked by a large tree. As a postscript to this, when carrying out a reconnaissance with Major Molloy on the following day, Pte. Saunders had to be restrained from making a lone entry into the position, and contented himself with removing a 'rattle-tin' from the wire.

The next three days were spent in patrolling and in harassing the Japanese with fire. At first they made several efforts to reconnoitre, stopped by mortar fire, but later on they became inactive and contented themselves with staying where they were, practically inaccessible to attack.

Eventually, on the morning of the 25th, a patrol found 'Bath' unoccupied. While the position was being searched, L/Cpl. Davies of No. 1 Company entered a deep dugout by a hole made in the roof. It was a brave act, for any occupant might have been armed, but, as it was, the Japanese he found at the bottom was too badly wounded to offer much resistance. So to the 48th went the honour of capturing the first live Japanese to be taken by any unit of the Corps.

In the position were found the bodies of only five of the enemy, though they had, undoubtedly, suffered much heavier casualties. This claim was substantiated by the large fires which had been seen burning during the preceding nights, caused in all probability by the cremation of the dead in

## THE 48th IN CEYLON AND BURMA. DEFENSIVE, 1943-1944

accordance with the Japanese custom. Further casualties were caused by ambushes which had been laid on the Japanese lines of withdrawal by other units.

It was now ascertained by patrols that the supposed enemy position at 'Wells' was, in fact, a myth. There were only the remains of two large wooden huts which had been destroyed by the bombing. Had this been known earlier the course of operations might well have been different, for it would have been possible to encircle the 'Bath' area and to establish blocks to the south of it to prevent the enemy's withdrawal, without fear of attack from the rear.

At this stage the 48th came once more under command of their own Brigade. The 9/14th Punjab Regt. went through them up the Dathwekyauk Chaung, while they remained in the captured position.

*Postscript to Kyaukchaw*

To anyone not conversant with the conditions of warfare in Burma, the fighting at Kyaukchaw against a position held by not more than a hundred of the enemy will seem but a minor affair compared to the battles of Western Europe and the Middle East, where the numbers involved ran into tens of thousands. But in Burma numbers meant little, for the nature of the country, where roads were almost non-existent and the rate of movement off the jungle tracks could be measured in yards, not miles, in the hour, prohibited the use of large forces. Consequently it was the action of the small sub-units, platoons and sections, or even of individuals, which decided the battle and had an effect which bore no relation to their size.

In Burma everything favoured the defence, and the Japanese, though in many respects unintelligent and certainly not the supermen which reports of the early fighting in the Far East made them out to be, were a difficult enemy to tackle in the circumstances. They fought fanatically, to the death, and no position could be considered as captured until it had been thoroughly searched and every Japanese in it, even though wounded, put out of action. They were adepts at concealing themselves in the jungle. Their defences were extremely strong. And they were very mobile, for though they could not live on the rumoured handful of rice a day they wanted little variety, and their supply arrangements were of the simplest. Consequently, the strength of an attacking force had to be greatly superior to that of the defence, and owing to the difficulties which accompanied the use of artillery and of armoured forces it was mainly an Infantryman's war.

The tenacity of the Japanese is well illustrated by the words of a war-correspondent who visited the Kyaukchaw position after its capture:[5]

> In a loop of the river where the jungle strides down to the water's edge, the wall of vegetation is broken by a startling scene of devastation.

A gap half the size of Trafalgar Square yawns in the solid forest. The jungle, which had been green since first it sprang from the primal ooze, is now bleached and grey. Tall teaks stand gaunt and leafless. More brittle trees lie shattered on the ground. Bamboo clumps are squashed flat. The earth is churned and pitted. This is what the Burma jungle looks like after bombing. It is the first time aerial attack has been concentrated on such a scale here.

This ruined space was once a Japanese bunker position. It is now occupied by our troops, the first strongpoint we have captured from the enemy on the new front. A surprising fact is that it was not captured as a result of the bombing. Many tons of explosives were rained upon this confined area. It was a warren of bunkers, trenches and foxholes, yet no vulnerable spot received a direct hit, though one bomb fell only four yards from the main ammunition dump. The enemy must have been badly shaken by such a terrific bombardment, but he was not driven from his holes by it. What finally forced him out and won us the position was a siege which cut off his water-supply.

The capture of the Kyaukchaw position was therefore an action of which the 48th could be proud, and this, their first experience of jungle warfare, proved the soundness of their earlier training. In it they had learnt lessons which were to stand them in good stead in the months to come: that the Japanese was a dour fighter, to be treated with respect; that in the jungle it was only by manœuvre that the point from which fire was coming could be located; that quick digging saved lives.

Before they ever went into action the Battalion had had to find a considerable number of men for extra-regimental employment, and for some unexplained reason these had never been replaced by reinforcements.[6] Consequently they went into battle only 402 strong, and their casualties, six officers and eighty other ranks, of whom two officers and fifteen other ranks were killed, were a high proportion of this strength. Yet their morale was high, and justifiably so, for they were the captors of the first Japanese bunker position and the first Japanese prisoner to be taken on this front.

*Round Kyaukchaw, 26th January–17th March*

While the Punjabis continued to drive against the enemy southwards along the Dathwekyauk Chaung, the 48th and the Gurkhas formed a strong base at Kyaukchaw and gave them flank protection, covering the approaches from the Chindwin. This entailed continuous patrolling, the establishment of 'stops' and the laying of ambushes on tracks used by the enemy.

The resistance of the Japanese to the advance of the Punjabis was stubborn and, in spite of the support given by medium artillery, firing from the Kabaw Valley, and by fighter-bombers, little progress was made. Enemy

Soldiers of the 48th in Jungle Battle-dress

*(From the painting by C. C. P. Lawson, Esq.)*

patrols were continually active, seeking to locate the flanks of the positions held, and occasionally minor attacks were made. This activity seemed to support the rumours and the reports which began to come in early in March, that a Japanese offensive was imminent on this front.

*The Japanese Offensive*

A month earlier, in Arakan, the enemy had begun the first phase of an offensive and had made some headway, including the encirclement of the Administrative 'box' of the 7th Indian Division. This the enemy had hoped would lead to the surrender of the garrison owing to lack of supplies, but they had reckoned without the power of the air-lift. By its aid the defenders were able to hold out, and by the middle of March the Japanese had been driven right back. They had failed to achieve their object—the capture of the port of Chittagong—nor had they succeeded in drawing reserves from, and so weakening, the central front against which the second phase of their offensive was to be staged.

The objectives of this phase were the capture of the bases of Imphal and Dimapur, and the severing of the Assam line of communication on which depended the supplying of China. Having achieved these objectives the Japanese hoped to set up a puppet government on Indian soil, under the traitor Subhas Chandra Bose, to create political unrest in India, and, ultimately, to march on Delhi. It was a grandiose plan, and the Japanese were confident of its success. In fact, in his Order of the Day the Japanese commander, General Mutaguchi, stated that its success would have a profound effect on the course of the war and might even lead to its conclusion. In addition to underestimating his opponents in the Fourteenth Army, he made other grave errors. He failed to appreciate the effect of the Allied ability to supply by air, which would allow garrisons to hold out even when isolated, and he failed to make adequate supply arrangements for his own troops, relying on capturing much of what was required.

The offensive opened on the 8th March with two thrusts from the south by the Japanese 33rd Division, the one up the Manipur River towards Tiddim, the other up the Kabaw valley towards Tamu. The first of these was opposed by the 17th Indian Division, which frustrated the enemy's efforts at encirclement and fought its way back along the road to Imphal. The second came against the 20th Indian Division, and it also began to carry out a fighting withdrawal, in accordance with the general plan which was to form a defensive ring round the southern portion of the Imphal plain.

*Withdrawal from Kyaukchaw, 18th March–1st April*

When the direction of the Japanese advances became known, the 32nd Brigade was ordered to pull out of its positions and to come in behind the other brigades of the Division in the Kabaw valley. The 48th were left at

Kyaukchaw for a few days, holding on to the ground which had been captured not long before and feeling somewhat lonely in this large area of jungle out of which numbers of Japanese might appear from almost any direction. However, they were now more up to strength, the arrival of reinforcements having allowed of the formation of a fourth rifle company under the command of Capt. Eales-White, and although patrols occasionally saw small parties of Japanese these were not aggressive.

On the 16th March orders came for the Battalion to withdraw, and after setting many booby-traps they started their march back, reluctant to give up the ground for which they had fought so hard just two months earlier, though not a little thankful to be leaving so isolated a position. Reaching the Kabaw valley in M.T. on the next day, they found that once more they were to be detached from their Brigade and were to move to the Moreh 'box' held by the 100th Brigade. There they arrived on the 18th, after a march which, though short, was exhausting due as much to the heat of the valley as to the stony road, a thing on which they had not set foot for three months. They took over that part of the perimeter which they had started to build when they were first at Moreh.

At this time the 32nd Brigade, less the 48th, was holding a rear-guard position at 'Charing Cross,' two miles to the south, in order to hit the Japanese hard should they press their advance too fast, and to give the 100th Brigade, and other units in the Moreh area, time to carry out their withdrawal to Palel.

Shortly after the Battalion had reached Moreh, Lieut.-Col. Taunton was ordered by Major-General Gracey to assume temporary command of the locality. The perimeter of this was held by the 48th, the Divisional Defence Battalion and G.T. Companies of the R.I.A.S.C. organised as rifle companies. Within the perimeter were units of the 100th Brigade, Field Companies, Gunners and Divisional H.Q., all getting organised for their withdrawal.

All went according to plan, except on one night when Japanese 'jitter-parties' created the effect which they wished and taught all who were in the 'box' a useful lesson. The incident is mentioned because it is a good example of Japanese technique and brings out the necessity for good fire-discipline training.

The tactics of these 'jitter-parties' were to worry points on the perimeter, firing, shouting remarks in English and Urdu, and generally making a noise, the object being to disturb the sleep of the garrison and to persuade the troops in the perimeter to return the fire and so disclose their positions. On this occasion they were assisted by other small parties which had managed to penetrate the defences, these, it was discovered later, being composed of 'Jifs,' traitor Indians who had joined the Japanese-sponsored Indian National Army.

For about forty minutes the defenders fired only an occasional burst at the enemy. Then, except for the 48th and the Defence Battalion, the strain became too great and fire was opened by all the other posts. This would not have been so bad had all the bullets been directed towards the outside of the perimeter, but the firing was indiscriminate as regards direction. Commanders were unable to stop, or even to reduce, its volume, and it ceased only when every round in these posts had been expended.

In their position at 'Charing Cross' the 32nd Brigade spent an anxious night, for it seemed to them, from the amount of fire which they heard, that they must have been by-passed by a large body of the enemy and that Moreh was withstanding a strong attack. However, their turn came later when a considerable force of enemy, with some tanks, came blindly up the road. They were stopped, five tanks being knocked out and about two hundred men killed. The carriers of the 48th, providing protection to the tanks supporting the Brigade, took part in this action. Two of them were destroyed by Japanese tanks.

Soon after this successful action the 32nd Brigade withdrew to Moreh, where Brig. Mackenzie assumed command.

The Japanese now started to probe the defences at various points and to worry the defenders with artillery fire, often at very short range. Fortunately they were very regular in the hours of these bombardments and the garrison was able to take shelter and avoid casualties. Patrols were very successful, inflicting satisfactory losses on the enemy at small cost to themselves.

By the end of March the Japanese advance was seriously threatening both the Imphal–Tiddim and the Imphal–Tamu roads, and the time had come for the 32nd Brigade to withdraw from Moreh. At dawn on the 1st April the 48th moved out, without interference on the part of the enemy, but after they had been on the march for about an hour the road came under heavy and accurate shell-fire. They were lucky, for at this point the road was on the reverse slope from the enemy and they suffered only a few casualties, including Lieut. Hughes, wounded again, but other units were less fortunate. At the end of a three hours' march the Battalion embussed in troop-carrying lorries, and reached its destination, Palel, early in the afternoon.

### Into the Naga Hills, 2nd–12th April

By now the 48th had been in action, more or less continuously, for over three months, and they had hopes of a few days in which they could rest, refit and absorb a draft of 120 men which was waiting for them at Palel and which brought them up to strength. But Fate ordained otherwise.

In the middle of March, a week after the 33rd Japanese Division had begun its advance to the south, two other divisions had crossed the Chindwin on a wide front. Briefly, one of these, the 31st, was directed on Kohima, the other, the 15th, on Imphal. They were lightly equipped and moved fast, and by the end of the month, in spite of some delay imposed on them at Ukhrul by an Indian Parachute Brigade, they had established a road-block on the Kohima–Imphal road and were approaching both these places. But the delay had been sufficient to allow of the reinforcement of the garrisons.

Such was the situation when, on the 2nd April, the 48th received orders to move into the Naga Hills between Imphal and the Chindwin, there to establish a road-block on the Japanese line of communication.

There was much to be done to prepare for the operation and little time in which to do it, but despite this a Battalion parade was held at which the C.O. read out the Army Commander's message announcing the posthumous award of the V.C. to Lieut. Horwood.

On the 3rd April the Battalion moved in M.T. to a concentration area some twenty miles to the north. Here they were joined by a troop of Mountain Artillery and received 472 mules, for by reason of the country into which they were going the operation had to be on a pack basis. The breaking-down of the seven days' rations and fodder into mule-loads was a work of considerable magnitude.

Next day they began their march, through country which was far harder than anything they had yet experienced, the hills rising to 6,000 feet with descents of 4,000 feet into the valleys. That evening they occupied a harbour area beyond Manwunyang. This had one great drawback. The watering-point was a mile and a half away, and it was found that the approach was so steep that mules could not be led down to it. So, early the next morning, working-parties went out to make a track, and in order to allow time for the watering of the large number of mules the C.O. decided to remain there for the day. The day's rest was also good for the new draft, who had no previous experience of real hills and no practical knowledge of jungle lore and had been tried severely by the march.

Another day's march brought the Battalion to Chungdaw, by a bad track which at points had to be widened before they could pass along it. Between this place and the objective lay two very deep valleys, and patrols, which were sent out to reconnoitre for positions from which artillery could support future operations, found that it would be impossible to get the guns up the hills. So, while further reconnaissances were being made of routes which might provide a better line of approach, No. 1 Company were sent to lay an ambush on the Japanese L. of C. Moving out on the afternoon of the 8th the Company halted for a few hours and established a base, and then made a night march to Meiring, which they reached at first light. The village was deserted, but the Naga villagers were found living in nearby caves. The indications were that the enemy had not been in the neighbourhood for about a week, and according to the Nagas they were using a track farther to the east. Patrols from the Battalion also failed to find any sign of the enemy.

The problem of what to do next was solved for the C.O. by a signal received that morning from Brigade, ordering the immediate withdrawal of the Battalion, a disappointing end to several days of very hard work. That evening No. 1 Company returned from Meiring and the next day, the 10th, was spent in making arrangements for the march back, No. 4 Company going out to establish a screen to cover the withdrawal.

The Battalion moved out early on the 11th, and after a midday halt reached the harbour area, from which they had set forth eight days previously, that evening. They had covered in one day the twenty miles of steep ascents and descents which had taken them twice that time, with a day's rest on the way, for the outward journey. It had not taken long for the new draft to become fit and accustomed to the country.

On the next day transport arrived and lifted the Battalion to a harbour area at Wangjing. Twenty-four hours later orders arrived for them to rejoin the 32nd Brigade at Bishenpur. That evening the Corps Commander addressed them in complimentary terms, which they well deserved. But in the weeks to come they had cause to doubt the strict accuracy of his statement that they were now going 'to face the disorganised remnants of the Japanese 33rd Division, floundering up the Tiddim road.'

*The Bishenpur–Silchar Track*

As the Tiddim road approached Imphal it ran across a plain, on which stood occasional villages hidden in dense woods. To the east of the road the plain was marshy, becoming a lake in wet weather. To the west the plain stretched for about two miles, the ground then rising through foothills to a main ridge, five to six miles distant from the road and averaging 5,000 feet in height. At Bishenpur, 17 miles south of Imphal, the ridge narrowed to a series of commanding spurs which met the main road. Ten miles to the north was an air-strip, of great importance to the garrison of Imphal.

Westwards, over the spurs from Bishenpur, a jeep-track had been constructed in 1943. After three and a half miles this track crossed the main ridge between two dominating features, Pt. 5846 to the north and Wireless Hill to the south. Thence it descended to Laimatak valley, crossing the river by a suspension bridge, and continued to Silchar 100 miles away in Assam.

To the north of Pt. 5846 the ridge went on to Laimaton, with important offshoots to Khoirok and Nunggang. South of Wireless Hill, and about one and a half miles from it, was a dominating ridge, the main features of which were known as Dome, Middle Ridge and Taylor Hill.

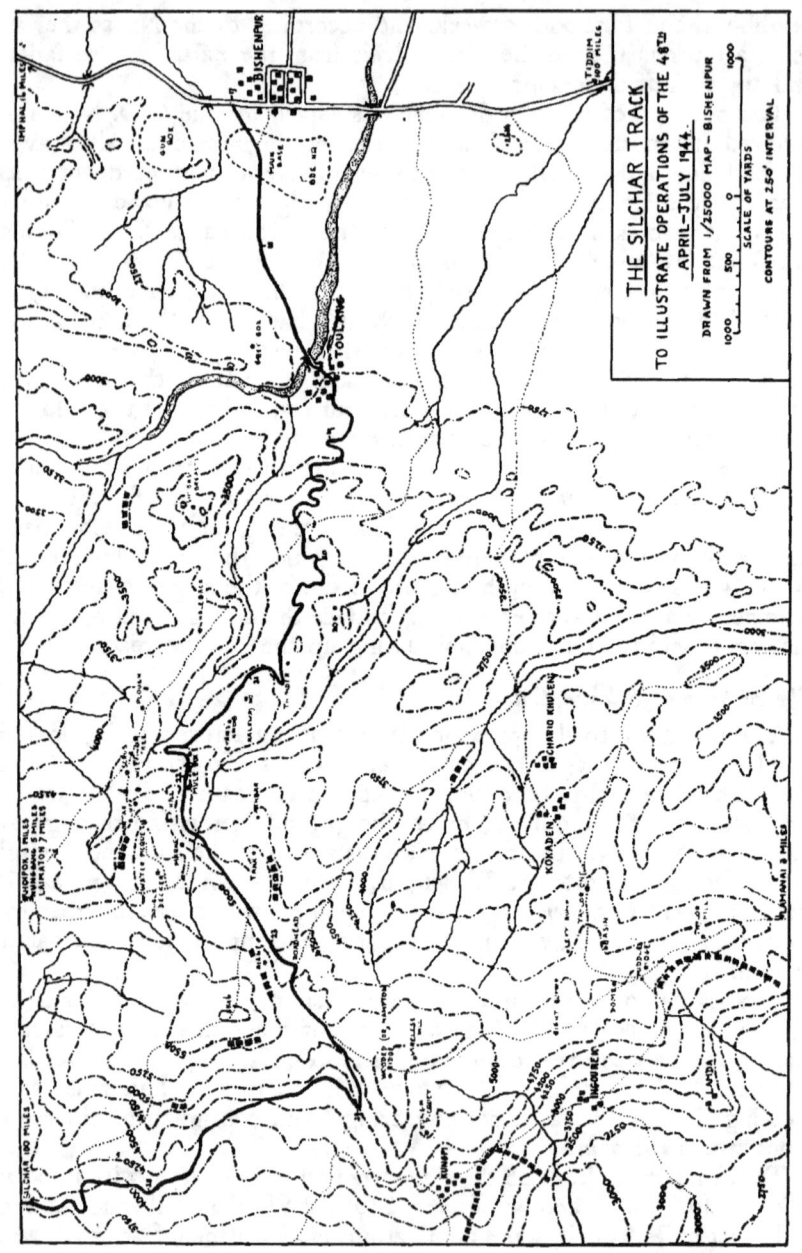

So much for the country in general. But for an understanding of the operations in which the 48th were to take part for the next three months, and of the complexity and the difficulties of fighting in this area of hills, valleys and jungle, some description of the country adjoining the track is necessary.

Between Bishenpur and Roadhead, below Pt. 5846, the track rose 2,500 feet. It was a typical hill-track, winding between, round the face of, and sometimes through, features, of which some were bare, some scrub-covered, some jungle-covered, some strewn with boulders, some covered with soft soil. From all these features effective fire could be brought to bear on some portion of the track or on each other, hence the fighting which took place for their capture or retention.

At intervals, particularly in the stretch between Evans's Knob and Marne, the track ran through close jungle. At other points, notably just to the east of Roadhead, the country immediately astride the track was much more open, and consequently exposed to artillery and mortar fire from the enemy positions on the Kokaden spur to the south.

This densely wooded spur ran from the main ridge eastwards towards the plain, parallel to, and at an average distance of 2,000 yards from, the Silchar track spur. Between the two spurs lay a deep ravine, covered with jungle, traversed by several approaches to the track. Of these, the most awkward from the British point of view was that which passed to the south of Evans's Knob and Mule Box, crossed the track, ran below and to the east of B.P. Hill and Water Piquet, and then joined the track to Khoirok and Nunggang. The whole of this route passed through jungle so thick that patrols could move within a few yards of each other without realising it. It was much used by the Japanese while they were building up their strength in the Nunggang–Laimaton area, providing them as it did with a much more direct route than the détour to the west, which the British activity forced them to use as an alternative.

From the British point of view, the most difficult area of country was the dense belt of jungle which stretched from the eastern slopes of Pt. 5846 through Double Deck and along the eastern upper slopes to near Khoirok. To reach this from the track meant crossing open, uphill ground, in the face of machine-gun and infantry-gun fire, and to get down to it from Pt. 5846 was equally difficult for the same reason.

*Topography and Tactics*

In order to secure the jungle corridor from Kokaden to Khoirok, the enemy's tactics were designed to seize commanding features within effective sniping distance of the track, and from these positions to despatch snipers and ambush parties. Against such tactics the remedy was to deny these features to the enemy, either by occupation or by fire, to send out counter-snipers and to lay counter-ambushes, and to patrol vigorously.

In the early stages of the operations, therefore, there was a race for the important features, piqueting tactics similar to those of mountain warfare being employed. Attacks were usually carried out in daylight, so as to get the full benefit of tank support. On no single occasion did the ground allow the deployment of more than one company of a battalion at a time. For the same reason, only small numbers of tanks could be used—one, or at the most two—and then by performing remarkable feats of hill-climbing.

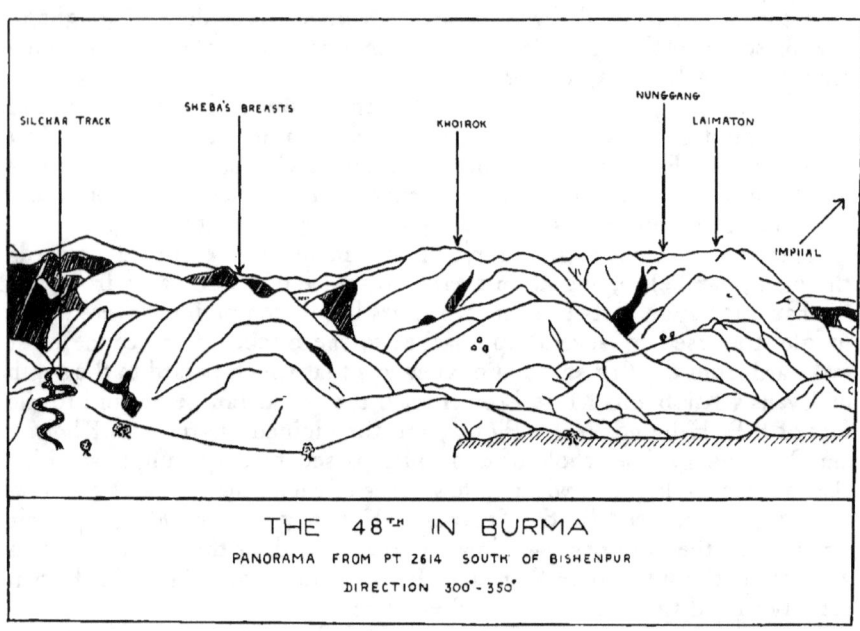

THE 48TH IN BURMA
PANORAMA FROM PT 2614 SOUTH OF BISHENPUR
DIRECTION 300°-350°

The co-ordination of attacks designed to encircle the Japanese positions was an extremely difficult problem. Wireless—the only means of communication—was unreliable, owing to the hilly nature of the country and to atmospherics, and it was difficult to arrange fire support and to ensure that friendly troops did not shoot at each other. Artillery support was further complicated by the fact that all the guns—25-pounders and 3·7 howitzers—were in the Bishenpur 'box,' from which they could not engage the reverse slopes of the hills on which the enemy was accustomed to take refuge from shell-fire; and while the 3·7s were the only guns which could have been brought up to engage Japanese bunkers, they were not a suitable weapon for the purpose. This had to be done by the tanks, blasting the ground-level bunkers from close range.

## THE 48th IN CEYLON AND BURMA. DEFENSIVE, 1943-1944

### Task of 32nd Brigade

After the 20th Indian Division had withdrawn from the Kabaw valley, the 32nd Brigade was placed under the command of the 17th Indian Division. This division, which consisted of two brigades only, was engaged to the north of Imphal. The 49th Brigade of the 23rd Division was holding a rear-guard position on the Tiddim road, sixteen miles south of Bishenpur, and the orders were for the 32nd Brigade to relieve it. However, a preliminary reconnaissance on the 12th April led Brig. Mackenzie, Commander of the 32nd Brigade, to the conclusion that this isolated position was but a liability; it could do nothing to stop the Japanese advance, which was obviously proceeding northwards through the hills to the west of the road. He therefore obtained permission for his brigade to occupy the Bishenpur position and for the 49th Brigade to withdraw through it and rejoin its own division.

### 48th reach Bishenpur

Early on the morning of the 14th April the 48th reached Bishenpur from Wangjing, and they and the 9/14th Punjab Regt. immediately started to dig in on the high ground to the west of the main road and south of the Silchar track. By dint of hard work, within three days bunkers and splinter-proof sleeping-positions had been built and a single-apron fence had been put up round the perimeter.

At the same time patrols went out daily into the hills to the west and south-west, seeing many signs of the enemy. On the 18th a patrol from No. 4 Company encountered a lone Japanese officer who, true to his creed, made a suicidal attack on a group of three men. On one of these he inflicted a severe cut with his sword, but the Bren gunner then dealt with him effectively and the patrol returned with his sword as a trophy. After the war this sword was presented to the Borough of Northampton, where it rests in the Guildhall.

### Operations of No. 1 Company

On the 13th April a company of the 3/8th Gurkha Rifles had been sent to occupy the high ground about Lamanai. Next day they reported that they were unable to make headway against opposition they had met short of their objective, this confirming the direction of the enemy's advance; so, within a few hours of the 48th's arrival at Bishenpur, No. 1 Company, under Capt. Cubey, were ordered to move up the Silchar track and then via Kungpi to seize the high ground north of Lamda. The Gurkhas were to hold on till nightfall, in the hope of delaying the enemy's advance on Kungpi, and were then to withdraw to Bishenpur.

As they reached the vicinity of Kungpi, the leading scout of the Company was shot dead and advanced elements of the enemy were encountered; so, since this place was overlooked from the north-east by Wooded Ridge, Capt. Cubey decided, very wisely it proved, to withdraw there after dark. On the night of the 15th/16th they were thrice attacked by about a platoon of Japanese and drove them off with considerable casualties.

At first light on the 16th the 3/8th Gurkha Rifles were sent to support No. 1 Company, with orders to drive the enemy back to the Lamda area and to establish the Company there in a position which would serve as a firm base for further operations against the enemy round Sadu. The Gurkhas made contact with the Company and went on to capture the dominating feature of Wireless Hill, two hundred yards to the south of Wooded Ridge. Unfortunately no wire was available to strengthen the position they had gained, and heavy counter-attacks during the night forced them off the top of the hill. Positions on the northern slopes were untenable and eventually they withdrew to Wooded Ridge.

Here, as a result of much hard work by the Sappers, a troop of General Lee tanks of 'Y' Squadron, 150 R.A.C., had arrived by the evening of the 18th. At 1930 hours that same evening the enemy began a determined attack. They managed to penetrate the perimeter at a few points and severe hand-to-hand fighting followed, particularly in the sectors held by the H.Q. of the 3/8th and by No. 1 Company. In the end, a strong counter-attack, aided by the tanks which switched on their headlights and brought their Brownings into action, succeeded in ejecting the enemy. The bodies of 23 Japanese, including three officers, were found within the position when daylight came, and, allowing for those taken away, the total enemy loss was estimated at not less than 100. The night's fighting cost No. 1 Company six killed and fourteen wounded.

In recognition of the gallant fighting of No. 1 Company, the C.O. of the Gurkhas named the feature 'Hampton Ridge' (for security reasons the word Northampton could not be used), and by this name it continued to be known.

To complete the story of Wireless Hill: after an attempt by the tanks to reach the summit, which failed five yards short of it, there followed a period of stalemate. Then, on the 20th May, after an intense bombardment by the guns which were then available, the 3/8th attacked and captured the hill at small cost, and it was never again lost.

*48th occupy Pt. 5846*

The Japanese pressure now made it necessary for Pt. 5846 to be occupied, since it commanded Wooded Ridge and Wireless Hill, and also afforded an uninterrupted view of part of the Silchar track and of the main road to Imphal. It had been occupied by a post of four platoons of the 7/10th Baluch Regt. early in April, and the original intention had been for a

Brigade of the 17th Division to arrive in that area on the 19th. But this move had to be postponed, so, late on the 18th, Lieut.-Col. Taunton was ordered to secure the feature with the Baluchi platoons under his command. A very sleepy collection of officers assembled to hear his orders at 0130 hours on the 19th, and in spite of their protests that they could never have their troops ready to move off at the early hour appointed the Battalion did, in fact, move off at that hour.

All three battalions of the 32nd Brigade were now committed, so the Brigade was reinforced by the 1/4th Gurkha Rifles and the 4/12th Frontier Force Regt. The former took over the Battalion's sector in the Bishenpur base, which also contained Brigade H.Q. and the artillery; the latter were despatched to the Khoirok area, north of the track, to prevent enemy infiltration towards the main road north of Bishenpur.

Pt. 5846 was no easy place to hold. The approaches to it were open, but the summit was covered with extremely dense bamboo jungle which greatly limited the field of view. The Battalion began to reach the position at 1700 hours; digging and wiring were immediately put in hand and continued throughout the night, and all companies sent out parties to try to familiarise themselves with the routes through the jungle in their immediate vicinity.

The enemy did not leave them undisturbed for long. The prelude was shelling by a long-range gun from the direction of Kokaden within a few hours of their arrival and this was followed, on the morning of the 20th, by two hours of l.m.g. and grenade fire against Company posts. Later in the day snipers were active, and a patrol from No. 2 Company had a surprise encounter with a large party of enemy near the Battalion waterpoint. 2/Lieut. Morris was wounded and one Japanese was killed.

Then the enemy started in earnest. After a heavy attack on No. 4 Company had been broken up in the evening, a second attack, delivered early on the 21st, managed to penetrate at a point where the wire had not been completed owing to lack of time and the activity of snipers, but this also was defeated. Lieut. Cufley managed to shoot the first two Japanese who got through, and then his platoon grenaded the remainder back down the hill. The Japanese, whom General Slim was wont to describe as 'insects,' were apt to behave as such and repeat the same process at the same hour and in the same place. Consequently, on the next night, when they attempted to rush the same point in the wire, all was ready for them, and a shower of grenades, hand-thrown and from cup-dischargers, broke up the attack while it was forming up.

There followed a period of comparative quiet, during which the enemy established posts on the slopes of the hill, some of them within forty yards of the 48th's positions. The thickness of the jungle made it impossible to prevent this, and attempts at encirclement of the Japanese failed, the bamboo clumps often making it impossible to deploy more than one section at a time. Meanwhile, enemy fire against the hill was causing a steady drain of casualties, including Major Molloy, succeeded in command of No. 2 Company by Capt. Veater, and Capt. Webb.

*Japanese Attempt to block the Track*

Before long patrols found that the enemy had thinned out, though positions to the north of Pt. 5846 were still firmly held. In the early morning of the 25th No. 1 Company at Roadhead was attacked by some thirty enemy, whom they drove off, and reports came in that the track near the 22nd milestone was being sniped from an enemy post just above Water Piquet.

All this activity indicated that the enemy probably intended to try to block the track and so isolate the 48th, and the 3/8th on Wooded Ridge; and though the daily convoy managed to get through to Roadhead on the 25th and 26th, by the next day the enemy had established a post south of the track near Half-way House. Other sections of the track were now commanded by fire, and until the enemy had been evicted the track was out of action.

On the 26th No. 3 Company moved out down the spur which led from Pt. 5846 towards Water Piquet, to try to clear the enemy away. They found a post dug in on the spur, and as they manœuvred to avoid having to attack uphill a party of six Japanese tried to rush them from lower down. All six were killed and it was found that they were wearing British uniforms and equipment, and carried British weapons.

Early on the day after this the 1/4th Gurkha Rifles moved up the track, with the object of relieving the 3/8th and of clearing any opposition met with on the way. They soon encountered enemy posts astride the track near Half-way House, and being unable to dislodge them called for a troop of tanks of the 3rd Dragoon Guards, who had relieved the 150th R.A.C. from Wooded Ridge.

In order to assist the 1/4th No. 4 Company were ordered to move down from Pt. 5846 and clear the enemy out of Water Piquet. This was under the direct observation of the Japanese guns in the Kokaden area, and the Company's final assault was broken up by their fire when they had actually reached their objective. As consolidation would have been impossible in the circumstances, the C.O. ordered the Company to pull back into dead ground on the track north of Half-way House.

During the withdrawal No. 4 Company flushed several parties of Japanese, inflicting casualties on them, and made contact with the troop of tanks. These gave invaluable moral support to the Company while they were collecting the wounded and reorganising. Unfortunately, one of the tanks crashed down a nullah beside the track; however, the crew dismounted the Browning gun and got it into action to help the Company in dealing with enemy posts which were still being cleared.

No. 4 Company's casualties in this action had been heavy, 15 killed and 25 wounded, three of the latter dying the next day; the wounded included Capt. Eales-White and Lieut. Hodges. Thirteen Japanese dead were counted, but the total was considerably greater than this, for there was neither time nor opportunity to count the bodies of those who had been shot as they bolted down the nullahs.

Great gallantry was shown by two American Red Cross drivers. Under heavy shell and machine-gun fire they brought their ambulance up the track to the main water-point, and took back seven wounded; then, returning with many bullet-holes in the ambulance and the back tyres flat, they made a second journey with four more casualties. One of the drivers later received a British decoration.

By the time that the tanks had reached the 1/4th, it was too late to stage an attack, so that battalion returned to Bishenpur, leaving a detachment to keep contact with the enemy.

After much good work by the Sappers to make the approaches to the Japanese positions 'tankable,' the 1/4th and tanks of the 3rd D.G.s again advanced to the attack on the 29th, and on that day and the next one succeeded in blasting the enemy out of their positions, including Evans's Knob and B.P. Hill. As an illustration of the difficulties confronting the tanks, on one occasion a tank had to move backwards along a spur, since there was not room for it to turn, and then had to be winched by a tractor down the hill to the track. No. 3 Company helped these operations by establishing a post near Water Piquet, where they captured a prisoner, a comparatively rare event in the war in the Far East. And as the enemy broke and ran in the face of the Gurkhas' final charge they were caught in the open by mortar and l.m.g. fire from Roadhead. The Japanese casualties in the two days were very heavy, and during April 281 dead were counted.

The track was now open, and a convoy carrying four days' supplies got through to Roadhead, taking back the wounded who had collected there. Its arrival was welcome, for though the 48th and the 3/8th both had two days' reserve rations they had been placed on half-rations on the 26th, when it had seemed that the opening of the road would take several days. They had been very short of water, too; the enemy had commanded the approaches to the water-point, and though a cloud-burst had helped matters the shortage was becoming acute.

Much hard fighting remained to be done on the Silchar track and it was not until the 20th May that the last remaining Japanese position, on Plough Hill, was taken by the 1/4th. But never again did the convoy fail to get through, though it often suffered casualties from shell-fire from Kokaden and from mines laid by the enemy.

*Keeping the Track open, 1st May–8th June*

Operations on the track now became a matter of seizing and holding the hill features in its vicinity, mostly within a radius of half a mile from Evans's Knob. The greater part of this work was done by the 1/4th, who successively attacked and built piquet positions on various points both north and south of the track. These included the features from Whaleback to Mortar Bluff, Tank and Akhbar. The 48th did likewise at Aisne and Marne, and the 3/8th at the Pimples, near Wooded Ridge.

Although the Japanese had been hit hard they were by no means disposed to give up the contest, and there were frequent clashes between them and the piqueting parties which went out every morning and returned in the evening. In one of these, on the 3rd May, a platoon under Capt. Hetherington saw a supply column of about forty of the enemy and, as the country was too precipitous to allow them to follow them up, engaged them with 2-inch mortars. Shortly afterwards a Japanese warrant-officer was found wandering up a track, apparently lost, and was shot by Capt. Hetherington at ten yards' range.

Two days later the piquet held by a platoon of No. 2 Company was attacked. The enemy managed to get inside the wire and hand-to-hand fighting ensued, in which six of each side were killed and the platoon also had six men wounded. As the Japanese remained in occupation of one section's post and the strength of the piquet was no longer adequate to hold it, the platoon was withdrawn, but the position was reoccupied after daybreak, when it was found vacated by the enemy.

At this time the company of the 7/10th Baluch Regt. was withdrawn to Bishenpur. The 48th were sorry to see them go; they had been of great help to them on and around Pt. 5846.

Patrols were continually reconnoitring, to keep in touch with the enemy's movements. By the middle of May they had found that the enemy had given up their post on the top of a prominent hill to the north. Longer-range patrols reconnoitred Tairenpopki, along the Silchar track to the west, and a Japanese road-block at Milestone 25, and as a result of the information they obtained, No. 3 Company, under Capt. Keily, carried out a sweep in that direction on the 18th/19th. They returned after killing eight enemy on the high ground north of the road-block.

The Battalion's snipers were active all this time, and the war diary records many successes by Ptes. Kelly and Brown. Up to the end of the 48th's time on the Silchar track Kelly, who later became Sniper Sergeant, had accounted for twenty-three Japanese, each success duly recorded by a notch on the butt of his precious rifle. He was an outstandingly good shot, some of his hits having been made at ranges of 800 yards. On one occasion, when waiting behind a large boulder with his rifle rested on top of it, stalking a Japanese machine-gun post, a discharger grenade landed on the rifle, blowing it to pieces. But he was undeterred and continued his sniping with another rifle until he was wounded in the leg some three weeks later. His fine work was rewarded by a D.C.M.

Towards the end of May the 1/4th Gurkha Rifles were withdrawn from command of the 32nd Brigade, and as a result there was a change in dispositions. The 48th took over responsibility for all the posts between Bishenpur and Roadhead, the 3/8th for Roadhead and Pt. 5846, in addition to Wireless Hill and Wooded Ridge which they already held. The 9/14th Punjab Regt., now only two companies strong, were in the Bishenpur 'box' and at Khoijuman, east of the main road.

From their new positions the 48th were responsible for patrolling southwards towards the Kokaden group of villages, and northwards to Khoirok. The latter was still held by the enemy, who showed little or no initiative, but, in the course of one of the patrols to it, Lieut. Hughes was wounded for the third time.

On the 8th June the 9th Border Regt. relieved the 48th, who then concentrated at Roadhead.

*Operations Elsewhere*

While all this fighting had been in progress along the line of the Silchar track, other no less important operations had been taking place around Bishenpur and to the north and south of it.

Mention has already been made of the presence of enemy forces in the area Nunggang–Laimaton, and of the despatch of the 4/12th F.F.R. to that area in the middle of April under command of the 32nd Brigade. So long as the enemy were there they constituted a threat to Imphal from the south-west, a threat which, as will be seen, became an actuality, and the task of the 4/12th was to stop any further progress northwards. Throughout April and May they had extremely hard fighting, but were unable to eject the enemy from the strong positions they held on knife-edged ridges. At the end of May this battalion was withdrawn and the 63rd Brigade assumed responsibility for the area; but they did not succeed in evicting the Japanese, who held on till the very last moment and only abandoned their positions after the main withdrawal southwards started in July.

Meanwhile, plans had been made for a counter-thrust by the 17th Division. Briefly, the 48th Brigade was to establish a block on the Tiddim road sixteen miles south of Bishenpur in the middle of May, by-passing the enemy to the north. Then the 63rd Brigade was to occupy positions in the foothills to the east of the road and about five miles south-west of Bishenpur, and was to send a force thence into the hills to the north to destroy the enemy in the Kokaden–Lamda area. To help these operations

32nd Brigade was to produce the greatest strength it could to operate southwards along the main ridge towards Lamda and was to endeavour to make the enemy believe that an attack was impending from the direction of Bishenpur and the Silchar track, and not from the south.

At the outset things went well. The 48th Brigade achieved complete surprise, established its road block firmly, and dealt severely with the efforts the enemy made to drive them from it. The 63rd Brigade moved forward on the 19th May and took its objectives in the foothills, but could make no further progress and was soon pinned to the ground. However, the result of these operations was to force the Japanese to thin out, especially in the Kokaden area. To the relief of the 32nd Brigade they removed the guns which had been harassing the Silchar track, and vacated the area between the track and Kokaden. In its diversionary operations this brigade at last succeeded in taking Wireless Hill, which had resisted capture for seven weeks, and cleared the enemy from Scrub and Plough.

The Japanese reaction to these operations was not, as had been hoped, to withdraw southwards. Instead, they staged a counter-stroke.

On the night of the 20th/21st May, two parties, each 150 to 200 strong, moved from the Nunggang–Laimaton area and crossed the main road north of Bishenpur.

One of these parties then turned north, blocked the main road about five miles north of Bishenpur, blowing a large crater in it, and was within an ace of overrunning 17th Divisional H.Q. before it was driven off after hard fighting.

The second party moved southwards, towards Bishenpur. Here, unknown to 32nd Brigade, some administrative units and large numbers of mules belonging to another brigade had set themselves down to the east of the main road, where not only were they outside the well-defended 'boxes' on the other side of the road, but had also failed to take proper defensive measures. It was upon them that the attack fell in the early hours of the 21st May, and the enemy succeeded in occupying a dug-in position astride the road at the northern end of Bishenpur, covering the end of the Silchar track. It was only after five days' hard fighting by infantry and tanks that the last of the enemy were killed and the battle of Bishenpur was ended.

While these events were in progress the two brigades to the south had become more and more isolated and their maintenance was a problem. Accordingly they were withdrawn in succession.

On the 7th June the 32nd Brigade was ordered to concentrate in the Wooded Ridge area. The 63rd Brigade took over their positions at Bishenpur and Khoirok, and the Silchar track piquets up to but excluding Roadhead. The 32nd Brigade was then disposed with Brigade H.Q. and the 48th at Roadhead, the 9/14th Punjab Regt. between Wooded Ridge

## THE 48th IN CEYLON AND BURMA. DEFENSIVE, 1943-1944

and Pt. 5846, and the 3/8th Gurkha Rifles between Wooded Ridge and Wireless Hill, with a piquet at Kungpi.

*First Attack on Dome, 10th–11th June*

The Brigade now had the task of capturing Dome, a hill nearly five thousand feet high, about a mile to the south of Wireless Hill.

From Wireless Hill the ground dropped fairly steeply, and in full view of Dome, to a deep nullah 600 yards away, and thence rose gently to a plateau which ended abruptly after 500 yards. At its eastern end the plateau descended steeply to the hill known as Taylor One and the woods in the Kokaden area. From the edge of the plateau a steep descent led, either

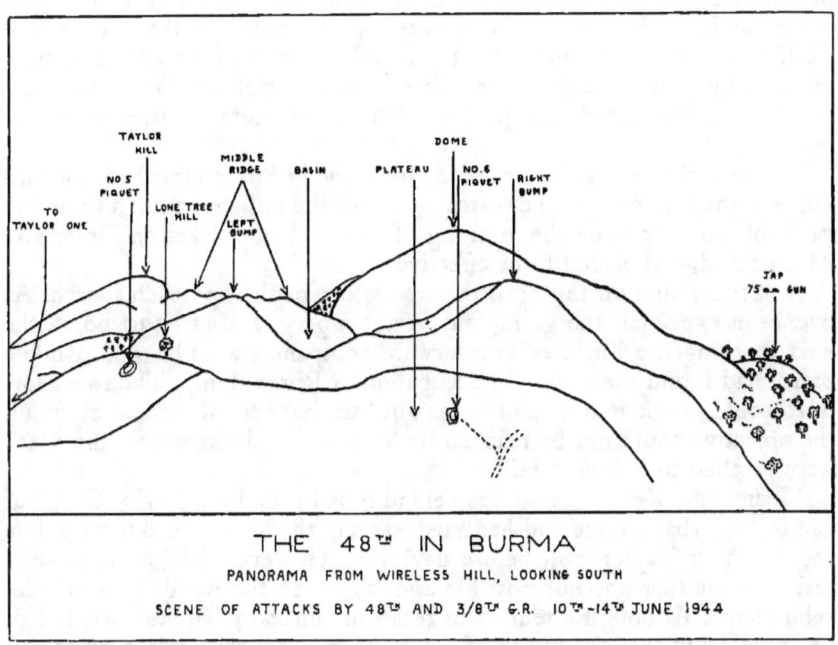

THE 48TH IN BURMA
PANORAMA FROM WIRELESS HILL, LOOKING SOUTH
SCENE OF ATTACKS BY 48TH AND 3/8TH G.R. 10TH-14TH JUNE 1944

over Right Bump to the ascent of Dome, 600 yards on, or over Left Bump, down into the Basin and then up to Middle Ridge. South of Wireless Hill the ground was devoid of jungle and boulders, and beyond the edge of the plateau any movement was exposed to fire from Dome.

It was a formidable objective to tackle, and, apart from the strength of the position, many other difficulties faced the Brigade. Weather conditions were at their worst, and in view of this, although the assault would have to be carried out by night, the distance to be covered in the darkness in the approach march would have to be as short as possible; no tanks were available and the weather rendered smoke unreliable; wireless was erratic and hindered the co-ordination of operations, both as regards infantry action and artillery support; the troops were now in their sixth month of daily contact with the enemy, they were never dry and the majority were suffering from diarrhœa; casualties had reduced the strength of rifle companies by about 40 per cent.; and, last but not least, on the withdrawal of the 63rd Brigade the enemy had reoccupied the Kokaden area, but the 32nd Brigade, which now disposed only of its own three battalions, could not spare the troops to engage that area while it attacked Dome.

The main attack was to be carried out by the 3/8th, passing to the west of Right Bump and thence up the north-western slopes of Dome. The enemy at Ingourek were to be masked by a company of the 9/14th, and 'Kelforce,' composed from Nos. 3 and 4 Companies of the 48th and commanded by Major Keily, was to move on Taylor Hill via Taylor One and put in a limited attack designed to distract the enemy's attention to the rear.

Between the 8th and the 10th June the 3/8th established forward piquets, the foremost on the plateau south of the nullah, within a thousand yards of Dome, and on the morning of the 10th air strikes on Dome and Middle Ridge appeared to be effective.

At 2100 hours on the 10th the troops began the approach march. As had been expected, the going was very slippery, and at 0230 hours the next morning the Gurkhas' two forward companies were bogged, while a patrol had found the enemy in occupation of Right Bump. The route forward could not be found, and it was obvious that even if it could be found the objective could not be reached under cover of darkness. So the 3/8th were recalled to Wireless Hill.

Meanwhile 'Kelforce' also was behind time in reaching Taylor One, but had left a layback there and had pushed on in the hope of making up time and reaching Taylor Hill before daybreak. However, Major Keily soon realised that this was not possible and lay up in the woods to await developments. Although attempts to recall his force by wireless had failed, he appreciated that the attack of the 3/8th had not taken place, as he had heard no sound of firing, so he rejoined his layback at Taylor One and made his way thence back to Roadhead in daylight under cover of the usual dense mist.

*Second Attack on Dome, 13th–14th June*

Few of the brigade had now had very much rest for three successive nights, so there was a pause while preparations were made for a second attempt. Two additional piquets were established on the southern edge of the plateau, No. 6 by the 3/8th and No. 5 by the 48th, to cover the advance which was, this time, to be made by the direct southerly route. In addition, a 2-pounder anti-tank gun was installed on Wireless Hill to deal with the enemy bunkers and 75-mm. guns, and two 3·7 howitzers on Wooded Ridge.

The new attack was to be on a two-battalion front. After concentrating on, and to the east of, Wireless Hill, the 3/8th were to assemble behind No. 6 Piquet, the 48th behind No. 5, so that both would start from the southern edge of the plateau. The objectives were, for the 3/8th Right Bump and Dome, for the 48th Left Bump and Middle Ridge, and then exploitation to Taylor Hill. The timing allowed for a rest of at least an hour in the assembly positions, and calculations were based on the first and second objectives being assaulted at 0330 hours and 0430 hours respectively, when the early-morning cloud and mist would help mopping-up and consolidation. Prospects of success seemed good, for the enemy had shown no sign of being aware of the first attempt and their patrols had been inactive; but much depended on the weather and on a continuance of the early-morning mist.

As ill luck would have it, it started to drizzle on the evening of the 13th, and this developed into torrential rain as the troops moved from the concentration areas. In the 48th only one company, No. 4, had reached the assembly area five minutes before zero hour; the rest of the Battalion was strung out along the track in rear, and the same applied to the 3/8th. The wonder is that the troops ever reached their first objectives at all, but they did, and at 0400 hours No. 4 Company, commanded by Major Thunder, reported that they had taken Left Bump without loss, killing a few of the enemy.

No. 3 Company then moved up on the left of No. 4, to push on towards Middle Ridge; but ill luck again intervened, for the dawn broke bright and clear, and every man and feature could be seen, though 500 feet below there was a dense layer of cloud.

As No. 3 went over the lip of the Basin they were met with fire from the front and from both flanks, and were pinned down where there was no cover except for grass a foot high. Nos. 13 and 14 Platoons then pulled out and tried to work round to the left via Taylor One. No. 13 got into position on a bare ridge and No. 14 approached Taylor One, the post on which was believed to be unoccupied. But when the Platoon Commander and the leading section were within about ten yards of the wire, a burst of fire killed him and four of his men. Attempts to reach their bodies led to more men being wounded, and the effort had to be abandoned.

Over on the right the 3/8th had had a similar experience, coming under intense machine-gun fire at a range of 300 yards after they had taken Right Bump. It was evident that Dome could not be taken, and so long as the enemy held it Left Bump was exposed to its fire; so at about 1000 hours a withdrawal was ordered, the 48th to hold the ground they had won so as to help the 3/8th to disengage.

The withdrawal of the 48th was carried out in a most praiseworthy and methodical manner. No. 3 Company had great difficulty in extricating themselves, as the Lone Tree Ridge over which they had to pass was in full view of the enemy, and was the target for machine-gun and snipers' fire and for the fire of a 75-mm. gun on Middle Ridge. However, they got across, with No. 15 Platoon acting as rear-guard, but suffered more casualties, including Major Keily who was wounded when standing beside the C.O. at an O.P. at No. 5 Piquet. No. 4 Company then had a similar experience, but finally the Battalion concentrated, No. 5 Piquet was pulled in, and the whole returned to Roadhead.

The casualties incurred by the two battalions totalled 104, of which number the 48th had lost one officer killed and four wounded, twenty-six other ranks killed and died of wounds, thirty wounded and four missing.

The attempt to capture Dome had been well planned and had been conducted with determination. No one could have foreseen the sudden change in weather conditions, on which so much depended and which was the principal reason for the failure.

*Final Attempt to block the Track, 16th–28th June*

On the 16th June the 48th moved into the Gref 'box' north of the Silchar track near Bishenpur, where they were in divisional reserve. No. 3 Company, under Capt. Clayton, remained at Roadhead under the 32nd Brigade, which was now responsible for the track westwards from Evans's Knob.

Farther to the north the battle of Kohima had been won. There were signs of a break-up in the Japanese offensive, and the general trend of enemy movement in the track area was from north to south. The 32nd Brigade, now reinforced by the 7/10th Baluch Regt., was ordered to act against the enemy's line of communication from Laimaton via Youyangtek to the south, and did it very successfully. It was probably this, and the need for a shorter route to Kokaden, which led to the enemy's final attempt to block the Silchar track.

Under cover of the early morning mist on the 21st June the Japanese attacked Mortar Bluff, Marne and the Water Piquet, and overran the Baluchis's garrison at the last-named post. The 48th, less two companies, were ordered up to Half-way House to recapture it, and at the same time the 32nd Brigade took over responsibility for the track from this point to the west.

After a long and arduous climb No. 2 Company went in to the attack, following on a heavy artillery concentration, while No. 1 occupied the B.P. Hill area. The attack reached the wire of Water Piquet, but was then stopped by machine-gun fire and had to withdraw, covered by No. 1 who then returned to Half-way House.

On the next day there was much enemy activity, including heavy attacks on Mortar Bluff, beaten off by the Baluchis. Then, on the 23rd, a strong enemy force attacked Dog, forcing the Baluchi garrison, and two sections from No. 2 Company which had been sent to strengthen them, to withdraw. The enemy were engaged with l.m.g. and mortar fire from Half-way House and, since they were reported to be vacating the post, a platoon of No. 2 Company was sent to reoccupy it. After they had started it was learnt that the tanks were to bombard the post in an hour's time; but it was too late to delay the attack, which went in without success. That night No. 4 Company came to rejoin the Battalion and established a piquet, christened Thunder, 150 yards from Dog.

Early on the 25th the Japanese captured the key piquet of B.P. Hill from the Baluchis. No. 1 Company of the 48th moved out quickly to retake it, failing only at the wire; however, they held on to nearby features, under cover of which preparations were made for a second attempt. Meanwhile the Brigade had asked for more troops, to cope with the vigorous enemy effort now in progress, and the 48th Brigade (less one battalion) was ordered up to Half-way House to recapture Water Piquet and B.P. Hill, and to clear the enemy away from the track.

As far as B.P. Hill was concerned, the 48th Regt. got in first. On the afternoon of the 25th a platoon of No. 1 Company followed up a heavy bombardment of medium artillery and took the hill, killing fifteen of the enemy at a cost of one man slightly wounded. They also recaptured two mortars and other equipment which the Baluchis had had to abandon. The Platoon Commander, Lieut. Franklin, was awarded an immediate Military Cross for this very successful action.

The Battalion now came under command of the 48th Brigade, and after the latter had retaken Mortar Bluff, captured by the Japanese on the night of the 25th/26th, and Water Piquet, No. 3 Company established a piquet at Double Deck. On the next day No. 4 Company attacked and took Dog, and, assisted by two platoons of the 1/10th Gurkha Rifles, held it against several counter-attacks; but, later, point-blank 75-mm. gun-fire from the Kokaden ridge compelled them to vacate it. They had killed at least 22 enemy, but had had four men killed and thirty-one wounded, the latter including Major Thunder and 2/Lieut. Phillips. As they withdrew towards Half-way House, an unlucky shell from a 105-mm. gun killed another five men and wounded two.

*Last Days on the Track, 29th June–13th July*

On the 29th June the Battalion rejoined its own brigade and took over the 3/8th positions on Wireless Hill, commanded by Major J. R. Britten in the absence of Lieut.-Col. Taunton. The orders now were that set-piece attacks were not to be attempted and unnecessary casualties were to be avoided—wise orders in view of the heavy losses, particularly in leaders, which had been incurred by all units—but steady pressure was to be kept up on the enemy. Patrolling was therefore very active, that of the 48th ranging to Ingourek, Kungpi, Dome, Middle Ridge, and Lamda. One patrol, setting out to ambush the enemy near Kungpi on the 29th June, was itself ambushed, but managed to break away after killing two Japanese. Two of the patrol were missing after the engagement, but returned to the Battalion on the 10th July, safe and sound. They had wandered all over the countryside in their efforts to get back without encountering the enemy, and had existed on two packets of biscuits, all the food they had with them. They brought back with them all their equipment and their l.m.g. which they had kept clean and serviceable by means of mosquito-cream, a good example of real discipline.

At last news came that the 32nd Brigade was to be relieved by a brigade of the 5th Indian Division. The 48th handed over their positions on the 14th July and assembled at Roadhead preparatory to moving back. Before they left, the 3/8th achieved their ambition, for they succeeded in occupying both Dome and Taylor Hill. Other troops made good progress towards Kokaden.

*Silchar Track: Retrospect*

The relief of the 32nd Brigade brought to an end seven months of daily and continuous contact with the enemy in some form or other.

During their three months on the Silchar track, they had gained no spectacular victories, nor had they won fame in the eyes of the public. But they had held the right flank of the defences of Imphal, which the enemy had determined to capture, hanging on sometimes by the skin of their teeth, always wet and tired, against the fiercest efforts of the 33rd Japanese Division, recognised as the best enemy formation in Burma.

This defence had cost them 931 casualties, of which the 48th's share had been more than one-third; but they had counted 1,133 enemy dead, so that for every casualty there was at least one Japanese who would never fight again—and this does not take into account the enemy killed by the guns of the artillery and the tanks.[7]

Besides the troops who bore the brunt of the fighting, there were many who contributed to the defence by their devotion to duty. Among these, special mention must be made of the mule leaders of the Animal Transport Platoon, commanded by Lieut. Adnitt, and those from the Pt. 5846 locality.

From mid-April to early June, day after day, the former brought up from Bishenpur the supplies and ammunition that were vital to the Battalion. Every journey demanded real courage, in cold blood, not in the heat of action, and with no chance of hitting back at the enemy. The casualties to men and mules from the fire of the Japanese artillery, machine-guns and snipers were heavy; but thanks to the gallantry and determination of the mule leaders, of the escorts which accompanied them, and of the piquets which went out from Pt. 5846 to afford them some protection they never failed to deliver a load. More than half of the mules were killed, but despite this their loads were retrieved under fire and man-handled to their destination.

The water-point for the Battalion was on the track, 1,000 feet below Pt. 5846, and the opening of the route to it for the collection of water meant daily fighting. The mule leaders who went down and brought the water back, and the escorts which preceded them and protected them at the water-point, showed courage beyond praise.

In addition to these, two individuals deserve special mention.

Sgt. Saunders, who had shown great gallantry at Kyaukchaw, had become Cook-Sergeant, but this did not prevent him from continuing his earlier activities, and on the track he was often seen rounding up cattle under fire, in order that the Battalion should have some fresh meat. One morning, early in June, the C.O. sent for him to congratulate him on the award of the D.C.M. for further gallant conduct. Returning to the cookhouse, he had sat down to a cup of tea to celebrate the occasion when a burst of machine-gun fire hit him in the chest and arms. However, he was back with the Battalion within three months, and served them well during the march back into Burma.

Another stalwart, Pte. Lee, a cockney costermonger, was a stretcher-bearer who was awarded the Military Medal. He had the utmost contempt for the enemy and was never seen to duck his head, let alone take cover, even under the hottest fire. By his influence on the other stretcher-bearers he was the means of saving many lives. He was never wounded and steadfastly refused to accept promotion until later.[8]

The British, Indian and Gurkha units, which had fought so well together, thoroughly deserved the praise of Major-General Cowan, Commander of the 17th Indian Division, in his farewell message, in which he commended their will to win and emphasised the pride of the Division in having fought beside such a fine fighting brigade.[9]

*The 48th rest and train, July–November 1944*

The 48th were very tired when they reached Wangjing on the 15th July, after a march down the Silchar track to beyond Bishenpur followed by a journey in lorries. Physically, but not morally, the Battalion was in a poor state, after weeks of living in the rain and the perpetual mist or cloud of the hills, and the majority were suffering from dysentery, jungle sores and other complaints. Heavily loaded as they were with packs and blankets, the march was trying, and the descent to the warmer atmosphere of the plain made them all very sleepy.

The first few days in camp were devoted to rest, cleaning-up, overhauling dress and equipment, amusements—they saw the first film for many months—and medical inspections; these last were particularly necessary, and more than a month was to pass before the numbers attending the daily sick-parade fell below twenty, a large proportion of whom were evacuated to hospital. Leave started and gave an opportunity for another sight of something resembling civilisation, but many were admitted to hospital whilst on leave and did not return for some time.

At the time that the Battalion left the Silchar track companies were only about fifty strong, No. 4 being almost entirely composed of M.T. and carrier drivers, and men from 'B' Echelon. Training was started after a week's rest, even though companies were still very weak; drill was most necessary as the Battalion now contained men from more than thirty different regiments,[10] and owing to the introduction of a new type of bayonet at home many of those recently drafted did not know how to fix the type in use in India.

Naturally, Talavera Day was celebrated in a style which was as near to tradition as circumstances would allow. A few days later the 48th were visited by Lieut.-General Scoones, Commanding 4th Corps, who addressed them and thanked them for what they had done; and by Lieut.-General Stopford, under whom the 58th had served for so long, who was the Commander of 33rd Corps in which the 20th Indian Division was now to serve.

Later on the Battalion paraded for even more distinguished visitors. On the 7th August the Viceroy, Field-Marshal Lord Wavell, presented medals to members of the Brigade, the only one of the 48th who was available being L/Cpl. Lee, awarded the Military Medal for gallantry on the Silchar track in April. On the 10th September they were addressed by the Supreme Commander, Lord Louis Mountbatten, who told them that they had done great things and had every reason to be proud of themselves.

Early in October Lieut.-Col. Taunton left the Battalion to join the pool of Brigade Seconds-in-Command. Major Snow, of the Somerset Light Infantry, who had joined them when they left Bishenpur, was appointed to command, and Major P. de C. Jones of the K.S.L.I. arrived as Second-in-Command. However, before the end of the month Lieut.-Col. Snow was posted to command the 1st Bn. The Devonshire Regt., and Lieut.-Col. Taunton came back to the Battalion until such time as there should be a vacancy for his promotion.

Throughout these months drafts, which included a proportion of men from disbanded Gunner units, had been arriving, and by the end of October the strength of the 48th was 32 officers and 677 other ranks. The age of many of the new arrivals was over thirty-five, which seems somewhat old for so arduous a theatre of war.

So rest and training went on, until November came and with it the time for the 48th to be on the move again to play their part in the offensive which was to drive the Japanese armies far to the south.

20th Indian Division

# CHAPTER XVIII

## THE 48th IN BURMA
## THE OFFENSIVE, NOVEMBER 1944–MAY 1945

General Situation in Burma—32nd Brigade's Problem—March to the Chindwin, 23rd–30th November 1944—Crossing the Chindwin, 2nd–5th December—Advance to Chingyaung, 9th–14th December—At Chingyaung, 15th–23rd December—Advance on Budalin, 24th December 1944–4th January 1945—Gaining of Contact, 4th–6th January—Capture of Budalin, 7th–10th January—Advance to Monywa, 13th–15th January—Fighting at Ywathit, 16th–19th January—Attack on Monywa, 20th–23rd January—The Advance Continues, 25th–28th January—The General Situation—The Plan—The 48th's Task—Resources—Preliminaries to the Irrawaddy Crossing—The Crossing, 12th–15th February—Japanese Attacks, 16th–17th February—Holding the Bridgehead, 18th–28th February—Relief of the Bridgehead—Advance to Kyaukse, 6th–19th March—Operations round Kyaukse, 23rd–30th March—Final Operations, 1st–25th April—The 48th leave Burma (*see* Maps on pp. 291 293, 297, 299 and 302)

## *General Situation in Burma*

AT the end of June 1944, at the time when the 48th were about to have a rest after their strenuous months on the Silchar track, the general situation in Burma had undergone a great change.

All attempts by the enemy to break through into the Imphal plain had failed, defeated by the tenacity of the defence which had been assisted, in the later stages, by the over-optimism of the Japanese High Command. The 31st Division, badly mauled at Kohima, was withdrawing precipitately towards Ukhrul. The 15th was distributed in three main groups, one on each of the exits from Imphal, in a wide arc stretching from the Kohima–Imphal road down to the Palel–Tamu road. The 33rd, the crack enemy division in Burma, was divided between the latter road and the Imphal–Tiddim road.

Meanwhile, the force under the command of General Stilwell had cleared all but a few pockets of the enemy from North Burma, and as it advanced southward had driven the Japanese before it into the central sector. The advance of the 15th Corps, which had cleared Arakan, had had a similar effect and had also opened up forward airfields for the support of the main body of the Fourteenth Army farther inland.

The Japanese were being hampered by the monsoon, but hoped that this would give them time to rebuild their forces and that it would equally

# THE 48th IN BURMA. THE OFFENSIVE, 1944-1945

affect the Fourteenth Army. However, contrary to their expectations, the Fourteenth Army disobeyed the rules and carried on, instead of waiting till the monsoon had ended.

In brief, the Allied plan was to draw as many as possible of the Japanese forces towards the centre of Burma, an object which was well on its way to achievement, to cut their line of retreat to the south and then to deliver a mortal blow against them.

In pursuance of this plan, by mid-November the 2nd, 17th, 20th and 23rd Divisions had driven the enemy over the Chindwin, east of Imphal, while to the south the 5th Indian Division had retaken Tiddim and had then joined up at Kalemyo with the East African Division, which had moved down the Kabaw valley from Tamu.

In the next phase, the 19th Division was to cross the Chindwin about a hundred miles north of Kalewa, and advance thence on Mandalay via Shwebo. The 5th and East African Divisions were to establish a bridgehead east of the Chindwin at Kalewa, through which the 2nd and 20th Divisions were to advance towards Mandalay, the 20th Division on the right.

In connection with this plan one of the problems was that of congestion on the Palel–Tamu road, the only one leading into the Kabaw valley. To relieve this, one brigade of the 20th was to march across country to the Kabaw River; having done this it was to cross the Chindwin at Mawlaik and, again moving across country, was to operate east of the river and so constitute a threat to the communications of the Japanese opposing the advance of the 2nd Division from Kalewa.

It was a compliment to Brig. Mackenzie and his 32nd Brigade that it was they who were selected to carry out this operation.

## 32nd Brigade's Problem

The problem confronting the 32nd Brigade was no easy one. The force under Brig. Mackenzie's command, besides the three battalions of the Brigade, included the 4/10th Gurkha Rifles of the 100th Brigade, a Mountain Battery, a Field Company, Animal Transport Companies R.I.A.S.C., and a Field Ambulance. The strength was some 5,300 men and 1,450 animals, and in single file, which would be necessary on many stretches of the route, the column would occupy a road space of about four and a half miles.

The first fifty miles of the route from Wangjing southwards, and the next thirty-six miles south-east of Sunle, were well-known, since the area was that over which operations had taken place earlier in the year. The route involved a severe climb west of Khengoi, but thence into the Kabaw valley at Sunle the going became easier, though only by comparison.

The second stage, the thirty-three miles from Sunle to Mawlaik, had been dominated by the enemy in the past, and little was known about the tracks and water-supply. But marching was likely to be easier, for the climb up to the Atwin Yomas was a gradual one and the descent to the river even more gradual.

East of the Chindwin nothing was known of the country, and it remained for the Brigade to discover its difficulties for itself.

Information regarding the enemy was, as so often the case in Burma, very conflicting, and the Brigade was to find that the only information upon which it could rely was that gleaned by its own patrols.

Naturally the column had to travel light. Baggage averaged ten pounds a head, and rations on the man and on pack-animals would allow the column to carry on for three days without replenishment. After crossing the Chindwin all supply was to be by air-drop. This arrangement worked admirably, for men and animals were not overloaded, and by putting the troops on a reduced scale of rations the column could carry on for four days without having to wait for supplies. This was an important point, in case the ground or the enemy interfered with the air-drop at any time.

*March to the Chindwin, 23rd–30th November 1944*

The 48th's four months' period of rest and training at Wangjing ended on the 21st November, and on the following day lorries conveyed them the forty-three miles to Chapki Karong. Next day the march began in earnest, and though the distance to the next camping site was only about eight miles it was a trying day, especially for some of those who had joined the Battalion recently. The weather was hot, there was no shade and the track climbed to over five thousand feet, being especially steep in the last four miles. On the 24th the track to Khengoi was a switchback, and though the Battalion started at 0800 hours it was not till eleven hours later that the leading company reached camp, and the mule transport did not get in till seven hours after that. No. 4 Company was held up on the track, and at 2330 hours, when still five miles from his destination, the Company Commander decided to camp where he was for the night. The last day's march of this stage, from Khengoi to Sunle, was easier, the track descending from four thousand feet to the five hundred feet of the Kabaw valley. The 'B' Echelon M.T., which had gone by the Palel–Tamu road, rejoined the Battalion here, and by the time that the marching column began to reach camp had hacked small clearings in the thick jungle which covered the site, and had a hot meal ready for the troops within half an hour.

Two days were spent at Sunle, during which No. 4 Company caught up with the Battalion, and the first leave-party for England—one officer and six men—found that their eastwards march into Burma was, for the time being at least, at an end.

Resuming the march on the 29th, the 48th reached Hmandaw, and Mawlaik on the following day. This stage was an easier one than those at the beginning of the march. There was evidence that the Japanese had used it for M.T. during their offensive, and there was also evidence of what they had suffered during their retreat, skeletons lying curled up in ground-sheets beside the track showing that those too weak to march had been abandoned to die by starvation or disease.

*Crossing the Chindwin, 2nd–5th December*

Before the march from Wangjing had started, a detachment of the 3/8th Gurkhas had been sent ahead to Mawlaik, to cross the Chindwin and patrol forward from there. There were no signs of enemy near the river, so the 48th, who had been the leading battalion, pressed on with arrangements for crossing, while the other units of the Brigade arrived at twenty-four-hour intervals.

The Chindwin at Mawlaik was at least five hundred yards wide and had a four-knot current. Even with the most modern types of craft the crossing would have been a formidable undertaking, but Burma came a bad second to the claims of other theatres of war for these, and had they been available the problem of getting them to the river would have been wellnigh insoluble. Rubber Ranger-boats had been dropped from the air, but a number of these were damaged on landing, and in the end only about a dozen were available, supplemented by local boats, many of the latter being 'mechanised' by the ingenuity of the Bombay Sappers and Miners.

These types of craft were, however, of little value for the transpoitation of mules, so other methods had to be tried. First free swimming, but most of the mules turned back after covering about a hundred yards. Then swimming accompanied by men also swimming, but this was a slow method, for the number of men who were strong swimmers was limited, and they tired quickly. Then towing behind a boat paddled by four men, while a fifth sat in the stern and held the mule's head in his lap; this worked fairly well, though on occasions the mule took charge, and either towed the boat round and round in circles or broke loose and returned to its starting-place. Finally the Sappers built two rafts, powered by outboard motors and christened 'Horrible Charlie' and 'Stinking Henry,' which supplemented the other means.

As far as the 48th were concerned, only six mules were got across on the first day and twenty-four on the second, but by the evening of the third day they had all been transferred to the east bank. Other units profited by the experiments of the 48th, for in the next five days all the mules of the Brigade Group were successfully across, about 1,450 in all. Only one was drowned, another went mad and disappeared into the jungle.

The 48th's crossing started on the 2nd December, when No. 3 Company went over and established a bridgehead on the far bank. They were followed on successive days by the remainder of the Battalion, and by 0100 hours on the 5th all were east of the Chindwin and had carried their stores into the bivouac area.

Thus they had the distinction of being the first battalion in the Fourteenth Army to form a bridgehead across the Chindwin.

*Advance to Chingyaung, 9th–14th December*

The orders now were for the Brigade to advance to Chingyaung, thirty miles south-east of Mawlaik, by the Pondaung Chaung, and not to move south of it until ordered. The 48th left the Chindwin on the 5th December for Kadu, a few miles to the south, and spent the next two days making an air-strip to take light aircraft and gliders; the work mainly consisted of clearing the stubble, assisted by labour provided by the local headman, and demolishing the bunds—the low banks—round the paddy-fields.

The Battalion was to move ahead of the rest of the Brigade on the 8th to a ford on the Pondaung Chaung. There it was to wait for a day, and thereafter the advance was to continue with the Brigade formed into two columns, moving at twenty-four-hour intervals, in order to lessen the delays inevitable for a long column moving, mostly, in single file. A 'pursuit column,' equipped with 48-sets, strong enough to have a complete company available to deal with any emergency and able to report on the enemy, the route, supply-dropping sites and bivouacs, was to precede the main body by a day's march.

The ford was reached after a march which for most of the way was along the line of the chaung, a stream about a hundred yards wide but only knee-deep, with a sandy bed. On arrival the usual slit-trenches were dug, and news came from a Gurkha patrol that there were Japanese in Chingyaung and that it was being bombed; so No. 4 Company and a platoon of the 9/14th Punjab Regt. were ordered to move there on the 9th to obtain confirmation.

On the 10th and following days the march was resumed up the Pondaung Chaung. The going was difficult and slow, the column winding its way, now on one bank, now on the other, and for long stretches through water varying from six inches to two feet in depth. The men were given the option of wearing either boots or slippers; in the wet sand slippers made for easier marching, though the added weight of the boots to the load in the pack was a disadvantage, for every additional pound told. Although the narrow defile of the chaung, with the ground sloping steeply upwards on both sides and covered by tall jungle trees, would have given Japanese snipers great opportunities, there was no sign of them, and as reports came in from the pursuit column that they had found no enemy, so was the main column able to open out on to a broader front, which made for greater ease of marching.

A danger which was more in evidence than the enemy was that of scrub (or tick) typhus, a disease caused by the bite of a minute insect, invisible to the naked eye, which lived in the long grass. To combat this, which usually proved fatal unless treated in good time, all clothing had to be smeared with an insecticide twice weekly, and it was only the few who neglected this precaution who contracted the disease.

Although there was no opposition from the enemy—the only occasion on which fire had to be opened was to remove a twelve-foot python from the track—the days were not without incident. Supplies were dropped almost daily, and one day the aircraft ignored the marked dropping-zone and, instead, loosed their cargoes over the camp area. Such packages as were dropped by parachute were none too pleasant to those at the receiving end, but free-dropped sacks of rice and grain were really dangerous. Fortunately, the camp was in forest country, and, by watching the aircraft and hugging the trees at the appropriate moment, the 48th escaped injury, except for minor bruises and one mule killed; eighty-pound sacks of rice hit the H.Q. Mess and the C.O.'s slit trench, damaging signal equipment, but the human occupants were, wisely, behind nearby trees. The 9/14th were less fortunate and had two men killed. However, this was the fortune of war, and had it not been for supply by air the operation could not have been undertaken, nor would the troops have had the good rations—sometimes including the luxury of apples—and the mail which they did.

After thirty-five miles the chaung began to widen, and on the 13th December the leading column reached Kyaunggyigon. Here contact was made with a patrol from No. 4 Company, which reported that on the previous day a small Japanese patrol had been encountered to the north of the place, but had got away with one man wounded. Another patrol reported that Chingyaung was clear of the enemy, so No. 3 Company were sent on to occupy it. On the next day the whole brigade column followed, and so completed the first 163 miles of its march according to programme.

## At Chingyaung, 15th–23rd December

The nine days spent at Chingyaung provided a welcome respite after the three weeks of hard marching, and an opportunity to replenish essential stores, more especially boots, of which many pairs had become unserviceable from the sand of the Pondaung Chaung.

There was plenty of work to be done, however, in the way of constructing defences and making a landing-strip. Dropping of supplies continued to be erratic sometimes and blame was, as usual, laid on the ground arrangements for recognition until one morning a Dakota dropped sacks on the air-strip on which the light aircraft of a R.A.F. liaison-officer happened to be standing, instead of on the proper dropping-zone. The effect of this incident on the subsequent accuracy of the Dakota pilots was most marked.

Patrols were sent out in all directions, remaining out for from four to seven days. The special preserve allotted to the 48th was the direct southern route to Pyingaing, soon known to all as 'Pink-Gin,' about twenty miles distant. It was in this area only that there was much Japanese activity, and it seemed that they were preparing to withdraw towards Shwebo in the face of the threat of an advance by the 2nd Division from the Kalewa bridgehead. On the 18th a No. 2 Company patrol met another of four Japanese about half-way to Pyingaing, killed the leader, a sergeant, and secured a useful identification.

*Advance on Budalin, 24th December 1944–4th January 1945*

The Divisional Commander, Major-General Gracey, had visited Chingyaung on the 17th December and had given the 32nd Brigade instructions for future operations. These were to move on Budalin, a small railway town about one hundred miles to the south, while the rest of the Division would follow the general axis of the Chindwin and concentrate at Budalin, which would by then have been secured by the Brigade. This would entail another cross-country march and the possibility of acute water shortage.

The 4/10th Gurkha Rifles were to leave the Brigade, and were to establish a road-block on the Japanese communications east of Pyingaing on the Ye-U–Shwebo road, a task which they carried out with great success, killing many hundreds of the enemy.

Meanwhile, the 2nd Division had crossed the Chindwin and was moving on Pyingaing, which it was expected to occupy on the 24th, and in order to avoid the possibility of confusion the 32nd Brigade was timed to pass through that place on Christmas Day.

The march began on the 24th December, along the Maukadaw Chaung to Pawlaw, a tiring twelve miles along loose sand, though this time there was little water in the chaung. Christmas Day was very hot, and reflections on better ways of spending that day than by marching sixteen miles through sand were not improved by the leading company of the 48th taking a wrong turning, and so wasting two hours, while the battalion behind them went ahead on the right route. However, as the Brigade moved through the rear elements of the 2nd Division, west of Pyingaing, the troops were rewarded by the welcome they received from their comrades, from whom they had been separated for so many weeks, and it was not long before they reached their camp.

Here the 48th's pursuit column had selected, perhaps not entirely by accident, a supply dropping-point very close to that already chosen by the 2nd Division's Corps Troops, and on Boxing Day they received from the air 'manna,' in the shape of turkey, tinned chicken and puddings. The ration was so lavish that a distribution could be made to the other units of the Brigade, and it was not until Christmas dinners were over that the 48th seem to have realised the cause of their good fortune: the 2nd Division was an all-British one, and, Christmas being essentially a Christian festival, special efforts had been made by those in rear to ensure that it could be properly observed as far as food went. However, there was enough for the Corps Troops as well, so the accident led to no ill feeling, and who shall say that the 48th did not deserve some reward after their long march from Wangjing?

The next stage of the march promised to be more than usually difficult. No one knew the route, but from the map it seemed that it would involve an ascent over a pass, followed by a difficult descent, and a single-file column through country ideally suited for snipers and ambushes.

So, on the 26th, the 48th were ordered to send ahead their pursuit column, No. 2 Company and a platoon fromNos. 1 and 3 Companies, under Major Jones, to get information at all costs about the route and the water situation at the end of it. By nightfall no information had been received, but in the early hours of the 27th two runners arrived with a message that the wireless would not work, that the route was most difficult but that the pursuit column were improving it, and that water had been found and was being protected by a platoon. This was welcome news, and much credit is due to the two runners, whose names unfortunately are not recorded, who had brought it back on a pitch-black night over six miles of very difficult country.

As a result of this information the Brigade was able to start later in the day, and a hard march it was, up a sandy nullah which narrowed as it neared the pass, with numerous huge fallen trees blocking the path at intervals and compelling détours and delays, with the result that the 48th did not reach their camp, thirteen miles away, until six and a half hours after they had started.

Then, day after day, the march continued, through Palusawa and other places to Kudaw, reached on the 3rd January.

There had been no opposition, only rumours of Japanese which usually proved to be incorrect, and this had led to carelessness in respect of those precautions which were always necessary even if there did not appear to be any sign of the enemy in the immediate neighbourhood. But this was soon put right by some well-chosen words from the C.O.

By now the type of country had changed, and was much more open, with frequent level stretches; and after they reached Kudaw the 48th had their first sight of a tarmac road since November. Gone was the jungle, which a year before had seemed strange and hostile, concealing an enemy in every tree, but had since become friendly and a cloak to movement. Now, in the comparatively flat plain, covered with scrub and occasional trees, the 48th felt very naked and conspicuous.

But the more open country had its advantages. Movement could take place on a much wider front and, from Palusawa, the Brigade could move by two tracks, while there was greater freedom of manœuvre for units and sub-units, as will be seen from the operations which followed. The farther south they got the farther they were from support, for the rest of the Division was struggling down the Chindwin to the west, while the 2nd Division was moving south-east on Ye-U. So pursuit columns were strengthened, to allow of patrolling well out to the flanks of the main axis of advance.

At Kudaw, after a cross-country march of 230 miles, the 32nd Brigade was within striking distance of the enemy in Budalin.

*Gaining of Contact, 4th–6th January*

By nightfall on the 3rd January the pursuit columns had reported that the line Nyaunggan–Aungbaunggyaung–Siba, about five miles from Budalin itself, was clear of the enemy. Next morning the three battalions of the Brigade moved up to this line and halted, while officers' patrols were sent forward for a close reconnaissance of the town.

There was every indication that the enemy, if in Budalin, was oblivious of the presence of so large a force in the neighbourhood, and it was hoped that it would be possible to encircle the place and kill any garrison there. Accordingly the plan, subject to the patrols' reports, was for the 9/14th Punjab Regt. to move across country from Nyaunggan and establish a road-block about Milestone 18, three miles south of the town; the 48th, supported by the 31st Mountain Battery, were to advance from Aungbaunggyaung, secure Hlwede and its water-supply, and move into Budalin from the north-west; the 3/8th Gurkha Rifles, from Siba, were to move round the east of the town and block the south-eastern approach at Ywashe.

Before long the 9/14th patrol reported the Thayogon area clear, and that battalion pushed on and established the road-block by nightfall.

Meanwhile a patrol commanded by Lieut. Stoddart, on approaching the road-junction of Hlwede, had drawn fire from about a platoon of Japanese which was dug in covering the road, and had withdrawn to a covered position between the two roads and about half a mile from the road-junction.

Lieut. Stoddart's report reached Battalion H.Q. at 1500 hours and at about the same time the 9/14th reported having seen Japanese in the Post Office and Dispensary areas of the town. This seemed to confirm the enemy's ignorance of their situation, so Brig. Mackenzie decided to move the 48th and the Gurkhas towards the town by night, in the hope of achieving surprise and at least blocking the enemy in, if not of rushing the positions which had been located.

Accordingly, at 1615 hours No. 2 Company moved out and joined Lieut. Stoddart's platoon. At dusk a 3-inch-mortar concentration was put

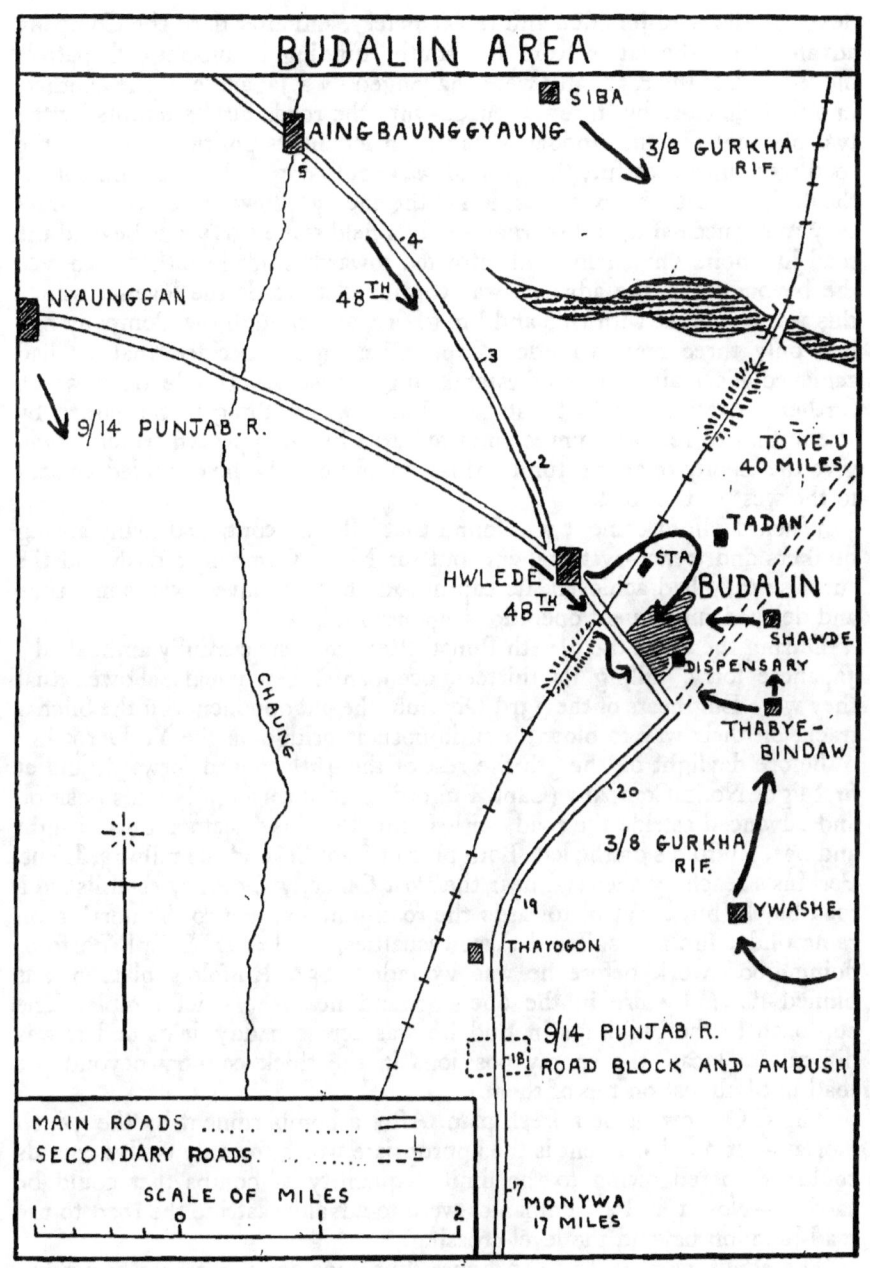

down on the road-junction and the cemetery, and after dark the Company advanced on the latter from the south. Finding it unoccupied, patrols moved east of the road, and were challenged by a Japanese, while another, in a foxhole close by, threw grenades into the road. First attempts by the two platoons (Lieut. Stoddart's had been left in its position) to cross the road were unsuccessful; the ground was confusing and it was difficult in the dark to locate the exact position of the enemy. However, by 0200 hours they were successful, and reorganised in a field some 350 yards beyond the road-junction. The enemy had retreated towards Budalin rather than face the bayonet, and the advance was continued towards the level-crossing; this was soon met with rifle and l.m.g. fire, and though the Company had had only three men wounded Capt. Cherrington decided that he had achieved his main object of establishing a base at Hlwede from which further operations could be staged. There was nothing to be gained by attempting to reach an unreconnoitred area by an approach which would give the enemy the opportunity to lay an ambush. So he occupied an area to the west of the road.

When daylight came it was found that Hlwede contained many strong bunkers and trench-systems, and but for No. 2 Company's dash and the surprise they had achieved, its capture might well have taken some time and delayed subsequent operations against Budalin.

During the night the 9/14th Punjab Regt. had successfully ambushed a Japanese lorry, killing its thirteen occupants. Documents showed that they were Engineers of the 33rd Division, the old opponents on the Silchar track, on their way to blow up an important bridge on the Ye-U road.

Before daylight on the 5th the rest of the 48th moved forward, and at first light No. 1 Company (Capt. Fulford) passed through No. 2's position and advanced astride the road, with Lieut. Perkins's platoon on the right and Sgt. Ruffold's on the left. Both platoons got beyond the railway, Lieut. Perkins's reaching the road near the Post Office, where they established a road-block, but a patrol towards the road-junction just to the north soon came under fire and suffered three casualties, the leader, L/Cpl. Barford, doing good work before he was wounded. Sgt. Ruffold's platoon was pinned down by fire in the open ground near the chief temple. The approach to the buildings in Budalin was across paddy-fields and it was difficult to locate the enemy positions in the thick country beyond the road until almost on top of them.

The C.O. now made a fresh plan. After a bombardment by the 3-inch mortars—if bombardment is the appropriate word, for only twelve rounds could be spared owing to the limited quantity of bombs that could be carried—Nos. 1 and 4 Companies were to advance astride the road to the road-junction beyond the level-crossing.

The attack went in at 1140 hours, but once again ran into heavy fire

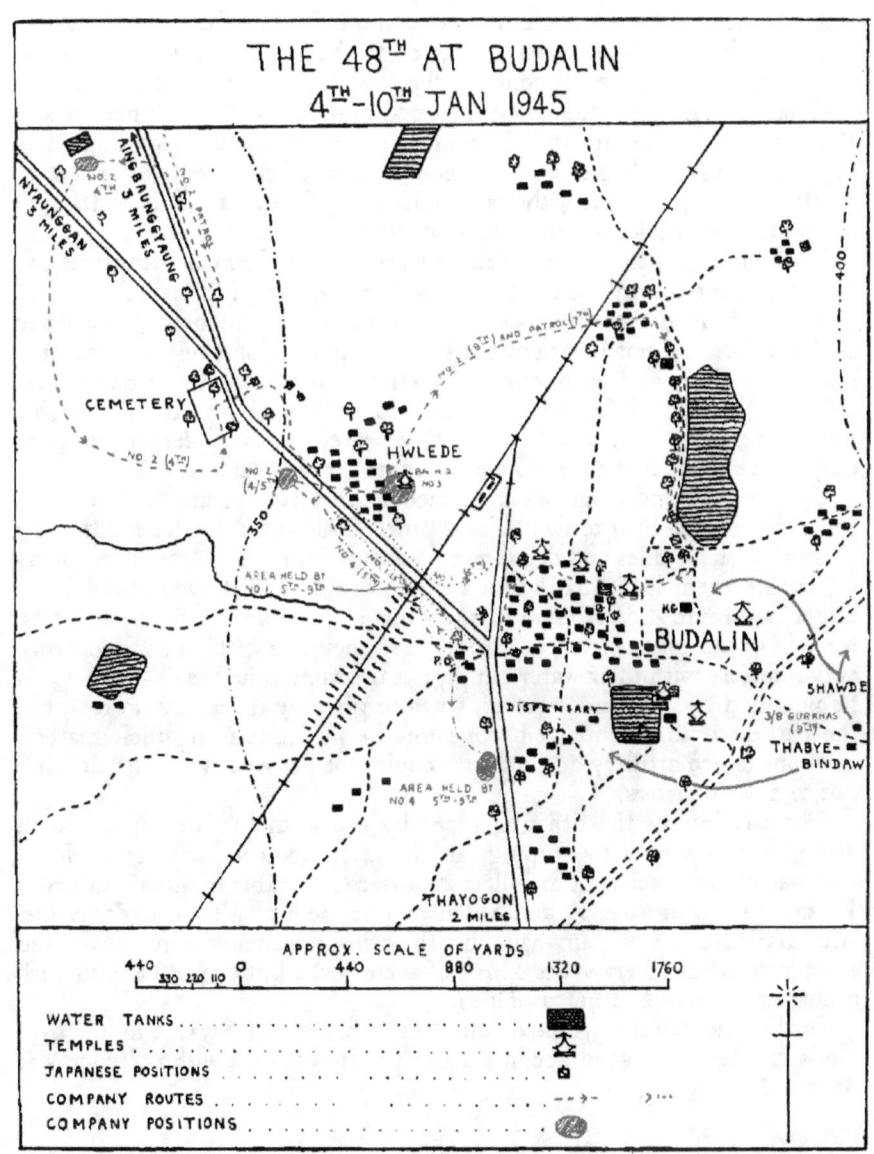

when crossing the open ground beyond the railway. After a pause for regrouping, No. 4 Company were diverted to the right, and took up a position on the road 400 yards south of the Post Office. At 1430 hours it was decided to hold on to the ground gained and attempt no further attacks that day, No. 1 Company occupying a 'box' at the level-crossing. The day's fighting had begun a closer encirclement of the enemy, at a cost of 2 killed and 24 wounded, the latter including Lieuts. Perkins and Leigh and four other ranks who remained at duty.

That night a 'jitter-party' tried to worry No. 1 Company, but was unsuccessful, for the troops kept calm and refused to be 'jittered.'

It now seemed that there were, at the most, one hundred Japanese in Budalin, holding not less than three well-dug positions, one covering the road and railway approach, one in the Dispensary area and one on the east side covering the Ye-U road, with numerous alternative positions to which they could move under cover. They appeared to have platoon weapons only, since there had been no sign of m.m.g.s, mortars or artillery.

By now the 32nd Brigade had formed an open ring round the town, and the problem was how to tackle its capture. This could be done, either by closing in on all sides and driving the garrison into one isolated area, or by separating them into small groups which could be destroyed in detail. In either case infiltration from as many points as possible was the best tactics, for this would force the enemy to disperse their strength and would probably interfere with their water-supply; at the same time the defences could be pounded by 3·7s and mortars, so as to give the defenders no rest, but the battle would essentially be one for the infantry, using their platoon weapons, since artillery and mortars could not be used when the fighting got to close quarters.

The daytime of the 6th was spent by the 48th in patrolling, and in worrying the enemy by sniping. In the afternooon a party from No. 4 Company which went out to collect a mortar O.P. cable found about seven Japanese bending over it, and killed two of them at fifteen yards' range. After dark No. 1 Company had a brush with some enemy who had worked a l.m.g. to within forty yards of one of their posts, but drove them off with grenades and suffered no casualties.

During the day the 3/8th advanced their base from Ywashe to Thabyebindaw, where they would be in a better position to deal with the enemy at Shawde.

*Capture of Budalin, 7th–10th January*

It was now decided to try to get another company into Budalin from the north, No. 2 (Capt. Cherrington) being selected for the task. The plan was to get the company in, and for them then to swing west, capture the water-point near the Kyaung [1] and work thence towards the railway station.

As a preliminary Lieut. Stoddart's platoon went out at about 0800 hours on the 7th, with the object of establishing a base south of the lake. Moving by Tadan they came under l.m.g. fire as they were working their way down the bund on the west side of the lake, and were held up for some time in open ground. Eventually, after killing one Japanese of an outpost which they dispersed, they reached their objective, but could not remain there and returned at 1700 hours with useful information.

Meanwhile the Gurkhas had pushed forward, and early on the 8th had established one company in the eastern outskirts of Budalin, while another had isolated the enemy at Shawde.

At 0900 hours on that day No. 2 Company, with Lieut. Perkins's platoon from No. 1 Company attached, moved from the area at the southern end of Hlwede where they had been with Battalion H.Q. Lieut. Stoddart's platoon led the way, and about an hour later, when they had reached the bund, Capt. Cherrington wirelessed that H-Hour should be 1015 hours.

At that hour supporting fire was brought down by mortars and a 6-pounder anti-tank gun. The Company moved forward, with some interference from Japanese grenade-dischargers but without casualties, and by about noon Lieut. Bacon's platoon had attacked and taken the area of the large temple south of the lake. Lieut. Stoddart's platoon then passed through them, with the large water-tank as their objective, but after they had gone fifty yards came under the fire of a light automatic. Lieut. Stoddart and one of his men were killed, and the platoon was held up.

By now the rest of the Company had come up and consolidated a position just east of the water-tank and commanding it, and after an hour's firing by a l.m.g. and snipers, the enemy's activity ceased. That evening Capt. Cherrington was outside the perimeter with Sgt. Lindsell and a small party, seeing to the laying of a telephone cable, when about seven Japanese were observed approaching the temple from the east. Accounts vary as to the sequel. One says that he killed three, another that he killed one but missed the remainder much to his annoyance, owing to the sights of his sniper's rifle having been pushed up to 900 yards when he was crawling through some bushes. In any case it was good shooting. Sgt. Lindsell went out into the open and removed the papers from the dead enemy's pockets, an act for which he was later awarded the Military Medal.

Towards dark a Japanese who attempted to reach the body of Lieut. Stoddart, lying in the open, was shot. The Company's casualties had been 3 killed and 6 wounded.

Patrols from the other companies were active during the day, and the snipers of No. 1 killed two of the enemy, one of them a tree-sniper. Yet another fell to the Bren gun of one of No. 4 Company's sections, when a small party of enemy approached their position during the night.

Early on the 9th a patrol from No. 2 Company made contact with the

Gurkhas and gave them information which enabled them to work farther into the town from the north-east. Farther to the south another Gurkha company was approaching the Dispensary.

On No. 2 Company's front no live Japanese were found, only some bodies. The area was searched methodically, a very necessary precaution against the Japanese, and a patrol went right through and gained touch with No. 3 Company which then occupied the road-junction. Documents found on the ground established the fact that the H.Q. of the 3rd Battalion 213th Regt. had been located there, this accounting for the resistance which the 48th had encountered in the area.

Before noon on the 10th January the whole of Budalin could be reported clear of the enemy. The 48th's casualties in the operation had totalled 42, most of them incurred on the first day, while in the whole area 44 enemy dead were counted; there were also many fresh graves. Although it had been impossible to form a continuous ring round the town, it was estimated from footmarks that only about fifteen or twenty Japanese had managed to slip through and make their escape.

All companies had done good work, especially No. 1 who had made the first contact astride the main road and had held the enemy while the others could manœuvre, but it was to No. 2 that the chief credit for the capture of Budalin was given. Their action on the 9th was the decisive one, and the D.S.O. which was subsequently awarded to Capt. Cherrington was well earned. Pte. Gannaway and two others of his Company were awarded the M.M.

Telegrams of congratulation were soon received by the Brigadier from Army, Corps and Divisional H.Q. for an action which proved that well-led troops could beat the Japanese at his own game of infiltration, using only their platoon weapons, providing that they used their eyes and were quick to shoot.

*Advance to Monywa, 13th–15th January*

With Budalin captured, the rest of the 20th Division came up fast and concentrated in the area. The town became a hive of activity, with Dakotas dropping supplies for the whole Division, and light aircraft using the landing-strip for the evacuation of casualties and other purposes.

The 32nd Brigade saw its M.T. once more, after having been without it for two months, and found that it was not without its disadvantages in the form of dust and noise.

The Brigade's next objective was Monywa, twenty miles to the south, an important railway junction and once a flourishing Chindwin port. It was practically certain to be occupied, and it was unlikely that the Japanese would give it up without a struggle, but the strength of the garrison was unknown. A simultaneous advance was to be made by the 80th Brigade on

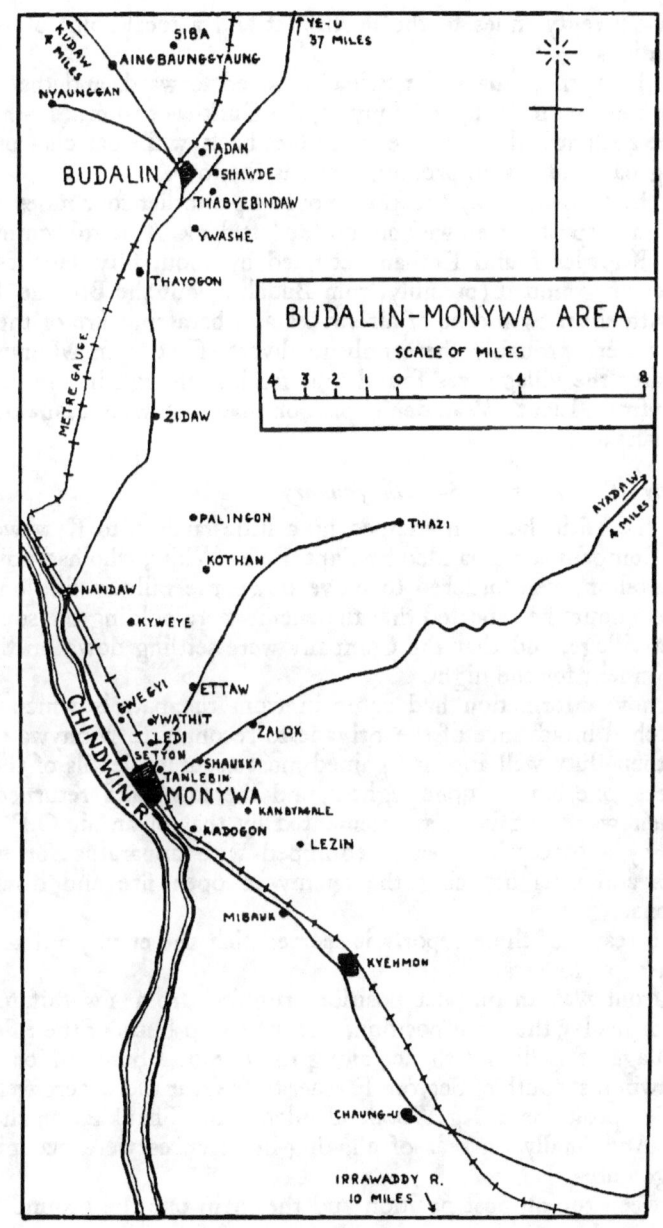

Ayadaw, twenty miles to the north-east and a focal-point of road communications.

On the 13th January the Brigade moved forward, and that night the 9/14th were six miles from Monywa, the Gurkhas two miles behind them, and the 48th at Zidaw, another five miles back, while patrols from the two leading battalions were probing towards the town.

On the following day the 48th moved up another four miles and established an outpost screen well out on the left flank. A patrol commanded by Lieut. Knowles found Kothan occupied by about fifty Japanese, with a number of wounded (possibly from Budalin), but the Brigade decided to deal with them by means of air-strikes and harassing fire of the artillery, as they were probably there only to divert effort from Monywa. Three days later the village was found undefended, though in the meantime a patrol from Lieut. Walkden's platoon had incurred casualties during reconnaissance.

*Fighting at Ywathit, 16th–19th January*

On the 16th the 48th stepped up a little farther, to Kywewe, whence No. 4 Company, commanded by Capt. Eales-White, who had now rejoined the Battalion, were ordered to move down the railway line on Ywathit. At 2000 hours he reported that the enemy were holding the southern end of that village, and that the Company were settling down on the railway embankment for the night.

By now information had come in from the patrols which had been despatched in advance of the Brigade to reconnoitre Monywa. They had done their duty well and had gained most accurate details of the enemy's defences, one having gone right round the town and returned through it. Their work had been supplemented by that of an air O.P. pilot and aided by a 'deception' party, equipped with apparatus for simulating attacks and thus inducing the enemy to open fire and disclose their positions.

As a result of these reports it seemed that the enemy's defences were organised as follows:

In front was an outpost position, running from Ywathit to Gwegyi. Behind this lay the main position, from the stop-butts of the rifle-range to the village of Ledi and thence along the line of a bund which led to the Chindwin just south of Setyon. Farther to the rear there were well-dug and occupied positions in Kg Wood,[2] Tanlebin and Shaukka, on the enemy's right. And finally, in rear of all, dug-in defences were occupied in the Kadogon area.

Between the outpost position and the main one the ground was fairly open, but there was a considerable amount of marsh grass, about a yard high, which would afford some cover from view, but none from fire.

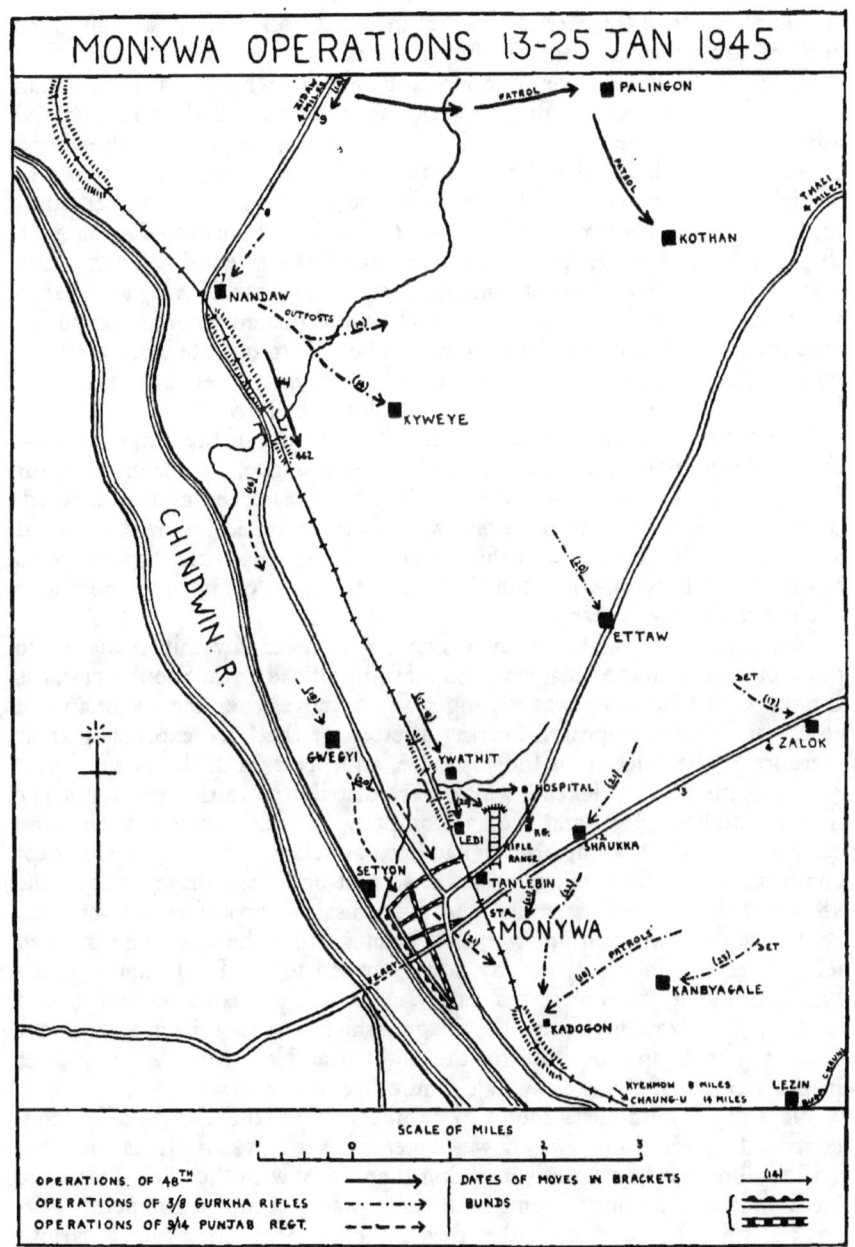

The strength of the garrison was estimated at 200 or more, with m.m.g.s and the usual platoon weapons, but no guns.

Apart from its superior numbers and morale (which was higher than ever after the success at Budalin), the 32nd Brigade had great material advantages over the enemy. As little fighting was in progress elsewhere, Ayadaw having been taken by the 17th January, abundant air support was available and was used to the best advantage thanks to the understanding of infantry problems displayed by the R.A.F. Squadron-Leader who directed it. The Brigade had the support of the guns of the 9th Field Regiment, and a squadron of armoured cars of the 11th Cavalry was placed under its command and was used for close and distant reconnaissance. In fact, for the first time the Brigade was to be able to operate with resources which, though regarded as a matter of course in most other theatres of war, had not hitherto been available in its operations in Burma.

The general plan of attack was, first, the capture of the outpost line—this was essential for further detailed reconnaissance, for forming-up for the subsequent operations and to enable the guns to be moved forward. Then the located enemy positions were to be softened by air-strikes and artillery. Finally, the 48th on the left and the 9/14th on the right were to advance on Monywa, while the Gurkhas carried out commando operations against the enemy's rear.

No. 4 Company of the 48th, which we left near Ywathit, managed to get a platoon into the village on the morning of the 17th. Soon afterwards the rest of the Battalion was getting ready to move when the headman and elders of Kywewe appeared bearing a letter for the C.O. expressing their pleasure at the eviction of the Japanese, and presents in the form of peanuts, hot milk and chickens, which were distributed to the men. At 1315 hours Battalion H.Q. and No. 3 Company had just started when news came from No. 4 that the platoon had been attacked by troops wearing cap-comforters, had been taken by surprise and had been driven out of the village with two men wounded and four missing, two of whom returned later. Lieut.-Col. Taunton, who had been visiting the Company but had left before this incident, had by now returned to his H.Q., and ordered No. 1 Company to reoccupy Ywathit. A patrol, preceded by mortar and artillery fire, drew fire from the village, which was then in flames, so the Company took up a position for the night near Nos. 1 and 4 Companies in the vicinity of the railway half a mile to the north-west.

Next day Ywathit was found to be unoccupied, and the Battalion concentrated there while Gwegyi was taken by the 9/14th after an air and artillery bombardment, thus bringing them level with the 48th. Patrols to Ledi and the rifle-butts found both these places occupied by enemy. Air-strikes were made during the day by Hurribombers against various known enemy positions, and were continued on the 19th.

## Attack on Monywa, 20th–23rd January

D-Day for the attack was the 20th. The air bombardment began at 0900 hours, when the first of the total of eighty-two Hurribombers, Mosquitoes and Thunderbolts started their timed programme, directed by the R.A.F. liaison-officer. Some twenty-five tons of bombs were dropped and the enemy bunkers in the rifle-butts were attacked by rocket-firing Hurricanes with good effect, for they formed an ideal target for them. The sight was a pleasing one for the 48th, even though they received some of the 'overs' from four Mosquitoes which engaged the rifle-butts with bombs and cannon, flying from south to north.

The 48th's first objectives were Ledi and the rifle-butts. To their right and west of the railway, the 9/14th had parallel objectives.

At noon companies moved to their start-lines. Forty minutes later yellow smoke gave the signal to the aircraft to cease their action, and at the same time the 9th Field Regiment and a troop of Medium Artillery put down a five-minutes' concentration on the objectives and then switched on to those of the 9/14th. The leading companies of the 48th (No. 4 under Major Eales-White and No. 1 under Capt. Fulford) then moved forward, following to within 150 yards of the shell-bursts.

On No. 4 Company's front, No. 10 Platoon had first to clear the White House area, which earlier patrols had found to be occupied. This they did without difficulty by about 1330 hours, and then went on to occupy Ledi without a shot being fired. Company H.Q. and No. 11 Platoon then moved up to the White House, but as they neared it came under fire from snipers; though they managed to reach it they found that the bunkers in the area, which had been searched by No. 10 Platoon, had been reoccupied by the enemy, and had three men killed. The enemy now tried to burn No. 4 out of the White House area by setting fire to the long grass, but a rapid attack, with flank protection by two platoons of No. 3, which had now moved up, forced the enemy to withdraw, leaving six dead behind them. In the course of these actions Major Eales-White was wounded and Capt. Noakes took over command of his company.

Meanwhile, west of the railway, the 9/14th had been held up by extremely strong positions sited in a stone-faced bund; so also had No. 12 Platoon, which was in touch with them on that side of the railway, and eventually it was withdrawn to Rear H.Q. after a platoon of No. 3 Company had helped in the evacuation of the casualties incurred.

In the centre No. 1 Company had about eight hundred yards of open ground to cover before reaching their objective—the rifle-butts. The right platoon had some trouble from sniping from the right, but this was neutralised by the action of the reserve platoon, and the left platoon made a détour to the left to avoid this fire. There was some small-arms and gren-

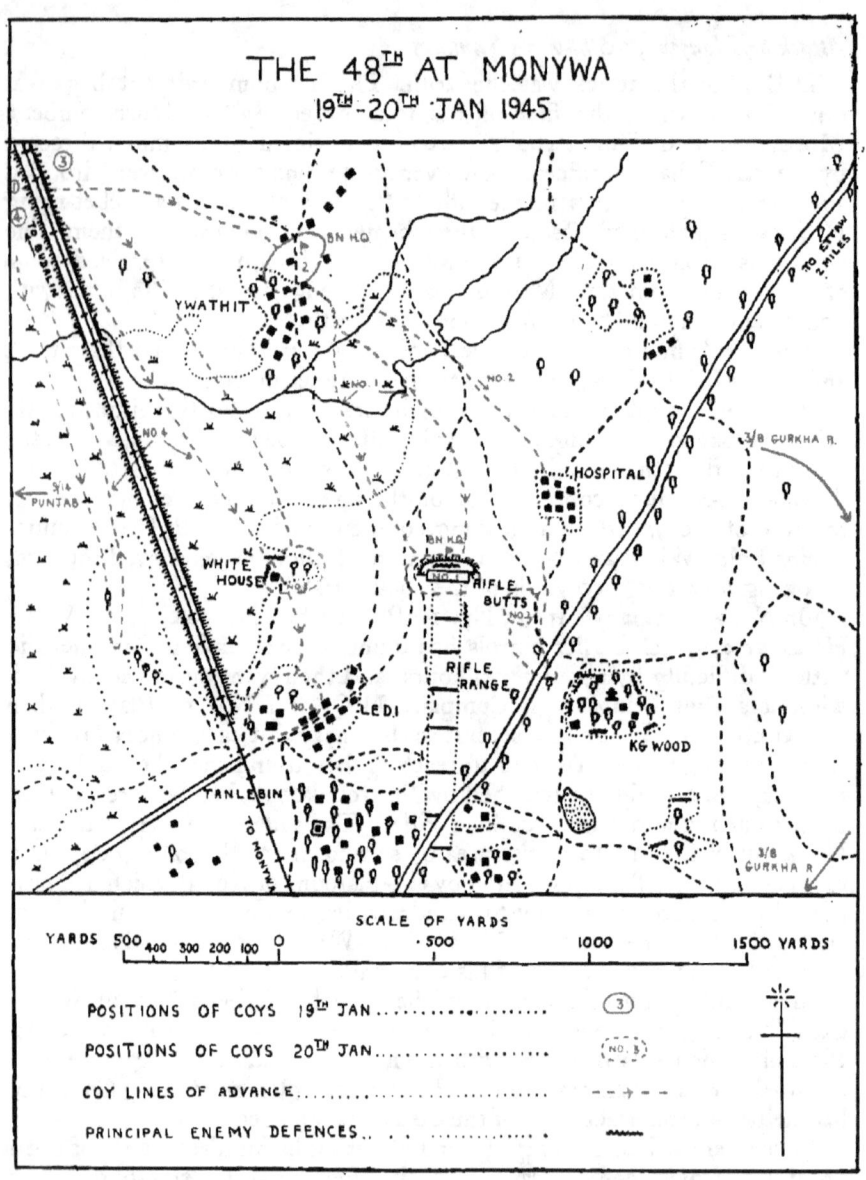

ade fire from the neighbourhood of the butts as the Company neared them, but they went on well and got to their objective to see the enemy running away as hard as they could. Much equipment and food was found in the strongly built bunkers around the butts. No. 1 had had only five casualties, Major Fulford slightly wounded and four other ranks wounded.

The remark made by one of his Company to Major Fulford, 'Why, Sir, this is just like an exercise!' as they advanced, firing from the hip, after the preliminary bombardment, is proof, if proof be needed, of the value of realistic battle-training. For this was the man's baptism of fire.

No. 2 Company, under Capt. Cherrington, which had been kept in reserve with Battalion H.Q. at Ywathit, were now ordered forward to take first the Hospital, then Kg Wood. A battery of 25-pounders was available in support, also some R.A. mortars and armoured cars.

The Hospital area was found to be clear of the enemy, and a short concentration was then put down on the Wood while Lieut. Bacon's platoon investigated a block on the road to the north-west. No Japanese were found there, so while the platoon occupied a covering position the rest of the Company moved up to the west side of the road opposite the Wood. The time was now about 1500 hours.

There was still no sign of the enemy, and there was no observation because between the road and the Wood lay a belt of very tall, thick bushes, closely matted together, which were, in most places, almost impassable. Company H.Q. and Lieut. Knowles's platoon remained by the road, while Lieut. Bacon's platoon on the left and Sgt. Solomon's on the right advanced on the Wood.

The former found a small gap in the bushes, but was soon fired upon and could not make much progress. However, a bunker in the Wood was located, and a belt of wire strung with booby-traps in the clearing between the bushes and the edge of the Wood. Sgt. Solomon's platoon had found a track and advanced down it, but was forced back by l.m.g. fire from the Wood.

At this stage there was a pause. Capt. Cherrington had disappeared and it was feared that he had been wounded. After a prolonged search he was found, and brought in by L/Cpl. Parker. He had, apparently, gone on alone to reconnoitre, and had been hit in the head when he had reached a point on the inner edge of the bushes only thirty yards from the Japanese positions. The enemy had removed his rifle and equipment, the latter being recovered on the next day. He died as he was being taken back to the R.A.P. A very gallant officer, he had already on several occasions displayed great fearlessness, and it was tragic that he fell before he knew that he had been awarded the D.S.O. for his leadership at the taking of Budalin.

Three armoured cars, with supporting infantry in trucks, were now sent up, and under cover of their fire a wounded man of the right platoon, who was lying in a spot dominated by enemy fire, was successfully got away. The cars then cruised round the bushes, firing their m.m.g.s and their 2-pounder guns, but were unable to locate the enemy positions with any certainty. They were followed by grenade fire which wounded their British officer, though they had the satisfaction of accounting for a Japanese officer in return.

Capt. Dyson, who had taken over command of the Company, continued to try to get definite information about the enemy's positions, and it was soon evident that nothing but a strongly supported attack would succeed against the Wood. So, after discussion by wireless with the C.O., it was decided at about 1630 hours to withdraw the Company a little way to the west of the road and establish a position there for the night. The withdrawal was successfully carried out under cover of artillery fire.

By now Battalion H.Q. had been established at the rifle-butts, and at 1700 hours they and No. 1 Company were assailed by a hail of bullets. Taking what cover they could, for they had not yet fully dug in, they stood to and awaited the Japanese counter-attack; however, they were relieved, though somewhat annoyed, when Capt. Veater's voice came over the air, and they discovered that the bullets were from No. 3 Company who were clearing small parties of enemy from the long grass between Ledi and the butts.

The night passed peacefully, and patrols out the next day found the level-crossing and the wood at the end of the rifle-range clear of enemy, though Kg Wood was still held. On the right the 9/14th made preparation for another assault on the extremely strong bund position, while to the left the Gurkhas tightened their ring to the south-east.

Early morning patrols on the 22nd found all these positions unoccupied, so at 0900 hours both battalions advanced till they reached a line running south-west and north-east through Monywa railway station. There they halted, so as not to interfere with artillery support for the Gurkhas who were clearing the southern half of the town, and spent that day and the next in collecting booty and in patrolling to maintain touch with the Gurkhas.

Investigation of Kg Wood showed it to have been a very strong position, especially on the side facing the road. On that side were two small bunkers linked by a deep crawl-trench, and at twenty-yard intervals all round the perimeter and within it was a series of well-concealed foxholes. A very deep and elaborate air-raid shelter had apparently been used as a Command Post, while other civilian shelters and banked enclosures had been converted into bunkers and provided with foxholes. Ladders led to two tree O.P.s. Round the whole perimeter ran a double-apron fence, with trip wires on either side. A Japanese officer's sword, later presented to the Battalion by the officers and men of Capt. Cherrington's company, and a considerable amount of ammunition, was found in the position, to say nothing of three unexploded 500-pound air-bombs; and in some pits were some old British mortar bombs, which, together with the evidence of the profusion of wire defences, suggested that it was possibly a position held by the British in the 1942 campaign.

The capture of Monywa, which had cost the 48th one officer killed and two wounded, seven other ranks killed, one died of wounds, and eighteen wounded, was another feather in the cap of the 32nd Brigade, and among the many messages of congratulation received none gave greater pleasure than that from the Commander of the Fourteenth Army, which spoke of 'the unexpectedly early capture' of the town. This brought home to them that their long march of 250 miles, the hard work of the patrols, which had covered a much greater distance, and the efforts of those who had kept them supplied had made a very material contribution to the defeat of the enemy and to the eventual reconquest of Burma.

The 48th could rest satisfied that the taking of Monywa—and of Budalin—would always be associated with the name of the Regiment, for at both places they had played a prominent part.

*The Advance Continues, 25th–28th January*

After a day's rest the 48th were ordered to resume the advance, moving via Lezin to Kudaw, six miles south-east of Kadogon, with the 9/14th on their right. Kanbyagale, described as being in a filthy state and full of fleas, flies and bad smells, was reached on the 25th. No. 2 Company then went ahead to another village, and a patrol from No. 1, under Lieut. Firth-Clark, reported that the enemy were still in the eastern part of Lezin. Next day this place was unoccupied, and the Battalion went on to Mibauk. Local information said that the enemy were in Kudaw, and this was confirmed by a patrol from No. 4 Company which lost a man killed in doing so.

Plans were made for an attack on the 27th, following an air-strike, but the aircraft were required to help the 9/14th and the operation was postponed. On the 28th, after air-strikes in which incendiaries were used with effect to burn the enemy out, Taungbon and Payitkon were taken by No. 1 Company, Kyehmon by No. 2 and Kudaw by No. 3. In no case were any enemy encountered. Next day the Battalion concentrated at Taungbon, a patrol went out to open the road to Chaungu, and the 80th Brigade went through and took up the chase.

A few days' rest followed, well-earned after a period of fighting which had lasted since the 4th January. There was still the inevitable patrolling to be done, some training and much attention to arms and equipment; but there was plenty of time to spare for relaxation, which included visits to places as widely contrasting as the mobile cinema and a great temple and monastery presided over by the chief Buddhist priest of Burma. Soon there were signs that the rest would not be a long one, and plans for the future began to be discussed. For ahead lay the Irrawaddy, and beyond it Mandalay.

*The General Situation*

When Monywa fell to the 32nd Brigade, the 100th Brigade was moving across country towards Myinmu, on the Irrawaddy, which was taken on the 23rd January after a stiff fight. By the 1st February the 80th Brigade had passed through the 32nd, and was operating against the enemy in the 'Ducksbill,' the area of country lying in the angle formed by the Chindwin and the Irrawaddy.

To the left of the 20th Indian Division, the 2nd Division, advancing from Shwebo, was approaching Sagaing, in the elbow of the river west of Mandalay, on the 26th January. On its left the 19th Indian Division had crossed the Irrawaddy to the east of Shwebo and had established bridgeheads in the face of fierce opposition.

Away to the west, and on the other side of the Chindwin, the 4th Corps had moved by way of the Gangaw valley, and by the end of January was nearing the Irrawaddy south of its junction with the Chindwin. The location of this Corps was not known to the Japanese, who, as a result, were concentrating all their efforts on containing the 19th Division in its bridgeheads and on preventing the 2nd and 20th Divisions from reaching the Irrawaddy.

In Arakan the last of the enemy had been cleared from the peninsula, and the islands of Ramree and Akyab had been taken by amphibious operations.

*The Plan*

The stage was now set for the assault on Mandalay and for the trapping and destruction of the main Japanese army.

Mandalay was to be taken by the 19th Indian Division, advancing east of the Irrawaddy. Meanwhile, the 20th Indian Division was to force a crossing of the Irrawaddy some forty miles to the west of Mandalay, advance eastwards, and block the enemy's line of withdrawal near Kyaukse. The 2nd Division was then to cross the river at Sagaing, about ten miles from Mandalay, and occupy the southern exits from the city. While these operations were in progress the 4th Corps was to cross the Irrawaddy at Pakokku and establish a block at Meiktila, thus firmly sealing the enemy's line of retreat southwards.

The 20th Division's plan, in more detail, was for the 100th Brigade to make the main crossing at Myinmu. The 32nd Brigade was then to pass through this bridgehead and move towards Myotha. The 80th Brigade, mechanised as far as was possible, was to follow the 32nd across and move rapidly to block the Mandalay–Meiktila road at Kyaukse.

# THE 48th IN BURMA. THE OFFENSIVE, 1944-1945

Until the time came for the 80th Brigade to carry out this task it was to continue to act against the enemy in the 'Ducksbill,' and prevent them from interfering with the crossing operations. In addition, one battalion of the 32nd Brigade was to be placed under its orders, and was to cross the Irrawaddy about seven miles to the south of Myinmu and then advance inland in order to prevent enemy reinforcements from moving up from the south and interfering with the 100th Brigade.

As will be seen, the course of events led to some modification of this plan.

## The 48th's Task

Brigadier Mackenzie selected the 48th for the task of making the subsidiary crossing, and it so happened that his choice was an appropriate one. Early in the planning stage Lieut.-Col. Taunton was ordered to 80th Brigade H.Q., prior to assuming temporary command of it while the Brigadier was on leave. The duty of making the preparations and of commanding the 48th during the actual crossing, fell therefore on Major P. de C. Jones, but at 80th Brigade H.Q. Lieut.-Col. Taunton naturally knew all the details of the plan, and this, as things turned out, was fortunate.

The Irrawaddy was a formidable obstacle, here 600 yards wide at its narrowest point and with a current which ran at five knots. This meant that, with the low-powered craft available, the take-off point on the west bank would have to be a matter of 1,500 yards above the point of landing on the east bank.

Considerable difficulty was experienced in reconciling the map with the excellent air photographs which were provided. The former depicted the river at its monsoon level, from which it had now fallen considerably. Consequently, it was not easy to establish without detailed ground reconnaissance whether islands were still surrounded by water, or whether they had become peninsulas and possible jumping-off places. At some points the river did contain undoubted islands, and these were a factor which affected the selection of the crossing-place; for in the dark their shores might well have been mistaken for the east bank of the river.

On the west bank an island-peninsula—christened Bog Island—was found to be a suitable jumping-off place. On it there was cover under which craft and stores could be assembled in daylight, within 150 yards of two small beaches which offered facilities for embarkation after dark. Much of it was covered with thick elephant-grass, and there were numerous nullahs which would give some protection from shelling and good positions for mountain artillery.

On the enemy's bank an expanse of sand gave way to a belt of elephant-grass, up to 1,000 yards in depth and six to eight feet high, presenting an obstacle through which it was difficult for a man to force his way, and impossible for him to see. Moreover, within this belt the ground was still sandy, and this added to the difficulty of the going, particularly for men laden with stores. The country was intersected with numerous hidden nullahs and several prominent chaungs. To the 48th the most important of the latter was that which ran north-westwards past Kyigon, known as the North Chaung.

Beyond the belt of elephant-grass lay a stretch of open, cultivated country, intersected by muddy creeks which were no obstacle to movement on foot but prevented any cross-country movement of M.T. Then the ground rose steadily, until, about four thousand yards from the river, it came to a ridge about one hundred feet above the surrounding country, which afforded the enemy good observation.

As regards the enemy, identifications had shown that troops of the 33rd Division were in the area. The 48th had met them in all their battles, from Kyaukchaw onwards, and knew them to be dour opponents. There was little doubt that they would do their utmost to stop the British from advancing east of the Irrawaddy.

After all the factors had been considered it was decided to make the crossing from Bog Island to a beach near Kyigon. On the 6th February the 80th Brigade handed over command of the operation to the 32nd Brigade, and at the instance of Brig. Mackenzie the Divisional Commander agreed to the plan being altered. The objective was to be Kyigon village, where a firm base was to be formed. But the advance to that place was not to take place until the beachhead had been put into a state of defence.

The crossing was to be a silent one, unless the wind got up and made the water choppy, in which case outboard motors would be used. Unfortunately, aircraft could not be made available to fly up and down the river to drown the noise of the crossing.

Zero hour was to be 2300 hours on the 12th February, at which hour the 100th Brigade crossing would also begin.

*Resources*

At the final Brigade conference on the 11th February it was decided that the 9/14th Punjab Regt., less one company, was to be prepared to cross the river as soon as the 48th had got over. One company was to cross a little farther to the north, and was to move on Inya,* there to act as a link between the 100th Brigade bridgehead and the Kyigon base.

The available artillery support was somewhat meagre, one Mountain Regt. R.A., but this was unavoidable since the main crossing by the 100th Brigade had to have priority. There were, in addition, a troop of 6-pounder anti-tank guns and a battery of 3-inch mortars, which were to be ferried across the river.

The craft supplied for the crossing were a strange assortment. There

* A mile north of Kyigon.

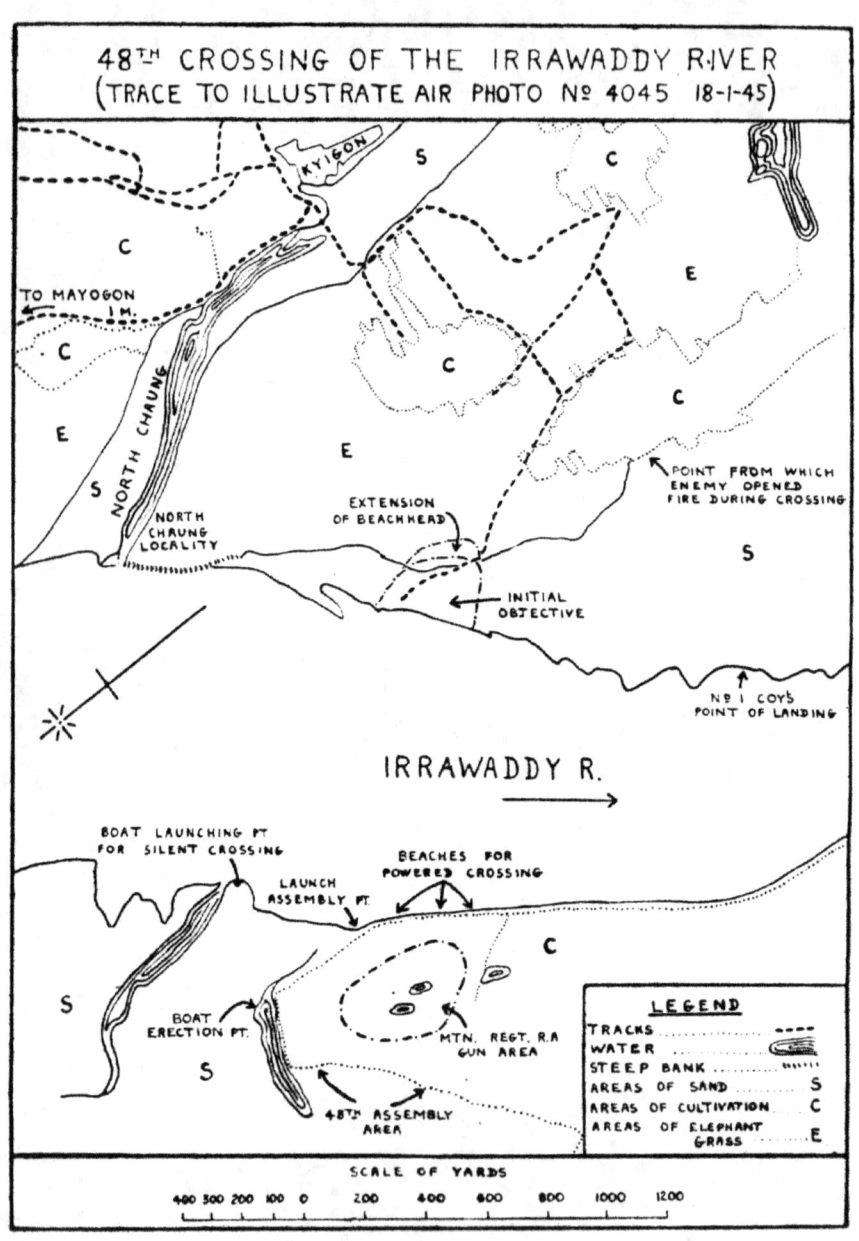

The Irrawaddy River

(*Air Ministry Photograph*)

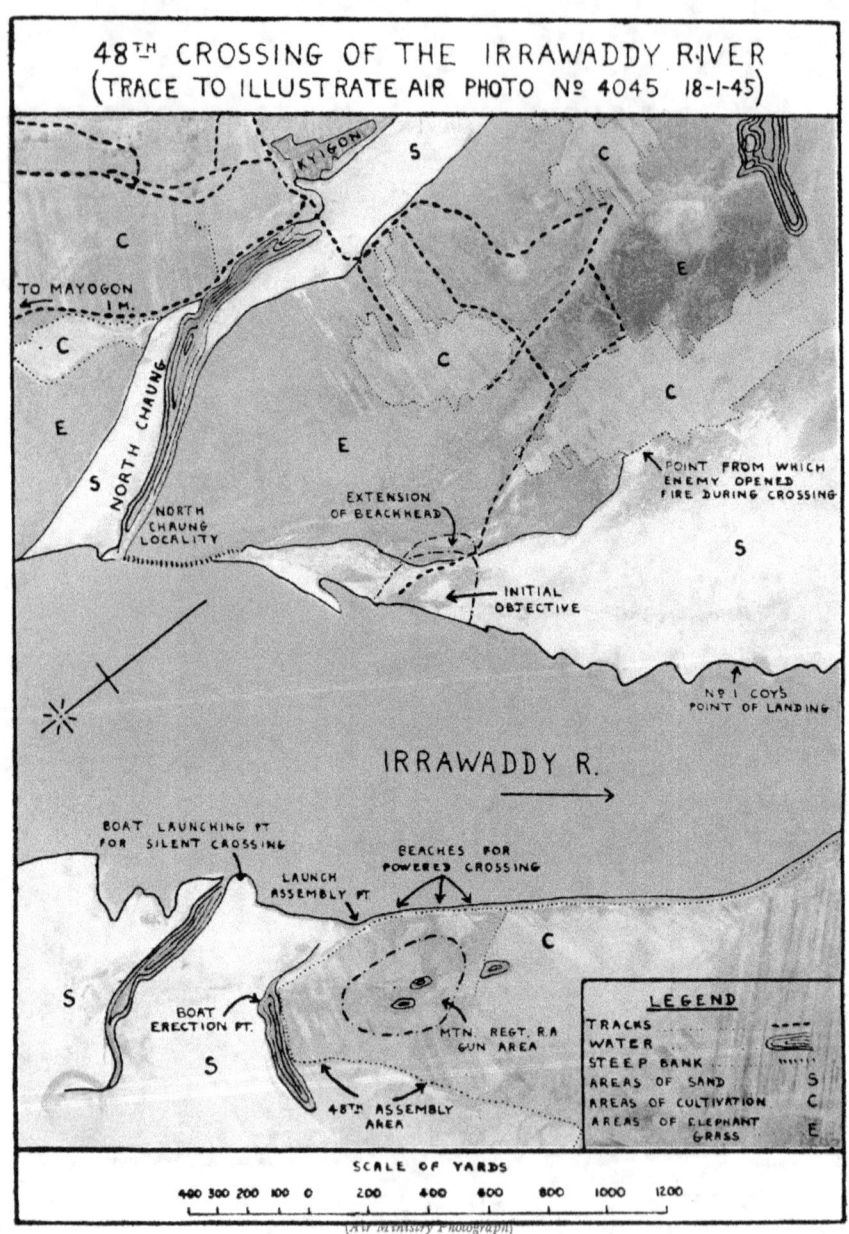

were about two dozen American Ranger craft, boats with inflated compartments, which held eight men each; three launches—Japanese iron boats powered by outboard motors; and two power-driven rafts constructed from local boats and timber. One launch could tow eight boats—the whole known as a 'crocodile'—though this number was reduced to five as a result of experience.

The six outboard motors, delivered as fit for service, proved to be far from serviceable, and it was only thanks to skilful 'cannibalisation' by the 92nd Field Company Sappers and Miners that three-quarters of them were eventually rendered reasonably reliable.

These resources can hardly be described as lavish, especially when it is remembered that they were to serve for the ferrying across a very wide, fast-running river of two battalions and their supporting arms, and for the maintenance in the bridgehead of this force for the three weeks which, it was estimated, would elapse before it could link up with the 100th Brigade. However, in Burma all had learnt to make the best of what was available.

*Preliminaries to the Irrawaddy Crossing*

On the 4th February the 48th left Taungbon, reached Letyetma on the 5th, and Myaung, near the western bank of the Irrawaddy, on the next day. There they relieved, and gained much useful information from, the 1st Bn. The Devonshire Regt., commanded by Lieut.-Col. Snow who had previously been Second-in-Command of the 48th.

There was much patrolling to be done before the operation. One party, under Lieut. Walkden, crossed the river and returned with valuable topographical information about the beachhead on the far bank. It was found that the sweep of the current was such that the outward journey took fifty minutes, the return journey only twenty-five.

It was an anti-climax that, at this stage, there arrived the voting papers for the General Election in Britain. It was hardly the moment for the voter to give earnest consideration to political matters.

At length, on the morning of the 12th, the necessary reconnaissances had been made, all details of boat-loads of men and stores had been worked out, and the 48th were as ready for the formidable operation which confronted them as careful planning and preparation could ensure.

*The Crossing, 12th–15th February*

By 2030 hours on the 12th the 48th were in their assembly area on Bog Island. No. 4 Company (Major Noakes) then prepared the boats—the Sappers were still having trouble with the motors—and carried them to the launching-point where Nos. 1 (Major Fulford) and 2 (Major Webb) Companies were waiting. Lieut. Phillips had set out for the beachhead, where he was to set up a guiding light on which the boats could steer.

Half an hour before zero a strong wind sprang up, and Major Jones decided that the choppy water would make a silent crossing impossible. It was a tribute to the flexibility of the plan that an alteration such as this could be made without causing confusion. The two companies embarked in their boats, coasted downstream to the launch assembly-point, picked up the launches and coasted onwards to the beaches selected for a power crossing.

Here there was some delay, for the motors, though emitting ear-splitting backfires, refused to start. However, at 2345 hours, forty minutes late, one motor was persuaded to start, and No. 1 Company set forth, only for their power to fail in mid-stream. When informed by the C.O. that the situation was that one company was heading for Rangoon, and that the second one had not yet started, Brigadier Mackenzie replied, consolingly but perhaps optimistically, 'Never mind, these things frequently turn out all right in the end.'

At this point there was a burst of firing from the far bank. It was known later that No. 1 Company, drifting downstream in their boats, had landed about a mile below the proper place. However, with commendable determination, they moved along the bank and linked up with No. 2, which had started soon after them and, thanks to the motors holding out, had landed at the correct spot. There had been a certain amount of fire from enemy automatics, but until daylight this was unaimed and caused no casualties.

At 0030 hours No. 3 Company (Major Veater) was ready to go. Again the motors refused to start, and when at last they did three of the boats were overturned. Then, to crown all, the power gave out when they were half-way across and they had to return to the west bank. No. 4 were slightly more fortunate and managed to get the best part of two platoons across.

So, when daylight came, the situation was that Battalion Tactical H.Q., two companies (at assault strength only) and part of a third were over the river, and clearly there could be no question of any advance on Kyigon.

A decision had now to be made, whether to try to continue the crossing in daylight or whether to wait until dusk. It was clear that the aimed fire of the enemy would cause serious difficulty. Then, by one of those strokes of fortune which do sometimes occur, there appeared at Brigade H.Q. an officer who proved to be an expert in the laying of smoke-screens by aircraft. Thanks to him arrangements were made for a screen to be laid across the river, under cover of which some 3-inch mortars, badly wanted to deal with enemy machine-guns, were to be ferried over. The screen was duly laid, but once again the motors failed when the 'crocodiles' were two-thirds of the way across. The strong wind blew the smoke away and the boats drifted down to a point about a quarter of a mile south of the beach-head. Accurate grenade fire and sniping forced the party to remain there until dusk, when they joined the remainder of the Battalion.

As soon as darkness fell the crossing was resumed, and by daylight on the 14th all the companies of the 48th, mortars, m.m.g.s and one jeep, were over the river. At this stage Lieut.-Col. Taunton returned and resumed command, as it had been found that he was not yet required to take over the 80th Brigade.

By now the Battalion held a semicircular bridgehead of about six hundred yards radius from the beach, and though there was some shelling and machine-gunning of the area casualties were few. They included Lieut. Walkden, killed when following up a mortar concentration on an enemy post.

One company of the 9/14th had got across the river about three miles to the north, but the opposition was too stiff for them to move on Inya, as planned, and they had to remain where they were for a fortnight, under command of a battalion of the 100th Brigade. By midnight on the 15th the rest of the 9/14th had joined the 48th, and the radius of the bridgehead had been enlarged to about eight hundred yards. Apart from patrols and the usual jitter-parties, the enemy had not been aggressive, but the defences, on which the troops had worked hard, were soon to be put to the test.

*Japanese Attacks, 16th–17th February*

Throughout the 15th it had become clear, from the reports of patrols, that the enemy had at least a strong screen of snipers in position round the bridgehead. Considerable movement had been seen in the direction of Yezin* and the nullah which led from it, and in order to watch the approach from this direction No. 4 Company were despatched to establish themselves on the near bank of the North Chaung, together with a section of m.m.g.s of the 9th Jat Regt. and an O.P. of the 23rd Mountain Regt. R.A.

At about 2200 hours, just as a 'crocodile' carrying reinforcements for the 9/14th had left the western bank of the river, a heavy attack developed against the north-eastern corner of the bridgehead, held by No. 4 Company of the 48th, and soon afterwards this was followed by another, against the 9/14th in the south-eastern corner.

Under cover of the noise of these attacks a party of about four officers and fifty men of the enemy managed to creep, unseen, through the edge of the water towards the beach where parties of the 48th and the 9/14th were waiting to receive the 'crocodile.' The enemy managed to capture a 6-pounder gun, and for a time there was considerable confusion in the dark as it was difficult to distinguish friend from foe, but fortunately all the Japanese officers were killed and the remainder of the enemy withdrew to hold a consultation, as was their habit when things did not go according to plan. This gave the beach parties time to act, and they were able to account for every one of the Japanese.

* Two miles north of Kyigon.

On the 48th end of the beach, the Battalion Command Post was very nearly involved. A line was established by the signallers and the police, and there incidents occurred which later, though not at the time, seemed amusing. The C.O., in his slit-trench, welcomed reinforcement in the shape of a burly Punjabi, complete with Bren gun. But when it was found that he had brought no magazines with him he was summarily evicted. The Second-in-Command, Major Jones, acting for the time being as a section commander in the telephone exchange, was forced to watch the efforts of the operator to extinguish the unpleasantly conspicuous lights on the switchboard as they came on when the companies called up to find out what was the cause of all the noise.

Unfortunately, before the enemy could be dealt with, they had managed to get a l.m.g. into action. This killed or wounded many of the men in the leading raft of the 'crocodile,' and would have caused heavier casualties but for the presence of mind of the officer in command. Cutting the tow-rope, he allowed the rest of the rafts to drift downstream out of harm's way.

The attack on No. 4 Company was beaten off, but on the 9/14th front the enemy penetrated the perimeter and were only driven out by the bayonet.

Apart from the casualties on the raft the losses were small, whereas 3 officers and 52 men of the enemy were counted dead, and other bodies were seen floating down the river. So the total number of enemy accounted for probably reached the satisfactory figure of about one hundred.

The 48th's trophies included three officers' swords, of which one was later presented to the Colonel-in-Chief of the Regiment, H.R.H. the Duchess of Gloucester.

On the 16th attempts by both the battalions in the bridgehead to reconnoitre outwards, towards Mayogon and Kyigon, were unsuccessful, for as soon as the troops debouched from the elephant-grass into the open they incurred casualties from heavy fire. During the day the shelling of the bridgehead by guns of all calibres increased, and could not be checked despite the best efforts of the supporting artillery, and of aircraft working on the 'cab-rank' principle—that is to say, airborne, and ready at call to engage indicated targets. Altogether it was obvious that the Japanese had been reinforced and that they were determined, not only to prevent any break-out from the bridgehead, but also to do their best to drive the garrison back into the Irrawaddy.

As soon as it was dark the enemy opened shell-fire from close range on the North Chaung post. How guns had been got into position to do this was rather a mystery until it was discovered that the fire came from two tanks which had been brought up to the far bank of the 100-yard-wide chaung. The Gunners were quick in getting on to them and they withdrew.

The next event was an attack on the 9/14th in the other corner of the bridgehead, but this, more noisy than dangerous, seemed to be a diversion, so No. 4 Company remained very much on the alert. Rightly too, for early on the 17th the Japanese came against them with great determination. Three successive attacks were made, and twice the enemy succeeded in entering one of the section posts. There was desperate hand-to-hand fighting, in which the whole garrison—48th, Gunners and Jat machine-gunners—distinguished themselves.

At 0430 hours No. 3 Company were ordered up to help in evicting some enemy who were still holding out. Their position was such that there was only room for one section to counter-attack, and soon after preparation by artillery and mortars, this small force went in with the bayonet. The enemy who stayed were killed in their foxholes; those who fled were dealt with, either by the l.m.g.s of the platoon or by the quick and accurate shooting of the Gunners.

The night's fighting had cost No. 4 Company 3 killed and 26 wounded, including Capt. Chandler and six men who remained at duty. The Jat M.G. section, which had done fine work, had had 3 killed and 5 wounded, while Major Byrne of the 23rd Mountain Regt., who received the immediate award of the D.S.O. for the splendid example he had set during the action, had also been wounded. Against this, 35 Japanese dead were found in and near the position.

For the rest of the day the troops were given as much rest as possible, for the strain of four successive nights without sleep and of hard work in patrolling and on the defences during the intervening days was beginning to tell on them. But there was little rest from Japanese shelling. This became intense in the evening, against the bridgehead and Bog Island, 105-mm. guns coming into action besides those of smaller calibre. In the North Chaung position all the automatic weapons and many rifles were out of action for a time, choked with sand and dust thrown up by the shelling. The same shell which killed the Second-in-Command of the 9/14th wounded Capt. Millar of the 48th, who died the next day.

After dark, an attack against the 9/14th was repulsed. The North Chaung post was the target for grenade-discharger and small-arms fire at intervals throughout the night, but the one attack which developed was held outside the wire which had been put up during the day, and any repetition was discouraged by the defensive fire of the mortars and the m.m.g.s. The deep trenches which had been dug in the post were the means of saving many casualties from the grenade fire.

*Holding the Bridgehead, 18th–28th February*

From the 18th February onwards the situation was one of stalemate. The Japanese made no more serious attacks; on the other hand, the garrison of the bridgehead was not strong enough, nor could the necessary support be given to them, to break out. So there they had to remain, incurring only light casualties from shelling by day, considering that the area they held presented such a good target; on the alert at night against possible attack, and having frequent patrol encounters with the enemy in the tall elephant-grass.

The strain to men cooped up in this small space was great. It would have been ever greater but for the valiant work of the boat crews of the 92nd Field Company, who nightly took their cargoes of supplies and ammunition across the river, almost always under shell-fire, and returned with wounded from the bridgehead garrison, who owed much to the devoted work of the 59th Field Ambulance.

During this period the Battalion welcomed the well-merited awards for earlier operations of the D.S.O. to Lieut.-Col. Taunton (who later was awarded a Bar for his part in the Budalin and Monywa fighting); the M.C. to Majors Molloy, Veater and Eales-White, and Lieut. Hughes; the M.B.E. to Lieut. and Quartermaster Howard, and the M.M. to Ptes. Cox and Stanley.

Towards the end of the month the amount of shelling decreased, the enemy's attention being distracted by events elsewhere which will be described later. On the 26th No. 1 Company moved across the North Chaung against a bunker position which had been located towards Mayogon. This was occupied without much difficulty, but the enemy then counter-attacked. Major Fulford, the Company Commander, was killed and, under command of the Gunner F.O.O., the only other officer, the position had to be evacuated.

By now the steady drain of casualties had made the 48th very short of men, so they were glad to receive a draft of 45. These were all straight from home and their first impressions of the war in Burma cannot have been very favourable. However, they were most welcome, and their arrival made it possible to bring companies up to a strength of about 90 other ranks. But there was still a great shortage of officers, and there were only two with each company.

*Relief of the Bridgehead*

By the 18th February the whole of the 100th Brigade, the 80th Brigade (less one battalion in the 'Ducksbill' dealing with the enemy still there), and the 3/8th Gurkha Rifles of the 32nd Brigade were over the river at Myinmu, but the 2nd Division nearer Mandalay and the 4th Corps to the south had not yet begun to cross. Consequently the enemy were able to concentrate their efforts on preventing a break-out from the Myinmu bridgehead, either eastwards or to the south to link up with the Kyigon bridgehead.

The situation became more favourable however when the 2nd Division began to cross the Irrawaddy on the night of the 24th/25th February and Brig. Mackenzie, who had moved with the rest of the 32nd Brigade into the main bridgehead, was able to make plans for the relief of the Kyigon bridgehead.

The operation would not be an easy one. It would involve the establishment of a corridor through the country east of the river, through Yezin, Inya and Mayogon, where the enemy were known to have strong positions, the piqueting of this corridor for the passage of some 250 mules, and the withdrawal through it of the 48th and the 9/14th with all their stores and equipment. Experience had shown that tanks would be essential, and one and a half squadrons of Lees and Stuarts were allotted. In addition, 'cab-rank' aircraft would attend to the enemy artillery.

The whole operation required very detailed planning. The necessary instructions were dropped by light aircraft on the Kyigon bridgehead, and Lieut.-Col. Taunton was, in turn, able to make his plan.

In due course Yezin was occupied, and on the 1st March the 3/8th Gurkha Rifles advanced on Mayogon. In co-operation with this, No. 1 Company of the 48th attacked the bunker position which they had engaged four days previously. Once again the attack was unsuccessful, and the Company had to withdraw after incurring casualties; the Commander, Capt. Perkins, was killed.

By the evening of the 2nd the Gurkhas had cleared Mayogon. Forty-eight hours later, with the aid of the tanks, which made a great difference to the duration of the Japanese resistance, they had taken the bunker position and had made contact with the 48th. Next day the mules arrived and the garrison of the bridgehead moved out through the corridor, leaving nothing behind, not even the one day's rations which was all that they had in hand from the stocks which had been built up. The 48th went to Yezin and the 9/14th to Kanlan, relieved to get into the 'open air' once more. The cost to the Kyigon garrison had been negligible, one Jat machine-gunner killed and one wounded. The 3/8th Gurkhas, to whom they owed their relief, had suffered the loss of both their C.O. and their Second-in-Command in the hard fighting in and round Mayogon.

The 48th and their companions of the 9/14th had had a hard three weeks in their bridgehead since they crossed the Irrawaddy—three weeks of sand, heat, boredom and incessant shelling. It was yet another of those actions in which the men of the Infantry had to play their part by 'sticking it' against the determined efforts of the enemy to destroy them. Not spectacular, but contributing in no small degree to the success of the main crossing of the Division which, in turn, contributed to the success of others who gained fame by their capture of Mandalay.

## Advance to Kyaukse, 6th–19th March

The time, and the opportunity, had now come for the 20th Division to begin the next phase of the operation, the advance eastwards to block the Japanese escape-route from Mandalay southwards. This began on the 9th March, with the 80th Brigade on the right and the 32nd on the left, directed respectively on Kyaukse and on the main road to the north of that place.

At the outset the 48th were left at Yezin. They wanted a few days of rest and comparative quiet to get the tired, strained look out of their eyes. And it was there, on the 8th March, that Lieut.-Col. Taunton left them, on promotion to command the 80th Brigade. Under him the Battalion had trained in Ceylon and in India, and had been in action, with only one four-months' break, continuously since December 1943. The successes which they had achieved and the reputation they had earned were very largely due to his inspiring leadership. Major P. de C. Jones took over command from him.

On the 10th March the Battalion left Yezin and caught up with the Brigade on the following day. The other two battalions were ahead, and continued to make rapid progress, for the enemy were pulling out fast and there was little opposition till the Panlaung River was reached. This they crossed on the 15th, and on the next day the 48th, who had meanwhile been marching steadily eastwards, followed them.

The operations for the capture of the city of Mandalay were now in their closing stages, and, south of it, the Japanese were occupying strong-points covering the main road which was the line of retreat for its garrison. Consequently, resistance began to stiffen, and on the 18th the 9/14th and the 3/8th Gurkhas met considerable numbers of the enemy. On that and the following day the 48th carried out a sweep some miles to the north, in the course of which they laid an extremely successful ambush, killing many Japanese.

At this stage the 32nd Brigade was ordered farther to the south, and the 48th came under the command of Brig. Taunton's 80th Brigade which was about to undertake operations for the capture of Kyaukse.

Almost at the same time Brig. Mackenzie left the 32nd Brigade to take up an appointment at Delhi. In 'Long Mac' the 48th felt that they had lost an old friend, for he had led the Brigade wisely and coolly throughout all the operations in Burma.

## Operations round Kyaukse, 23rd–30th March

The capture of Kyaukse was no easy matter. Lying as it did at the junction of several main roads, it was important for the enemy to hold it for as long as was possible. There was a strong defensive screen in the many villages on the approaches to the town, and every village had to be fought for. Furthermore, the country thereabouts was irrigated by a system of canals, of which the enemy had opened the sluice-gates with the result that many of the paddy-fields which should have afforded good going for tanks were flooded and impassable.

Gradually the enemy were driven back. The task of the 48th for several days was patrolling, protective duties and the holding of captured villages to prevent their reoccupation by the enemy. Then, on the 29th March, they prepared to mount an attack on Kyaukse, with the 9th F.F.R. But patrols the next morning reported that the town was clear of the enemy, and the two battalions entered it unopposed.

*Final Operations, 1st–25th April*

Two days later the 48th rejoined their own brigade on the Rangoon road ten miles south of Kyaukse. On arrival there they found that the next operations were to be carried out largely in M.T. This entailed re-forming the M.T. Platoon with drivers for some fifty vehicles, no easy matter after so long a period without M.T. However, fifty men who claimed to be able to drive were found and managed to deliver the vehicles intact to the Battalion.

News also came that all British battalions serving in Indian divisions were to be transferred to the 36th Division, which would then become all-British, but for the time being the 48th were to be lent to the 80th Brigade.

The next objective of the Fourteenth Army was Rangoon, the 33rd Corps advancing on it on the Irrawaddy axis, and the 4th Corps, which had secured Meiktila as planned, on the axis of the main road and railway. The 20th Indian Division was to move south, concentrate near Meiktila and then advance in a south-easterly direction.

During the operations on the Irrawaddy, at Mandalay and at Meiktila, the Japanese had suffered a decisive defeat, having lost their main line of communication and most of their armour. They were short of artillery, and their complete administrative breakdown meant that they had very inadequate stocks of all essentials, including ammunition, equipment and medical supplies. Their forces were very disorganised, but with the Japanese there was no question of a general surrender and there was little doubt that they would oppose an advance to the best of their ability.

On the 9th April the 48th received orders to move by M.T. on the next day with the rest of the 80th Brigade to near Meiktila. A draft of 90 men arrived, most opportunely, for it allowed of the re-formation of No. 3 Company which had had to be disbanded owing to shortage of men.

The original orders for operations on the 11th were that the 48th would protect the flank of the 20th Division as it turned south at Zayotkon. But on reaching that place this plan was changed and they were given the task of operating independently to open up the road leading westwards to Kyaukpadaung. A squadron of armoured cars of the 11th Cavalry, a battery of 25-pounders, and a deception unit known by the appropriate name of 'Smart Alec,' were placed under Lieut.-Col. Jones's command for the purpose. It was not an easy task, for on the one hand the orders were that the speed of advance was to be consistent with safety and that unnecessary casualties were to be avoided. On the other hand, Divisional H.Q. kept on pressing for the advance to be speeded up. The country was such that most of the length of the road was dominated by hill features, affording ideal positions for the enemy to fight delaying actions. The weather was extremely hot, especially for fast marching, and there were many cases of heat-exhaustion.

At the outset of operations, on the 12th April, Nos. 1 and 4 Companies were at Milestone 31 (the milestone distance along the road from Meiktila), with the remainder of the Battalion four miles behind them. On reaching the Causeway at Milestone 39 the armoured cars halted, as they were suspicious of mines, moving on as soon as No. 1 Company had examined it. They then made contact with some enemy and No. 1 Company occupied a feature from which exploitation could begin next morning. Here, joined by No. 2, they spent the night. There was some sniping from bunkers which had been located.

With the help of some tanks which had come up, and after an artillery and mortar bombardment, No. 4 Company advanced on the 13th, occupied the position which had held up the armoured cars, and went on to exploit further. There was continuous sniping from the other side of the road. The Gunner F.O.O. working with a No. 2 Company patrol was wounded, and it was only thanks to Capt. Lodge and three volunteers, who followed his line up the hillside after dark, that he was brought in that night.

The two days which followed were spent in clearing a road-block where the road had been cratered, lifting mines (up to Milestone 41 a total of ninety-three mines of five different types were lifted), securing positions which commanded the road and patrolling to various villages to the north and south. By the evening of the 15th the road was open as far as Milestone 42, the limit given in the original orders. But the 48th were then told to go on, open the road to Kyaukpadaung and keep it open. At the same time the tanks and the 25-pounders were withdrawn and were replaced by a battery of 3·7-inch howitzers, one of which was unserviceable.

The new orders led to days of difficult fighting in rocky, broken country, where every feature had to be fought for against an enemy who, though weak in numbers, was strong in determination to delay. The strength of the Battalion, too, was steadily decreasing, more from heat-exhaustion, especially among the recently joined reinforcements, than from battle casualties, though these occurred daily in small numbers; the average platoon strength was now only eighteen.

At last, on the 18th, a patrol got through to Kyaukpadaung and made contact there with the 268th Infantry Brigade, which was operating under command of the 7th Indian Division in the Mount Popa area to the north. But there was more fighting to be done before the road was officially declared open on the 22nd, and until the 25th patrolling was continued over a wide area and ambushes were laid to mop up enemy stragglers and small parties trying to make good their escape from Mount Popa.

On the 25th April the 48th sent an advanced party to Meiktila and the Brigade Commander visited them to bid them good-bye. That night saw them carrying out their last operational task, the laying of an ambush; justice would have allowed this to produce a good bag of Japanese, but no Japanese appeared.

As far as the 48th were concerned the Burma campaign was over.[3] They were nearly, but not quite, in at the death. Rangoon fell on the 2nd May, and four months later, on the 2nd September, just as the great assault on Singapore was about to be launched, the Japanese Commander signed the order for the capitulation of all his forces in South-east Asia.

*The 48th leave Burma*

On the 27th April the Battalion moved to Meiktila and there, on the next day, the Divisional Commander, Major-General Gracey, paid them a farewell visit. Three days later, on the 1st May, they moved to Imphal, the journey which had required so many weary weeks of foot-slogging taking little more than two hours to complete by air in the opposite direction.

After a night at Imphal the Battalion went on to railhead at Dimapur by M.T. and there prepared to leave for India.

Of all the campaigns fought during the war, two—those in Burma and New Guinea—stand out by reason of the demands which they made upon the individual, both morally and physically.

Both were fought in country largely covered by jungle; where roads and railways were practically non-existent and hundreds of miles had to be traversed on foot; where the climate, both in the rains and in the dry season, was extremely trying to the white man; where there was little or no chance of leave to some place in which there would be an opportunity for relaxation, still less of leave to home; where a battalion could never rest for months on end, for there was no battle-front, and for many miles behind the positions held by the foremost troops every unit had to be continually on its guard against an enemy who, screened by the features of the country, might appear at any point without warning. They were fought in countries where, however sound the Commander's plan, success or failure depended as a rule upon the skill, courage and initiative of sections, or even of individual men, against a foe of whose presence the first warning would be a shot fired or a grenade thrown, at a range of a few yards.

New Guinea, where one of the Regiment's Allied Battalions, the Australian 48th, so distinguished themselves, does not enter into this history. But in Burma, while great events were in progress in Libya and Tunisia, in Sicily and Italy, in Normandy, through France and Belgium to Germany, the men of the Fourteenth Army had, almost unnoticed, first held, then beaten back, and finally destroyed the Japanese armies.

Of this great Army the 48th had been worthy members, and in it they had conducted themselves in such a way as to add much honour to the name of the Northamptonshire Regiment.[4] In the words of the man who had commanded the 20th Indian Division throughout its existence, Lieut.-General D. D. Gracey, they had 'earned a magnificent reputation for efficiency and courage.'[5,6]

East Anglian Brigade Group

# CHAPTER XIX

## THE BATTALIONS AT HOME AND THE I.T.C., 1943-1945

The 4th Battalion, February 1943–February 1944—Exercise 'Flake,' February–August 1944—Move to Cornwall, September 1944–January 1945—The 4th Mobilise, February 1945—The 6th Battalion, 1943-1945—The 70th Battalion, 1943—The I.T.C., 1943-1945—Death of Major A. Hill-Walker, V.C., April 1944—The Comforts Fund

### The 4th Battalion, February 1943–February 1944

EARLY in February 1943, after more than two and a half years in Northern Ireland, the 4th Battalion moved with the rest of the 61st Division to England and was stationed first at Rayleigh and then at High Wycombe, where training continued until October.

During this period, Lieut.-Col. Buszard relinquished command, handing over to Lieut.-Col. Furminger. A notable event was the visit, on Talavera Day, of the Colonel-in-Chief of the Regiment, who took the salute at a march-past.

In October the Division moved to Kent and the 4th, stationed at Hythe and Folkestone, were responsible for the defence of the coast at those places until they were transferred to Dover at the end of January 1944.

### Exercise 'Flake,' February–August 1944

From February onwards the Battalion was called upon to despatch parties of 150 men at a time to Ipswich, to train for an operation designated Exercise 'Flake.' The precise nature of this was shrouded by a thick veil of secrecy, made even thicker by the imposition of postal censorship at the beginning of April.

In the middle of that month the advanced party of a Canadian Division arrived to relieve the Battalion, which moved to Broadstairs on the 19th. Two days later the C.O. attended a conference in London, at which he heard that Exercise 'Flake' was to be carried out almost immediately.

'Flake' was, in fact, part of a large-scale deception scheme, designed to distract the attention of the Germans from the landings on the coast of Normandy. In it the Battalion's rôle was the erection, launching and maintenance of a number of 'mock-up' landing-craft, on the River Deben at Ipswich, at Oulton Broad in Norfolk, at Lowestoft and at Yarmouth. Battalion H.Q., the H.Q. Company, Support Company and 'D' Company were to be at Ipswich; 'C' Company at Lowestoft; 'A' and 'B' Companies, under the command of Major Webb, at Yarmouth.

After selected individuals had been trained in their task by experts from 21st Army Group, they in turn trained the rest of the Battalion, and then the operation began.

The 'Fleet' consisted of about 150 craft, the buoyancy of which was provided by large airtight drums to which was attached the superstructure, composed of tubular scaffolding covered by canvas affixed by cordage. The construction of each craft took about eight hours and they then had to be pushed, with many a heave and groan, to the launching-site, whence they were towed to their moorings by a motor-vessel. Thirty men were required to launch a craft, and on an average four were launched nightly at Ipswich and Yarmouth and two at Lowestoft. All this work had to be carried out during the hours of darkness and any craft not completed and launched by dawn had to be dismantled and hidden, though after a few initial failures this was seldom necessary.

The task was by no means finished when the craft had been launched. Maintenance had to be carried out continuously during daylight, this involving the tightening of thousands of bolts and the replacement of miles of cordage as it became rotted by the salt water. Furthermore, deception had to be made complete by devices such as smoke issuing from the dummy funnels, oil seeping from the sterns, washing flapping in the breeze and men rowing from craft to craft. The general effect was imposing and realistic. So much so that on one occasion, when Lieut.-Col. Furminger was flying over the River Deben, the pilot of the aircraft drew his attention to two of the craft, saying that they must have just come into harbour because of the oil-track at their sterns. It was only then that the C.O. realised that the pilot was not in the secret, a tribute to security since his airfield was but a short distance away.

The work was not without its trials and tribulations. The canvas superstructures were very vulnerable to high winds and on one morning the fleet presented a sorry spectacle. A gale had broken many of the craft from their moorings, and had beached them up creeks and on mudbanks, with buckled sides, torn canvas and funnels awry, damage which had to be repaired without delay lest suspicions should be aroused in the mind of the pilot of any enemy aircraft which might fly over.

However, there were compensations. A large number of the Battalion learnt how to handle a rowing-boat, to swim, and even to fish—though their catch was mainly of eels. They realised that their work was of more than usual importance and of direct help to the Normandy landings.

## THE BATTALIONS AT HOME AND THE I.T.C., 1943-1945

### Move to Cornwall, September 1944–January 1945

At the end of August, having completed their 'Flake' task, the 4th moved to Bake House Camp at St. Germans, in Cornwall. There, with the 1st Cheshire Regt. and the 30th R. Berkshire Regt., they formed the 115th Independent Infantry Brigade. This was under orders to recover the Channel Islands from the Germans, consequently intensive training in landing operations was the order of the day.

As the year wore on, and the tides and currents round the Islands became more violent, plans were continually changed and it was probably just as well that the operation never materialised. The needs of 21st Army Group for additional man-power led to the drafting overseas of all but one of the units of the Brigade.

### The 4th Mobilise, February 1945

At the end of January the Battalion was warned to be ready to move overseas on the 9th February. The date originally given had been the 15th, consequently the 600 men on embarkation leave had to be recalled hurriedly. It says much for morale that when the Battalion finally embarked there was only one absentee.

Busy days followed. Lieut.-Col. Furminger paid a flying visit to H.Q. 2nd Army in Holland to receive orders, and the Battalion mobilised. On the 8th the drivers went far afield to collect their vehicles, the last of which did not reach St. Germans until the 10th. Simultaneously, drafts from many different units came, to bring the Battalion up to war-establishment. The state of British man-power at this stage of the war is shown by the fact that many of these men were of such low medical categories that they were excused the wearing of steel helmets or equipment. Some were even excused shooting. The value of such men to a unit which expected to be given the task of holding a portion of the line in Holland was, to say the least of it, dubious, and the C.O. was able to make arrangements for their transfer elsewhere.

On the 9th and 10th the vehicles set out on their long road journey to the Dagenham marshalling-area, the last to arrive being greeted by a couple of V-2 rockets. On the 11th the rest of the Battalion entrained at Launceston and reached Tilbury the next morning. The long period of training and service at home had come to an end and the 4th were at last to have the privilege of taking part in active operations. The story of these will be told in a later chapter.

### The 6th Battalion, 1943–1945

Early in 1943, the 6th Battalion, still at Sheringham, changed its rôle for the less spectacular, but none the less essential, one of draft-finding. In this they were responsible for ensuring a supply of trained men for units overseas, and as a result the officers and men were continually changing. Despite this they managed to achieve considerable distinction in athletics, notably in the 2nd Corps cross-country running championship, and in the half-mile relay race at the White City A.A.A. Meeting. In 1944 the Battalion's teams won both the mile and the half-mile relay races at the Inter-Services Athletic Meeting and also the 77th Division's 12-miles road-walking championship.

In May 1944 Lieut.-Col. Growse relinquished command, handing over to Lieut.-Col. R. R. C. Cox, who in turn was relieved by Lieut.-Col. P. O. B. Sherwood in July 1945.

From Sheringham the Battalion moved to Aylesbury in November 1944, and thence to Blandford at the end of 1945.

The strength of the Battalion, over 900 at the beginning of 1945, had dwindled to 350 by the end of the year, and finally, on the 11th April 1946, came disbandment. Though never privileged to serve overseas, the 6th were one of the many units which had to be content with the task of keeping other more fortunate units up to strength in trained men, a task which they had performed most thoroughly.

*The 70th Battalion*, 1943

Before the end of 1943 the Young Soldiers' Battalions had fulfilled the object for which they had been raised, and in addition the man-power situation in the country made it necessary to economise wherever possible. As a result, in common with all the other battalions of this type, the 70th Battalion of the Regiment was disbanded, having carried out the duties for which it had been formed quietly and efficiently.

*The I.T.C.*, 1943–1945

In November 1943 No. 2 I.T.C. at Norwich, with which the Northamptonshire I.T.C. had been amalgamated two years before, was disbanded. By then Talavera Camp, Northampton, had been vacated by the A.T.S. Training Centre, and there the Northamptonshire I.T.C., now renamed No. 14 I.T.C., was established, under the command of Lieut.-Col. W. E. Carrick, M.C. Instead of serving the Regiment only, however, it also served the Royal Hampshire and Devonshire Regiments.

As a mark of appreciation of the kindness and hospitality of the Royal Norfolk Regiment during the two and a half years' sojourn of the I.T.C. at Norwich, a cup was presented to the former, with the request that it should be known as 'The Northamptonshire Cup.'

*Death of Major A. Hill-Walker, V.C., April* 1944

On the 21st April 1944 the death occurred, at his home in Yorkshire, of Major Alan Hill-Walker, who had won the Victoria Cross at the Battle

The Granting of the Freedom of the Borough of Northampton, 8th June 1946
(See p. 351)

*Northampton " Chronicle and Echo"*

of Laing's Nek more than sixty-three years before and had for many years been the senior holder of that decoration in the Army. Though it was many years since he had retired, he was never absent from Regimental functions until prevented by ill health. At his funeral the 'Last Post' and 'Reveille' were sounded by a party of buglers found, most fittingly, by the band of the 58th, the battalion with which he had been serving when he won his decoration.

*The Comforts Fund*

Mention should here be made of the organisation set up in Northamptonshire to provide comforts for all units connected with the County.

At the outset of the war the local branches of the Red Cross Society, St. John's Ambulance and other voluntary organisations made arrangements for the supply of woollen clothing to the troops. Then, largely as a result of representations made by General Sir Harry Knox, it was decided to expand this work and to form a branch which would provide other comforts. A Committee got to work and, mainly as a result of the appeal launched by the Northampton *Chronicle and Echo*, were able to despatch Comforts to the value of £10,000 before the end of the war.

The gratitude of the Regiment is due to the Colonel-in-Chief, as Patron of this Comforts Branch, and to all those who devoted so much time to a work which was so highly appreciated. They were many, but especial mention should be made of Mr. Cowper Barrons, Mr. and Mrs. Arthur Rice and Mr. H. Talbot Butler.

# CHAPTER XX

## THE 58th AND THE 4th BATTALION IN HOLLAND AND GERMANY, 1945

The 58th move to Belgium, 8th March–15th April 1945—Move into Germany, 15th–20th April—Operations on the Elbe, 22nd–30th April—The Elbe to the Baltic, 1st–6th May—The Aftermath of Victory, 6th May–1st July—The 4th move to Holland, 11th–16th February—On the Maas, 17th February–2nd March—Across the Maas, 2nd–6th March—Preparations for the Rhine Crossing—The Rhine Crossing—Various Tasks, 25th March–8th May

*The 58th move to Belgium, 8th March–15th April 1945*

THE 58th, whom we left on board ship on the Mediterranean, landed at Marseilles on the 8th March 1945. After a stay in a section of a large American transit-camp they entrained on the 13th and reached their destination, Zotteghem in Belgium, three days later. The wheel had turned full circle, and, after their wanderings through many lands, some of them had returned to the country which they had seen nearly five years before.

Soon after they arrived they paraded by the roadside for a visit by Field-Marshal Montgomery, who welcomed them to 21st Army Group. Then, while leave to the U.K. started at the rate of eleven men a day, there was much to be done in the way of drawing new vehicles and weapons and training.

*Move into Germany, 15th–20th April*

The Allied forces began to cross the Rhine south of the Dutch border on the 23rd March. Within a week the Ruhr had been encircled, the Americans were streaming eastwards into Germany and the British north-eastwards towards the Baltic coast. To all intents and purposes the power of resistance of the German armies had been broken, and their final defeat was near.

On the 15th April the 58th left Ghent by train for Goch, just across the German border to the south of Nijmegen, and from there moved on in T.C.V.s or by march-route until, on the 21st, they were approaching the River Elbe.

## Operations on the Elbe, 22nd–30th April

The first operation which the Battalion was called upon to undertake was the clearance of a portion of the forest of Gohrde, in which they encountered but slight opposition and took a few prisoners. On the next day, the 23rd, Katemin was captured without difficulty and with no casualties. Positions were taken up to the west of the town, patrols to the bank of the Elbe seeing no sign of any enemy.

After a few days on the defensive, uneventful except for the enemy shelling which followed two deception attacks, the Battalion was relieved by an American unit and moved back in readiness to exploit the success of the crossing of the river farther to the north by the 15th Division.

## The Elbe to the Baltic, 1st–6th May

On the 1st May orders were received for Operation 'Volcano,' in which the 58th were to be the reserve battalion to the 17th Brigade in the advance to Lübeck on the Baltic.

Starting just after midnight there was considerable delay owing to the number of vehicles waiting to cross the Elbe, but by about noon the Battalion had concentrated to the north of the river and began to move on in convoy. Tactically the day was without incident, except for an attack on the column by a solitary German fighter aircraft, in which two men were wounded—the last casualties to be incurred by the 58th in the war. But in the course of the afternoon they had to wait for the surrender of the remnants of the German 245th Infantry Division, and when the rest of the Battalion continued the advance later 'C' and 'D' Companies were left behind to deal with more prisoners who were coming in.

Next morning Lübeck was reached after a fast journey along a motor road, and at 1500 hours the 58th began to debus at Travemunde, on the Baltic coast, where they relieved units of the 11th Armoured Division. The two days which followed were spent in shepherding the thousands of surrendering Germans, of all ranks and of all Services, and in patrolling. In the course of one of these patrols, carriers of the Support Company were successful in bringing in one Meissner, reported to be secretary to the infamous Heinrich Himmler.

On the 6th May the Battalion moved back to Lübeck, charged with the duty of guarding dumps and maintaining order, and there on VE-Day, representatives attended a parade at which the Divisional Commander took the salute.

The war was over for the 58th, and they could feel, not only that they had worthily represented the Regiment in many lands, but that they had, at long last, had their revenge for the defeats of 1940.

### The Aftermath of Victory, 6th May–1st July

On the 17th May Lieut.-Col. Ballard, who had led the Battalion in so many operations, left to join the Allied Mission to Denmark and was succeeded, temporarily, by Major Purton. Soon afterwards there was a move to Kletzin, where the Battalion held a sector of the 'stop line,' the boundary between the Allied and the Russian occupying forces. Their task was to prevent the movement of German civilian or military refugees across the line, and of Russian soldiers except those on official business. As regards the latter the instructions were that the greatest care was to be taken to avoid unpleasant incidents, and apparently the 58th displayed much tact, for there is no record of the occurrence of any such incidents. These were to come later when peace was more firmly established.

A fortnight later there was another move, to take over duties from the Americans at Schwerin, and it was not until the 1st July that the 58th finally settled down at Göttingen, a place which can fairly be regarded as their first post-war peace-time station.

### The 4th move to Holland, 11th–16th February

The road party of the 4th Battalion embarked at Tilbury in two L.S.T.s on the 11th February.[1] One of these reached Ostend on the following day, but the other developed a defect soon after she had sailed and had to return. The troops and vehicles were transferred to another ship and they eventually disembarked at Ostend on the 13th, shortly before the main body which had embarked in S.S. *Biarritz* on the 12th.

On the 14th and 15th the Battalion left by road and rail for Helmond, whence they went into billets at Asten, south of Eindhoven. There they received orders to relieve an American battalion on the line of the Maas on the night of the 19th/20th.

### On the Maas, 17th February–2nd March

Preparations for taking over the sector and reconnaissances occupied the next two days, but this was one of the rare occasions on which time spent in reconnaissance was wasted, for on the 18th, after Lieut.-Col. Furminger had left his H.Q. with Company Commanders and Platoon Sergeants to arrange final details of the relief, the orders were cancelled. The 115th Independent Infantry Brigade was to take over the complete sector held by the 377th U.S. Regt., with the 4th in reserve at Homberg, six miles north-west of Venlo, to which place they moved on the following day.

The Battalion's tour in reserve did not last for long. On the 23rd they relieved the 30th R. Berkshire Regt. on the Maas. Four days later their first important patrol was carried out very successfully. At 0125 hours on the 28th a party under Lieuts. Shaw and Burbidge left the west bank in assault boats, clearly visible from the C.O.'s O.P. in the bright moonlight, but invisible to the enemy. They succeeded in locating four German posts, but these were so close together that it was not possible to secure a prisoner and they had to return at 0400 hours with useful information only. On the following night these two officers set out again, but though they managed to land on the east bank they found the enemy on the alert (due, possibly, to the careless talk with civilians of a Dutch sergeant attached to the 4th) and had again to return empty-handed.

These patrols had suffered no casualties, but a third on the night of the 1st/2nd March was less fortunate.

At 2200 hours a reconnaissance patrol (Lieut. Bell and two men) and a bridgehead party (Lieut. Smith and nine men) from 'B' Company started to cross the river. As the bridgehead party got out of the boat on reaching the east bank they were met by a burst of spandau fire from a copse to their front so, as they had evidently been seen, they re-embarked and paddled off. Very soon a burst of fire hit the boat, forcing those who could to abandon ship and swim, no easy matter as the river was quite seventy-five yards wide and the current was strong.

By degrees members of the patrol began to reach the west bank. The first to arrive, L/Cpl. McGrann, had swum the river fully clothed. He was followed by Lieut. Smith, who had started to swim with two of the men. Next was Sgt. Parker, who ran, completely naked, from the point at which he landed to his Company H.Q. Finally Cpl. Sharpe, who had begun to swim across with Lieut. Bell but had lost him about half-way across.

To conclude the story of this patrol. On the 4th March an 'A' Company patrol searched the area where it had landed and were glad to find Sgt. Kirkton lying in a small pit in the river bank, alive but suffering from exposure. In the boat, which had beached itself in the mud, they found the body of Pte. Bradshaw who had been killed instantaneously when the boat had been hit. He was the first member of the Battalion to lose his life in action.

A fortnight later a seventh member of the patrol, L/Cpl. White, was accounted for. He had had considerable adventures. To start with he had swum two hundred yards upstream, had hidden in some long grass, and had then made his way to some woods. He then decided to try to make contact with the American troops who were advancing northwards from Venlo, and on the third day hid in an empty barn containing dried peas and potatoes on which he lived until, on the 9th March, a Dutchman told him that the Germans had left the neighbourhood. He then emerged and eventually fell in with some British troops.

On the 6th May the body of Pte. Barrett, a signaller, was recovered from the river and the grave of Pte. Carless was discovered. A few days later a letter was received from Pte. Burn, announcing his liberation from a prisoners-of-war camp. Early in July the Battalion was notified that Ptes. Byne and Meadows were back in England, having been prisoners of war. Thus the only one of the patrol who was never traced was Lieut. Bell and he, it must be assumed, lost his life.

*Across the Maas, 2nd–6th March*

For a few days it had been evident that the troops to the north and south were advancing steadily, and at midday on the 1st elements of the 9th U.S. Army were only eight miles from the Battalion's right flank, having captured Venlo. During the afternoon of the next day troops of the 75th U.S. Division could be seen moving into Lomm, on the far side of the river opposite 'D' Company's front, and on the afternoon of the 3rd, as the information was that the enemy had withdrawn from their positions, 'A' Company prepared to throw a party over the river to cover a bridging reconnaissance by the R.E. The Corps Commander, Lieut.-General E. H. Barker, was watching them carry their boats down to the river when there was a burst of machine-gun and rifle fire from the position which had caused Lieut. Bell's patrol so much trouble. The covering party returned the fire with Brens and 2-inch mortar within thirty seconds, and the enemy replied with their mortar. The Corps Commander gave orders that the patrol was to postpone its crossing, and the party dispersed as best they could under enemy observation. Some, including Major Newman, the Second-in-Command, had to remain on the river bank under most inadequate cover until after dusk. Later, the enemy post was mopped up by the Americans, with whom 'A' Company established a liaison post the next day when the R.E. began to bridge the river. Mines were plentiful, and the Pioneer Platoon unfortunately lost Cpl. Orton who was severely wounded.

*Preparations for the Rhine Crossing*

The battle front had now moved away from the Maas towards the Rhine. The 4th Battalion soon moved back to billets near Brussels, where training was carried out until the 13th. Many took the opportunity to visit the battlefield of Waterloo. The diary records, with much appreciation, the arrival of a consignment of canned beer from Major Rice of Northampton, who never failed in his efforts to provide comforts.

On the 15th there was a move at short notice to Venraij, in Holland. The Brigade had by now been very split up and consisted only of its H.Q. and the 4th Battalion, and the latter soon began to be detailed to provide various detachments. The first to go was the Anti-tank Platoon, placed under command of the 1st Cheshire Regt. who were attached to the 1st

Commando Brigade. They started to train for an unknown operation, but the fact that they were practising with 'Buffaloes'—amphibious tanks—was significant. Then 'D' Company left to join the 1st Royal Dragoons and, finally, 'C' Company and a section of carriers were attached to H.Q. 2nd Army for defence of that headquarters against paratroops.

Throughout these days there were many signs that a big operation was afoot. Traffic filled the roads leading towards the Rhine day and night, vast dumps of bridging and other stores were accumulating, and all the inhabitants had been cleared from the area. Then, on the morning of the 24th March, a continuous stream of aircraft passed overhead—bombers, Dakotas carrying airborne troops, and towed gliders. Those who were left with the 4th spent the day in inspections and playing football, for they had no rôle allotted to them in the crossing of the Rhine.

*The Rhine Crossing*

When 'D' Company joined the Royals they were attached to 'D' Squadron, one platoon being allotted to each half-squadron. Their task was the control of the traffic for the two assaulting brigades of the 51st Highland Division and for the follow-up troops. Some of the remaining platoon were given traffic-control duties on the west bank of the Rhine, others were used for guarding prisoners of war.

In the initial assault several of the Company crossed the river in storm-boats, establishing the first traffic-control post on the east bank, and later the whole Company crossed. Their task was no light one, for the 3rd, 43rd and 3rd Canadian Divisions passed through their posts. To give an idea of its magnitude, on the first bridge to be constructed in this sector No. 16 Platoon checked through 2,500 vehicles on the first day. One man, L/Cpl. Thornton, crossed the river thirty-one times in a storm-boat and jumped in eleven times to rescue men who had fallen in. The Company had only one casualty during the day.

The 1st Commando Brigade, to which the Anti-tank Platoon was attached, was to assault the town of Wesel, east of the Rhine. The Platoon was to be called forward to the area where it was likely to find targets.

H-Hour was 2200 hours on the 23rd March. As the Platoon at that time was located in the middle of a Medium Artillery Regiment's area, all troops had to be underground throughout the bombardment, which began at 1800 hours. They then stood by to cross the river, but the damage done to Wesel by the preliminary bombing had blocked the roads for transport, and it was not until two days had passed that they were called forward. They then occupied various positions, but the enemy had been so thoroughly beaten that they had no targets at which to shoot. On the 28th they rejoined the Battalion, having at least had a front-row view of the great operation.

*Various Tasks, 25th March–8th May*

As the Allied advance moved swiftly towards the interior of Germany there was much work to be done by the troops who remained on the Rhine, and the 4th found that the daily round did not lack variety. To start with, there was the guarding of many bridges and ferries, mainly to prevent the unauthorised movement of civilians across the river. Then came the task of maintaining the internal security of some 160 square miles of the 1st Corps District, this involving many jeep patrols to search houses for stocks of firearms and food. Meanwhile the Pioneer Platoon, under Capt. Gardiner, began the disposal of the dumps of mines in the Reichswald. By the end of April this had been completed, except for actual minefields which were marked and left. This work, which gave excellent training in the location of booby-traps, was not without its dangers, and when it had nearly been finished Sgt. Outhwaite of 'A' Company was mortally wounded by the mysterious explosion of a stick-grenade, the last of a heap in which none of the grenades had contained detonators.

Apart from these there were tasks such as the guarding of a 25-mile-long ammunition depot in Holland and of various supply depots, which were liable to pilfering. 'C' Company, still attached to 2nd Army H.Q., did everything, from clearing areas in which the headquarters were to be established to stopping strife between Russian labourers, Italians and German civilians.

In their spare time the Battalion ran a training cadre in various subjects for the 2nd North Brabant Regt. of the Netherlands Army.

Then, on the 8th May, came VE-Day, duly celebrated by the 4th Battalion. Though it had not fallen to their lot to take part as a unit in any of the final battles of the campaign, they had carried out many essential tasks during and after the crossing of the Rhine. And, after their long spell of training and home defence in the United Kingdom, it was satisfying to them to have been the first battalion of the Regiment to have had the privilege of joining 21st Army Group, and to have been the second Territorial Battalion of the Regiment to serve overseas.

# CHAPTER XXI

## THE REGIMENT AFTER THE WAR, 1945–1948

The 48th in India, May–December 1945—The 48th in Malaya, January 1946–February 1947—Homecoming of the 48th, April 1947—Final Ceremonies—The 58th at Göttingen, July 1945–June 1947—The 58th in Berlin, June 1947–January 1948—The Return of the Colours, October 1947—The 58th move to Austria, January 1948—The 4th Battalion in Germany, May 1945–February 1946—The 5th Battalion move into Austria, May 1945—Occupation, July 1945–September 1946—Disbandment, September 1946—Re-formation of the 5th Battalion—585 Searchlight Regt. R.A. (T.A.)—The I.T.C., 1945–1946—No. 48 P.T.C., 1946–1948—The Depot—The Comrades' Association—Post-war Reorganisation—The Reasons—The Solution—The Revised Solution—The Colonel of the Regiment—The Regimental War Memorial—Freedom of the Borough of Northampton, 8th June 1946

### The 48th in India, May–December 1945

WE left the 48th about to entrain for India, having said good-bye to Burma. Their long journey ended at Visapur, between Poona and Ahmednagar, on the 9th May, and there, after a period of rest and leave, they began training for what was to be the final assault on Singapore. However, the dropping of the atom-bomb on Hiroshima obviated the need for this operation and after VJ-Day, the 16th August, had been celebrated, the Battalion concentrated on preparations for occupational and internal-security duties.

Shortly before this, on the 5th August, a Parade Service had been held in memory of the 221 members of the 48th who had given their lives during the Burma Campaign. A copy of the form of service, which included the Roll of Honour, was sent to the next-of-kin of the fallen.

In October the 36th Division was amalgamated with the 2nd to form a new 2nd Division, and the 48th found themselves in the 6th Brigade. All officers and men who were due for release, or repatriation, were transferred to the 36th Division, the 48th thus losing many who had seen much service in Burma.

At the end of November Lieut.-Col. Jones gave up command and was succeeded by Lieut.-Col. J. R. Britten.

The Battalion was now warned to prepare to move to Hong Kong, and left for Bombay on the 12th December. The *Highland Chieftain* in which they embarked, 32 officers and 660 other ranks strong, sailed on the 15th, but was delayed by engine trouble in the bay and did not really start on her voyage until the 21st.

As the ship was passing Sumatra, on the 26th, a signal was received ordering the 48th to Singapore, and there they disembarked on the 29th.

### The 48th in Malaya, January 1946–February 1947

In 1889 Rudyard Kipling visited Malaya in the course of a voyage from India to Japan and, in an account of his visit wrote: 'The 58th (Northamptonshire) live in these parts; so Singapur is quite safe, you see.' [1] On the 29th December, fifty-seven years later, the 48th disembarked there to follow in the footsteps of the 58th.

To begin with the Battalion was dispersed over a very wide area, with Headquarters at Mersing, a village on the east coast of the Malay Peninsula about 110 miles north of Singapore, but during January all except 'C' Company moved into Gillman Barracks, west of the city of Singapore. These were comfortable quarters, having been completed just before the war.

Until the beginning of April 'C' Company remained at Pengerang, on the extreme tip of the Malay Peninsula, in an area of dense jungle apart from a few coastal villages and rubber plantations. Until the Company arrived there little had been done to show the British flag, or restore order, in the area. As a result of searches, some of which were carried out by landing-craft along the rivers, much property stolen from European bungalows during the Japanese occupation was recovered, and a stop was put to a flourishing contraband traffic in rice from Siam.

Whilst at Gillman Barracks the Battalion had little time for training, owing to their internal-security duties. They did, however, assist in the training of troops of the Royal Netherlands Army. As a memento of this the 1/12th Battalion presented them with a pair of drums which had been buried in Holland during the German occupation and recovered after the liberation of the country.

Among other tasks the 48th were called upon to find firing-squads for the execution of Japanese war-criminals. The first of these in the Command was carried out on the 27th April, the criminal being Lieut.-General Fukei Shempei, who, as senior officer in charge of prisoners-of-war camps in Malaya in the latter part of 1942, had been found guilty of responsibility for the murder of two British and two Australian prisoners of war. Appropriately he was executed on the exact spot on which these murders had been committed, and the firing-squad was composed of men who had been wounded in the fighting in Burma.

Towards the end of June the Battalion was relieved and returned to the former stations in the Mersing area, but within three weeks there was a move to Changi Gaol, on Singapore Island, except for a small detachment which remained at Pengerang until September.

Changi Gaol housed between two and three thousand Japanese, either awaiting trial or execution, serving long sentences of imprisonment, required as witnesses at trials or held pending repatriation to Japan. Guard duties were extremely heavy, so much so that employed men such as M.T. drivers, sanitary squad men, and Pioneers had to be used, their work being done by Japanese under escort. The standard of turn-out of the guards had to be, and was, extremely high, and earned the 48th much praise. Alertness against attempts at suicide by the prisoners was essential and succeeded in averting the two attempts which were made.

On the 7th October the 48th were glad to be relieved by the 2nd Bn. Durham L.I. The novelty of the duties had then worn off, and the men had wearied of being locked up in the Gaol for two days out of every three, duty in the watch-towers round the walls having been particularly monotonous.

The new station was Seremban, the capital of the State of Negri Sembilan, 200 miles up-country from Singapore. Rasah Camp was but partially completed, the huts being made of the roughest timber. Such drains as existed were incapable of carrying away the water which flooded the camp whenever it rained, a daily occurrence at that time of year. There were no amenities such as a N.A.A.F.I. in the camp, but fortunately for the troops welfare organisations existed in the town. 'A' Company, at Port Dickson, was more comfortably housed in billets.

For several months it had been rumoured that certain battalions were to be placed in 'suspended animation' for a period of years, as part of the scheme for the reorganisation of the Army. On the 20th December a letter from the Adjutant-General informed the Colonel of the Regiment that the 48th would be one of these, and on Christmas Eve the news reached them in Malaya.[2]

During the post-war period many officers and men had left the Battalion on release from the Forces; now only a small cadre was to go home with the Colours and the Regimental property, the remainder were to complete their service with units serving in the East.

In January 1947 Lieut.-Col. Taunton returned from his Brigade to take command of the 48th. There was much to be done in the way of checking and packing the Regimental property, most of which had only just been returned to the Battalion from its war-time store in Bombay, but there was time for a 48th 'week' before the dispersal began. This included inter-company cricket and football and matches against the State and other units, an Officers' Mess guest-night from which a telegram 'Best wishes from 48th dining regimentally to-night for the last time' was sent to the Colonel of the Regiment, and a final dinner for all below the rank of sergeant.

By the 28th February disbandment had been finished in Malaya and the Cadre of the Battalion[3] embarked for England, their sadness somewhat relieved by the messages of praise and encouragement which had been sent to them by the Colonel-in-Chief and the Colonel of the Regiment, and by Lieut.-General Gracey who had been their Divisional Commander in Burma.[4]

*Homecoming of the 48th, April 1947*

The Cadre reached Liverpool on the 15th April. Two days later they detrained at Northampton, the train drawn by the locomotive 'The Northamptonshire Regiment,' a gesture for which the Regiment owes gratitude to the L.M.S. Railway.

The Colonel of the Regiment and many former members of it were on the platform to greet them. After detraining, accompanied by the playing of the Regimental March, the Cadre formed up and were welcomed by the Colonel of the Regiment. In his address, Major-General Robinson said:

'Colonel Taunton, officers and men of the 48th.

'For reasons of which we are all aware, you come back, after just twenty years abroad, to this your county town. Not, as we would have wished, with a full Battalion, but as a Cadre. Fate has ordained that you represent this Cadre, and as such you must feel great pride and honour, so that for years to come you will remember this day.

'The fact that we see here only the Cadre does not in any way dim the warmth of the welcome we give you. This is borne out by the many old officers and men of the Regiment you see here, apart from your relations and friends.

'Your last tour abroad has been an historic one. You have visited seven countries and two islands, and fought most gallantly in a major campaign in Burma. During your twenty years' foreign tour you have brought, in peace and in war, added fame to your Battalion and Regiment. In peace you were foremost in shooting, in war you have conducted yourselves like our Talavera ancestors. With pride and affection we give you a special welcome home.'

Outside the station, an Escort Company from No. 48 P.T.C. was waiting. To the strains of the Regimental Slow March the Colours were marched on to parade and the column then moved off to the Guildhall, exercising the Regiment's privilege of marching through the town with Colours flying and with bayonets fixed.

On reaching the Guildhall the parade formed up with the Colour Party facing a platform on which were standing the Mayor and officials of the Corporation. After he had inspected the parade the Mayor welcomed the Cadre of the 48th, referring to the past deeds of the Battalion and concluding with some words from the epilogue to the Regimental History.

Handing over of the Colours of the 48th at Northampton, 1947
(See p. 337)

*Northampton "Chronicle and Echo"*

In reply, Lieut.-Col. Taunton thanked the Mayor for his address and expressed the gratitude of the Battalion for the gifts which had been received from the county while they were in the Far East. In conclusion he presented to the Mayor a Japanese sword, captured in action by the 48th, the mount bearing an inscription.[5]

*Final Ceremonies*

From the Guildhall the column marched to Talavera Camp and formed up in line facing the Officers' Mess. The Colours and their Escort moved out in front of the line to the Royal Salute. Lieut.-Col. Taunton then took the King's Colour from the hands of the officer carrying it, turned to the Colonel of the Regiment and handed him the Colour, saying:

'Sir, I hand over to you the King's Colour of the 48th Regiment.'

General Robinson then handed the Colour to Major J. R. Wetherall, Commanding the Depot, saying:

'Major Wetherall, I hand over to you for safe custody the King's Colour of the 48th Regiment, for safe keeping until such time as the 48th shall again re-form.'

With similar ceremonial and with similar words, the Regimental Colour was then handed over and the two were placed in the Officers' Mess, side by side with those of the 58th for the first time in the history of the Regiment.

Then, with Lieut.-Col. Taunton's word of command, '48th Dismiss,' the 48th received their final order on parade as a single battalion, possibly for ever.

The ceremony had been short and simple. There was none of the pageantry which would have marked such an occasion in the past. Instead of a full battalion of Infantry in the blaze of scarlet tunics, the 48th were represented by a small group of officers and men wearing battle-dress and the slouch hats of the Burma Campaign. The sole sign of pageantry was in the Colours, and when they were handed over all those who were present felt that they had witnessed the passing of a Battalion which for more than two hundred years, in many lands both in peace and war, had worthily upheld the honour of its Country and of its Regiment.

That night, at the Regimental guest-night which was held, the Colonel of the Regiment ordained that annually in the future, on a guest-night nearest to Talavera Day, all battalions of the Regiment should drink a toast—'To the 48th!'

In a speech, Lieut.-Col. Taunton reminded those who had come through the Burma Campaign of what they owed to those who had given their lives there. He concluded by saying that the traditions of the 48th would be kept alive by those who had recently left, and by those who still belonged to the Battalion, and that they would undoubtedly be added to by the new generation who would form the 48th when the period of 'suspended animation' had ended.

By a decision of the Regimental Council, the Silver and other property of the 48th was to be divided between the 58th and the Depot, for safe keeping, so that their historical significance should be kept alive and the memory of the 48th not forgotten.

## The 58th at Göttingen, July 1945–June 1947

Göttingen, to which the 58th had moved at the beginning of July 1945, was a pleasant old town, practically untouched by the war, in Hanover Province, close to the meeting-point of the British, American and Russian zones of occupation. At the end of the month Lieut.-Col. Osborne-Smith arrived to assume command.

There were many duties to be performed, such as guards on frontier-posts and dumps, curfew and area patrols, and periodical road-checks. The refugee problem was ever-present. Many German civilians were trying to return to their homes in Western Germany from the Russian zone. Theoretically they should have been turned back, but the difficulty was that, whereas the Russian posts were on the frontier line, those of the British lay some five hundred yards from it. Consequently, once the refugees had passed the Russian posts they were in the British zone and the Russians declined to allow their return. So Göttingen had more and more people to look after and more mouths to feed.

Despite the number of duties there was plenty of variety for the Battalion. There were good facilities for sport, including the rarer one of boar-shooting, to say nothing of a cinema and a good opera-house.

The release of men to civil life proceeded with regularity, but the strength of the Battalion was kept up by the arrival, early in 1946, of a large draft from the disbanded 4th Battalion, and by a steady flow of reinforcements of men of the higher age-and-service groups. Nevertheless, when extra duties, such as the finding of guards for Corps H.Q. at Luneberg and on the Brunswick–Berlin ration-train, fell to the 58th they were forced to give up the guard at Battalion H.Q.

In June, Lieut.-Col. Osborne-Smith relinquished command, leaving for a staff appointment at Rhine Army H.Q., and was succeeded by Major Melsome.

As 1946 drew out it was possible to start training in earnest. The rifle companies were nearly up to strength, and though the Battalion included officers and men of many different units these settled down well among the permanent members of the Regiment, and there was a feeling that the end of the lean post-war period was in sight. A German rifle-range was not far distant, and when part of this had been cleared of mines the Battalion fired its first rifle course. A shooting team was organised and achieved its first success by winning the Brigade and Brigade Group championships at Brunswick in October.

Soon after the 58th's arrival at Göttingen, life had been made more pleasant by a relaxation of the strict rules regarding fraternisation with the German people. This, no doubt, helped towards the report made by a high German official of Göttingen to the Regional Commissioner. In it he said that the town had been accustomed to having a German regiment there for the past fifty years, and that they now regarded the British one, the 58th, with equal pride and affection. The difference between the conduct and the discipline of the soldiers of the two had been much appreciated, and he considered that the British soldiers were the best propaganda for democracy.

*The 58th in Berlin, June 1947–January 1948*

In due course the time came for the 58th to leave Göttingen, to take their turn as part of the garrison of the British sector of Berlin. The first rail party reached that city on the 1st June, and by the 6th the whole Battalion was in its new quarters at Kladow. This place, some ten miles from the centre of the city, was in the country, surrounded by pine-woods and cultivated land. Montgomery Barracks, where the 58th lay, were a relic of the days when Hitler was expanding the armed forces of the Reich. They were therefore of modern design, though many of the amenities had been spoilt by the Soviet troops who had been the first to occupy them after the German surrender.

Shortly after their arrival Lieut.-Col. Taunton took over the command of the Battalion from Lieut.-Col. Melsome.

In Berlin guard duties were very heavy, and the 58th set themselves, and achieved, a high standard of turn-out and discipline which was not to pass unnoticed by the many Commanders who visited them. Although previously they had had no opportunity of training an athletic team, this was soon remedied and a month after their arrival they distinguished themselves by winning the championship for the British troops stationed in Berlin, held in the Olympic Stadium.

At the first post-war meeting of the Army Rifle Association at Bisley, the 58th team went to the fore, as they had been before the war. They were second to their old rivals, the Rifle Brigade, in the King's Royal Rifle Corps Cup, the unit championship. Worthy of note is the fact that one of the members of the sergeants' team in the Worcestershire Cup (second in the event) was Sgt. Wilmott, who, though he had only come back to the Battalion a fortnight before the team left for Bisley, was remembered by someone as having fired in the same event in 1934, though then with that forgotten weapon, the Lewis gun.

Next came the British Army of the Rhine meeting at Paderborn. This closely resembled the pre-war Aldershot Command event, many of the cups being the identical ones which the 58th had won in those palmy days. The Battalion tied for third place, thirty units competing, and deemed this result to be below their usual standard. It came as somewhat of a shock, before the meeting, to find that the Young Soldiers' team, which had shot so well at Bisley, was ineligible to compete at Paderborn. Under A.R.A. rules, those with less than two years' service were eligible, but the B.A.O.R. conditions specified one year. So, in the space of about two months, a new team had to be found and trained, and it says much for the efforts of Lieut.-Col. G. V. Britten and Major Ogle, and their assistants, that at the meeting the team won both the Rifle and the L.M.G. event, and the Inter-Unit Championship in its class.

In the same month, at the meeting for the British Troops in Berlin, the 58th won all the events except two, and in these they gained second place.

After this there only remained the firing of the competitions for the Queen Victoria Trophy, which the 58th were determined to win and so maintain the reputation which the 48th had earned in India in the years before the war. They were not disappointed, and for the first time in their history they became the holders of the Trophy.[6]

### The Return of the Colours, October 1947

The occasion of the visit of the Colonel of the Regiment to the 58th in October 1947 was marked by a ceremonial parade, at which he handed back to them their Colours, which had been laid up at the Depot since September 1939.

On the morning of the 21st October, headed by the Band, which had arrived from England only four days earlier, and escorted by 'C' Company, the Colours were marched on to the parade-ground and were deposited cased on a pile of drums. The remainder of the Battalion then marched on parade, formed hollow square, and received Major-General Robinson with the General Salute.

After inspecting the parade he moved to the dais where, after the Colours had been uncased by the Drum-Major, he handed them over in turn to Capt. Newby and Lieut. Yates. As the Battalion presented arms the Colours were then marched into the ranks to the tune of the Slow March.

Major-General Robinson then addressed the Battalion. After referring to the fine reputation which the 58th had in Berlin, he reminded them of the history of the Colours, the last in the Army to have been carried into action. Then, 'I charge you,' he said, 'do nothing by deed or by action that will sully the proud traditions and the historic background of your Colours. Indeed, I am confident that you will not do so, knowing how well you are maintaining the proud traditions of your Regiment.

'This day all old members of the Regiment at home will, you may be

THE REGIMENT AFTER THE WAR, 1945-1948    341

sure, learn of what has been happening, and with pride when they hear how good I consider your turn-out was this morning. I would like to congratulate you on that, and ask you to maintain, and even improve on, the fine reputation you have got for yourselves so far.'

The Battalion then marched past the Colonel, and, after they had re-formed hollow square, the Colours and their escort marched off parade.

Thus was 1947 marked by two impressive ceremonies: the one at Northampton, when the Colours of the 48th were sadly handed over to the care of the Depot; the other in Berlin, when the Colours of the 58th were gladly welcomed back by the Battalion. Both were historic days.

*The 58th move to Austria, January 1948*

When the 58th went to Berlin it was understood that after their tour of duty there they would return to Göttingen. Later, this was altered to Essen, and then this was cancelled and they were warned that they would be transferred to the United Kingdom in December 1947. In the end, on Christmas Eve, news came that their destination would be Austria. The main body left Berlin in two trains on the 28th January 1948, and ended their long journey across Central Europe at the town of Spittal.

Spittal lies high up in the Austrian Alps, not far from Italy's northern border. A small, pleasant town, surrounded by magnificent scenery, the 58th found it a very welcome change from the devastation and the flatness of Berlin.

One Company, 'C,' formed a detachment at the small town of St. Jakob's close to the Jugoslav border, its main tasks being the keeping of a watch on the Rosenbach Tunnel through which ran one of the main railways between the two countries, and the carrying out of patrols in the Prohibited Frontier Zone. In March the Company was withdrawn to Velden, some thirty-five miles from Spittal, continuing the same tasks until the middle of the year, when patrolling ceased. Then, reduced to a cadre, they began to prepare for their new duty, the intensive training for six weeks' periods of National Service men, on arrival from the United Kingdom and before they were posted to Companies, due to start in 1949.

In April Lieut.-Col. Taunton gave up his short tenure of command of the 58th, on promotion, and was succeeded by Lieut.-Col. Ballard, who had already commanded for two lengthy periods during the war.

The 1948 Bisley meeting found the Battalion high up in all the team and individual events. Four months later, at the meeting for the British Troops in Austria and at Trieste, they were the winners of the Unit Championship, the Individual Rifle and L.M.G. Championships, and many other team events. These successes, however, seemed comparatively small when the result of the Queen Victoria Trophy became known. This year, being in Austria, the Battalion came into the 'abroad' category, which included all units other than those in the United Kingdom and the British Army of the Rhine. Not only did they win the Trophy (for the first time as the 48th/58th, for reasons which will be seen later), but also every one of the separate events which contributed towards it.[6]

So, at the end of this period in our history, the Regiment's reputation for good shooting remained firm. Nor will it ever be forgotten, for the Army Rifle Association accepted from the Regiment the gift of a cup, to be known as 'The Northamptonshire Cup,' for an Infantry Team Match to be fired at the Central Meeting at Bisley.

## The 4th Battalion in Germany, May 1945–February 1946

After VE-Day the 4th Battalion remained in the Rees area, finding various guards and carrying out salvage duties. Here they were rejoined by 'C' Company, which had been at H.Q. 2nd Army since March. Early in June, as a result of the adjustment of boundaries between zones, the Battalion moved to take over the Mors Kreis (or District), covering about two hundred square miles, from American troops. Battalion H.Q. was in the town of Mors, on the east bank of the Rhine some three miles from Duisburg; companies were billeted in neighbouring towns.

Duties were many and varied, and included the guarding of several Rhine bridges, a salt-mine and a pipe-line; the clearance of battlefields within the Kreis; 'potato patrols,' to stop the transportation of potatoes across the Rhine from west to east for purposes of barter, as much as five tons being confiscated in a day; and, in general, the maintenance of order.

The last-named task was made all the more difficult by the presence of large numbers of Russians, formerly slave-workers under the Nazis, who made a habit of raiding farms and killing or wounding the inhabitants. One of the least pleasant duties which fell to the Battalion's lot was the guarding of a camp containing 8,000 Russians, who were confined to camp owing to their lawless behaviour and who frequently committed murder among themselves.

At the beginning of August the first party of men to be released from service left the Battalion, and, as the rate of release accelerated, it was evident that it would be only a matter of time before orders came to disband, for the 4th was classified as a war-time unit.

These orders were received on the 8th January, and during the next few days all operational commitments were handed over and the Battalion settled down to the depressing task of preparing to disband. Lieut.-Col. Furminger soon left to take up another appointment, leaving Major Newman to command during the closing days of the Battalion's existence. In his farewell message to the Battalion Lieut.-Col. Furminger told them that they were regarded by the Brigade and Divisional Commanders as the best battalion under their command, and added that this was not said for sentimental reasons but as an honest statement of fact, a statement which was supported by a later message from the Colonel of the Regiment.[7]

By the end of January only a few men who were due for release were left, the majority of the remainder having been drafted to the 58th, and by the 5th February disbandment was complete. The 4th Battalion of 1939–1945 had completed its task and had carried it out in a manner which was worthy of their predecessors who had served before, during and after the 1914–1918 War.

## The 5th Battalion move into Austria, May 1945

After the surrender of the German armies in Italy, the 5th Battalion were soon on the move northwards, and at 1500 hours on the 8th May, at the precise moment that Mr. Winston Churchill was announcing the unconditional surrender of Germany, they crossed the frontier into Austria. On reaching Spittal they received a great welcome from the British who had been liberated from the civil internment camp there, and then began to deal with the numerous problems which arose, the result of five years of Nazi occupation.

However, more urgent work lay ahead, this being to deal with the multitude of Germans who were coming in from the north-east to surrender. So, on the 11th the Battalion moved on to Tamweg, finding a continuous stream of enemy transport, both horsed and motorised, entering the town. It was here that they received, through the Colonel of the Regiment, the congratulations of the Colonel-in-Chief on having seen the fulfilment of their efforts.

Early in June, patrols on foot, in jeeps and on horse-back searched the whole of the Battalion area for concealed enemy troops and equipment; hard work, as it necessitated the covering of every square mile of the country.

At the same time a major task, that of the evacuation of the enemy troops in the area, was put in hand. First priority was given to the German Cavalry Corps, the troops of which were moved out of the Battalion area in groups of about 3,000. Within a week, and a day ahead of schedule, the whole of the 3rd Cavalry Division had been cleared. They were followed by the 23rd Panzer Division and some 4,500 men of the Luftwaffe, and by the time that the Battalion handed the area over to an American Airborne Division they had dealt with over 50,000 enemy troops, estimated to amount to about one-fifth of the total for the Eighth Army, no mean feat of organisation.

## Occupation, July 1945–September 1946

After two months spent at Trefling and Mallnitz, the latter a well-known winter resort, the 5th moved up to the Volkermarkt area at the beginning of September. Here their duties included the manning of posts on the Jugoslav border. Mounted patrols were much used, and for these, and for less military purposes, the Battalion managed to collect a very good 'stable.' In fact it would have been strange if they had not, considering that they had had a good opportunity to make their selection from the Cavalry Corps horses. Ski patrols were also employed during the winter, and many made use of the opportunity to become good skiers. Another feature was wood-cutting, carried out by companies to ease the fuel shortage. They seem to have worked with a will, for between the middle of October, when this work was started in earnest, and the middle of December the amount cut totalled 1,192 tons.

Throughout this period the Battalion lost many men through release, but the strength, 973 at the end of 1945, was kept up by drafts of young soldiers from home.

In November the first number of a fortnightly Battalion newspaper, *Tally-Ho!*, appeared. Another feat was the production of a very comprehensive history of the Battalion's achievements in the Italian campaign, compiled by the Adjutant, Capt. McKee, and admirably printed and bound by various members of the Intelligence Section of the German Cavalry Corps on its mobile printing press.

*Disbandment, September 1946*

Late in July 1946 the 5th heard the sad news that, owing to the policy of reducing the size of the Army in Austria, the 78th Division was to lose its identity and that the Battalion, together with all other Territorial Army units, was to be disbanded. From then on drafts left for other units, the majority to Italy.

Talavera Day was duly celebrated in traditional style and then, on the 12th August, before too many members of the Battalion had been drafted away, the final ceremonial parade was held in the main square of Volkermarkt. It was a tribute to the 5th that the Burgomaster of the town declared the day a holiday so that the citizens could witness the parade. And, in a subsequent letter, he expressed his thanks to the Battalion for all that they had done.

A few days later duties were handed over to the 1st Bn. The R. Irish Fusiliers, and the remnants of the Battalion moved into a nearby town. There, on the 25th September, the 5th were placed in 'suspended animation.'

It is fitting to close this chapter in the Battalion's history with an extract from a farewell letter, written by Major-General R. K. Arbuthnott, Commander of the 78th Division.

> I shall always remember the good humour, courage and endurance of the men during the hard days of the Italian Campaign, and their excellent behaviour and restraint during the occupational days.

## THE REGIMENT AFTER THE WAR, 1945-1948

These things could never have been achieved had not the Battalion always had at its disposal a team of Officers who showed the highest degree of leadership, particularly devotion to duty in action and tireless care of their men at all times.

The Battalion can well be proud of its war record, and successive Commanding Officers . . . can look forward with every satisfaction to their period of Command.

### Re-formation of the 5th Battalion

The period of 'suspended animation' of the 5th Battalion was brief. One of the main future tasks of the Territorial Army was to be the training of National Service men after they had finished their Regular Army service. Accordingly, early in 1948 the 5th began to raise a cadre of officers, instructors and key men against the day when general enlistment in the T.A. would be reopened.

This was not long delayed and, although when it started recruiting was not as good as it should have been, by the end of the year the Battalion was firmly established under the command of Lieut.-Col. R. K. McMichael, T.D. Its stations were at Peterborough, Huntington, Ramsey, Oundle and Rushden, and it had completed its first post-war annual training in camp. And there we must leave the 5th, preparing for the first intake of National Service men in 1950.

### 585 Searchlight Regt. R.A. (T.A.)

Earlier in this volume mention was made of the conversion of the old 4th Battalion into a Searchlight Battalion R.E. Three years later they were transferred to the Royal Artillery, under the title 50th A.A. Searchlight Regt. R.A. (T.A.) and served as such throughout the war. In 1945 the Regiment underwent yet another change, becoming the 637th Garrison Regt. R.A. (T.A.) and reorganising on an Infantry basis for garrison duty in Norway.

This continued until, in February 1947, they were placed in 'suspended animation,' but two months later they came to life again, re-forming as 585 Searchlight Regt. R.A. (T.A.), with Headquarters in the old 4th Battalion drill-hall in Northampton. The link with the Regiment is still maintained, for not only do the words 'Northamptonshire Regiment' continue to appear in brackets after their title, but all ranks wear the cap-badge and buttons of the Regiment.[8]

### The I.T.C., 1945-1946

No. 14 I.T.C. remained in Talavera Camp until March 1945, when these quarters were required for a Dispersal Unit. Accordingly the I.T.C. moved, and was accommodated in the Old Barracks, Quebec Barracks (still but partially completed) and some large houses in the neighbourhood.

Soon after the move Lieut.-Col. Carrick relinquished command and was succeeded by Lieut.-Col. Cadoux Hudson of the R. Hampshire Regt. A year later Talavera Camp again became available and the I.T.C. returned there, leaving only the Primary Training Wing in Quebec Barracks.

## No. 48 P.T.C., 1946–1948

In November 1947, as part of the general reorganisation of the Army, the I.T.C. was replaced by No. 48 Primary Training Centre, under the command of Lieut.-Col. Watts.

The P.T.C. consisted of a Headquarter Company and two Training Companies, one of the latter being housed in Quebec Barracks. Its duty was to train men during the first few weeks of their time in the Army. On arrival, all recruits wore the badge of the General Service Corps. After six weeks' training, those selected for service in the Infantry were posted to the Regiment and went to the East Anglian Group I.T.C. at Colchester for further training, those for other arms to the appropriate Training Centre. The intake averaged 90 men a fortnight, the actual figure rising sometimes to 120.

Early in 1948 there was more reorganisation, and news came that the P.T.C. was to be disbanded, that Talavera Camp was to be demolished and the site returned to the Borough. The Permanent Staff were dispersed, and on the 21st April the unit which, under various names and in various places, had trained so many men, ceased to exist.

During its brief life the P.T.C. had contributed to the shooting successes of the Regiment by winning the A.R.A. Match for P.T.C.s in the only year (1947) in which it was fired.

### The Depot

Throughout the war years the Regimental Depot—a small body of officers and men who, under Major Dipper, looked after purely regimental affairs such as the Comrades' Association and the war-time *News-letter*°— had remained in the Old Barracks at Northampton. When these were vacated at the end of 1946, the Depot moved to Talavera Camp and was affiliated to the P.T.C.

On the disbandment of the P.T.C. the Depot was established in Quebec Barracks, and there, with an establishment of four officers and twenty-two other ranks, it resumed its old rôle as the home of the Regiment, always busy with regimental affairs, but never more so than at the time of the Annual Reunion.

### The Comrades' Association

Before the end of the war the Colonel of the Regiment had drawn up a scheme for the reorganisation of the Comrades' Association on a sound basis, and as a result, after thorough consideration at Regimental Meetings, a Trust Deed and Rules were approved early in 1947.

The management of the affairs of the Association was vested in a Council, of which the Colonel of the Regiment was President, and the Members were the Commanding Officers of each Battalion and the Depot, the President of the London Branch of the Association, the Secretary of the T.A. Association, and others appointed to serve for a term of years either by the Colonel of the Regiment or by co-option by the Council. This body was also responsible for other matters, such as the Annual Reunion, the Journal, the Museum, and Regimental Memorials and History.

A major alteration as compared with the pre-war organisation was the division of the funds into two—the General Fund and the Benevolent Fund. The former received all subscriptions and other moneys which were available. The Benevolent Fund was established as a Charitable Trust Fund, thus gaining considerable financial advantage, and derived its resources from sums transferred from the General Fund and from gifts from other sources.

As a result of the steps taken the Comrades' Association was placed on a firm basis, and the funds available for its principal object—the assistance of members of the Regiment who were in need—became greater than they had ever before been.

*Post-war Reorganisation*

The sequel to every war is reorganisation, in a greater or a lesser degree, but never before has this affected Regiments of the Infantry as did that which followed the Second World War of 1939–1945.

As the reader will already have seen, the Northamptonshire Regiment was no exception, so this portion of the chapter which tells of the Regiment in the years immediately after the war also gives the reasons for the reorganisation which took place and the scheme itself, in some detail.

*The Reasons*

In the later years of the First World War the uneven distribution of casualties made the system under which the Infantry was divided into more than sixty different regiments largely a failure for reinforcement purposes, and both officers and men had frequently to be posted to Battalions other than those of their own Regiment.

During the years between the two world wars the Cardwell system, under which one battalion of a regiment normally served at home while the other was abroad, worked well, though at times, such as the Shanghai crisis, the balance was upset owing to both battalions having to be abroad simultaneously. A great advantage of the system was that, generally speaking, it did ensure that officers and men served with a battalion of their own regiment, thus maintaining the *esprit de corps* which is so essential at all times, and especially in battle.

The conditions of the Second World War intensified the reinforcement problem of twenty years before. Many regimental officers realised the drawbacks of the system, but others, who had never served as Infantry officers in war, began to argue that complete flexibility was required, and advocated the formation of a Corps of Infantry.

Fortunately this argument was killed, and for this Field-Marshal Montgomery was mainly responsible, for in 1943 he had written:

> We must be very careful what we do with the British Infantry. They are the people who do the solid fighting and the killing. If we mess them about we may lose the war. Their fighting spirit is based largely on morale and regimental *esprit de corps*. On no account must anyone be allowed to tamper with this.

After the war ended other factors introduced themselves and affected the solution of the problem. It would be necessary for a larger proportion of Infantry battalions to serve outside the United Kingdom than had been the case in the past, and this would upset the balance of the Cardwell system even if service in the Armies of Occupation in Europe were to be treated as home service. The introduction of the shorter term of Colour service, five years in place of seven, and of the overseas tour of about three and a half years, would lead to bigger demands for drafts from the home battalions. And the possibility that India would no longer require a British garrison made it probable that fewer Infantry battalions would be required than before the war.

The conclusion was reached that it would probably be necessary for officers and men to serve in more than one regiment, and this not only in war time but also in peace, but that traditions and territorial connections could best be preserved by organising regiments into small Groups. As time went on and it became clear that most, if not all, regiments would have to consist of one Regular battalion only, it was realised that these Groups would have to form centres for the training and holding of recruits, and for the officers and men of the solitary Regular battalion (if this were serving overseas) during their tour of home service.

*The Solution*

So it came about that in 1947 the East Anglian Group was formed, consisting of the Royal Norfolk, Suffolk, Bedfordshire and Hertfordshire, Essex, and Northamptonshire Regiments. The Group Training Centre was established at Colchester and consisted of one company for each regiment of the Group. The task of the Centre was to conduct the more advanced training of recruits, to draft them to battalions of the Group and to hold officers and men who had come home from overseas.

Feeding the Group Training Centres were the Primary Training Centres, of which we are concerned with No. 48 P.T.C. at Northampton. This more or less filled the rôle of the pre-war Regimental Depot, but there was one big difference, due to the introduction of National Service as a peace-time measure.

The Labour Government which had come into office in 1945 had introduced a Bill which provided that, at or after the age of eighteen, all men should be liable to undergo a period of eighteen months' service in the Regular Armed Forces, followed by a period of training in the Territorial Army, unless exempted for other essential work. This Bill was supported by the majority of all political parties in the House of Commons, but met with considerable opposition from some of the members of the Labour Party. To pacify this opposition, the Minister of Defence abruptly reduced the period of service to one year. The amended Bill was passed, but before long the period of service was raised to the originally-proposed eighteen months.

Consequently, the P.T.C. not only dealt with the initial training of volunteer Regular soldiers, but had also to train the National Service men as they were called up. These, at the end of their basic training at the P.T.C., might be sent for more advanced training either to the Group I.T.C., if they had enlisted and been judged suitable for Infantry, or to the Training Centre of another Arm of the Service.

Then came the reduction in the number of Infantry battalions. In order to effect this various alternatives had to be considered, but all had great disadvantages excepting that finally adopted—the placing of battalions in turn in 'suspended animation.' This was to be combined with the periodical relief of battalions serving overseas, and envisaged each battalion of a regiment serving at home for 8–10 years, abroad for 10–15 years, and then being placed in 'suspended animation' for another 10–15 years. In the last-named category a battalion would have no officers or men on its strength, and the Colours and regimental property would be stored at the Depot. It would then be for the active battalion of the regiment to ensure that the traditions of such battalions were not forgotten, as well they might in such a space of time.

This was the chain of events which had, early in 1947, put an end to the existence of the 48th in any way other than as a memory, after a life of 207 years. Fortunately, however, this state of affairs was not to last for long.

*The Revised Solution*

Towards the end of 1947 the 'suspended animation' project underwent considerable alteration and regiments were told that the non-existent battalion could either be completely disbanded or that it could be amalgamated with the battalion in being. If the latter course were adopted the resulting battalion would be named the 1st Battalion.

There was little doubt regarding the choice to be made as far as the Regiment was concerned, and as a result, on the 30th August 1948, there came into existence the 1st Battalion The Northamptonshire Regiment (48th/58th). The amalgamation of the two Battalions was marked, as a token, by the arrival in Vienna of a small cadre from the Depot representing the 48th.

So the new Battalion was born, the trustee for the future of the Colours, the traditions and the customs which the 48th and the 58th had each guarded so jealously for so many bygone years. And there, in Vienna, before many months had passed, the 48th/58th were proud to welcome the Colonel-in-Chief and the Colonel of the Regiment, a visit which set the seal on the union of the two Battalions.

Simultaneously with this amalgamation, both I.T.C.s and P.T.C.s were abolished. In their place arose Brigade Basic Training Battalions, one for each Group. These were to be the Regular battalions of the Regiments of the Group, in turn, and in the case of the East Anglian Group the first to perform this rôle was the 1st Battalion The Essex Regiment, stationed at Colchester.

The abolition of the P.T.C.s did not entail the loss of all territorial connections, for the Regimental Depot remained at Northampton, guardians of Regimental affairs and all that that implies.

*The Colonel of the Regiment*

On the 5th November 1943 General Sir Harry Knox reached the age-limit of his appointment as Colonel of the Regiment which he had held for twelve years, and handed over to Major-General G. St. G. Robinson.[10] It fell to the latter, therefore, to receive and to reply to the gracious message sent to the Regiment by the Colonel-in-Chief at the end of the war.[11]

*The Regimental War Memorial*

The Regimental War Memorial in St. Sepulchre's Church took the form of additions to the existing Memorials of the 1914–1918 War in the St. George's, or Warriors', Chapel. To the Book of Remembrance were added the names of the 55 officers and 890 other ranks of the Regiment who gave their lives in the Second World War.

Panels were added to the screen, bearing on the left the words: 'In Proud and Glorious Memory, World War 1939–1945.' And on the right the words: 'Dedicated to the Officers and Men of The Northamptonshire Regiment who Gave their Lives in the Service of their Country.'

Reproduction of the Title Deed conferring the Freedom of the Borough of Northampton, 8th June 1946

# THE REGIMENT AFTER THE WAR, 1945-1948

These Memorials were dedicated by the Vicar, the Rev. G. P. H. Rowson, at the Comrades' Parade Service on the 27th June 1948.

*Freedom of the Borough of Northampton, 8th June 1946*

On the 8th June 1946 the Regiment was accorded an honour, and a privilege, such as can fall to any regiment once only in its history—the presentation of the Freedom of its county town, and the right to march through it with bayonets fixed and Colours flying.

On that morning a Guard of Honour from the Regiment, many former members of it, and a contingent of the Army Cadet Battalion, headed by the Band of the 58th, marched into position in the Market Square of Northampton, under the command of Major C. J. M. Watts.

Soon afterwards the civic party arrived. This included the Mayor, Councillor Watts, members of the Corporation, the Lord-Lieutenant, the Colonel of the Regiment and many others. Also the officers and men of H.M.S. *Loch Insh*, the ship adopted by Northampton after H.M.S. *Laforey* had been sunk off Anzio. Having been received with the General Salute, the Mayor inspected the parade. Then, returning to the platform, behind which were panels bearing the Regimental badge and the words 'Talavera' and 'Gibraltar,' he addressed the parade and the concourse of many thousands of the people of the Borough.

At the conclusion of his speech, in which the Mayor referred to the past deeds of the Regiment and to the achievements of the Battalions in the recent war, the Town Clerk read the Title Deed conferring the Freedom of the Borough upon the Regiment:

> Whereas we, the Mayor, Aldermen and Burgesses of the County Borough of Northampton, appreciating the famous record and glorious traditions created by the Northamptonshire Regiment over many years of loyal and devoted service to the Sovereign of this realm, and in recognition of the very long association and cordial relations which have existed between the Corporation and the Regiment, in which so many of our citizens have been proud to serve, do by these presents confer upon the Northamptonshire Regiment the title, privilege, honour and distinction of marching through the streets of the Borough of Northampton on all ceremonial occasions with bayonets fixed, Colours flying and bands playing.

With the words 'Those who follow after will know the great esteem in which the town holds the Regiment' the Mayor then handed the case containing the Title Deed to Major-General Robinson, who proceeded to read a message from the Colonel-in-Chief of the Regiment, then in Australia:

I deeply appreciate the distinction accorded to my Regiment in receiving the freedom of the Borough of Northampton in recognition of its magnificent war record.

I feel sure that this will cement for ever the good comradeship which already exists between all ranks of the Regiment and the citizens of Northampton.

Then, replying to the Mayor's speech, Major-General Robinson said that though the Regiment had no battalion serving at home it was worthily represented on parade, where those present made a picture of the past, the present and the future. The past was represented by the ex-Servicemen, whose devotion to duty had earned the Regiment the honour which it was now receiving. The present (and he turned towards the small group of officers and men facing the platform in the centre of the parade) by young men still in uniform, some of whom had served in the last world war, others had not been old enough to do so. The future was represented by the Cadets, whose bearing made him feel that the honour of the Regiment would be safe in their hands.

After the General Salute had been given and the Regimental flag broken from the flagstaff, the troops marched to the Guildhall, exercising their newly-granted right to do so with bayonets fixed and Colours flying. At the Guildhall the Mayor took the salute, and afterwards entertained the Colonel of the Regiment, and many others, to luncheon in the Town Hall.

So ended a day which will always be outstanding in the history of the Regiment. Although this chapter tells of some events which occurred later in time, it seems fitting that it, and this new volume of the Regimental History, should close with an account of the honour done to the Regiment on that day, since it then received from the capital town of the county with which it has been linked since 1779 the reward for more than two hundred years of service to its Sovereign and to its Country. A reward which had been earned by the men who had fought at Quebec, Gibraltar and Talavera; in France and in Belgium; in India and Tunisia; in Sicily, Italy and Burma. A reward of which the Regiment of the future will always strive to be worthy, if only in grateful memory of those who fell.

The lines which follow are inscribed on a memorial to those who gave their lives in the First World War.[12] They might well refer to any of the campaigns in which the Regiment has fought down the years:

> These died in war, that we at peace might live;
> These gave their best, so we our best should give.

# NOTES ON CHAPTERS

## CHAPTER I

[1] Pages 2, 5, 6
For details of shooting results, see Appendix VII.

[2] Page 2
The Silver Jubilee Medal was awarded to the following members of the Regiment:

### 1st Battalion
Lieut.-Col. F. W. L. Bissett, D.S.O., M.C.
Lieut. & Q.M. J. Holmes
R.S.M. E. Johnson
Bdmr. H. Hope
C.S.M. A. Cletheroe
C.S.M. O. Franklin
C.S.M. C. Wilkinson, M.M.
Cr./Sgt. W. Ford
Cr./Sgt. W. Papworth
Sgt. G. Allen
Sgt. H. Gibson
Sgt. T. Loveland
Sgt. F. Masters
Sgt. P. McInerny
Sgt. L. Nurser, M.M.
Sgt. H. Stock
Cpl. B. Hearn
L/Cpl. C. Arnull
L/Cpl. V. Dyson
L/Cpl. H. Goulty
L/Cpl. P. Ham
Pte. H. Dicks
Pte. A. Matthews
Pte. A. Reubens

### 2nd Battalion
Lieut.-Col. G. St. G. Robinson, D.S.O., M.C.
Lieut. & Q.M. H. Payne
R.S.M. F. R. Carrington, M.M.
Bdmr. T. Adams
C.S.M. F. Wilkes
Pte. F. Wagstaffe

### 4th Battalion
Lieut.-Col. H. N. Scott-Robson
Capt. & Q.M. F. G. Bowtell
R.Q.M.S. G. Abbott
O.R./Sgt. A. E. Fiddy
Pte. C. Ekins

### 5th Battalion
Lieut.-Col. W. E. Green, D.F.C.
Capt. & Q.M. A. E. King
C.S.M. W. Cunningham, M.M.
Sgt. J. Armer
Dmr. A. L. Baker

### Regimental Depot
Major (Bt. Lieut.-Col.) E. G. Warren
Capt. & Q.M. C. E. Downs
R.S.M. V. Farrell
Pte. T. Whurr
Mr. E. E. Howard

[3] Pages 5, 6

The teams which represented the 58th in the competitions for the Duke of Connaught's Cup were:

### 1932
Lieut.-Col. W. D. Barber, M.C.  
Capt. W. C. Ratcliffe, D.S.O.  
Lieut. G. P. Clark  
Major (Bt. Lieut.-Col.) F. W. L. Bissett, D.S.O., M.C.  
Capt. W. G. Dipper  
Lieut. G. A. Hill-Walker  

### 1933
Major (Bt. Lieut.-Col.) F. W. L. Bissett, D.S.O., M.C.  
Major H. W. Jackson  
Capt. R. R. Flood  
Capt. J. A. F. Barthorp  
Major E. G. Warren  
Capt. W. G. Dipper  
Lieut. G. A. Hill-Walker  

### 1934
Major W. G. A. Coldwell, D.S.O.  
Capt. R. R. Flood  
Capt. J. Lingham, M.C.  
Capt. W. V. Marshall  
Major H. W. Jackson  
Capt. W. G. Dipper  
Capt. E. L. Percival  

### 1935
Capt. A. A. Crook  
Capt. E. L. Percival  
Lieut. C. J. M. Watts  
2/Lieut. N. R. Ogle.  
Capt. W. V. Marshall  
Lieut. H. L. R. Fuller  
Lieut. J. T. Ennals  

[4] Page 8

Each plate bears the Regimental badge and the inscription:
'Colours of the Northamptonshire Regiment entrusted to the care of the Church of the Holy Sepulchre.'

Beneath these words is written on the plate on the north side of the church:

| Queen's Colour | Colour | Colour | King's Colour |
| --- | --- | --- | --- |
| 1st Bn. | 1 (Gar) Bn. | V (S) Bn. | 3rd Bn. |
| 1923 | 1921 | 1921 | 1925 |

and on the plate on the south side:

| Regimental Colour | Colour | Colour | Regimental Colour |
| --- | --- | --- | --- |
| 1st Bn. | VII (S) Bn. | VI (S) Bn. | 3rd Bn. |
| 1923 | 1919 | 1919 | 1925 |

[5] Page 9

The following letter of thanks was received from the Burgomaster:

MONS.  
*le 30 Septembre 1935.*

Monsieur le Lieutenant-Colonel,

Nous avons l'honneur d'accuser réception de votre aimable lettre du 24 août dernier, ainsi que des badges et boutons utilisés en 1914 par votre bataillon, et que vous avez bien voulu nous adresser pour notre musée de guerre.

Ces souvenirs ont été exposés à la section de la 'Bataille de Mons due 23 août 1914', dans le cadre réservé aux insignes de la I⁰ division britannique (2ᵉ brigade), dont le 1ᵉʳ bataillon du Northamptonshire faisait partie.

Une notice mentionne succintement la position occupé par cette unité au cours de la première bataille de Mons.

Veuillez croire, Monsier le Lieutenant-Colonel, à nos vifs remerciments, ainsi qu'à nos sentiments distingués.

Par le Collège.             Le Bourgmestre.
Pr. le Secrétaire:
    Le Chef de division délégué.

A Monsieur le Lieutenant-Colonel commandant le 1ᵉʳ bataillon du 48ᵉ Northamptonshire, Wellington Barracks, Jullundur (Inde).

## CHAPTER II

[1] Page 11

The names of the officers who moved from Jullundur to Razmak are given below. Those who accompanied the Battalion at the outset of the Khaisora Valley operations are marked *:

| | |
|---|---|
| Lieut.-Col. W. G. A. Coldwell, D.S.O. | Commanding |
| Major H. K. F. Nailer * | Second-in-Command |
| Capt. P. F. A. Growse | Adjutant |
| Lieut. R. E. Osborne-Smith | Acting Adjutant |
| Lieut. J. Holmes | Quartermaster |
| Lieut. W. J. Feehally * | Sig. Officer |
| Lieut. F. R. Wilford * | Tpt. Officer |
| Capt. C. H. Marsden, R.A.M.C. | Med. Officer |
| Capt. W. B. Spencer * | H.Q. Wing |
| 2/Lieut. W. P. P. Cleverton, U.L.I.A. | |
| Major A. O. F. Winkler * | 'A' Company |
| Lieut. N. J. Dickson | |
| Lieut. B. E. Hastings-Thomas * | |
| 2/Lieut. J. G. McGowan, U.L.I.A. | |
| Capt. W. C. Furminger, M.C.* | 'B' Company |
| Capt. M. F. F. Buszard * | |
| Lieut. W. J. Bennett * | |
| Capt. L. O. A. Hunt * | 'C' Company |
| Lieut. H. G. Metcalfe * | |
| Lieut. R. F. H. Philpot-Brookes * | |
| 2/Lieut. P. S. Thunder * | |
| 2/Lieut. R. K. Constantine, U.L.I.A. | |
| Capt. H. N. Drake | 'D' (S) Company |
| Lieut. J. R. Britten * | |
| Lieut. P. W. P. Green * | |
| 2/Lieut. A. G. H. Moore | |

The following officers joined, or were attached to, the Battalion during its service in Waziristan:

| | |
|---|---|
| 2/Lieut. G. R. Shipway, U.L.I.A. | 12th November 1936 |
| Capt. & Q.M. H. Payne | 22nd November 1936 |
| P/O. K. N. Lees, R.A.F. | 23rd November 1936 |
| 2/Lieut. J. C. Wood, U.L.I.A. | 24th November 1936 |
| 2/Lieut. R. F. T. Tyers, U.L.I.A. | — |
| 2/Lieut. J. W. A. Meredith, U.L.I.A. | — |
| 2/Lieut. P. M. D. H. McLaughlin, U.L.I.A. | — |
| 2/Lieut. R. H. Barber | 28th November 1936 |
| Capt. J. V. Brewin, M.C. | 22nd December 1936 |
| Major (Bt. Lieut.-Col.) E. G. Warren | 11th January 1937 |
| 2/Lieut. J. B. Hickson | 13th June 1937 |
| Lieut. J. W. Rawlins | 23rd July 1937 |
| 2/Lieut. J. A. Girdwood | 12th October 1937 |
| Capt. D. E. Taunton | — |
| Lieut. D. W. Spooner | — |

² Page 16

Extract from a letter received by the Colonel of the Regiment from General Sir John Coleridge, G.O.C.-in-C. Northern Command, India:

'The Northamptonshire Regiment have done uncommonly well since they came to Waziristan, and especially well during these Operations. The fighting during 25th November was pretty hot, but the Battalion appeared to enjoy it; since then they have faced dreary piqueting and road-making, to say nothing of three days' drenching rain, cheerfully. You can well be proud of them.'

With this letter was enclosed another from Major-Gen. D. E. Robertson, G.O.C. Waziristan Force, which read:

'The Northamptonshire Regiment have done very well indeed, especially in view of the fact that they are new arrivals, and hence not well up to the tricks of this hill fighting. But they make up for this by their admirable spirit and dash. Twice their Brigadier had to make special use of them to capture hills on which piquets were finding difficulty in establishing themselves, and on both occasions they went up with a will, so much so that the tribesmen cleared off. . . . The fact that recently only two men of this Battalion reported sick after three hard days of continuous rain and cold, tells a tale which needs no embellishment to an old soldier. All Officers did excellently.

'Their Colonel can rest assured that the old 48th reputation has been fully maintained.'

In the Battalion's Annual Inspection Report for the year 1936–1937, the same Commander wrote:

'An excellent Battalion. Traces of its fine spirit are evident from its team of Officers downwards. It comes out in their absence of sickness during Operations under severe conditions, and again in its skill with the rifle, as in its discipline.'

³ Page 16

For details of shooting results see Appendix VII.

# NOTES ON CHAPTERS

⁴ Page 21
Letter dated 26th August 1937, to Lieut.-Col. Coldwell from Brig. J. S. Marshall, Commanding Razmak Brigade. (Original in 48th Documents Book.)

'Before leaving Razmak I want to express to you, your officers, and all ranks of the 48th Regt., my great appreciation of the splendid service the battalion has rendered whilst in my Command.

'You arrived just before the present disturbances in Waziristan broke out, and have been in every operation carried out since by Razcol.

'I have at all times felt nothing but admiration for the splendid fighting spirit and keenness of the battalion, and for the efficient and cheerful manner in which they have carried out every task they have been called upon to do—no matter how arduous.

'I would like you to let all ranks know that I am very proud and pleased to have had the battalion with me during the operations, and thank them on my behalf for the fine work they have done and which I know they will continue to do....'

⁵ Page 25
The following letter accompanied the statuette:

1/9TH GURKHA RIFLES,<br>DEHRA DUN.

Dear P.M.C.

We have sent you a small statuette of one of our men, which the British Officers of this Battalion hope the Officers of the 48th will accept, not only as a rank of esteem in which we hold your Battalion, but also in memory of the friendship between all ranks of both Battalions, which we all sincerely hope will not be forgotten, and may be renewed at some not too distant date.

(Signed) R. O. FAWCETT.

⁶ Page 26
For list of honours awarded for the campaign, see Appendix XIV.

⁷ Page 26
Extract from the Battalion's Annual Inspection Report for 1937–1938.

## CHAPTER III

¹ Pages 28, 29, 30, 31, 33, 34
For details of shooting results, see Appendix VII.

² Pages 32, 36
The Coronation Medal was awarded to the following:

*1st Battalion*

Lieut.-Col. W. G. A. Coldwell, D.S.O.

| | |
|---|---|
| Capt. & Q.M. H. Payne | C.S.M. W. Ford |
| R.S.M. H. Freshwater | C.S.M. O. F. Franklin |
| Bdmr. H. Hope | C.S.M. T. W. Loveland |
| R.Q.M.S. E. E. Howard | C.S.M. C. H. Wilkinson, M.M. |
| C.S.M. J. T. Eden | C.S.M. (O.R.S.) W. Johncock |

C.Q.M.S. W. C. Papworth  Sgt. H. W. Stock
C.Q.M.S. W. L. Spalding  L/Sgt. B. Hearn
Sgt. R. J. Brown  Cpl. P. McInerney
Sgt. L. Nurser, M.M.  Cpl. W. Partridge
Sgt. T. D. Slinn

### 2nd Battalion
Lieut.-Col. O. K. Parker, M.C.
Capt. W. G. Dipper  Cr./Sgt. H. Willmott
Lieut. & Q.M. J. Holmes  Cpl. D. Jakins
R.S.M. F. R. Carrington, M.M.  Bdsm. H. Wilding
Sgt. W. Pettican

### 4th Battalion
Lieut.-Col. H. N. Scott-Robson
Major J. W. Heywood  C.S.M. K. Goff, D.C.M.
Capt. M. Jelley  L/Cpl. Rich
C.S.M. Cashmore

### 5th Battalion
Lieut.-Col. W. E. Green, D.F.C.
Major R. K. McMichael  Drum-Major A. Barber
R.Q.M.S. A. Stimpson  Pte. J. W. Stimpson

### Regimental Depot
Major A. St. G. Coldwell
Capt. & Q.M. R. Downs  Pte. P. Seery
Sgt. C. Geary

² Page 36

The following correspondence is connected with the conversion of the 4th Battalion to an anti-aircraft unit:

(1)    THE WAR OFFICE,
                   WHITEHALL.
20/A.A./75 (A.G.1)    14th May 1937.
Sir,

I am commanded by the Army Council to inform you that it has been decided that the 4th Battalion The Northamptonshire Regiment, Territorial Army, be invited to convert to an anti-aircraft rôle, and to form an Anti-Aircraft Battalion, Royal Engineers (Territorial Army) of Battalion Headquarters and four Anti-Aircraft Companies.

It is the intention that the unit, on conversion, will become part of the Corps of Royal Engineers, but it will retain its identity and distinctive title and at the same time be affiliated to the Regular Infantry Corps to which it belonged in the past.

The responsibilities which the Army Council are asking this unit to undertake are of outstanding importance. An exceptionally high standard of efficiency will be necessary since the duties may entail the unit being in action immediately on the declaration of war, or even earlier. In fact the degree of readiness must be considerably greater than that of the Field Army. Unlike the latter, no opportunity for the completion of training after mobilisation can be expected.

The Council realise that this proposal involves the severance of ties that have long existed between this unit and the Regular unit of whose Corps it formed a part. The Council are, however, confident that they may rely in the future, as in the past, on the readiness of Officers and other ranks of the unit, even at the cost of cherished sentiments and the loss of valued associations, to adapt themselves to forms of defence necessitated by changes in modern conditions.

A copy of this letter is enclosed for distribution to the Commanding Officer of the Unit concerned.

I am, Sir,
Your obedient Servant,
(*Sgd.*) A. E. WIDDOWS.

General Sir Harry H. S. Knox, K.C.B., D.S.O.,
Colonel, The Northamptonshire Regiment.

(2)                                                                                                       18*th May* 1937.
Dear Scott-Robson,

I enclose for your information a copy of a letter which I have received regarding the conversion of your Battalion to form an Anti-Aircraft Battalion, Royal Engineers (Territorial Army).

In forwarding this letter to you I should like, on behalf of The Northamptonshire Regiment, to wish you all good fortune and success in your new rôle. The regret which the whole Regiment will feel at losing the 4th Battalion will, I hope, be to some extent mitigated by the maintenance of a close affiliation.

Yours sincerely,
(*Sgd.*) H. KNOX, Colonel,
The Northamptonshire Regiment.

Lieut.-Col. H. N. Scott-Robson,
4th Bn. The Northamptonshire Regiment.

(3)                                                                                                       20*th May* 1937.
Dear Sir Harry,

On behalf of all ranks of the 4th Battalion, I want to thank you very much for your kind letter wishing us all good fortune when we become an Anti-Aircraft Battalion.

We are very glad indeed that the Battalion will be affiliated to The Northamptonshire Regiment. Many thanks again for your letter.

Yours sincerely,
(*Sgd.*) N. SCOTT-ROBSON.

⁴ Page 38

The following correspondence passed between the Colonel of the Regiment and H.R.H. the Duchess of Gloucester, on her appointment as Colonel-in-Chief of the Regiment:

(1)                                                                                        THE WAR OFFICE,
                                                                                               WHITEHALL,
                                                                                               LONDON, S.W.1.
                                                                                               10*th May* 1937.
Madam,

I have the honour, as Colonel of The Northamptonshire Regiment, to write on behalf of all Battalions to thank you for honouring the Regiment by becoming our

Colonel-in-Chief. It is an honour which every Officer and man in the Regiment, down to the last-joined recruit, highly appreciates, and it is one of which I trust we will prove ourselves worthy.

The connection of the Regiment with the county of Northamptonshire has existed for over 150 years. It is a connection which is highly valued by the Regiment, and that Your Royal Highness should have honoured your County Regiment will, I feel sure, be warmly welcomed by many families in Northamptonshire whose sons have served in the County Regiment.

Through nearly 200 years of strenuous service your Regiment has taken a proud place in the service of the Crown and of the Empire. It is our earnest hope, that honoured by your presence at our head, we may give ever-increasing proof of our loyalty and devotion to duty.

I have the honour to be, Madam,

Your Royal Highness's most obedient Servant,
(*Sgd.*) H. KNOX, Colonel,
The Northamptonshire Regiment.

(2)
YORK HOUSE,
ST. JAMES'S PALACE.
13*th May* 1937.

Dear General,

The Duchess of Gloucester directs me to thank you very much indeed for your letter.

Her Royal Highness is very proud indeed to become Colonel-in-Chief of a Regiment which has such a great and honourable record, and she wishes me to assure you that she will always follow with keen interest all that your Regiment does.

Her Royal Highness would like me to say how happy she is that the Regiment belongs to her own county of Northamptonshire.

Yours sincerely,
(*Sgd.*) WINIFRED CECIL,
Lady-in-Waiting.

⁵ Page 39

The following correspondence is connected with the presentation of the brooch:

(1)
8*th December* 1937.

Madam,

I have the honour to present my humble duty, and on behalf of all ranks of The Northamptonshire Regiment to ask Your Royal Highness to accept the accompanying regimental badge. The badge is a gift from all ranks, past and present, of all Battalions of Your Royal Highness's Regiment, and it is tendered as a token of their loyal and dutiful respect for their Colonel-in-Chief.

I have the honour to be, Madam,

Your Royal Highness's obedient Servant,
(*Sgd.*) H. KNOX, Colonel,
The Northamptonshire Regiment.

## NOTES ON CHAPTERS

(2)
YORK HOUSE,<br>
ST. JAMES'S PALACE.<br>
*9th December*, 1937.

Dear General,

I am desired by the Duchess of Gloucester to convey to you and to all ranks of The Northamptonshire Regiment her very warmest thanks for the beautiful regimental badge. She is delighted with it and hopes to wear it often. It is a very beautiful token of the loyalty of the Regiment.

Yours sincerely,<br>
(*Sgd.*) EVA SANDFORD,<br>
Lady-in-Waiting.

⁶ Page 39

The instructions issued by the Colonel of the Regiment for the honouring of this toast were:

1. The toast will be drunk on all Regimental Guest-nights after the toast of 'The King' has been honoured.
2. The President will say: 'Mr. Vice—Our Colonel-in-Chief.' The Vice-President will say: 'Gentlemen—Her Royal Highness The Duchess of Gloucester.'
3. Those dining will stand, the band will play the appropriate Regimental Call, followed by a few bars of the Regimental Slow March.
4. Those dining will say: 'The Duchess of Gloucester,' and will drink the toast.

The following is the music of the portion of the Regimental Slow March approved for the toast:

MUSIC FOR THE TOAST
COLONEL-IN-CHIEF OF THE NORTHAMPTONSHIRE REGIMENT

⁷ Page 39

The following correspondence is connected with the alliance with the Regiment de la Rey:

(1)

THE WAR OFFICE,
WHITEHALL.
*7th April*, 1937.

Sir,

I am commanded by the Army Council to inform you that His Majesty the King has been graciously pleased to approve of an alliance between The Regiment de la Rey, Active Citizen Force, Union of South Africa Defence Forces, and The Northamptonshire Regiment. A notification of this alliance will appear in Army Orders in due course.

I am, Sir,
Your obedient Servant,
(*Sgd.*) H. CREEDY.

General Sir Harry H. S. Knox, K.C.B., D.S.O.,
Colonel, The Northamptonshire Regiment.

(2)

*9th April* 1937.

Dear Colonel van Noorden,

I have before me the formal notification of the King's approval to the alliance of The Regiment de la Rey and The Northamptonshire Regiment. As Colonel of The Northamptonshire Regiment I write to assure you how greatly we appreciate the fact that we are allied to The Regiment de la Rey. The Northamptonshire Regiment has in the past served many years in South Africa, and the Officers and men in the Regiment during those years of peace and war learnt to appreciate the high qualities of the South African people. We therefore specially value the alliance of your Regiment, which gives official recognition to the friendship of our respective Armies.

I know that I express the wish of the whole of The Northamptonshire Regiment when I say that I trust that our alliance will bear fruit in mutual assistance and many friendships.

Yours sincerely,
(*Sgd.*) H. KNOX, Colonel,
The Northamptonshire Regiment.

Lieut.-Col. M. P. van Noorden,
Officer Commanding Regiment de la Rey,
Rustenburg,
Transvaal,
South Africa.

(3)

HEADQUARTERS,
REGIMENT DE LA REY,
RUSTENBURG.
*17th July*, 1937.

Dear General Knox,

Owing to a prolonged absence I have not been able to reply to your letter of the 8th April before.

NOTES ON CHAPTERS 363

The alliance of The Northamptonshire Regiment and The Regiment de la Rey has now been published in the Force Orders of the Union Defence Forces.

The alliance is greatly appreciated by us and especially by our Colonel-in-Chief, General J. C. G. Kemp, who was Second-in-Command of General de la Rey's forces during the Anglo-Boer War.

I am sure that the alliance will bear fruit, and particularly with regard to the splendid co-operation between the two races in South Africa in all military affairs.

I am, Sir,

Yours truly,
(Sgd.) M. P. van Noorden,
Lieut.-Colonel.
In Command Regiment de la Rey.

A brief history of The Regiment de la Rey is given in Appendix XIII.

⁸ Page 40

The boomerang bears the inscription:
'Greetings to The Northamptonshire Regiment from 43/48th Battalion, 1937, Adelaide, South Australia.'
and the following signatures:

*Headquarters Wing*

C.O., Lieut.-Col. M. J. Moten; Second-in-Command, Major A. Pope; Adjt., Major C. R. V. Wright; A/Adjt., Lieut. J. G. Dobbs; Tpt. Offr., Capt. L. G. Bruer; R.M.O., Lieut. N. C. Adams; Sig. Offr., T. Garrard Moore.

*'A' Company*

O.C., Major T. M. Conroy; Second-in-Command, Capt. B. G. Davies; Lieuts. A. Anderson, M. L. Jeans, C. T. Hearn.

*'B' Company*

O.C., Capt. R. L. Batten; Second-in-Command, Capt. L. R. McPhee; Lieuts. H. A. Wood, G. T. Winton, L. D. Spence.

*'C' Company*

O.C., Capt. H. F. Beaney; Second-in-Command, Lieut. F. A. Ligertwood; Lieuts. F. A. Stretton, A. G. K. Haupt, M. L. Smith.

## CHAPTER V

¹ Page 56

A return dated 18th May 1940 shows the following officers on the strength of the 58th:

Lieut.-Col. J. W. Hinchcliffe (C.O.); Major J. R. Wetherall (Second-in-Command); Majors R. M. G. Wetherall (O.C. H.Q. Coy.), C. J. M. Watts (O.C. 'B' Coy.); Capts. R. G. W. Melsome (O.C. 'A' Coy.), D. J. B. Houchin (O.C. 'D' Coy.), A. L. Norman (O.C. 'C' Coy.), J. Holmes (Q.M.); T/Capts. P. W. P. Green (Adjt.), A. W. B. Symonds (M.T. Offr.), R. F. H. Philpot-Brookes (2 i/c 'B' Coy.),

G. M. C. Anderson (Attd. H.Q. 5 Div.); Lieuts. G. R. W. Cobb (Bde. Liaison Offr.), E. W. Evans-Evans (2 i/c 'D' Coy.), A. de V. Gibson (2 i/c 'A' Coy.); 2/Lieuts. G. S. Drew (O.C. Fighting Patrol), R. P. S. Erskine-Tulloch (on leave in U.K.), J. C. Richardson (2 i/c 'C' Coy.), R. C. R. Roche (O.C. Carrier Pl.), J. A. Brittain (Int. Offr.), H. E. Oswald * ('C' Coy.), R. G. W. Fitzwilliam * (Asst. M.T. Offr.), J. S. Reddy * ('B') Coy.). *Attached:* Lieut. J. W. Dowzer, R.A.M.C.; Rev. D. W. Hoare, R.A.Ch.D.

* Then with First Reinforcements.

² Page 61

Among those mentioned in despatches for gallantry during the campaign was Capt. Houchin. Towards the end of 1940 Lieut.-Col. Hinchliffe received a letter from Lieut. Evans-Evans, then a prisoner of war in Germany, in which he described Capt. Houchin's gallantry at the Battle of Arras. This was used to support a further recommendation, and as a result Capt. Houchin received the award of the Military Cross.

³ Page 67

The officers at Battalion H.Q. at the time were:

Capt. Melsome, Capt. Symonds, 2/Lieut. Drew, Lieut. Thompson (Bde. Anti-Tank Coy.), 2/Lieut. Webb (R.A. Liaison Offr.).

⁴ Page 67

The following Special Order was published:

The Commander 2nd Corps has asked me to convey his warm congratulations and thanks to the 5th Division and to other troops who fought so gallantly in co-operation with the 5th Division on May 27th and 28th. It is his opinion that it was entirely due to our action that the whole Corps was able to effect a withdrawal and that unless we had held the YPRES–COMINES Canal so successfully the safety of the whole B.E.F. might have been put in serious danger. I am confident that this fact will be confirmed by History.

It is a matter of great satisfaction to all of us that we were able to carry out such a vitally important task with complete success. It was not done without heavy loss: this must be so always when Troops are asked to hold wide frontages to the last.

It is sad to see such fine Units reduced by casualties to their present small numbers but it would be much worse if they had not achieved a vital task and inflicted far heavier losses on the enemy.

I am indeed proud to have under my command such a splendid body of Troops and to all Commanders and Troops I offer my sincere congratulations and thanks.

FIELD,
29th *May* 1940.

(*Sgd.*) H. E. FRANKLYN,
Major-General,
Commander 5th Division.

## CHAPTER VI

¹ Page 71

A return dated 12th May 1940 shows the following officers on the strength of the 5th Battalion:

NOTES ON CHAPTERS 365

Lieut.-Col. W. E. Green, D.F.C. (C.O.); Majors R. K. McMichael * (Second-in-Command), R. K. Lamplugh (Attd. H.Q. 4 Div.), W. V. Marshall † (Adjt.); Capts. J. H. W. Cobbing ‡ (O.C. H.Q. Coy.), B. G. A. Measures (O.C. 'B' Coy.), T/Capts. J. H. Johnson (O.C. 'C' Coy.), W. V. Hart (O.C. 'A' Coy.), J. H. Heard, E. A. Pashley (O.C. 'D' Coy.); Lieut. R. C. Cawdell; 2/Lieuts. A. Brown, H. M. Knee (O.C. Carrier Pl.), P. K. Hill § (Int. Offr.), K. Halton, S. S. Stanley, K. G. Hunnybun ||, P. D. Passmore, V. A. Pemberton, J. F. Myers, J. Orr (O.C. Mortar Pl.), W. D. Hilton-Johnson (Sig. Offr.), R. C. Greener ¶, R. R. Macrory ¶, J. Perry, F. A. Norton, F. P. Sutton, D. H. Truckle, M. H. R. King, J. G. Henderson; Major A. E. King (Q.M.). *Attached:* Capt. G. A. F. Holloway, R.A.M.C.; Rev. J. E. G. Quinn, R.A.Ch.D.

NOTES:

\* On leave. Did not rejoin the Battalion until after its return to England.

† Commanded temporarily after Lieut.-Col. Green was killed. Became Second-in-Command when Lieut.-Col. Anstee took over command.

‡ Became Second-in-Command temporarily after Lieut.-Col. Green was killed.

§ Became Adjt. vice Major Marshall.

|| Rejoined the Battalion on the Escaut from leave. Became Intelligence Officer vice Lieut. Hill.

¶ Left the Battalion on 12th May.

## CHAPTER VII

¹ Page 84

During the period 1st April 1940–1st March 1941 the following numbers of other ranks were posted away from the 48th, either to the United Kingdom or to extra-regimental employment in the Far East:

|        |     |         |     |
|--------|-----|---------|-----|
| C.S.M. | 3   | L/Sgt.  | 1   |
| P.S.M. | 1   | Cpl.    | 9   |
| C.Q.M.S. | 4 | L/Cpl.  | 23  |
| Sgt.   | 11  | Pte.    | 78  |

On the 31st March 1940 the strength of the Battalion was 31 officers and 733 other ranks.

² Page 84

A photograph of the officers of the 48th taken on the occasion of the 200th Anniversary gives the following names:

Major D. E. Taunton; Capts. D. W. Spooner, P. S. Thunder, J. W. Rawlins, N. R. Ogle, T. R. Molloy, W. J. Feehally, R. R. Greaves; Lieut. G. V. Martin; 2/Lieuts. B. C. Withers, M. R. Haselhurst, A. H. Reynes, P. F. Keily, M. H. Harris, D. S. Clarke, H. R. Johnston.

And absent from the Battalion at the time:

Lieut.-Col. A. O. F. Winkler, Major J. V. Brewin, M.C., 2/Lieut. H. W. Morgan.

### 366   HISTORY OF THE NORTHAMPTONSHIRE REGIMENT

³ Page 94

The following officers were serving with the 6th Battalion on its formation on the 9th October 1940:

Lieut.-Col. W. C. Furminger, M.C. (C.O.); Majors B. A. E. M. Hall (Second-in-Command), R. D. Lake, D.S.O. (O.C. H.Q. Coy.), H. K. F. Nailer, A. M. Hutchinson; Capts. J. H. W. Cobbing (O.C. 'A' Coy.), F. H. Hamer (O.C. 'D' Coy.), W. D. Yeomans (O.C. 'C' Coy.), A. G. H. Moore (O.C. 'B' Coy.), D. Baxter (Adjt.); Lieuts. H. J. Pitt, F. A. Andrews, T. Phillips; 2/Lieuts. G. A. C. Danby, A. H. Wilkinson, T. J. Pepper, W. Griffiths-Elsdon, C. A. Sanders, A. G. Gray, R. C. Rickett, J. D. Monkman; Lieut. C. P. Ward (Manchester Regt., Q.M.); Lieut. E. P. Morley (R.A.M.C.).

## CHAPTER VIII

¹ Page 98

The following officers embarked with the 58th:

Lieut.-Col. J. W. Hinchcliffe, D.S.O. (C.O.); Majors L. O. A. Hunt (Second-in-Command), D. J. B. Houchin, M.C. (O.C. H.Q. Coy.), G. M. C. Anderson (O.C. 'C' Coy.); Capts. H. J. Wood (Adjt.), R. Whitaker, Som. L.I. (O.C. 'R' Coy.), G. M. Darbyshire, Som. L.I. (O.C. 'A' Coy.), J. B. Hickson (O.C. 'B' Coy.), R. C. R. Roche, M.C. (O.C. 'D' Coy.), J. A. Purton, Som. L.I., R. W. Careless, R. J. Hornsby, E. W. Kitchen; Lieuts. G. M. Godall, M.B.E. (Q.M.), B. G. Saunders, J. R. Robb, M. R. Barry, J. M. Taylor (A.D.C. to Comd. 5 Div.), A. J. Roberts; 2/Lieuts. A. N. Soutar (Int. Offr.), H. G. T. Gill, S. J. Allen, V. D. Godley, L. H. Roberson, J. K. Munday, A. C. Mullins, S. Maxwell, R. A. Whitney, S. C. Hamer, P. B. Kehoe, A. Gill, R. O. Tear, J. H. York, J. L. Large, R. T. Webb, C. K. Walker, R. F. Adams. *Attached:* Capt. J. W. Dowzer, R.A.M.C.; Rev. D. W. Hoare, R.A.Ch.D.

## CHAPTER IX

¹ Page 110

The following officers embarked with the 5th Battalion for North Africa:

Lieut.-Col. A. A. Crook (C.O.); Major G. A. Hill-Walker (Second-in-Command); Capt. M. C. Benett (Adjt.); Lieut. D. V. Emmerton (Int. Offr.); Lieut. P. McLoughlin, Border R. (Q.M.).

*H.Q. Coy.:* Major H. V. Hart, M.C.; Capts. M. W. Hunt, R. W. Cook (A.A. Pl.), E. Grant (M.T. Offr.); Lieuts. P. K. Tighe, F. W. N. Farrow, J. H. Andrews (Sig. Offr.).

*'A' Coy.:* Capts. B. C. Withers, J. R. Rayment; 2/Lieuts. S. N. H. Roberts, P. H. Tue.

*'B' Coy.:* Capts. D. H. Truckle, J. A. Girdwood; 2/Lieuts. W. E. Garner, C. C. Needle (The Loyal Regt.), S. J. Hawthorn.

*'C' Coy.:* Capt. T. L. Beagley; Lieuts. F. P. Sutton, T. P. L. Villiers (Som. L.I.), P. A. Brown.

## NOTES ON CHAPTERS

'D' *Coy.*: Major E. A. Wright; Lieut. E. N. Willetts; 2/Lieut. W. H. Fulford (W. Yorks. Regt.).

'R' *Coy.*: Capt. H. W. Morgan; Lieuts. Ricketts, P. C. Swarman, M. E. Handon; 2/Lieuts. F. H. Broad, S. W. P. Cox (R. Norfolk Regt.), D. Woodhouse (R. Norfolk Regt.).

*Attached:* Capt. E. J. Kerr, R.A.M.C.; Rev. A. Guthrie, R.A.Ch.D.; Major D. V. Rosen, U.S. Army; Capt. J. M. Swanley, U.S. Army.

² Page 122

'The distances covered and the feats achieved by the brigades of 78 Division (in particular 36 Brigade) operating with a very reduced scale of first and second line transport and with no third line, were one of the features of the early stages of the campaign.' (From the Official Despatch.)

³ Page 122

'Algiers. Sunday, December 6th, 1942.

'... While General Anderson was at Algiers conferring with Ike [*Note*: General Eisenhower], he reported that his forces had had a "nasty setback." Heavy losses had been suffered by his Infantry Brigade Group, several U.S. medium tanks had been knocked out, and a large number of guns, mainly six-pounder anti-tank and Bofors were lost. Anderson said that this action, coming on top of previous heavy fighting and the prolonged strain caused by four weeks of ceaseless effort and hard living, had exhausted the fighting value of the Infantry Brigade until it can be rested, reinforced and refitted. He said that the Surreys and Northamptons are down to only about 350 all ranks, the Lancashire Fusiliers is only about 450 strong, while two Hampshires, sent ahead with the 1 Guards Brigade, have been wiped out, only ninety all ranks remaining. The defeat has been caused by heavy dive-bombing attacks.... (It is obvious that we have lost the race for Tunis.)' From *Three Years with Eisenhower*, by Harry C. Butcher (Wm. Heinemann Ltd.).

⁴ Page 130

The 11th Brigade diary, dated 27th December, gives the casualties of the Battalion, presumably those incurred between the 23rd and 26th as: Killed—11 other ranks. Wounded—2 officers, 14 other ranks. Missing—1 officer, 16 other ranks.

⁵ Page 131

From *The Turn of the Road*, by Bartimeus (Chatto & Windus).

## CHAPTER X

¹ Page 136

Order of the Day by Gen. Sir H. R. L. G. Alexander:

'23 Feb. 1943.

'The enemy is making a desperate bid to break through the iron ring which is closing round him in North Africa.

'Stand firm, fight and kill the enemy.

'A great Allied victory is within our grasp if every soldier does his duty.'

² Page 142

The following narrative, written later by Capt. Emery, commanding 'A' Company, describes these events graphically:

'Just before dark on the 14th I was called to Bn. H.Q. where I found the C.O. with Jim Hudson of the Lancashire Fusiliers and Tom Beagley. We were briefed for the capture of Tangoucha, which the Brigadier had ordered to be taken before midnight. For this important task the two Battalions could only raise between them two weak companies and one half company (Tom Beagley's). We had no time for reconnaissance and not much for passing orders on and, at about 8 p.m., the mixed force, under Jim Hudson's command, started off for its objective. . . .

'We had not been marching for half an hour before we plunged into a thick fog, and almost immediately contact was lost between the three companies. With "A" Company I floundered about the valley for more than an hour. From the direction of Heidous we could hear the sounds of digging and occasionally voices. . . .

'Eventually we climbed what I took to be Tangoucha until I stumbled on some bodies which proved on inspection to be wearing the Bn. flash. One of them I recognised as a man of my old platoon in "C" Company. I knew then that we must be on the saddle between Ang and the elusive Tangoucha, so we lost no time in finding our agreed company position and settling in as well as one can on solid rock. It was now about 0030 and there was no sign of Jim Hudson or of Tom Beagley. From time to time we could hear the despondent notes of a hunting-horn which we knew belonged to one of the platoon commanders in Jim's company, and which did much to encourage the men of my company. They felt an immense superiority in knowing where they were. . . .

'About 2 a.m. Matthew Hunt came up with some mules carrying a mortar and a Vickers, but not a great deal of ammunition. He promised to do his best to get us some more and, after a Sapper detachment had blown some weapon-pits for us with "beehives" this party returned to Bettiour.

'About 4 a.m. the Lancashire Fusiliers arrived and started to dig in on the saddle. I had a talk with Jim, who said he had seen no sign of Tom and "B" Company, and a quick survey of the ground we had to hold sent our morale down to zero. Tangoucha's rocky spine ran east and west, which made the top and the eastern end untenable (another good reason against holding it turned up in the night in the discovery that the enemy was already doing so!); the southern side was untenable because the enemy held Longstop on that side; the northern side came under observation from Djebel Ang, which we thought was in enemy hands (how right we were we did not discover for three hours); the western slopes of Tangoucha were in full view of Heidous, which we guessed from what we had heard earlier that night to be in enemy hands. We decided that all we could do was to try and find a position which was not overlooked by the enemy, dig in and hope for the best. . . .

'There was a small depression in the western end of the top of Tangoucha, about 25 yards in diameter and well studded with large boulders. Into this depression we managed to get the whole company, less two sections hidden in the rocks towards the pinnacle where they could give warning of enemy approach. The rest of the night we spent in building sangars and trying to make ourselves inconspicuous.

'While going round the platoons and across to the Lancashire Fusiliers I became somewhat alarmed at the number of odd Germans who seemed to be walking about.

Because of the poor visibility it was almost impossible to identify an enemy till one had peered closely at his uniform; this method of identification placed a premium on the rapidity of one's reflexes, and my batman, Henson, and myself became very quick in the uptake after a few of these encounters. Sgt. Goodman of 8 Platoon looked up from his digging and saw an apparently idle member of his platoon leaning on a spade watching him. He administered a sharp rebuke to the idler, who gaped, turned and ran into the mist making guttural noises of surprise.

'Soon after dawn the visibility increased to about 50 yards and the landscape hummed with activity. The Lancashire Fusiliers came under steady fire from the eastern end of Tangoucha and from Djebel Ang and, by 8 a.m., it was impossible to maintain contact with them because the hundred yards of open ground between us was covered by snipers, who infiltrated steadily into our position as the morning wore on. Between 9 a.m. and 10 a.m. the Fusiliers were under constant fire at very close range from an invisible enemy, and shortly after 10 a.m. their position was overrun. All this we learned after we, in our turn, had become prisoners. At the time we had our hands too full to pay much attention to anything else.

'At dawn "windows" began to appear infrequently in the fog, and through one of these gaps we looked down on the scrubby ridge of Longstop. I ordered the mortars and the Vickers detachments to range, and this seemed to irritate the tenants considerably, for they replied with a steady drizzle of mortar bombs that soon rendered our shallow basin very uncomfortable. At the same time they sneaked on us to their big brothers in Heidous, who had an infantry gun with which they never tired of playing and, before long, they had made our mortar and our Vickers look like a couple of wrecked bedsteads.

'About this time we heard considerable numbers of troops moving past us in the mist and, when I reported this to Bn. H.Q., they told me that an attack seemed to be developing on Bettiour. We fired blind into the mist with everything we had (and later were gratified to see the results of our efforts laid out in rows at German H.Q., like the bag at a fashionable shoot), and this caused the enemy to decide to remove us altogether. Before that they seemed to be concentrating on pinning us down and waiting till they had finished their main course before they turned on us for dessert.

'The sniping and mortaring began to work up in intensity until it became impossible to move in the company area at all. Several mortar bombs registered direct hits on slit-trenches, which then seemed to become death-traps—yet to move from them was certain death. It is a striking commentary on the morale and discipline of the men that no panic resulted from what was a most uncomfortable situation.

'About noon, when things looked about as black as they possibly could be, we were given a demonstration of the axiom that in the infantry nothing is ever so bad that it couldn't be worse; our own artillery put down a divisional concentration on Tangoucha. The originator of this happy thought was Bill Williams, F.O.O. with Jim Hudson. When he saw that capture was inevitable he indicated the Djebel as a divisional target before destroying his wireless set.

'The concentration lasted nearly three-quarters of an hour. . . . When the heavy and medium shells began to arrive they tossed boulders weighing four or five tons about like ping-pong balls and struck showers of jagged splinters off the rock face, quite apart from filling the air with flying scrap-iron. The noise was ear-splitting, echoing off the rock walls and reverberating in the valleys, but after a time we became deafened by it and only felt the force of the explosions in the pit of the stomach. After 45 minutes the concentration came to a ragged halt and the enemy, who had been gleeful spectators from secure positions behind the pinnacle, rushed our little circle.

'We discovered that the German Bn. H.Q. was less than 50 yards from my Company H.Q., and there we found the officers of this Austrian Mountain Bn. (which incidentally came from Carinthia) drinking coffee and reading the local papers from home while their platoons were led in action by *feldwebels*. "My dear fellow," one of them said to me in English, "you have no idea what it is like to be in a civilised climate fighting human beings—we have just come from the Russian front." They treated us most correctly, attending to our wounded simultaneously with their own, and making arrangements to bury our dead. That evening we marched to Tunis, where we were handed over to the Italians. They kept us in appalling conditions in the notorious shoe-factory, where for ten days they omitted the formalities of food, hygiene or medical attention.

'The prisoners in the shoe-factory were a mixed bag, consisting of some 500 members of the First and Eighth Armies, together with Senegalese, Goums and Indo-Chinamen. Their discipline was non-existent and, on the two occasions when the French Red Cross came to feed us, there were degrading scenes reminiscent of the Zoo. Porky Young of the Bedfords and myself were the only officers who still had some remnants of their companies left and, with the help of our N.C.O.s and men, we succeeded in knocking some sort of shame and self-control into the rabble. I cannot speak too highly of the magnificent courage and cheerfulness of our men under the most trying conditions and of the fine example they set of how a British soldier should behave.'

[3] Page 142
From the Official Despatch.

[4] Page 147
From the Official Despatch.

[5] Page 147
The war diary of the 11th Brigade gives the 5th Battalion's casualties for the campaign from 8th November 1942–12th May 1943 as:

|  | *Killed* | *Wounded* | *Missing* | *Total* |
|---|---|---|---|---|
| Officers | 7 | 27 | 8 | 42 |
| Other Ranks | 68 | 336 | 294 | 698 |

The number of wounded was greater, the number of missing less, than in any other unit of the brigade.

[6] Page 147
In addition to the officers who landed in North Africa with the Battalion (see Notes on Chapter IX), the following can be traced as having joined later:
January 1943: Rev. E. Elworthy, R.A.Ch.D.
February 1943: Capt. Hertzberg, Canadian Army; Major T. A. Buchanan, M.C.

NOTES ON CHAPTERS 371

March 1943: Capt. I. A. McKee; Lieuts. Edwards-Hogg, C. A. Emery, J. McNeill, M.C., K. I. Coullie; 2/Lieuts. W. Taylor, A. Dupre, C. Robertson, L. B. Gunn.

April 1943: Major E. A. S. Brett; Lieuts. D. L. S. Ap Ivor, J. Pearcey, — Craddock, D. A. Lee; 2/Lieuts. J. Cox, E. W. Taylor, W. Wright.

June 1943: Majors J. W. Rawlins, D. Baxter, E. K. Wherry.

Not known: Capts. H. H. Wilkinson, M. H. R. King; Lieuts. H. E. Coulter, E. Woolvern; 2/Lieuts. R. G. Burkley, J. F. Clarke.

## CHAPTER XII

[1] Page 156

The following officers were serving with the 58th at the time of the landing in Sicily:

Lieut.-Col. J. A. W. Ballard, M.B.E. (C.O.); Major D. J. B. Houchin, M.C. (Second-in-Command); Capt. A. N. Soutar (Adjt.); Lieut. R. A. Whitney (Int. Offr.); Capt. G. A. Goodall, M.B.E. (Q.M.).

*H.Q. Coy.*: Major J. B. Hickson; Capt. H. G. T. Gill (M.T. Offr.); Lieuts. S. L. Clark (Sig. Offr.), J. L. Large (Mortar Pl.), R. F. Adams (Carrier Pl.); Capt. R. Whitaker (A/Tk. Pl.); Lieuts. R. O. Tear, R. Batiste.

'*A*' *Coy.*: Capts. R. J. Hornsby, E. W. Kitchin; Lieuts. J. O. Gaze, F. Howlett, A. C. Garner.

'*B*' *Coy.*: Major J. A. Purton, M.C.; Capt. A. J. Roberts; Lieuts. S. C. Hamer, P. B. Kehoe, J. R. Sydall.

'*C*' *Coy.*: Major A. de V. Gibson; Capt. B. G. Sanders; Lieuts. H. Mossop, J. H. York, V. Godley.

'*D*' *Coy.*: Capts. R. C. R. Roche, M.C., R. W. Careless; Lieuts. R. Webb, G. P. Hofman, V. K. Walker.

*Rear Party*: Lieuts. A. C. Mullins, G. C. A. Leguen de Lacroix.

*Attached*: Capt. R. J. Benians, R.A.M.C.; Rev. T. A. Thornton, R.A.Ch.D.

[2] Page 162

A roll of officers dated 7th August 1943 shows the following officers as serving with the 5th Battalion:

Lieut.-Col. T. A. Buchanan, M.C.; Major J. F. Connolly; Majors M. Crocker, M. W. Hunt, R. W. Cook, E. K. Wherry; Capts. T. J. Pepper, D. Baxter, E. Grant, A. H. Rawlins, D. V. Emmerton, F. N. W. Farrow, J. F. Pearcey, M.C., K. Coullie, I. A. McKee; Lieuts. M. E. Handon, R. P. T. Cave-Brown, A. S. H. Vickers, S. J. Hawthorn, J. H. Smith, J. K. Mayhew, M.M., D. A. Lee, D. L. S. Ap Ivor, A. Brown, J. Murphy, K. S. Griffiths, E. W. Taylor, R. R. Morgan, J. A. Woolford, V. D. Mayer; 2/Lieuts. M. Pulleyn, C. C. Balle. *Attached*: Capt. V. R. Macleod (R.A.M.C.); Rev. E. Elworthy (R.A.Ch.D.).

In addition, the following officers, who were killed between the date of landing in Sicily and the date of this roll:

Lieut. Beardsall; 2/Lieuts. A. Domminey, J. W. Metson.

³ Page 164
Special Order of the Day by Major-General V. Evelegh, Cmd. 78 Div., dated 5th August 1943:

'Today I showed General Sir Bernard Montgomery, our Army Commander, around Centuripe and explained to him how the Division had captured this feature. The Army Commander has asked me to tell all ranks that he considered the Division had, by capturing the position, performed a wonderful feat of arms, and he doubted if any other division in his Army could have carried out this operation successfully. This is indeed high praise for the Division on its first battle in Eighth Army.

'In First Army we had the reputation of being the finest division in the Army, and we are now well on the way to earning the same reputation in the Eighth Army. . . .'

⁴ Page 166
For list of awards, see Appendix XIV.

⁵ Page 166
Personal Message from the Army Commander. To be read to all troops:

1. Having captured SICILY as our first slice of the Italian home country, the time has now come to carry the battle on to the mainland of Italy.

2. To the Eighth Army has been given the great honour of being the first troops of the Allied Armies to land on the mainland of the continent of Europe.

We will prove ourselves worthy of this honour.

3. I want to tell all of you, soldiers of the Eighth Army, that I have complete confidence in the successful outcome of the operations we are now going to carry out.

We have a good plan, and air support on a greater scale than we have ever had before.

There can only be one end to this next battle, and that is: ANOTHER SUCCESS.

4. Forward to Victory!
Let us knock ITALY out of the war!

5. Good luck. And God Bless you all.

(*Signed*) B. L. MONTGOMERY,
SICILY, Gen.,
*Sept.* 1943. 8 Army.


## CHAPTER XIV

Page 179

The following officers were serving with the Battalion at the time of the landing in Italy:

Lieut.-Col. J. A. W. Ballard, M.B.E. (Comdg.); Major D. J. B. Houchin, M.C. (Second-in-Comd.); Capt. A. N. Soutar (Adjt.).

*H.Q. Coy.*: Capts. L. D. Groundsell (O.C.), H. G. T. Gill (M.T. Offr.), G. A. Goodall, M.B.E. (Q.M.); Lieuts. S. L. Clark (Sig. Offr.), J. L. Large (O.C. Mortars), R. F. Adams (O.C. Carriers); Capt. R. Whitaker (O.C. Anti-Tank); Lieuts. R. O. Tear, R. Batiste (Anti-Tank Pl.).

'*A*' *Coy.*: Major J. A. Purton, M.C.; Capt. E. W. Kitchin; Lieut. J. O. Gaze.

'*B*' *Coy.:* Capts. R. P. S. Erskine-Tulloch, A. J. Roberts; Lieuts. S. C. Hamer, J. R. Syddall.
'*C*' *Coy.:* Major A. de V. Gibson; Capt. B. G. Sanders; Lieuts. J. H. York, V. Godley, A. A. T. Parratt.
'*D*' *Coy.:* Capts. R. C. R. Roche, M.C., R. W. Careless; Lieut. G. P. Hofman; 2/Lieut. L. D. Tonkin.
*And:* Lieuts. M. C. Benett, M.C., A. C. Mullins, G. C. A. Leguen de Lacroix; Capt. W. Lamb, R.A.M.C.; Rev. K. W. Jones, R.A.Ch.D.

² Page 187
Battalion Orders show that the following officers were serving with the 58th on the 1st January 1944:
Lieut.-Col. J. W. A. Stephenson, D.S.O. (Comdg.); Major D. J. B. Houchin, M.C. (Second-in-Comd.); Capt. A. C. Mullins (Adjt.); Lieut. R. A. Whitney (I.O.).
*H.Q. Coy.:* Capts. L. D. Groundsell (O.C.), H. G. T. Gill (M.T. Offr.), S. L. Clark (Sig. Offr.), G. A. Goodall, M.B.E. (Q.M.).
*Sp. Coy.:* Major R. J. Hornsby (O.C.); Capt. J. H. York (O.C. Mortars); Lieut. R. F. Adams (O.C. Carriers); Capt. R. Whitaker (O.C. Anti-Tank Guns); Capt. A. J. Roberts (O.C. Pioneers); Lieut. S. C. Hamer (O.C. Fighting Patrol).
'*A*' *Coy.:* Major J. A. Purton, M.C.; Major G. M. C. Anderson (Attd.); Capt. R. S. Wallis; Lieuts. J. L. Large, A. J. Cushion.
'*B*' *Coy.:* Capts. R. W. Careless, V. D. Godley; Lieuts. G. C. A. Leguen de Lacroix, R. J. Gregory.
'*C*' *Coy.:* Major A. de V. Gibson; Capt. A. C. Garner; Lieuts. R. O. Tear, J. Thompson.
'*D*' *Coy.:* Major R. C. R. Roche, M.C.; Capt. B. G. Sanders; Lieuts. C. G. Ahlquist, J. R. Syddall, L. Tonkin; Major R. R. Greaves (Attd.).
*And:* Capt. W. Lamb, R.A.M.C.; Rev. T. D. T. Jones-Evans, R.A.Ch.D.

³ Page 201
The following letter, addressed later to units of the 5th Division, shows the importance of the 'Fortress' to the Anzio beachhead:

Tonight we are deliberately pulling out of the Fortress, having held it, under most trying conditions, since 6th March. As long as the Germans had reserve divisions opposite to us, it was necessary to retain the Fortress as one of the first steps to a converging attack directed against 1 Div. on our right.
We were therefore ordered to hold it; and it has been held by the pluck and determination of every battalion in the Division in succession. It has become a name which we shall remember with admiration for those who held it.
The reserve divisions have now been moved to meet our main attack in the south and we are therefore vacating the Fortress in favour of prepared positions slightly farther to the rear.
I wish all ranks to know that we are pulling out voluntarily and have NOT been driven out. Our task there has been fulfilled.

(*Sgd.*) P. G. S. GREGSON-ELLIS,
Major-General,
24th *May* 1944.              Commander 5th Division.

⁴ Page 205

A copy of Battalion Standing Orders (Operations) issued at this time shows, among other things, the organisation of Battalion and Company 'R' (Reconnaissance) and 'O' (Order) Groups; the variation of the organisation of the Battalion from that laid down in War Establishments; and the normal allotment of Wireless Sets within the Battalion.

### Battalion 'R' Group
C.O. Sig. Offr. O.C. Support Coy. Os. C. any supporting Arms.

### Battalion 'O' Group
Second-in-Command. I.O. Os. C. Rifle Coys. Pioneer Offr. Os. C. Support Platoons (if ordered).

### Company 'R' Group
Company Commander and Orderly.

### Company 'O' Group
Company Commander. Three Platoon Commanders. Four Orderlies. (In withdrawal the Company Second-in-Command would take the place of the Company Commander.)

### Battalion Organisation

|  | W.E. | Bn. W.E. |  |
|---|---|---|---|
| Battalion H.Q. | 58 | 78 | Extra clerks, batmen, snipers and defence section. |
| Sigs. | 36 | 36 | |
| Support Coy. H.Q. | 8 | 9 | |
| Mortar Platoon | 43 | 42 | 6 Mortars. |
| Carrier Platoon | 63 | 58 | 4 Carriers. |
| Anti-Tank Platoon | 55 | 42 | 3 Secs. each of 2 guns. |
| Pioneers. | 22 | 21 | |
| Rifle Company H.Q. | 14 | 15 | |
| Platoon H.Q. | 7 | 10 | 3 Piat men. |
| Section | 7 | 7 | |
| Total Coy. | 125 | 121 | |

(This total includes Company L.O.B.s—men not taken into battle without the C.O.'s orders.)

### Allotment of W/T Sets

18-*sets:* C.O.—2; Control—1; Rifle Companies—4; Carriers—1; Mortars—1; H.Q. Company—1.

38-*sets:* C.O.—1; Rifle Companies—12; Carriers—5; Mortars—9; Pool—4.

⁵ Page 206

It has not been possible to show on the map, with any clarity, the route of the Battalion, nor all of the places mentioned in the text. Below is given a list of the places through which the Battalion passed or at which it was stationed:

# NOTES ON CHAPTERS

**1943**

| | | |
|---|---|---|
| September | 3rd | . Messina–Gallico Marina (3 miles north of Reggio)–Sambatello. |
| | 4th | . San Stefano. |
| | 5th | . San Giovanni. |
| | 7th | . Scilla—by sea to Gioja. |
| | 8th/9th | . Pizzo–Nicastro. |
| | 9th/14th | . Nicastro. |
| | 15th | . By sea to Scalea. |
| | 16th/18th | . Scalea. |
| | 19th/20th | . Lagonegro–Nemoli–Buonabitacoli. |
| | 21st/30th | . Atena. |
| October | 1st/5th | . Avigliano–Minervino–Troia. |
| | 7th/10th | . Foggia. |
| | 11th/24th | . Troia. |
| | 25th/26th | . Vinchiaturo. |
| | 30th/31st | . Point 1385–Macchiagodena. |
| November | 1st/2nd | . Macchiagodena. |
| | 3rd/19th | . Castelpetroso. |
| | 20th/26th | . Alfedena–Point 1086. |
| | 27th/30th | . Castel di Sangro. |
| December | 1st/7th | . Castel di Sangro. |
| | 8th/9th | . Isernia. |
| | 10th/11th | . Liscia–Atessa. |
| | 12th/21st | . R. Moro. |
| | 22nd/31st | . Lanciano. |

**1944**

| | | |
|---|---|---|
| January | 1st/2nd | . Lanciano. |
| | 3rd/6th | . Via Casalbordino–Lucera–Ariano–Avellino–Cicciano (east of Naples)–Mondragone–Cellole. |
| | 7th/13th | . Cellole and Capua. |
| | 14th/21st | . R. Garigliano. |
| | 22nd/31st | . Minturno Ridge. |
| February | 1st | . Minturno Ridge. |
| | 2nd/4th | . Sorbello (south of R. Garigliano). |
| | 5th/18th | . Tufo area. |
| | 19th/22nd | . Sorbello. |
| | 23rd/29th | . M. Damiano. |
| March | 1st/2nd | . M. Damiano. |
| | 3rd/8th | . Pozzuoli (Naples area). |
| | 9th | . By sea to Anzio. |
| | 10th to | } Anzio Bridgehead ('Starfish'; 'Lobster Claw'; 'The |
| May | 9th | } Fortress'). |
| | 10th/25th | . Anzio Bridgehead, R. Moletta. |
| | 26th to | } R. Moletta–R. Torto. |
| June | 4th | } |

### 1944

| | | | |
|---|---|---|---|
| June | 5th | . | Advance to R. Tiber. |
| | 6th/12th | . | Area south of R. Tiber. |
| | 13th/28th | . | Naples area. |
| | 29th | . | To Taranto. |
| July | 5th/9th | . | By sea to Port Said. |
| | 10th to | | ⎫ |
| | **1945** | | ⎬ In Egypt, Palestine and Syria. |
| February | 9th | | ⎭ |
| | 10th/15th | . | By sea, Haifa–Taranto. |
| | 15th/28th | . | Bari. |
| March | 1st/5th | . | Salerno. |
| | 6th | . | Embarked Naples. |

## CHAPTER XV

Page 207
The following officers were serving with the 5th Battalion on the 24th September 1943:

Lieut.-Col. J. F. Connolly, D.S.O., The Buffs (C.O.); Major L. Wigram, R. Fus. (Second-in-Command); Capt. E. Grant (Adjt.); Capt. R. P. T. Cave-Brown, R.W. Fus. (Int. Offr.); Capt. I. A. McKee, K.O.S.B. (A/Q.M.).

*H.Q. Coy.*: Capt. J. H. Andrews, Lieut. S. J. Hawthorn (Sig. Offr.); Capt. D. L. S. Ap Ivor, R.W. Fus. (M.T. Offr.).

'*S*' *Coy.*: Major M. H. Crocker, Essex R.; Capt. K. I. Coullie, K.O.S.B. (A/Tk. Pl.); Lieuts. J. Murphy, Dorset R. (Pioneer Pl.), D. D. Beynon, S.W.B. (Mortar Pl.).

'*A*' *Coy.*: Major T. J. Pepper; Capt. R. N. W. Farrow; Lieut. R. R. Morgan, S.W.B.

'*B*' *Coy.*: Major H. M. A. Hunter, Wilts. R.; Capt. H. W. Rawlins; Lieuts. D. A. Lee, K.S.L.I., M. Pulleyn, Beds. & Herts. R., B. C. Balle, Welch R.

'*C*' *Coy.*: Major R. W. Cook, M.C.; Capt. J. F. Pearcey, M.C., Recce Corps; Lieuts. J. F. Griffith, R.W. Fus., J. A. Woolford, W. Yorks. R.

'*D*' *Coy.*: Capts. D. V. Emmerton, M.C., V. D. Mayer, R. Norfolk R.; 2/Lieut. C. Spicer, R. Sussex R.

*Attached*: Capt. J. R. McLeod, R.A.M.C.; Rev. E. Elworthy, R.A.Ch.D.

² Page 216
In the year 529, St. Benedict went to Cassino to destroy idolatry in the temple on the hill. He founded the Abbey, which became the monastic centre of the West. It was destroyed and rebuilt five times during its history.

³ Page 218
A typical night's mule-train carried:

| | |
|---|---|
| Water | 400 galls. |
| Petrol | 32 „ |
| Washing | 4 sacks |
| Sandbags | 300 |
| Newspapers and mail | 1,640 lb. |
| Tommy cookers | 145 |
| Candles | 144 |
| Anti-louse powder | 4 tins |
| Rations for | 380 men |

⁴ Page 225
The following officers were serving with the 5th Battalion on the 2nd July 1944:
Lieut.-Col. J. F. Connolly, D.S.O., The Buffs. (C.O.); Major R. Wasey, Middx. R. (Second-in-Command); Capt. I. A. McKee, K.O.S.B. (Adjt.); Lieut. J. R. S. Michell, Rifle Brigade (Int. Offr.); Capt. D. Ord, Lon. Scot. (Q.M.).

*H.Q. Coy.*: Capts. J. H. Andrews, D. L. S. Ap Ivor, R.W.F. (M.T. Offr.); Lieuts. S. J. Hawthorn (Sig. Offr.), S. N. H. Roberts (P.R.I.).

'*S*' *Coy.*: Major M. H. Crocker; Capts. R. N. Ruddock, S.A.A.C. (A/Tk. Pl.), W. H. Fulford, W. Yorks. R. (M.M.G. Pl.); 2/Lieut. A. C. Hodgkiss, S.A.A.C. (A/Tk. Pl.); Capt. G. J. Hards (Mortar Pl.).

'*A*' *Coy.*: Major D. V. Emmerton, M.C.; Capt. K. I. Coullie.

'*B*' *Coy.*: Capts. A. B. Mountjoy, R. Berks. R., K. R. Ennals; Lieut. W. A. Hillian, M.C., Kensingtons.

'*C*' *Coy.*: Major R. H. Newby, R. Berks. R.; Capt. D. S. McLeod, H.L.I.; Lieut. A. F. Large.

'*D*' *Coy.*: Major M. W. Hunt; Capt. H. W. Rawlins; Lieuts. J. C. Bayes, N. H. Tallis, Worc. R.

*Attached*: Capt. B. C. E. Richardson, R.A.M.C.; Rev. E. Elworthy, R.A.Ch.D.

The following officers also served with the Battalion between 24th September 1943 (see Note 1 above) and 2nd July 1944:
Major R. G. Rosser, M.C., Imp. Light Horse; Capt. K. O. Carpenter; Lieuts. G. W. R. Terry, A. A. Sharp, S.A.A.C., J. C. Pearson, R. Warw. R., F. S. Farrar, Manch. R., W. C. Giblett, Wilts. R., A. A. Prinsloo, S.A.A.C., G. W. S. Jewell, R. Glos. H., M. Mattinson.

⁵ Page 225
The following statistics referring to the period 25th March–2nd July 1944 are of interest:

(*a*) On the latter date there were still serving 147 members of the Battalion who had been with it since the landing in North Africa.

(*b*) The average age of the Battalion was $26\frac{1}{4}$ years. Thirty-four per cent. were married.

(*c*) The battalion transport had covered a distance of 65,448 miles, and had consumed 15,100 gallons of petrol.

(*d*) Twenty thousand postage stamps had been issued for airmail and airgraph letters.

### ⁶ Page 226

Extracts from the letter written by Lieut.-General Sir Oliver Leese, Comd. Eighth Army, to the Comd. 78th Division, dated 8th June 1944:

'... Now that the 78th Division is out of the line I should like to send you my best congratulations on the tremendous energy and drive your Division showed throughout its successive fights.

'The excellent training of the Division has more than proved itself on the day. Its excellent attacks towards Highway Six, supported by tanks and artillery, led decisively to the fall of Cassino and Monastery Hill.

'I am very grateful for the quick contact your troops gained along the Hitler Line, and for your flank march through Arce, as well as the general speed of movement achieved.... Throughout the hard fighting in the mountains the spirit and toughness of the troops was beyond all praise.

'All this I expected from the great traditions of your Division, with its fine record in North Africa, Sicily and Eastern Italy. I well realise the hard and difficult fighting the Division has had all through the winter and the severe casualties suffered in those months. To have succeeded soon after the hard-fought actions of the last three weeks is a great achievement and reflects the greatest credit on all ranks.

'My personal congratulations and heartfelt thanks to yourself and your fine Division.'

### ⁷ Page 227

It has not been possible to show on the map, with any clarity, the route of the Battalion, or all the places mentioned in the text. Below is given a list of the places through which the Battalion passed, or at which it was stationed:

```
1943
September 22nd/24th   .   Taranto.
          25th/28th   .   Giovinazzo.
          29th        .   Trani.
          30th        .   San Severo.
October   1st         .   Serracapriola.
          2nd/3rd     .   San Martino–Portocannone.
          4th/19th    .   R. Biferno–Larino.
          19th/22nd   .   San Martino.
          23rd        .   Via Campamorina and Termoli to Pettaciato.
November  3rd         .   Crossed R. Trigno to San Salvo.
          5th         .   Montederisio.
          8th         .   Crossed R. Osento.
          15th/20th   .   Casalbordino.
          21st        .   R. Sangro.
December  1st         .   Fossacesia.
          2nd         .   Casalbordino.
          3rd         .   Campobasso.
          10th/30th   .   Montenero.
          31st        .   Campobasso.
```

## 1944

| | | |
|---|---|---|
| January | 11th | Pescolanciano. |
| | 21st/31st | Capracotta–S. Pietro–Vastogirardi. |
| February | 1st | Agnone. |
| | 4th | Via Castiglione, Carunchio, Attesa, R. Sangro to Lanciano. |
| | 5th/11th | Lanciano. |
| | 12th | Castelnuova (Foggia). |
| | 15th | Via Lucera to Motta. |
| | 16th | Via Vinchiaturo and Isernia to Alife. |
| | 17th | San Secondino (Capua). |
| | 23rd | Mignano (R. Rapido). |
| March | 15th/22nd | R. Rapido (for Cassino attack). |
| | 23rd | Mignano. |
| | 25th | Cassino area. |
| April | 25th | Capua area. |
| May | 14th | R. Rapido (Cassino area). |
| | 25th | Aquino. |
| | 26th | R. Melfa. |
| | 30th | Highway Six. |
| June | 2nd | Alatri. |
| | 3rd | Fumone. |
| | 8th | Via Highway Six, Valmontone, Rome. |
| | 9th/13th | Rignano. |
| | 14th | Viterbo. |
| | 15th | Via Orvieto to north of R. Chianti. |
| | 16th | Via Ficulle to Montegabbione. |
| | 18th/19th | Via Piegaro to Panicale. |
| | 19th/23rd | Panicarola. |
| | 24th | West of Lake Trasimene. |
| | 30th | Piana. |
| July | 2nd | Panicarola. |
| | 4th | Tivoli (Rome area). |
| | 11th/14th | By train to Taranto. |
| | 17th | Embarked for Egypt. |

## CHAPTER XVI

[1] Page 228

The following officers were serving with the 5th Battalion on 16th September 1944:
Lieut.-Col. J. F. Connolly, D.S.O. (C.O.); Major R. Wasey (Second-in-Command); Capt. I. A. McKee (Adjt.); Lieut. J. R. S. Michell (Int. Offr.); Capt. D. Ord (Q.M.).

*H.Q. Coy.:* Capts. J. H. Andrews, D. L. S. Ap Ivor (M.T. Offr.); Lieut. S. J. Hawthorn (Sig. Offr.).

'S' *Coy.*: Major M. H. Crocker; Capts. K. I. Coullie (A/Tk. Pl.), W. H. Fulford (M.M.G. Pl.), L. F. Hailey, R.A. (Mortar Pl.); Lieuts. G. Fellows, R.A. (Carrier Pl.), N. H. Tallis (Pioneer Pl.).
'A' *Coy.*: Major D. V. Emmerton, M.C.; Capt. N. S. Ballam, R.A.; Lieuts. A. C. Hodgkiss, A. C. Prinsloo; 2/Lieut. H. Gentles.
'B' *Coy.*: Capts. A. B. Mountjoy, S. F. Saunders; Lieuts. W. A. M. Hillian, M.C. E. E. Orchard, R.A.
'C' *Coy.*: Major E. H. Newby; Capt. B. W. H. Shankland, R.A.; Lieut. A. F. Large.
'D' *Coy.*: Major M. W. Hunt; Capt. M. J. Wise, R.A.; Lieut. M. R. S. Phillips, R. Berks. R.; 2/Lieut. F. J. Griffith, U.D.F., S.A.
'R' *Coy.*: Capts. K. R. Ennals, B. A. Jenkinson, R.A., G. J. Hards; Lieuts. S. N.H. Roberts, A. T. Unwin, R.A., J. W. R. Kennedy, U.D.F., S.A., J. C. Hayes.
*Attached*: Capt. J. A. Petrie, R.A.M.C.; Rev. E. Elworthy, R.A.Ch.D.
The following officers are not shown against any particular company: Capt. R. P. T. Cave-Brown; Lieuts. F. S. Farrer, J. C. Pearson, W. C. Giblett.

² Page 241
The following message was addressed by the Commander, Eighth Army, to all ranks of the 5th Corps, in which the 78th Division was serving:

You have played a decisive part in this great Eighth Army offensive. You have driven the enemy north of the River Po in disorder. You have all shown a splendid determination and fighting spirit, and a fine endurance in two and a half weeks of continuous battle. Your attack across the River Senio, so carefully prepared, succeeded so well that the enemy was unable to stand on the River Santerno. After capturing bridgeheads over this river, you exploited rapidly northwards, and in combination with outflanking operations executed with great skill along the shores of Lake Comacchio, you succeeded in forcing the formidable Argenta position. The enemy was protected by extensive floods on both flanks, and by deep minefields covering the gaps; but you attacked him by day and by night, and broke out into the more open country towards Ferrara. This success was decisive for the whole plan of operations of 15th Army Group.

Your subsequent determined and relentless advance to the River Po both East and West of Ferrara drove the enemy back over the river, with heavy losses in tanks, guns, M.T. and equipment. Only remnants of his fighting Units succeeded in escaping, and our aim to destroy the enemy south of the river has been largely successful.

All arms have played an equally important part in this great victory. Good leadership has resulted in the close co-operation between the infantry, tanks, artillery and engineers, which is the secret of success.

I send my warmest congratulations to every man in 5 Corps. I know that you will continue a relentless pursuit to finish off the enemy and to prevent him organising on any further defensive line.

(*Sgd.*) R. L. McCreery,
Lieut.-General,
G.O.C. Eighth Army.

Main H.Q. Eighth Army.
26*th April*, 1945.

## NOTES ON CHAPTERS

³ Page 241

Message to the 5th Battalion from the Colonel of the Regiment, published in Battalion Orders of the 26th May:

'On behalf of our Colonel-in-Chief, Her Royal Highness the Duchess of Gloucester, and all ranks of the I.T.C., I send congratulations on your share of the magnificent achievements of the Armies of the C.M.F. which have now led to the surrender of the German forces in Italy. For many months you of the 5th Battalion have faced great difficulties in climate and terrain, and now you have seen the fulfilment of your efforts. Well done and good luck.'

Message to the 5th Battalion from the Earl of Sandwich, Lord Lieutenant of Huntingdonshire:

'Now that hostilities are finished, I would like to take the opportunity of congratulating you and your officers and men of the 5th Territorial Battalion of The Northamptonshire Regiment for your remarkable services throughout the campaigns in Africa, Sicily and Italy, and thanking you on behalf of the Hunts. Territorial Association and indeed all in our county.

'Your Battalion was engaged in constant and heavy fighting throughout several campaigns, that in itself constituting a fine record.

'These years now show only too well how the Battalion has lived up to its old reputation.

'Once more I send you our warm congratulations, and if you have the opportunity I hope you will convey the thanks of the county of Huntingdonshire to both officers and men.'

Special Message, dated 3rd May, from the Army Commander to all ranks of the Eighth Army:

'On 9th April the Eighth Army started the last great battle in Italy. Twenty-three days later, on 2nd May, the enemy surrendered unconditionally. We achieved our object of destroying the enemy south of the River Po. North of the Po a relentless pursuit prevented the remnants of the enemy from making any further stand. This final and decisive victory in the history of the Eighth Army was achieved only after hard and bitter fighting. In the first seventeen days the enemy's best troops were smashed and reduced to remnants. The enemy had great advantages of ground, strong defences on a succession of river obstacles, extensive flooding and deep minefields, but all difficulties were overcome by the splendid fighting spirit, skill and endurance shown by All Ranks, and the excellent co-operation of all Arms. In this battle, as always, the decisive factors have been the magnificent fighting qualities of our soldiers and good junior leadership. . . .'

⁴ Page 241

The following officers were serving with the 5th Battalion at the end of the campaign, on 8th May, 1945:

Lieut.-Col. D. J. B. Houchin, D.S.O., M.C. (C.O.); Major R. Wasey (Second-in-Command); Capt. J. K. Smith (Adjt.); Lieut. J. R. S. Michell (Int. Offr.); Capt. D. Ord, M.B.E. (Q.M.).

*H.Q. Coy.*: Capt. J. H. Andrews; Lieuts. E. W. Culwick (M.T. Offr.), S. J. Hawthorn (Sig. Offr.)

'*S*' *Coy.*: Major F. D. Mordin; Capt. W. C. Giblett (Mortar Pl.); Lieuts. C. J. Lambert (Carrier Pl.), N. H. Tallis (Pioneer Pl.), R. H. Coppack (M.M.G. Pl.); Capt. B. W. H. Shankland (A/Tk. Pl.).

'*A*' *Coy.*: Capts. G. J. Hards, S. J. Allen; Lieuts. D. J. Davies, C. E. R. Chapman, F. G. Green.

'*B*' *Coy.*: Major A. B. Mountjoy; Capt. B. A. Jenkinson; Lieuts. S. Toone, J. K. Crerar.

'*C*' *Coy.*: Major M. J. Wise; Capts. N. S. Ballam, L. F. Hailey; Lieuts. K. J. Batterson, P. H. Sewell.

'*D*' *Coy.*: Major F. P. Tindall; Capt. I. A. McKee; Lieuts. J. N. Sturton, J. C. Bayes.

*Attached*: Capt. D. Pottinger, R.A.M.C.; Rev. E. Elworthy, M.C., R.A.Ch.D.

*Left out of Battle*: Major H. W. Rawlings; Capt. J. V. Kent, M.C.

The following officers, not shown in the above list, or in Note 1 to Chapter XVI, also served during the period:

Capt. R. N. Ruddock, U.D.F., S.A.; Lieuts. F. Gray, U.D.F., S.A., J. P. Merryweather, R. Berks. R., S. Martin, S. Drake, O. Kelf, A. E. Bennett; 2/Lieut. J. T. Clarke.

The casualties of the 5th Battalion during the Italian Campaign are given in their history as:

|          |   |   |   |   |                       |
|----------|---|---|---|---|-----------------------|
| Killed   | . | . | . | . | 108 (inc. 9 officers) |
| Wounded  | . | . | . | . | 346 (inc. 18 officers)|
| Missing  | . | . | . | . | 44 (inc. 1 officer)   |
| Total    | . |   | . |   | 498                   |

⁵ Page 241

The route followed by the Battalion during this period was:

1944
September 16th . . Disembarked Taranto.
          26th/28th . Via Foggia, San Severo, Termoli, Ortona, Pescara, Ancona, to Bellochi (near Fano).
October 3rd/4th . Via Fano, Jesi, Fabriana, Perugia, Arezzo, to Figline (near Florence).
          5th/11th . By stages, via Spiero, Scarperia, Firensuola, to Castel del Rio.
          12th . . Pessola.
          14th/16th . M. Pieve (Point 508).
          16th/20th . Area M. Pieve.
          21st . . M. della Tombe.
          24th/25th . Attack Point 362.
November 1st to
    1945 } M. Spaduro–Travellata–Castel de Rio.
February 12th
          14th/23rd . La Caldine (near Florence).
          24th . . Across Apennines to Forlimpopoli.

|  | 1945 |  |
|---|---|---|
| March | 26th | To R. Senio. |
| April | 1st | Russi. |
|  | 11th | Cotignola. |
|  | 14th | Pastorella. |
|  | 16th/19th | Argenta Gap. |
|  | 23rd | R. Po di Volano. |

## CHAPTER XVII

¹ Page 242
The Company Commanders were:
No. 1.—Capt. J. B. Cubey.   No. 2.—Major T. R. Molloy.
No. 3.—Capt. P. F. Keily.   H.Q.—Capt. D. J. Eales-White.
             Adm.—Capt. M. S. Hall.

² Page 247
'Bunker' was the term used for the emplacement in a Japanese position which sheltered heavy Infantry weapons and l.m.g.s. It was constructed by digging a large hole below ground-level, and roofing it with extremely thick overhead cover of tree-trunks and earth. It was usually very well concealed and proof against a direct hit by anything smaller than a 25-pounder field-gun.

A 'foxhole' was a one-man weapon-pit, often provided with a small dug-out shelter with overhead cover.

Bunkers and foxholes were normally connected with communication-trenches, thus forming a post with all-round defence.

³ Page 250
The distribution of the Battalion at the time of the Kyaukchaw attack was:

*Main H.Q.*: C.O., Lieut.-Col. D. E. Taunton; Adjt., Capt. E. F. Smith; I.O., Capt. R. A. Clayton; Sig. Offr., Lieut. K. H. Malby; No. 3 Pl., Lieut. A. G. Horwood, D.C.M.; No. 5 Pl., Lieut. G. C. Pile.

*Rear H.Q.*: Battle 2 i/c, Major N. R. Ogle; Capt. H. L. Webb; M.O., Capt. M. Cram, R.A.M.C.

*No. 1 Coy.*: Major J. B. Cubey; Lieuts. J. E. A. Hopkins, E. D. W. Davies, D. J. Andrews.

*No. 2 Coy.*: Major R. Molloy; Capt. P. R. Cherrington; Lieuts. M. E. Walton, R. E. M. Hughes, P. W. Smith.

No. 3 *Coy.*: Major P. F. Keily; Capt. N. F. Veater; Lieuts. R. A. Bucher, J. S. Hincks, G. C. Hetherington.

*Attached*: 114 Fd. (J) Reg. R.A., Capt. Beer, Lieut. Furlonger; 23rd Mtn. Regt. R.A., Majors Hollick, Lamb; No. 2 Coy. 3/8th Gurkha Rifles, Capt. Clements; G(R) Pl. 9/14th Punjab Regt., Capt. Wilson; 92nd Fd. Coy. R.E., Lieut. Riddell.

*Left out of Battle:*
At rearward posts: 2 i/c Major C. A. Southey; Capts. D. J. Eales-White, W. J. Morris; Lieuts. P. R. Noakes, J. M. Knowles, G. L. Levy; All Colour-Sergeants;

2 Cooks for H.Q. Coy., 1 for each Rifle Coy., 4 from H.Q. Coy., 12 mule drivers. Animal Tpt. Offr. Lieut. G. C. Adnitt and remainder of platoon.

    At roadhead: A/Q.M. R.S.M. L. Howard and 10 other ranks
    In 'B' Echelon area: Capt. M. S. Hall, Lieut. D. C. Cufley, 39 other ranks.
    In F.M.C. Area: 1 N.C.O. and 2 other ranks.
    The strength of the Battalion forward was:
    Main H.Q. 6 officers, 98 other ranks.

| | | | | |
|---|---|---|---|---|
| Rear | ,, 3 | ,, 45 | ,, | ,, |
| No. 1 Coy. | 4 | ,, 85 | ,, | ,, |
| No. 2 ,, | 5 | ,, 83 | ,, | ,, |
| No. 3 ,, | 5 | ,, 91 | ,, | ,, |

Plus 2 signallers and 4 stretcher-bearers attached.

Total forward: 23 officers, 402 other ranks.
  ,, in rear: 9 ,, 100 ,, ,, (approx.).

**⁴ Page 253**

An extract from the *London Gazette* notifying the award of the Victoria Cross to Lieut. Horwood is given in Appendix XIV.

    After the announcement of the award, the 48th received the following signals:

From H.Q. 14th Army.

    Army Commander and all ranks of 14 Army wish to convey to Officer Commanding 1 Northamptons their regret at the death of Lieut. A. G. Horwood. His gallantry and devotion to duty have earned for him the award of the Victoria Cross and the admiration of the whole 14 Army. Lieut. Horwood's example is not only testimony of his gallantry but shows the fine spirit of all ranks of the Bn. The award of the Victoria Cross will be an inspiration to all ranks of the 14 Army.

From H.Q. 20th Indian Division.

    From Div. Comdr. My heartiest congratulations on the award of the V.C. to Lieut. Horwood. His Majesty's recognition of his supreme gallantry and sacrifice will I know be an inspiration to All Ranks to do their duty unflinchingly and unselfishly in the face of all the dangers of this war.

From General Sir Ivo Vesey, Colonel, The Queen's Royal Regt.:

    On behalf of the Queen's Royal Regiment I send you most sincere congratulations on award of Victoria Cross to late Lieut. Horwood whilst serving under your command, and deep sympathy on the loss of a most gallant officer.

**⁵ Page 255**

From an article by the *Daily Telegraph and Statesman* war-correspondent, published in the *Statesman* of the 5th March 1944.

**⁶ Page 256**

The following note appears in the 48th war diary for the 17th January 1944:

    'The Bn. went into battle 402 B.O.R.s strong instead of some 574 strong which should have been the case if man-power had been available to form the fourth Rifle Coy. and fill Specialist Pls.

    'This lack of man-power due to milking * and repatriation puts too great a strain on those effectives left to fight. Man-power is still too large a responsibility to the comd.

## NOTES ON CHAPTERS

on the spot. It is strongly urged that the cure is to provide reinforcements BEFORE repatriation personnel are taken away from a fwd. bn.

'* Milking refers to early demands to provide men for new employments such as P.O.W. Staffs and for whom replacements have never been received in full.'

⁷ Page 278

The Brigade's losses were 254 killed, 653 wounded, 24 missing. Total 931.

Included in the above, those of the 48th were 1 officer and 113 killed, 15 officers and 206 wounded, 8 missing. Total 343.

⁸ Page 279

For complete list of honours and awards see Appendix XIV.

⁹ Page 279

Extracts from the message sent by the Commander 17th Indian Division to the Commander 32nd Indian Infantry Brigade:

'It has been my privilege to have had under command 32 Ind. Inf. Bde. 20 Div. for the past three months. Our partnership has ended and I therefore take the opportunity of congratulating and thanking the Comd. and all ranks on the high-grade manner in which they have fought throughout. You have had a strenuous time with no let-up. But in spite of this you have overcome the many difficulties which have confronted you. All ranks 17 Div. are proud to have fought by the side of such a fine fighting brigade. For all practical purposes we have liquidated ten and a half Jap bns. strongly supported by arty. and tanks. . . . I thank you all for your ever-willing support. On behalf of all ranks 17 Ind. Div. I wish you the best of luck in the future.'

¹⁰ Page 280

A return, in which some of the particulars are illegible, shows that, in June 1944, men of the following Regiments were serving with the 48th:

| Regiment | Number | Regiment | Number |
|---|---|---|---|
| Northamptonshire | 221 | R. Warwickshire | 196 |
| Worcestershire | 1 | N. Staffordshire | 34 |
| Suffolk | 8 | Leicestershire | 4 |
| W. Yorkshire | 1 | R. Fusiliers | 26 |
| Hertfordshire | 31 | | 2 |
| Oxf. & Bucks. L.I. | 6 | S. Lancashire | 40 |
| K.O.S. Borderers | 2 | Seaforth Highrs. | 3 |
| Q.O. Cameron Highrs. | 20 | R. Scots Fus. | 3 |
| Cameronians | 3 | R. Innisk. Fus. | 5 |
| R. Norfolk | 10 | Beds. & Herts. | 18 |
| Lancashire Fus. | 1 | | 1 |
| Pioneer Corps | 3 | E. Lancashire | 5 |
| Dorsetshire | 12 | Devonshire | 2 |
| E. Yorkshire | 4 | R.A.S.C. | 2 |
| R. Welch Fus. | 2 | Cheshire | 1 |
| Sherwood Foresters | 1 | R. Berkshire | 4 |

## CHAPTER XVIII

**¹ Page 294**
'Kyaung' (pronounced in almost the same way as 'chaung') was the Burmese name for the house in which the local priest lived. Since these priests were, as a rule, the best educated of the local population, their houses were the best in a town or village. The priests were often extremely pro-Japanese.

**² Page 298**
'Kg' was the map abbreviation for 'Kyaung' (see Note 1 above).

**³ Page 319**
The casualties incurred by the 48th in the various phases of the campaign were:

|  | Killed | | Wounded | | Missing |
| --- | --- | --- | --- | --- | --- |
|  | O. | O.R. | O. | O.R. | O.R. |
| Kyaukchaw | 2 | 15 | 4 | 63 | — |
| Moreh | — | 9 | — | 6 | — |
| Silchar Track | 1 | 113 | 15 | 206 | 8 |
| Ops. Nov. 1944–May 1945 | 6 | 77 | * | * | * |
| Total | 9 | 214 | 19 | 275 | 8 |

\* Details of the number of wounded and missing during the final period cannot be ascertained. The number of killed has been extracted from the Roll of Honour printed by the 48th for the In Memoriam service held in July 1945.

**⁴ Page 320**
For list of honours and awards to individuals, see Appendix XIV.

**⁵ Page 320**
From the farewell message sent to the 48th in February 1947.

**⁶ Page 320**
The following list gives the names of the officers who served with the Battalion in Burma, and the operations in which they took part. It has been made as complete as is possible from available records, and the author apologises for any omissions.
The abbreviations used denote operations as follows:

| K | . | . | . | Kyaukchaw. | M | . | . | . | Monywa. |
| S | . | . | . | Silchar Track. | I | . | . | . | Irrawaddy. |
| B | . | . | . | Budalin. | L | . | . | . | Later operations. |

| Lieut.-Col. D. E. Taunton, D.S.O. | . | K.S.B.M.I. |
| „ „ P. de C. Jones. | . | B.M.I.L. |
| Major N. R. Ogle | . | K.S. |
| „ C. A. Southey | . | K.S. |

## NOTES ON CHAPTERS 387

| | | |
|---|---|---|
| Major | J. B. Cubey . | K. |
| ,, | T. R. Molloy | K.S. (wounded 21st April 1944). |
| ,, | P. F. Keily, M.C. . | K.S. |
| ,, | P. S. Thunder, M.C. | S. (wounded 27th June 1944). |
| ,, | H. L. Webb | K.S.B.M.I.L. |
| ,, | P. R. Noakes | K.B.M.I.L. |
| ,, | N. F. Veater, M.C. | K.S.B.M.I. |
| ,, | A. W. Dyson | S.M. |
| ,, | J. R. Britten, M.C. | S. |
| ,, | L. Fulford | M.I. (killed 26th February 1945). |
| ,, | R. A. Paddock | L. |
| ,, | H. F. Fergusson | L. |
| ,, | J. F. Snow | (14th July to 22nd October 1944). |
| Capt. | D. J. Eales-White, M.C. | K.S.B.M. (wounded 27th April 1944 and 20th January 1945). |
| ,, | R. A. Clayton | K.S.B.M.I.L. |
| ,, | K. H. Malby | K.B.M.I.L. |
| ,, | G. C. Pile | K.B.M.I.L. |
| ,, | E. F. Smith | K.S. |
| ,, | J. M. Knowles | K.B.M.I.L. |
| ,, | W. J. Morris | K. |
| ,, | M. S. Hall | K.B.M.I.L. |
| ,, | R. A. Bucher | K. (wounded 18th January 1944). |
| ,, | P. R. Cherrington, D.S.O. | K.B.M. (killed 20th January 1945). |
| ,, | C. W. Chandler | S.B.M.I.L. |
| ,, | G. C. Hetherington | K.S.B.M.I.L. |
| ,, | R. L. Cutler | S.I.L. (wounded 14th June 1944). |
| ,, | M. H. Nott | S.L. |
| ,, | J. Millar | S.I. (killed 18th February 1945). |
| ,, | G. V. James | S. |
| ,, | G. S. Franklin, M.C. | S.L. |
| ,, | E. K. Perkins | B.M.I. (killed 1st March 1945). |
| ,, | Lodge | L. |
| Lieut. | A. G. Horwood, V.C., D.C.M. | K. (killed 20th January 1944). |
| ,, | T. Phillips | S.I.L. (wounded 27th June 1944). |
| ,, | L. A. Howard, M.B.E. | K.S. |
| ,, | J. E. A. Hopkins | K. |
| ,, | E. D. W. Davies | K. |
| ,, | D. J. Andrews | K. (killed 18th January 1944). |
| ,, | M. E. Walton | K. (wounded 20th January 1944). |
| ,, | R. E. M. Hughes, M.C. | K.S. (wounded 1st April 1944 and 31st May 1944). |
| ,, | P. W. Smith | K.B. |
| ,, | J. S. Hincks | K. (wounded 18th January 1944). |
| ,, | G. L. Levy | K. |
| ,, | G. C. Adnitt | K.S. |
| ,, | D. C. Cufley | K.S. (wounded 14th June 1944). |

388  HISTORY OF THE NORTHAMPTONSHIRE REGIMENT

| | | |
|---|---|---|
| Lieut. T. N. S. Hodges | . . . | S. (wounded 27th April 1944). |
| ” F. Stoddart | . . . | S.B. (wounded 12th May 1944, killed 8th January 1945). |
| ” A. G. Bacon. | . . . | S.B. |
| ” J. P. Walkden | . . . | B.M.I. (killed 14th February 1945). |
| ” J. T. Firth-Clark | . . . | M. |
| ” Leigh | . . . | B. (wounded 5th January 1945). |
| ” J. E. Lewis | . . . | L. |
| ” H. A. Payne. | . . . | L. |
| ” R. A. Durrant | . . . | L. |
| ” Weightman | . . . | L. |
| ” Crump | . . . | L. |
| ” G. J. E. H. Freeman | . . . | L. |
| ” E. W. R. Tebbell | . . . | B.M.I.L. |
| ” A. E. Goddard | . . . | L. |
| ” G. Allen | . . . | L. |
| 2/Lieut. W. Coleman | . . . | S. (wounded 14th June 1944). |
| ” R. G. Morris | . . . | S. (wounded 20th June 1944). |
| ” D. Buckley | . . . | S. (wounded 2nd May 1944). |

Details of the operations in which the following took part cannot be traced: Major M. R. Hazelhurst, Capt. C. L. Patterson, Lieut. F. P. Hitchins.

## CHAPTER XX

[1] Page 328
The following officers went overseas with the 4th Battalion:

*Battalion H.Q.:* Lieut.-Col. W. C. Furminger, O.B.E., M.C. (C.O.); Major J. G. Newman (Second-in-Command); Capts. R. Shearer, M.B.E. (Adjt.), W. G. Wright (Int. Offr.), N. Bending (O.C. H.Q. Coy.); Lieut. R. Pugh (Sig. Offr.); Capts. G. W. Tyrell (M.T. Offr.), R. J. Brown (Q.M.).

*'S' Coy.:* Major A. H. Timpson (O.C.); Capts. R. W. Dunn (A/Tk. Pl.), A. E. Atkinson (Carrier Pl.); Lieuts. Hon. J. H. Darlington (Mortar Pl.), R. Bowmer; Capt. G. T. Gardiner, M.B.E. (Pnr. Pl.).

*'A' Coy.:* Major G. A. C. Danby; Capt. F. Decamps; Lieuts. W. E. Boezalt, J. Sykes, A. L. Gittins.

*'B' Coy.:* Major A. C. Webb; Lieuts. J. Bell, W. Griggs, A. G. Smith, A. P. Ricketts.

*'C' Coy.:* Major V. A. Harding; Capt. R. M. Burnett; Lieuts. C. H. Shaw, J. Burbidge, N. Coop.

*'D' Coy.:* Major P. M. Kemp-Gee; Capt. H. C. G. Harding; Lieuts. F. L. Billing, R. Palmer, P. A. Moore.

*Attached:* Capt. J. G. Howells, R.A.M.C.; Fr. T. A. Whittle, R.A.Ch.D.

## CHAPTER XXI

[1] Page 334
From *From Sea to Sea*, by Rudyard Kipling (Macmillan & Co.).

[2] Page 335
The letter from the Adjutant-General to the Forces read:

THE WAR OFFICE,
20th December 1946.

Dear Robinson,
You will remember that at the Colonels of the Regiments' conference at Warminster in September last all Colonels of Regiments were informed that owing to the reduction in the number of Infantry battalions in the post-war Army it would be inevitable that some regular battalions would have to be placed in suspended animation.

As I informed you at the time all regular battalions would undergo this process in their turn on a system of *roulement*.

The time has now come when certain regular battalions must lapse temporarily. You will, I am sure, appreciate that the order in which battalions are selected depends entirely upon the circumstances existing in the theatres in which they are located together with the situation of all the other regular battalions of the same group.

I am very sorry to have to tell you that your 1st Battalion which, as you know, is serving in SEALF, must now lapse into suspended animation and instructions to that effect are being issued.

I think you will be glad to know that I have arranged for a cadre to be sent home with the Regimental property and funds, and I will let you know when this cadre is due to arrive and its destination on arrival.

Yours sincerely,
(*Sgd.*) R. N. O'CONNOR.

[3] Page 335
The cadre was composed of:
Lieut.-Col. D. E. Taunton, D.S.O. (C.O.), Major R. R. Greaves (Second-in-Command), Major J. S. Jones, Capt. F. H. Uren (Q.M.), 2/Lieut. L. Robinson, R.S.M. D. Jakins and 22 W.O.s, N.C.O.s, and men.
Colour Party: Capt. J. L. Boe (Adjt.), Capt. J. N. Sturton, C.S.M. G. Gibbs, Sgt. J. Patchett, Pte. G. Barratt.

[4] Page 336
From H.R.H. the Duchess of Gloucester, then in Australia.

'I am so sorry to hear that you are amongst the Battalions to be placed in "Suspended Animation," particularly as I have never had the opportunity of seeing you.

'Had I been accompanying the Duke on his journey home, I would certainly not have missed the opportunity of saying "Farewell" to you all in person. As it is, I can only say that I have read with interest of all your exploits during the war, and would like to congratulate you all on your achievements.

'I send to all ranks my best wishes for the future.'

From the Colonel of the Regiment.

'As your Colonel it is with very great regret that I have to send you this message of farewell. . . . I well know what it means to break up a Bn. like the 48th with its great traditions of over 200 years, its past wars and its achievements this last war in the Burma Campaign. I know too that while in Malaya you have well maintained the high standard of the Regiment both at work and in sport. Friendships and all that go to make a fine team must now disappear for a space. I myself, while commanding the 48th on the Rhine after the First World War, had the sad task of reducing them to cadre, and did not like it one bit.

'You can all rest assured that your services with the 48th will not be forgotten by the Regiment. . . .

'I know that you will accept the order in the proper spirit, and in the way we of the Northamptonshire Regiment have always faced up to unpleasant duties. To you all I say "Thank you" for the way you have conducted yourselves while in the Regiment, and to those who still have to serve elsewhere I wish Godspeed—may good luck and good fortune attend you and bring you a quick return to your homes over here.'

From Lieut.-General D. D. Gracey. Farewell message to all ranks, the 48th Regiment.

'As the Commander of 20th Indian Division under whom the 48th served from July 1942 till April 1945—in Ceylon, Assam and Burma—I hope that you will all grant me the privilege of sending this message, not only because I commanded the Division, in which the 48th fought so well and earned a magnificent reputation for efficiency and courage, but also as a very old friend of the battalion. It is with the greatest sorrow that I have heard from Colonel Taunton that the battalion is being put into suspended animation and I hope most sincerely that this will not last for long. I do know this, that however long this may last, the grand spirit of the 48th will stay alive. You must never let that die, as it is something that all of those very gallant lads of yours who fell round Bishenpur, Budalin, Monywa, the Irrawaddy Bridgehead, Kyaukse and Mount Popa kept alive and which you all, since the war has finished, have carried on by your discipline, cheerfulness and all those fine British qualities, which we are shy of discussing in public.

'For myself, I welcome this opportunity of thanking you all, and especially those officers and men who fought with 20 Division, for the great part the 48th played in the victories at Imphal and in the recapture of Burma.

'I wish you all the very best of luck in the future, and ask you to take with you the cheerful happy discipline in which all the units of 20 Division took such great pride.'

The originals of these messages are in the 48th Burma scrapbook.

[5] Page 337
In a letter of thanks for this gift the Town Clerk of Northampton said:
'I can assure you that the good will which prompted the presentation is much appreciated and reciprocated. The Sword will fill an honoured place with the plate and historic possessions of the Borough.'

[6] Pages 340, 342
For full details of shooting results, see Appendix VII.

### ⁷ Page 343
In his farewell message to the 4th Battalion the Colonel of the Regiment said:

'I have always received the highest praise of your efficiency, your discipline and your smartness. Your energy in training has been watched and approved, and thus you earned for yourselves the name of a first-class Battalion. In Northern Ireland you gained the reputation of being one of the best Battalions in the District. In January I hear you spoken of as the best Battalion in your Division. You may well be proud of your record during the war years, which reflects the greatest credit on all ranks of the Battalion. That, by fate, you did not have to undergo to the full the trials of battle does not in any way take away from that credit, for I know well that you could have proved yourselves as worthy in the final test as you did in preparing for it.'

### ⁸ Page 345
For fuller details of the history of 585 Searchlight Regt., see Appendix VIII.

### ⁹ Page 346
From the outbreak of war in 1939 the *Regimental Journal* had to cease production, for security reasons and owing to difficulties of publication. There was, however, a need for some means of keeping battalions and individuals in touch with regimental affairs, in so far as the censorship would allow. The Depot, therefore, undertook the publication of a *Newsletter*, of which ten numbers appeared between May 1940 and October 1945. In August 1946 the *Journal* resumed regular publication.

### ¹⁰ Page 350
On the occasion of the change in the Colonelcy of the Regiment, the following letters were sent to all Battalions:

By General Sir Harry Knox, K.C.B., D.S.O.

'On 5th November, on reaching the age of seventy, I hand over to Major-General G. St. G. Robinson, D.S.O., M.C., the proud office of Colonel of the Northamptonshire Regiment.

'I have for over 50 years had the honour of being an Officer of the Regiment, and I leave with great regret.

'All Battalions are proving in this war, as they have done in the past, that The Northamptonshire Regiment is second to none.

'In saying good-bye to your Battalion, I wish you and ranks under your Command long life and happiness.'

By Major-General G. St. G. Robinson, D.S.O., M.C.

'On taking over the duties of Colonel of the Regiment I wish to say how much I appreciate the honour that has been done me by my selection to hold that proud position.

'In succeeding our late Colonel, General Sir Harry Knox, K.C.B., D.S.O., I well realise that I will not have an easy task. He has, as always, set a high standard and we owe him a very great debt of gratitude for all that he has done for us, not only during his tenure as Colonel, but also throughout his long service of 50 years. The welfare and interests of the Regiment and its members, both past and present, have alwaysv been his chief aim and object. For my part, I can assure you that I will do my best to follow that example and to further the good of the Regiment in every way.

'I take up my responsibilities knowing that I can rely on the same loyal co-operation and support that you have given your previous Colonel.

'Difficult days lie ahead. The present is a time for action not words, and therefore I can but end by asking Old Comrades to stand by until happier days are with us once more, while to those who are still serving with our Battalions at Home and throughout the Empire I wish good luck, good fortune and a speedy and safe return.

'I know well that the proud history and traditions of the Regiment are in safe hands and that they are both upheld in a manner worthy of our Comrades of long ago.'

[11] Page 350

At the end of hostilities, the following cables were exchanged between the Colonel-in-Chief and the Colonel of the Regiment:

(1)
To Major-General G. St. G. Robinson,
Colonel, The Northamptonshire Regiment,
The Barracks, Northampton.

On the momentous occasion of the end of the war, I send to all ranks of my Regiment my best congratulations for the outstanding work they have done during the past six years. By their devotion to duty and their courage they have made a wonderful contribution to the victory which has now been achieved. They have added splendid pages to their previous illustrious record. I am proud to be your Colonel-in-Chief.

ALICE, Colonel-in-Chief.

(2)
Secretary to
Her Royal Highness, The Duchess of Gloucester,
Government House, Canberra, Australia.

Please convey to Her Royal Highness on behalf of all ranks The Northamptonshire Regiment our grateful thanks and appreciation for her inspiring message to her Regiment on the conclusion of hostilities. In presenting our humble duty to our Colonel-in-Chief we look forward to the time when Battalions of her Regiment can again have the honour of parading before her in the ceremonial of peace.

GENERAL ROBINSON,
Colonel, The Northamptonshire Regiment.

[12] Page 352
On the Glasgow War Memorial for the 1914–1918 War.

# APPENDIX I

## THE COLONELS-IN-CHIEF AND THE COLONELS OF THE REGIMENT

#### COLONELS-IN-CHIEF OF THE REGIMENT
I. H.R.H. The Duchess of Gloucester, G.B.E., 11th May 1937.

#### COLONELS OF THE REGIMENT
VI. Major-General G. St. G. Robinson, C.B., D.S.O., M.C., 5th November 1943.

# APPENDIX II

## BIOGRAPHICAL NOTES ON COLONELS

### VI. MAJOR-GENERAL GUY ST. GEORGE ROBINSON, C.B., D.S.O., M.C.

Guy St. George Robinson, son of St. George C. W. Robinson of Sligo, Ireland, was born on the 2nd April 1887, and was commissioned from the R.M.C., Sandhurst, on the 7th May 1907. After joining the 2nd Battalion, in 1908 he was posted to the 1st Battalion, serving with it at Poona, Aden and Devonport. Accompanying the Battalion to France in August 1914, he was wounded at Ypres in November. In January 1915 he was awarded the Military Cross, being one of the first recipients of this decoration in the Army. He was Adjutant of the 1st Battalion in France from the 19th April 1915 to the 14th February 1916, and then served as an instructor at the R.M.C., Sandhurst, until April 1917. Returning to the 1st Battalion he commanded it in France and subsequently in the Rhine Army, from the 25th July 1917 until April 1919. He was awarded the D.S.O. in December 1919. After holding the appointment of Assistant Adjutant at the R.M.C., Sandhurst, from May 1919 to December 1923, he passed into the Staff College, Camberley. After completing the course there he held appointments as G.S.O. Weapon Training, Small Arms School, G.S.O.2 War Office and G.S.O.2 H.Q. China Command. Returning to the 2nd Battalion he served as Second-in-Command from May 1932 to March 1933. Promoted Lieutenant-Colonel on the 14th March 1933, he commanded the Battalion at Aldershot until the 7th May 1935, when he was appointed Assistant-Commandant of the Small Arms School.

In 1937 he was given a Brigadier's appointment in Burma, and commanded the Rangoon Brigade Area until 1940. On his return to England, he commanded the 210th (Buffs) Infantry Brigade until October 1941, and the Essex and Suffolk Area until November 1942, when he was appointed to command of the East Riding and Lincolnshire District as a Major-General. He held this command until his retirement in October 1944. He was appointed Colonel of the Regiment on the 5th November 1943 and was awarded the C.B. in 1945.

# APPENDIX III

## SUCCESSION LIST OF LIEUTENANT-COLONELS

### 1ST BATTALION

| | |
|---|---|
| W. G. A. Coldwell | 27th February 1936 |
| W. J. Jervois | 1st August 1939 |
| A. O. F. Winkler | 20th May 1940 |
| J. V. Brewin | 24th December 1940 |
| D. E. Taunton | 15th October 1942 |
| P. de C. Jones | — March 1945 |
| J. R. Britten | — November 1945 |
| D. E. Taunton | — January 1947 |

### 2ND BATTALION

| | |
|---|---|
| O. K. Parker | 8th May 1935 |
| E. G. Warren | 7th May 1939 |
| J. W. Hinchcliffe | 6th February 1940 |
| J. A. W. Ballard | 28th November 1942 |
| J. W. A. Stephenson | 15th October 1943 |
| J. A. W. Ballard | 1st August 1944 |
| R. E. Osborne-Smith | — June 1945 |
| R. G. W. Melsome | — June 1946 |
| D. E. Taunton | 17th June 1947 |
| J. A. W. Ballard | 8th June 1948 |

(Officers who commanded temporarily for short periods during the Second World War were: R. M. G. Wetherall, C. J. M. Watts, L. O. A. Hunt, J. A. Purton.)

### 4TH BATTALION (TERRITORIAL) ARMY

| | |
|---|---|
| J. G. Lowther | — April 1939 |
| J. Lingham | 19th March 1940 |
| W. B. Spencer | 22nd April 1942 |
| M. F. F. Buszard | — August 1942 |
| W. C. Furminger | 29th July 1943 |

### 5TH BATTALION (TERRITORIAL ARMY)

| | |
|---|---|
| G. A. Anstee | — May 1940 |
| A. A. Crook | 16th October 1942 |
| T. A. Buchanan | 1st May 1943 |
| J. F. Connolly | 9th August 1943 |
| D. J. B. Houchin | 18th December 1944 |
| R. K. McMichael | — February 1947 |

## 6TH BATTALION

| | |
|---|---|
| W. C. Furminger | 9th October 1940 |
| P. F. A. Growse | 11th May 1942 |
| R. R. C. Cox | — May 1944 |
| P. O. B. Sherwood | — July 1945 |

(From the 12th June 1940 until the 9th October 1940 this Battalion was entitled The 50th (Holding) Battalion. It was disbanded in April 1946.)

## 70TH BATTALION

| | |
|---|---|
| W. E. Carrick | 19th January 1941 |

(This battalion was disbanded in 1943.)

# APPENDIX IV

## SUCCESSION LIST OF ADJUTANTS

### 1ST BATTALION

| | |
|---|---|
| R. E. Osborne-Smith | 18th February 1937 |
| W. J. Feehally | 18th February 1940 |
| M. R. Haslehurst | — June 1941 |
| A. Spencer | 5th November 1942 |
| E. F. Smith | — March 1943 |
| J. L. Boe | — 1947 |

### 2ND BATTALION

| | |
|---|---|
| J. A. W. Ballard | 15th May 1936 |
| P. W. P. Green | 21st January 1939 |
| G. S. Drew | 22nd May 1940 |
| H. J. Wood | — March 1941 |
| A. N. Soutar | 7th May 1942 |
| A. C. Mullins | 22nd November 1943 |
| H. G. T. Gill | — |
| J. S. Drew | — April 1946 |
| D. Baxter | — August 1947 |

### 4TH BATTALION

| | |
|---|---|
| H. C. R. Cochrane | — |
| J. S. Simpson | — |
| L. J. Jennings | — |
| J. M. Boardman | — |
| R. Shearer | — 1943 |
| W. G. Wright | — September 1945 |

### 5TH BATTALION

| | |
|---|---|
| W. V. Marshall | 15th May 1936 |
| P. K. Hill | — May 1940 |
| W. Hilton-Johnson | — |
| J. Henderson | — |
| E. Grant | — 1943 |
| I. A. McKee | — 1944 |
| J. K. Smith | 20th January 1945 |
| J. V. Kent | 8th June 1945 |
| N. P. Bailey | 19th January 1946 |
| G. C. Hetherington | 8th June 1946 |

# APPENDIX V

## THE MESS PLATE

In the days when the Regiment had two Regular Battalions in being, each kept and treasured its own Mess Plate, of which some details were given in the first volume of the Regimental History.

When, however, the two Battalions were amalgamated, it was evident that the amount of Mess Plate would be excessive for the one to maintain, and that this would mean that much of it would never see the light of day, much less appear on the Mess table. The matter was therefore considered by the Regimental Council, and what follows is the result of the decision made by them.

In October 1948 all the Mess Plate of the 48th and 58th, less that already with the Battalion in Austria, was collected at the Depot, unpacked, sorted and labelled. On the 14th of that month, a further sorting was made by a Board of Officers, consisting of Lieut.-Col. O. K. Parker, Brig. W. J. Jervois and Major D. W. Spooner, with Major N. R. Ogle representing the Battalion.

On the following day the Colonel of the Regiment was present, and under his presidency the Board made final decisions. Briefly, these were as follows:

(i) All articles of regimental historical or sentimental value were retained, to be divided between the Battalion and the Depot, and held in Trust for former 1st and 2nd Battalions.

(ii) The 'Weallens Bowl,' presented to the 48th in 1906, was to be given to the Army Rifle Association on long loan, for a competition to be called 'The Northamptonshire Cup.'

(iii) A cup was selected for presentation on long loan to the Guildhall, Northampton.

(iv) Twenty silver beer-goblets were to be lent to the Officers' Mess, School of Infantry.

(v) Certain Cups and Trophies were lent to the 5th Battalion and the County Cadet Battalions.

(vi) All surplus items were purchased by the Goldsmiths and Silversmiths Company. The proceeds of this sale were devoted towards the purchase of a replica of the Queen Victoria Trophy for the Battalion, to commemorate the shooting successes of the 48th and the 58th.

As far as the Mess Plate of the 3rd Battalion is concerned, this must remain in store, For the War Office ruling was that the Battalion had never been officially disbanded. although it had ceased to carry out any form of duty, or training, since 1919 and, although the Army List had shown it to possess one officer for the next seventeen years, thereafter it seems to have had none.

# APPENDIX VI

## NOTES ON ORGANISATION AND CONDITIONS OF SERVICE, UNIFORMS, ARMS AND EQUIPMENT, AND WIRELESS

### ORGANISATION AND CONDITIONS OF SERVICE

**1937.** In June, a first draft of 29 *Supplementary Reservists* joined the 58th from the Depot, where they had completed twelve weeks' training. After six months with the Battalion they had the choice, either of continuing in the Army on a Regular engagement, or of returning to civil life and doing fourteen days' training a year.

In the course of the year, Mr. Duff-Cooper, the Secretary of State for War, announced the introduction of certain improvements in conditions of service, mainly connected with *Messing* and *Kit*. Among these were:

> The issue of an allowance, to be drawn by the unit, which would provide suppers for men in Mess.
> The provision of a proportion of butter in the ration, and of a daily issue of milk to boys.
> The improvement of cookhouse and dining-hall equipment.
> An increase in the kit-allowance issuable to recruits in their first year's service, in order to reduce the former hardship of their having to pay for items such as washing, hair-cutting and cleaning materials, and the free issue of certain articles of small kit.
> The free issue of a third suit of khaki-drill to soldiers serving abroad, and of socks, a shirt and a plate to Territorial Army soldiers when in camp.

The Army Estimates for 1937 made provision for considerable reorganisation and re-equipment. Most of the Infantry units serving at home were to become either *Rifle* or *Machine-Gun Battalions*, with mechanised first-line transport. In Rifle Battalions (of which the 58th was one) a *Mortar Platoon* and a *Light Machine-Gun Platoon* were added to the Headquarter Wing, which was henceforth to be named the *Headquarter Company*. The Support Company, as such, was abolished and became a *fourth Rifle Company*.

**1938.** Army Order 197 of this year authorised a new grade of Warrant Officer Class III, to be known as *Platoon Sergeant-Major*.

The object of this was to enable a reduction to be made in the proportion of junior officers to each Lieut.-Colonel, thus increasing their prospects of promotion in the latter rank in due course, and also to improve the prospects of promotion for N.C.O.s. These Warrant Officers were to be trained as officers, rather than as N.C.O.s.

With the resulting changes in establishment there was to be an increase in the powers of all Warrant Officers, to enable them to replace in nearly all respects the junior officers whom they displaced. They were to be allowed to handle public money, and to be in charge of certain regimental accounts.

Promotion above the rank of Sergeant was, in future, to be on a regimental, as opposed to the former battalion, basis. The avenue of promotion to W.O. Class II would be, either through W.O. Class III, or through C.Q.M.S. or equivalent rank.

The first promotions to the new grade were made on the 1st October 1938.

Army Order No. 39 introduced *increased rates of pay* for all other ranks who had enlisted, or re-enlisted, on or after 26th October 1925. These included *Special Proficiency Pay*, for which two-thirds of the Lance-Corporals and Privates in a battalion were eligible. The effect of this increase was that a Private, if in receipt of Special Proficiency Pay, would receive 3s. 9d. a day as against 3s. a day under the old rates.

Army Order No. 66 introduced revised scales of *Marriage Allowances* for all other ranks from 30th April.

Army Order No. 169 introduced new *scales of pay and conditions of service for combatant officers*. Briefly, this meant time promotion from Subaltern to Captain after 8 years' service, and from Captain to Major after 17 years' service, with rates of pay slightly increased. The new conditions came into force from the 30th August.

**1939.** Parliament passed the *Military Service Bill*, which compelled all men between the ages of 20 and 21 to register, and made them liable to undergo six months' training in the year following registration, unless exempted.

A War Office Letter of 11th January promulgated a *Revised Peace Establishment* for Infantry Battalions at home and in the colonies. In it the old appointments of Pioneer Sergeant, Farrier and Saddler were abolished, and those of Sergeant M.T. Stores, Pioneer Corporal, Motor Cyclist, Motor Mechanic, Storeman (Technical) and Equipment Repairer were introduced.

The quota system, under which only a limited number of soldiers were allowed to *extend their service*, was suspended, subject to revision after six months. Meanwhile, there was to be no limitation to the number of soldiers who could extend their service to complete 12 years with the Colours.

Under A.C.I. 154 the *length of tour of Foreign Service* for other ranks was reduced from six to four years.

**1939–1945.** Many changes in organisation were made during these war years. These are too many to state in detail, but those which follow are of interest.

Early in the war it was realised that the H.Q. Company of a battalion, some 470 strong, was too large to be a satisfactory unit. It contained six platoons—Signal, A.A., 3-inch Mortar, Carrier, Pioneer and Administrative, numbered from 1 to 6, and an Anti-Tank Platoon.

Before the invasion of North Africa a directive was issued, asking units to evolve an organisation which would overcome the difficulty of having this one unwieldy company, greater in strength than three rifle companies, under the command of one Major. The resultant organisation, though for the time being unofficial, received the approval of the higher command. It is interesting to note that the 5th Battalion of the Regiment was one of the first to adopt it, and that the post-war organisation resembled it very closely.

A division was made into an *Administrative Company* and a *H.Q. Company*.

The Administrative Company consisted of the Signal, A.A., and Administrative Platoons, and was commanded by a Captain.

APPENDICES 401

The H.Q. Company comprised the Mortar, Carrier, Pioneer and Anti-Tank Platoons, and was commanded by a Major.

In April 1943 this organisation was officially recognised throughout the Army, but the names of the two companies were changed to *H.Q. Company* and *Support Company* respectively. Soon afterwards, the A.A. Platoon was abolished, and the others were numbered—No. 1, Signal; No. 2, Administrative; No. 3, Mortar; No. 4, Carrier; No. 5, Anti-Tank; No. 6, Pioneer.

At the end of June 1943 it was recognised that the battalion establishment of three Majors—of whom one was Second-in-Command, one commanding the H.Q. Company, and one a Rifle Company—was inadequate. Furthermore, it did not recognise the fact that command of a Rifle Company was a most responsible task, fairly justifying a rank higher than that of Captain for its commander. The establishment of Majors was therefore raised to five.

At the outset of the war the battalion *Pioneers'* duties consisted mainly of carpenters' work, though they were also trained as the Anti-Gas experts. As the war progressed, however, and mine warfare assumed greater prominence, it was realised that the R.E. were too few in number to be able to cope with the task of mine-laying, detection and lifting, and it became one of the Pioneers' main duties to assist them in these.

Eventually, the Pioneers were organised into two Assault Sections, each of one N.C.O. and three men, transported in a jeep which towed a trailer carrying minedetectors, tools and explosives. In addition there was a Tradesmen's Section, carried in a 3-ton lorry.

**1946.** In this year it was announced that the conditions of *Voluntary Service* would be, either 5 years with the Colours and 7 with the Reserve, or 12 years with the Colours and 7 with the Reserve, or 12 years with the Colours. Soldiers could re-engage after 12 years to complete 22 years with the Colours.

*Short Service Engagements* of 3 or 4 years with the Colours were opened to men who had completed at least 2 years Colour service after 1st September 1939 and were between 30 and 40 years of age.

The policy was to be that normal tours of duty overseas would be 3 to $3\frac{1}{2}$ years, and long-service soldiers serving for 12 years would have 3 years at home between foreign tours.

UNIFORM

**1935.** In the 48th, new *Dress Cords* and *Bugle Cords* were taken into use by the Drums. The former consisted of separate cords of black and buff, with tassel to match. The latter were black, with a buff tassel. At the same time, the bugles were silver-plated.

In December, the privilege of wearing plain clothes when not on duty, hitherto accorded only to N.C.O.s holding the appointment of Lance-Sergeant and above, was extended to all ranks of the 48th in India. Corporals and Lance-Corporals were allowed to wear them at any time, Privates when on leave outside the station, subject to the C.O.'s approval.

**1939.** For some years prior to this, experiments and trials were carried out with a view to the introduction of a design of Service Dress which would be more practical for training and for active service than that which had been in use for nearly forty years.

In 1939 *Battle-dress* was adopted and issued. This consisted of a khaki blouse and trousers, provided with ample pockets for the carriage of maps, papers, first field-dressing, etc. It had no brass buttons, which required cleaning and were conspicuous. Puttees were abolished, and were replaced by anklets, made of webbing material, into which the bottoms of the trousers were tucked.

**1939–1945.** In the Middle and Far East the khaki-drill jacket was replaced by the loose-fitting *Bush Shirt.*

In the later stages of the war in Burma all clothing was coloured *Jungle Green* in place of Khaki, and the Australian pattern *Bush Hat* replaced other forms of head-dress.

A feature of the war, as far as service in hot climates was concerned, was the belated discovery that, once troops were reasonably well acclimatised, the precautions against the effect of the sun which had been the rule for many years were, in fact, unnecessary and that the troops were fitter without them. Consequently, the wearing of topees was virtually abolished, and it ceased to be a military offence not to wear them between sunrise and sunset, and the same applied to the baring of the upper parts of the body.

Other innovations, common to the Army as a whole, were the introduction of the *Beret*, which replaced the old 'Fore and Aft' or Field Service Cap in battle-dress, and the granting of permission to other ranks to wear a collar and tie in place of the collarless shirt.

**1944.** As a result of representations made to the War Office by the Colonel of the Regiment, A.C.I. 692 authorised the wearing of the *Silver Cap Badge* by officers on all forms of regulation headdress. It was stipulated that it was not to be worn in battle-dress.

### ARMS AND EQUIPMENT

**1936.** The Army in India decided to adopt the *Vickers-Berthier Light Machine-Gun*, to replace the Lewis Gun, in preference to the *Bren Gun* which was adopted by the War Office. Twelve of these weapons were issued to the 48th in March.

**1937.** In April, the 58th were selected to fire an *Experimental Weapon-Training Course*, a compliment to their high standard of shooting. This Course involved more shooting at moving and figure targets, under conditions approaching those of battle, than did the old Course.

The reorganisation of Infantry battalions at home was accompanied by the introduction of new weapons. The *Bren Gun* replaced both the Lewis and the Vickers Gun, those in the Light Machine-Gun Platoon being transported in *Carriers* intead of in horsed limbered wagons. A ·5-inch Anti-Tank Rifle was adopted as a platoon weapon.

**1939–1945.** During the war the *Carrier* was employed in many rôles other than that for which it had originally been issued.

In the campaign of 1940, in France, they were often used as armoured reconnaissance vehicles and, in emergencies, even as light tanks.

In later campaigns it became the normal practice to employ them as spearheads of vanguards, in which rôle it was found that the Bren had insufficient range. So, in some cases, these guns were replaced by Brownings, acquired unofficially. They were also largely used for the carriage of battalion and company stores and R.E. equipment.

Towards the end of the war, in Italy and in North-West Europe, some carriers were equipped with medium machine-guns, others with 'Wasp' flame-throwers.

# APPENDICES 403

Although the *2-pounder Anti-Tank Gun* had been issued to a few selected units for the Army Manœuvres of 1938, the majority of units had only 'mock-up' guns, and went to France at the beginning of the war with the ·5-inch rifle as their only means of anti-tank defence. This rifle proved to be ineffective against the German tanks, and by degrees battalions received 2-pounder guns. Anti-Tank Regts. R.A. were issued with the new 6-*pounder*. Later in the war, the 17-pounder was produced in response to the demand for a still more powerful anti-tank weapon, and Infantry battalions then received the 6-pounder.

There was still a need for an effective close-range anti-tank weapon, and this was filled by the Projector, Infantry, Anti-Tank (commonly known as the '*Piat*'), produced in 1942 and issued to the whole Army by 1944. The Piat was a tubular, one-man weapon, weighing 34¼ lb. and was fired from the shoulder. It fired a 2½-lb. hollow-charge bomb. In an anti-tank rôle its maximum range was 115 yards, at which range it could penetrate the armour of most of the existing types of tank. It was also used against houses, with a maximum range of 350 yards, and for high-angle fire against trenches.

At the beginning of the war, the establishment of *3-inch Mortars* was two per battalion. This was increased to four after the campaign in France, and to six in 1941.

In the early stages of the war they were normally used singly, and were controlled by voice, but when the number in a battalion became six, they were invariably used in pairs, and frequently as a complete battery, control between the O.P. and the mortar position being by 38-set.

They were normally carrier-borne, but in theatres of war where this was impracticable, they were carried on mules or man-handled.

Improvements in the propelling charge increased their effective range to 2,800 yards.

The *Jeep*, a four-wheel-driven vehicle, of American origin, with a very good cross-country performance owing to its light weight, powerful engine and emergency gears, was first used by the British in the Middle East about the beginning of 1941. Thereafter it was used in all theatres of war, and was of the greatest value in areas where roads were either non-existent or very bad. Its uses included the carriage of stores and supplies in the forward area and the evacuation of casualties.

The S.M.L.E. Rifle in use before the war had the drawback that it was not designed for mass-production. To remedy this, during the war a new version of it was produced, known at first as the S.M.L.E. Mark VI, later as the *No. 4 Rifle*.

The main differences between it and its predecessor were: a heavier barrel, giving greater accuracy; aperture sights instead of open ones; and lighter weight, 9 lb. 3 oz. without bayonet. The bayonet was 8 inches long, and weighed 7 oz., and was fitted to the rifle by means of a turning lock, a reversion to a design of more than a century earlier. What was lost in length of reach with the short bayonet was compensated for by the greater lightness and handiness of the whole weapon.

## WIRELESS

Before the outbreak of war in 1939 there had been much research into the problem of communication in the field within the Battalion. As units and formations became more highly mechanised and battle conditions more fluid, so the pre-war methods had to change in order to meet the requirements of fast-moving troops. Consequently, in 1938 and 1939, experiments were made with the object of producing a one-man Pack

Set, but it was not until 1941 that a satisfactory set had been produced and issued to units.

Throughout the war the types of sets changed from time to time, and the establishment within the battalion varied, as experience showed the need for alteration, or to suit particular conditions of warfare.

The following notes give particulars of the sets used in Infantry battalions:

18-*set*. A portable set, carried on a man's back. Weight 34 lb. Designed for speech or for Morse up to a maximum distance of 5 miles. Used for communication between Battalion H.Q. and Companies, and as O.P. sets in the Mortar Platoon. A set was often allotted to the Carrier Platoon. First used in action in Libya in 1942. In the later stages of the war the establishment was sixteen sets per battalion.

38-*set*. A small, and very portable, set, carried in place of a pouch on the equipment. Weight 14 lb. Designed for two-way speech up to a distance of $1\frac{1}{2}$ miles. First used in Tunisia in 1942. Ultimately, each battalion had 28 of these sets.

46-*set*. A portable, semi-waterproof set, very simple to tune. Weight 25 lb. Designed for speech and Morse up to a range of 10 miles. Originally designed for use in combined operations, it was first used in the Sicily landings in 1943. It was also issued to battalions to replace the 18-set in certain operations, such as the crossing of the Rhine in 1945.

48-*set*. An American-built version of the 18-set, with the same appearance and performance. Used in place of the 18-set in Italy and the Far East from 1943 onwards.

19- *and* 22-*sets*. Long-range sets, carried in a vehicle, and only man-packed in exceptional circumstances. Not issued to battalions, but, communications between Battalion and Brigade H.Q. being the latter's responsibility, a set of this type was normally sent up to Battalion H.Q. to act as the rear link.

# APPENDIX VII

## REGIMENTAL SHOOTING RECORDS, 1931–1948

These records include the placings of Regimental teams, and of individuals who were placed in the first three of their event. In the case of the Army Hundred Cup and the Army Championship, all placings are included.

Some of the records are those of the years before this volume of the Regimental History opens. They are included in order to present a complete record, and to show the progress made from year to year.

### 48TH

#### ARMY RIFLE ASSOCIATION

#### NON-CENTRAL MATCHES—ABROAD

NOTE: The Queen Victoria Trophy was awarded on the scores obtained in the following matches: King George Cup, Royal Irish Cup, Young Soldiers' Cup, Company Shield, Machine-Gun Cup, Duke of Connaught Cup.

Excepting where specified, competitions were open to units in all stations abroad, including India.

### 1931—MOASCAR

| Competition | No. of Entries | Place Gained | Team |
|---|---|---|---|
| Young Soldiers' Cup | 51 | 11 | Regimental |
| Company Shield | 38 | 3 | H.Q. Wing |
|  |  | 6 | 5 Pl. |
| 1st Army Cup | 14 | 1 | 7 Pl. |
| Hopton Cup | 134 | 32 | 15 Pl. |

### 1932—MOASCAR

| King George Cup | 49 | 16 | Regimental |
|---|---|---|---|
| Young Soldiers' Cup | 51 | 8 | Regimental |
| Company Shield | 34 | 3 | H.Q. Wing |
| 1st Army Cup | 21 | 1 | 7 Pl. |
|  |  | 3 | 1 Pl. |
| Hopton Cup | 144 | 27 | 7 Pl. |
|  |  | 35 | 1 Pl. |

### 1933—JULLUNDUR

| Competition | No. of Entries | Place Gained | Team |
|---|---|---|---|
| King George Cup | 47 | 2 | Regimental |
| Young Soldiers' Cup | 49 | 4 | Regimental |
| Company Shield (India) | 68 | 2 | 'B' Coy. |
| Duke of Connaught Cup | 63 | 15 | Regimental |

Queen Victoria Trophy (India). 23 entries. 6th

### 1934—JULLUNDUR

| Competition | No. of Entries | Place Gained | Team |
|---|---|---|---|
| King George Cup | 39 | 3 | Regimental |
| Royal Irish Cup | 55 | 3 | Regimental |
| Young Soldiers' Cup | 47 | 1 | Regimental |
| Company Shield (India) | 63 | 5 | 'B' Coy. |
|  |  | 6 | 'A' Coy. |
|  |  | 8 | H.Q. Wing |
|  |  | 18 | 'C' Coy. |
| Machine-Gun Cup | 80 | 7 | 'D' (S) Coy. |
| Hopton Cup | 134 | 3 | 8 Pl. |
| India Cup | 29 | 2 | 8 Pl. |
|  |  | 3 | 1 Pl. |

Queen Victoria Trophy (India). 23 entries. 1st

### 1935—JULLUNDUR

| Competition | No. of Entries | Place Gained | Team |
|---|---|---|---|
| King George Cup | 46 | 7 | Regimental |
| Royal Irish Cup | 54 | 4 | Regimental (A Team) |
|  |  | 5 | Regimental (B Team) |
| Young Soldiers' Cup | 46 | 2 | Regimental |
| Company Shield (India) | 81 | 1 | 'C' Coy. |
|  |  | 2 | 'B' Coy. |
|  |  | 3 | 'A' Coy. |
|  |  | 4 | H.Q. Wing |
| Machine-Gun Cup | 77 | 3 | 'D' (S) Coy. |
| Duke of Connaught Cup | 56 | 5 | Regimental |
| Hopton Cup | 121 | 7 | 1 Pl. |
|  |  | 9 | 9 Pl. |
|  |  | 11 | 8 Pl. |
| India Cup | 22 | 1 | 8 Pl. |
|  |  | 5 | 11 Pl. |

Queen Victoria Trophy (India). 29 entries. 1st

### 1936—JULLUNDUR

| Competition | No. of Entries | Place Gained | Team |
|---|---|---|---|
| King George Cup | 45 | 12 | Regimental |
| Royal Irish Cup | 53 | 5 | Regimental |
| Young Soldiers' Cup | 48 | 2 | Regimental |

## APPENDICES

| Competition | No. of Entries | Place Gained | Team |
|---|---|---|---|
| Company Shield | 81 | 1 | 'B' Coy. |
| | | 4 | H.Q. Wing |
| | | 5 | 'C' Coy. |
| | | 9 | 'A' Coy. |
| Machine-Gun Cup | 82 | 4 | 'D' (S) Coy. (B Team) |
| Duke of Connaught Cup | 57 | 12 | Regimental |
| Hopton Cup | 122 | 13 | 'B' Coy. |

Queen Victoria Trophy (India). 26 entries. 1st

### 1937—RAZMAK—DINAPORE

| Competition | No. of Entries | Place Gained | Team |
|---|---|---|---|
| King George Cup | 42 | 3 | Regimental |
| Royal Irish Cup | 47 | 9 | Regimental (B Team) |
| | | 12 | Regimental (A Team) |
| Young Soldiers' Cup | 43 | 6 | Regimental |
| Company Shield | 60 | 4 | H.Q. Coy. |
| | | 5 | 'B' Coy. |
| | | 11 | 'D' Coy. |
| | | 14 | 'A' Coy. |

Queen Victoria Trophy (India). 23 entries. 1st

### 1938—DINAPORE

| Competition | No. of Entries | Place Gained | Team |
|---|---|---|---|
| King George Cup | 31 | 2 | Regimental |
| Royal Irish Cup | 39 | 5 | Regimental |
| Company Shield | 84 | 3 | 'B' Coy. |
| | | 8 | 'C' Coy. |
| | | 12 | H.Q. Coy. |
| | | 18 | 'D' Coy. |
| Duke of Connaught Cup | 48 | 5 | Regimental |

Queen Victoria Trophy (India). 24 entries. 2nd

### CENTRAL SMALL-ARMS MEETING (INDIA)
### 1939

| Competition | Place Gained | Team |
|---|---|---|
| Northern Command Cup | 1 | P.S.M. Wilson / Sgt. Carswell |
| Southern Command Cup | 3 | Regimental |
| Birdwood Vase | 10 | Regimental |
| Carnatic Gold Cup | 3 | Regimental |
| Army Hundred Cup | 19 | Pte. Duckett |
| | 79 | 2/Lieut. McDowell |
| | 81 | L/Cpl. Worsfold |
| | 92 | Sgt. Carswell |
| | 96 | Pte. Parsons |
| Army Championship—Class 3 | 2 | Pte. Duckett |

## OTHER EVENTS

| Competition | Place Gained | Team |
|---|---|---|
| **1934** | | |
| Powell Cup (Jullundur Bde.) | 1 | Team of Officers |
| **1935** | | |
| Powell Cup (Jullundur Bde.) | 1 | Team of Officers |
| **1936** | | |
| Powell Cup (Jullundur Bde.) | 2 | Team of Officers |

## 58TH

### ARMY RIFLE ASSOCIATION
### NON-CENTRAL MATCHES—AT HOME

#### 1932—ALDERSHOT

| Competition | No. of Entries | Place Gained | Team |
|---|---|---|---|
| Duke of Connaught Cup | 54 | 7 | Regimental |

#### 1933—ALDERSHOT

| Competition | No. of Entries | Place Gained | Team |
|---|---|---|---|
| King George Cup | 43 | 9 | Regimental |
| Duke of Connaught Cup | 58 | 9 | Regimental |

#### 1934—ALDERSHOT

| Competition | No. of Entries | Place Gained | Team |
|---|---|---|---|
| King George Cup | 47 | 14 | Regimental |
| Royal Irish Cup | 67 | 11 | Regimental |
| Machine-Gun Cup | 98 | 7 | 'D' (S) Coy. |
| Duke of Connaught Cup | 50 | 6 | Regimental |

#### 1936—BALLYKINLER

| Competition | No. of Entries | Place Gained | Team |
|---|---|---|---|
| Royal Irish Cup | 53 | 6 | Regimental |
| | | 11 | Regimental |
| Company Shield | 62 | 11 | 'B' Coy. |
| | | 14 | 'A' Coy. |

#### 1937—BALLYKINLER

| Competition | No. of Entries | Place Gained | Team |
|---|---|---|---|
| King George Cup | 33 | 2 | Regimental |
| Royal Irish Cup | 48 | 6 | Regimental (A Team) |
| | | 12 | Regimental (B Team) |
| Young Soldiers' Cup | 28 | 2 | Regimental |
| Company Shield | 56 | 4 | 'C' Coy. |
| | | 8 | H.Q. Coy. |
| | | 10 | 'B' Coy. |
| Duke of Connaught Cup | 40 | 4 | Regimental |

Queen Victoria Trophy (At Home). 18 entries. 2nd

# APPENDICES

## 1938—BALLYKINLER

| Competition | No. of Entries | Place Gained | Team |
|---|---|---|---|
| King George Cup | 27 | 3 | Regimental |
| Royal Irish Cup | 46 | 2 | Regimental |
| Company Shield | 54 | 3 | 'B' Coy. |
|  |  | 7 | 'D' Coy. |
|  |  | 8 | H.Q. Coy. |
| Duke of Connaught Cup | 33 | 3 | Regimental |
| Hopton Cup | 40 | 2 | 16 Pl. |
| Revolver Cup (Individual) | 108 | 3 | Lieut. N. J. Dickson |

Queen Victoria Trophy (At Home). 15 entries. 3rd

## 1939—BALLYKINLER

| Competition | No. of Entries | Place Gained | Team |
|---|---|---|---|
| King George Cup | 17 | 2 | Regimental |
| Royal Irish Cup | 25 | 2 | Regimental (A Team) |
|  |  | 7 | Regimental (B Team) |
| Company Shield | 44 | 4 | H.Q. Coy. |
|  |  | 5 | 'A' Coy. |
| Hopton Cup | 34 | 4 | 1 Pl. |
|  |  | 10 | 7 Pl. |

Queen Victoria Trophy (At Home). Not awarded this year

## 1947—GERMANY

| Competition | No. of Entries | Place Gained | Team |
|---|---|---|---|
| King George Cup | 10 | 4 | Regimental |
| Royal Irish Cup | 10 | 2 | Regimental |
| Young Soldiers' Cup | 9 | 1 | Regimental |
| Company Shield | 18 | 2 | 'A' Coy. |
|  |  | 4 | 'C' Coy. |
| Duke of Connaught Cup | 15 | 2 | Regimental |

Queen Victoria Trophy (At Home). 8 entries. 1st

## ALDERSHOT COMMAND SMALL-ARMS MEETING

### 1933

| | | |
|---|---|---|
| H.Q. Wing Match | 2 | H.Q. Wing |
| Company Match | 3 | 'A' Coy. |
| Revolver Team Match | 4 | Regimental |
| Rapid Fire Match | 1 | Regimental |
| Evelyn Wood Challenge Cup | 1 | Regimental |

Command Inter-Unit Championship. 20 Battalions entered. 6th

### 1934

| | | |
|---|---|---|
| Sergeants' Match | 3 | Sgt. Marshall |
| H.Q. Wing Match | 1 | H.Q. Wing |
| Company Match | 3 | 'A' Coy. |

| Competition | Place Gained | Team |
|---|---|---|
| Rapid Fire Match | 7 | Regimental |
| Command Match | 4 | Regimental |
| W.O.s' and Sergeants' Match | 7 | Regimental |
| Young Soldiers' Team Match | 2 | Regimental |
| L.A. Match | 10 | Regimental |
| A.A.L.A. Match | 1 | 'C' Coy. |
| | 2 | H.Q. Wing |
| | 5 | 'A' Coy. |
| | 10 | 'B' Coy. |
| Revolver Team Match | 6 | Regimental |
| Revolver Individual Championship—Class C | 1 | L/Cpl. Malpas |
| Evelyn Wood Challenge Cup | 3 | Regimental |

Command Inter-Unit Championship. 20 Battalions entered. 3rd

### 1935

| Competition | Place Gained | Team |
|---|---|---|
| Sergeants' Match | 3 | Sgt. Ganley |
| Corporals' Match | 1 | L/Cpl. Stapleford |
| | 2 | Cpl. Murdin |
| Young Soldiers' Match | 1 | Pte. Horn |
| | 3 | Pte. Jones |
| H.Q. Wing Match | 2 | H.Q. Wing |
| Company Match | 2 | 'A' Coy. |
| Platoon Match | 1 | 10 Pl. |
| Rapid Fire Match | 1 | Regimental |
| Command Match | 2 | Regimental |
| Young Soldiers' Team Match | 2 | Regimental |
| L.A. Match | 9 | 'B' Coy. |
| A.A.L.A. Match | 2 | 'A' Coy. |
| Revolver Team Match | 9 | Regimental |
| Machine-Gun Match | 5 | 'D' (S) Coy. |
| Machine-Gun Knock-Out Match | 2 | 'D' (S) Coy. |
| Rifle Knock-Out Match | 1 | 'D' (S) Coy. |
| Revolver Individual Championship—Class C | 2 | L/Cpl. Malpas |
| Evelyn Wood Championship | 1 | Regimental |
| W.O.s' and Sergeants' Match | 9 | Regimental |

Command Inter-Unit Championship. 1st

### British Troops in Berlin Rifle Meeting

#### 1947

| Competition | Place Gained | Team |
|---|---|---|
| Inter-Unit Rifle Match | 1 | Regimental |
| Inter-Unit L.M.G. Match | 1 | Regimental |
| L.M.G. Individual Pairs Match | 1 | { Pte. Davies<br>Pte. Gusterson |
| | 2 | { Sgt. Wilmott<br>Pte. Allen |

APPENDICES 411

| Competition | Place Gained | Team |
|---|---|---|
| Inter-Unit Sten Match | 2 | Regimental |
| Inter-Unit Pistol Match | 2 | Regimental |
| Individual Rifle Match | 1 | Pte. Allen |
| | 2 | Pte. Steadman |
| Individual Pistol Match | 2 | Lieut.-Col. Taunton |
| | 3 | Major Britten |
| Inter-Unit Championship. 1st | | |

## ARMY RIFLE ASSOCIATION
### CENTRAL MEETING—AT HOME

#### 1932

| Competition | No. of Entries | Place Gained | Name |
|---|---|---|---|
| Roupell Cup—Class C | 749 | 1 | L/Cpl. Murdin |
| Worcestershire Cup—Class A | 38 | 2 | { Sgt. Marshall<br>{ Sgt. Felce |
| Army Hundred Cup | 100 | 39 | Sgt. Marshall |
| | | 56 | Sgt. Felce |
| | | 85 | 2/Lieut. G. V. Britten |
| | | 88 | Pte. Arnull |
| Army Championship | 700 | 22 | Sgt. Marshall |
| King's Medal | | 12 | Sgt. Marshall |

#### 1933

| Competition | No. of Entries | Place Gained | Name |
|---|---|---|---|
| Army Hundred Cup | 102 | 8 | C.Q.M.S. Felce |
| | | 13 | Sgt. Marshall |
| | | 90 | C.Q.M.S. Bradley |
| Britannia Trophy | 45 | 8 | Regimental Team |
| Army Championship | 742 | 21 | C.Q.M.S. Felce |
| | | 34 | Sgt. Marshall |
| King's Medal | | 3 | Sgt. Marshall |
| | | 11 | C.Q.M.S. Felce |

#### 1934

| Competition | No. of Entries | Place Gained | Name |
|---|---|---|---|
| Rhine Army Shield | 30 | 3 | Regimental Team |
| Army Hundred Cup | 109 | 42 | Lieut. G. V. Britten |
| | | 50 | C.S.M. Felce |
| | | 59 | L/Cpl. Payne |
| | | 68 | L/Cpl. Malpas |
| | | 105 | Sgt. Dixon |
| | | 106 | Sgt. Marshall |
| Army Championship | 680 | 40 | Lieut. G. V. Britten |
| | | 50 | L/Cpl. Payne |
| King's Medal | | 17 | L/Cpl. Payne |
| | | 22 | Lieut. G. V. Britten |

## 1935

| Competition | No. of Entries | Place Gained | Team |
|---|---|---|---|
| Roupell Cup—Class B | 767 | 2 | L/Cpl. Malpas |
| King's Royal Rifle Corps Cup | 28 | 9 | Regimental Team |
| Small Arms Cup | 29 | 4 | Regimental Team |
| Army Hundred Cup | 100 | 64 | L/Cpl. Malpas |
|  |  | 93 | L/Cpl. Stapleford |

## 1936

| Competition | No. of Entries | Place Gained | Team |
|---|---|---|---|
| Britannia Trophy | 33 | 3 | Regimental Team |
| Army Hundred Cup | 100 | 48 | Capt. A. A. Crook |
|  |  | 72 | Sgt. Sherwood |
| Army Championship * | 628 | 47 | Sgt. Sherwood |

## 1937

| Competition | No. of Entries | Place Gained | Team |
|---|---|---|---|
| Roberts Cup—Class C | 681 | 3 | L/Cpl. Gould |
| King's Royal Rifle Corps Cup | 22 | 2 | Regimental Team |
| Worcestershire Cup—Class A | 26 | 2 | { L/Sgt. Palmer<br>L/Sgt. Smith |
| Class B | 37 | 3 | { Cpl. Jakins<br>Cpl. Ball |
| All Classes | 63 | 2 | Teams as above |
| Britannia Trophy | 33 | 4 | Regimental Team |
| Army Hundred Cup | 100 | 28 | Pte. Pollard |
|  |  | 43 | Cpl. Moore |
| Army Championship | 634 | 17 | Pte. Pollard |

## 1938

| Competition | No. of Entries | Place Gained | Team |
|---|---|---|---|
| Roupell Cup—Class B | 591 | 1 | Cpl. Malpas |
|  |  | 3 | Pte. Pollard |
| All Classes |  | 2 | Cpl. Malpas |
| Roberts Cup—Class B | 590 | 2 | Pte. Pollard |
| King's Royal Rifle Corps Cup | 24 | 2 | Regimental Team |
| Worcestershire Cup—Class B | 50 | 1 | { Cpl. Malpas †<br>Pte. Ludlow † |
| All Classes | 76 | 2 | { Above pair, and L/Sgts. Smith and Ariss, Cpls. Jakins and Stapleford |
| Small Arms Cup | 23 | 4 | Regimental Team |
| Britannia Trophy | 30 | 2 | Regimental Team |
| Rhine Army Shield | 25 | 5 | Regimental Team |

\* NOTE: From this year, inclusive, the King's Medal was awarded to the winner of the Army Championship. Previously there had been a separate competition for the Medal.

† This pair won A.R.A. Medium Silver Medals for making the highest score in the Match, irrespective of Class.

| Competition | No. of Entries | Place Gained | Team |
|---|---|---|---|
| Army Hundred Cup | 100 | 5 | Lieut. N. J. Dickson |
| | | 20 | Cpl. Malpas |
| | | 24 | Pte. Pollard |
| | | 48 | Sgt. Davison |
| | | 77 | Cpl. Moore |
| Army Championship—Class B | 530 | 1 | Cpl. Malpas * |
| | | 2 | Pte. Pollard |
| All Classes | | 4 | Cpl. Malpas |
| | | 6 | Pte. Pollard |
| | | 19 | Lieut. N. J. Dickson |
| | | 31 | Sgt. Davison |

1947

| Competition | No. of Entries | Place Gained | Team |
|---|---|---|---|
| King's Royal Rifle Corps Cup | 8 | 2 | Regimental Team |
| Worcestershire Cup—Class A | 15 | 2 | { Sgt. Wilmott<br>{ Sgt. Bonney |
| Small Arms Cup | 10 | 5 | Regimental Team |
| Britannia Trophy | 15 | 3 | Regimental Team |
| Army Hundred Cup | 100 | 36 | Major N. R. Ogle |
| | | 43 | R.S.M. Pilgrim |
| | | 86 | C.S.M. Golden |
| Army Championship † | 431 | 45 | Major N. R. Ogle |

1948

| Competition | No. of Entries | Place Gained | Team |
|---|---|---|---|
| Roupell Cup—Class C | 470 | 2 | Pte. Allen |
| | | 3 | Pte. Steadman |
| Roberts Cup—Class B | 470 | 3 | Cpl. Harris |
| Class C | | 3 | Pte. Allwood |
| Worcestershire Cup—Class A | 45 | 2 | Sgt. Wilmott |
| King's Royal Rifle Corps Cup | 12 | 3 | Regimental Team |
| Small Arms Cup | 12 | 3 | Regimental Team |
| Britannia Trophy | 20 | 5 | Regimental Team |
| Army Hundred Cup | 100 | 26 | Capt. D. Baxter |
| | | 32 | Pte. Allen |
| | | 37 | Major G. V. Britten |
| | | 43 | R.S.M. Pilgrim |
| | | 48 | Cpl. Harris |
| | | 61 | Cpl. Ward |
| | | 73 | Pte. Allwood |
| | | 85 | S/Sgt. Lancashire |
| Army Championship | 470 | 23 | Major G. V. Britten |
| | | 32 | R.S.M. Pilgrim |
| | | 47 | Capt. D. Baxter |
| | | 50 | Pte. Allen |

\* Winner of the Manchester Regiment Challenge Cup, as the Champion Shot of Class B.

† NOTE: In this year the King's Medal and the Army Championship were won by R.Q.M.S. Malpas, formerly of the 58th. See results from 1934 onwards.

## OTHER MEETINGS
### LONDON AND MIDDLESEX RIFLE ASSOCIATION
#### 1934

| Competition | Place Gained | Team |
|---|---|---|
| Parnell Cup (Team) | 3 | Regimental Team |
| H.M.S. President's Cup | 1 | Regimental Team |

#### 1935

| | | |
|---|---|---|
| Stock Exchange Cup | 1 | Regimental Team |
| H.M.S. President's Cup | 1 | Regimental Team |
| Service Rifle Championship | 1 | Sgt. Sherwood |

### R.E. (ALDERSHOT) SMALL-ARMS MEETING
#### 1935

| | | |
|---|---|---|
| Open Match | 1 | Regimental Team |

### 2ND BN. THE BUFFS, SMALL-ARMS MEETING
#### 1935

| | | |
|---|---|---|
| Open Match | 1 | Regimental Team |

### 1ST BN. THE NORTHAMPTONSHIRE REGT. (48TH/58TH)
### ARMY RIFLE ASSOCIATION
### NON-CENTRAL MATCHES—ABROAD
#### 1948
##### AUSTRIA

| Competition | No. of Entries | Place Gained | Team |
|---|---|---|---|
| King George Cup | 7 | 1 | Regimental |
| Royal Irish Cup | 5 | 1 | Regimental |
| Company Shield | 7 | 1 | 'A' Coy. |
| | | 2 | 'D' Coy. |
| | | 3 | 'C' Coy. |
| 1st Army Cup | 9 | 1 | 'C' Coy. |
| | | 2 | 'C' Coy. |
| Hopton Cup | 6 | 1 | 'A' Coy. |
| Sniper Cup | 1 | 1 | Regimental |

Queen Victoria Trophy * (Abroad). 3 entries. 1st

* NOTE: For this year the Trophy was awarded on the aggregates of the first four of the above Matches. The Young Soldiers' Cup was in abeyance, owing to the shortage of men in this category in units serving abroad.

## APPENDICES

### BRITISH TROOPS IN AUSTRIA AND TRIESTE RIFLE MEETING
#### 1948

| Competition | No. of Entries | Place Gained | Team |
|---|---|---|---|
| Victory Match (Team Rifle)— | | | |
|   1st Stage | 23 | 1 | Regimental |
|   2nd Stage | 3 | 1 | Regimental |
| Young Soldiers' Rifle and L.M.G.— | | | |
|   1st Stage | | 1 | Regimental |
|   2nd Stage | 4 | 3 | Regimental |
| Bren Test— | | | |
|   1st Stage (Team) | | 2 | Regimental |
|   2nd Stage (Individual) | 24 | 1 | Sgt. Wilmott |
| Sten— | | | |
|   1st Stage | 96 | 2 | C.S.M. Shotbolt |
|   Team | | 2 | Regimental |
| Inter-Command Anglo-American Match (Rifle and L.M.G.) | | 1 | Regimental |
| Falling Plate Competition | | 1 | Regimental |
| Crusader Shield (Individual Rifle Championship)— | | | |
|   1st Stage | 217 | 5 | Pte. Peake |
| | | 11 | R.S.M. Pilgrim |
| | | 15 | Major G. V. Britten |
| | | 19 | Capt. D. Baxter |
| | | 23 | { Capt. R. W. Careless<br>Pte. Saville |
|   2nd Stage | 23 | 1 | Capt. D. Baxter |
| | | 3 | Capt. R. W. Careless |
| | | 5 | Major G. V. Britten |
| | | 9 | R.S.M. Pilgrim |
| | | 11 | Pte. Peake |

Inter-Unit Championship (Steele Cup). 4 entries. 1st

### REGIMENTAL DEPOT
### ARMY RIFLE ASSOCIATION
### NON-CENTRAL MATCHES
#### 1936

| Competition | No. of Entries | Place Gained | Team |
|---|---|---|---|
| Prince of Wales' Cup | 22 | 6 | Depot Team |

#### 1937

| | | | |
|---|---|---|---|
| Prince of Wales' Cup | 17 | 2 | Depot Team |

## No. 48 P.T.C.
### Army Rifle Association
### Non-Central Matches
#### 1947

| Competition | No. of Entries | Place Gained | Team |
|---|---|---|---|
| P.T.C. Match | 11 | 1 | P.T.C. Team |
| P.T.C. 30-yards Match | 11 | 7 | P.T.C. Team |

### Central Meeting—At Home
#### 1947

| Competition | No. of Entries | Place Gained | Team |
|---|---|---|---|
| Roupell Cup—Class B | 420 | 1 | Cpl. Dickerson |
|  |  | 3 | Cpl. Crawford |
| Army Hundred Cup | 100 | 58 | Sgt. Humphries |
| Army Championship | 431 | 50 | Sgt. Humphries |

# APPENDIX VIII

## THE 585th SEARCHLIGHT REGIMENT (NORTHAMPTONSHIRE) R.A. (T.A.), 1937-1948

As has been told in the text of this volume, the 4th Battalion The Northamptonshire Regt. (T.A.) was converted into a Searchlight unit in 1937, and assumed the title of 50th A.A. Battalion R.E. By the following year there were four companies in the Battalion, Nos. 400 and 401 at Northampton, No. 402 at Peterborough, and No. 403 at Kettering and Wellingborough.

The Munich Crisis of 1938 brought sudden mobilisation. Nos. 401 and 403 Coys. were allotted a searchlight rôle in Northamptonshire and Huntingdonshire, while Nos. 400 and 402 were despatched to the Cardiff area, armed with Lewis guns, for the anti-aircraft defence of the docks.

The period of mobilisation ended after ten days, and thereafter came a time of intensive training. Recruits poured in, together with new equipment, and drill-hall accommodation was doubled. By June 1939 the unit was nearly at full strength.

On the 25th August 1939 the Territorial Army was mobilised, and the Battalion deployed to its war stations. By the time that war was declared, on the 3rd September, it was well established, with all digging of positions completed, forming a forty-mile-long section of the twenty-mile-wide searchlight belt which stretched from the Humber to Dover.

The rôle of the searchlights was to co-operate with night-fighter aircraft, which patrolled the area ready to attack any enemy bombers which were picked up by the lights. Although the early days of the war produced few raids, a high state of alertness had to be maintained all night and every night, while the days were fully occupied in the care of equipment. To this work was added, in the hard winter of 1939-1940, the task of building hutted camps for their own occupation.

At this stage in its career the unit again changed its name, in common with all searchlight battalions, and became the 50th A.A. Searchlight Regiment (Northamptonshire Regiment) R.A. (T.A.).

The system of defence against night-flying enemy aircraft, with its intricate network of operation rooms and radar, was excellent, but the equipment in use soon proved to be too inaccurate to deal with the fast German aircraft. New and elaborate sound-location and searchlight equipment, soon to prove inefficient, was hurriedly made and issued, and much time was spent in the spring of 1940 in training to use it, and in building large searchlight emplacements.

In June 1940 the threat of invasion was accompanied by the start of air-raids in earnest, and soon the 50th were moved to the important gun-defended area of Nottingham and Derby. The new locations of batteries were: No. 400, Newark; No. 401,

Nottingham and Tuxford; No. 402, Nottingham and Grantham; No. 403, Derby. The main task of the searchlights was to illuminate aircraft for the many regiments of Heavy A.A. guns deployed in the area, but detachments were also stationed at many gun-sites, helping to increase the volume and accuracy of the fire by providing data from the sound-locators. Batteries soon had experience against the enemy during the raids on Coventry, Derby, Nottingham, Sheffield, Manchester and Liverpool.

Towards the end of 1940 Lieut.-Col. Hogsflesh took over command, when Lieut.-Col. Scott Robson was promoted.

As new radar equipment became available for the guns the searchlights on the gun-sites could revert to their proper rôle. This entailed the moving of many huts and the building of new emplacements, but hardly had this work been completed than an alteration of policy demanded the clustering of searchlights in groups of three, so, during the winter of 1941, every detachment, and almost every one of their huts, had to move again.

In 1942, when preparations were being made for the raid on Dieppe by the Canadian troops, it became necessary to strengthen the A.A. defences of the Isle of Wight, and thither went Nos. 401, 402 and 403 Batteries at short notice. At the same time No. 400 Battery was detached for training as an Independent Searchlight Battery. Later it proved that they were to take part in the campaign in North Africa.

After operating against enemy raids and mine-laying in November 1942 the Regiment left the Isle of Wight and occupied stations south-east of London, in Hampshire and Surrey. They had plenty of work to do against the German bombers which passed over this area on their way to raid London. Many aircraft were shot down when in the beams of the searchlights, and several detachments were officially credited with having brought down aircraft with their A.A. l.m.g.s. Other important work was the guiding home by searchlight beams of British disabled bombers.

In 1943 Lieut.-Col. Davis took over command from Lieut.-Col. Hogsflesh.

With the start of the flying-bomb attacks in 1944 the Regiment was fully engaged. The H.Q. of No. 401 Battery at Leatherhead was hit by one of these missiles, fortunately without suffering serious casualties. At this time, too, many detachments were posted in south-coast towns, to thicken up the defence against the enemy's low-level 'hit and run' raids.

In 1945 Mixed Heavy A.A. Regiments, manned partly by men, partly by A.T.S., were taking over A.A. defences in order to release men for duty overseas. At the same time the flying-bomb attacks were increasing from an easterly direction, while, with the cessation of night bombing, there was less need for searchlights. Accordingly the 50th were moved to the Frinton-Clacton area, where, for the first time since 1939, they were concentrated, and non-operational at night, spending some weeks on building roads, huts and emplacements for the gun-sites. Soon there came a demand for more Infantry units and the 50th gladly downed tools and once again took up Infantry weapons, training first at Littlehampton, then in the Southampton-Bournemouth area, under the title of the 637th Garrison Regiment, R.A.

On May 29th the Regiment embarked at short notice in H.M.S. *Berwick*, at Rosyth, sailed, and reached Bergen, in Norway, on the 30th. Here they were detached from their brigade, with the task of providing guards for food and clothing stores, U-boat pens and other military installations, and other duties such as searching for hidden arms and checking Fifth Column activity.

# APPENDICES

At the end of July the Regiment rejoined the brigade, which was responsible for a large area of northern Norway up to the Russian border. They went by sea to Narvik and thence to Bardu Foss, where their duties were similar to those performed at Bergen, with the addition of responsibility for a camp of Germans who were being repatriated, and for the despatching of many thousands of displaced persons, including Poles Russians and Italians. One battery was despatched to Finmark territory, and helped in the erection of huts and the building of roads and bridges in the area which had been 'scorched' by the Germans when they retired.

In October the Regiment was transferred to Oslo, where, besides finding guards at German prisoners-of-war camps, they had the task of escorting thousands of Poles to Gdynia.

Lieut.-Col. Davis now relinquished command and was succeeded by Lieut.-Col. Ripley, whose father had been, firstly Adjutant, then Commanding Officer, of the Volunteer Battalion which was the forerunner of the 4th Territorial Battalion.

As time went on the strength of the Regiment dwindled through demobilisation, and on the 26th December, after a farewell parade and inspection by H.M. the King of Norway, the remainder left for England, being among the last of the Allied troops in Norway.

On arrival in England the Regiment was stationed at Much Hadham, and there, on the 16th February 1946, it was placed in 'suspended animation.'

A year later, on the 1st May 1947, it was re-formed under the title 585th Searchlight Regiment (Northamptonshire) R.A. (T.A.). Lieut.-Col. M. Jelley, O.B.E., T.D., who had served for thirteen years before the war with the old 4th Battalion, was appointed to command. Many former members of the Regiment rejoined and were followed by volunteers who wished to serve in the new Territorial Army. An innovation was the attachment to the unit of a Company of A.T.S.

Training soon began at the drill-halls at Northampton, Kettering and Wellingborough, and in 1948 the Regiment attended its first post-war annual camp. It was preparing for the reception, in 1950, of the first intake of National Service men.

# APPENDIX IX

## THE NORTH AUCKLAND REGIMENT, 1935-1948

At the beginning of this period in its history the North Auckland Regiment, in common with all the other forces of the British Empire, relied upon voluntary enlistment to fill its ranks. But, as was the case both in Great Britain and elsewhere, despite the enthusiasm of officers and N.C.O.s the number volunteering was disheartening and this affected the building up of an efficient and adequate reserve.

As no improvement had been shown by 1937, the authorities decided to form Composite Battalions in each Military District. In the North Military District the 1st Battalions of the North Auckland, Hauraki and Waikato Regiments combined to form the 1st Composite Battalion.

On the 2nd May 1937 there occurred an event of great importance in the history of the North Auckland Regiment: the presentation of Colours by the Governor-General of New Zealand, Viscount Galway. The ceremony was held at Dargaville, at the end of the annual training camp prior to the change to Composite Battalion training.

The Regimental Colour, in Cambridge blue, bore a replica of the badge of the Regiment, the numerals '15' being prominent, and the Battle Honours awarded for service in the 1914-1918 War.

When the Second World War broke out in 1939 it was a great disappointment that the order of battle of the 2nd New Zealand Division did not include, by name or by number, any of the existing units of the Defence Forces, nor were representative companies formed into battalions, as had been the case in the First World War. However, practically all officers and N.C.O.s qualified to do so by age volunteered for service overseas, and were posted to the 18th, 21st, 24th and 27th (M.G.) Battalions. These were all recruited from the Northern Military District, except the 27th, which drew its members from machine-gunners throughout the Dominion.

Serving thus, many of the Regiment distinguished themselves on active service, notably Brig. R. W. Harding, D.S.O., M.M., who won his D.S.O. when commanding the 21st Battalion at Halfaya Pass; Lieut.-Col. H. McElroy, D.S.O., who, serving in the same unit, won his decoration at the Battle of Ruweisat Ridge, and a bar to it at Cassino; and Lieut.-Col. R. J. Lynch, M.C., who, having won his award as a Company Commander in the 18th Battalion in Crete, later died of wounds in an Italian prisoners-of-war camp.

In 1940 New Zealand reintroduced compulsory military training, suspended since 1929. The 1st Battalion of the Regiment was mobilised with men of the 18-21-years age-group, and carried out three months' training, ending in Brigade exercises. Throughout 1941 this battalion was not fully mobilised, and carried out only week-end training.

## APPENDICES

With the entry of Japan into the war the Battalion was again mobilised, and formed part of a Brigade Group, which had the task of the defence of Auckland. Its station was Okaihu where, nearly one hundred years before, some of the 58th had been engaged in an action against the Maoris.

A 2nd Battalion was then formed, with the initial task of providing coast-watching stations in the North Auckland Peninsula. Later it was to be available to join the main striking force. This battalion was recruited from men of the National Military Reserve, most of whom had seen service in the First World War.

A 3rd Battalion, consisting of Maori personnel, was to have been formed early in 1942, but this project did not materialise as the men were drafted to an independent Maori Battalion not allied to the North Auckland Regiment. However, a 4th Battalion was formed of men of the 18–21-years age-group who were not eligible for service in the Expeditionary Force, and was stationed in the Waitangi area of North Auckland.

As the Japanese were driven back, officers and men of the battalions were gradually released, some to return to civil life, others to be drafted to the 3rd N.Z. Division in the Pacific. Disbandment was finally completed in November 1945.

So, though not privileged to take part in operations against the enemy as a unit, the North Auckland Regiment played its part in the war, while many of its members distinguished themselves on active service with other units.

In 1948 the New Zealand Government realised the need for a reorganisation of the military forces of the Dominion and, although many of the old regiments had to give way to more modern units, the North Auckland Regiment continued to exist. The 1st Battalion began to reorganise in December of that year, and although it was not then known whether the basis of service was to be voluntary or compulsory, for a decision on this point was to be the subject of a referendum in 1949, many officers came forward and volunteered to serve with their old Regiment.

# APPENDIX X

## THE 48th AND 2/48th BATTALIONS,
## AUSTRALIAN MILITARY FORCES, 1934-1948

During the years preceding the Second World War the 48th Battalion continued to be linked with the 43rd, under the title 43/48 Battalion. Early in 1937 Lieut.-Col. M. J. Moten assumed command, and it was he who was responsible for the presentation to the Regiment of a boomerang inscribed with the names of his officers, an account of which has been given elsewhere in this history. It was in this year that Pte. E. W. Potter of the Battalion won the King's Medal for shooting in the meeting at Melbourne for the second year in succession.

As was the case in England, Hitler's aggressive attitude acted as a stimulant to recruiting, and the Battalion mustered 800 strong for the annual camp in March 1939. At the same time it was rumoured that the 48th Battalion might resume its separate identity, as in fact it did.

For an understanding of what then occurred, some account of the organisation of the Australian Military Forces (A.M.F.) is necessary.

The A.M.F., when first formed, was essentially a Militia force, with a sprinkling of permanent officers and instructors. Until 1929 there was universal training, under the provisions of the Defence Act, but these were then suspended and training continued on a voluntary basis. The compulsory clauses of the Act could be put into force to raise the A.M.F. to a war footing for Home Defence only.

In the First World War units composed of volunteers were raised for service overseas. These were named the First Australian Imperial Force (A.I.F.) and when disbanded the existing Militia units took over their numerical designations. Thus it was that the Torrens Regiment added the words '48th Battalion' to its title.

In the Second World War a Second A.I.F. was formed in a similar manner, all units bearing the prefix '2/,' and so it was that the 2/48th came into being. When Japan entered the war the compulsory clauses of the Defence Act were enforced, and the Militia, which included the 48th Battalion, was put on a war-time footing for Home Defence, this later being held to include service in the islands north of Australia.

### THE 48TH BATTALION

The 48th Battalion spent the first year of the war in various camps. Then, when Japan declared war in December 1941, they were linked with the 10th Battalion under the title 10/48th. They were then ordered to supply reinforcements to two other battalions which were being moved into the Northern Territory. Every available man was transferred, and as a result only a nucleus of officers and N.C.O.s were left.

APPENDICES 423

Large batches of reinforcements and equipment were then received, and by the end of April 1942 the unit was up to war establishment. It was moved to New South Wales, and after large drafts had left for the A.I.F. at the end of August, the whole Battalion was transferred to form a new Light A.A. Regt., the 108th. Later this became the 101st Higher Composite Regt., of Heavy and Light Batteries, and served in the defence of airfields in the Northern Territory from September 1943 until December 1944, when it returned to New South Wales and was disbanded, the officers and men being transferred to various A.I.F. units.

In 1948 the Militia again began training on a voluntary basis, but South Australia, which had hitherto raised four battalions of Infantry, was called upon to raise only two. Consequently, by the end of that year, neither the 43rd nor the 48th Battalions had been re-formed.

### THE 2/48TH BATTALION, A.I.F.

The 2/48th Battalion was formed at Wayville Camp, South Australia, on the 16th August 1940, under the command of Lieut.-Col. W. V. J. Windeyer, and was in the 26th Brigade of the 7th Australian Division. On the 17th November the Battalion embarked for the Middle East, and continued training in Palestine until early in March 1941. By this time the 26th Brigade had been transferred to the 9th Australian Division, and continued to serve with it for the remainder of the war.

In March the 9th Division moved into the Western Desert and relieved the 6th Division, the 2/48th getting as far as Barce, near Benghazi. Then came Rommel's drive eastwards and the Battalion, blocking the track leading from Mechili to Tmimi, had their first contact with the enemy before they withdrew to Tobruk.

Here they were in the western sector of the perimeter defences, and it was not long before they were attacked by Italian troops. These, however, were no match for the men of the 2/48th, even when the attacks were supported by German tanks, and during a period of eighteen days in the line the Battalion took the remarkable number of 1,375 prisoners for the loss of 15 men killed and 20 wounded. On one day alone, the 16th April, 26 officers and 777 men were captured at the cost of 1 man killed and 1 wounded, mainly by the action of three carriers and a small patrol which rounded up practically an entire Italian battalion, from the C.O. downwards.

But there was harder fighting to come, especially in April and May, when Rommel launched the attack which was intended to capture Tobruk. The German attack penetrated the Australian defences, and the 2/48th were called upon to counter-attack. Although they failed to reach their objectives, and suffered considerable casualties, they forced the enemy on to the defensive, and gave time for fresh infantry and anti-tank guns to establish themselves on the flanks of the enemy salient.

Eventually Tobruk was relieved, having withstood a siege of 242 days, 55 days longer than that of Mafeking in the South Africa War. The part played in it by the 9th Australian Division was commemorated by the adoption by them of a 'T' as the Divisional sign.

After a time spent in Palestine and Syria, during which Lieut.-Col. H. H. Hammer took over command from Lieut.-Col. Windeyer, promoted to command of a Brigade, in June 1942 the 2/48th went back to the Western Desert. This was when Rommel's drive on to Egypt was expected, and the Division's first task was to hold a defensive line covering Alexandria. Then the enemy were held at El Alamein, and the Battalion moved up and took part in the first of the successful counter-attacks at Tel el Eisa, on the 19th July.

From now on the 2/48th were continuously in action until the end of the great battle of El Alamein early in November. There is not the space to tell the full story here, but it is one of great gallantry and heavy losses. In the closing stages of the battle the strength of the Battalion was reduced to 3 officers and 40 other ranks. Three of the Battalion—Ptes. A. S. Gurney, P. E. Gratwick and Sgt. W. H. Kibby—were awarded the Victoria Cross, having lost their lives in winning it.

By now Japan was threatening Australia, and troops were wanted for her defence. So after a short period in Palestine the 2/48th returned home with the rest of the Division, reaching Australia in February 1943. There, on the big training ground of the Atherton Tableland in North Queensland, they reorganised, re-equipped and learnt the art of jungle warfare. There Lieut.-Col. Hammer left them, on promotion, and was succeeded by Lieut.-Col. R. I. Ainslie.

At this stage of the war in the South-west Pacific, the Japanese attempt to capture Port Moresby, in New Guinea, had been driven back by a magnificent effort on the part of Australian troops, fighting in appallingly difficult country. But the enemy still held key-points all round the east and north coasts of the island, and were determined to continue to hold them.

In August 1943 the 2/48th sailed for New Guinea, and early in September took part in the very successful airborne and seaborne operation which resulted in the capture of the small, but important, seaport of Lae, situated on the east coast.

This paved the way for another landing at Finschhafen, at the north-east end of the island, towards the end of September, and when this had been accomplished the 2/48th moved inland and played a major part in the extremely bitter fighting which took place for the Sattelberg heights. Here yet another Victoria Cross was won, by Sgt. T. C. Derrick, D.C.M.

After the successful conclusion of the operations to drive the Japanese from this part of New Guinea, the 9th Division was moved back to Australia, and spent a long time on the Atherton Tableland, training and re-equipping.

While the American forces were clearing the enemy from the Philippines, the task allotted to the Australians was the attack on Borneo, the first phase of which was to be the capture of the oil-bearing island of Tarakan, off the north-east coast. In April 1945 the 2/48th sailed for Morotai, a small island south of the Philippines, and, after rehearsing the operation there, landed on Tarakan Island on the 1st May. The campaign which followed, though a minor one, was of intense ferocity, but on the 21st June all effective resistance had been overcome. Unfortunately Sgt. Derrick, V.C., promoted to commissioned rank since the Sattelberg operations, lost his life in the fighting.

Victory Day in the Pacific came on the 10th August, and thereafter the Battalion carried out garrison duties on Tarakan Island until it was disbanded there on the 19th October 1945.

In the operations in which they had taken part the 2/48th had been awarded more than a hundred honours and awards, and had earned the name of the most decorated battalion in the A.I.F. Among these were 4 V.C.s, 4 D.S.O.s, 12 M.C.s and 21 M.M.s. Truly a remarkable record of gallantry for a battalion whose operational life lasted for little more than four years.

# APPENDIX XI

## THE 58th BATTALION (ESSENDON RIFLES), AUSTRALIAN MILITARY FORCES, 1934–1948

In the years preceding the Second World War, the 58th Battalion A.M.F. continued its normal training. Evidence of the high state of efficiency that was reached is provided by the fact that at the end of 1934, in the matches organised by the Militia Union Rifle Association, the Battalion was the best, both in the rifle and the Lewis gun, and produced the best individual Vickers gun shot.

In 1938 the strength of the forces in Australia was increased from 35,000 effectives to 70,000, and this led to considerable reorganisation. The country centres of the 58th Battalion were transferred to the 59th Battalion, in exchange for the latter's metropolitan centres in and near Melbourne. At this time, Lieut.-Col. N. F. Wellington, M.C., V.D., handed over command to Lieut.-Col. W. G. Cannon, E.D. As affairs in Europe became more critical so did recruiting improve, and by the end of the year the 58th mustered about 600 of all ranks, and were stronger than at any time since the suspension of universal training in 1929.

The summer of 1939 was marked by a visit to the Battalion of Brig. G. St. G. Robinson, D.S.O., M.C., then commanding a brigade in Burma and later to become Colonel of the Northamptonshire Regiment.

Just before the declaration of war one company was called up for security duties. As soon as the Second A.I.F. was formed, a number of officers and N.C.O.s were transferred to A.I.F. units and training battalions, and early in 1940 the 58th went into camp for three months, in order to train the 600 men who had been called up for service and who had joined them. Training continued throughout 1941 and the early months of 1942, under Lieut.-Col. F. W. H. Hale, who had succeeded Lieut.-Col. Cannon, appointed to command an A.I.F. Battalion.

In 1942, when the Japanese threat to Australia became very real, the 15th Brigade of the 3rd Division, in which the 58th Battalion was serving, was given the task of defending the Tweed Valley in New South Wales against possible invasion. In August, when the situation had improved, the Battalion was moved to the Brisbane area where, owing to a reorganisation of the order of battle, it was amalgamated with the 59th Battalion, under the command of Lieut.-Col. R. P. Whalley of the latter unit. The 58/59th then organised on the new jungle-warfare establishment, and spent the next six months in training accordingly.

In March 1943 the Battalion embarked for New Guinea and continued their training at Port Moresby for the next two months. Then the time came for them to go into action against the enemy and they were moved northwards by air to Wau, under the command of Lieut.-Col. P. D. S. Starr.

At this time the Japanese had been driven back in their offensive against Port Moresby, had been evicted from the Wau valley in the Owen Stanley Mountains in February, and had then fallen back to strong positions covering the port of Salamaua. Many of these positions had been chosen to cover the all-important tracks, little more than jungle trails, used for supply purposes. Any movement off these tracks had to be through extremely difficult country.

Having moved up from Wau to a point about five miles west of Salamaua, the first task of the 15th Brigade was to harass the enemy and to gain information of their strength and positions. Then, on the 29th June, the Australian offensive began. The 58/59th went in on the 30th and gained a footing on the important Bobdubi Ridge. This led to fierce Japanese counter-attacks, in which, strongly supported by mortar and machine-gun fire and with a fanatical disregard for casualties, no fewer than six separate attempts were made on the 21st and 22nd July. The last of these attacks got to within six yards of the Australian positions, but the 58/59th stood firm and drove the enemy back. After the failure of these attacks, 'A' Company, supported by bomber aircraft, succeeded in capturing a feature known as Old Vickers, which had resisted all previous attacks.

Slowly and methodically the advance continued, and with the fall of Lae, to the north of Salamaua, it became possible to put full pressure on the defenders of the latter. Salamaua was captured on the 11th September and the 58/59th, under the command of Major G. R. Warfe, M.C., moved to occupy the heights to the north of the isthmus on which it stood, in order to be in position to fall upon the flank of the retreating Japanese.

By now the Battalion was only about 300 strong, so it was withdrawn from operations for rest and reinforcement, moving by sea to Milne Bay and thence to Port Moresby, where Christmas was spent. In the arduous Salamaua campaign, the 58/59th had been in direct contact with the enemy for seventy-seven consecutive days.

In January 1944, the 15th Brigade was moved by air to the valley of the Ramu River, which runs inland from Lae westwards. Thence the brigade moved on foot to the north-west, with the object of forcing the enemy back from their positions in the mountains and making contact with the American forces moving along the coast from Saidor. To the 58/59th fell the task of protecting the right flank of the advance by long-range offensive patrolling through intensely difficult country. Many bitter engagements were fought, in which heavy casualties were inflicted on the Japanese.

Eventually the Brigade achieved its object, and was then moved by sea to near Madang, a small port on the north-eastern coast of New Guinea. It took no further part in the operations, and returned to Australia in August for home leave, having spent a very hard seventeen months in the tropics.

The leave period ended, the Battalion concentrated for training on the Atherton Tableland for two months, and on Christmas Eve 1944 embarked at Townsville for Bougainville in the North Solomon Islands.

Two months earlier American forces had landed at Torokina, on Bougainville Island, and had established a small beachhead within which they had constructed three air-strips. Later in November the Australian 2nd Corps had assumed responsibility for further operations against the main Japanese force, known to be concentrated in the south of the island. The 3rd Australian Division came under command of that Corps.

After a period of intensive training, which included practice in co-operation with tanks, from a camp near Torokina, the 15th Brigade moved to relieve another brigade which had had four months of hard fighting. The 58/59th were now under command of Lieut.-Col. W. M. Mayberry, Lieut.-Col. Warfe having been appointed to command of an A.I.F. Battalion.

From the middle of April until the end of the war the Battalion took part in a series of operations, a feature of these being a series of attacks against strong Japanese positions on river lines, which drove the enemy farther and farther towards the southern end of the island. After hostilities ended the 58/59th returned to Torokina for disbandment, which was completed early in 1946.

If evidence is wanted of the active part played in the Pacific War by the 58/59th, it is provided by the casualties they suffered and the decorations won. The former totalled 144 killed and 345 wounded, and of these about 60 per cent. were incurred in the Salamaua Campaign. The decorations included 1 D.S.O.; 11 M.C.s; 1 Bar to the M.C.; and 17 M.M.s.

Early in 1948 the 58th and 32nd Battalions (the latter from the city of Footscray) were reconstituted under the title of 'The Melbourne Rifles,' and were included in the active list of the Citizen Military Forces, forming part of the 4th Infantry Brigade of the 3rd Division.

On the 1st April Lieut.-Col. B. J. Callinan, D.S.O., M.C.; was appointed to command. The first parade of newly selected officers was held on the 28th May, and recruiting of other ranks began a month later. As this part of the Battalion's history ends, its Headquarters, 'A' Company and the Support Company are located at Moonee Ponds, 'B' and 'C' at Footscray, and 'D' at Brunswick, thus maintaining touch with the pre-war centres.

# APPENDIX XII

## THE LAKE SUPERIOR REGIMENT, 1940-1948

The Lake Superior Regiment, as it was then known, mobilised on the 2nd June 1940 at Port Arthur, Ontario, as a rifle battalion of the 4th Canadian Division. Training was carried out at various places, and then, with the conversion of the Division to an armoured one, the Regiment changed its rôle, becoming the Divisional Motor Battalion under the title 'Lake Superior Regiment (Motor).'

In August 1942 the Regiment embarked at Halifax, Nova Scotia, for England and there, mainly in Sussex, continued training for the next two years.

On the 26th/27th July 1944, seven weeks after the invasion of Normandy had begun, the Regiment landed near Graye-sur-Mer as one of the units of the 4th Canadian Armoured Brigade.

Nine days later the Regiment took part in its first action, a raid on La Hogue, south of Caen, and thereafter was heavily engaged in the break-out from the Caen bridgehead and the closing of the Falaise Gap. Then followed the pursuit through France, across the Seine at Elbœuf on the 28th August, and the Somme near Abbeville six days later. Then Belgium was reached, and the last days of September were spent in overcoming the strongly held German positions south of the Leopold Canal, Holland was entered in October, and during operations there 'B' Company of the Regiment surprised a German naval flotilla in Zijpe harbour on the 5th November. Using every available weapon the Company managed to sink four vessels before they could take effective defensive action.

The months which followed were spent in a holding rôle on the Maas, near s'Hertogenbosch, the monotony of this period being broken by a successful attack, on the 9th December, on Fort Crevecœur, the only remaining enemy foothold south of the Maas, and frequent raids across the river.

The Regiment's next major operation was in Germany, in the Hochwald, and on the 26th February, riding in to the assault on tanks, the Regiment successfully captured a ridge north-east of Udem. Two days later the advance was continued to the gap between the Hochwald and the Balberger Wald, where opposition was strong. On the 9th March the Regiment encircled a wood near Winnenthal, taking a large number of prisoners without loss to themselves, and assisting, on the next day, in overcoming desperate resistance in Winnenthal itself.

After crossing the Rhine on the 1st April the Regiment took part in the operations for clearing north-east Holland and the German coast west of the Weser, which included many stiff actions. Eventually there came the break-out from the Justen Canal bridgehead south of Osterscheps, from which started the slow grind to Bad Zwischenahn which fell on the 1st May. When VE-Day came the Regiment was fighting in the vicinity of Oldenburg.

The total casualties suffered by the Regiment during its service in North-west Europe were 767, of which 191 were killed. The awards received by members of the Regiment included 3 D.S.O.s, 6 M.C.s, 3 D.C.M.s, 21 M.M.s, 1 B.E.M. and 10 Mentions in Despatches.

While awaiting repatriation the Regiment was stationed in Holland, until, on the 9th December 1945, it left for Canada, where it was disbanded on the 15th February 1946.

In the post-war reorganisation of the Canadian Forces, the Regiment became a unit of the Reserve Force and assumed a new title, 'The Lake Superior Scottish Regiment (Motor).' With it the Regiment adopted the MacGillivray tartan, and new badges and buttons were authorised. The cap badge is described as 'A wreath of maple leaves ensigned with the Imperial Crown, within the wreath an annulus inscribed "The Lake Superior Scottish Regiment," in the centre of the annulus a maple leaf charged with a beaver couchant facing dexter. Below, a scroll inscribed "Inter Pericula Intrepidi." ' The buttons bear the Imperial Crown above the letters LSSR in cypher.

# APPENDIX XIII

## THE REGIMENT DE LA REY, 1934–1948

The Regiment de la Rey was created as an Active Citizen Force unit of the Union Defence Forces of South Africa by a proclamation dated the 7th September 1934.

The Regiment derived its name, as did others of the Citizen Force, from one who was prominent in the history of his country. General Herklas Jacobus de la Rey was a leader in the South African War of 1899–1902 who was famous for his raiding tactics, as was well known by the 58th when they were serving in that war, and was one of the last of the Republican generals to surrender. He was known as 'The Lion of the Western Transvaal.' His death in 1914 was untimely. The driver of his car failed to hear the challenge of the police manning a road-block, who were trying to stop a gang of criminals, and a shot which was fired killed General de la Rey instantaneously. His daughter, Mrs. de la Rey Morkel, is Honorary Colonel of the Regiment.

As is fitting, the badge of the Regiment is a half-lion, with the motto 'Ons Waarsku,' which, literally translated, means 'We Warn,' but is generally accepted as meaning that it is unwise to meddle with the lion's cubs.

The service dress was veldt green, the mess-kit a red jacket with black facings and waistcoat.

The South African defence system was based on the Active Citizen Force, a force somewhat similar to the British Territorial Army, which drew its recruits from the youth of the country, boys of between seventeen and twenty-one years of age. These served for three years, during which a certain number of hours' non-continuous training, and training in annual camp, was obligatory. Instructors were provided by the Permanent Force, or Regular Army.

Before 1934 several Active Citizen Force units had existed for some years, mostly drawn from the towns and all English-speaking. So when, in 1934, the South African Government decided to strengthen its defence forces, it was natural that they should turn to a new source. These were the young Afrikaans-speaking men who, bred in the veldt and used to hunting and shooting, were excellent material who had, hitherto, received no form of military training. It was from this source that the Regiment de la Rey drew its recruits, its area being the whole of the Western Transvaal, covering some 20,000 square miles. The five companies came from the districts of Rustenburg, Brits, Ventersdorp, Klerksdorp and Potchefstroom, the Regiment only coming together for annual camp.

The first Commanding Officer was Lieut.-Col. H. P. van Noorden, E.D., who was succeeded, in 1939, by Lieut.-Col. W. Basson, E.D.

On the 18th July 1940 the Regiment was mobilised, and for nearly three years undertook various internal-security duties. In February 1943 the General Service

Oath was offered, and the response being satisfactory, the Regiment became an Infantry Battalion of the 12th S.A. Motorised Brigade of the 6th S.A. Armoured Division, under the command of Lieut.-Col. J. B. Bester.

Having equipped and reorganised, the Battalion embarked at Durban on the 18th April 1943, landed at Suez, and went into camp near Cairo. A lengthy period of training followed, in the course of which the Division paraded before Field-Marshal Smuts. One of his remarks, 'You will be there,' was well remembered later.

Shortage of man-power now caused difficulties in maintaining the strength of the Division, and it became necessary to amalgamate certain units. So on the 7th July the Regiment de la Rey and the Witwatersrand Rifles united to form one battalion, known henceforth as the WR/DLR, or the WitsdelaRey, under Lieut.-Col. Bester's command. The Witwatersrand Rifles prided themselves on being the only Rifle Regiment of the Union Defence Forces, and also on their prowess at shooting, of which their record both in South Africa and at Bisley was proof.

Almost a year after leaving South Africa the WR/DLR sailed for Italy, reaching Taranto on the 20th April 1944. Early in May they had their battle inoculation, when their brigade was attached to the 2nd New Zealand Division and held a sector of the line in the Cassino area.

Soon after this the Germans withdrew, and the 6th S.A. Armoured Division was in the forefront of the pursuit. After passing through Rome and taking part in many engagements, on the 4th August the Battalion entered Florence, thus distinguishing itself by being the first unit to gain the final divisional objective at the end of the 300-mile race from south of Rome.

Moving on north of Florence, the Battalion took part in severe fighting. Then, aided by the mountainous country and the advent of winter, the Germans managed to resist any further advance. Static warfare ensued, the Battalion alternately holding the line and resting in billets in rear. During the winter Lieut.-Col. Bester was promoted to command of a brigade, and was succeeded by Major W. R. van der Riet, who had left South Africa with the Regiment de la Rey as a Company Commander.

After four months in the Apennines the Division was taken out of the line for rest and training. Then came the beginning of the final offensive. On the 15th April 1945 the WR/DLR went into the attack against a very strong German position in the mountains north of Florence, capturing it after bitter fighting which included a most gallant bayonet charge up a mountain-side against a well-dug-in enemy.

The enemy's resistance now broke, and the Allied Armies swept northwards into the valley of the River Po. After passing through the outskirts of Bologna the Battalion led the way for the brigade, and established a bridgehead over the River Panaro to the north of that city.

This was the last organised resistance to be encountered. From then on it was a matter of advancing rapidly and rounding up numbers of surrendering Germans. When the German Armies in Italy capitulated on the 2nd May the WR/DLR had reached a town a few miles to the west of Venice.

The end of hostilities did not mean idleness, and the Battalion was soon transferred to the Milan area, with the task of keeping order between various Italian factions. This accomplished, the next station was Aosta, near the French frontier. From there repatriation to South Africa began, was continued at a faster rate from Turin, and ended at Alassio.

The wartime union of the Regiment de la Rey and the Witwatersrand Rifles had ended, and in the future they were to resume their separate identity. But the union will not be forgotten, and to commemorate it two memorials were unveiled in South Africa in 1947, the one at Potchefstroom, in the territory of the Regiment de la Rey, the other at Johannesburg in that of the Witwatersrand Rifles. Both bore the name of the WR/DLR.

When unveiling the former, Major-Gen. W. H. E. Poole, Commander of the 6th S.A. Armoured Division in Italy, said: 'The gallant deeds and great achievements of the WR/DLR cost our country 797 casualties, of whom 151 were killed—a tremendous sacrifice worthy of a remembrance that inspires those of us who are spared, and one that will nourish generations of our sons in the years to come.'

The honours won by the WR/DLR included 2 D.S.O.s, 10 M.C.s, 1 D.C.M., and 18 M.M.s.

In January 1946 the Regiment de la Rey was re-established under the command of its first Commanding Officer, Col. van Noorden. It was organised as a Machine-gun Battalion, on the basis of one Mortar and three Vickers Machine-gun Companies. Headquarters were at Rustenburg, other stations being Potchefstroom, Klerksdorp and Lichtenburg. In July recruits were called up for training, and approximately 80 attended their first continuous training-camp at Potchefstroom.

During the Royal visit to South Africa in 1947 the Regiment had the honour of finding the guard at Government House, a memento of this being a guard-report signed by H.M. The King. On the following day new Colours were received from the King at Voortrekkershoogte.

Early in 1948 Col. van Noorden retired, and was succeeded by Major Knowles-Williams.

# APPENDIX XIV

## HONOURS AND AWARDS, WAZIRISTAN, 1936–1937, SECOND WORLD WAR, 1939–1945

### 1ST BATTALION
#### WAZIRISTAN, 1936–1937

*Order of the British Empire*
  Lieut.-Col. W. G. A. Coldwell

*Distinguished Conduct Medal*
  Pte. A. R. Letts

*Military Medal*
  Pte. A. Clarke
  Pte. S. Lee
  Pte. C. A. Millard
  Pte. W. W. D. J. Rose

*Mentioned in Despatches*
  Lieut.-Col. W. G. A. Coldwell
  Major H. K. F. Nailer
  Capt. W. C. Furminger
  Capt. J. W. Rawlins
  2/Lieut. J. W. A. Meredith
  C.S.M. O. Franklin
  Sgt. A. Newton
  Sgt. F. Sheppard
  Sgt. S. Stringer
  L/Sgt. S. Hughes
  Cpl. P. Allen
  L/Cpl. G. Thorpe

*Army Commander's Certificate for Services Rendered*
  Sgt. A. Casey
  L/Sgt. A. Tempest
  L/Sgt. A. Wilson
  L/Cpl. J. Hurwood
  L/Cpl. J. Kerr
  L/Cpl. J. Whiffen
  Pte. G. Grazier
  Bdsm. F. Lee

#### BURMA, 1943–1945

*Victoria Cross*
  Lieut. A. G. Horwood

*Distinguished Service Order*
  Lieut.-Col. D. E. Taunton
  Capt. P. R. Cherrington

*Bar to Distinguished Service Order*
  Lieut.-Col. D. E. Taunton

*Military Cross*
    Major P. F. Keily
    Major T. R. Molloy
    Major P. S. Thunder
    Major N. F. Veater
    Major D. J. Eales-White
    Capt. G. C. Hetherington
    Lieut. G. E. Franklin
    Lieut. R. E. M. Hughes

*Member of the Order of the British Empire*
    Lieut. & Q.M. L. A. Howard

*Distinguished Conduct Medal*
    Sgt. P. E. Kelly
    Sgt. W. Saunders

*Military Medal*
    C.S.M. W. F. Cairncross
    Sgt. F. Pottinger
    Sgt. G. Thurley
    L/Sgt. A. Linzell
    Cpl. J. Smith
    L/Cpl. H. Barford
    L/Cpl. R. Lee
    L/Cpl. J. W. G. Plain
    Pte. A. W. Cox
    Pte. W. C. Gannaway
    Pte. W. Jarvis
    Pte. A. C. Kemp
    Pte. G. Stanley

*Mentioned in Despatches*
    Lieut.-Col. P. de C. Jones
    Lieut.-Col. D. E. Taunton
    Major A. Dyson
    Major L. Fulford
    Major P. F. Keily
    Major P. R. Noakes
    Major H. L. Webb
    Capt. E. D. Wynne-Davies
    Capt. M. S. Hall
    Capt. G. C. Pile
    Capt. K. H. Malby
    Capt. S. J. Moult
    Lieut. J. S. Jones
    Lieut. A. D. Lytle
    Lieut. E. E. E. Miller
    W.O. II G. S. Harley
    C.Q.M.S. F. J. Lee
    Sgt. H. French
    Sgt. W. G. Guest
    Sgt. J. Jennings
    Sgt. A. Leese
    Sgt. L. Weston
    L/Sgt. D. N. Bennett
    Cpl. R. Bloor
    Cpl. G. H. Boxall
    Cpl. J. Rand
    Cpl. W. Saunders
    L/Cpl. J. E. Day
    L/Cpl. W. Gilbert
    L/Cpl. G. H. Green
    L/Cpl. R. A. Magee
    L/Cpl. A. W. Prince
    Pte. R. R. Clarke
    Pte. F. E. Scott

*Certificate of Gallantry*
    Sgt. R. Bloor
    Sgt. G. H. Boxall
    L/Cpl. R. A. Magee
    Pte. W. Saunders

## 2ND BATTALION
### FRANCE AND BELGIUM, 1939–1940

*Distinguished Service Order*
    Lieut.-Col. J. W. Hinchcliffe

*Military Cross*
    Capt. D. J. B. Houchin                        2/Lieut. R. C. R. Roche

*Member of the Order of the British Empire*
    R.S.M. G. A. Goodall

*Military Medal*
    Sgt. C. Ashdown

*Mentioned in Despatches*
    Lieut.-Col. J. W. Hinchcliffe             L/Cpl. T. K. Bird
    Major C. J. M. Watts                    L/Cpl. G. Greenfield
    Capt. & Q.M. J. Holmes               L/Cpl. J. Harlock
    Capt. R. F. H. Philpot-Brookes      L/Cpl. G. Haydon
    Capt. D. J. B. Houchin                  Pte. W. H. Fishenden
    P.S.M. J. Harris                           Bdsm. A. L. Gutteridge
    Sgt. W. J. Cobb

### MADAGASCAR, 1942

*Bar to Military Cross*
    Major D. J. B. Houchin

*Military Cross*
    Major J. A. Purton

*Mentioned in Despatches*
    Sgt. H. S. Heward                      Pte. N. E. Merryweather
    Cpl. R. T. Walker

### SICILY, 1943

*Distinguished Service Order*
    Lieut.-Col. J. A. W. Ballard

*Military Medal*
    Cpl. N. Smith                              Pte. J. Smith
    L/Cpl. S. Swepson                    Pte. H. Wilks
    Pte. G. Davies.

*Mentioned in Despatches*
    Capt. A. N. Soutar                    Lieut. S. L. Clarke

### ITALY, 1943–1944

*Military Cross*
    Major J. C. Denny                     Capt. A. C. Garner
    Major E. W. Kitchin                   Capt. S. C. Hamer
    Capt. S. L. Clarke                      Capt. C. Lamb (R.A.M.C.)

*Bar to Military Cross*
    Capt. S. C. Hamer

*Member of the Order of the British Empire*
    Major R. S. Wallis       R.S.M. R. Batchelor

*Distinguished Conduct Medal*
    Sgt. V. Bell      Sgt. R. Underwood
    Sgt. H. Heward      Pte. A. McDonald
    Sgt. P. Organ

*Military Medal*
    R.S.M. A. A. Pilgrim      Cpl. J. Hurrell
    Sgt. V. Bell      Cpl. L. Jeynes
    Sgt. J. Dodman      Cpl. G. McReedy
    Sgt. W. McNicol      Cpl. G. Reade
    Sgt. J. Manners      Cpl. C. Wilford
    Cpl. M. Alden      Cpl. I. Wright
    Cpl. H. Doubleday      Pte. C. Simmonds
    Cpl. W. Hume

*Mentioned in Despatches*
    Major J. C. Denny      Sgt. F. Wiles
    Capt. & Q.M. G. A. Goodall      Cpl. H. L. Doubleday
    Capt. A. C. Mullins      Cpl. F. Thomas
    Capt. A. J. Roberts      L/Cpl. L. Peacock
    C.S.M. A. A. Pilgrim      Pte. W. Craven
    C.S.M. E. Willmott      Pte. A. McDonald
    C.Q.M.S. W. E. Pritchard

*Commander-in-Chief's Certificate for Gallantry*
    Major R. J. Hornsby      Sgt. L. Bell
    Capt. R. O. Tear      Sgt. C. Stennett
    Capt. J. York

*Foreign Decoration*
    U.S.A. Silver Star—Sgt. F. Morris

## NORTH-WEST EUROPE, 1944–1945

*Mentioned in Despatches*
    Major R. W. Careless      Sgt. D. Jackson
    Capt. H. G. T. Gill      L/Cpl. J. Thurnham
    2/Lieut. G. S. Drew      Pte. G. Blanchard
    Sgt. G. England      Pte. J. Woodcock
    Sgt. L. Harris

*Foreign Decoration*
    U.S.S.R. Medal for Valour—Sgt. R. Walker

## 4TH BATTALION
### NORTH-WEST EUROPE, 1944–1945

*Mentioned in Despatches*
    Major A. C. Webb      Capt. W. G. Wright

## 5TH BATTALION

### FRANCE AND BELGIUM, 1939–1940

*Military Cross*
- Capt. W. V. Hart
- Rev. J. E. G. Quinn (R.A.Ch.D.)

*Military Medal*
- Pte. W. Sharpe
- Pte. H. Herbert

*Mentioned in Despatches*
- Major W. V. Marshall
- Capt. J. H. W. Cobbing
- 2/Lieut. P. K. Hill
- 2/Lieut. J. Orr
- C.S.M. F. Parkinson
- Sgt. L. O. Groundsell
- Pte. A. J. Harrison

### NORTH AFRICA, 1942–1943

*Military Cross*
- Major R. W. Cook
- Major J. R. Rayment
- Capt. M. C. Benett
- Capt. D. V. Emmerton
- Capt. J. F. Pearcey
- Capt. E. J. Kerr (R.A.M.C.)

*Military Medal*
- C.S.M. L. Wade
- C.Q.M.S. K. Nixon
- Sgt. E. R. Barber
- Sgt. H. T. Pollett
- Cpl. G. Allen
- Cpl. T. L. Baker
- Cpl. S. F. Brown
- Cpl. J. Williams
- Pte. M. Gillett
- Pte. T. Tovey
- Pte. J. Welton

*Mentioned in Despatches*
- Lieut.-Col. A. A. Crook
- Major H. M. A. Hunter
- Capt. T. L. Beagley
- C.S.M. N. S. W. Mann
- Cpl. H. W. Panter
- Pte. C. H. Moody

### SICILY AND ITALY, 1943–1945

*Distinguished Service Order*
- Lieut.-Col. J. F. Connolly
- Lieut.-Col. D. J. B. Houchin

*Bar to Distinguished Service Order*
- Lieut.-Col. J. F. Connolly

*Military Cross*
- Major M. W. Hunt
- Major A. B. Mountjoy
- Major M. J. Wise
- Lieut. W. A. M. Hilliam
- Lieut. R. R. Morgan
- Lieut. J. C. Pearson
- Rev. E. Elworthy (R.A.Ch.D.)

*Member of the Order of the British Empire*
- Major E. Wasey
- Capt. D. Ord

*Distinguished Conduct Medal*
    R.S.M. M. Surkitt                  L/Cpl. L. Childs

*Military Medal*
    Sgt. H. Rayment                 Pte. J. Barnacle
    Sgt. J. Stanley                   Pte. A. Clements
    Sgt. H. N. Thompson           Pte. L. Dalton
    Cpl. F. Raison                    Pte. N. Hutchins
    L/Cpl. R. Allkin                 Pte. C. Lunn
    L/Cpl. R. Lovell

*Bar to Military Medal*
    Sgt. H. Rayment

*Mentioned in Despatches*
    Major E. H. Newby             Cpl. A. L. Jelliss
    Capt. J. H. Andrews            Cpl. S. W. King
    Capt. M. H. R. King            Cpl. H. W. Panter
    Capt. H. M. Knee              L/Cpl. R. Bradbury
    Capt. D. H. Truckle            L/Cpl. R. J. Bull
    Lieut. M. E. Handon           L/Cpl. W. A. Burrell
    Lieut. S. J. Hawthorn          L/Cpl. H. B. Davis
    Lieut. W. A. S. Salisbury      L/Cpl. R. C. Lovell
    C.S.M. A. S. Beeson            L/Cpl. C. Milliner
    C.S.M. W. Eassom             Pte. T. A. Bird
    Sgt. G. J. Baxter                Pte. T. C. Bull
    Sgt. W. Baxter                    Pte. B. Dewberry
    Sgt. A. W. Doe                   Pte. F. Draper
    Sgt. H. Dowbekin              Pte. R. E. Driver
    Sgt. H. Gibson                   Pte. D. W. Facer
    Sgt. C. Shaw                      Pte. A. J. Harrison
    Sgt. J. A. Siddals               Pte. S. W. McRobert
    Sgt. G. Webster                 Pte. H. Mitchell
    Sgt. F. Wiles                     Pte. H. V. Moore
    L/Sgt. J. W. Potter            Pte. A. Munton
    Cpl. J. Balmer                   Pte. S. C. Pead
    Cpl. A. J. Hickling

*Foreign Decoration*
    U.S.S.R. Medal for Valour—Major M. W. Hunt

The following officers and other ranks received honours and awards when extra-regimentally employed or when serving with other regiments.

*Commander of the Bath*
    Major-General G. St. G. Robinson

*Commander of the Order of the British Empire*
    Brig. F. W. L. Bissett          Brig. E. G. Warren
    Brig. M. A. Green             Wing-Cmdr. H. L. Maxwell

APPENDICES 439

*Distinguished Service Order*
   Brig. A. A. Crook　　　　　　　　Lieut.-Col. N. J. Dickson
   Brig. H. Essame　　　　　　　　　Lieut.-Col. R. E. Osborne-Smith
   Brig. J. Lingham　　　　　　　　　Major G. P. Clark
   Wing-Cmdr. H. L. Maxwell

*Officer of the Order of the British Empire*
   Col. G. V. Britten　　　　　　　　Lieut.-Col. W. C. Furminger

*Military Cross*
   Major J. R. Britten　　　　　　　　Major A. M. N. Rice
   Major G. V. Martin　　　　　　　　Lieut. F. J. Berridge

*Member of the Order of the British Empire*
   Major W. H. Brindell　　　　　　　Capt. J. T. Ennals
   Major H. M. Knee　　　　　　　　Capt. G. Gneditch
   Capt. J. A. W. Ballard　　　　　　　Lieut. E. N. Willetts
   Capt. G. V. Britten　　　　　　　　W.O. II S. K. Benford

*Military Medal*
   Sgt. G. E. Thurbey

*Foreign Decoration*
   Officer, U.S.A. Legion of Merit—Brig. W. J. Jervois

*Mentioned in Despatches*

The names of the following officers and other ranks appeared in the *London Gazette*. They are either known to have been serving away from the Regiment at the time, or else cannot specifically be traced as serving with a particular battalion of the Regiment.

FRANCE AND BELGIUM, 1939–1940

Major G. P. Clark　　　　　　　　Capt. A. B. Coote
Major R. D. Lake　　　　　　　　Capt. H. F. Perkins

NORTH AFRICA, 1942–1943

Major J. G. S. Hobson　　　　　　Major R. K. Lamplugh

PERSIA–IRAQ, 1943

Col. J. W. Hinchcliffe

BURMA, 1943–1945

Brig. A. A. Crook　　　　　　　　Capt. N. L. Geary
Brig. D. E. Taunton　　　　　　　Lieut. J. P. Walkden
Lieut.-Col. P. W. P. Green　　　　　Lieut. J. L. Williams
Lieut.-Col. P. K. Hill　　　　　　　W.O. II R. A. Gell
Lieut.-Col. F. R. Wilford　　　　　Cr./Sgt. E. Knights
Major J. B. Hickson　　　　　　　Sgt. R. L. Taylor
Major P. Marriage　　　　　　　　L/Cpl. H. Brocklebank
Major J. L. Young　　　　　　　　Pte. K. Grigg
Capt. S. C. Burt　　　　　　　　　Pte. A. Stockwell

## ITALY, 1943–1945

Lieut.-Col. G. V. Britten
Major F. N. W. Farlow
Major R. D. Foot
Major E. Grant
Major G. V. Martin
Capt. M. R. Barry
Capt. M. A. W. Davies
Capt. G. Gneditch
Capt. R. Blyth
Lieut. F. W. Howlett
Lieut. R. C. Rickett
C.Q.M.S. K. W. Goodhead
Sgt. R. Burrows
Sgt. F. J. Day
Sgt. R. J. White
Sgt. H. P. Wood
L/Cpl. A. H. King
L/Cpl. H. E. G. Rose
Pte. E. R. Moody

## NORTH-WEST EUROPE, 1944–1945

Lieut.-Col. A. B. Coote
Major J. E. Dulley
Major A. G. Grey
Major W. D. Hilton-Johnson
Capt. J. M. Boardman
Capt. C. H. Searle
Capt. F. P. Sutton
Capt. D. J. Wiltsher
W.O. II G. J. Wigley
C.Q.M.S. G. W. Rust
Cr./Sgt. A. Smith
Sgt. S. Gregory
Sgt. A. Lilley
Sgt. D. R. Steele
L/Cpl. J. W. Fuller
L/Cpl. A. Myford
L/Cpl. W. D. R. White

## MALAYA

Major C. J. M. Watts
Capt. E. F. D. Hyde

## MIDDLE EAST

Lieut.-Col. R. J. Dinsmore

## THEATRE OF WAR NOT STATED

Major P. L. Burgin
Capt. D. A. ffrench-Kehoe
Sgt. S. E. Radage
Pte. A. E. Cullip

# APPENDIX XV

## THE VICTORIA CROSS

LIEUTENANT ALEC GEORGE HORWOOD, D.C.M. (165583),
THE QUEEN'S ROYAL REGIMENT (WEST SURREY),
ATTACHED THE NORTHAMPTONSHIRE REGIMENT

At Kyauchaw on 18th January 1944 Lieutenant HORWOOD accompanied the forward company of the Northamptonshire Regiment into action against a Japanese defended locality with his forward mortar observation post. Throughout that day he lay in an exposed position, which had been completely bared of cover by concentrated air bombing, and effectively shot his own mortars and those of a half-troop of another unit while the company was manœuvring to locate the exact position of the enemy bunkers and machine-gun nests. During the whole of this time Lieutenant HORWOOD was under intense sniper, machine-gun and mortar fire, and at night he came back with most valuable information about the enemy.

On 19th January he moved forward with another company and established an observation post on a precipitous ridge. From here, while under continual fire from the enemy, he directed accurate mortar fire in support of two attacks which were put in during the day. He also carried out a personal reconnaissance along and about the bare ridge, deliberately drawing the enemy fire so that the fresh company which he had led to the position and which was to carry out an attack might see the enemy positions.

Lieutenant HORWOOD remained on the ridge during the night 19th/20th January and on the morning of 20th January shot the mortars again to support a fresh attack by another company put in from the rear of the enemy. He was convinced that the enemy would crack and volunteered to lead the attack planned for that afternoon. He led this attack with such calm, resolute bravery that the enemy were reached, and while standing up in the wire, directing and leading the men with complete disregard to the enemy fire which was then at point-blank range, he was mortally wounded.

By his fine example of leadership on the 18th, 19th and 20th January when continually under fire, by his personal example to others of reconnoitring, guiding and bringing up ammunition in addition to his duties at the mortar observation post, all of which were carried out under great physical difficulties and in exposed positions, this officer set the highest example of bravery and devotion to duty to which all ranks responded magnificently. The cool, calculated actions of this officer, coupled with his magnificent bearing and bravery which culminated in his death on the enemy wire, very largely contributed to the ultimate success of the operation which resulted in the capture of the position on the 24th January.

*London Gazette*,
30th March 1944.

# INDEX

References to the more important events will be found in the body of the Index under the appropriate initial letter. For greater detail the reader is advised to consult the heading 'Battalions of the Regiment.'

Adams, Lt., 158; Capt., 196
Adjutants, succession list of, 397
Adnitt, Capt., 278
Ahlquist, Lt., 193
Air, supply by, 257, 284, 287–9; smoke-screen, 312; support of operations, 240, 249–50, 256, 274, 300–1, 310; lack of in N. Africa, 121–2
Airborne troops in Sicily, 154, 157
Alexander, Gen. Sir H., 135, 145–6, 177, 241
Algiers, 5th Bn. at, 111–14
Allen, P.S.M., 63
Allied Regts.: De la Rey, 39, 430–2; Lake Superior, 40, 428–9; 43/48th Bn., 40, 320, 422–4; 58th Bn., 40, 425–7; North Auckland Regt., 420–1
Allkin, L/Cpl., 220
Andaman Islands, 48th in, 27, 82
Anderson, Lt.-Gen., 76, 110
Anderson, 2/Lt. G. M. C., 30, 33; Major, 103, 191
Andrews, Lt., 251
Anstee, Lt.-Col., 77, 91
Antanambao, 58th attack at, 105
Anti-Aircraft, conversion of 4th Bn. to, 35–6
Antsirane, 58th at, 102–5
Anzio, 58th at, 194–202
Arbuthnott, Brig., 207, 237; commends 5th Bn., 344
Armoured cars, action in Burma, 300, 303–4, 318
Arms, notes on, 402–3
Army Reorganisation, post-war, 347–50
Arras, 58th at Battle of, 56–61

Bacon, Lt., 303
Ballam, Capt., 232
Ballard, Major, 148, 150; Lt.-Col., 180–1, 204–5, 328, 341
Baluch Regt., 7/10th, 266, 270, 276–7
Bannu, 48th at, 25
Barford, L/Cpl., 292
Barnacle, Pte., 224
Barrett, Pte., 329
Batchelor, R.S.M., 182
Batiste, Lt., 191
Battalions of the Regiment:
  48th
    Jullundur: training at, 1; success in shooting, 2; in boxing, 2; award of Silver Jubilee medals, 3; farewell messages to, 4
    Razmak: move to, 10–11; operations in Khaisora valley, 11–16; awards for gallantry, 13; road-making, 14–15; casualties, 16; work commended, 16; shooting, 16; Razmak isolated, 17; operations of Razcol, 18–23; gallant platoon action, 21–2; retrospect of campaign, 24; friendship with Gurkha Rifles, 24–5; leave Razmak, 25
    Dinapore: move to, 27; further shooting successes, 28–9; reorganise as rifle battalion, 28; commended by G.O.C., 29; preliminary war measures, 29–30; internal security duties, 81–2; Patna guard of honour, 82; leave Dinapore, 82; behaviour commended, 82
    Jhansi: move to, 82; training at, 83–4; equipment difficulties, 83; at Babina Camp, 84; celebrate bi-centenary, 84; return to Dinapore, 84–5; mobilise, 85; embark at Calcutta, 85; back to Dinapore, 85; to Secunderabad, 86
    Ceylon: move to, 86; training in, 86; leave for India, 242
    Burma: move to, 243; to Moreh, 244; advance towards Kyaukchaw, 244–6; difficulties, 246; work of patrols, 246–7; the Kyaukchaw position, 247; preliminaries to attack, 247–9; air-bombing, 250; attack, 18th Jan., 250–1; Lt. Horwood's gallantry, 251–2; attack, 19th Jan., 251–2; attack, 20th Jan., 252–3; Lt. Horwood wins V.C., 253; subsequent operations, 253–4; comments on operations, 255–6; lack of reinforcements, 256; the Japanese offensive, 257; withdrawal to Moreh, 257–8; in the Moreh 'box,' 258–9; into Naga Hills, 259–61; withdrawal, 261; the Silchar Track, 261–2; topography and tactics, 262–4; task of 32nd Bde., 265; first patrol operations, 265; No. 1 Coy.'s action, 265–6; occupation of Pt. 5846, 266–7; Japanese attacks, 267–9; tanks give help, 269; defence of Track, 270; work of snipers, 270–1; first attack on Dome, 273–4; second attack, 274–5; more Japanese attacks, 276–7; 48th counter-attacks, 277; patrol operations, 278; retrospect of operations, 278–9; work of supply echelon, 278–9; rest and training, 279–81; situation in Burma, 282–3; rôle of 32nd Bde., 283–4; advance to Chindwin River, 284–5; difficulties in crossing river, 285; march up Pondaung Chaung, 286–7; patrol operations at Chingyaung, 287–8; advance on Budalin, 288; Christmas dinners, 288–9; closing in on Budalin, 290; capture of town, 280–6;

# INDEX

Battalions of the Regiment—*continued*
48th (Burma)—*continued*
advance on Monywa, 296–8; action at Ywathit, 298; description of defences, 298; the attack, 301; action at White House, 301; action at Rifle Butts, 301–3; attack on Kg Wood, 303–4; Capt. Cherrington's gallantry, 303; occupation of Monywa, 304–5; advance to Irrawaddy River, 305–6; situation in Burma, 306; British plan, 306–7; task of 48th, 307; the river and country, 307–8; resources for crossing, 308–9; preliminaries, 309; the crossing, 309–10; the bridgehead, 311; Japanese attacks, 311–14; awards for gallantry, 314; plan for bridgehead relief, 315; work of 3/8th Gurkhas, 315; relief, 315; advance on Kyaukse, 316; operations round it, 316–17; plans for further advance, 317; task of 48th, 317–18; difficulties, 318–19; 48th leave Burma, 319; comments on operations, 319–20; praise by Gen. Gracey, 320
India: at Visapur, 333; memorial service, 333; sail for Far East, 333
Malaya: arrival at Singapore, 334; execution of war criminals, 334; at Changi Gaol, 335; at Seremban, 335; notification of disbandment, 335; cadre embarks, 335; reception at Northampton, 336–7; handing over the Colours, 337; disposal of Mess silver, 338, 398

48th/58th
Birth of, 350

58th
Aldershot: successes in sports and shooting, 5–6; Royal review, 6; commended, 6; return to on mobilisation, 51
Ballykinler: successes in boxing, athletics and shooting, 30–4; reorganisation, 31; trooping the Colour, 32; pre-war training, 34–5; mobilisation, 35–51
With B.E.F.: reach France, 52; at Halluin, 53; training, 53–4; advance into Belgium, 55; withdrawal, 55–6; join 'Frankforce,' 56–7; fighting at Maroeuil, 58–9; losses, 61; to St. Eloi, 61–2; 'Q' arrangements, 63; German attacks, 63–5; counter-attack, 65; Battalion H.Q. overrun, 65–7; withdrawal to coast, 67–8; on the beaches, 68; leave Dunkirk, 69
In U.K.: in Scotland, 86–7; at Northwich, 87; bi-centenary celebrations, 87; duty at Liverpool, 87; in N. Ireland, 87–8; loss of Mess property, 87; at Caterham, 88; embark for overseas, 88
Madagascar: voyage to, 98–9; at Durban, 99; plan of assault, 99–100; landings, 100; advance inland, 101–2; night attack on Antsirane, 102–5; commended, 105; French surrender, 106; occupation duties, 106; embark, 107
India and Middle East: stay in India, 148–9; join Paiforce, 149; move to Persia, 149–50; in Teheran, 150; to Egypt, 151; training, 151; embark, 151–2; voyage to Sicily, 152
Sicily: landing, 156; advance to Syracuse, 156–7; capture Priolo, 158–9; advance to Augusta, 159–60; on the Simeto, 160–1; final operations, 165–6; training, 166; embark, 167
Italy: landing near Reggio, 179; advance to Nicastro, 179–80; at Foggia, 180–1; at Macchiagodena, 181–2; maintenance problems, 183; on Sangro River, 183–5; cross Moro River, 185–6; join 5th Army, 186–7; cross Garigliano River, 187–90; Minturno Ridge battle, 190–3; Mt. Damiano position, 193–4; supply arrangements, 194; move to Anzio, 194–5; in the 'Starfish,' 195; the 'Lobster Claw,' 195–6; the 'Fortress' position, 196–7; enemy attack, 197–9; counter-attacks, 199–201; praise for gallantry, 201; Moletta River crossing, 202–3; advance to Rome, 203–4; leave Italy, 204; return from Middle East, 205
North-west Europe: reach Belgium, 326; on Elbe River, 327; to the Baltic, 327; to Göttingen, 328
After the war: at Göttingen, 338–9; in Berlin, 339; shooting successes, 339–42; return of the Colours, 340–1; move to Austria, 341

4th Battalion
At Home: activities in peace, 7, 35; conversion to Anti-Aircraft, 35–6; re-raised, 37–8; service in England, 88–9; move to N. Ireland, 89; return to England, 321; Exercise 'Flake,' 321–2; mobilise, 323
In North-west Europe: move to Holland, 328; on the Maas, 328–30; at Rhine crossing, 330–1; various duties, 342; disbanded, 342–3

5th Battalion
At Home: peacetime activities, 7, 36–7; mobilise, 37, 70
With B.E.F.: land in France, 71; in Maginot Line, 71; move into Belgium, 71–2; withdraw, 72; on the Escaut River, 73–6; on the Lys River, 77; to Ypres, 77; withdrawal to the coast, 78–9; leave Dunkirk, 79
In U.K.: at Winchester, 90; 'Cromwell' alarm, 90; at Christchurch, 90–1; commended by C.-in-C., 90; visited by the King, 91; to Scotland, 91–2; Exercise 'Dryshod,' 92; embark, 92–3
North Africa: voyage to, 110–11; landing near Algiers, 111–15; task of 78th Div., 114;

## INDEX

Battalions of the Regiment—*continued*
  5th Battalion (North Africa)—*continued*
    'Hart Force,' 114–15; advance on Tunis, 115–17; capture of Medjez, 117–18; attacks on Djedeida, 120–2; at Longstop Hill, 123; patrol activities, 124–5; the Christmas offensive, 125–9; difficult withdrawal, 129–30; on Goubellat plain, 133–4; German offensive, 134–7; British attack, 137–40; assault on Tanngoucha, 141–2; final offensive begins, 143; attacks on Sidi Ahmed, 144–5; advance to Tunis, 145–6; training in Tunisia, 147
    Sicily: landing, 162; attack Catenanuova, 162–3; at Centuripe, 163; praise for capture, 164; take Bronte, 164; near Randazzo, 165; final operations, 166; training, 167
    Italy: landing at Taranto, 207; take Serracapriola and Termoli, 207–8; on the Trigno River, 209; advance to Sangro River, 210; fighting there, 211–13; move to central sector, 213; patrol successes, 214; return to coast, 214–15; move to Cassino area, 215; plan of operations, 216; 'The Bowl,' 217; supply arrangements, 218; at Capua, 219; assault on Gustav Line, 219–21; advance to Rome, 221–2; action at Montegabbione, 222–5; near Lake Trasimeno, 225; to Taranto, 226; rest and training in Egypt, 226–7; return to Italy, 228; attacks on Pt. 508, 229–33; on Monte Spaduro, 233–7; reorganisation, 236; on Senio River, 238; force the Argenta Gap, 239; advance to Po River, 240–1; earn congratulations, 241
    After the war: in Austria, 343–4; in suspended animation, 344; Battalion reformed, 345
  6th Battalion
    Formation as Holding Battalion, 93; change of title, 94; coast-defence duties, 94; draftfinding, 323; disbanded, 324
  50th (Holding) Battalion
    See under 6th Battalion above
  70th Battalion
    Formation of, 94–5; service in Cornwall, 95; disbanded, 324
Beagley, Capt., 121, 141
Beard, C.S.M., 196
Beardsall, Lt., 162
Belgian Army, surrender of, 49
Bell, Lt., 329
Bell, Sgt., 190, 203
Bennett, Lt., 13
Beynon, Lt., 214
Bi-centenary of Regiment, 84, 87
Bihar, Governor of, commends 48th, 82, 84
Bissett, Lt.-Col., 3
Black Watch, 6th Bn. The, 74

'Blade Force,' 117–18, 122–3
Boshell, Lt., 86
'Bowl,' 5th Bn. in the, 217–19
Boxing: in 48th, 2, 16, 28–9; in 58th, 5, 30–1; in 4th Bn., 7
Bradshaw, Pte., 329
Brewin, Major, 84, 86
B.E.F.: strength of, 43; shortcomings, 44, 54; plans for action of, 45–6; advance of, 46–7; withdrawal of, 47
Brittain, Lt., 66
Britten, Lt.-Col. G. V., 340
Britten, Major J. R., 277, 333
Brooke, Lt.-Gen., 71, 90
Brown, Lt.-Gen. Sir J., 41, 89
Brown, Pte., 270
Browne, Major-Gen. G. F., 9
Buchanan, Major, 138, 144; Lt.-Col., 147, 164
Bucher, Lt., 251
Budalin, 48th at, 288–96
Burbidge, Lt., 329
Burghley, Lord, 37
Burkley, Lt., 140
Burma, 48th in, *see* under Battalions; situation in, 243–4, 257, 282–3, 306, 319
Burn, Pte., 330
Buszard, Major, 89; Lt.-Col., 321
Butterworth, Major-Gen., 227
Byne, Pte., 330
Byrne, Major (R.A.), 313

Carless, Pte., 330
Carrick, Lt.-Col., 95, 324, 346
Carrier, introduction of, 31
Carrington, Lt., 38
Cass, Brig., 92, 207
Cassino, 5th Bn. at, 215–21
Caterham, 58th at, 88
Centuripe, 5th Bn. attack, 163–4
Ceylon, 48th in, 85
Chandler, Capt., 313
Cherrington, Capt., 254, 292, 294–6, 303
Chindwin River, crossing by 48th, 283–6
Clark, Capt., 195
Clarke, 2/Lt., 140; Lt., 238
Clarke, Pte., 22
Clayton, Capt., 276
Cobbing, Capt., 75–6
Coldwell, Lt.-Col. W. G. A., 3, 29
Coldwell, Major A. St. G., 96–7
Coleridge, Gen. Sir J., commends 48th, 24
Colonel-in-Chief: appointment of H.R.H. the Duchess of Gloucester as, 38; presentation to, 39; toast of, 39; messages from, 52, 84, 352; visits battalions, 87, 89, 90, 321, 350; accepts Japanese sword, 312
Colonel of the Regiment: *see* under Knox and Robinson

# INDEX

Colours, The: centre device for, 8; in Invalides, 8–9; trooping, 32; handing over of 48th, 337; return of to 58th, 340–1
Comforts Fund, County, 325, 330
Comrades' Association, 346–7
Connolly, Lt.-Col., 164, 166, 219, 330
Cook, Major, 141, 220
Coullie, Capt., 210
Cowan, Lt., 197
Cox, Lt.-Col., 324
Cox, Pte., 314
Crocker, Major, 223–4
'Cromwell' alarm, 90, 94
Crook, Lt.-Col., 91, 118, 121–2, 138–9, 144, 164
Cubey, Capt., 246, 265
Cufley, Lt., 267
Cushion, Capt., 193

Damiano, 58th on Mt., 193–4
Davies, L/Cpl., 254
Day, C.S.M., 195
Deception parties, work of, 298, 318, 321–2
De la Rey, Regt., *see* under Allied Regiments
Denny, Major, 195, 197, 203
Depot, Regimental, 40–1; new barracks, 41; renamed I.T.C., 95; post-war duties, 346; *see also* under I.T.C. and P.T.C.
Diego Suarez, attack on, 100
Dipper, Major, 346
Djedeida, 5th Bn. attack, 120–2
Dodman, Sgt., 201
'Dome,' 48th attack, 273–6
Domminey, 2/Lt., 163
Doubleday, Cpl., 203
Dowzer, Capt., 151
Duke of Connaught's Cup, 58th win, 5–6
Dumais, P.S.M., 133
Dunkirk: 58th at, 68–9; 5th Bn. at, 79; effect on I.T.C., 96–7
Dupre, Lt., 146
Durban, 58th at, 99
Dyson, Capt., 304

Eales-White, Capt., 258, 269, 298, 301, 314
Eassom, C.S.M., 233
East Surrey Regt., 1st Bn. The, 71, 118, 120, 130, 138, 140, 143, 147, 164, 210, 229, 233–4
Eisenhower, Lt.-Gen., 110, 135, 147
Elworthy, the Rev., 142, 223–4
Emmerton, Capt., 144, 210, 224, 229–30
Equipment, notes on, 402–3
Escaut River, battle of, 73–6
Evans-Evans, Lt., 61
Evelegh, Major-Gen., 92, 164, 214; commends 5th Bn., 130
Exercises: 'Bumper,' 90; 'Character,' 149; 'Dryshod,' 92; 'Flake,' 321–2; 'Nocturne,' 91; 'Snowdrop,' 88

Field, P.S.M., 59
5th Battalion: *see* under Battalions
58th: *see* under Battalions
58th Battalion A.M.F.: *see* under Allied Regiments
Finlinson, Brig., 196
Firth-Clark, Lt., 305
Fitzwilliam, 2/Lt., 63
Foggia, 58th at, 181
'Force 121,' 99
'Fortress' position, 58th in, 196–202
48th: *see* under Battalions
48th Battalion A.M.F.: *see* under Allied Regiments
48th/58th, formation of after the war, 350
4th Battalion: *see* under Battalions
France and Flanders, outline of campaign in, 43–50
'Frankforce,' 58th with, 56–61
Franklin, Lt., 277
Franklyn, Major-Gen., 48, 53
Freedom of Northampton, granting of, 351–2
Frontier Force Regt., 5/12th, 11, 18, 19
Frontier Force Rifles: 2/13th, 15; 6/13th, 11, 18, 19, 21
Fukei Shempei, Gen., execution of, 334
Fulford, Capt., 292, 301–3, 314
Furminger, Capt., 11; Lt.-Col., 93–4, 321–3, 342

Gannaway, Pte., 296
Gardiner, Capt., 332
Garigliano River, 58th cross, 187–8
Garner, Capt., 193
German Army: invasion of Poland, 45; invasion of Low Countries, 45–9, 54; attack at St. Eloi, 63–7; counter-offensive in Tunisia, 122–3; offensive in Tunisia, 136–7
Gibson, Major, 157, 192
Gibson, 2/Lt., 62
Gloucester, H.R.H. the Duchess of: *see* under Colonel-in-Chief
Goodall, R.S.M., 60, 86, 194
Gould, L/Cpl., 32
Gracey, Lt.-Gen., 86, 288, 319, 336; commends 48th, 320
Greaves, Major, 192
Green Howards, 1st Bn. The, 202
Green, Lt., 21; Capt., 60
Green, Lt.-Col., 7, 71, 75–6
Grenadier Guards, 2nd Bn. The, 78
Group, East Anglian, 348–9
Growse, Lt.-Col., 94, 324
Gurkha Rifles: 1/3rd, 15, 18–20; 1/4th, 267–9, 271; 2/4th, 3, 19; 3/8th, 86, 253, 255–6, 265–6, 268, 270–1, 273–6, 278, 290, 295, 298, 300, 304, 314–16; 1/9th, 11, 13, 21–2, 23–5; 1/10th, 277; 4/10th, 283, 288
Gurney, Col., 51

Hamer, Lt., 182, 186, 192, 197, 203
Hampshire Regt., 2nd Bn. The, 122
Hampton Ridge, 266

# INDEX

Harris, L/Cpl., 253
Hart, Capt., 73, 114, 121
'Hart Force,' 114–18, 120
Hasdell, Pte., 66
Haselhurst, 2/Lt., 82
Hatcher, Sgt., 253
Hayman, Sgt., 182, 200
Heard, Capt., 78
Herbert, Pte., 73
Hertzberg, Capt., 136–7
Hetherington, Capt., 270
Heward, Sgt., 200–1
Hickson, Capt., 105
Hill, 2/Lt., 76–7
Hillian, Lt., 220
Hill-Walker, Major A., V.C., 38, 324–5
Hill-Walker, Major G. A., 112–13
Hinchcliffe, Lt.-Col., 53–4, 60–1, 86, 98, 102, 150
Hincks, Lt., 247, 253
Hodges, Lt., 269
Hodgkiss, Lt., 231–2, 236
Hofman, Lt., 33, 182
Holding Battalion, 50th, 93
Holmes, Capt., 63
Honours and Awards, 433–41
Horn, Pte., 6
Hornsby, Capt., 151, 158
Horwood, Lt., V.C., 251–3, 441
Houchin, Capt., 58, 66–7; Major, 100, 102–5, 148, 181, 189, 195; Lt.-Col., 237
Houston, L/Cpl., 253
Howard, Lt., 314
Howard, R.S.M., 64–5
Hughes, Lt., 249, 251–2, 259, 271, 314
Hunnybun, Lt., 79
Hunt, Major L. O. A., 102
Hunt, Major M. W., 144, 164, 230, 232

I.T.C., 96–7; moves to Norwich, 97; returns to Northampton, 324; after the war, 345–6; see also under P.T.C.
Invalides, 48th Colours in, 8–9
Irrawaddy River, crossing of by 48th, 306–15
Italian Campaign: Allied plan for invasion, 168; course of, 169–78; result of, 178

Japanese: offensives, 243, 257; fighting ability, 255; advance on Imphal, 259; withdrawal, 282–3; surrender, 319
Jarvis, L/Cpl., 21
Jervois, Lt.-Col., 29, 53, 84
Jewell, Lt., 214
Jhansi, 48th at, 82–3
Jitter-parties, Japanese, 258–9, 294
Johnson, Capt., 75
Jones, Major, 280, 289, 307, 310; Lt.-Col., 316, 318, 333
Jones-Evans, the Rev., 184, 202

Keightley, Major-Gen., 214, 227
Keilthy, C.S.M., 146
Keily, 250, 274, 276
Kelly, Pte., 270
Kennedy, Lt., 237
Kerr, Capt., 130
King, 2/Lt., 76
King George VI, H.M., inspects 58th, 88; inspects 5th Bn., 70, 91, 147
Kirkton, Sgt., 329
Kitchin, Capt., 192–3
Knowles, Lt., 298, 303
Knox, Lt.-Gen., 9, 39, 52, 88, 325, 350
Kyaukchaw, 48th attack at, 244–56

*Laforey*, H.M.S., 190, 351
Lake Superior Regiment: see under Allied Regiments
Lamb, Capt., 182, 184, 202
Lamplugh, Major, 77
Lancashire Fusiliers, 2nd Bn. The, 77, 112, 118–19, 122, 141–2, 164, 225, 233
Large, Capt., 195
Lee, L/Cpl., 279–80
Lee, Sgt., 182
Leigh, Lt., 294
Letts, Pte., 22
Lieutenant-Colonels, succession list of, 395–6
Lincolnshire Regt., 1st Bn. The, 29, 82
Lindsell, Sgt., 295
Lingham, Lt.-Col., 89
'Lobster Claw,' 58th in the, 195–6
Locomotive, 'The Northamptonshire Regiment,' 9, 30, 336
Lodge, Capt., 318
'Longstop Hill,' 123–4, 127, 130, 140–1, 144
Lowther, Col., 37, 89
Ludlow, Pte., 33
Lys River, 5th Bn. on the, 77

Mackenzie, Brig., 242, 265, 283, 307, 310, 315–16
McDonald, Pte., 201
McGill, Pte., 220
McGrann, L/Cpl., 329
McKee, Capt., 344
McLoughlin, Lt., 140
McMichael, Major, 91; Lt.-Col., 345
McNeill, Capt., 141
McTighe, Sgt., 200–1
Madagascar, assault on, 98–107
Maginot Line, 5th Bn. in, 71
Maintenance: in France, 63; in Italy, 183, 194, 217–18
Malaya, 48th in, 334–5
Maloney, R.S.M., 162
Malpas, Cpl., 33
Manners, Cpl., 190
Marks of Esteem, 78 Div., 238
Maroeuil Wood, 58th at, 57–60

# INDEX

Marshall, Major, 75–7
Marshall, Sgt., 5
Mattinson, Lt., 224
Mayhew, Lt., 164
Mead, Cpl., 158
Meadows, Pte., 330
Meager, Lt., 197
Measures, Capt., 75
Mechanisation, 28, 31, 35, 83
Mellows, Lt.-Col., 7
Melsome, Capt., 58, 65; Lt.-Col., 338
Mercer, Pte., 237
Meredith, 2/Lt., 21–2
Mess Plate, notes on, 398; decision on 48th, 338
Metson, 2/Lt., 163
Millar, Capt., 313
Millard, Pte., 13
Minturno, 58th at, 190–3
Mobilisation of 48th, 30, 85; of 58th, 35, 51; of 5th Bn., 37; of 4th Bn., 323
Moletta River, 58th cross, 202–3
Molloy, Major, 246–7, 252–4, 268, 314
Mons, 48th emblems in museum at, 9
Montgomery, Lt.-Gen., 90, 147, 152
Monywa, 48th attack on, 296–305
Morgan, Capt., 104
Morgan, Lt., 212
Moro River, 58th cross, 185–6
Morris, 2/Lt., 267
Mountbatten, Lord Louis, commends 48th, 280
Muirhead, Col., 8, 35
Muzzaffarpur, 48th at, 27

Nailer, Major, 11, 17
Needle, Lt., 120
Neill, Pte., 66
Newby, Lt., 196; Capt., 340
Newman, Major, 330, 342
Nicholls, Pte., 190
Nind, Pte., 22
Noakes, Capt., 309
Norfolk Regt., R., 97, 324
Norman, Capt., 58, 60
North Africa: 5th Bn. in, *see* under Battalions; comments on campaign in, 146–7
Northamptonshire Cup, presentation to A.R.A., 342, 398
North Auckland Regiment: *see* under Allied Regiments
Northern Ireland: 58th in, 87–8; 4th Bn. in, 89
Northfield, 2/Lt., 182
Northumberland Fusiliers, R., 74, 76

Ogle, Major, 340
Operation: 'Avalanche,' 168; 'Baytown,' 168; 'Dynamo,' 96; 'Husky,' 151–2; 'Peasoup,' 181; 'Torch,' 92, 109; 'Volcano,' 327
Organ, Sgt., 200–1
Organisation, notes on changes in, 399–401

Orr, 2/Lt., 74
Orton, Cpl., 330
Osborne-Smith, Lt., 11; Capt., 82; Lt.-Col., 338
Outhwaite, Sgt., 332
Owens, Pte., 158

Pack, Pte., 94
Paiforce, 58th in, 148–51
Parachute Bn., 1st, 120
Parker, L/Cpl., 303
Parker, Lt.-Col., 6, 35
Parker, Sgt., 329
Parratt, Capt., 182
Pashley, Capt., 76
Patna, 48th at, 81–2
Pearson, Lt., 224
Perkins, Lt., 292, 294; Capt., 315
Phillips, 2/Lt., 277, 309
Philpot-Brookes, Capt., 60, 65
Pieve, 5th Bn. at Monte, 229–33
Pollard, Pte., 32
Pondaung Chaung, 48th advance up, 286–7
Presland, Pte., 13
P.T.C., No. 48: formation of, 346; disbandment, 346; duties, 349
Prinsloo, Lt., 235
Priolo, action by 58th at, 158–9
Pulleyn, Lt., 224
Punjab Regt.: 4/8th, 15, 21; 9/14th, 86, 265, 271, 274, 286, 290–2, 298, 300–1, 305, 308, 311, 313, 315–16
Purton, Capt., 105, 158, 183, 195, 204

Quebec Barracks, Northampton, 41, 345–6
Queen Victoria Trophy, 2, 16, 28–9, 30–2, 34, 340–1
Quinn, the Rev., 75, 78

Raisborough, Pte., 185
Rangoon, 48th sail for, 85
Rawlins, Lt., 22; Major, 240
Rayment, Capt., 136–7, 139
Reddy, 2/Lt., 65, 67
Richards, Lt., 182, 185
Rickett, Lt., 124, 208
Roberts, Capt., 201
Robinson, Lt.-Col. G. St. G.: leaves 58th, 6; Major-Gen.: addresses 48th, 335; appointed Colonel of the Regiment, 350; addresses 58th, 340; biographical note on, 394
Roche, 2/Lt., 57, 61, 66–8; Capt., 157; Major, 189
Rome, advance on, 203–4, 221–2
Rose, Pte., 13
Rosser, Major, 217
Ruffold, Sgt., 292
Ryder, Major-Gen., 110, 113

Saar, 5th Bn. in the, 71
St. Eloi, 58th at, 62–7
St. Sepulchre's Church, Northampton, 8, 350–1

## INDEX

Sangro River, 58th on, 183-5; 5th Bn. on, 211
Saunders, Pte., 254; Sgt., 279
Scotland, 58th in, 86-7; 5th Bn. in, 91-3
Scots Fusiliers, 2nd Bn. R., 55, 57, 62-3, 68, 102, 156-7, 159, 183, 187-91, 203
Scott-Robson, Lt.-Col., 7, 39
Seaforth Highlanders, 6th Bn. The, 55, 57, 62, 68, 102-3, 156, 158-9, 182, 187-92, 197-9, 202-3
Searchlight Battalion, 50th, formation of, 36; later career, 345; notes on, 417-19
70th Battalion: *see* under Battalions
Sharpe, Pte., 73; Cpl., 329
Shaw, Lt., 329
Sherwood, Lt.-Col., 324
Shooting: in 48th, 2, 16, 28-9; in 58th, 5-6, 30-4, 338-42; at Depot, 41-2; at P.T.C., 346; Regimental records, 405-16
Sicily: invasion of, 153-4; plan for, 154; progress of operations in, 160-2; end of campaign in, 166; *see* also under Battalions—58th and 5th Battalion
Sikh Regt., 2/11th, 15
Silchar Track, description of, 261-2; defence of, 262-79
Silver, Regimental, notes on, 338
6th Battalion: *see* under Battalions
Slim, Brig., 83
Smith, Lt. (58th), 164
Smith, Lt. (4th Bn.), 329
Snipers, work of, 195
Snow, Lt.-Col., 280, 309
Solomon, Sgt., 303
Spaduro, 5th Bn. at Monte, 233-7
'Speedy Express,' 216
Spencer, Earl, 35
Spencer, Major, 89
Stanley, Lt., 78
Stanley, Pte., 314
'Starfish,' 58th in the, 195
Steadman, R.Q.M.S., 162
Stephenson, Lt.-Col., 181, 184, 189, 204
Stoddart, Lt., 290-2, 295
Stopford, Brig., 51, 62, 65, 68, 87; Lt.-Gen., 280
Sturges, Major-Gen., 99
Supply arrangements: 58th in France, 63; 5th Bn. in Italy, 217-18; 48th in Burma, 284
Surkitt, R.S.M., 221
Suspended Animation, 48th in, 335, 349
Syddall, Lt., 189
Symonds, Lt., 33, 63-4

Talavera Camp, Northampton, 97, 324, 345-6
Tanngoucha, Djebel, 5th Bn. at, 141-2
Tarleton, Brig., 87, 181
Taunton, Lt.-Col., 84, 86, 254, 258, 278, 280, 300, 307, 311, 314-16, 335-7
Teheran, 58th at, 150

Terry, Lt., 214, 223
Thirkhill, Sgt., 222
Thornton, L/Cpl., 331
Thubron, Brig., 237
Thunder, Major, 275, 277
Toasts: to Colonel-in-Chief, 39; to 48th, 337
Tovey, Pte., 37
Truckle, Capt., 114, 120, 181-2
Tunisia, description of country, 115
Turnbull, P.S.M., 65

Underwood, Sgt., 200-1
Uniform, changes in, 401-2
U.S.A.: officers with 5th Bn., 92, 112-13; tanks support 5th Bn., 119-22; forces in Sicily, 153-4, 160; gallantry of ambulance drivers with 48th, 269

Veater, Major, 268, 304, 310, 314
Vickers, Lt., 111, 164
Victoria Cross, Lt. Horwood's, 253, 260, 441
Villis, Lt., 111

Wade, C.S.M., 137
Walkden, Lt., 309, 311
Walker, Lt., 182
Wallis, Major, 196
Walters, L/Cpl., 252
Walton, Lt., 252
War Memorial, Regimental, 350-1
Ward, Brig., 181, 196
Wardell, 2/Lt., 161
Warren, Lt.-Col., 35, 53
Wasey, Major, 218, 225
Watts, Major, 58, 60, 64-8, 346, 351
Waziristan: 48th in, 10-26; retrospect of campaign in, 24
Webb, Capt., 268, 309
Webb, Lt., 157, 159
Wetherall, Major J. R., 55, 60-1, 337
Wetherall, Major R. M., 60, 65
Wherry, Major, 164
Whitaker, Capt., 106, 196
White, L/Cpl., 329
Wilford, Cpl., 203
Wilkinson, Capt., 141
Wilks, Pte., 158
Winkler, Major, 13, 28, 84
Wireless, notes on, 403-4
Wood, Capt., 105
Woolvern, Lt., 140
Wright, Major, 122
Wyatt, L/Sgt., 13

Yates, Lt., 340
Young, Sgt., 140
Young Soldiers' Battalion, 70th, 94-5
Ypres-Comines Canal, 62

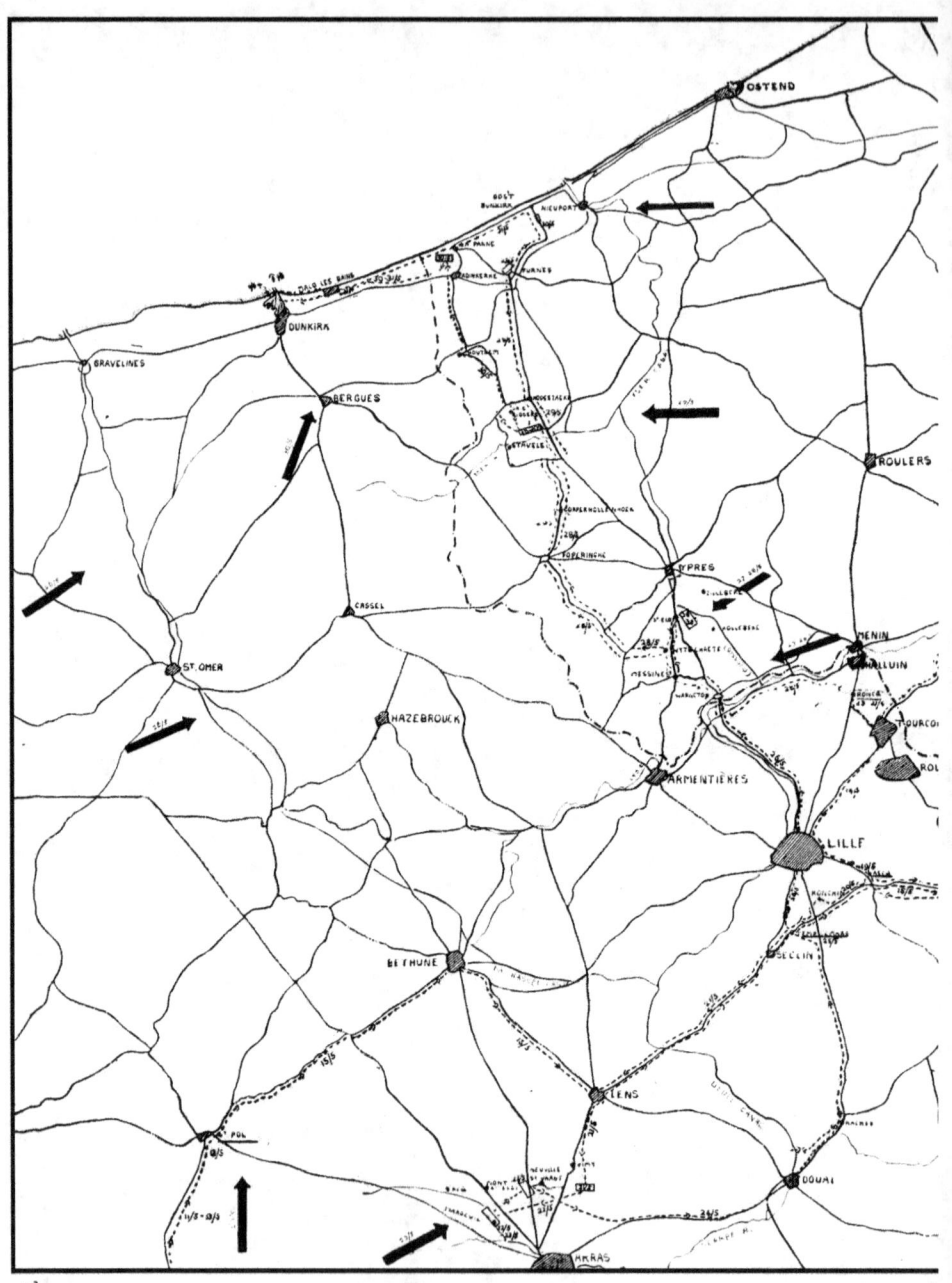

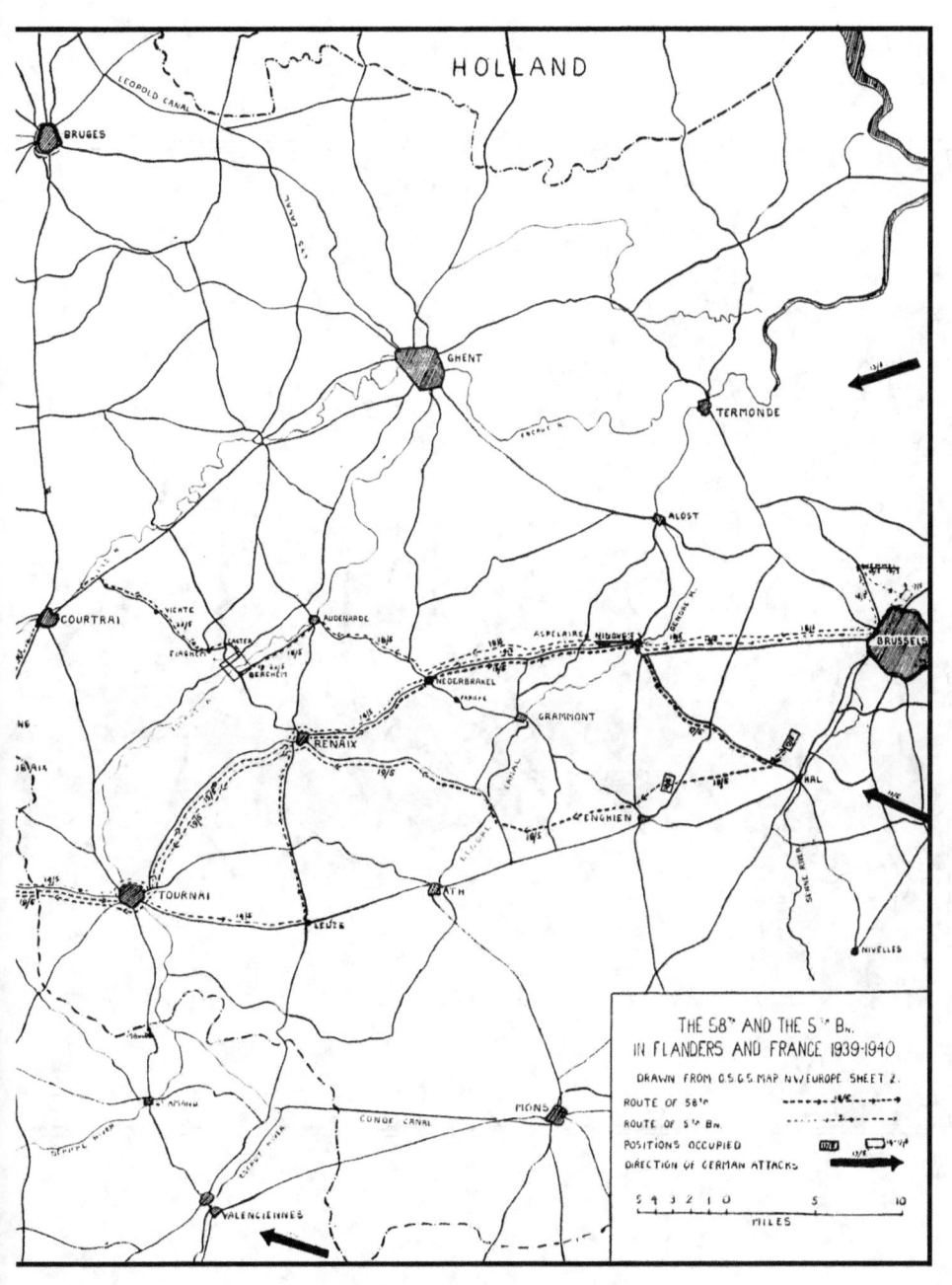

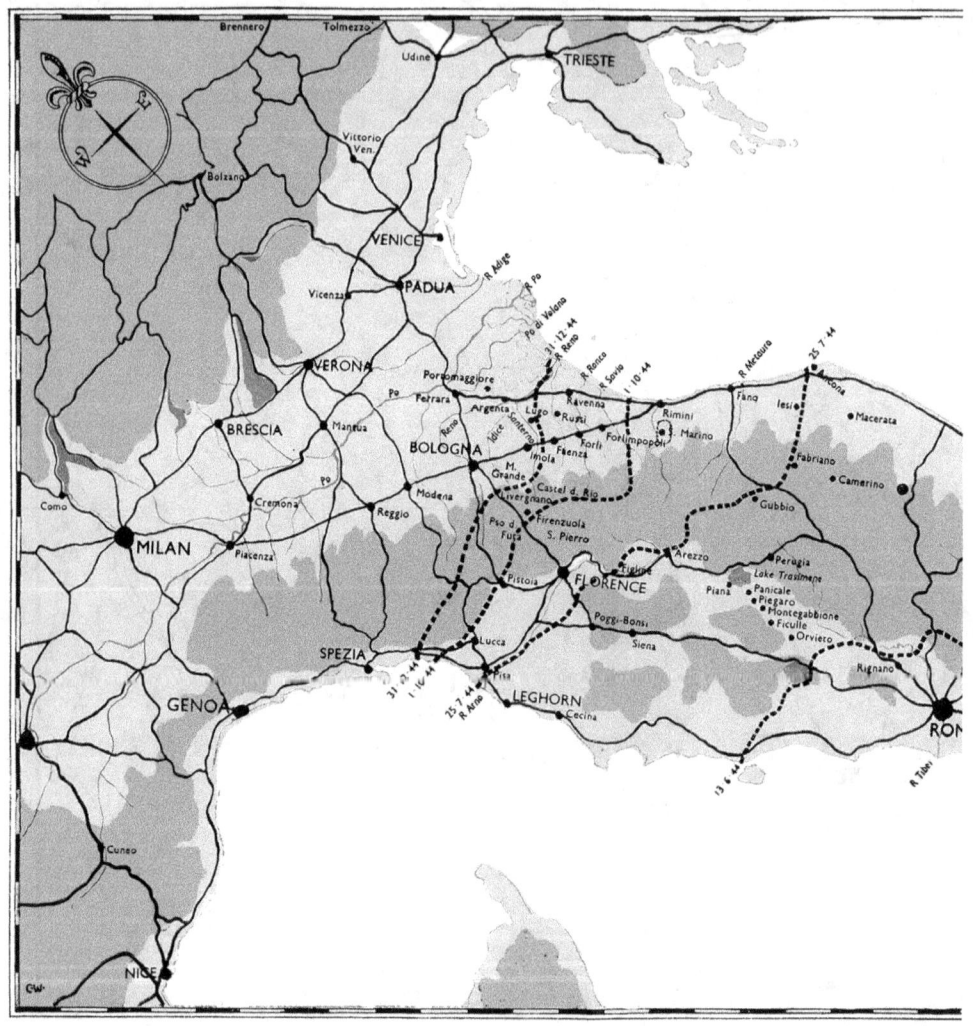

# REGIMENTAL HISTORIES OF THE BRITISH ARMY

## A SELECTION OF N&MP REPRINTED TITLES
## ALWAYS AVAILABLE ALWAYS IN PRINT

READ THE REAL HISTORY OF THE SECOND WORLD WAR IN THE STORIES OF THE REGIMENTS, CORPS, DIVISIONS, & BATTALIONS THAT FOUGHT IT.

## CLUB ROUTE IN EUROPE
### The Story of 30 Corps in the European Campaign.
**9781783311033**

30 Corps was heavily involved in the closing campaigns of the Second World War in Europe, starting when its 50th (Northumbrian) Division landed on Gold Beach on D-day. It helped to clear the Cotentin peninsular in Operation Bluecoat and, after General Brian Horrocks took over command, it took part in Operation Market Garden at Arnhem, and the crossing of the Rhine into the German heartland. A superb unit history of these often difficult and bloody operations.

## SEVENTH ARMOURED DIVISION
### October 1938 - May 1943
**9781474539180**

## 2nd BATTALION SOUTH WALES BORDERS 24th REGIMENT
### D-DAY TO VE-DAY
**9781474539012**

Describing the campaign from D-Day onwards, this excellent contemporary battalion history is divided into two parts. The first contains an outline of the activities of the 2/24th during the campaign in Europe from D-Day to VE-Day, and the second is a detailed narrative of some of the more important actions in which the battalion fought. Complete with a list of awards. Originally printed in Hamburg in 1945.

## THE HISTORY OF THE CORPS OF ROYAL MILITARY POLICE
**9781783310951**

Excellent history of this corps, almost entirely devoted to WW2 on all fronts, including Middle East, North-West Europe and Burma. Complete with a Roll of Honour.

## HISTORY OF THE ARGYLL & SUTHERLAND HIGHLANDERS
### 7th BATTALION
### From El Alamein To Germany
**9781781519653**

## 49 (WEST RIDING) RECONNAISSANCE REGIMENT
### Royal Armoured Corps
### - Summary of Operations June 1944 to May 1945
### 9781474536677

Rare Reconnaissance unit history that was completed immediately after the war had ended. Following the D-Day invasions, the 49th Reconnaissance Regiment fought as Montgomery's left flank, and played vital roles in the capture of Arnhem, and the liberation of Holland. They are honoured annually in Utrecht to this day. The book is completed with 2 good coloured maps.

## THE STORY OF
## THE 79th ARMOURED DIVISION
## OCTOBER 1942 - JUNE 1945
## 9781783310395

A magnificent and fully illustrated official history of Britain's 79th Armoured Division - the specialised unit which developed and operated 'Hobart's Funnies', the adapted tanks which carried out a range of tasks on D-day and after ranging from mine clearance to bridge laying. Follows the unit from its formation to victory in Europe.

## THE ESSEX REGIMENT 1929 - 1950
## 9781781519813

Comprehensive history of both regular & territorial force battalions, mainly Middle East (inc. Tobruk & Alamein), North-West Europe & 1st Bn. with Chindits in Burma 1944. Rolls of Honour and awards.

## THE STORY OF THE ROYAL ARMY SERVICE CORPS,
## 1939-1945
## 9781474538251

A complete history of the RASC in all theatres throughout the Second World War. This a model unit history originally published under the direction of the Institution of the Royal Army Service Corps, it is excellently produced, and arranged by theatre of war. The narrative is full with technical information, and the many photographic plates record visually British military vehicles in service situations.

## HISTORY OF THE IRISH GUARDS IN THE SECOND WORLD WAR
## 9781474537094

A fine history of a proud regiment; The Irish Guards played their part gallantly during campaigns in Europe, North Africa and Italy during the Second World War, claiming two Victoria Cross recipients during that conflict. The basis of this history was the War Diaries kept by Battalion Intelligence Officers, along with individual records and papers.
A Roll of Honour, Honours Awards down to Military Medal, and 22 good maps complete this very good WW2 Regimental.

## OPERATIONS OF THE EIGHTH CORPS

The River Rhine to the Baltic Sea. A narrative account of the pursuit and final defeat of the German Armed Forces March-May 1945.
## 9781474538176

## THE HISTORY OF THE 51st HIGHLAND DIVISION 1939-1945
## 9781474536660

The 51st Highland Division fought and lost in France in 1940, was reborn, and fought and won in the North African desert, Sicily and finally in North Western Europe from D-Day to the end of the war. As a division the men earned the respect of friend and foe alike, and this is their story. Amply illustrated with 36 photographs, 18 maps and battle plans (many coloured) that help the reader to follow the course of the conflict. A good index (persons, units and place names) and a statistical battle casualties list complete this good WW2 Divisional History

## THE HISTORY OF THE FIFTEENTH SCOTTISH DIVISION 1939-1945
### 9781783310852

Formed at the outbreak of war in September 1939, the 15th (Scottish) division served in North-western Europe after landing in Normandy soon after D-day on 14 June 1944. It fought on the Odon River, at Caen, Caumont, Mont Pincon, the Nederrijn, the Rhineland, and across the Rhine. On April 10, 1946, the division was disbanded. The total number of casualties it sustained during the 12 months of fighting was 11,772.

## ALGIERS TO AUSTRIA
### The 78th Division in the Second World War
### 9781783310265

## F COMPANY 8th BATTALION THE RIFLE BRIGADE
### 9781474541299

This is a Regimentally published title that covers an individual company of the Rifle Brigade, is compiled from memory, and is a day-to-day account of men of F Company in the heat of battle – taking part in the Normandy landings in June 1944 and the subsequent advance across North West Europe. A Roll of Honour, List of Wounded, H&A and – unusually – an Address list complete this excellent history. Written so shortly after the cessation of hostilities, this account has an immediacy that modern histories lack. F Company, along with G and H Companies, were mobile infantry companies (or 'motor companies') with a strength of 175 officers and men each. Each company consisted of one scout (reconnaissance) platoon (in Bren Carriers) and three mobile infantry platoons (using International Harvester half-tracks).

## E COMPANY 8th BATTALION THE RIFLE BRIGADE
## Through the France and Germany campaign, 1944-1945
### 9781474541282

This is a Regimentally published title that covers an individual company of the Rifle Brigade, is compiled from memory, and is a day-to-day account of men of E Company in the heat of battle – taking part in the Normandy landings in June 1944 and the subsequent advance across North West Europe. Written so shortly after the cessation of hostilities, this account has an immediacy that modern histories lack. E Company were a support company of 198 officers and men, delivering heavy weapon support to F, G and H Companies. E Company was divided into five platoons, of which three were Anti-Tank platoons (equipped with 6-pounder A/Tk. guns) and two were MMG platoons (equipped with water-cooled Vickers .303 Medium Machine Guns). A nominal roll of officers and men showing KIA and DOW concludes this interesting history.

## FROM NORMANDY TO THE BALTIC
### 9781474541800

The Story Of The 44th Lowland Infantry Brigade Of The 15th Scottish Division From D Day to The End Of The War In Europe
A fine Infantry Brigade history covering heavy fighting including Operation Epsom, Hill 112, Operation Jupiter and Operation Bluecoat. One of the scarcer World War II unit histories of the type that were published just after the German surrender, this originally printed in the region of Holstein during 1945.

## HISTORY OF THE FIRST DIVISION
### Anzio Campaign, January-June 1944
9781474541572

The First Division delivered - immediately after leaving Italy and transferring to Palestine - two first-class Divisional Histories detailing its role in the allied advance in Italy and the capture of Rome. The first covered the "Anzio campaign, January-June 1944" and the second completed its story with the breaking of the Gothic Line in "Florence to Monte Grande: August 1944-January 1945". Both of these Mediterranean Theatre Histories have now been reprinted by N&MP.

The division landed at Anzio on 22 January 1944 under the command of the US VI Corps. It sustained heavy casualties during the battle for Anzio. It remained in the Anzio beach-head until the breakout. It then rested and refitted after its long period of front-line duty. The division was involved in the battle for the Gothic Line between 25 August and 22 September 1944.

## HISTORY OF THE FIRST DIVISION
### Florence to Monte Grande: August 1944-January 1945
9781474541305

This, the second volume of the excellent and thoroughly professional 1st Divisional History, covers the period from early August 1944 to the end of January 1945. Split into three parts, the first covers operations from Florence to the end of the advance following on from the breaking of the Gothic Line. Part 2 deals with the static period of holding Monte Grande through the winter. Part 3 contains descriptions of work of supporting arms etc, and important matters not forming part of the general narrative.

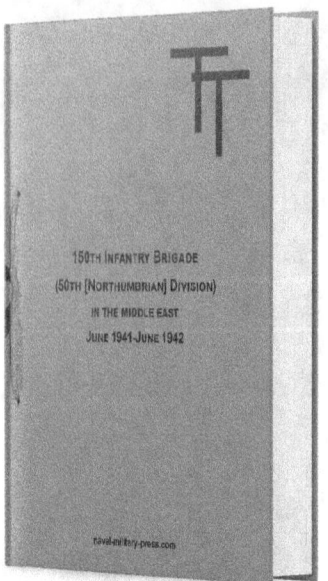

### 150th INFANTRY BRIGADE (50th [Northumbrian] Division) in the Middle East June 1941-June 1942
### 9781474541862

A rare Western Desert Brigade history in its original printing (1946). The brigade served in the Middle East and was overrun and forced to surrender after suffering heavy losses during the Battle of Gazala in the North African Campaign. Many British tanks were lost and the Panzerarmee had regained the initiative. Compiled by officers in PoW camps in Italy and revised in Switzerland in 1944.

---

## naval-military-press.com

www.ingramcontent.com/pod-product-compliance
Lightning Source LLC
Chambersburg PA
CBHW051332230426
43668CB00010B/1240